Y0-BCW-172

AN INTRODUCTION TO CONTEMPORARY BUSINESS

Second Edition

AN INTRODUCTION TO CONTEMPORARY BUSINESS

Second Edition

WILLIAM RUDELIUS
University of Minnesota

W. BRUCE ERICKSON
University of Minnesota

WILLIAM J. BAKULA, JR.
Anne Arundel Community College

 HARCOURT BRACE JOVANOVICH, INC.
New York   Chicago   San Francisco   Atlanta

© 1973, 1976 by Harcourt Brace Jovanovich, Inc.

All rights reserved. No part of this publication
may be reproduced or transmitted in any form or by
any means, electronic or mechanical, including
photocopy, recording, or any information storage
and retrieval system, without permission in writing
from the publisher.

DECIDE acronym © 1973 by William Rudelius.

The devices used on the cover of *An Introduction
to Contemporary Business,* Second Edition, are trademarks
belonging to the respective companies. Their use
here in no way indicates an endorsement of the contents
of this book by those companies.

ISBN: 0-15-541648-0
Library of Congress Catalog Card Number: 75-39368

Printed in the United States of America

Illustrations by EH Technical Services

Pages 573–79 constitute a continuation of the copyright page.

PREFACE

American business. It is more than concepts, techniques, opportunities, decisions, problems. American business is men and women. To capture the vigor, the vitality, and the human drama that is American business demands a narrowing of the gap between what is conventionally presented in textbooks and what occurs in real life. In *An Introduction to Contemporary Business,* Second Edition, students will discover real people, places, and events side by side with the modern principles and practices that are necessary to understand contemporary business and that are so important in career selection.

Like its predecessor, the Second Edition of *An Introduction to Contemporary Business* provides a complete, lively, and career-oriented introduction to modern American business. Particular features of the text include:

Up-to-date content: Current business concepts and practices are highlighted. Examples include a discussion of the impact of equal employment opportunity legislation on business (Chapter 3); market-product grids (Chapter 7); the role of computers in accounting (Chapter 11); how businesses use funds (Chapter 13); and the development of multinational business (Chapter 20). The applications and limitations of carefully defined key traditional and contemporary business concepts are illustrated by actual business examples. The Second Edition also contains two new chapters: "Understanding Financial Markets and Financial News" (Chapter 14) and "International Business" (Chapter 20).

A functional framework: The functional areas of business—management and personnel, marketing, production, accounting, finance, and data processing—are the hub of modern business operations. *An Introduction to Contemporary Business,* Second Edition, opens with discussions of the American business system (Chapter 1), the various forms of business ownership and the role of the private enterprise system (Chapter 2), and the legal, social, and ethical responsibilities of business (Chapter 3). These are followed by a thorough examination of the business functions of management (Chapters 4–6), marketing (Chapters 7–9), production (Chapter 10), accounting and budgeting (Chapter 11), finance (Chapters 12–13), financial markets (Chapter 14), and data processing (Chapter 15). The two remaining parts in the Second Edition explore small businesses and small-business ownership (Chapters 16–17), and government and business (Chapter 18), labor unions (Chapter 19), and international business (Chapter 20). The Epilogue examines the current global issues that are expected to affect the business community in the next two decades: economic growth, the quality of life, resource shortages, ecology.

The organization of *An Introduction to Contemporary Business,* Second Edition, permits an unusually complete presentation of the functional areas of business. The social and environmental factors that influence business are carefully examined in Chapter 3 and in the Epilogue. A systematic method for making, implementing, and evaluating business and personal decisions — what we have called the DECIDE process — is presented in detail in Chapter 6.

Practical orientation: An Introduction to Contemporary Business, Second Edition, abounds with practical business examples. Concepts, decisions, applications, successes, failures — and the men and women responsible for them — enrich the text. A series of boxed inserts (some serious, some humorous, all functional) describe actual business situations and often ask students to participate in making business decisions by applying principles discussed in the text. As in the first edition, each chapter in the Second Edition of *An Introduction to Contemporary Business* ends with a "Critical Business Decision" that presents the facts regarding an important decision confronting a well-known business personality. Based on this information, students are asked either to make a decision or to evaluate the decision that was made.

An emphasis on careers: The links between business concepts and prospective business careers for students are carefully developed in the text. In many of the functional chapters, business concepts specifically relate to the individual or to the unit of the firm that is most likely to utilize them. In addition, preceding each "Critical Business Decision" is a "Career Selection" section presenting the alternative job opportunities. "Career Selection" sections at the end of Chapters 4–19 include relevant information relating to individual careers: occupational titles, educational prerequisites, required skills, average salaries, future employment opportunities, and sources of additional career information. The "Career Selection" sections at the end of Chapters 1–3 contain general information about career selection; the "Career Selection" section at the end of Chapter 20 discusses job hunting and handling the initial job interview.

Recent public opinion polls reveal that many Americans are misinformed about business and that some are even hostile to our private enterprise system. One crucial test of an introductory business textbook is whether it gives students a sense of the way business *really* functions. In *An Introduction to Contemporary Business,* Second Edition, we have attempted to portray American business as objectively and as fully as possible and to present a fair description of its successes as well as its failures. If this text corrects even some of the current public misinformation about American business — and sparks interest and enjoyment in the process — we will be fully satisfied.

William Rudelius
W. Bruce Erickson
William J. Bakula, Jr.

ACKNOWLEDGMENTS

Any textbook that examines the broad subject of contemporary business necessarily involves contributions from many sources. *An Introduction to Contemporary Business,* Second Edition, could not have been written without the assistance of the many business leaders and scholars we consulted.

Contributions from the members of the business faculty at the University of Minnesota proved invaluable. Professors Michael F. Barrett, Mario F. Bognanno, Gary W. Dickson, Richard Gaumnitz, Ivan Ross, Alan R. Solem, Roger B. Upson, Orville C. Walker, and Albert K. Wickesberg provided outstanding help in their specialized fields as well as general guidance in detailing business operating concepts. We also gratefully acknowledge the contributions of Professors Roy R. Grundy, College of DuPage; Judith Furrer, Inver Hills Community College; Bipin B. Ajinkya, The University of Florida; Robert A. Brechner, Miami-Dade Community College; Harold Hartzell, Skyline College; John D. Palmer, Anne Arundel Community College, and Raymond Tewell, American River College. We also extend our thanks to Professors Rachel Anderson, University of North Colorado; John E. Bates, Oregon State University; Peter J. Boone, Tidewater Community College; Ronald A. Chapman, Tidewater Community College; Jesse L. Jordan, College of Steubenville; Thomas Nolan, Pierce College; Peter Parker, Jr., Keene State College; and Charles Thompson, Jr., El Camino College.

In addition, we have benefited from the suggestions of several members of the business community. In particular, Henry A. Brown of the Pillsbury Company helped to identify key factors in career planning and résumé preparation, and H. Alvin Domholdt of the U.S. Small Business Administration, Minneapolis, and Glen R. Walters of the First National Bank of Minneapolis provided valuable assistance in the preparation of the discussion of small-business operations in Chapters 16 and 17.

We are also grateful to Thomas R. O'Connell, whose contributions substantially improved both the text and the supplements, and for the assistance of Joyce R. Hegstrom, LuAnne Moe, and Catherine M. Spreigl. And we extend our deep appreciation to the following members of the staff of Harcourt Brace Jovanovich, Inc., for their thoughtful and timely aid: Helen Faye, Lois Paster, Alice Sánchez, and Sandra Weisband. Designer Harry Rinehart provided countless helpful suggestions that are reflected throughout the book. Finally, special thanks go to Mary George and Gary Burke, our editors, who agonized through countless drafts — while retaining both a sense of purpose and a sense of humor.

CONTENTS

ix

MANAGEMENT: MAKING EFFECTIVE DECISIONS, 142

6

PART THREE   MARKETING AND PRODUCTION

MARKETING: CONSUMERS AND THE PRODUCT ELEMENT, 172

7

MARKETING: THE PLACE AND PRICE ELEMENTS, 198

8

THE AMERICAN LABOR MOVEMENT, 496

19

INTERNATIONAL BUSINESS, 520

20

ECONOMIC GROWTH AND THE QUALITY OF LIFE, 544

EPILOGUE

GLOSSARY OF BUSINESS TERMS, 556

REFERENCES, 573

INDEX, 580

PART ONE

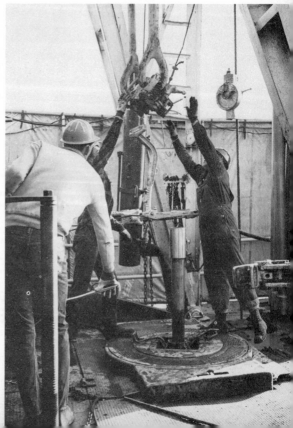

THE AMERICAN
BUSINESS SYSTEM

Every day, American consumers witness an economic miracle: the enormous variety of goods and services that are available to them in unprecedented abundance at times and places largely consistent with their needs. Americans have attained the world's highest standard of living and can afford to satisfy many of their material desires.

Part One provides an overview of the American economy and identifies some of the key principles underlying its remarkable performance. At the same time, this portion of the book probes honestly into the occasional shortcomings of American business. Chapter 1 examines the growth of the U.S. economy since colonial times and then assesses business challenges in the 1970s and 1980s. The organization of American business and the economic role of the private enterprise system are explored in Chapter 2. Finally, Chapter 3 is concerned with the legal effects and the influence of all Americans—both as consumers and as employees—on business. This leads to a discussion of the social responsibility of American business today.

First they tell you you're wrong, and they can prove it. Then they tell you you're right, but it's not important. Then they tell you it's important, but they've known it for years.

Charles F. Kettering

CHAPTER 1

AMERICAN BUSINESS: AN OVERVIEW

Nothing ever came easily for Chester F. Carlson. There were no flashes of genius, no thunderbolts of brilliant inspiration. What successes he achieved were the result of dogged determination, often in the face of repeated and discouraging failures.

Profiles of a Man, an Idea, and a Business

The Man

He received part of his early education in a country school—a school in which he was the only student.* At 12, Chester F. "Chet" Carlson —along with the county welfare board—became the main support of his family. Chet's father had crippling arthritis, and both his parents had contracted tuberculosis. The jobs Chet found in California's San Bernandino Valley were the family's principal source of income.

80 tries, 0 successes

When Chet was 17, his mother died. At 20, he entered the California Institute of Technology and emerged four years later—exhausted from studying, working at odd jobs, and nursing his father—with a B.S. degree in physics. The year was 1930, the start of the deepening national depression. Chet wrote over 80 letters applying for work. He received two replies, both from firms saying they could not use him.

The Idea

After his father's death, Chet moved to New York, where he found a job in the patent department of P.R. Mallory and Company. One night, he worked until midnight on a patent application with a colleague, a job made longer by the extreme difficulty of reproducing the drawings and documents. Chet Carlson turned wearily from his desk to say, "There must be a quicker, better way to make these copies!"

"There must be a . . . better way . . ."

"Sure," the colleague agreed. "But nobody has ever found it."

"Maybe nobody has ever tried to," Chet responded.

So Chet tried. First in his kitchen and then in a dingy room behind an Astoria, New York, beauty parlor. He eventually focused his efforts on an electrophotographic process in which a powder adhered to spots on a

* Sources of information, quotations, and references cited in the text are listed by chapter and page number at the end of the book.

Two people looked at this smudged message that had been transferred onto a piece of waxed paper in Astoria, New York, on October 22, 1938. But each had an opposite reaction: one saw it as a success; the other saw it as a failure. Who was right? (For the answer, see the text.)

surface charged with static electricity. On October 22, 1938, he managed to use this process to transfer the inscription *10-22-38 Astoria* from a glass slide to a piece of waxed paper.

Two differing views

Only two men observed the experiment, but each had a different reaction to it. Chet Carlson was overjoyed. His assistant, looking at the primitive, smudged message, became discouraged; he joined International Business Machines (IBM) instead.

Chet Carlson patented his invention. But he realized he had to find a company that could improve, manufacture, and market his design. During the next six years, he showed his invention to scientists and technicians at 21 major companies, including IBM, Radio Corporation of America, Remington Rand, A.B. Dick, and General Electric.

Not one company was interested.

The Business

A 25-line abstract describing the process appeared in *Kodak's Monthly Abstract Bulletin*. German immigrant John H. Dessauer, a research scientist for the tiny Haloid Company in Rochester, New York, saw the abstract; Haloid, looking for new products to market, was interested. Dessauer and Joseph C. Wilson, Haloid's president, agreed that the process was worth a closer look. After talking to Chet Carlson and to other scientists, Dessauer and Wilson decided to proceed with the project, even though several company experts predicted that it would take ten years and tens of millions of dollars to produce a marketable machine. And Haloid's profits at that time were a mere $138,000 per year.

As late as the 1950s, the prospects for producing and marketing a workable photocopier appeared grim. Not only did technical and financial

ONE FACE OF SUCCESS: PERSISTENCE

In their efforts to obtain sharp photocopies, Chet Carlson and the Haloid Company faced two technical problems that illustrate the dogged persistence which is often the main ingredient of success:

● Chet Carlson originally used sulphur or anthracene powder to adhere to spots on a surface charged with static electricity. But the scientists he consulted, seeking a powder that would improve the quality of the copies, selected selenium—a nonmetallic element whose electrical resistance varies with the influence of light rays. Initial experiments with selenium produced fuzzy copies, and the consulting scientists were ready to conclude that selenium was useless.

But fate smiled. All of the tests using selenium powder had been conducted under ordinary laboratory lights. One scientist—whether by accident or design we still do not know—decided to make a last test using only a dim red lamp. To his amazement, the selenium in combination with the red light produced clear, sharp prints. Today, selenium remains a key component in the photocopying process.

● The consulting scientists also sought to improve Chet Carlson's original method of rubbing a surface with cotton cloth or rabbit fur to develop the necessary static electricity. The scientists tried a bank of sewing needles, with poor results.

Discouraged, they wanted to toss the needles aside. But Chet, who had been observing the experiment, said, "I think you've been holding them too close to the plate. Try increasing the distance."

One of the scientists wearily assured him that it was common knowledge that the further the needles were from the plate, the weaker the charge that they generated would be. Nodding, Chet remained insistent. "I know, but please try it my way. You've got nothing to lose."

To humor him, the experiment was repeated with the needles positioned further from the plate. To everyone's astonishment, Chet's theory—which flew in the face of "common knowledge"—proved correct. The method produced a sharper image and was immediately incorporated in the design.

problems often seem insurmountable, but the market for an effective office copier appeared small. Haloid hired large, reputable, New York marketing research agencies to conduct a series of market surveys. One survey questioned a large number of businessmen about the potential market for such a copier. Their projection: not more than 5000 copiers could be used in American offices. If this estimate were correct, Haloid could never even recover its original investment in Chet Carlson's idea.

The Results

And what became of the man, the idea, and the company in this American business drama? Perhaps you know or can guess the answer.

The man, Chet Carlson, became wealthy. He quietly donated untold fortunes to charitable and public service organizations, including millions of dollars to his alma mater, the California Institute of Technology.

The idea of using photoelectrical principles to provide paper copies was given a name. It was called "xerography," which is Greek for "dry writing" or "dry copying."

The firm was renamed. The Haloid Company became Haloid–Xerox, Inc., and then simply the Xerox Corporation. By the mid-1970s, the company had grown from a few hundred people in Rochester, New York, to

105,000 employees who were scattered in 40 plants around the world. Fortunately for Xerox, the original market estimate of a total of 5000 copiers was wrong, as evidenced by the 26 billion Xerox copies produced annually by its 580,000 copiers in operation.

Today, Xerox is considered one of the best managed and one of the most socially responsible firms in American business. Its $300,000,000 in annual profits place Xerox among the 20 most profitable American corporations—a far cry from the $138,000 in annual profits it was earning when it first invested in Chester Carlson's primitive idea.

Chet Carlson, xerography, and the Haloid Company, respectively, represent the three major concepts underlying the study of business in this book—the people, the ideas, and the businesses that in combination have produced our present standard of living in the United States. Chet Carlson's story also provides an introduction to the three topics to be covered in this chapter: (1) the major developments in American business, (2) the structure of the American economy today, and (3) the vital issues facing business in the future.

John H. Dessauer, Chester F. Carlson, and Joseph C. Wilson of Haloid (later Xerox) demonstrate an early dry-copying machine in Rochester, New York, 1948.

Source: Alex Groner, *The American Heritage History of American Business* (New York: American Heritage Publishing, Co., Inc., 1972), p. 307.

Major Developments in American Business

Business, broadly understood as all private economic activity undertaken for profit, literally came to the United States with the *Mayflower*. The Pilgrims arriving at Plymouth Rock in 1620 sought religious freedom. But the boats that carried these and later colonists to the New World were launched by joint stock companies—the forerunners of today's corporations—and were manned by merchant adventurers. By the time the Declaration of Independence was proclaimed in 1776, the 2.5 million Americans along the eastern seaboard had already displayed considerable aptitude for commerce and industry. Wages were higher in America than in Europe, the exploits of American skippers and their crews were famous, and colonial businessmen produced a seventh of the world's iron.

The early American economy: primitive but promising

Yet the American economy was primitive: most staples—salt and woolens, for example—had to be imported. During the Revolutionary War, the wise Benjamin Franklin found himself arguing that American bows and arrows could defeat English muskets—a good bowman could shoot four arrows in the time it took a marksman to load and fire a single shot! The probable explanation for Franklin's awkward position: the colonists produced no potassium nitrate, an essential ingredient of gunpowder.

Private business, which is responsible for 60 percent of all economic activity, has played a vital role in the transformation of American society. In short, business has been central to the development of American society and, as such, must share the credit for the nation's accomplishments as well as the blame for its shortcomings. Let us briefly identify the mind-boggling accomplishments of the American business system over the past two centuries, as well as the business-related problems we face in today's society.

From Independence to the Civil War

Whatever their reasons for emigrating, the first settlers faced one common, all-absorbing problem: wresting food from an often unfriendly land. Yet, in time, the colonists developed other interests as well. An early traveler in the Boston of 1744 noted that talk focused "on commerce and trade" and that other economic activities included "shipping, lumber, and fish."

Agriculture dominated the colonial economy

The colonial aristocracy, whose members read like the players in a historical pageant, clearly illustrates the principal ways in which the early colonists made their livings: George Washington, probably the wealthiest Southerner, was a Virginia plantation owner; John Hancock inherited a fortune based on merchant trade; Stephen Girard and Robert Morris

helped to finance the Revolutionary War through their banking and merchant connections; John Jacob Astor began to build America's first great fortune through fur trading and real-estate speculation. Agriculture, fishing, whaling, fur trading, commerce, banking, and land speculation were the colonists' main economic pursuits.

✔ **The industrial revolution.** Then one of those extraordinary events occured that irrevocably alters age-old patterns of thought and behavior. The *industrial revolution* has been described as "the replacement of hand tools by power-driven machines." Begun in England around 1760, it reached the United States about 30 years later. Typical of the early stages of the industrial revolution was the widespread use the the power loom, the spinning jenny (which permitted the simultaneous spinning of several yarns), the machine lathe, and the steamboat.

Ironically, the term "industrial revolution" is a misleading way to describe the ecomonic and technological events that began in America around 1790 and that continue to exert a profound influence in this country today. Also, the revolution was as much agricultural as industrial. During the colonial period, farm families comprised more than 95 percent of the population; even as late as 1850, four out of every five families lived in rural areas (Figure 1-1). Such agricultural innovations as the iron plow, the mechanical planter, and the corn reaper, which were introduced in the 1830s, freed the economy from an overwhelming dependence on the land and facilitated industrial growth.

The industrial revolution: both industrial and agricultural

The pace of agricultural progress has continued to accelerate. By the 1970s farmers accounted for only 5 percent of the American population.

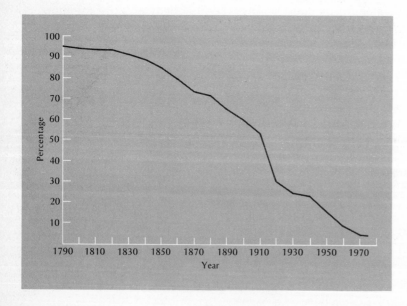

1-1

Percentage of U.S. population in agriculture, 1790–1975. This figure shows that the number of Americans living and working on farms has declined over the years from 95 percent in 1790 to less than 5 percent in 1975.

Source: *Statistical Abstract of the United States.*

Yet they were able to provide more than enough food for the nonagricultural majority, who were freed to become specialists in manufacturing, retailing, and other business activities.

Thus, the industrial revolution can be viewed as a gradual but an accelerating process of change that began in 1790 and that extends to the present. In this sense, Americans of the 1970s are both its beneficiaries and its participants.

In its formative years, the industrial revolution was a product of three interrelated changes: the rise of science and technology, mass production, and improved transportation.

✔ The rise of science and technology. During the nineteenth century, the pace of scientific discoveries accelerated to an unprecedented degree, particularly in the 1830s and 1840s. These years saw the advent of the telegraph, the mechanical harvester, the sewing machine, the Colt revolver, vulcanized rubber, and a hundred other innovations, all of which were designed to improve everyday life. Samuel F.B. Morse, inventor of the telegraph, established the Magnetic Telegraph Company, the forerunner of Western Union; Cyrus McCormick created the mechanical harvester, the first of International Harvester's many farm implements; and I.M. Singer developed the sewing machine and founded the Singer Company. The modern corporation, with its specialized research laboratories, is a logical continuation of the fruitful cooperation between business and science that evolved during the early stages of the industrial revolution.

The rise
of technology:
applying science
to everyday life

✔ Mass production. The foundation for today's system of mass production was laid in 1799, when business pioneer Eli Whitney received an order for 10,000 muskets from the U.S. Army. On the basis of the reputation for mechanical genius he earned when he invented the cotton gin, the Army also advanced Whitney $5000, even though he had never built a musket before.

Snowstorms and trouble in obtaining further financing delayed plant construction. As a result, Whitney missed the delivery date for the first load of muskets. According to one story, army inspectors appeared one morning at his plant to find not one completed musket—just boxes of parts. They were dumbfounded. Whitney told them to select ten pieces from each box and then assembled ten muskets in front of the astonished inspectors. This experience so impressed them that Whitney was allowed to retain the contract. The musket pieces had been manufactured by ordinary metalworkers using fixtures and gauges to produce *interchangeable* or *standard parts*—parts so similar in physical characteristics as to be indistinguishable. Thus, a skilled gunsmith who could work on only one gun at a time and who could not produce two identical guns was not needed. Whitney's interchangeable or standard parts were to provide the foundation for mass production.

Mass production:
a new approach
to increasing output

✔ **Improved transportation.** The Constitution took the first decisive step toward creating mass markets by granting the federal government sole authority in regulating trade between the states. Over the centuries, the United States became what has been called "the world's greatest Common Market."

In the early 1800s, however, the problem was not a legal but a physical one—the inability to transport goods over a long distance at a reasonable cost. Roads were exceedingly primitive, and ships could reach only the coastal cities and towns. Quick to recognize the problem, federal and state governments first subsidized a round of frenzied road construction and later embarked on a frantic race to build canals, several of which proved to be financial disasters. Steamboats and the famous clipper ships substantially improved water transportation.

Railroads paved the way to mass markets

But it was the advent of the railroads in 1830, and especially the second wave of railroad construction around 1850, that heralded modern mass markets. The changes brought about by the railroads were swift and dramatic: by 1863, Civil War armies and their supplies were largely transported by rail.

✔ **An inadequate financial system.** Despite notable progress during the post-Revolutionary War period, the United States was handicapped by its inadequate financial base. Capital was in extremely short supply, and eventually more than half the money needed to finance American farms and factories was borrowed from England. Currency shortages were chronic, and private banks were permitted to issue their own (often worthless) paper bills. As a result of America's weak financial structure, a series of *panics*—sharp recessions in economic activity—descended like plagues about every five years.

Weaknesses of the pre-Civil War economy

From the Civil War to World War I

The post-Civil War era in the United States has been described as "the age of electricity" or "the age of Edison." Especially noteworthy were the advances in the processing of industrial raw materials and in mass communication. The Bessemer process and its refinements revolutionized steel production. Widespread use of the telegraph, the telephone, and later still the radio ushered in an era of instantaneous communication that produced shattering long-term economic and social consequences.

The age of electricity and mass communication

In short, the industrial revolution was a cumulative process. The three basic changes that spurred the revolution—the rise of science, mass production, and improved transportation—continued to operate after the Civil War with undiminished intensity. In addition, four new facets of the industrial revolution came into play.

✔ **Finance capitalism** The post-Civil War era saw the rise of a new force in American economic life—"the money power," centered largely in

Wall Street in downtown Manhattan. Fear of this new power prompted many Americans to label businessmen "robber barons."

Finance capitalism marked America's economic and financial maturity

Popular mistrust of Wall Street power and of robber baron manipulations was not entirely misplaced, but it fails to tell the whole story. The growth of New York City as a financial center was largely a sign that the young American economy was beginning to generate enough capital internally to finance both factory and farm. No longer would American businessmen and farmers be dependent on London financiers for funds.

Public suspicion, however, was not without foundation. The notorious Erie Ring, led by Jim Fisk and Jay Gould, frequently used advance inside information to bilk unsuspecting investors and sometimes initiated rumors to further the Ring's stock manipulations. The financial giant of the era was the aloof J. Pierpont Morgan, who performed many of the duties of a modern Secretary of the Treasury from his famous office at Broad and Wall Streets. Presidents of the United States received Morgan's help when financial panic threatened.

The financier still suffers from a "bad press"

In many respects, the efforts of eastern financiers were beneficial. Morgan himself took great pains to see that the businesses he financed were soundly capitalized and competitively viable. Morgan's money enabled Thomas A. Edison to build the world's first central power station —a development that advanced the spread of electricity by many years.

Americans idolize an inventor like Thomas Edison or Chester Carlson who realizes millions from his discovery of a new product. But many Americans still view the financier who makes it possible to produce and market an invention with a mixture of distrust and fear. Yet for every Edison or Carlson, many financiers and other investors have lost billions of dollars on inventions that failed to sell in the marketplace.

✔ **The factory system.** The post-Civil War years ushered in an unprecedented period of expansion in the size of business. In many industries, larger firms were able to take maximum advantage of the economies mass production offered by using money provided by finance capitalism. Thus, the *factory system* was born. Men and machines were gathered in large manufacturing establishments known as factories or plants. A business (or a firm) might own and operate a single plant or a complex of plants distributed throughout the world. The factory system so successfully provided goods of comparatively high quality at reasonable prices that it quickly replaced the older *handcraft system,* comprised of highly skilled craftsmen employed in small shops.

For most of us, the word "factory" brings an automobile assembly line to mind—and with good reason. Improvements in both the factory system and mass production were accelerated by the *moveable assembly line,* introduced by Henry Ford in the early twentieth century. Ford, observing that a typical worker in a metal shop spent most of his time moving materials from job to job, had a flash of insight one day: why not send the job to the man rather than the man to the job? In 1913, Ford's Highland Park plant introduced the moveable assembly line, in which incomplete

WHY STUDY BUSINESS?

Although business is the dominant economic institution in the United States, not everyone wants to be in business. In planning a business career, it is obviously necessary to study the field carefully. But why should anyone who is unsure of an occupational choice or who is planning another career study business? In addition to the fact that plans may change, there are four main reasons why an understanding of business is important:

1. *Personal challenge:* For many people, business is intellectually challenging. Business concepts are often in the forefront of knowledge, introducing ideas that are adopted later by government and educational institutions.
2. *Social awareness:* Today — as never before — Americans are asking difficult business-related questions such as "Are corporations 'ripping off' consumers?" and "Are giant labor unions too powerful?" Reasoned answers to such questions require an understanding of the critically important private sector.
3. *Solving practical, everyday problems:* Applying techniques for analyzing business problems to personal day-to-day situations can yield substantial benefits. For example, topics discussed in this book can help the reader, as a consumer

and as an investor, to make rational choices between alternatives, such as deciding whether to go to college on a full-time or on a part-time basis.
4. *Personal economic gain:* Education beyond high school can increase an individual's lifetime earnings. A recent study, for example, suggests that one to three years of college will add 14 percent to a person's lifetime earnings and that four years of college will add 57 percent. Many experts believe that skills such as the ability to work with, motivate, and coordinate others will be scarce in the 1970s and 1980s. Traditionally, business has tried to develop skills in precisely these areas, which suggests that understanding and applying such skills may improve a person's job opportunities.

This book encourages the reader to achieve these four benefits of studying business. In addition, because personal economic gain is closely related to choosing a career wisely, each chapter closes with a "Career Selection" section that describes what factors to consider in selecting an occupation or that discusses career opportunities currently available in the major business fields.

products were carried past men and machines whose positions were fixed and who performed carefully specified operations on the products as they passed through the various production stages. The moveable assembly line quickly became the heart of production in twentieth-century factories.

But in some instances, Americans paid a stiff price: one or a few large businesses occasionally dominated an industry — eliminating competition, controlling output, and artificially raising prices. And workers were often given boring, repetitive jobs.

✔ **Scientific management.** As the size of the average plant grew, it soon became physically impossible for a small group of people to control all aspects of the business. Specialization in the corporate office became as essential to efficiency as specialization in the shop. In addition, as stock markets developed and as many companies became publicly owned, few individual shareholders were willing to assume the day-to-day responsibility of managing a business operation. These two forces, the growing complexity of business and the spread of stock ownership, produced a

The rise
of professional
management
and specialized
management
techniques

new business breed: the professional *executives* or *managers,* who special-ize in knowing how to run a business and who may even specialize fur-ther by becoming expert in a particular *functional area* such as accounting, finance, or marketing.

One of the pioneers in professional management was Frederick W. Taylor, who developed his famous ideas about *scientific management* in the 1890s. Taylor's stress on planning led to the establishment of business management as a separate field of study. Like a modern "efficiency ex-pert" in a factory, Taylor undertook detailed, on-the-job studies of blue-collar workers: what they did, their interactions with machinery, and the conditions under which they worked. Taylor's goal was to institute changes that would not only increase production but that would also be humane.

✔ **Mass-marketing systems.** Improvements in transportation and communication systems following the Civil War were highlighted by the completion of the first transcontinental railroad in 1869. And the com-bined factors of mass production, the factory system, and scientific man-agement contributed to the ever more efficient manufacture of products.

The result of these forces was the beginning of a genuine mass market for manufactured goods in the United States. Innovative mass-marketing sys-tems soon followed. Prior to the Civil War, most products were sold in general stores or trading posts in local communities. But large department stores carrying many different products soon emerged. Later, people purchased merchandise by mail from mail-order houses: Montgomery Ward began operating in 1872. These were among the first systems designed to distribute products efficiently to mass markets throughout the United States. They were followed in the nineteenth and the twentieth centuries by "five-and-ten-cent stores," chain stores, self-service super-markets, discount houses, and automatic vending machines.

From World War I to the 1970s

By 1920, the average American could look on the world with complacency. The United States stood at the pinnacle of world economic power, and an even brighter future loomed ahead.

Amazingly, not even the Great Depression of 1929-39 could prevent America's bright economic prospects from being realized. Robert A. Brady, one of the foremost experts on the application of science to contem-porary business, identifies four fundamental twentieth-century revolu-tions that have profoundly affected the American economy.

✔ **The chemical revolution.** The chemical industry arose in Ger-many around 1900. Given its impetus by the lack of access to German chemicals during World War I, the chemical industry in the United States grew by leaps and bounds after 1920. Today, chemical processing ranks among the nation's most dynamic industries. Witness the bewildering variety of new labels confronting the modern consumer: orlon, dacron, Teflon, fiberglass, and so on; each label represents a highly useful, entirely man-made product.

✔ **The standards revolution.** When Eli Whitney began production of his new musket, he established *standards* for each interchangeable part —tolerances or limits from which a given part would not be allowed to deviate. Each firing pin, barrel, trigger, or other part that Whitney produced was honed to an accuracy of hundredths of an inch—a high standard in the early phase of the industrial revolution.

Technological improvements in the twentieth century enabled industry to build parts that were accurate to thousandths of an inch and in many instances to integrate hundreds of parts into a single product. The incredibly narrow tolerances involved in the thousands of components in an Apollo spacecraft represent the success of the standards revolution. Today, American business faces the ultimate test in the standards revolution: whether to adopt the metric system or to continue with the British measurement system of feet and pounds. The conversion, if undertaken, will cost American industry billions of dollars.

✔ **The electronics and automation revolution.** Since World War II, the electronics industry has made notable progress, especially in the use of transistors and integrated circuits to miniaturize its products. Even after a quarter of a century, the effects of its most spectacular product, the computer, are not totally clear.

But the electronics industry's most significant achievement lies in its contribution to mass production. In the early 1900s, pioneering businessmen began to develop primitive gauges and control devices that utilized electrical impulses to measure the level and quality of a factory's output. After World War II, the effectiveness of electronic control devices improved steadily. In its most recent phase, mass production is based on the emerging concept of *automation*—the mechanical control, usually by electronic impulses, of many aspects of production. The central idea underlying the principle of automation is that the entire factory is treated as if it were a single giant machine. Thus, the ultimate implication of complete automation is the elimination in the factory not only of workers but of most managers and executives.

✔ **The energy revolution.** The substitution of inanimate for human and animal energy contributed greatly to the efficiency of mass production. Water and steam were used to power early machines, but today coal, oil, and natural gas supply more than 95 percent of the energy consumed by industry.

Since known fossil-fuel reserves are limited, atomic power could

WHY IN AMERICA?

Why did the industrial revolution have such an impact in the United States? Historians have offered many explanations—ranging from America's temperate climate to its Puritan emphasis on frugality and hard work. But Swedish novelist Wilhelm Moberg may have provided the keenest insight in his famous trilogy, *The Emigrants:*

A price was demanded for the liberty of the new country; much thought, a great deal of labor. From the irresponsible, responsibility was extracted; from the selfish, unselfish effort; from the arbitrary, willingness to listen to the opinions of others. . . . Through the new country's demands

on the immigrants, powers within them would be developed that they had no use for in the homeland. They changed America, and America changed them.

It probably can never be conclusively established that business "made America great." But throughout the short history of the United States, most Americans have found challenge and opportunity in business and private agriculture. If, as Moberg suggests, America extracted previously hidden abilities from its citizens, business and private agriculture made an immense contribution to America's human as well as to its economic development.

Harnessing atomic and solar power for industry

prove to be the most important aspect of the energy revolution. If, as some experts predict, atomic fusion or solar energy is harnessed for peaceful uses within the next two decades, an unlimited supply of energy could become available. But the "energy crisis" of the 1970s illustrates how precarious the balance between energy supplies and demands are. Since mass production requires great quantities of energy, the twentieth-century energy revolution is one of man's greatest continuing needs.

The American Economy Today

In the two centuries after the Declaration of Independence, the American economy underwent a remarkable transformation: what was an infant in colonial times had become a giant by the 1970s. The population swelled from 2.5 million to 210 million, while the settled geographic area expanded tenfold. In the 1970s, the United States accounted for 6 percent of the world's land mass and for 7 percent of its population, producing and consuming a third of the world's supply of goods and services.

Vastness, variety, and changeability characterize the U.S. economy

In the mid-1970s, the United States produced goods and services valued at nearly 1.4 trillion dollars—a sum equivalent to a stack of dollar bills that would reach the moon and return part way back to earth. This vast output is divided among hundreds of thousands of different kinds of goods and services produced by the nation's 10 million businesses. New products are introduced constantly. For example, only three years after its development, indoor-outdoor carpeting was in the homes of millions of consumers.

Since economic and noneconomic aspects of life intermingle, the

American economy cannot be treated in isolation. Nevertheless, several trends—mainly economic, but to some degree social and cultural—warrant attention.

The Affluent Society

One of the effects of the industrial revolution was to raise living standards enormously. By conventional standards, the quality and usefulness of products improved dramatically. The life expectancy rose due to improved medicine and better housing; labor-saving appliances and central heating increased personal comfort. Many economists believe that the quality of products rises at least 1 or 2 percent per year.

The most dramatic effect of the industrial revolution was to increase the quantity of goods and services available to every American. The key statistical measure of quantity is *gross national product* (GNP)—the money value of all goods and services produced in a given nation during a designated time period (usually one year).

GNP:
the money value
of production
in an economy

The GNP for the United States in 1974 was $1.4 trillion. When GNP is expressed in this form, it is often described as GNP in current dollars, or *money GNP*. If GNP has been adjusted to reflect changing price levels, it is usually called GNP in constant dollars, or *real GNP*. Real 1974 GNP, based on 1967 prices, amounted to $946 billion. Another important measure of economic growth is *per-capita GNP*—the money value of all goods and services produced for each member of the population. In 1974, per-capita money GNP amounted to $6592.

Since 1800, per-capita real GNP—a measure of general living standards—has grown at an average annual rate of approximately 2 percent; since 1945, the annual rate of increase has been about 3 percent. Thus, as a result of the industrial revolution, the quantity of goods produced in the United States has grown both absolutely and on a per-capita basis.

Figure 1-2 illustrates three ways of viewing GNP. The *output approach* shows the economic sector that produces the goods and services. Manufacturing heads the list with 25 percent of GNP, while agriculture accounts for 5 percent of GNP. The *final-demand approach* indicates who buys the goods and services. In the American economy, private consumers purchase the bulk of output (62 percent), with federal and state governments second (21½ percent). The *income approach* shows who earns the receipts from the sale of the goods and services. Labor, as the recipient of wages and salaries, accounts for 61 percent of GNP, while total profits (proprietary and corporate) account for 15 percent.

Three perspectives on GNP

Some experts maintain that the average person has acquired more than a necessary amount of material possessions and that the United States should redirect its energies from raising production to meeting more important noneconomic goals. This view merits further attention and will be examined in the Epilogue. While the consequences of afflu-

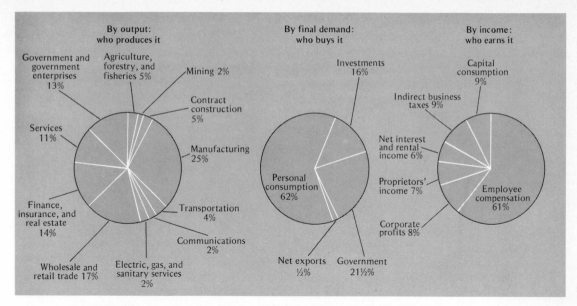

By output:
who produces it

Government and government enterprises 13%
Agriculture, forestry, and fisheries 5%
Mining 2%
Contract construction 5%
Services 11%
Manufacturing 25%
Finance, insurance, and real estate 14%
Transportation 4%
Wholesale and retail trade 17%
Electric, gas, and sanitary services 2%
Communications 2%

By final demand:
who buys it

Investments 16%
Personal consumption 62%
Net exports ½%
Government 21½%

By income:
who earns it

Capital consumption 9%
Indirect business taxes 9%
Net interest and rental income 6%
Proprietors' income 7%
Employee compensation 61%
Corporate profits 8%

1-2 Three ways to slice a trillion-dollar economy:
by who produces it, who buys it, and who earns it.

Source: *Survey of Current Business,* July 1974, U.S. Department of Commerce.

ence are controversial, America's relative affluence has been well established. Data on the actual quantities of goods that consumers own and on per-capita GNP reveal that the United States is indeed an affluent society.

The Service Economy

Business experts often contrast goods and services. *Goods* normally refer to material items: home appliances, machinery, and other tangible products. *Services* are intangible items: repairing a television set, taking an ocean voyage, administering a government program. The service economy encompasses transportation, communication, public utilities, trade, finance, government, and private household and other services. Currently, services as defined above constitute about 60 percent of GNP. In 1975, 65 percent of all workers were employed in services.

Services dominate the modern American economy

In its relatively short history, the American economy has undergone two sweeping changes: from an agricultural to an industrial base in the 1800s, and from a product to a service orientation in the last two decades. Mass production techniques are not widely used in services. As a result, output per worker has grown at less than half the industrial rate, while rapidly increasing labor costs have forced the price of services to rise more than twice as fast as general prices.

Thus, the shift to services—one of the most important contemporary economic changes—creates both problems and opportunities. As services become more important in the American economy, the relatively low output of service workers increasingly constrains a rise in living standards. Moreover, rewards for those able to apply mass production concepts to services are considerable.

The Rise of the Public Sector

Government is of increasing importance in the American economy. Government spending on goods and services advanced from 8 percent of GNP in 1929 to 21½ percent of GNP in 1974. If welfare, social security payments, subsidies, and the like are included, government activities account for nearly 40 percent of GNP. Moreover, through laws and regulations, taxes and stockpiles, government influence over the American economy has grown sharply during the past four decades.

The private sector dominates the production of goods and services

Economists customarily distinguish between the private and the public sector. The *private sector* refers to all economic institutions—business firms, foundations, cooperatives, and so on—that are not owned by the government. The *public sector* includes all federal, state, and local government activities. In terms of total production, the private sector is by far the dominant economic force, controlling more than 87 percent of GNP. While the public sector generates less than 13 percent of the physical production of the United States, it purchases vast quantities of goods and services directly from business and transfers income from group to group

The public sector is important in the distribution of goods and services

(through the social security system, for example). The result is that spending and taxation by the public sector have important effects on the American economy. The public sector, then, has been a large and growing force in the American economy of the 1970s, especially in determining who has the purchasing power to buy the goods and services produced in the private sector.

The Interest-Group Society

The American scene is dominated by *interest groups* (sometimes referred to as pressure groups)—people or organizations bound together to achieve similar objectives. The "big three"—big business, big labor, and big government—are often viewed as the most important interest groups.

The "big three" interest groups: business, labor, and government

Big business first emerged in the post-Civil War era. Today, giant corporations like General Motors and American Telephone and Telegraph employ hundreds of thousands of workers and generate revenues larger than the GNPs of many nations in the world. In fact, seven companies—General Motors, Ford, American Telephone and Telegraph, Exxon, Texaco, Gulf Oil, and IBM—normally realize a quarter of all U.S. corporate profits.

Big labor soon followed big business. Although there had long been stirrings in the labor movement (the first workers were organized shortly after the Revolutionary War), labor became a dominant interest group with the advent of the New Deal in 1933. Millions of workers, both skilled and unskilled, were organized into unions. Today, the AFL-CIO represents nearly a fifth of all employees in the United States, and membership in the nation's largest union, the International Brotherhood of Teamsters, is almost 1.9 million.

Big government also gained momentum under the New Deal. By the 1970s, the federal government alone employed more than 3 million people, and the federal budget exceeded $350 billion. One-fourth of all U.S. employees work for the federal, state, or local governments.

Highly specialized and sometimes very powerful interest groups have also prospered: the American Medical Association, the National Rifle Association, and the U.S. Army Corps of Engineers are examples. The American people have come a long way from a nation of self-sufficient farmers; today, most Americans look to well-organized and often militant pressure groups to advance their interests.

The Knowledge Society

Because knowledge tends to become more useful as it accumulates, it is a critical factor in modern industrial economies. The United States has experienced an explosion in what many experts call the *knowledge industries* of scientific research and education. Between 1940 and 1970, research expenditures expanded from less than $1 billion to approximately $28 billion—a high tribute to the value of knowledge.

Education expenditures have grown as rapidly—from $2.5 billion in 1940 to more than $77 billion in 1970. Although educational expenditures have not grown as rapidly since 1974, education and scientific research are *Since 1941* still rated among the fastest-growing sectors in the American economy. *the knowledge* Knowledge has joined mass production in the forefront of the new indus-*industries* trial revolution. *have expanded*

spectacularly These growing trends in the U.S. economy, from affluence to concern with knowledge, indicate how far the American people have traveled since their colonial beginnings. Business and America have literally grown up together.

Business Challenges of the 1970s and the 1980s

In his book *Future Shock,* Alvin Toffler quotes a Chinese saying that "To prognosticate is extremely difficult, especially with respect to the future." But in spite of the difficulties, a vital task of all leaders in business, education, and government is to anticipate the future and to take necessary actions to deal with it. In 1970, 120 men and women—business experts selected from eight sectors of society—identified the key business-related problems that they saw in the future. Surprisingly, neither the 120 experts who contributed to this study nor Toffler in his 1968 book *Future Shock* even *hinted* at the energy problems that became a dominant concern of business and the general public in the mid-1970s. Concerns about energy, inflation, and unemployment—in addition to severe food shortages in many underdeveloped nations—would certainly change the problems appearing in any study undertaken today.

Only change is a constant in today's world

In summary, Americans are confronting many potentially serious challenges in the late 1970s and in the 1980s: inflation, unemployment, environmental decay, the energy crisis, the quality of life, participation in the world economy—issues which we will discuss in later chapters. But change is the one constant factor in today's world. Making history our guide, then, the American public and the American business system will overcome these challenges only to confront a future series of problems and opportunities.

KEY POINTS TO REMEMBER

1. Business is all private economic activity undertaken for profit.
2. Four major events influenced American business between Independence and the Civil War: the industrial revolution; the rise of science and technology; the introduction of mass production; and improved transportation.
3. Major events shaping American business between the Civil War and World War I include: finance capitalism; the factory system; scientific management; and mass-marketing systems.
4. Since World War I, four "revolutions" have dramatically influenced American business: those in chemistry, standards, electronics and automation, and energy.
5. Today's American economy is characterized by greater affluence; an increasing importance of special-interest groups; and dramatic growth in services, in the public sector, and in the "knowledge industries" (scientific research and education).
6. Gross national product (GNP) is the money value of all goods and services produced in a nation during a designated time period (usually one year). Two related measures are real GNP and per capita GNP.
7. The study of business offers four potential benefits: the personal challenge and excitement a business career provides; a social awareness that can lead to improvements in the business system; help in solving day-to-day personal problems; and an opportunity for personal economic gain.

8. The American people and the American business system face key problems in the 1970s and 1980s: inflation, unemployment, environmental decay, the energy crisis, the quality of life, and participation in the world economy. But as these problems are overcome, others will emerge—for constant change is a way of life in today's world.

QUESTIONS FOR DISCUSSION

1. What is the industrial revolution? In what ways is its name misleading?

2. Mass production concepts are often difficult to apply to the service sector. For example, have mass production concepts been applied to your education so far? If so, in what ways? What characteristics of education make it difficult to use mass production techniques effectively?

3. Critics of the industrial revolution and of the role of business in it focus their attacks on five areas: (a) the disadvantages of mass production; (b) the "exploitation" of workers, including long hours, child labor, and low pay; (c) the unequal distribution of wealth; (d) the mistreatment of minorities, especially blacks and Indians; and (e) the destruction of natural resources through such practices as strip mining. What is your assessment of each of these criticisms?

4. What is gross national product? Distinguish between money, real, and per capita GNP. Why is each important?

SHORT CASES AND PROBLEMS

1. Write a memorandum to yourself on your "personal career evaluation," listing (a) your goals, (b) your assessment of your strengths and weaknesses, (c) your experience, and (d) whether or not you believe a career in business is for you.

2. The following data for the years 1972–74 are taken from official government reports:

Statistic	1972	1973	1974
Money GNP (billions of dollars)	1158	1295	1397
Consumer price index (1967 = 100)	125.3	133.1	147.7
Population of the United States (millions)	208.9	210.4	211.9

(a) Using the consumer price index when appropriate, calculate real GNP, per-capita money GNP, and per-capita real GNP for 1972–1974.

(b) Make the same calculations for each year between 1975 and the last calendar year. (*Hint:* You can find the appropriate data on GNP, prices, and population in the *Statistical Abstract of the United States,* various publications of the U.S. Department of Commerce, the *Federal Reserve Bulletin,* and the latest *Economic Report of the President.*)

CAREER SELECTION: OBJECTIVES AND SPECIFIC STEPS

"How do I want to earn my living?" During the next ten years, about 34 million young men and women will answer this question as they join the American labor force. Each day, tens of thousands of young people make vital decisions about careers and employers that will affect them for the rest of their lives.

THE OBJECTIVE AND THE IMPORTANCE OF PROPER CAREER SELECTION

The process of choosing a career may involve informal conversations with friends and relatives or a formal in-school guidance course. But the objective of both informal and formal career counseling is the same: to match an individual's talents and goals with those required in a given career.

Selecting the right career is important. It can mean the difference between personal and professional fulfillment or a long series of bad working experiences evidenced by "job hopping" and unemployment. Indeed, personnel experts identify three key benefits resulting from effective career selection: greater personal satisfaction, greater financial rewards and responsibilities, and a greater contribution to society. Yet, while students like you spend thousands of hours in school and college, their career choices may often be hit-or-miss decisions that are based on only a few minutes or hours of thought.

STEPS IN CHOOSING A CAREER

A systematic approach to career selection will increase your chances of obtaining a challenging and a satisfying position. We will therefore identify five key steps in career selection and relate them to the information presented in this book.

1. *Assessing your personal characteristics.* In selecting a career, it is essential to evaluate your personal strengths and weaknesses in terms of aptitudes, interests, mental ability, manual dexterity, and personality. These characteristics can be related to key self-appraisal questions. For example, "Would I prefer to work with things, with ideas, or with people?" "Do I want to see the physical results of my work?" "Would I rather work independently or be one part of a team?" "Could I handle a job that requires physical stamina?" "A supervisory position?" The answer to these questions must be found jointly through self-appraisal, career-guidance testing, and counseling.

2. *Assessing employment and industry trends.* No one can predict future employment opportunities precisely. Yet, being aware of expected industrial demands for various skills may help you to identify the types of occupations you should pursue and those you should avoid. Employment and industry trends will be discussed in the Career Selection sections at the end of Chapters 2 and 3.

3. *Matching careers and personal characteristics.* People who like to work with numbers may become engineers or accountants. Yet, a more careful assessment of mathematical abilities suggests other career opportunities in statistics, market research, and computer programming. The job opportunities for people who enjoy direct public contact are innumerable, ranging from personnel counseling to industrial or retail buying or selling. Thus, a key goal in career selection is to consider a variety of jobs — not just one or two — that complement your own personal characteristics. Each Career Selection section at the end of Chapters 4 through 19 relates various career opportunities to the chapter topics. Where information is available, each job is described in terms of the nature of the work, the educational and/or experience requirements of the position, recent earnings, expected employment outlook, and sources of additional information. In preparing this material, we have drawn largely on the two references cited below.

4. *Obtaining the necessary education and training.* Some jobs discussed in Chapters 4 through 19 are open to high-school graduates; others are open to people with two-year or four-year college degrees; and still others are open to people with graduate degrees. Some are entry-level positions; others require years of experience. To plan your career effectively, you must (1) recognize these facts, and (2) acquire the necessary education and training to secure the position you desire.

5. *Securing the desired position.* Campus recruiters visit many colleges to interview prospective employees. You can take advantage of such opportunities, but you may also find it necessary to go beyond the assistance of your college placement office to obtain interviews with other employers for whom you might like to work. In either case, selling yourself effectively is essential to securing a job. Steps in "selling oneself" vary from developing an effective personal resumé (to be discussed in Chapter 5) to knowing how to ask and answer questions in a job interview. Some job-hunting and interviewing tips appear at the end of Chapter 20.

Following these five steps may not guarantee you an ideal job, but they will certainly increase your chances of undertaking a satisfying career.

Business Career References

1. *Occupational Outlook Handbook, 1974–75 Edition,* Bulletin 1785 (Washington: U.S. Government Printing Office, 1974).
2. Don Dillon, "Toward Matching Personal and Job Characteristics," *Occupational Outlook Quarterly* (Spring 1975), pp. 3–18.

A CRITICAL BUSINESS DECISION

—made by C. Peter McColough

THE SITUATION It is 1974, and the Xerox Corporation faces a crucial test. Leadership of the company that converted Chester Carlson's xerographic technique into an actual office photocopier has passed into the hands of C. Peter McColough, Xerox's Chairman of the Board. Born in Halifax and graduated from Dalhousie University Law School, Dalhousie, Canada, McColough received a master's degree from the Harvard Business School. He joined Haloid (Xerox's predecessor) in 1954 at the age of 31, and rapidly moved up through the marketing department to become sales vice president and, in 1966, Xerox's president.

McColough insists "I've tried, I think successfully, to decentralize decision making"—to allow important decisions to be made at lower levels in the firm. Yet, he often goes deep into the organization to find out what people think. About reports, he says, "I don't pay a lot of attention to them because I came that route." Instead, McColough observes, "I know what a salesman can say, and before I see the reports, they go through 15 hands and I know what they do to them." As a result, he gets deeply involved in the "important decisions that are really critical to the business." But not all decisions turn out perfectly. In July 1975, Xerox announces it is withdrawing from the production of large-scale computers and writes off $84 million in losses from its computer business.

THE DECISION In 1974, McColough faces a critical business decision: what equipment to design and market for the "office of the future." *Business Week* magazine observes that "The office is the last corporate holdout to the automation tide that has swept through the factory and the accounting department. It has changed little since the invention of the typewriter 100 years ago."

However, in the mid-1970s, office systems may be ready for dramatic changes. In the past, the four key pieces of equipment in a typical, large corporate office operated separately from one another: typewriters, dictating machines, copiers, and facsimile machines (for transmitting letters or pictures by wire to other offices). But in 1964, International Business Machines Corporation (IBM) had started a revolution in office equipment with the introduction of its magnetic-tape Selectric typewriter. Basically, this Selectric was an electric typewriter wired to a tape recorder, which permitted a typist to make corrections directly on a tape without retyping an entire document. Once any changes were made, the typist pressed a button and the machine produced a perfect final copy. Not until the late 1960s did

You can probably name the best known automatic typewriter. Guess who makes one that's twice as fast?

We've hidden a clue in the picture below. Surprised?
Well, you're looking at the new Xerox 800 electronic typing system.
An automatic typewriter with a memory, that can type by itself at the incredible rate of up to 350 error-free words per minute.
And our typewriter has a combination of features that the other automatic typewriter doesn't.

Features like automatic carriage return. Reverse printout. Right margin justification. And pica, elite, and proportional spacing. All on one machine.
All of which means that typing gets done faster, and looks better than it ever did before.
The new Xerox 800 electronic typing system. Years ahead of its time. And about 175 words per minute ahead of the best known automatic typewriter.

XEROX

IBM realize how unusual its product was, and for marketing purposes, coined the phrase "word processing" to describe the technique involved in its new Selectric.

To promote word processing—and the eventual linking of the four key office machines—IBM now recommends the complete reorganization of the standard office. The traditional secretarial job is abolished and divided into two parts. The typing is now handled by "correspondence secretaries" in a centralized word-processing center. Managers dictate messages by phone to the center and receive typed letters and reports in return. The much-reduced secretarial staff—without typewriters—deals with the administrative aspects of the job, each staff member handling a group of managers.

Since Xerox presently produces both copying and facsimile equipment, McColough concludes that the company must introduce its own word-processing machine and gives production the go-ahead. But he wonders if IBM's approach to office reorganization will offset the "people problems" that may affect potential customers' willingness to adopt and use the new equipment.

QUESTIONS

1. What advantages and what disadvantages for Xerox can you see in C. Peter McColough's decision to build word-processing equipment for the "office of the future"?

2. What personnel problems do you think IBM's approach to reorganizing traditional office procedures will produce?

There can be no economy where there is no efficiency.

Benjamin Disraeli

Unlike Chester Carlson, Joseph C. Wilson, and the Xerox Corporation, Alex Manoogian's story is far from legendary. A penniless immigrant to the United States from Turkey in 1921, he started his own small business as a parts supplier to the automobile industry in 1929. Alex was beset with problems during the Depression, and to raise funds, he incorporated his struggling business as the Masco Corporation. In 1936, stock in his corporation sold to the public at a dollar a share.

The Masco Corporation grew slowly, remaining a minor automobile-parts supplier until 1953, when Alex became interested in a new product—the single-handed faucet. Intrigued by the concept, Alex recalls asking himself the question, "Why wouldn't people want to do something with one hand instead of with two?" Purchasing the manufacturing rights to the single-handed faucet from its four inventors, the Masco Corporation began manufacturing the new product in 1955. But unexpected problems arose. The plumbing industry refused to buy "the outrageous thing." Stubbornly, Alex decided that Masco would market as well as manufacture the single-handed faucet. It was the best decision he ever made.

Dull products for a family-owned proprietorship . . .

Alex's persistence paid off handsomely. Consumer demand for single-handed faucets was spectacular, and the product became Masco's most consistent profitmaker. Richard Manoogian, who inherited the business from his father in 1968, reports sales of $250 million each year. Under its 40-year-old president and from its facilities in Taylor, Michigan, Masco has acquired more than 15 other companies. The Masco Corporation now manufactures such diverse products as single- and double-handed faucets, trailer hitches, cold-forged golf-club heads, and drum shafts for copy-machine manufactures like Xerox. Of the products manufactured by Masco, Richard Manoogian says, "They're dull. People look at these little mundane industries and say 'What can anyone do with them?'"

. . . led to a profitable small corporation

By concentrating their efforts on little-known products such as the single-handed faucet, Alex Manoogian and his family have accumulated a $100-million fortune. Original investors in the Masco Corporation stock have also benefited. By 1974, their investments had risen 700-fold in value. The evolution of the Masco Corporation from a family-owned proprietorship to a highly profitable small corporation parallels the development of many successful small businesses.

Alex Manoogian's career and the rise of the Masco Corporation are outstanding examples of the vitality of American business. But in recent years, private businesses like the Masco Corporation have been subjected to a variety of pressures from government, from the public, from organized labor, and from foundations and educational institutions.

Alex and Richard Manoogian, with the single-handed faucet
that made them millionaires.

Consequently, the modern American business system is usually
described as a *mixed economy*. It includes a wide variety of organizations—business, government, labor, agricultural, and nonprofit—and is
ruled according to no fixed ideology. Elements of private enterprise, wel-
fare-statism, and even socialism exist side by side, although sometimes
somewhat uneasily.

This chapter discusses three central aspects of the American business
system: (1) major forms of business ownership; (2) the development of the
modern corporation; and (3) the private enterprise system. A concluding
section describes the principles on which the American economy's two
main competitors, socialism and communism, are based.

Forms of Business Ownership

In examining the modern American economy, it is useful to divide
business ownership into two broad classes: nonprofit organizations and
profit-making businesses. Let us briefly examine nonprofit organizations
before concentrating on profit-making businesses, which have become
central to the American economy.

Nonprofit Organizations

Governments, most hospitals, foundations, and other semipublic organizations receive all or a significant part of their financial support from taxes or from charitable contributions made by individual citizens. Although profit is not an important goal of such organizations, they often apply relevant business principles to operate more efficiently.

Several kinds of businesslike organizations do not seek profits as a primary goal. *Profits* represent the difference between the sales revenue of a business and the costs of producing the goods and services it sells. Two of the most important types of nonprofit businesslike organizations are the cooperative and the publicly owned corporation.

A cooperative seeks to serve its members

✔ **The cooperative.** A *cooperative* is a business chartered under state laws that seeks to better its members economically. It is owned by its members, who elect a board of directors. Each member has a single vote and may purchase limited shares in the cooperative. Interest is paid to those providing capital in relation to the size of their investments. Profits of the cooperative are allocated to members in proportion to their purchases. The most common form of cooperative in the United States is the agricultural cooperative. Credit unions, many savings and loan associations, and mutual insurance companies are modifications of the cooperative concept.

In the past five years, numerous consumer cooperatives have sprung up near college campuses and in low-income areas across the United States. These organizations have sought to provide members with quality food at low prices. Many have stressed "natural foods" that are grown and processed without the use of artificial fertilizers or preservatives. Members of cooperatives divide end-of-year profits and are often required to work at their store for several hours each month.

A publicly owned organization seeks to serve the public good

✔ **The publicly owned organization.** A publicly owned organization is a business established by government to achieve goals felt to be in the public good. Profits accruing to the organization are retained for use in future operations; in the case of federally authorized organizations, profits are returned to the U.S. Treasury.

The Tennessee Valley Authority (TVA) is an example of a publicly owned organization. It was created by the U.S. Congress in 1933 to provide for the systematic development of a variety of economic resources along the Tennessee River. Dams and other projects undertaken by the TVA have led to improved river shipping, reforestation, flood control, low-cost electric power, and better fertilizers. The TVA has provided an improved standard of living for thousands of Americans in the Tennessee Valley area.

Another example of a publicly owned organization is Amtrak, which was established by Congress in 1971. Amtrak is responsible for the operation of nearly all passenger rail service in the United States and receives subsidies for this purpose from the U.S. Treasury.

Profit-Making Businesses

The most important form of business ownership in the United States is the private business run for profit. Even the ancient Egyptians and Greeks conceived business to be a private profit-seeking enterprise. Two of the oldest forms of business organization are the sole proprietorship and the partnership. In the late eighteenth century, the industrial revolution was instrumental in developing a type of business that neither the early Egyptians nor the early Greeks had recognized — the modern corporation.

Private businesses are run for profit

✔ **The sole proprietorship.** The simplest form of business is the *sole proprietorship,* a business owned and usually managed by one person (for example, Alex Manoogian's business before it was incorporated as the Masco Corporation). Such owner-managers are often classified as self-employed. A sole proprietorship can be formed without a written agreement, charter, or other legally binding document. The business is simply begun by an enterprising individual who wants to follow a particular pursuit. The owner of a sole proprietorship assumes *unlimited liability;* that is, he is legally obligated, if necessary, to use his entire business and personal wealth to pay any debts accumulated by the business.

Sole proprietorships are small and numerous

Sole proprietorships can range from a child's summer lemonade stand to a neighborhood laundry or shoe repair shop. As Figure 2-1 shows, sole proprietorships are numerous but normally small in size. In 1971, their combined revenues of $255 billion accounted for only 11 percent of the total revenues of all business. The average receipts of an individual sole proprietorship in 1971 were only about $26,000.

The small size of the average sole proprietorship is not surprising. Mass production and high-volume sales frequently require huge outlays of capital. Because the typical sole proprietor is dependent on personal (and usually limited) financial resources, he or she is frequently short of capital and is, therefore, unable to use mass production techniques or specialized management effectively.

Despite these disadvantages, the sole proprietorship is an attractive form of business ownership. Because of its simplicity and flexibility, few if any legal formalities are required. Legal expenses and delays are minimal, and written commitments restricting future actions can be avoided.

✔ **The partnership.** Another ancient form of business organization is the *partnership,* in which two or more persons are associated owners.

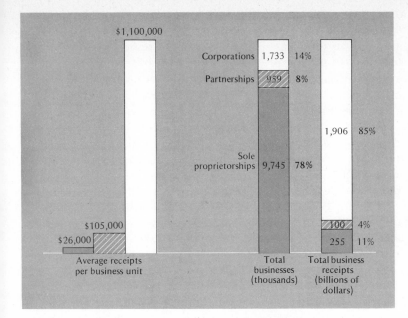

2-1

U.S. sole proprietorships, partnerships, and corporations, 1971. Although small in number compared to proprietorships and partnerships, corporations dominate American business.

Source: *Statistical Abstract of the United States.*

**Co-owners
of a business
are bound together
by legal contract**

Two types of partnerships can be distinguished. In the *general partnership,* as in the sole proprietorship, each partner is exposed to unlimited liability for all actions of the business. In the *limited partnership,* one or more general partners continue to be personally liable for all partnership debts, but the limited partners risk only their own investments.

Unlike the sole proprietorship, the partnership is subject to several legal formalities, beginning with the *partnership agreement* (or contract). This agreement defines the terms of the partnership. It is usually drawn up by attorneys and includes the following information:

1. Description of the business (name, location, and type).
2. Description of each partner (name, type: general or limited partner, responsibilities, salary, initial investment, and portion of profits).
3. Designation of business practices (the partnership's fiscal year and accounting system, and the amount of funds that can be withdrawn from the business).
4. Provisions for changes in the partnership (length of partnership, renewal of partnership, admission of new partners, and treatment of partnership upon withdrawal or death of a partner).
5. Signatures of the partners.

The provisions of the partnership agreement dealing with the compensation and the responsibilities of each partner are crucial. A *secret partner,* who often provides capital for the business, assumes some of the partnership's profits but takes no active role in the business. (The role of the secret partner is typically concealed from the public.) A *nominal partner* assumes an active role in the partnership but receives none of its profits. *Senior partners* receive a greater profit share than do *junior partners*.

The partnership has two major advantages over the sole proprietorship. First, because the financial resources of several partners can be consolidated, a partnership has potential access to larger quantities of capital. Second, partners can contribute varied talents to a business, since each specializes in the area in which he is most skillful. Thus, partnerships are often better adapted to the requirements of modern business than are sole proprietorships.

Advantages of a partnership: greater financial resources and managerial skill

Yet partnerships are the least popular form of business ownership in the United States. In 1971, their combined revenues of $100 billion represented only 4 percent of the total business receipts for that year, and individual partnerships in 1971 averaged a mere $105,000 in receipts. Almost three-quarters of all partnerships have only two partners, and nearly nine in ten have three or fewer.

What accounts for the relative unpopularity of partnerships? To begin with, the general partner is exposed to unlimited personal financial liability for all partnership transactions, including those undertaken by other partners with or without approval. Moreover, divided authority can create many problems: important decisions may be delayed; employees may have mixed loyalties when conflicts arise; and mutual suspicion and distrust may develop among partners. For a partnership to be successful, the partners must be compatible and must have full confidence in one another's integrity and ability.

✔ **The corporation.** The corporation is by far the most influential form of business ownership. The first organization truly comparable to a modern corporation was chartered by the New Jersey legislature on November 22, 1791. Supported by Alexander Hamilton, the Society for Establishing Useful Manufacturers began to operate in 1793, producing cotton prints in Paterson, New Jersey—the "new city" it helped to form. Interestingly, America's first corporation was a financial failure.

The first American corporation: a financial failure

The explosive growth in corporate influence began in the 1840s and 1850s, when state legislatures adopted general incorporation laws. To attract new business to their states and to collect incorporation fees, many states—particularly Delaware and New Jersey—engaged in a competitive scramble to simplify the incorporation process. Post-Civil War changes in mass production, transportation, and finance also aided the formation of corporations.

Figure 2-1 shows that in 1971 America's 1.7 million corporations represented only 14 percent of all business organizations. Yet corporate revenues totaled 1.9 trillion, or 85 percent of all business receipts. Revenues of the average corporation amounted to $1.1 million in 1971, a figure significantly larger than that for the average sole proprietorship or partnership. Giant corporations like General Motors and American Telephone and Telegraph are the world's largest private organizations.

What Is a Corporation?

In 1819, U.S. Chief Justice John Marshall described a corporation as "... an artificial being, intangible. ... Being the mere creature of law, it possesses only those properties which the charter of its creation confers upon it, either expressly or as incidental to its existence." The *corporation*

2-2 Basic corporate structure.

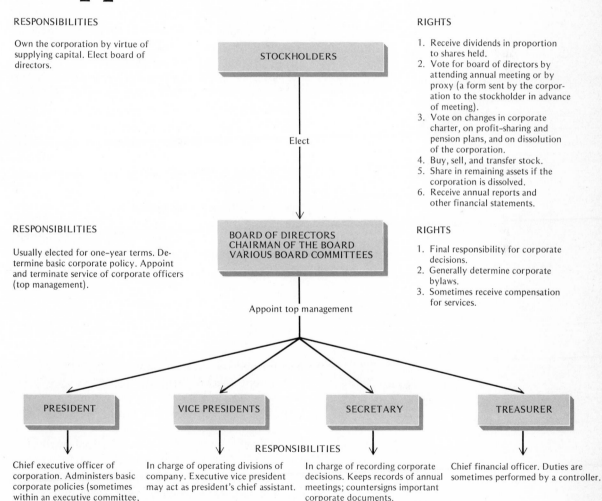

RESPONSIBILITIES

Own the corporation by virtue of supplying capital. Elect board of directors.

STOCKHOLDERS

Elect

RIGHTS

1. Receive dividends in proportion to shares held.
2. Vote for board of directors by attending annual meeting or by proxy (a form sent by the corporation to the stockholder in advance of meeting).
3. Vote on changes in corporate charter, on profit–sharing and pension plans, and on dissolution of the corporation.
4. Buy, sell, and transfer stock.
5. Share in remaining assets if the corporation is dissolved.
6. Receive annual reports and other financial statements.

RESPONSIBILITIES

Usually elected for one–year terms. Determine basic corporate policy. Appoint and terminate service of corporate officers (top management).

BOARD OF DIRECTORS
CHAIRMAN OF THE BOARD
VARIOUS BOARD COMMITTEES

Appoint top management

RIGHTS

1. Final responsibility for corporate decisions.
2. Generally determine corporate bylaws.
3. Sometimes receive compensation for services.

PRESIDENT   VICE PRESIDENTS   SECRETARY   TREASURER

RESPONSIBILITIES

Chief executive officer of corporation. Administers basic corporate policies (sometimes within an executive committee, which includes the directors).

In charge of operating divisions of company. Executive vice president may act as president's chief assistant.

In charge of recording corporate decisions. Keeps records of annual meetings; countersigns important corporate documents.

Chief financial officer. Duties are sometimes performed by a controller.

has three key characteristics. First, ownership may vary from one individual to several million people who purchase stock in the company. Second, the corporation is managed according to written principles that are generally much more detailed than the typical partnership agreement. Third, corporate owners are exposed to limited liability and at most can lose only their investments in the business.

Corporate Structure

Figure 2-2 illustrates in simplified form the basic structure of the modern corporation. The owners of a corporation, called its *stockholders* (or shareholders), elect a *board of directors*—usually a group of stockholders who are responsible for the overall direction of the corporation. Senior managers of the firm are frequently on the board, either as voting or as nonvoting members. The board may also include *outside directors,* nonstockholders whose special skills, knowledge, or contacts are useful to the business. For example, several major corporations have recently named nonbusiness directors to represent outside consumer interests.

The board of directors has two major responsibilities: to make the final decisions on basic corporate objectives and policies, and to select the *officers* or top managers of the corporation (the president, vice president, secretary, treasurer, and others). In large corporations, several vice presidents are normally in charge of special areas within the firm; their appointments are approved by the board of directors.

The officers of the corporation are responsible for carrying out the objectives and policies set forth by the board of directors. In practice, officers often initiate and develop basic policies, which are eventually approved by the board of directors. For their efforts, corporate officers receive compensation through large salaries, pension benefits, and expense accounts.

Corporate Charter and Bylaws

A corporation is formed by submitting a formal application to the appropriate state government official, typically the secretary of state. The contents of the application, which becomes the *corporate charter,* are governed by state law but usually include the following information:

1. Name, address, duration (if necessary), and principal purpose of the company.
2. Names and addresses of company directors and stockholders.
3. Number of shares, privileges, and voting rights assigned to each type of stock authorized.
4. Procedures for amending the charter.

**The corporate charter
and bylaws
are governed
by state law**

Within the framework provided by state law and by the corporate charter, the board of directors (or, in some instances, the stockholders by direct vote) establishes the *corporate bylaws,* which normally contain the following provisions:

1. Designation of stockholder meetings (time, place, method of notice, and provisions for special meetings).
2. Description of the board of directors (number of members, responsibilities, organization, compensation, and provisions for filling vacancies).
3. Description of officers (titles, duties, and selection procedure).
4. Statement of financial procedures (stock issuance and transfer, accounting methods, and required accounting statements and their timing).

The bylaws of a corporation establish the internal rules under which the company is to operate. The charter and the bylaws are legally binding under state law. A corporation that violates its internal rules — for example, by failing to notify stockholders of an annual meeting — can be sued in the courts.

Because of these formalities, it is more expensive to organize and operate a corporation than a sole proprietorship or partnership. The formal organization of a corporation may take several months. Legal fees, occasionally running into tens of thousands of dollars, and state incorporation fees and taxes must be paid. In addition, depending on state law, the corporation may be forced to pay annual license fees and to submit various reports and accounting statements at designated intervals..

These restrictions and expenses, however, can often be surmounted. Attorneys draft corporate charters and bylaws so broadly that few corporate actions are overly restricted. In most states, incorporation of a small, uncomplicated business can be completed for as little as $1000. An especially common method for avoiding many of the legal expenses normally associated with incorporation is to form a *close* (or privately held) *corporation,* in which stock is issued only to a small group of investors, often in a single family. *Open* (or publicly held) *corporations* are more expensive to form and maintain, since the publicly held business must conform to state and federal laws designed to protect the investing public. Operation of small businesses that might be sole proprietorships, partnerships, or corporations will be discussed in Chapters 16 and 17.

Advantages of Corporations

One of the key advantages of corporations is their access to large amounts of capital. Investors are attracted by the potential marketability of the stock, by the limited financial liability in purchasing corporate stock, and by the opportunity to participate in a large business by making a small initial investment at a limited risk. The corporate form is unique in its potential to secure huge quantities of capital from investors of modest means.

Although the charter usually specifies an initial life for the corporation (often 35 years), a corporation can remain vigorous for generations. This advantage arises because the corporation's structure, charter, and bylaws provide for the continuity of both management and ownership. When corporate officers and managers die or leave the company, the board of directors and top management seek to replace them with other capable individuals. Ownership, represented by possession of stock in the company, can be transferred without difficulty by selling or giving stock to another person. In contrast, sole proprietorships and partnerships generally lack a formal, practical means of transferring ownership. Major characteristics of sole proprietorships, partnerships, and corporations are described in Figure 2-3.

Effects of the Rise of Corporations

A legacy of the industrial revolution and the liberalized nineteenth-century incorporation laws, the corporation has become America's most important economic institution. Although sole proprietorships and partnerships can attain the size of large corporations, nearly all large U.S. businesses are organized as corporations. Clearly, the corporate form has benefited mass production, but it has also produced some unexpected consequences.

✔ **Separation of ownership and management.** Because large corporations are owned by thousands of stockholders, ownership is necessarily divorced from management—from the daily operations of the business. Except in cases of obvious failure, stockholders at annual meetings routinely vote to retain management. More and more candidates for the board of directors, which theoretically represents the stockholders, are being chosen by management and are being approved without question by stockholders. In addition, widespread stock ownership often means that management, which acquires stock through bonuses and options, controls a larger percentage of shares than any other single owner. In a careful study of U.S. corporations, economist R.J. Larner found that 89 of the 200 largest corporations were management controlled in 1929 and that 169 of the 200 were management controlled in 1963.

When management gains control of a corporation, it may regard the interests of stockholders as coequal with the interests of other groups: employees who seek higher wages, consumers who desire lower prices, and government agencies that enforce various regulations. Once the expectations of each of these groups are met, management may elect to pursue its own interests at the expense of the stockholders.

2-3 Characteristics of three major forms of business ownership.

Characteristic	Sole proprietorship	Partnership	Corporation
Legal status of owners	No legal formalities; unlimited liability.	Partnership agreement; unlimited liability of general partners.	Formal charter and bylaws; limited liability.
Ability to secure capital	Limited to wealth and borrowing capacity of proprietor.	Limited to wealth and borrowing capacity of partners.	Potentially very large because of the number of possible investors.
Life of organization	Limited to life span of proprietor, unless business can be sold.	Limited to period when partnership agreement is in force.	Ownership can be transferred by sale of stock; no real limit on corporate life.
Flexibility and secrecy	Complete	Flexibility limited by provisions of partnership agreement; secrecy restricted to partners.	Flexibility limited by provisions of corporate charter; most corporations must make financial information publicly available.
Taxes	Personal income tax; heirs must pay inheritance tax, often forcing sale of business.	Personal income tax; inheritance taxes similar to proprietorship.	Corporate profits tax on earnings; personal income tax on dividends; inheritance taxes do not jeopardize business, since deceased owner's stock can be sold in the market.

↙ **Changing business goals.** Traditionally, the major objective of business has been *profit maximization*—achieving the highest financial return possible. Profit maximization can be either a short-range or a long-range goal. A business that chooses to emphasize *short-term profits* seeks immediate returns within the next few months or within the coming year. Such a business operates on the conviction that "a bird in the hand is worth two in the bush." A firm that decides to maximize *long-term profits* is concerned with returns a year or more in the future. The Japanese government encourages businesses to realize very low initial profits when exporting products to a new market. Once Japanese dominance in a particular market has been established, then businesses can raise prices and secure very high profits on their foreign trade. Sometimes, however, market conditions change so drastically that future profits promised by long-term profit maximization are never realized.

The rise of corporations and the resulting separation of ownership and management have led many large firms to stress nonprofit goals. Empirical studies indicate that management-dominated businesses have four major nonprofit goals. First, a firm may emphasize *survival* at the expense of higher profits. A safe action promising a moderate return might be preferable to a risky venture with a potentially high payoff, especially if the failure of the venture would bankrupt the company. Second, a firm may strive to maintain or to increase its *market share*—the proportion of the

Management-dominated companies may stress nonprofit objectives

total sales of the product that is controlled by the business. Even when profits remain high, a declining market share is a danger signal for a firm, since high profits often reflect a good year for the industry as a whole. Third, once a firm has achieved an acceptable profit level, it may seek to *expand sales,* even at the risk of losing profits. Larger sales can lead to an increase in the size of business units, which adds to executive power and prestige. Fourth, a firm may make *social responsibility* a major goal. Management may focus its efforts on balancing the claims of stockholders, consumers, employees, and other groups. It may even devote a portion of the corporation's resources to searching for solutions to social problems. Advocates of the doctrine of corporate social responsibility believe that business has a moral obligation to promote the general welfare of the public, even at the expense of profits.

But profits remain a key business goal

Nonetheless, a satisfactory profit level remains a major goal for most businesses. Survival, market-share maintenance, and expanded sales are often the means to an end—acceptable profits. Vigorous competition also forces many firms to concentrate on profits. Finally, high profits may generate the financial resources needed to contribute to socially worthy projects. The rise of management-controlled businesses has made the pursuit of nonprofit goals more likely, but the drive for satisfactory profits still dominates American business.

The Private Enterprise System

The millions of sole proprietorships, partnerships, and corporations in the United States form the private sector of the American economy. Unlike socialism or communism, the American business system relies on the private decisions of its 212 million consumers and of its 10 million businesses.

Characteristics of Private Enterprise

The *private enterprise system* is the dominant institution in the American economy. It is often described by other names: capitalism, the free enterprise system, the voluntary exchange economy, the market system, and the profit system. An effective private enterprise system displays four major characteristics which will now be described.

✔ **Private ownership of business.** In a private enterprise system, businesses or private enterprises are owned by individuals rather than by the government. Most sole proprietorships, partnerships, and corporations are in private hands. Private or free enterprise also implies that business owners have certain rights:

1. The right to operate the business with a minimum of outside interference. In particular, business owners can select the products to be made, determine how to produce them, price and market the products as they please, buy raw materials and other supplies freely, and hire and discharge employees without restriction.
2. The right to retain control over most profits generated by the business.
3. The right to compete freely with other businesses for raw materials, personnel, customers, new products, new production techniques, and so on.

Private ownership
of business implies
three basic rights

Of course, it is true that the U.S. government can restrict these rights. Federal regulations and union contracts limit management's right to hire or to discharge employees at will. Firms may not discriminate among customers on the basis of age, race, or sex. Federal taxation takes nearly half of business profits. However, despite government regulation, the basic principles of private ownership have survived.

✔ **Private property.** Private property refers to the right of individuals or groups to own and to control physical resources as well as personal possessions. In the United States, most land, minerals, buildings, machinery, farms, and personal goods are privately owned.

The right
to private property
is an economic incentive

The right to private property has been justified on both ethical and practical grounds. Americans believe that they have a right to most of what they have earned "by the sweat of their brow." Ownership of private property provides incentive and promotes responsibility. In general, people work harder and more effectively if they are allowed to accumulate private property than they do if they are forced to relinquish the property they acquire. People also take better care of the things they own than they do of other people's things; for example, note the contrast between the way most people take care of their own homes and the way they abuse public property.

✔ **Freedom of choice.** In a private enterprise system, managers and workers are free to choose their occupations, to enter or leave a business, to change jobs, and to negotiate salaries, wages, and other benefits. With a minimum of government or social pressure, consumers are also free to select the goods they buy.

The federal government places relatively few restrictions on freedom of choice. In some instances, federal laws do prevent employees from negotiating individually with employers. In addition, federal agencies have been established to keep unsafe or dangerous products off the market.

✔ **Limited role of government.** In a private enterprise system, the role of the government is limited to such traditional objectives as adminis-

39 *The Private Enterprise System*

tering justice, protecting individual freedom, and providing for national defense. Government also establishes "the economic rules of the game" by developing and maintaining a domestic currency and a national banking system, by encouraging commerce, and by enforcing private contracts in the court systems. As government activities go beyond these limits, the private enterprise system begins to include the components of a mixed economy.

Government sets the economic rules of the game

The Basic Economic Problem: Allocation of Resources

Every society must solve a basic set of economic problems that economists call the *allocation of resources.* The need to allocate resources arises from the ever-present tension between the level of wants in a society and that society's ability to satisfy them. Human desire for material goods and services is unlimited. Once an individual's or a society's basic needs for food, clothing, and shelter have been met, desires for better clothing, luxuries, and convenience goods arise.

Yet, a society's ability to produce goods and services at any given time is limited by resource scarcities. *Resources,* or factors of production, include all items that are useful in producing goods and services. Resources are frequently classified into basic categories like land, labor, capital, and technology. As an example of resource limitations, total farm production in the United States today is affected by such resources as the quantity of cultivated land, the amount of seed and fertilizer available, the capacity of farm machinery to plant and harvest crops, and the numbers and skills of American farmers.

Resource allocation: unlimited demand versus limited supply

The tension between unlimited human wants and limited resources forces every society to be concerned with the allocation of resources. This involves four basic questions:

1. What goods and services are to be produced?
2. To whom are the goods and services to be distributed?
3. How are the goods and services to be produced?
4. How much should the resource base be expanded each year to secure increased future production?

How a society resolves these questions reflects its economic system.

Resource Allocation Under Private Enterprise

On the whole, the American business system is extraordinarily efficient at allocating resources. Even in a private enterprise system, however, resource allocation can be improved by better understanding and more considered actions on the part of both businesses and consumers.

The private enterprise system allocates resources extraordinarily well

How well the private enterprise system works depends on four key factors: consumer sovereignty, profits, competition, and productivity.

✔ **Consumer sovereignty.** The freedom of private consumers to select whatever products they desire is central to the private enterprise system. In effect, whenever consumers make purchases, they are voting on what products should be produced. The total number of votes each consumer has is proportional to the number of dollars that that consumer has available to spend. Consumer sovereignty refers to the primacy of the consumer in a private enterprise system.

Informed consumers can improve the private enterprise system

One obvious way to improve the efficiency of private enterprise is for all Americans to become better consumers. If purchase decisions are reasoned, the private enterprise system will meet real consumer needs. But if consumers purchase carelessly or without adequate information, the American economy will be less responsive to their needs. The goods and services produced in a private enterprise system are, therefore, a fair reflection of the quality of its consumers.

Profits: an incentive to private business and a measure of its performance

✔ **Profits.** Profits represent the difference between what a business receives for the products sold and what must be paid to produce and market these products. Profits play a vital role in efficient resource allocation by encouraging businesses to produce the goods and services that consumers want. If consumer desire for a product — say, bicycles — increases, then bicycle manufacturing will be profitable and bicycle manufacturers will be tempted to expand production. Other producers, attracted by the high profits of bicycle manufacturers, will be encouraged to enter the business until the consumer demand for bicycles is precisely met.

Profits are the carrot that induces business to be efficient and to be responsive to consumer demand. Efficient business owners who correctly anticipate future changes are rewarded with higher profits and therefore have a strong incentive to be even more efficient and forward-looking in the future.

PROFITS AND PEOPLE

The famous British economist J.M. Keynes once observed that great periods of economic, social, and cultural progress are characterized by high business profits. Profits — the difference between business revenues and business costs — are largely used to expand industry, to support government through the taxes business enterprises and their owners pay, and to subsidize cultural and philanthropic projects. Many Americans, however, appear to believe that profits primarily enrich high-income families at the consumers' expense.

The well-known pollster Louis Harris recently asked a random sample of 2000 Americans two questions about profits:

1. After taxes what percentage of each sales dollar do you believe represents the profits of American businesses?
2. In terms of the percentage of an average sales dollar, what do you believe is a reasonable after-tax profit for a typical business?

What do you think the average responses were to these two questions? How much are *actual* profits in a typical business as a percentage of the average sales dollar? For the answers see the text.

Profits also provide the private enterprise system with an objective standard of performance. Although there are limitations to evaluating the success of a business on the basis of profits alone, profit comparisons can be useful in assessing the performance of a business over time, in determining which part of a business to expand in measuring management performance in various locations, and in comparing the performance of a firm with that of its competitors. No other institution in American society has developed as clear a measure of performance as has business.

Most Americans overestimate profits earned by American businesses. For example, those questioned in a recent Louis Harris poll described in "Profits and People" believed profits represent 28 percent of the average sales dollar. The largest portion felt 10 percent was a reasonable return on sales. Business actually earns about 4 percent (*not* 10 or 28 percent) on the average sales dollar. Therefore, a complete elimination of profits would temporarily reduce prices by about 4 percent. Price-conscious consumers should be much more concerned that business operate efficiently in order to reduce its costs to a minimum on the other 96 cents of each sales dollar!

Profits play a major role in determining a nation's living standards. A basic source of economic growth in every society is the accumulation of plants and machinery—the *physical capital* of a nation. Physical capital includes all material resources used to produce goods or services. Since physical capital makes production possible, this capital must be selected carefully and must be used wisely. The more physical capital a business can accumulate, the greater its potential output will be.

High business profits ultimately improve living standards

But in order to accumulate physical capital, a firm must acquire *financial capital*—monetary resouces that can be used to purchase plants and machinery. (The word "capital" is often used for both physical and financial resources.) A firm obtains financial capital mainly by retaining the profits it earns from its own operations.

The importance of profits in the acquisition of physical and financial capital cannot be overstated. To the extent that they contribute to economic growth, high profits benefit both business and labor. Americans display little understanding of the role of profits.

✔ **Competition.** Competition can refer either to pure competition or to rivalry. *Pure competition* exists in an industry when a large number of firms produce identical products, when each firm is free to enter or to leave the industry as it chooses, and when government interference is absent.

If there are only a few firms in an industry (say, less than 20), competition becomes fundamentally different and is often designated as *rivalry*. In an industry comprised of only a few competitors, each firm is affected by the actions of the other firms. Consider two gas stations on a corner. If one lowers its gasoline price substantially, the other must follow suit or lose sales. A price war often becomes so bitter and so personal that both businesses end up selling the product below cost.

But low consumer prices are hardly a typical result of industry rivalry. Rivals soon learn that starting a price war is highly unprofitable, especially in industries that produce automobiles, cigarettes, steel, and aluminum, where most firms have sufficient strength to withstand a prolonged price war. In product areas where there are few sellers, either prices are stabilized or other sellers follow suit if one bold seller raises prices. To prevent a damaging price war, rivals rarely lower their prices.

Large rivals stress nonprice competition

Forced to shift attention away from price, most large firms engage in *nonprice rivalry* (or nonprice competition). Product quality improvements, advertising campaigns, new models and styles, better service, puzzles and contests, and other devices are used to lure customers from one firm to another. Some aspects of nonprice rivalry are clearly beneficial to consumers (for example, the development of automatic transmissions in the automobile industry); others (such as costly annual model changes) are of dubious advantage.

Whatever form it takes, competition tends to raise the efficiency of the private enterprise system in several ways:

Benefits of vigorous competition

1. It induces businesses to seek out new or improved products that might appeal to consumers.
2. It encourages businesses to market a high-quality product at a reasonable price in order to retain customers.
3. It pressures businesses to use the most efficient production methods available. An inefficient producer is soon weeded out of the competition.
4. It forces businesses to respond quickly to changes in consumer desires and in the economy.
5. It rewards the efficient and the hard working and penalizes the idle.

Many experts believe that present-day rivalry is less satisfactory than competition among a large number of firms in a single industry. Economist F.M. Scherer estimates that the excessive dominance of large rival firms in many industries reduces U.S. gross national product by about 6.2 percent. Thus elimination of the waste in resource allocation resulting from excessive rivalry could restore at least $80 billion to the annual GNP —more than enough money to eradicate all major forms of pollution. Restoring vigorous competition would therefore improve the private enterprise system substantially.

✔ **Productivity.** In any economic system, increased productivity is essential to higher living standards, to a growth in GNP, and to an increase in leisure time. By providing incentives and rewards, the private

HOW TO ALLOCATE RESOURCES INEFFICIENTLY

There have been radio and television bloopers, newspaper bloopers, and sports bloopers—some of them serious; most of them humorous. Here are four candidates for worst allocation-of-resources bloopers in the 1970s.

The right-footed shoe problem: The manager of the Communist shoe factory was pleased. He had been ordered by the Soviet government to produce an astounding quantity of shoes and had been given inadequate resources to do the job. His brilliant solution: improve efficiency and output by using mass production technology to produce only right-footed shoes!

The missing railroad car problem: The experts were ecstatic. The federal government had just allowed the New York Central and the Pennsylvania railroads to merge to form the world's largest privately owned railroad. Only a few obscure voices warned that large companies were not automatically more efficient than small enterprises. But slowly the evidence came in: adding one inefficient management to another produced chaos. In the bankruptcy courts, evidence was revealed of fraudulent accounting statements, price manipulation of Penn Central stock by its officers, and—most incredibly of all—Penn Central's loss of 10,000 railroad boxcars! As one observer noted, "The managerial skill required to lose 10,000 railroad boxcars boggles the imagination."

The Swiss postal problem: Burghers in all the little villages were amazed. All of their postal boxes were being rented by Italians who would drive up to Switzerland to send and pick up their mail. Finally, the truth came to light. The government-run postal system in Italy, never known for its efficiency, had broken down. Many post offices literally had undelivered mail running out of the windows. In contrast, several post offices were completely free of stacked mail, and the Italians marveled at the efficiency of their postmasters—until it was discovered that they were selling all of the unopened mail to paper companies at enormous profits!

The discount-store problem: The Comrades were amazed. Could this be happening in Communist Russia? The Soviet Union had discovered that nearly $40 billion in unwanted goods—commodities that could not be sold at regular prices because they were of poor quality, the incorrect size, or the wrong kind of product—were cramming the shelves of the state-owned stores. What could be done with these goods? Why, of course—sell them at a discount! But how would the consumers know about the sale? Of course, advertise! But weren't discount sales and advertising what the hated capitalists did? Why no, explained the government: in Western countries, the discount stores advertise to make a profit for private individuals who exploit their economic position; in Russia, the stores are owned by the government, which represents the workers.

The Moral? Is there a moral to these situations? Perhaps. The allocation of resources is imperfect under all economic and social systems and among all institutions. A key goal is to make the allocation of resources as efficient as possible in an imperfect world and to choose an economic system that does the best possible job of allocating resources.

---

enterprise system can increase worker output. In the final analysis, of course, no system can prosper unless its workers and its managers are motivated, efficient, and competent.

Increased productivity is essential to economic progress

Productivity is defined as real output per working hour and is usually expressed in percentage terms. Thus, an increase in productivity of 10 percent between 1977 and 1978 means that the average employee is 10 percent more productive during each working hour in 1978 than he or she was in 1977. Since World War II, productivity in the United states has grown at an annual rate of about 3 percent. In contrast, employee productivity in Japan and in many western European nations has risen more than 4 percent annually.

An Overview of Resource Allocation

A private enterprise system achieves an efficient allocation of resources when it meets all of the following conditions:

Conditions for efficient resource allocation under private enterprise

1. Consumers are sovereign and use their sovereignty wisely and rationally to make informed purchase decisions.
2. Profits are adequate to finance future growth in GNP and are sufficient to encourage businesses to produce the goods and services that consumers want.
3. Competition rewards efficient businesses and forces inefficient businesses into insolvency.
4. Productivity is high, both because competition encourages businesses to use resources wisely and because employees are willing to work hard and well.

Advocates of socialism and communism object to consumer sovereignty, believing that in most cases the government is more knowledgeable about long-term consumer needs than consumers are themselves. Some Socialists and Communists also believe that government-owned businesses can produce goods and services more efficiently than private businesses can. In practice, all economic systems display imperfections in resource allocation (see "How to Allocate Resources Inefficiently"), and supporters or opponents of the private enterprise system debate the merits of their positions endlessly.

Alternatives to Private Enterprise

Many economies throughout the world have not adopted the private enterprise system. In the United States, a small minority rejects the principles of private enterprise completely, and most Americans support sufficient modifications in the private enterprise system to maintain a mixed economy in the United States. Since socialism and communism are the primary alternatives to private enterprise, it is important to become acquainted with these two economic systems.

Before doing so, however, it should be noted that every economic system is amazingly varied: Communist Yugoslavia and Communist Russia represent very different economies. Moreover, every national economy is a mixed one to some extent. For example, Soviet farmers are allowed to cultivate small private plots that exceed state farms fivefold in production per acre.

Socialism

Socialism is a broad term that applies to two quite different economic approaches. *Traditional socialism,* still popular in western Europe, involves state ownership and control of the basic means of production: major raw materials (for example, coal, iron, and oil), utilities, transportation, finance, communication, and other important industries. Recently, many Socialist nations in western Europe have sought to organize industries as independent, publicly owned corporations with government-appointed directors.

Socialism:
an increased
government
role in business

Another form of socialism is the *welfare state,* in which the government sponsors extensive programs to protect and promote the welfare of the individual. In Sweden, more than 90 percent of business, including most basic industry, is privately owned. Swedes enjoy a long list of government-paid benefits, such as free medical care, inflation-protected pensions, and free university education. They also pay the highest taxes in the world.

Communism

Communism as practiced in the Soviet Union involves government ownership of nearly all business and agriculture. Communism differs from traditional socialism not only in the extent of government ownership but also in the degree of government control over economic activity.

Communism:
central planning,
little
private business

The Soviet Union is a centrally planned economy with no significant private sector. Central planning as practiced in the Soviet Union involves the following steps:

1. The Communist party sets basic economic objectives. In the past, the party has stressed military power and the industrial manufacture of heavy-duty materials like steel.
2. A government bureaucracy translates basic policies into specific production targets for a five-year period. Careful determination is made of the types, quantities, and prices of the goods and services to be produced.
3. National production targets are translated into output goals for individual plants. The local manager is given a target output and the quantities of each resource to be used in the production process.

Managers who successfully meet or exceed their assigned targets are rewarded with bonuses and medals signifying government approval.

The Soviet Union has experienced many difficulties with central planning. Planned targets expressed in physical units often induce harassed managers to reduce the quality of output in favor of greater quantity. Even specifying targets in terms of weight presents problems: some Russian nail manufacturers recently achieved their target tonnages by producing easily manufactured spikes rather than the small tacks and nails that were required. In addition, central planners often misjudge the requirements of the large Soviet economy, sending too much steel to Siberia or too little coal to the Ukraine. Pilferage and poor maintenance of state property are chronic. Because of these difficulties, recent Soviet economic growth has not matched past achievements or planned targets.

Figure 2-4 presents a synopsis of the differences between the private enterprise system and traditional socialism and communism.

In a private enterprise system, both management and labor enjoy high levels of personal incentive and economic freedom of choice. These

2-4 Comparison of major economic systems.

Economic characteristics	Private enterprise system	Socialism	Communism
Basic features	Private ownership of business; freedom of choice.	Basic industries owned by government; freedom of choice.	Industry and agriculture owned and controlled by government.
Goals	Decided by individual consumers and businessmen.	Considerable state modification of business goals.	Individual goals subordinate to state goals.
Status of management	Independent; freedom to choose jobs.	State control of publicly owned enterprises.	Management selected by state.
Status of labor	Independent; few restrictions by state	Restricted right to strike in public enterprises.	State-controlled unions; restrictions on occupational choice.
Status of consumers	Independent; freedom to purchase limited by consumer incomes.	Must accept prices established in public enterprises.	Prices of goods and income levels set by state.
Economic role of government	To foster private enterprises.	To direct basic industries according to government plans.	To own and operate industries and agriculture.
Main economic advantages	Private initiative; economic freedom.	Possible full employment, if unemployed placed on government payroll in basic industries.	Government can direct resources toward specific goals; wages can be depressed to accumulate capital.
Main problems	Possible business cycles; some waste from competition.	Lack of incentives in public enterprises; inefficient government-run businesses.	Lack of incentives; inefficiencies; limited freedom of choice; resource allocation errors can be serious.

characteristics are consistent with the individualistic stress typical of Western culture. The private enterprise system has served the American people well, and at present it seems unlikely that they will abandon it. Undoubtedly, the main economic alternative to challenge private enterprise in the future will be an economic system other than socialism or communism.

KEY POINTS TO REMEMBER

1. The United States is a mixed economy containing business, government, nonprofit organizations like cooperatives, and publicly owned corporations.
2. Privately owned businesses include sole proprietorships, partnerships, and corporations.
3. Sole proprietorships are easy and inexpensive to organize, but owners are exposed to unlimited liability and often experience difficulty in raising capital.
4. Partnerships combine the capital and the skills of two or more business owners. Partners are exposed to unlimited liability for their own actions as well as for their partners' actions.
5. Corporations can accumulate large quantities of capital from many small investors, who are thus exposed only to limited liability.
6. The stockholders own a corporation and elect its board of directors. This board is then formally responsible for setting basic corporate objectives.
7. Top management includes the president, the vice-presidents, the secretary, and the treasurer, who are usually the main officers in the corporation.
8. A major goal of most businesses is to maximize profits. Profit maximization may be either long- or short-term.
9. A central goal of all economies is the efficient allocation of resources, which involves channeling scarce resources into high-priority economic and social needs.
10. The private enterprise system is characterized by private ownership of business, private ownership of property, individual freedom of choice, and a limited government role in the economy and in society.
11. Consumer sovereignty, competition, and the motivation to achieve high profits and productivity are the basic tools the private enterprise system uses to obtain an efficient allocation of resources without resorting to the use of physical force.
12. Socialism and communism attempt to efficiently allocate resources by increasing the government's economic role.

QUESTIONS FOR DISCUSSION

1. Publicly owned corporations are designed to meet important public needs. What public needs is Amtrak, a publicly owned corporation, designed to meet?

2. Define limited and unlimited liability. As a potential business investor, why would you be interested in liability?

3. What is the corporate charter? What are corporate bylaws? What legal significance do they have?

4. Who really controls the large corporation—its stockholders or its management? Discuss the reasons for your answer.

5. What are the four main characteristics of a private enterprise system?

6. Define the following terms and explain their significance in a private enterprise economy: (a) consumer sovereignty; (b) competition; (c) profits; (d) productivity.

7. There are only five automobile repair shops in a small town, and they all agree on a common price of $29.95 for a tuneup. Is this an example of pure competition or of rivalry? Explain your answer.

8. A steel plant manager is told to produce 100,000 tons of steel and to use 1000 employees to do it. All profits are returned to the government, which also owns nearly all private property. Under what economic system is the manager working?

9. Distinguish between traditional socialism and welfare-state socialism.

SHORT CASES AND PROBLEMS

1. After World War II and again in the middle 1970s, many types of steel were in very short supply. At both times, the large American steel companies—knowing of the worldwide steel shortage—could have raised prices faster than they did. Based on your knowledge of corporate goals, can you explain why U.S. steel companies raised prices less rapidly than they could have?

2. There are two major airlines in Hawaii: Hawaiian and Aloha. Both fly similar routes among the five Hawaiian Islands, and both are financially strong enough to withstand a fairly long price war. Recognizing the distinction between competition and rivalry, would you recommend a fare cut to the top management of Aloha Airlines in order to secure a larger share of the passenger market?

3. "High productivity is a very bad thing," a worker argued. "If we work hard and produce a lot, there will be fewer jobs and some of us will be unemployed." "Nonsense," a companion muttered angrily. "If everyone followed your suggestion, we would produce so few goods and services that our standard of living would decline." Which of these two views do you think is correct? Why?

CAREER SELECTION: EMPLOYMENT TRENDS BY INDUSTRY

No one can forecast the future precisely. Yet, in making important career choices, it is helpful to know what past employment trends have been by industry and occupation and what they are likely to be in the future. The *1974–75 Edition of the Occupational Outlook Handbook,* published by the U.S. Department of Labor, provides such data. It is the source of the employment trends by industry described here and of the employment trends by occupation presented in the Career Selection section at the end of Chapter 3.

KINDS OF INDUSTRIES

Industries may be viewed as either goods-producing or as service-producing. The four main goods-producing industries are manufacturing, agriculture, construction, and mining. The five main classes of service-producing industries are wholesale and retail trade; government (local, state, and federal, including education); repair and maintenance services; transportation and public utilities; and finance, insurance, and real estate. In 1950, goods-producing and service-producing industries employed about 27 million Americans apiece. By 1972, jobs in service-producing industries had almost doubled (to 50 million), but employment in goods-producing industries had remained unchanged. Figure 2-5 shows the 1972 employment in the nine sectors of goods- and service-producing industries.

FUTURE EMPLOYMENT IN GOODS-PRODUCING INDUSTRIES

In recent years, the number of available jobs in goods-producing industries has not grown perceptibly, largely because automation and improved worker skills have led to large increases in output without corresponding increases in employment. The total number of jobs in all goods-producing industries are expected to increase by about 3 million to 30 million between 1972 and 1985. Projected employment changes from 1972 to 1985 for each of the four types of goods-producing industries appear in the right-hand portion of Figure 2-5. Note that while employment in manufacturing and construction is expected to grow substantially, employment in agriculture and mining is actually expected to decline. The mining estimate indicates how difficult it can be to forecast the future. If petroleum and natural-gas supplies are adequate through 1985, this forecast seems reasonable. But if coal becomes a more important energy source in the next decade, mining employment will increase dramatically, making the current forecast erroneous.

FUTURE EMPLOYMENT IN SERVICE-PRODUCING INDUSTRIES

The greatest employment growth is expected in the service-producing industries: about 18.5 million new jobs should be available between 1972 and 1985. But, as shown in the right-hand portion of Figure 2-5, each of the five types of service-producing industries will grow at a substantially different rate. Employment in service and miscellaneous industries is expected to increase dramatically (by about 7 million jobs); this industrial class includes a variety of services, such as maintenance, repair, advertising, and health care. Government employment is expected to increase more than five million during this period, virtually entirely at the state and local levels. From 1972 to 1985, jobs in wholesale and retail trade are expected to increase by more than 4 million. Employment in finance, transportation, and related areas is also expected to increase, but not as much in terms of total number of jobs as the other types of service-producing industries.

Employment by industry in 1972 and projected employment changes from 1972 to 1985.

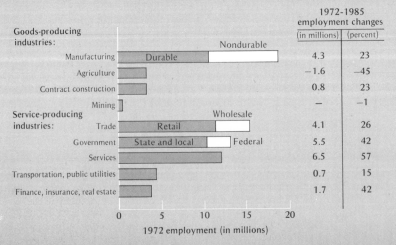

	1972-1985 employment changes	
	(in millions)	(percent)
Goods-producing industries:		
Manufacturing	4.3	23
Agriculture	−1.6	−45
Contract construction	0.8	23
Mining	—	−1
Service-producing industries:		
Trade	4.1	26
Government	5.5	42
Services	6.5	57
Transportation, public utilities	0.7	15
Finance, insurance, real estate	1.7	42

1972 employment (in millions)

Source: U.S. Bureau of Labor Statistics.

A CRITICAL BUSINESS DECISION

—made by Margaret Rudkin

THE SITUATION   It was August 1937, in the midst of the Great Depression, when Margaret Rudkin discovered that her youngest son was suffering from asthma. Mrs. Rudkin said later, "The doctor suggested that natural foods and natural sugars and the wheat germ contained in old-fashioned whole wheat bread might help this child who needed special food."

Although she had never baked bread before, this 40-year old woman from Fairfield, Connecticut believed that good food was the key to good health. "I got down an old cookbook and looked up a recipe for homemade bread," she said. "The ingredients it called for came as a bit of a shock —especially stone-ground flour. But I decided to make bread just that way, even to obtaining the whole wheat from a local feed store and grinding it in a coffee mill."

Rudkin's initial attempt was disasterous: her first "loaf" of bread was rock hard and one-inch high because she had used the yeast incorrectly. But she continued to experiment.

When she told her family doctor she was making bread from stone-ground whole wheat, he said it would be too coarse unless she added some white flour to the recipe. To convince the doctor, she brought him some samples of her bread and her list of ingredients. Impressed by both the bread's nutrition and its taste, the doctor ordered some for himself and for his patients. With his letter of introduction, Margaret Rudkin soon had a flourishing mail-order business going.

THE DECISION   In describing her business decision, Rudkin later wrote, "Businessmen and women agree with me in thinking that if I had talked to experts in our line of business in 1937, I would never have begun. A business expert would surely have said that without experience and without ample available capital, no one could successfully enter the food market with one of the oldest and simplest articles in man's diet—a loaf of bread." But she was too modest about her own capabilities: college majors in mathematics and finance and six years in the banking and brokerage business before her marriage.

She also had a practical problem: the income of her husband, Henry Rudkin, a stockbroker, had been cut dramatically. A serious accident had kept Mr. Rudkin out of the office for six months and at home—in a house they called Pepperidge Farm because of the pepperidge trees on the property.

So Margaret Rudkin went into the retail bread business by taking six loaves of her bread to a local Fairfield grocery store on August 15, 1937. She told the owner that her 20-

Some of the products Pepperidge Farm sells today.

ounce loaf was to retail at 25 cents, even though other breads were selling at 10 cents. Her sales pitch consisted of giving the owner a buttered slice of her bread. The six loaves were sold before she returned home. Within a week, several local stores called with requests to market the bread.

By September, Rudkin had outgrown her kitchen and had moved her baking operations to the garage. She had also hired her first employee, who still works for the firm. After weeks of experimenting, Rudkin added a "new" product to the Pepperidge Farm line: whole wheat bread with raisins. Her formal New York City debut occurred when she sold an order of two dozen loaves to a specialty food store there.

The rest of the story is history. The first modern Pepperidge Farm bakery, designed by Margaret Rudkin, began operations in Norwalk, Connecticut, in 1947. To serve the growing Philadephia and Washington markets, the Downington, Pennsylvania bakery was opened in 1949. To meet the Midwestern demand, a bread, roll, and stuffing bakery was built outside Chicago in 1953. These plants were soon producing an additional line of frozen turnovers, strudels, and puff pastries.

In 1961, Pepperidge Farm merged with the Campbell Soup Company. As president of Pepperidge Farm, Margaret Rudkin joined Campbell Soup's board of directors. From 1937 to 1961 she had seen Pepperidge Farm grow from a kitchen bakery in which two employees prepared 100 loaves a week to several plants which produce over 1,000,000 loaves a week and employ about 2000 workers.

QUESTION

In merging with the Campbell Soup Company, a much larger firm than Pepperidge Farm, what do you think the potential advantages and disadvantages would be for Margaret Rudkin, for Pepperidge Farm stockholders, and for consumers who buy Pepperidge Farm products?

A corporate executive's responsibility is to make as much money for his stockholders as possible so long as he operates within the rules of the game.

Milton Friedman

A large corporation these days may not only engage in social responsibility, it had damn well better do so.

Paul Samuelson

CHAPTER

3

LAW, ETHICS, AND THE SOCIAL RESPONSIBILITY OF BUSINESS

For more than 33 years, the Federal Communications Commission (FCC), the government agency in charge of regulating the communications industries, has tried to resolve a dispute between radio stations WABC in New York City and KOB in Albuquerque, New Mexico. The two stations were assigned the same radio frequency in 1941, and their radio waves have interfered with each other ever since—especially at night, when signals travel longer distances. According to Frank Fletcher, a KOB lawyer, the stack of legal briefs that make up the FCC's record of this case is "tall enough that a couple of giraffes couldn't kiss over it."

Regulatory delay plagues government agencies like the FCC. "Many people have died before they got what they sought from us," comments FCC member Robert E. Lee. More seriously, he observes, "The incredible delay is terrible. It's something you can't defend, but you can't pinpoint the blame either."

Business must adjust to pressures from outside the firm

As the handling of the WABC-KOB dispute suggests, government intervention in business has not always been successful. But neither has business always shone—as evidenced by the pollution, shoddy products, unfair employee practices, and poor public relations displayed by some businesses. Consequently, the contemporary manager is exposed to pressures from all sides: from the government, from consumers, from employees, and from society as a whole (see Figure 3-1).

In Chapter 3, we will examine: (1) the legal framework governing relationships among businesses; (2) the influence of consumers and consumerism on business behavior; (3) the impact of more affluent and educated employees, including women and minorities, on business decisions; and (4) the effects of new standards of business ethics and of corporate social responsibility.

Legal Considerations in Business

Business (or commercial) *law* encompasses all statutes, codes, rules, regulations, and court actions that govern interactions among businesses. It provides an explicit framework for the conduct of business affairs and for the settlement of disputes that arise in connection with business transactions.

Statutory law consists of written constitutions, codes, statutes, and regulations enacted by the people or their elected representatives. Antitrust and regulatory laws (discussed in Chapter 18) are good examples of

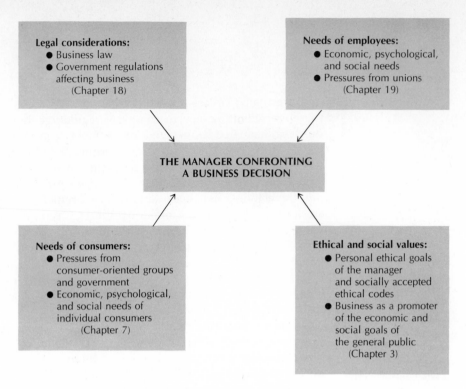

Legal considerations:	Needs of employees:
● Business law	● Economic, psychological, and social needs
● Government regulations affecting business (Chapter 18)	● Pressures from unions (Chapter 19)

THE MANAGER CONFRONTING A BUSINESS DECISION

Needs of consumers:	Ethical and social values:
● Pressures from consumer-oriented groups and government	● Personal ethical goals of the manager and socially accepted ethical codes
● Economic, psychological, and social needs of individual consumers (Chapter 7)	● Business as a promoter of the economic and social goals of the general public (Chapter 3)

3-1 The manager making an important business decision considers many legal and social factors that are external to the business.

Two kinds
of law exist:
statutory and
common law

statutory law. *Common law* consists of past court decisions that establish precedents for deciding similar cases. The law of contracts, for example, has developed out of a large number of court decisions concerning what specific types of agreements are legally enforceable. As new legal principles are established through a series of court decisions, they are often incorporated into written statutes. New laws may also be written to cover newly developed practices or situations not adequately covered by existing law. After new laws are passed, however, they must be interpreted through subsequent court decisions.

There is an old saying that a man who serves as his own lawyer has a fool for a client. Because so many codes and subsequent court interpretations apply to business, it is usually unwise for managers to make their own legal decisions. Some knowledge of business law is necessary, however, if managers are to be aware of their legal rights and are to avoid making serious legal blunders. As a result of pioneering efforts by the National Commissioners on the Uniform State Laws and by the American Law Institute, most areas of business law have been codified in the Uniform Commerical Code (UCC). Knowledge of the UCC and its subsequent court

The UCC applies
to most businesses

interpretations in various states is essential in many businesses. In the following section, we will examine three frequently encountered aspects of business law: the law of contracts, the law of agency, and the law of bankruptcy.

The Law of Contracts

Almost every transaction involves a *contract* — an agreement between two or more individuals or firms that is enforceable by court action. Many common transactions involve contracts of one kind or another. Examples are: using a credit card at a gas station; buying a ticket to a concert; paying a fare and riding a bus. Clearly an agreement does not have to be written and signed to be a contract. However, many states have enacted statutes of fraud requiring that certain types of contracts be written before they are considered enforceable. These include contracts for the sale of land, contracts for the sale of personal property valued in excess of some specified amount (usually $500), and contracts that are to be in force for more than one year.

To be enforceable, a written or an unwritten contract must meet several legal conditions:

1. There must be an offer.
2. There must be an acceptance.
3. There must be a consideration.
4. The parties must be competent.
5. The contract must have a lawful purpose.

✔ There must be an offer. An *offer* is a proposal by one party (the offeror) to enter into a contract with a second party (the offeree). The offer

---

BUSINESS LAW AND YOU

A working knowledge of the law of contracts and the law of agency can be as useful to consumers as it is to managers. Consider the following two situations.

The problem of the no-smoking contract: James has a very rich but eccentric uncle named Horace. While visiting James one day, Horace says, "James, your are my favorite nephew, but I think you smoke too much. If you'll stop smoking for six months, I'll give you $60,000." James quickly agrees to the offer. In your opinion, have James and Horace entered into a legally binding contract?

The problem of the undervalued house: The Birches have a lovely old house overlooking a beautiful lake. But both husband and wife have been transferred, and they must sell their home. The real estate agent values the house at $75,000, but finds a purchaser who is willing to pay $85,000. Without informing the Birches, the real estate agent closes the sale and pockets the $10,000 difference as a "finder's fee." Six months later, the Birches discover that the bill of sale for $75,000 did not include the finder's fee. Can they recover the $10,000 from the real estate agent?

Answers to both of these problems can be found by carefully applying the basic principles of business law described in the text. When you have formed your answers compare them with those given at the close of the business-law section.

must be made in definite terms and with the specific intention of creating a contract. For example, the courts have ruled that advertisements and store window displays are not offers because the terms they specify do not necessarily propose a contract with potential customers. Rather, advertisements are invitations to customers to offer to buy merchandise.

✔ **There must be an acceptance.** An *acceptance* is an acknowledgment by the party to whom an offer is made that the terms of the offer are satisfactory and that the person is willing to be bound to a contract. The acceptance must conform to the terms of the original offer. If a party attempts to change the terms of the original offer after it is made, that party is actually rejecting the offer and making a counteroffer.

Offers and acceptances can be spoken, written, or in the form of an action. Thus, the presence of a bus on a city street is an offer by the bus company to carry passengers; the action of getting on the bus and putting money in the coin box is an acceptance of the bus company's offer.

The offer of a contract and its acceptance must be made voluntarily by both parties. A contract is not valid if one party is forced into the agreement. The contracts signed at gunpoint in the movies would never hold up in court. The agreement of both parties must also be based on a reasonable understanding of the facts. If one party signs the agreement under a mistaken impression of the situation, the contract may not be valid.

✔ **There must be consideration.** For a contract to be enforceable, each party must give *consideration*—something of value in exchange for the agreement of the other party to the contract. Consideration may be in the form of money, goods, an action, or an agreement to refrain from an action. For example, if Mrs. Leary sells her dry-cleaning business, she may receive an additional $5000 for the "goodwill" associated with the business—the reputation the firm has earned over the years. In return she may agree to refrain from starting a similar business in the same city for five years so as not to draw old customers away from the firm she has sold. In this case, not starting a new business is the consideration that Mrs. Leary gives in return for the $5000.

✔ **The parties must be competent.** Four classes of people are considered legally incompetent to enter into contractual agreements: minors (in most states, persons under 21 years of age), emotionally unbalanced persons, aliens, and intoxicated people. Most agreements made by such persons are voidable, although these people do have a legal right to contract necessities such as food, clothing, shelter, and medical care.

Legal contracts
must be made
by competent people
for lawful purposes

✔ **The contract must have a lawful purpose.** A contract is not enforceable if the parties have agreed to something that violates a statute or that is not in the best interests of society. Thus, contracts that restrain free competition or that involve unfair trade practices are illegal. In states where gambling is against the law, for example, contracts involving wagers or the payment of gambling debts are not enforceable.

The Law of Agency

Agency is a legal relationship in which one party (the agent) is authorized to act on behalf of another (the principal) in transactions with a third party. Virtually all types of transactions, except voting and making a will, can be negotiated by an agent, and agents are used in a wide variety of business situations. Insurance representatives who make policy agreements with clients are agents of their company. Manufacturers' representatives are agents of their clients, as are real estate brokers.

✔ The principal's obligations to the agent. The principal grants the agent the authority to make, modify, or terminate contracts with a third party on behalf of the principal. The principal usually compensates the agent for services performed and expenses incurred. In addition, if the agent suffers a loss or is sued for unintentionally injuring a third party while following the principal's instructions, the principal must reimburse the agent.

Agents represent others in making contracts

✔ The agent's obligations to the principal. The agent must be loyal to the principal and cannot use agency powers to further the agent's own interest or the interests of a third party at the principal's expense. The agent is expected to follow the principal's instructions carefully and cautiously. An agent who fails to follow instructions can be forced to reimburse the principal for any losses suffered. The agent is also legally responsible for all money or property received on behalf of the principal and must keep the principal informed of facts relevant to his or her business interests.

The agent should represent the principal fairly

✔ The difference between agents and employees. An agent is given specific powers to act on behalf of a principal. As a result, the principal legally forfeits some degree of control over the agent's behavior. In contrast, an employee may be free to act, but the employer always has the legal right to control employees activities. This distinction between agents and employees is important in determining who is ultimately responsible for the behavior of an individual. If an agent acts negligently while conducting a principal's business (by driving recklessly and causing an accident, for example), the agent is responsible for the consequences of the action. If an employee commits the same negligent act while working, the employer is responsible because employers are legally in control of their employees.

Agents are legally responsible for their actions; employees may not be

The Law of Bankruptcy

Just as there are a wide variety of laws to guide and protect people while they conduct business, there are laws to guide and protect them if their business fails. In the eighteenth and nineteenth centuries, people who were unable to pay their debts were thrown into debtors' prison. Since even the most honest and hard-working managers may fail in a competitive economy, modern law provides a way to relieve debtors of financial obligations so that they may make a fresh start. The Chandler Act of 1938, an amendment to the Federal Bankruptcy Act of 1898, protects both parties in a bankruptcy proceeding by providing rules for fairly distributing the bankrupt debtor's assets among the debtor's creditors.

Bankruptcy may be either *voluntary* or *involuntary*. The debtor initiates voluntary bankruptcy; the creditors initiate involuntary bankruptcy. Bankruptcy procedures begin with the filing of a petition in federal district court. If the court judges the debtor named in the petition to be bankrupt, the case is referred to a bankruptcy court, where a referee is appointed. The referee calls a meeting of the creditors, who elect a trustee to manage the bankrupt's estate while their claims are determined and the assets are distributed.

Priority of claims against a bankrupt's assets

The assets available in a bankrupt's estate are used to pay claims in the following order: (1) expenses of the court incurred in preserving and managing the estate after the petition is filed; (2) wages owed to employees; (3) expenses incurred by creditors in developing a plan to discharge the bankrupt's assets; (4) taxes owed to the government; and (5) any debts given priority by state or federal law. After these claims are paid, the remaining funds are divided among the creditors. Each creditor's share of the remaining funds is determined by assessing the type of debt involved and then negotiating with the other creditors.

Effects of Business Law

A well-developed body of business law is essential to the orderly conduct of business, just as traffic laws are vital to the orderly flow of

---

"BUSINESS LAW AND YOU" (Answers)

Applying the text discussion of business law to the two questions asked in "Business Law and You" provides the following answers.

The problem of the no-smoking contract: Under the law of contracts, both James and his uncle must be legally competent for the contract to be completely valid. If we assume that both are at least 21 years of age, that both are U.S. citizens, that neither

is mentally incompetent, and that neither was intoxicated at the time of the agreement, James and his uncle have entered into a legally binding contract.

The problem of the undervalued house: Under the law of agency, agents must be loyal to their principals. Thus, the agent cannot benefit personally at the expense of the principal. Clearly, the Birches' agent violated this trust, and the Birches can recover their $10,000 from the agent.

traffic. Imagine the confusion that would arise if drivers had no rules to follow and did not know what kind of behavior to expect from other drivers. Business law prevents the same kind of confusion from arising in business relationships by providing a basic set of rules and regulations to guide business behavior. The law also insures that all businessmen play by the same rules, so that each one knows what to expect from the others and so that minor details concerning the rules of the game do not have to be renegotiated in every transaction. If a businessman violates the rules and injures another party financially, the law and the court system provide a mechanism for reimbursing the injured party and for punishing the lawbreaker. If two parties disagree over their rights and obligations in a particular transaction, the legal system can help to settle the dispute. Finally, business law provides a way for society to communicate with and to enforce its will on those who run business institutions.

Business law promotes orderly business conduct

Business and Consumers

In a broad sense, American business exists to serve the consumer. The production of goods and services is its means, but the consumption of commodities is its end. Consumers merit detailed study for at least three other reasons.

Business exists to serve consumers

First, consumers spend an enormous amount of money each year on goods and services. In 1975, consumer spending amounted to more than one trillion dollars, about five-eighths of the U.S. gross national product. Consumer dollars often determine whether products and business firms succeed or fail.

Second, the pattern of consumer spending is unpredictable. Immediately after World War II, massive consumer expenditures helped to prevent the severe recession many economists forecast. In 1974-1975, consumers spent an unexpectedly low part of their incomes on goods and services, thus contributing to a recession and to high unemployment.

Third, consumers as a group are becoming better informed and more active and influential in the economic community. The voices of consumers—somewhat muffled in the past—are now loud and clear enough to be heard even by top management.

In this section, we will examine two important aspects of consumer influence on business: consumer sovereignty and consumerism.

Consumer Sovereignty

Consumer sovereignty refers to the concept that consumers direct the types of goods and services that are produced in a private enterprise system. The effectiveness of consumer sovereignty has been challenged in the 1970s for several reasons:

1. *Are consumers sufficiently intelligent and informed to make wise purchase decisions, or are they excessively influenced by the advertising claims of giant corporations?* Will the average consumer, for example, eat a heavily advertised, highly sugared cereal for breakfast or a more healthful, less-advertised food, ("Will the Real Consumer Please Stand Up?")?
2. *Should intelligent and informed consumers be allowed to buy products that are detrimental to their health or safety?* Clear-cut restrictions are placed on the excessive use of drugs and alcohol, but what about products like cigarettes or aerosol cans?
3. *Should consumers be permitted to use products that may ultimately be harmful to others?* Should soft-drink manufacturers be allowed to provide nonreturnable bottles for consumers who are willing to pay a premium for them, even though nonreturnable bottles are a major source of litter along highways and streets? Should the violence on children's television programs remain uncensored even though many psychologists feel the medium's emphasis on violence is linked to rising crime?

Americans, through their elected representatives in government, have addressed themselves to these questions, have placed legal limitations on the claims advertisers can make, and have attempted to place restraints on the harm consumers can do to themselves and to others. But the danger exists that government may overstep its jurisdiction and impose decisions on consumers that consumers can better make themselves.

Consumerism

In 1962, President John F. Kennedy presented a message to Congress that emphasized four basic consumer rights:

1. *The right to safety:* To be protected against hazardous products.

WILL THE REAL CONSUMER PLEASE STAND UP?

"The consumer is king!" John Wanamaker reputedly proclaimed in 1875. In the century between John Wanamaker and Ralph Nader, the American consumer appears to have progressed from being king in name only to being king in fact. Attitudes toward the consumer vary dramatically. One view holds that consumers who make careful, reasoned decisions are the dominating force in the American economy. Another view argues that the careless, illogical buying habits of consumers make them easy prey to the manipulations of big business. On one hand, the consumer is assumed to have a computer-like ability to assimilate vast amounts of information and to make wise purchase decisions. On the other hand, the consumer is considered too dumb to even benefit from readily available information. Will the real consumer please stand up?

2. *The right to be informed:* To be protected against fraudulent or misleading information, advertisements, and labeling, and to be
given the facts necessary to make informed purchase decisions.
3. *The right to choose:* To have access to a variety of products at competitive prices.
4. *The right to be heard:* To affect the formulation and the execution of
government policy.

President Kennedy's message reflected emergence of *consumerism* — the
view that government and business have a joint responsibility to educate,
to inform, and to protect the consumer. Prominent consumer advocates
like Ralph Nader argue that the old attitude of *caveat emptor* ("let the
buyer beware") is outmoded in an age where many products are technically so complex that the average person has no reasonable chance of in-
telligently judging their safety or quality.

Consumerism aids the consumer before (the prepurchase stage),
when (the purchase stage), and after (the post-purchase stage) a product is
purchased. An extensive body of federal and state legislation is available
to aid the consumer. But no amount of government intervention can protect consumers as they make millions of individual purchases each hour.
Much of the credit for the increased responsiveness to consumer complaints by business must go to private firms, most of which have established consumer affairs departments to handle consumer relations. Figure 3-2 lists some of the major government and business changes that
consumerism has already produced. Some of these changes are also
reviewed below in more detail.

🖙 **Prepurchase assistance to consumers.**   Prior to the point of sale,
actions that reduce and correct misleading advertising are of the greatest
value to consumers. In the past, advertising copywriters have often gone
out of their way to make product claims that were difficult either to prove

Dear GE:
Prove that
GE air conditioners
produce air
as clean as
mountain air!
Sincerely,
The FTC

or to disprove. The Federal Trade Commission (FTC), the government
agency charged with protecting consumers from misleading advertising,
has ordered manufacturers of cars, air conditioners, electric shavers, television sets, toothpastes, and cold and cough remedies to prove their advertising claims. For example, General Electric has been asked to document its statement that its air conditioners give "the clean freshness of
clear, cool mountain air." Similarly, Schick has been asked to explain its
statement "No more nicks and cuts" in reference to the Lady Schick. When
asked to back up its claims that its cars were quieter than expensive imports, Ford submitted test data dating back to 1966. The Ford tested then
was quietest. It was also new; the losers included a 1964 Jaguar which had
been driven more than 20,000 miles and a 1963 Daimler registering 37,225
miles.

If a claim is ruled to be misleading, the FTC can request that the advertiser run a *corrective advertisement* to clear up any misconceptions the

consumers may have about the product. A milestone was reached when Profile bread ran a corrective ad explaining why each slice of its bread had fewer calories than competing brands: Profile bread was sliced thinner!

✔ **Purchase assistance to consumers.** Another major problem is the inadequate information about interest charges on installment loans that is made available to the consumer. In 1968, a federal truth-in-lending law was passed stating that buyers must be informed of the annual simple interest they pay on installment loans and on revolving charge accounts.

The information supplied on a product or its package for the consumer's benefit has also been criticized. For example, government quality ratings have been a source of confusion to consumers. How many people

3-2 Consumer problems and how consumerism has helped business and government become increasingly responsive to consumer complaints and needs.

Purchase stage	Consumer problem	Action taken to protect consumer
Before the sale	Misleading advertising.	The Federal Trade Commission (FTC) can ask advertisers to prove their claims; if claims are untrue, the FTC may require corrective advertising. The advertising industry is now attempting to regulate itself by developing precise advertising guidelines and by reviewing questionable ads.
During the sale	Inadequate product information on package or product.	The 1965 Fair Packaging and Labeling Act ("truth in packaging") regulates the packaging and labeling of consumer goods and encourages voluntary packaging standards in industry. Food stores must provide unit pricing, open dating, and nutritional labeling on grocery products.
	Incomplete information on actual interest paid on installment loans and charge accounts.	The 1968 Consumer Credit Protecting Act ("truth in lending") requires the full disclosure of annual simple interest rates and other finance charges on consumer loans.
	High-pressure, door-to-door selling.	Many states require a cooling-off period of 3–5 days, during which consumers can amend their purchase decisions.
	"Unavailable" advertising specials in food stores.	Grocery specials advertised at stated prices must be stocked and be made available to consumers on the sale days indicated.
	Credit denial because of incorrect credit reports.	The 1970 Fair Credit Reporting Act gives consumers access to their own credit reports.
After the sale	Better quality and safer products.	Federal legislation on product quality and safety includes the National Traffic and Motor Vehicle Safety Act (1966), the Child Safety Act (1966), the National Commission of Product Safety Act (1967), and the Child Protection and Toy Safety Act (1969).
	Lack of effective business reaction to consumer complaints.	Manufacturers have installed toll-free "hot lines" to handle consumer complaints. Some trade associations review customer complaints.

"And now listen to what 'Consumer Reports' has to say about your Model 1211 Electric Train: 'Extremely noisy, poor rail grip on curves at even moderate speeds, offers only fair protection against shock, and displays an utter lack of historical accuracy in recreating B. & O. circa 1890.' "

Drawing by Dedini; © 1974 The New Yorker Magazine, Inc.

When U.S. No. 1 is third best

really know that a U.S. No. 1 apple is one grade below U.S. Fancy, which in turn is one grade below U.S. Extra Fancy? And how many consumers know that U.S. No. 1 is the second grade in grapes (behind Fancy) and in dinnerware (behind Select)? Problems like this have prompted consumer advocates to request that three kinds of information appear on grocery products:

1. *Unit pricing:* Giving price information in cents per ounce or cents per pound. This permits a consumer to make a best-buy decision in terms of price. For example, the choice may be between brand A's 20-pound "giant size" box at $5.14 and brand B's 5-pound, 11-ounce "king size" box at $1.61.
2. *Open dating:* Indicating the latest date the consumer should buy or use a product.
3. *Nutritional labeling:* Giving information in common household units (per bowl, cup, or glass) about the proportion of recommended daily allowances of vitamins, minerals, and proteins contained in the product.

Critics of proposals requiring that business provide additional information to consumers question (1) the increased cost of providing this information, which is usually passed on to consumers in the form of higher prices, and (2) the number of consumers who use the information. Unfortunately, research suggests that consumer information is most often used by better-educated consumers and has little effect on consumers who have less education and income.

✔ **Post-purchase assistance to consumers.** Beginning with the book *Unsafe at Any Speed,* Ralph Nader has raised questions about automobile safety, inflammable and dangerous toys, and radiation hazards. Such publicity has resulted in three consumer benefits. First, business is giving more attention to product quality at the product design stage. Second, industry is acknowledging its responsibility for product quality by recalling problem products; in 1971, General Motors recalled 6,700,000 Chevrolets (1965-1969 models) because of engine mount failures that could have resulted in loss of vehicle control. Third, consumers may take their grievances either directly to the business in question or to court. However, few consumers can mount the frontal attack of movie producer David Merrick, who placed an ad on the front page of *The New York Times* that read "My Chrysler Imperial is a piece of junk." Grievances may be pressed either through individual claims or (in some states) through *class action suits* — the pooling of claims by consumers who are economically injured by fraudulent business practices.

Aids after purchase better products and warranties

Virginia Knauer, one-time special assistant to the President of the United States for consumer affairs, summed up the business challenge of the consumer movement: "Consumerism is nothing more and nothing less than a challenge to business to live up to its full potential . . . and to return to the basic principle upon which so much of our nation's business was structured — 'satisfaction guaranteed or your money back.' " A number of business- and government-sponsored groups are available to assist consumers who are unfairly treated by business.

The business challenge: "satisfaction guaranteed"

Business and Employees

In the mid-1970s, increasingly affluent and educated blue- and white-collar workers began to demonsrate a growing dissatisfaction with their working conditions. In addition, militant groups representing women and ethnic minorities, often backed by federal and state laws, began to pressure business for more and better job opportunities.

The Dissatisfied Employee

The founder of scientific management, Frederick W. Taylor, once told a group of workers: "Each day, year in and out, each man should ask himself over and over again two questions. First, 'What is the name of the man I am working for?' and having answered that definitively, 'What does this man expect of me?' " Taylor accurately forecast that modern mass production would involve the division of work into specialized, routine tasks that workers could carry out quickly and with little thought.

Recent evidence, however, suggests that the routine, specialized jobs typical of many occupations no longer satisfy most blue- and white-collar employees or their bosses. *Work in America*, a study sponsored by the fed-

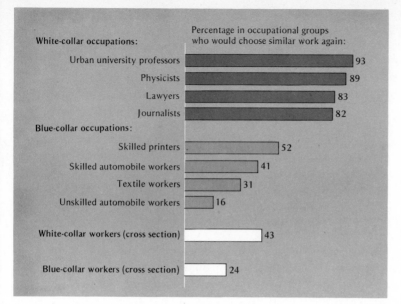

Percentage in occupational groups who would choose similar work again:

White-collar occupations:

Urban university professors	93
Physicists	89
Lawyers	83
Journalists	82

Blue-collar occupations:

Skilled printers	52
Skilled automobile workers	41
Textile workers	31
Unskilled automobile workers	16
White-collar workers (cross section)	43
Blue-collar workers (cross section)	24

3-3

Job satisfaction among various occupations in the United States. Note that the degree of job satisfaction varies greatly by occupation.

Source: James O'Toole (ed.), *Work and the Quality of Life: Resource Papers for Work in America,* prepared under the auspices of the W. E. Upjohn Institute for Employment Research (Cambridge, Mass.: MIT Press, 1974), p. 204.

eral government and prepared by the Upjohn Institute for Employment Research, found substantial job dissatisfaction among all economic, occupational, racial, religious, and ethnic groups.

Rising job dissatisfaction

For example, throughout the American economy, only 43 percent of white-collar workers and 24 percent of blue-collar workers said that they would choose the same occupation if given a second chance (see Figure 3-3). Moreover, job discontent appears to be increasing at all occupational levels. Many middle managers in large impersonal corporations are unhappy at their apparent loss of authority, influence, and responsibility.

Employee discontent has seriously damaged many businesses. Employees' high absenteeism, drug and alcohol problems, indifference to quality of output, and poor performance have all been costly to business in terms of output, product quality, and profits.

Business has responded to worker dissatisfaction in a number of ways:

. . . What can be done

1. *Better use of personnel* by improving screening and testing methods so that job assignments are based on individual abilities and needs.
2. *Participative management* by fostering communication within the business, encouraging employees and supervisors to meet jointly to discuss problems and to assign goals.
3. *Job enrichment* by redesigning jobs so that the individual employee is given a greater variety of tasks to perform and is assigned additional responsibilities. As examples: automobile

workers may be responsible for assembling a whole subsection of a car; the jobs of secretary and assistant to a manager may be combined.

4. *Greater job flexibility* by allowing employees, at their discretion, to spread their 40-hour week 4 or 5 days and to select their own working hours.

As former General Motors Chairman Richard C. Gerstenberg has observed, "Personnel development is probably the most imporant part of our business. Every problem we have gets back to what I call a 'people problem'."

Equal Employment Opportunities

In the last two decades, women and ethnic groups have won increased employment opportunities from business and from the public sector. Articulate feminists like Kate Millett and Gloria Steinem have helped to secure wider job opportunities for women. Blacks and Chicanos have been represented by prominant leaders like Martin Luther King, Jr., Leon Sullivan, and César Chavez. Advocates of *equal employment opportunities* (EEO) have sought such goals as: (1) equal pay for equal work, regardless of the sex, race, national origin, or age of the employee; (2) more jobs for women and ethnic minorities; (3) representation of women and minorities in high-pay, high-prestige professional and supervisory occupations in approximante portion to their numbers in the population; and (4) recognition of the special job-related problems faced by women and minorities.

Equal job opportunities

✔ **Women in business.** Since 1947, the number of working women employed largely in business has risen more than 80 percent, while the number of working men has increased about 10 percent. In 1975, females constituted 46 percent of the civilian labor force (all nonmilitary persons employed or seeking work). Yet, on the average, women earn about 20 percent less than men do for the same work, even after educational background and work experience are taken into account.

A waste of feminine brainpower . . .

Female employment is also concentrated in the clerical and service areas (see Figure 3-4), where low-pay, low-prestige jobs are traditional. The large discrepancy between occupations held mainly by women and those held mainly by men indicates a potential waste of human abilities of considerable scope.

Most feminists believe that the effective use of women in business requires that both sexes make several basic adjustments in attitudes and behavior. First, women themselves must be free to choose whether they want a career, a family, or both. To achieve freedom of choice, women must be able to resolve their own internal problems produced by the sometimes conflicting demands of career and family. And both women

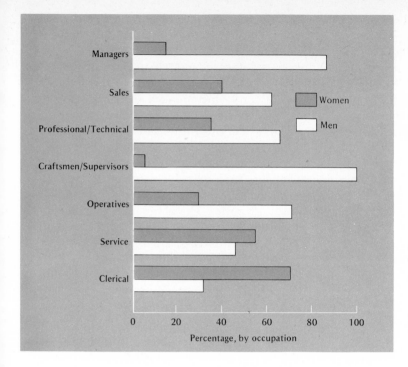

3-4

Occupational distribution of men and women. Male occupations are clustered in managerial, professional/technical, and craftsmen/supervisors areas. Women usually work in clerical-, service-, and sales-related occupations.

Source: U.S. Bureau of Labor Statistics.

and men must be prepared to make appropriate compromises in such aspects of their lifestyles as location of living quarters and sharing child-care responsibilities. Second, stereotypes about women must be overcome. Contrary to popular opinion, careful research indicates that female employees are as emotionally stable as male employees and that an employee's sex has no effect on job turnover or on absenteeism. Finally, women and men should meet equal performance standards. A woman should not have to do better work than a man to reach the same occupational level. Aggressiveness and initiative, regarded as desirable qualities in a male employee, should not be considered unfeminine or detrimental qualities in a woman employee.

... which business can help to cure

Business can help to provide equal opportunities for women and men by searching out, identifying, and promoting qualified women and providing them with "role models" — examples of successful and productive female employees. Business should also seek to meet the special needs of women employees by providing fexible work schedules, day-care facilities, and leaves of absence to care for children, when necessary.

✔ **Ethnic minorities.** Black workers constitute about the same proportion of the labor force as white workers do, but the unemployment rate among blacks averages more than twice that among whites. Unemployment among blacks, Chicanos, Indians, and most other ethnic minorities is greatest among the teenage population. A nonwhite wage-earner is more than three times as likely to earn an income of less than $4,000 as is a white wage-earner. Jobs held by ethnic minorities are heavily concentrated in the operative, service, and laborer categories. Since 1947, however, nonwhite-family incomes have increased more than white-family incomes. In 1973, the typical nonwhite family received an income of $7,600, 60 percent of the equivalent white-family income (see Figure 3-5).

Ethnic minorities of all types confront many similar employment problems. The lifestyles and cultures of ethnic minorities frequently differ substantially from white middle-class norms. As a result, minority employees may find it difficult to preserve their cultural heritages and succeed in business simultaneously. The effects of past racial discrimination have placed minorities in an unfavorable position to take advantage of potential employment opportunities. Discrimination in housing, for example, has forced minority populations to concentrate in urban downtown areas, away from expanding suburban job markets. Thus, minority employees frequently lack experience and cultural familiarity with business. Minorities, then, often enter the job market with substantial disadvantages unrelated to their potential abilities and, as employees, find themselves confronted with an overt or unconscious racial bias.

Business can help to remove minority bias by hiring qualified minority employees, by redesigning jobs so that entrance requirements correspond to actual job requirements and not to nonminority, middle-class attitudes, by financially supporting those minority employees who wish to receive more education, and by placing minority employees in mainstream business areas where rapid promotion based on ability is feasible. Business has already made notable contributions to *minority entrepreneurship* — the development of businesses owned and operated by ethnic

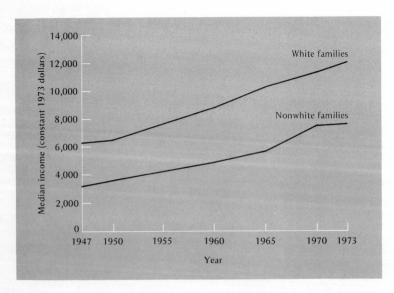

3-5

Income of white and nonwhite families in constant 1973 dollars. Purchasing power of all families has risen since 1947.

Source: *1974 Statistical Abstract of the United States*, p. 383.

minorities. Many firms have encouraged top management to aid in the development and operation of minority enterprises and have ordered purchasing departments to buy a designated percentage of items from minority-operated businesses. General Motors, for example, has trained and financed several hundred new automobile dealerships operated by black businessmen.

✔ **EEO and the law.** The rights of women and ethnic minorities to equal employment opportunities have been advanced by series of statutes, court decisions, and executive orders of the President of the United States:

Keys to improving equal employment opportunities

1. *Equal Pay Act* (1963) prohibits discrimination on the basis of sex and orders equal pay for equal work.
2. *The Civil Rights Act* (1964) prohibits discrimination in compensation, terms, or conditions of employment on the basis of an employee's race, color, religion, sex, or national origin. The Equal Employment Opportunities Commission, an agency of the federal government, enforces this act.
3. *Executive Order 11246* (1965) requires that all federal contractors establish "affirmative action" programs. As subsequently defined by this Presidential order, affirmative action programs are to be in written form and are to show that the business is actively seeking women and minority employees. Percentage targets for both groups are to be established at each plant for each occupational category. If the established targets are not met, an effort at compliance in good faith must be demonstrated or the affected business loses its federal contracts and its potential right to bid on future federal contracts.

Most businesses have direct or indirect commercial dealings with the federal government and are required to file affirmative action programs. All businesses must conform to the Equal Pay Act and to the Civil Rights Act. The costs of violating these statutes can be high. American Telephone and Telegraph Company, for example, agreed to pay millions of dollars in settlements to female employees who alleged that they were subjected to unfair treatment by the company.

Ethical and Social Responsibilities of Business

Business decisions are frequently influenced by ethical and social considerations. Modern techniques of mass communication have made fraud, bribery, open conflicts of interest, and ruthless selfishness much more noticeable. Business behavior that would have been ethically, legally, and socially acceptable 50 years ago is more than likely questionable today.

Business Ethics

Business ethics provide guidelines as to what is right, good, or moral in commercial relationships. Should a business pay bribes to public officials? (Bribes are a way of life in many nations and are regarded by the Internal Revenue Service as legitimate business expenses in most areas outside the United States.) Should an employee accept every order from the boss without question, no matter how many fellow workers or consumers will be hurt if it is carried out? Most business decisions have ethical implications; managers conscientiously or unconscientiously follow ethical guidelines.

Ethics: taking the moral action

✔ **Personal ethical convictions.** An ethical decision may be based upon an absolute set of moral standards, some form of situational ethics, or perceived self-interest. *Absolute ethical standards* are moral principles that a person attempts to follow consistently, regardless of the situation. Thus, a manager may follow such rules as never giving gifts to business associates and accepting all merchandise returned by customers without question.

Absolute standards: rules that apply all the time

Absolute moral standards are usually drawn from religious convictions. At times during the Middle Ages, for example, the Church was permitted to designate "just prices" and "just wages"; prices, wages, and profits were set by religious directive and tradition rather than in the marketplace. All types of religious demoninations have established ethical guidelines for their members — many of which are potentially applicable to business.

Situational ethics provide guidelines to moral behavior that may vary with the particular circumstance. For example, offering a gift to a business associate may be considered a bribe in some circumstances; in others, it may be a humane and thoughtful act. Guidelines commonly applied in situational ethics include:

Situational ethics: rules that depend on circumstances

1. Always behave in a way that produces the greatest amount of good for the greatest number of people.
2. Always behave in a way that does people more good than harm.
3. Never behave in a way that produces unfair gains for yourself at someone else's expense.

Situational ethics are often difficult to apply in practice, since the benefit and the harm resulting from such actions are typically difficult to predict or measure.

Self-interest frequently guides moral behavior. A business that maximizes its profits in a competitive industry ultimately benefits consumers and the general public , as we saw in Chapter 2. Consumers who selfishly purchase goods and services may improve general public welfare through the dollar votes they cast. Thus, in many instances, expressing selfish desires can best communicate real consumer needs to society.

✔ **Codes of ethics.** Many firms have formulated their own ethical codes for their employees. Company codes are usually established in the belief that sound ethics is good business in the long run—that fair and just treatment of employees, suppliers, and customers will lead to more profitable, long-term business relationships.

A company's ethical code, however, has little effect on employee behavior unless it is openly supported and enforced by the firm's top executives. Ethical standards often break down when superiors put pressure on employees to increase sales and profits. In the absence of a clear ethical policy supported by top executives, employees may attempt to please their superiors and to relieve job pressure in any way they can. Many professions, such as those in accounting and marketing, have also established ethical codes for their members.

A firm's ethical code
means little unless
top executives
support it

It is difficult for a firm to establish and to enforce a code of ethics if its competitors do not follow similar codes. Thus, firms in some industries have devised industry-wide ethical codes. One advantage of industry codes is that all companies are provided with the same ethical guidelines. No particular firm is placed at a competitive disadvantage because it follows higher ethical standards than other firms in the industry. Furthermore, industry codes simplify the detection of unethical behavior by competitors and employees and provide a rationale for reprimanding unethical behavior.

✔ **Ethics and the law.** Law enables society to communicate and to enforce its will—including its views on ethical conduct—on business. Consequently, some people in business believe that they can fulfill their ethical obligations simply by strictly adhering to the law. For example, the chief executive of a firm accused by the government of manufacturing a cheap and possibly dangerous mouthwash commented:

> We broke no law. We're in a highly competitive industry. If we're going to stay in business, we have to look for profit wherever the law permits. . . . Then why do we have to put up with this "holier than thou" talk about ethics? . . . We're not in business to promote ethics. . . .

Such people use the law as their ethical code and argue that "if it's legal, it's ethical."

As a guide to ethical behavior, however, the law is a very imperfect instrument. Only the principles that society feels demand compliance from everyone are embodied in the law. Were all businesses to equate ethics and law, the private sector would be entangled in a maze of laws and regulations.

THE CASE FOR A RESTRICTIVE VIEW OF SOCIAL RESPONSIBILITY

Business can best meet its obligations to society within a framework of private enterprise by securing the highest possible profits because:

1. If business seeks the greatest profits, in a competitive economy maximum social welfare is usually achieved.
2. Socially responsible businesses usually sacrifice profits. Less responsible domestic and foreign competitors who produce similar products can therefore charge lower prices and achieve higher profits at the expense of socially responsible firms. To ask business to be socially responsible is to punish the conscientious business.
3. A business elite of giant corporations should not be granted the sole power to make important social decisions. Social decisions should be made by democratically elected governments.
4. Business leaders have been trained to make decisions involving profits, prices, and costs. Expecting them to make important social decisions as well may not make full use of their specialized experience and may result in poor social performance.
5. Business profits are too small, too widely distributed among hundreds of businesses, and too volatile over time to be used to attack social problems effectively.

For a contrasting view, see the opposite page.

The Social Responsibility of Business

The growing debate: profit or social concerns

As a society evolves, it develops a number of *social institutions*—mechanisms for organizing the efforts of its members toward the acheivement of common goals. These mechanisms include family, religious, educational, military, government, and business institutions. Almost everyone agrees that the purpose of business institutions is to organize group efforts toward achieving the goals of material well-being and higher living standards. However, argument centers on what social groups business is primarily responsible to and how far that responsibility should extend beyond purely material concerns.

✔ **The restrictive view of business responsibility.** Most Western societies have maintained separate social institutions: the separation of church and state, the separation of church and business, and, as much as possible, the separation of government and business. Traditionally, Americans believe that the business of the church is religion, the business of government is government, and the business of business is business, and that each institution should tend its own garden and not interfere with the others.

The traditional view of business responsibility is that the primary obligations of management are to provide a good return for the owners or stockholders and to continue to provide jobs for employees. Any activity that interferes with the achievement of these goals should be avoided.

Professor Theodore Levitt of Harvard University writes: "The governing rule in industry should be that something is good only if its pays. Otherwise it is alien and impermissible."

✔ **The expansive view of business responsibility.** A broader concept of the social responsibility of business has emerged in recent years. Proponents of this view argue that business has helped to create so many social problems—such as pollution, discrimination, and the destruction of natural resources—that it should be actively involved in solving them. The expansive view of social responsibility requires that business: (1) respond to the economic and social pressures exerted by government, consumers, environmentalists, minorities, and other social groups; and (2) act affirmatively in a manner consistent with the public interest even in the absence of economic and social pressures from sources external to the firm.

Social objectives: less important to business during hard times

Conflict over the definition of the social responsibility of business reflects basic disagreement about the role business can and should assume in modern society (see the two opposing views of corporate social responsibility given here). Evidence from recent recessions suggests business is likely to be deeply concerned with profits in adverse economic circumstances. Polls of executives, however, reveal that most managers agree that business responsibility extends beyond the pursuit of profit and that younger executives are in the forefront in advocating greater social responsibility for business.

How Socially Responsible Is Business?

Talk is cheap; action dear. To what extent has business been willing to back up its feelings of social responsibility with programs of social action? In recent years, many companies have undertaken programs

---

THE CASE FOR AN EXPANSIVE VIEW OF SOCIAL RESPONSIBILITY

Business has an ethical and practical obligation to consider social as well as economic factors in its actions because:

1. It is often profitable to be socially responsible. For example, when downtown merchants promote a shopping mall, the mall may also help their businesses.
2. Business has an important stake in a workable society. If social needs are not met, disruptions like strikes and riots will damage both business and the American economy.
3. When business does not meet social needs, people turn to the government. Government regulation is often inefficient and damaging to business.
4. Because business is partially to blame for many social problems, it has a moral responsibility to help alleviate them.
5. As "good, social citizens," business firms—like other organizations—have an ethical obligation to help solve pressing social problems.

As the quotations at the beginning of this chapter indicate, the social responsibility of business is a controversial topic. The "right" answer to the question "How can business best be socially responsible?" is a matter of opinion. What are your views?

aimed at solving a variety of social problems. It is impossible to completely outline these programs here, but most businesses have been engaged in several of the following areas:

1. *Pollution control:* Water, air, and noise pollution are significant social problems, and many businesses have cooperated with the federal and state governments on these ecological issues. Soft-drink manufacturers encourage the use of returnable bottles by their pricing policies; several progressive mining firms landscape their strip-mining sites.

2. *Consumer responsiveness:* Consumer pressure has revolutionized the marketing practices of many businesses. Firms like Whirlpool and American Motors have installed consumer "hotlines" and consumer-relations departments to deal more effectively with consumer complaints. Many businesses have attempted to make their product warranties and service contracts more complete and more readable.

3. *Employee relations:* Employee discontent has caused many changes in business practices. Both Xerox and IBM, for example, sponsor "loaned executive" programs which grant employees up to one year's paid leave to work in various social service areas.

Examples of socially responsible business actions

4. *Employment of women and minorities:* Feminist and civil-rights organizations have pressured business to produce significant changes in hiring and promotion procedures. A major shoe company has established a free day-care center for its employees' children; several major banks provide special lending programs to high-risk, minority-run businesses.

5. *Poverty and the central city:* The decay of urban centers has prompted a wide range of responses from business. Three of Control Data Corporation's large plants are located in major urban ghettos. The JOBS program, sponsored by the National Alliance of Businessmen, secures hundreds of thousands of jobs for the disadvantaged.

6. *Corporate philanthropy:* For many years, business has donated about 1 percent of its after-tax profits to educational and charitable organizations. The Dayton-Hudson Corporation, a giant national retailer, has established a foundation which recieves 5 percent of the corporate profits. The Dayton-Hudson Foundation has supported the development of downtown urban areas and has promoted local symphony orchestras.

Such socially related activities have not always been profitable for the business involved. Their continuation by many businesses suggests that a great number of managers have accepted a rather broad concept of social responsibility.

Business and Its Environment: An Overview

The executive of the future must understand the business environment

Most business experts believe that the federal and state governments will increasingly regulate the areas of business decision-making that are traditionally the domain of management. Pressures from consumer, environmentalist, minority, and other groups seem to go through phases: the initial recognition that a problem exists, an extremely activist stage, and a period of declining activity. Even after the decline, however, a residual of changed popular attitudes and formal legislation remains. Activist groups may also rapidly change their views and concepts of the social responsibility of business.

The result is that the business leader of the future will need to be extraordinarily sensitive to social and ethical change. Unfortunately, the ways in which the external environment influences a firm are not well understood; consequently, the field of environmental management of business is still in its infancy.

KEY POINTS TO REMEMBER

1. The business environment—reflecting business law, pressures from social groups like consumers and employees, and changed ethical views and conceptions of the social responsibility of business—is becoming more important in business.
2. Business law includes statutes and regulations that affect relationships among businesses and relationships between business and its customers and employees. Three important aspects of business law are the law of contracts, the law of agency, and the law of bankruptcy.
3. Business exists to serve its customers, and failure to do so will eventually undermine the firm. Consumerism is an organized movement to pressure business to educate, to inform, and to protect the consumer.
4. Employees have become increasingly dissatisfied with dull, highly specialized jobs. A firm's "people problems" require increasing attention from management at all levels. Women and ethnic minorities, backed by the American legal system, are pressuring business to provide equal employment opportunities.
5. Mass communication has caused the public to question the ethical standards and social responsibilities of business. Ethical standards are ultimately set by the individual. Ethical guidelines may be influenced by personal beliefs or by the ethical codes of individual firms, professional

associations, or industry trade groups. To some, ethical and legal behavior are identical.

6. Social responsibility in its narrowest sense argues that business can best serve the public interest by securing high profits. In its broadest sense, social responsibility asserts that business ought to serve the social as well as the economic needs of the general public, even if social action produces lower profits. Proponents of both views can be found both inside and outside the business field.

QUESTIONS FOR DISCUSSION

1. What is the function of business law? Why is it important to a person in business?

2. What consumer rights did President Kennedy propose? Do you agree with them?

3. In what ways has consumer sovereignty been challenged in recent years?

4. How has consumerism aided the consumer?

5. How can business deal with the discontented employee?

6. What legal requirements must a business meet with regard to the employment of women and minorities?

7. Distinguish between business ethics and the social responsibility of business.

8. In what practical ways can business implement an expansionist view of social responsibility?

SHORT CASES AND PROBLEMS

1. A manufacturing firm is considering hiring and training ten physically handicapped workers. Some members of management are reluctant to approve the program because it will increase the firm's costs; in addition, plant productivity may be reduced while the new workers are being trained.
   (a) What reasons can you think of for going ahead with the program?
   (b) What reasons can you think of for opposing the program?

2. You are in charge of the design of a new American Motors car. The company is under pressure to build a car that is safe, provides excellent gas mileage, produces few noxious emissions, and is powerful and comfortable enough to appeal to American consumers. You have been asked to come up with the best design you can, but you have been given no directions from top management.
   (a) Since it is technically impossible to meet all of the requirements simultaneously, how would you decide which ones to emphasize?
   (b) What factors external to American Motors would you take into account in reaching your decision?

3. Most people have their own views of the ethical standards of various occupations and professions.
   (a) In terms of ethics and honesty, rank the following occupations from highest to lowest:

automobile repairers	judges	politicians
executives	union leaders	TV repairers
clergy	columnists	generals
professors	physicians	salespeople

   (b) How does your ranking compare with the rankings of other members of your class?
4. Using literature available from the library and clearly stating your definition of the social responsibility of business, write a brief (3–5 page) paper on one of the topics listed below. Emphasize how a medium or a large corporation should implement socially responsible policies in the area you select:

   advertising
   corporate ethics
   credit practices
   employment of women
   employment of minorities
   job fulfillment
   job safety
   employee participation in community affairs
   employee participation in politics
   philanthropy
   pollution control
   poverty
   product pricing
   product quality
   product safety
   resource use

   Did your views on the social responsibility of business change as a result of your paper?

CAREER SELECTION: EMPLOYMENT TRENDS BY OCCUPATION

Occupations are normally divided into four broad groupings: white-collar jobs; blue-collar jobs; service jobs; and farm jobs. Government economists rank employment outlooks for these four groupings over the next decade in the following order, from best to worst: white-collar, service, blue-collar, and farm occupations.

WHITE-COLLAR OCCUPATIONS

Professional and technical workers numbered almost 12 million in 1972. This category includes such highly trained personnel as teachers, doctors, engineers, accountants, and the clergy. As Figure 3-6 indicates, professional occupations are expected to reflect the greatest growth from 1972 to 1985: employment in this group should increase by almost half during that period.

Managers, officials, and proprietors numbered about 8 million in 1972 and these jobs are expected to increase by about 30 percent over the 1972–1985 period. The *Occupational Outlook Handbook* notes that the demand for managers is likely to continue to increase rapidly because of the future needs of businesses and government agencies.

Clerical workers were the largest occupational group in 1972, totaling over 14 million. Clerical workers keep records, take dictation, type, and operate computers and office machines. The need for such workers is expected to increase by almost 40 percent from 1972 to 1985. A particularly strong demand should exist for clerical personnel who are qualified to handle jobs created by electronic data-processing operations.

Salespeople sell goods and services for retail stores, wholesale firms, insurance companies, real-estate agencies, and door-to-door merchandising operations. More than five million salespeople were employed in 1972. Since sales are augmented by increases in population and in new products, selling occupations are expected to continue to grow.

SERVICE OCCUPATIONS

Service workers maintain law and order, assist hospital professionals, cut hair and give beauty treatments, serve food, and clean and care for homes. Employment in this diverse occupational group totaled about 11 million in 1972; it is expected to increase by more than one-fifth between 1975 and 1985.

BLUE-COLLAR OCCUPATIONS

Craftsmen accounted for almost 11 million workers in 1972. Craftsmen include carpenter, tool and die makers, instrument makers, general machinists, electricians, and typesetters. The number of craftsmen is also expected to increase by about one-fifth by 1985. *Operatives* (sometimes called *semiskilled workers*) may assemble goods or operate machines in factories or may drive vehicles like trucks, buses, and taxis. Over 13 million operatives were employed in 1972, and the number of jobs in this occupational area is expected to increase by about 13 percent by 1985. *Laborers* (excluding miners and farmers) totaled about 4 million in 1972 but will grow only slightly in the future.

FARM OCCUPATIONS

Farm workers, including farmers and farm managers, laborers, and supervisors, totaled about 3 million in 1972. By 1985, continued advancements in farm mechanization are expected to almost halve this number.

Thus, in general, the more education or occupational training men and women have, the brighter their employment outlooks will be in the coming decade.

Employment by occupation in 1972 and projected employment changes from 1972 to 1985.

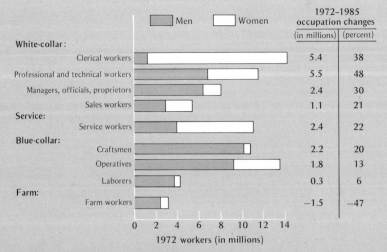

Source: U.S. Bureau of Labor Statistics.

A CRITICAL BUSINESS DECISION

—made by Searle Lawson and Kermit Vandivier

THE SITUATION The date is June 18, 1967. The LTV Aerospace Corporation places an order with the B.F. Goodrich Company for 202 brake assemblies for a new Air Force fighter plane—the A7D. At the company plant in Troy, Ohio, one of B.F. Goodrich's most capable engineers is assigned to the project. His preliminary design for the brake calls for four disks and a total weight of only 106 pounds. Weight is a critical factor in aircraft design, since the lighter the aircraft part, the greater the plane's potential payload. When the preliminary design is completed, major subassemblies are ordered from Goodrich suppliers.

THE DECISION Late in 1967, 26-year-old Searle Lawson, a newcomer to Goodrich, is assigned the task of converting the preliminary design into the final production design. Just two years out of the Northup Institute of Technology, Lawson is elated at his new assignment and plunges into his work. Before the A7D brake will be produced in quantity, Lawson must subject it to quality-control testing, select the best materials for the brake linings, and identify any minor adjustments that might be needed in the brake design. When Lawson completes his work, an entire brake assembly constructed according to the production specifications will be subjected to Air Force qualification tests in the Goodrich laboratory. The Air Force specifies the details of the qualification tests, a series of grueling braking stops designed to simulate actual landing conditions.

Because time is crucial—LTV has scheduled flight tests for the A7D for mid-1968—Lawson decides to begin testing immediately. The brake housing and other parts have not yet been delivered by suppliers, but the brake disks have arrived. Using a brake housing and other parts similar to those proposed for the A7D brake design, Lawson builds a prototype and begins a series of lab tests by "landing" the wheel at the A7D's landing speed and braking it to a stop. The main purpose of these tests is to determine what temperatures will develop inside the four-disk brake and to evaluate proposed lining materials.

In a normal aircraft landing, the temperatures inside a brake can reach 1000 degrees or slightly higher. To Lawson's astonishment, in the first simulated landing, the A7D brake glows a bright red and the temperature rises to 1500 degrees. After several such stops, Lawson dismantles the brake and finds that the brake linings have almost disintegrated.

Lawson orders new brake-lining materials and tries again. The second and the third tests are carbon copies of the first. Inexperienced though he is, Lawson recognizes the seriousness of the problem. It is not defective parts or unsuitable lining materials that are at fault but a bad brake design. The brake is too small—there is simply not enough surface area on the disks to to stop the A7D without generating the excessive temperatures that cause the brake linings to disintegrate. The solution is obvious: scrap the four-disk design and start from scratch on a new design using five disks—a costly process that would involve discarding the subassemblies that have begun to arrive from suppliers.

Lawson takes his results to both his boss and his boss's boss. Both refuse to recognize that a problem exists and order Lawson to find better brake-lining materials. Indeed, LTV has already been told that the preliminary tests have been successful.

During the formal Air Force qualification tests, the brake meets with 12 successive failures. On April 4, 1968—less than three months before the scheduled flight tests—the thirteenth qualification attempt is begun in the Goodrich lab. Engineers are instructed to "nurse" the brake through 50 simulated stops so that it will meet the Air Force's qualification requirements. Even though the brake is not subjected to established military tests (the test equipment is deliberately miscalibrated), it fails. The fourteenth attempt also fails.

Company managers order Lawson and Kermit Vandivier, a 42-year-old technical writer at Goodrich, to prepare the qualification report, fabricating whatever data are necessary to demonstrate that the brake has met all Air Force requirements. The two men are aware of the implications of their assignment: if the report is accepted and the brake is flight-tested, the test pilot will be exposed to possible injury or death.

QUESTIONS

1. What alternative courses of action are open to Lawson and Vandivier?
2. Which course of action would you choose? Justify your decision.

PART TWO

MANAGEMENT

Management is sometimes referred to as "what managers do." The basic management functions include planning how to achieve specific goals, organizing and staffing business operations, communicating ideas and directing and controlling the activities of the firm. In an efficiently run firm, management can usually overcome unfavorable business developments — such as a decline in sales or a change in competitor's tactics — by anticipating potential difficulties and by taking fast, corrective action. Efficient managers can also motivate employees and can infuse a business with a sense of direction. On the other hand, managers who make poor decisions or who delay timely action can quickly destroy even a well-established firm. Inefficient management has been a primary cause of failure in both large and small businesses throughout the United States. Chapters 4 and 5 will examine the six basic functions of modern management, which are vital to both private and public organizations. Chapter 6 will then focus on decision making and business information — factors that influence most managerial activities.

As for the best leaders, the people do not notice their existence. The next best, the people honor and praise. The next, the people fear;. and the next, the people hate. When the best leaders' work is done, the people say, "We did it ourselves!"

Lao-tzu

enry Ford started with nothing in 1905. By 1920, he had built the world's largest and most profitable manufacturing firm. Ford's accomplishments were due to his personal genius for invention and manufacturing: one example of this genius was his introduction of the moveable assembly line. Yet by 1927, Ford's business empire was a shambles. Management theorist Peter Drucker states that "Ford failed because of his firm conviction that business did not need managers and management." Ford believed that all a business needed was an owner and some "helpers." In fact, Drucker notes that Ford fired or sidelined "any one of his helpers, no matter how able, who dared act as a 'manager,' make a decision, or take action without orders from Ford."

Business is too large for one decision maker so . . .

Meanwhile, in Michigan in the early 1920s, Alfred P. Sloan, Jr., realized that the automobile business had become too complex to depend on the orders of one man, so he assembled a group of small automobile companies that were all for sale because they couldn't stand up to Ford's competition. Sloan turned over authority in day-to-day operations to the management of each of these firms, which became divisions in his new company. Sloan built a strong central staff and devised a series of forecasts against which the performance of each division was measured. *Fortune* magazine observes that Sloan "dealt effectively with one of the problems of modern life: how to achieve cooperation among men who were—and who needed to be—too individualistic to be commanded in the old sense, but who would accept an orderly framework of policy making." Within five years, Sloan's firm became the world's leading automobile manufacturer—a position it still holds today. The firm is General Motors.

. . . we have managers and management

Sloan and General Motors pioneered many of the management concepts now applied throughout industry. We will discuss these concepts in Chapters 4, 5, and 6.

What Is Management?

Two Meanings of Management

The term *management* can describe either a group of people or a process. In the first sense, "management" refers to a specific group of people who direct efforts toward common objectives by using available resources: employees, supplies, plants and equipment, and money. The

Management is both a group of people . . .

management group in a business firm achieves its objectives primarily by utilizing the other four resources effectively.

... and a process

In its second sense, "management" refers to the process by which a cooperative group directs actions toward common goals. Today, there are specialized management groups in all the functional areas of large business firms (marketing, accounting, finance, manufacturing, and so on), although management in each area tends to stress one of the four basic resources more than the others. Also, almost all jobs have some managerial content, such as planning, even though the management of other employees is not involved.

Functions of Management

The management process involves techniques that coordinate available resources as well as basic functions that provide the foundation for studying management. These functions are listed below in the sequence in which they normally apply to management decisions:

Planning: The process by which a manager sets objectives, assesses the future, and designs a program of action to achieve the objectives.

Six functions of management

Organizing: The process by which the structure and the allocation of jobs are determined.

Staffing: The process by which managers select, train, promote, and retire subordinates.

Communicating: The process by which ideas are transmitted to others for the purpose of effecting a desired result.

Directing: The process by which the performance of subordinates is guided toward common goals.

Controlling: The process by which actual results are compared with planned performance and corrective action is taken when necessary.

All of these functions are related and are part of the continuing activities of a manager. This chapter will focus on the first two functions of manage-

---

MANAGEMENT STYLES OF SOME TOP EXECUTIVES

In a recent analysis of the personal management styles of several top executives in American corporations, *Business Week* magazine concluded: "There are thousands of corporations in the United States, and no two are managed exactly alike. Each company has its own strengths and weaknesses, and each chief executive officer brings his own background and temperament to the job." In Chapters 4 and 5, the management styles of six top executives are profiled: we begin with George E. Johnson (opposite page). Each of the top executives in these six profiles stresses one of the six management functions we will discuss in this and in the following chapter. We picked these particular executives because they have markedly different management methods.

GEORGE E. JOHNSON OF JOHNSON PRODUCTS COMPANY: PLANNING AND GOAL-SETTING

Using $500 of borrowed money, George E. Johnson founded his cosmetics company in 1954. Today, he is President of Johnson Products Company, Inc., a black-owned manufacturing company. To date, Johnson Products has concentrated on cosmetic products for black consumers, largely because Johnson feels—and his research indicates—that ''social change just hasn't been great enough for my company to make any real impact on the general market at this time.''

In its early years, Johnson's fledgling company came precariously close to failure. ''The year 1960 was a most fateful one for this company,'' Johnson recalled in a 1973 interview. ''I projected three goals that year, in three segments covering 15 years: a million in sales by the end of 1964; $10 million by the end of 1969; and $50 million by the end of 1975. We exceeded 1964 by 25 percent; 69 by 12 percent. We're still working on the 1975 goal. . . .''

But Johnson's management style affects company decisions on far deeper levels than the planning and goal setting stages of organization. While not authoritarian, Johnson's personal style is to keep abreast of all vital aspects of the firm's operations. An associate observes: ''George is very much the boss of his company—from the production of his merchandise to the creation of his advertising program. Nothing goes out without his approval.''

ment—planning and organizing. The other four management functions will be discussed in Chapter 5.

Some experts identify a seventh management function: *decision making*—the process of choosing a course of action from available alternatives to achieve designated objectives. Indeed, some management special-

4-1 Six functions of management. The six functions of management, discussed in Chapters 4 and 5, are performed in a framework that involves decision making and business information, which will be discussed in detail in Chapter 6.

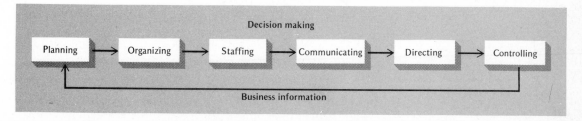

Decision making

Planning → Organizing → Staffing → Communicating → Directing → Controlling

Business information

ists consider that management *is* decision making. Decision making and the business information necessary to make decisions are present in all six basic management functions. Thus, decision making and business information are shown in Figure 4-1 as the framework that surrounds the six basic functions. Decision making and business information will be discussed in Chapter 6.

Planning

The definition of planning emphasizes its three key steps. *Planning* is the process by which a manager (1) sets objectives, (2) assesses the future, and (3) designs a program of action to achieve the objectives.

Planning for business and other organizations can be compared to a football's "game plan," but planning is generally a more complex process. A football team has one objective (to win), normally anticipates its future only in terms of the actions its opponent is likely to take in the next game, and has a limited choice of available actions defined by the strengths and weaknesses of both it and its opponents ("Because of their inexperienced secondary, we will pass 60 percent of the time"). A business must choose among several objectives, plan over a considerable period of time (often five years or more) and design a program of action after considering many alternatives. In both cases, the basic purpose of the planning is the same: setting objectives, assessing the future, and designing a program of action to meet the objectives.

Business planning: a version of football's "game plan"

Setting Objectives

Setting objectives both for the organization and for the individuals comprising it is essential to the effective management of any business. An important reason for this is that human behavior is purposive: people act in ways that enable them to attain certain objectives or goals. Management behavior is also purposive: managers seek to attain organizational objectives by making decisions and directing people effectively. Thus, a major management task is to help employees realize that they can best achieve their personal goals by working toward organizational goals. To understand the job of setting objectives, we will examine (1) the nature of organizational objectives; (2) the relationship between organizational and personal objectives; and (3) the use of guidelines in achieving organizational objectives.

Behavior is goal-oriented

Subgoals of lower units should be consistent with overall organizational goals

✔ **Nature of organizational objectives.** Organizational objectives seek to direct the efforts of all members of the firm. As Professor Joseph L. Massie of the University of Kentucky points out:

There is a hierarchy of objectives in an organization: at the top, the entire organization aims in a given direction: each department, in turn, directs its efforts toward its own sets of goals; each subdivision of each department has its own meaningful aims. Each of the subgoals should be consistent with and contribute toward the goals of the next higher level.

Organizational objectives have two important dimensions: general versus specific goals, and long-range versus short-range goals. In general, the lower the organizational level, the greater the likelihood that goals will be more specific and short-term in nature. Goals for different units in an organization sometimes conflict. For example, suppose that an appliance manufacturer's principal corporate goal is profit maximization. Subordinate goals might include corporate responsibility, personnel development, and a profit increase on the sales of a new line of dishwashers. With respect to the last goal, the marketing department might believe that profitability could best be achieved by increasing the number of dishwasher styles to appeal to more diverse consumer tastes. Manufacturing might believe that the opposite policy would be effective and recommend reducing the number of styles to increase the production run of each style and thereby reduce costs. In general, conflicts in subgoals are reconciled by having the next higher level of the organization determine what subgoals are appropriate in light of overall corporate goals. In the case of the conflict between the appliance firm's marketing and manufacturing departments, the problem might be resolved by the company president.

✔ **Personal and organizational objectives.** People in an organization have individual objectives that motivate them and that make their behavior purposive. As with organizational goals, some of an individual's objectives are primary, and others are secondary; some are short-run, and others are long-run; some are consistent, and others conflict. Generally, individuals in an organization are most highly motivated when they see that the organization's goals are consistent with their own goals. For example, employees who wish to have higher incomes will be motivated to achieve greater productivity by a compensation plan that includes profit sharing — a system that has produced spectacular results in many firms. When personal and corporate goals diverge, conflicts result; thus a salesperson with a large sales territory who wishes to spend more time at home with the family may choose to leave a company rather than to accept a promotion to a position which involves even more travel. Between these extremes, there is a gray area in which corporate and personal goals are largely independent and neither support nor conflict with one another; in such a situation, the individual is neither spurred to greater effort nor placed under strong pressure to find a new job. Management by objectives — a method of translating organizational goals into terms that will motivate and elicit teamwork from all members of the organization — will be discussed in Chapter 5 as part of the management function of controlling.

When subgoals conflict, the next higher level of the organization may reconcile them

Individual motivation increases when personal and company goals agree

BUSINESS FORECASTING: AN EXAMPLE OF EXTRAPOLATION

Extrapolation is a business forecasting technique that makes projections about the future by extending observed trends in past data. For example, suppose you had wished to forecast the U.S. population for 1973 and 1974 early in 1973 from actual data available for the years from 1960 to 1972. As shown at right, you could fit a straight line to the past data by eye (although more elaborate statistical methods are available). Extending the trend line to 1973 and 1974 would yield the estimates indicated by the black dots. These data are quite close to the population values that actually occurred (indicated by the circled ×s).

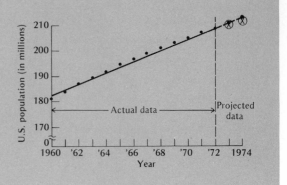

Assessing the Future: Business Forecasting

Until World War II, most businesses did not systematically project and plan for the future, except on a short-range (often year-to-year) basis. Since that time, producing and marketing a product has become a complex process. Today, a single business decision can involve millions or even billions of dollars. IBM, for example, reportedly risked more than $3 billion on its "360" line of computers, which depended on technology that was not yet available when the decision to produce and to market the product was made. Even in relatively small businesses, managerial decisions can involve gaining or losing thousands of dollars. Thus, businesses need to project economic, social, and political forces that are likely to influence their current and future decisions. The importance of making accurate and timely business decisions has created a need for *business forecasting* — assessing and projecting the future to aid in corporate planning.

Most business decisions involve projections whether the decision maker is aware of them or not. For example, a manager at Procter & Gamble who decides to market a new hair tonic without projecting future sales may simply feel that the product will be a good seller. Implicitly, however, through experience or intuition, managers make assumptions about the future — assessments which may turn out to be right or wrong and for which they will probably be held responsible. Systematic projection techniques can help these managers to make better decisions, but they do not always do so. For example, the Edsel, a Ford disaster, was one of the most carefully researched new products in American business history.

A variety of forecasting techniques are used to estimate future business activities. Steelmaker Andrew Carnegie is alleged to have stood on a hill just outside Pittsburgh to see how many stacks were belching smoke before he estimated future steel orders. More traditional techniques

Business decisions require forecasts of the future

include: (1) judgmental methods; (2) statistical methods; and (3) surveys of experts, salespersons, purchasing agents, consumers, and others. We will discuss one example of each of these techniques.

✔ **Lost-horse forecasting.** To a certain extent, all business forecasting involves subjective assessments of the future based on the forecaster's past experience and on any planned events in the future that seem likely to affect the forecast. Judgmental forecasts can range from spur-of-the-moment ''guesstimates'' to more formal methods such as *lost-horse forecasting* — a technique that derives its name from the common-sense procedure assumed to underlie the search for a lost horse. To find a runaway horse, you go to the last place the horse was seen, assess the factors determining where the horse went next (hunger might have driven it to the hayfield; thirst might have driven it to the river; and so on), and proceed in that direction to find the horse.

Using lost-horse forecasting to estimate tennis racket sales

The same procedure can be applied in business forecasting problems. For example, if a firm that produces tennis rackets wishes to forecast sales for 1976 early in the year, the sales manager (1) takes the last known value (1975 sales); (2) identifies the factors determining 1976 sales and their probable effects (increased public interest will tend to increase racket sales; the longer life of the metal rackets will decrease replacement sales; and so on); and (3) forecasts 1976 sales by assessing the net dollar change of these factors over 1975 sales. The lost-horse method incorporates the major factors affecting the forecast in the final estimate.

Extrapolation: extending past trends into the future

✔ **Extrapolation** Most statistical forecasting techniques use past information to extend former trends into the future. One such technique, known as *extrapolation,* can be very direct, as in the case of a businesswoman who finds that her sales rose about $8 million each year from 1955 to 1975 and who concludes that her 1976 sales will be $8 million higher than they were in 1975. Extrapolation is usually represented graphically by fitting a straight line to past data and then extending the line into the future.

GAZE INTO YOUR CRYSTAL BALL

Large corporations need to know when certain major technological breakthroughs are likely to occur. Such estimates enable management to undertake active programs that can utilize the new technology. One technique used in technological forecasting is the Delphi method described in this section. You can compare your ability to forecast technological breakthroughs with those of some of the experts. Just estimate the year you think each of the following events will occur:

1. Reliable weather forecasts.
2. Production of 20 percent of the world's food by ocean farming.

3. Growth of new organs and limbs through biochemical stimulation.
4. Use of telepathy and ESP in communications.

The estimates of a panel of experts can be found in Figure 4-2. (Daggers indicate the estimates that are to be compared to your own.) The experts were polled in 1963, and their forecasts were imperfect. For example, half the panel estimated ''reliable'' weather forecasts would be available by 1975. Many of us might question whether today's weather forecasts can be termed ''reliable'' — although they are far better than they were a decade ago.

The business forecasting example on page 88 illustrates how this technique is used to forecast the U.S. population.

✔ **The Delphi method.** The *Delphi method* is a business forecasting technique that relies primarily on surveys of experts rather than on the use of past data. The technique, initially classified as secret when it was developed 20 years ago by mathematicians at the Rand Corporation, is now in regular use by over 100 large corporations. The Delphi method works in this way:

The Delphi method:
collecting estimates
from experts

1. A panel of experts from both within and without the organization is assembled. Each expert is asked to prepare an anonymous estimate (often by mail) of the probable date or value of a future event. (For example, the McDonald-Douglas Corporation asked a panel to estimate the date when air cargo revenues would equal airline passenger revenues.)
2. Each panelist is given a composite (a summary) of the panel's views and is asked to make a second, anonymous estimate, based on the information in the composite. The composite may also include a summary of the reasons individual panelists have given for their initial estimates.
3. The process in step (2) is repeated one or more times, and a final summary is then made. This composite is the one used by the businessman. Generally, bias is compensated for in the final summary. (In the McDonald-Douglas case, for example, aerospace experts were found to forecast earlier dates than the company's own executives.) Extreme estimates are removed.

A major advantage of the Delphi method is that it allows the expert to remain anonymous. This frees the decision maker from the obligation of defending his or her own views or of agreeing with a supervisor's estimate, thus making a more objective analysis possible.

Controlled experiments using Delphi—that is, surveys for which verifiable data are available (for example, asking a group of people to estimate the price of wheat in 1924)—indicate that the technique produces reliable results and that estimates become better as the experiment progresses. A modified form of the Delphi technique was used to develop the estimates about scientific breakthroughs shown in Figure 4-2.

Designing a Program of Action

Once objectives have been set and the future has been assessed, the final step in planning is to design a program of action to achieve the desired objectives. The remaining functions of management—organizing, staffing, communicating, directing, and controlling—should all be used to implement the selected programs of action. After comparing strategic and tactical planning, this section will describe three methods commonly used

4-2 Projected dates for scientific breakthroughs according to a 1963 Rand Corporation panel.

Breakthrough	Projected year		
	Opinion of one-quarter of panel*	Opinion of half of panel*	Opinion of three-quarters of panel*
Economical desalination of sea water	1964	1970	1980
Ultralight synthetic construction materials	1970	1971	1978
Automated language translators	1968	1972	1976
Reliable weather forecasts†	1972	1975	1988
Implanted plastic or electronic organs	1975	1982	1988
Popular use of personality-control drugs	1980	1983	2000
Economical ocean-floor mining (other than offshore drilling)	1980	1989	2000
Limited weather control	1987	1990	2000
General immunization against bacterial and viral diseases	1983	1994	2000
Production of 20 percent of the world's food by ocean farming†	2000	2000	2017
Growth of new organs and limbs through biochemical stimulation†	1995	2007	2040
Use of drugs to raise intelligence levels	1984	2012	2050
Direct information recording on the brain	1997	2600	3000+
Use of telepathy and ESP in communications†	2040	3000+	3000+

* Projecting the most rapid breakthrough in this area.
† The breakthrough you were asked to estimate in the box on p. 89.
Source: Reprinted from *Business Week* by special permission. © 1970 by McGraw-Hill, Inc.

in implementing the programs of actions: management guidelines, scientific management, and scheduling with Gantt charts.

✔ **Strategic and tactical planning.** *Plans* are the means by which an organization achieves its objectives. Thus, planning for any organization can be classified according to (1) the nature of the objectives to be achieved, and (2) the period of time allotted to fulfill these objectives. *Strategic planning* for organizations involves planning to achieve composite

PLANNING IN THE DEPARTMENT OF DEFENSE THAT DIDN'T DOVETAIL— BECAUSE ADMIRALS DIDN'T SPEAK TO GENERALS

Effective planning requires talents ranging from an ability to formulate broad statements of objectives to a meticulous concern over detailed programs of action. It has been said that half of genius is the ability to recognize the obvious. Effective planning also involves this skill. In 1961, Robert McNamara left his job as president of the Ford Motor Company to become U.S. Secretary of Defense. Shortly thereafter, the Navy arranged an elaborate, top-secret briefing for him concerning possible wartime targets for its submarine-carried Polaris missiles. The briefing was typical of what some observers have come to call a Pentagon art form: a presentation replete with pictures, flip charts, movies, and impressive narration.

Halfway through the briefing, McNamara asked the obvious question: How did Navy Polaris targets tie into Air Force targets? The assembled admirals were aghast and told McNamara that the targets the Air Force hit were strictly their own business, not the Navy's, and vice versa. McNamara rose to his feet, made clear that such strategic plans were of concern to Navy admirals and Air Force generals alike, and stormed out of the room.

"So much for Plan A."

Drawing by Richter;
© 1974 the New Yorker Magazine, Inc.

Strategic planning involves achieving long-term company objectives organizational goals over a long-range period of time, generally two or more years. An example from Exxon (formerly Standard Oil of New Jersey) vividly illustrates the nature and the importance of strategic planning in making a decision that the firm's present chief considers probably the most important planning decision in the firm's history. This key decision illustrates the three elements of planning:

1. *Setting objectives:* In 1960, M.J. Rathbone became head of Standard Oil of New Jersey. One key company objective was to maintain a continuous supply of crude oil, from which gasoline and other petroleum products could be refined.
2. *Assessing the future:* At the time, the company faced what seemed to be a minor problem: too much oil on the market. However, as Rathbone assessed the future, he saw trouble—trouble based on two key projections he had made: (1) with the demand for oil outrunning new oil discoveries, oil would become scarce, and (2) seeing this situation, oil-producing countries in the Middle East would be able to restrict the oil supply and raise consumer prices.
3. *Designing a program of action:* Rathbone convinced the top management of Standard Oil to accept his assessment of the future.

From this assessment, management developed a logical but tremendously expensive program of action: to embark on an immediate search for oil outside the Middle East.

The oil exploration program cost $700 million, but today Exxon has 19.3 billion barrels of proven oil reserves outside the Middle East—a far greater supply than any of its major competitors.

**Tactical plans
must dovetail with
strategic plans**

Tactical planning in an organization generally involves planning to achieve organizational subgoals over a period of less than two years. Examples of tactical planning include weekly or monthly plans for the entire company, for specific departments or plants, or for particular projects. Just as the main goals of an organization are achieved by implementing strategic plans, so the subgoals of the various units in the organization are achieved by developing and carrying out detailed tactical plans. And just as subgoals must be consistent with overall organizational goals, so tactical plans must dovetail with strategic plans.

Plans can involve any or all of the firm's resources. The distinguishing characteristic of all plans, however, is *time*. A key to effective strategic planning is to establish milestones in tactical plans that subunits are required to meet. For example, shortly after taking office in 1961, President John F. Kennedy set a major U.S. objective of landing on the moon before 1970. The success of the 1969 moon landing can be attributed to the fact that thousands of tactical plans of manufacturers dovetailed with the strategic plans of the National Aeronautics and Space Administration.

✔ **Implementing plans: the use of guidelines.** To help different people in an organization handle the same problem in the same general way, management develops *guidelines*. Guidelines enable members of an organization to make decisions that achieve objectives more quickly, easily, and consistently.

**Guidelines
increase the speed
and consistency
of decision making**

Management sets four important kinds of guidelines, which exist in a hierarchy: policies, practices, procedures, and rules. Moving down the hierarchy from policies to rules, the guidelines become more precise and give the decision maker less latitude. For example, a *policy* is an understanding by members of an organization or a group that makes the actions of any one member under a given set of circumstances more predictable to the other members; a policy allows the decision maker some flexibility under certain circumstances. A *practice*, which is often informal and developed by trial and error, is the usual way a given problem is handled. A *procedure* is a system that describes in detail the particular steps that must be taken in order to accomplish a job; sometimes when each detail is of crucial importance—as in starting up a new nuclear power station or launching a spacecraft—the procedure is put in the form of a detailed, written checklist. The guideline that allows the decision maker no flexibility whatever is called a *rule*; a rule states precisely what is to be done (or not to be done) in a given situation, without deviation. Because rules are

**The decision-maker's
latitude varies
with the kind
of guideline**

so fixed, they are often given to machines to handle; in fact, computer instructions consist exclusively of rules. But when judgment and flexibility are required, the task must be handled by people, not machines.

Figure 4-3 illustrates each of these guidelines with a statement that a college might develop for admitting students to advanced courses. Few managers are able to distinguish between the four guidelines. More important than distinguishing between guidelines is recognizing that (1) a hierarchy of guidelines exists that permits subordinates differing degrees of judgment in making decisions, and (2) both superiors and their subordinates must be clear about the degree of flexibility subordinates are to have in addressing each kind of problem they face.

In the ranking of guidelines, policies are most important because they set constraints on the remaining practices, procedures, and rules. Clear statements of policy provide a framework for the decisions of subordinates and facilitate the delegation of decisions to lower levels in the organization. For example, a personnel policy on vacations might stipulate only that adequate clerical support be provided for the firm throughout the year. Thus, an office manager can exercise some flexibility in approving vacations for employees, provided that this clerical requirement is met. Policies enable subordinates to handle the vast bulk of the questions they face and to move routine decisions to lower levels in the firm. Effective policies also allow the members of the organization closest to the problems to exercise judgment in making decisions, rather than restricting the decision makers with rigid rules. In a well-managed organization, then, the four types of guidelines are carefully designed to advance the objectives and plans of the firm.

Good policies help to move decisions to lower levels in the firm

✔ **Implementing plans: the use of scientific management.** As a result of the pioneering efforts of Frederick W. Taylor, Frank and Lillian

---

AN EXAMPLE OF SCIENTIFIC MANAGEMENT: INCREASING A BRICKLAYER'S OUTPUT

The use of scientific management to increase productivity is illustrated by a bricklaying study conducted by Frank Gilbreth. While working as a bricklayer's apprentice, Gilbreth was puzzled by the innumerable ways that experienced bricklayers laid bricks. He reasoned that since bricklaying dated back to biblical times, trial and error should have produced a "best method" for laying bricks, but this was not the case.

Gilbreth analyzed each phase of the bricklaying process: the bricklayer, the tools, the physical positions of the bricklayer and the bricks to be laid, how the worker selected the bricks to be used, and the mortar. Then, taking the best elements of the various methods bricklayers used, Gilbreth developed his own system. For example, he designed a scaffold that placed the bricklayer, the bricks, and the mortar at three different levels, so that they were always properly positioned relative to the structure being built. Traditionally, bricklayers obtained their own bricks and then studied each brick to find its best side before laying it. Gilbreth specialized this function by having a separate worker carry the bricks to the bricklayer and place each brick with its best face up. Finally, to insure consistency in construction, Gilbreth developed a standard formula to be used for the mortar.

As a result of Gilbreth's changes, the number of movements made by a bricklayer decreased from 18 to 5, and individual output increased from 120 to 250 bricks per hour. Thus, Gilbreth's scientific approach accomplished in several weeks what the trial-and-error method had failed to achieve in over 2000 years.

Guideline	Definition and explanation	Example for admission to a college course
Policy	An understanding by members of a group that makes the actions of each member more predictable to other members. A policy is a guide for making decisions.	"Students are encouraged to take those courses they find challenging and for which they are adequately prepared."
Practice	The usual mode of handling a given problem. A practice stresses expediency and things as they are; a policy stresses direction and things as they should be.	"A student not having taken the prerequisite for a course can talk to the instructor, who will consent to registration if the student is adequately prepared."
Procedure	A system that describes in detail the steps to be taken in order to accomplish a job. A procedure emphasizes details; a policy concentrates on general approaches.	"1. Transcripts of students applying for advanced courses will be checked. 2. Those having completed the prerequisites at this college will be admitted to the course. 3. A student who wishes to be admitted without the necessary prerequisites must talk to the course instructor, who will then make an admissions decision based on whether the student's past work is equivalent to the course prerequisites."
Rule	A statement of precisely what is to be done (or not to be done) in a given situation, without deviation. A rule allows no flexibility in decision making; a policy encourages decision making by offering guides.	"Psychology 122 is open spring semester to only those students who took Mr. Jones' Psychology 121 fall semester and received a grade of B or better."

Source: Definitions and explanations are taken from Joseph L. Massie, *Essentials of Management,* Second Edition (Englewood Cliffs, N.J.: Prentice-Hall, 1971), p. 59.

Gilbreth, and Henry L. Gantt, the scientific management approach to developing and implementing plans for individual projects is widely used today. *Scientific management* is an entire school of thought that emphasizes ways to increase productivity through the careful planning and execution of corporate objectives. The four key principles of scientific management, as applied by Frank Gilbreth to increasing the output of bricklayers (see page 94), are listed below:

1. *Develop an ideal or best method:* Analyze each job to determine the best way of doing it. Once a best method has been determined, set a standard for average performance and an incentive to be paid for work beyond that standard. Thus, analysis might show that under Gilbreth's method of laying bricks an average bricklayer could lay 200 bricks per hour. A rate of 4 cents per brick might be established, so that the typical bricklayer would earn $8 per hour.

95 *Planning*

Workers who achieved a level of 250 bricks per hour would receive hourly wages of $10.

2. *Select workers properly:* After identifying the best method for a given task, a manager should find the right workers to do the job. Thus, those considered for the job of bricklayer would be screened to determine if they had the necessary manual dexterity and strength. The same would apply to the job of brick carrier.

3. *Train workers to use the best method:* This principle emphasizes greater specialization of and collaboration among workers rather than individual effort. Under Gilbreth's plan, some workers would be trained to lay bricks and others to carry and stack the bricks properly. If one brick carrier served two bricklayers, cooperation could be encouraged by relating the brick carrier's incentive pay to the number of bricks laid by the two bricklayers.

4. *Separate the planning and the preparation of work from the actual execution of the task:* In essence, this extends the third principle to managers as well as to workers. Taylor reasoned that each group would perform the duties to which it was best fitted—managers would plan and workers would carry out the plans—with an attendant increase in efficiency. Although workers would not be allowed to choose their own methods, close cooperation between management and workers would be assured because of the greater incentive earnings workers would receive. Hence, under Gilbreth's plan, bricklayers would be able to increase their income with the incentive pay they received when they surpassed bricklaying standards.

In summary, Taylor's ideas reduced wasted effort and developed standards of performance, better methods for selecting and training workers, and greater specialization, including planning by someone other than the worker.

↙ **Implementing plans: scheduling with Gantt charts.**   Plans must be converted into a program of action to be meaningful and tangible to the people who must execute them. Preparing a program of action involves (1) identifying the principal tasks necessary to execute the plan and the time required to complete each of these tasks, and (2) arranging the activities in a way that meets the required deadline.

An example will clarify the process. Suppose that three students in a college class are asked to undertake a term project on the following problem: "How can the college increase dwindling attendance at home football games?" The instructor places the following constraints on the project on the first day of class:

Constraints on a student term project

1. The project must involve (a) a search to determine how other colleges have addressed the problem, and (b) a mail survey of a sampling of students on campus to determine their attitudes toward the problem.

2. The project must be completed and the final report must be submitted by the end of the 11-week quarter.

In carrying out the project, the students must first identify the various tasks involved and estimate the time they can allot to each task in light of their other activities and classes. As indicated in Figure 4-4, it would take the students 21 weeks to complete the project if they undertook all the tasks in sequence. If the students are to complete their project within the eleven-week quarter, two conditions must be met: (1) each student must work on different project activities concurrently at least part of the time, and (2) some activities must be independent enough to overlap in time.

Running project activites in parallel requires specialization of workers . . .

The first requirement relates to Frederick Taylor's principle of specialization and cooperation of workers. Suppose that of the three students (A, B, and C) only student C can type; student A has done considerable library research, and student B has constructed questionnaires and conducted mail surveys. The need for efficiency suggests that the students should specialize in the areas in which they are experienced; at the same time, whenever possible, they should learn about unfamiliar areas from one another. For example, student A might be primarily responsible for collecting library information (task 1), while student B contracts and tests a questionnaire (task 4) with student C's help. All three students could cooperate in writing the final report which student C could type.

. . . and tasks that are largely independent of one another

The second requirement for completing the project involves identifying the degree to which the various tasks are independent—that is, distinguishing activities that must occur sequentially from activities that can occur concurrently with other activities. In Figure 4-4, it is clear that task 5 (constructing, typing, and mimeographing the final questionnaire) must be completed before task 7 (mailing the questionnaire). However, task 6

4-4 Tasks required to complete a term project.

Task	Time (in weeks)
1. Check library to find (a) other colleges with the same problem, and (b) how they handled it.	3.0
2. Collect information from ten colleges that have a similar problem but that have no information as to how the problem was handled.	4.0
3. Summarize information obtained from other colleges.	1.0
4. Construct, type, and test a rough-draft questionnaire for clarity (in person, not by mail) on friends.	2.0
5. Construct, type and mimeograph a final questionnaire.	1.0
6. Randomly select the names of 200 students from the school directory.	0.5
7. Address and stamp envelopes; mail questionnaires.	0.5
8. Collect returned questionnaires.	3.0
9. Tabulate data from returned questionnaires.	2.0
10. Write final report.	3.0
11. Type and submit final report.	1.0
Total time necessary to complete all activities:	21.0

(selecting the names of the 200 students to receive the questionnaire) might easily be done before, at the same time as, or after task 5. Hence, task 6 is independent of task 5 and both tasks might be undertaken at the same time if they are conducted by different students. Finally, most projects involve activities that depend on one another to some degree and that might be carefully correlated, recognizing that extra costs might be incurred. For example, student C might start typing the final draft of the report before the rough draft of the report is completed, even though additional information obtained at the last minute might necessitate changing and retyping some early pages of the final report.

Henry L. Gantt developed a method of charting various kinds of management and production activities. The Gantt chart remains the basis for most of the scheduling techniques used today, including elaborate computerized methods. Figure 4-5 employs one version of the Gantt chart

Gantt charts display both sequential and parallel tasks . . .

4-5 Gantt chart showing the planned schedule to complete a term project on time and the status of the project after the second week.

	Task	Students involved in task	Week of quarter										
Number	Description		1	2	3	4	5	6	7	8	9	10	11
1	Check library to find (a) other colleges with the same problem, and (b) how they handled it.	A											
2	Collect information from ten colleges that have a similar problem but that have no information as to how the problem was handled.	A											
3	Summarize information obtained from other colleges.	A											
4	Construct, type, and test a rough-draft questionnaire for clarity (in person, not by mail) on friends.	B, C											
5	Construct, type, and mimeograph a final questionnaire.	B, C											
6	Randomly select the names of 200 students from the school directory.	B, C											
7	Address and stamp envelopes; mail questionnaires.	B, C											
8	Collect returned questionnaires.	B											
9	Tabulate data from returned questionnaires.	B											
10	Write final report.	A, B, C											
11	Type and submit final report.	C											

Current date

Key:

△ Planned completion date
▲ Actual completion date
▢ Planned period of work
▬ Actual period of work
Ⓐ Planned completion date missed
▽ Rescheduled completion date
▼ Rescheduled completion date met

which the General Electric Company uses to schedule aerospace projects to illustrate the scheduling of the student term project just discussed. With the rows representing tasks and the right-hand columns representing weeks, the chart shows which of the tasks required to complete the term project occur sequentially and which of the tasks are accomplished concurrently with other activities. On one hand, tasks 5, 6, and 7 occur in sequence and do not overlap in time. On the other hand, task 2 (which requires four weeks to complete) is accomplished at the same time that portions of six other activities—tasks 1, 4, 5, 6, 7, and 8—are occurring. It is the paralleling of appropriate tasks that will enable the students to complete the term project within the 11-week quarter. Of course, other schedules besides the one in Figure 4-5 could be designed to meet the deadline.

Ultimately, the actual results of any project or activity must be compared with the planned results. Figure 4-5 assesses the status of the term project at the end of the second week. Note that task 4 has been completed according to schedule. Task 1, however, has run into trouble; its completion, originally set for the end of the third week, has been rescheduled for the end of the fourth week. Measuring the project status on the same schedule with the original plan indicates the flexibility of a Gantt chart. When actual performance does not meet planned performance, some corrective action is appropriate. This is the essence of the management function of control, which we will discuss in the next chapter.

. . . and compare planned and actual performance

In summary, scheduling a program of action—perhaps with the aid of a Gantt chart—does three things. First, it translates plans into specific tasks that can be understood clearly by those who must execute them. Second, it forces planners to distinguish sequential from parallel activities, thereby providing a faster way to meet the plans. And third, it forces people to allot their time as needed to specific tasks. Without such a program of action, people tend to concentrate on the tasks they like and do best and to neglect the other activities. For example, if student B loves to design questionnaires, she could spend two months doing this if left to her own devices. Faced with a precise schedule that allots a maximum of two weeks for this task and that assigns student B additional specific tasks, she will generally budget her time to prepare a questionnaire to meet the schedule.

Organizing

Organizing is the process by which the structure and the allocation of jobs are determined. To understand the organizing function of management, we will first consider organizational structure and then organizational practice.

Organizational Structures

➤ **Principles of organization.** Most successful businesses attempt to structure and to allocate jobs systematically. Management experts have identified six principles of organizational structure that are generally accepted and that are employed by many firms:

1. *Unity of command:* This concept is simple: no man can serve two masters. In organizational terms, no member of an organization should report to more than one superior. Unity of command makes it impossible for a subordinate to receive conflicting orders from two different superiors.
2. *Span of control:* There is a limit to the number of subordinates who should report to one superior, since a supervisor has only a certain amount of time, energy, and attention to devote to supervision. An acceptable span of control is often set at four to eight people. However, factors such as the routine of the job influence the span of control; the more routine the job, the greater the number of people who can be supervised effectively.
3. *The exception principle:* Routine problems that recur frequently should be handled by lower-level personnel; only unusual, nonroutine problems should be referred to higher-level managers. This principle leads to a successive filtering of problems: the most important problems are handled by the president of the firm, the next most important problems are handled by the vice presidents, and so on down the organization.
4. *The scalar principle:* Known in the military as "chain of command," this principle holds that authority and responsibility should flow in a continuous line from the highest person in an organization to the lowest person. Authority is the right and power to issue an order; responsibility is the obligation to perform and to take action when ordered. To effectively deal with subordinates, a manager must be both authoritative and responsible.
5. *Departmentation by groups:* People and activities may be grouped together in an organization when they have similar functions, when they have the same objectives, or when they need to be coordinated. Departmentation is often established on a geographic, product, or functional basis, or on a combination of these bases. Thus, salespeople for a computer company might be grouped on the basis of region (geography), kinds of computer sold (product), or customer business, such as retailing or manufacturing (functional).
6. *Decentralization:* Really an extension of the exception principle,

Six principles
for developing
the organizational
structure of a firm

decentralization refers to moving decision making to lower organizational levels that are independent enough of one another to be evaluated objectively. In the 1950s, Ralph Cordiner, President of the General Electric Company, developed an effective way to measure the performance of each of the company's various product areas: he decentralized the company into about 100 departments (small steam turbines, major appliances, and so on), and measured each department by its profit contribution to the entire company. General Electric simply extended the ideas that Alfred Sloan used to organize General Motors (the example that opened this chapter).

Subsequent thought and analysis have revealed that although these principles are not universal — there are many exceptions to them, and several principles conflict under some circumstances — they provide a useful guide for developing an organizational structure for a business firm.

✔ **Types of formal organizational structures.** The task of management is to translate the principles of organization into a workable organizational structure. Three formal organizational structures have been used as models for actual organizations: (1) line organization, (2) functional organization, and (3) line-and-staff organization.

EDWIN H. LAND OF POLAROID: ORGANIZING WITHOUT AN ORGANIZATION CHART

"Seldom, if ever, has a large American company so faithfully reflected the substance and the style of one man as does Polaroid Corporation," says *Business Week* magazine. The "man" is Dr. Edwin H. Land, Polaroid's founder, board chairman, director of research, and 15-percent owner. A Polaroid vice president comments, "This company reflects Land's personality, his interests, his dedication to science, his liberal social views, and his way of working."

Land thrives on informality, so the company has no organization chart. Land is extremely secretive; so is Polaroid. Land works prodigious hours; so do key employees, who are resigned to receiving phone calls from Land at all hours.

When he tackles a project, Land assumes that none of the conventional rules apply — for example, his refusal to believe that an inch-thick SX-70 could not be built. When a new project is launched, Land's leadership style is "crisis management": he concentrates on what he sees as the most critical company problem, attending to the most minute details until the problem is solved; then he goes on to the next problem. Perhaps this management style works at Polaroid because Land tends to set very high goals, to hire talented people whom he pays well, and to hold them to account.

"Line" and "staff," two important organizational terms, may be distinguished by the nature of the authority present in each. As we noted earlier, authority is the right and power to act. Thus, *line authority* is a general power over the subunits below that authority level in the organization, while *staff authority* is purely advisory to the line structure and has no power to execute line-authority recommendations. With respect to the work activities in an organization, *line functions* relate to activities that contribute directly to the primary service objective of the organization. For a manufacturing firm, line functions include the manufacturing of the firm's product and the sale of the product to ultimate consumers. *Staff functions* serve secondary objectives concerned with organizational support and maintenance. Examples of staff functions are machine maintenance and legal advice to management. In general, when line functions are performed poorly, the firm's ability to generate revenue is affected quickly; conversely, poor performance of staff functions may not be felt for years, if ever. Groups that perform line functions and staff functions are termed *line units* and *staff units,* respectively. In practice, it is often difficult to classify every unit in an organization neatly into a given category. For example, are accounting, finance, and production control best described as line units or as staff units? In terms of achieving organizational goals, it is more important to be able to recognize line versus staff authority than it is to be able to categorize line and staff units precisely.

4-6   Three types of formal organizational structures.

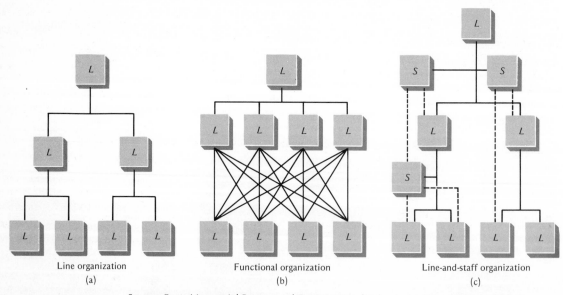

Line organization
(a)

Functional organization
(b)

Line-and-staff organization
(c)

Source: From *Managerial Process and Organizational Behavior* by Allan C. Filley and Robert J. House, pp. 258-59. Copyright © 1969 by Scott, Foresman and Company. Reprinted by permission of the publisher.

The simplest type of formal business organization is *line organization* [Figure 4-6(a)], in which each position has general authority over the positions below it in accomplishing the firm's objectives. This type of organization is widely used in small businesses, but it is rarely found in medium-sized or large businesses. For example, Figure 4-6(a) might represent the line organization of a small restaurant that is open from 8 A.M. to midnight. Each *L* in the figure indicates a line position, and solid lines indicate line authority. The single box at the top of the structure represents the owner. A day manager and an evening manager report to the owner and wait on customers (represented by the second row in the figure). A cook and a dishwasher (represented by the bottom row) report to each of these managers. The advantages of such an organization are simplicity, clear-cut devision of authority, and quick decision-making ability. However, these advantages must be balanced against two major disadvantages: the absence of advisory specialists and an overreliance on managers at the highest levels. In a line organization, top managers may be expected to master such diverse activities that they spread themselves too thin and are overworked; yet the success of the firm depends upon their performance. For example, the restaurant owner must serve as purchasing agent, accountant, advertising specialist, production scheduler, and so on. If the owner becomes ill, the firm could fail quickly.

In the line organization, formal authority is equated with technical expertise. Frederick Taylor recognized that formal authority in an organization differs from technical expertise and supervision, and he designed a *functional organization* [Figure 4-6(b)] to handle the situation. In his functional organization, workers report to a number of different supervisors, each of whom is competent in a particular technical area. Taylor applied this organizational structure to a manufacturing shop, making each worker responsible to eight different specialized supervisors, among them a repair boss, a work scheduler, a time-and-cost clerk, and a disciplinarian. Taylor also believed that specialization would make each supervisor more effective. Although Taylor's functional organization recognizes the importance of technical expertise in supporting a supervisor's formal authority, it has never gained real popularity, largely because of the ambiguity a worker faces when the unity-of-command principle is violated so blatantly.

The *line-and-staff organization* [Figure 4-6(c)] attempts to compromise the best features of the other two organizational structures: (1) the unambiguous supervisory authority of the line organization, and (2) the specialized technical support of Taylor's functional organization. Each *S* in Figure 4-6(c) represents a staff position, and the dotted lines represent lines of advisory communications. Workers at the two lower levels shown in the figure receive daily supervision from a line supervisor in addition to advice and specialized direction from staff personnel. Against the advantages of direct supervisory authority and the use of advisory specialists must be weighed the problems of conflicting orders and advice from line and staff

Line organization: one boss for each worker

Line-and-staff organization: one boss and several advisers for each worker

personnel and the lack of authority of staff members to carry out their recommendations.

Organizational Practices

Organization charts
show formal authority
relationships . . .

✔ **Formal organization charts.** The authority relationships in a business firm can be diagramed in a *formal organization chart,* such as the one in Figure 4-7 for a hypothetical manufacturing firm. In most large companies, organization charts are made available to employees through company handbooks or are posted on bulletin boards. They answer such questions as "To whom does each person report?" and "Which units have staff (advisory) authority?" In Figure 4-7, for example, each lathe operator reports to the lathe supervisor, who in turn reports to the manager of the machine-shop section, and so on. Groups like the legal staff and the methods-improvement staff are clearly shown to be separate from the line units and to have only advisory duties.

4-7 Formal organization chart for a hypothetical manufacturing firm, showing a detailed breakdown of a portion of the manufacturing department.

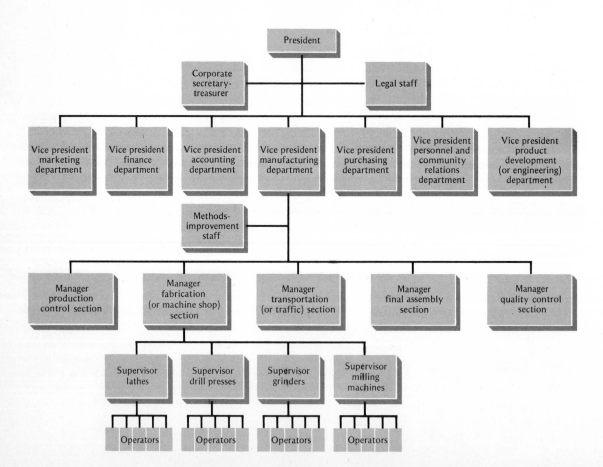

Organization charts may be described as formal in the sense that they indicate relationships intended by the organization. In practice, however, there are many informal relationships in a firm that are equally important or more important than the relationships indicated in formal charts. Thus, in Figure 4-7, although all the vice presidents who report to the president appear to be of equal importance, the president of a particular firm may rely primarily on the opinions and advice of the vice president of finance. *Informal organizations*—groups of people drawn together by common interests—also cut across the formal organizational structure of a firm. For example, two lathe operators, a grinder operator, and the supervisor of the drill-press unit may bowl together; in this informal group, they may agree that some recently developed work rules are a good idea. If this group has earned the respect of the other operators and supervisors, such a favorable opinion may facilitate implementation of the new rules.

. . . but tell nothing about informal influences in the firm

✔ **Levels of management.** Top management in a firm is usually interpreted to mean the president and the vice presidents who report to the president. *Operating management* (also called first-line supervision) refers to supervisors whose major job is the immediate direction of people performing clerical or shop work. In Figure 4-7 the four supervisors within the machine shop are first-line supervisors. *Middle management* is a somewhat vague term that refers to managers in the organization who lie between top management and operating management. Figure 4-7 shows one level of middle management within the manufacturing department; large companies may have two or even three such levels of middle management.

KEY POINTS TO REMEMBER

1. Management may be viewed both as a group of people and as a process.
2. Six functions of management can be identified: planning, organizing, staffing, communicating, directing, and controlling. In addition, decision making and business information underlie and are present in all of these six management functions.
3. Planning is comprised of three key steps: setting objectives, assessing the future, and designing a program of action to achieve the objectives.
4. In setting organizational objectives, management must recognize that individuals within the organization have their own personal objectives. Thus, management must help employees realize that they can achieve personal goals by working toward organizational goals.
5. Management develops guidelines—such as policies, practices, procedures, and rules—that enable members of the organization to make

decisions that achieve objectives more quickly, easily, and consistently.

6. Making business decisions has become more and more expensive, and more emphasis has been placed on assessing the future with business forecasting techniques in recent years. Examples of such techniques are lost-horse forecasting, extrapolation, and the Delphi method.

7. The final step in planning is to design a program of action to achieve the objectives.

8. Management can make plans more meaningful to subordinates by translating them into a program of action using such scheduling aids as management guidelines, scientific management, and the Gantt chart.

9. Strategic planning normally involves planning to achieve organizational goals over a long-range period (usually two years or more). Tactical planning generally involves achieving lower-level objectives in a shorter time period.

10. Organizing is the process that determines the structure and allocation of jobs.

11. Management experts have developed principles of organization that can be used as guides for establishing and analyzing formal organizational structures. Three such structures are the line, the functional, and the line-and-staff organizations.

12. Formal organization charts clarify authority relationships for employees but do not take into account the influence of informal groups or lines of communication.

QUESTIONS FOR DISCUSSION

1. List four or five personal goals that you have set for yourself. Which goals would be most consistent with and most in conflict with (a) one another; (b) the organizational goals of a large corporation; and (c) being in business for yourself?

2. Many colleges have credit-distribution requirements (for example, at least six credits of English and nine credits of science) that a student must satisfy to be awarded a degree. Develop policy, practice, procedure, and rule statements for these requirements that are comparable to the statements developed in the right-hand column of Figure 4-3.

3. "Clear statements of policy facilitate the delegation of decisions to lower levels in the organization." Explain this statement. Why is delegation desirable?

4. Specialization often acts as a barrier to people who are specialists but who wish to broaden themselves, perhaps by seeking a better job or more responsibility. How might this apply to the activities of the three students working on the term project shown in Figure 4-5?

5. In Figure 4-5, the task of writing the final report is begun in the middle of the seventh week. If the schedule is to be completed as planned, what

parts of the report can be written at this stage of the project? What parts cannot yet be written?

6. Edwin H. Land, founder and President of the Polaroid Corporation, insists that the firm's structure follow no formal organization chart. What are the advantages and disadvantages of this procedure?

SHORT CASES AND PROBLEMS

1. With the class as a whole serving as the panel, use the Delphi method, repeating the process twice and giving reasons for your estimates, for the following projections: (a) the total popular vote received by Lincoln in the 1860 presidential election, and (b) the number of students enrolled during the fall term of 1970 in colleges and universities across the United States. (Have the class select a committee to gather and distribute the information.)

2. Suppose that between 1960 and 1970, automobile sales for one manufacturer grew by an average of 20,000 units per year. In 1970, total domestic sales were 800,000 units.
   (a) Using extrapolation, estimate car sales for 1980. What difficulties do you find in this estimation method?
   (b) What other estimation methods might be considered?

3. Motion study is intended to economize the movements of workers and to increase their productivity. Lillian Gilbreth extended these concepts to activities in the home, such as washing dishes, mowing grass, and making home repairs. Suppose that you are writing a term paper and that you have assembled appropriate magazines and books on the subject that you are writing about. If you are going to cite your data sources in an appendix to the paper:
   (a) Diagram the best way to lay out the materials (references, writing paper, and so on) on your desk to economize your motions and to reduce the problem of misplacing reference books and papers.
   (b) What adjustments could you make in your planning and work layout to reduce the problem of having to run to the library to collect additional information?

CAREER SELECTION: POSITIONS IN MANAGEMENT AND PLANNING

MANAGERIAL AND ADMINISTRATIVE CAREERS

Hotel managers *and* **assistants** are responsible for the profitable operation of their establishments—a task that requires both social and business skills. Managers coordinate and supervise accounting, housekeeping, kitchen, personnel, and maintenance functions, and make decisions regarding room rates and credit policy. In large establishments, managers have a staff of **hotel assistants** (often management trainees) who head various departments. Managers are usually recruited on the basis of experience, although a bachelor's degree or a community-college degree in hotel and restaurant administration is becoming increasingly important. Positions are generally filled by employees who have demonstrated their competence as front-office clerks and as assistant managers. Yearly salaries range from $8000-$12,000 for hotel-manager trainees who are graduates of specialized college programs up to $50,000 for experienced managers at top hotels. (*Additional information:* The Educational Institute of the American Hotel and Motel Association; 77 Kellogg Center; Michigan State University; East Lansing, Michigan 48823.)

City managers are experts on urban problems who work for cities with council-managerial forms of government. Managers are appointed by public officials and assume such specific responsibilities as preparing the annual budget, coordinating departmental activities, and planning urban population and industrial growth. Managers must possess sound decision-making abilities as well as social finesse. City managers usually acquire experience in small communities before working in larger cities. Such positions require a bachelor's degree, but a master's degree in public or municipal administration is preferred in many cities. Yearly salaries range from $12,000 to $35,000, depending on the size of the community. Because of the growing number of cities converting to the city-managerial type of government, the number of future available jobs is promising. (*Additional information:* International City Management Association; 1140 Connecticut Avenue, N.W.; Washington, D.C. 20036.)

Hospital administrators perform an amazing number of managerial duties: coordinating and supervising departmental activities, determining personnel and equipment needs, planning future facility expansion, preparing the budget, and raising funds. Positions are generally filled by promoting experienced assistant administrators. A master's degree in health and hospital administration qualifies an applicant for a hospital's highest executive position. Middle-management jobs require a bachelor's or an associate degree. Hospital administrators' salaries vary from $20,000 to over $40,000. The expansion of existing health facilities will provide additional employment opportunities for applicants with graduate degrees. (*Additional information:* American College of Hospital Administrators; 840 North Lake Shore Drive; Chicago, Illinois 60611.)

CAREERS IN PROFESSIONAL PLANNING

Economists study the production, the distribution, and the consumption of goods, analyze supply and demand factors, and formulate policies for the efficient utilization of scarce resources. Many economists work for business organizations, providing management with planning information essential to resource allocation, marketing, and pricing decisions; others work for government agencies or teach at colleges. Their specialized competence requires a thorough understanding of statistical techniques and good communication skills. Educational qualifications vary: college teaching positions generally require a doctoral degree; most business and governmental positions require a bachelor's degree. Annual salaries range from $12,000 to $23,000. Competition for jobs is expected to increase as the number of qualified college applicants continues to exceed available positions. (*Additional information:* American Economic Association; 1313 21st Avenue South; Nashville, Tennessee 37212.)

Geographers analyze the interrelationship of physical variables, (such as climate and terrain) and human population characteristics. For example, economic geographers focus on the geographical distribution of manufacturing, farming, mining, and communication activities. Urban geographers investigate human activities within city environments. Many geographers teach in educational institutions, but a growing number are filling planning jobs in private industries like market-research organizations. Their skills are also useful in analyzing new business locations. Businesses require a bachelor's degree; teaching and governmental research positions require one or more graduate degrees. Annual income ranges from $10,000 to $25,000. Employment opportunities for geographers with doctoral degrees are expected to increase due to the growing emphasis on ecological issues. However, geographers with master's and bachelor's degrees will face stiff job competition. (*Additional information:* Association of American Geographers; 1710 16th Street, N.W.; Washington, D.C. 20009.)

A CRITICAL BUSINESS DECISION

—made by Henry G. Parks, Jr.

THE SITUATION It is the late 1930s. Henry G. Parks, Jr., a black student majoring in marketing, graduates with honors from Ohio State University. As an undergraduate, Parks has already earned a reputation for careful, brilliant planning, followed by decisive action.

In 1939, Parks begins to work as a salesman for the Pabst Brewing Company, trains his own sales force, and eventually becomes Pabst's top salesperson. Occasionally, Parks encounters snags: he and several other businesspeople attempt to market a soft drink that they hope will become the new Coca-Cola; but the drink loses its color in the sun, and the venture fails miserably. Parks then buys a share in a sausage company in Cleveland and 18 months later decides to go into business for himself. He raises $60,000 by selling his interest in the Cleveland firm, mortgaging his home, and borrowing on his life insurance.

Moving to Baltimore in 1951, Parks starts his own business—grinding sausage in an old dairy. He recognizes that there are special problems confronting the black business owner, and he tries to anticipate such problems before they arise. "There are people who are self-starters," Parks says, "and I am one of them. . . . I've gotten used to getting thrown out of places and then going back." During the first years of his new business, Parks' self-starting and planning abilities pay big dividends. Anticipating prejudice about his meat products from white merchants, Parks insists on having his products federally inspected, even though only state inspection is required. He stresses quality and codes each package of sausage and scrapple with the date it leaves the plant. This code dating permits both retailers and consumers to verify freshness—a policy that puts Parks years ahead of other meat manufacturers. If the meat doesn't move off grocers' shelves in a reasonable time, Parks pulls it back and takes the loss. Even the growth of his company presents challenges. Forestalling union trouble, Parks chooses not to wait for them to demand recognition but to invite them in instead. Encountering difficulty attracting experienced management personnel because he is black, Parks trains his top-level managers himself.

THE DECISION It is now 1960. Parks analyzes his broad markets with an eye toward continued expansion. At

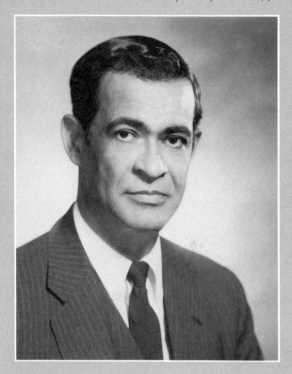

the heart of his analysis is his understanding of the black consumer. Parks notes that "the ghettos have traditionally been the dumping ground for bad products," and that black consumers typically respond with two strategies: (1) relying on national brand names to insure quality, and (2) doing a considerable portion of their shopping in supermarkets outside predominantly black neighborhoods. Parks feels that he has the first problem beaten: his "Parks" brand meats have achieved an outstanding reputation for quality. It is the second problem over which he agonizes. How can his understanding of his present customers be used to increase the number of retail outlets carrying Parks meat products?

QUESTIONS

1. How do some of Henry Parks' actions illustrate the planning function discussed in this chapter?
2. Specifically, what plan of action might Parks develop to increase the number of retailers who market his product?

The best executive is the one who has sense enough to pick good men to do what he wants done, and self-restraint enough to keep from meddling with them while they do it.

Theodore Roosevelt

CHAPTER

5

MANAGEMENT: OPERATIONS AND PERSONNEL

STAFFING AND PERSONNEL MANAGEMENT
Preemployment Staffing Activities
Postemployment Staffing Activities

COMMUNICATING
Bases of Effective Communication
Barriers to Effective Communication

DIRECTING
Motivation
Leadership

CONTROLLING
Essentials of Control
Management by Objectives

A young radical stepped onto U.S. soil for the first time in 1848. He had a revolutionary faith in "the improvement of mankind." Andrew Carnegie began working in a cotton mill for $1.20 a week. Later, earning $25 million a year as president of the Carnegie Steel Company, he was to lead the steel industry into its period of greatest expansion.

As a manager, Carnegie assumed all of the duties the word implies in terms of judging, motivating, and controlling people. To reflect this, he even wrote his own epitaph: "Here lies the man who was able to surround himself with men far cleverer than himself." In later life, Carnegie found personal fulfillment donating money to build 2500 libraries in English-speaking countries. His desire to improve mankind is even present today in the grants the Carnegie Foundation gives to colleges.

The stress Carnegie placed on selecting the right employees illustrates one part of the management function of staffing. The four management processes that will be discussed in this chapter—staffing, communicating, directing, and controlling—may be described collectively as the operating functions of management, since they are all part of the day-to-day operations of a business firm. In the past, management concentrated on the structure of an organization and left the staffing to its personnel department. In today's modern business firms, this distinction has been de-emphasized; thus, this chapter will relate the important role of personnel management to the general management function of staffing.

Staffing and Personnel Management

The staffing role is shared by the personnel department and individual managers

Staffing is the process by which managers select, train, promote, and retire subordinates. This function is shared by the personnel department of a business firm and the immediate manager for whom a subordinate works. Figure 5-1 divides staffing activities into those occurring before a prospective employee is offered a job and after he or she is hired. To understand how the staffing function operates, let us assume that Roger Kerin, a graduating college senior, wishes to obtain a job selling office equipment, such as electronic calculators or duplicating machines. By following Roger's activities before and after he is employed by the ABC Office Equipment Corporation, we can identify the ways that both the personnel department and the immediate manager affect the staffing function.

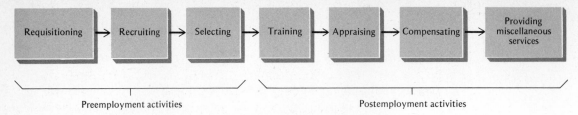

Requisitioning → Recruiting → Selecting → Training → Appraising → Compensating → Providing miscellaneous services

Preemployment activities   Postemployment activities

5-1 Sequence of activities in staffing.

Preemployment Staffing Activities

The staffing process includes three activities that precede actual employment: requisitioning, recruiting, and selecting needed personnel.

✔ **Requisitioning needed personnel.** *Requisitioning* personnel involves identifying and specifying future manpower needs. An office equipment manufacturer might employ the requisitioning process in several ways. For example, top management at ABC might have a favorable business outlook and conclude that 20 new salespeople are needed during the next three months to staff all of its field sales offices. Or one of ABC's field sales managers might have an opening as a result of a retirement, transfer, promotion, or resignation and might initiate the requisition. For every position in a firm, the personnel department and the appropriate manager perform a *job analysis* to determine what detailed tasks the person holding that position should perform. Then they develop a detailed *job description*—an explicit written statement of the duties and responsibilities of the position. Using these data in the job description, the personnel department and the manager may also develop a *job specification* describing the skills, work experience, and education a prospective employee must have to perform the job satisfactorily.

(margin note) Requisitioning: identifying and specifying manpower needs

✔ **Recruiting needed personnel.** With the job description, the job specification, and an estimate of the number of salespeople needed, the personnel department undertakes the task of *recruiting*—a systematic search to meet a firm's manpower requirements. The firm can fill a job from either an inside or an outside source. When feasible, management will probably adopt a policy of "promotion from within"—the transfer or promotion of another employee into the open position. For example, ABC might fill its open sales positions by promoting those equipment maintenance personnel who have demonstrated an ability to deal with customers effectively. Promotion from within motivates employees and improves company morale.

(margin note) Recruiting: searching for qualified personnel

Let us assume that ABC can fill five positions internally by promotion or by transfer; the remaining 15 positions must be filled from outside sources. Prospective employees may be sought by contacting colleges and universities, state and private employment services, and technical institutes. The company may also place recruitment advertisements and review unsolicited job applications.

For the job applicant, an important step in seeking employment is to develop a clear, concise résumé that provides information on personal history, educational background, job experience, and employment goals. The personal résumé for Roger Kerin, our hypothetical applicant for an ABC sales position, appears in Figure 5-2. A résumé should provide enough information to give a potential employer a favorable first impression and to gain the applicant a personal interview.

At a glance, the résumé in Figure 5-2 reveals the background information of interest to potential employers. One unique part of the résumé is headed "Personal Qualifications Illustrating My Potential," a section recommended by Henry A. Brown, manager of recruiting and placement at the Pillsbury Company. Brown advises college students seeking jobs to

WOULD YOU HIRE THE FOLLOWING MEN?

Selecting a future employee is a difficult job: some individuals perform beyond a manager's wildest hopes; others are total failures. The personal sketches below contain more information than is often available when a hiring decision is to be made. Decide whether or not you would hire each of the following four people. The actual names of these people and the ways employers seek to collect more systematic information about prospective employees are revealed in the text.

Applicant A: He dreamed of being an inventor, but he had had only three months of formal schooling—he was expelled because the schoolmaster considered him "retarded." In early life, his biggest joy was planning pranks designed to anger his father, who once beat the boy in public in the village square. He was fired from his first job for accidentally starting a fire. In his 30s, he paid little attention to his family, neglected his dress, chewed tobacco, was rejected by "polite society," and was ridiculed by theoretical scientists as an "anti-intellectual." He was egotistical and, to fellow workers, both a tyrant and their most entertaining companion.

Applicant B: At the age of 21, he was of medium height and thin. He wore glasses, had an unpleasant toothy grin and affected flashy clothes. He spoke indistinctly, stumbled, hesitated, appearing to have almost a speech impediment. His companions thought he was queer and eccentric, and his seniors were irritated by him. He was a particular nuisance in class—bumptious, cocky, boyishly positive, know-it-all. He

was earnest, outspoken, and tactless. His hot temper, nervousness, and childish manner made an unfavorable impression. He was a good student, making Phi Beta Kappa in his senior year in college. He had an array of interests, and for some time after college graduation he was unable to decide what he wanted to do in life.

Applicant C: He was born in a middle-class residential section of a large midwestern city. His father was a stern, religious, scrupulously honest man. He was a bright youngster with a piercing goal to become rich and famous. He had a prodigious mechanical aptitude and manual dexterity. According to his first boss, he was "very fast and accurate . . . sober, honest, and very industrious." He was very popular with young people in the local church. He was fond of baseball, and he spent some time in the U.S. Navy.

Applicant D: He was red-haired, sturdy, and not handsome. He had a distinct speech impediment, which was a combination of a stammer and lisp. He was uncommonly self-assured, obstinate, bumptious, and arrogant. He was foolhardy, often taking unnecessary chances with his life. He hated school, he refused to absorb anything that didn't interest him. When students were listed according to scholastic achievement, he was always at the bottom. In the army, he was a wild and careless soldier, but he did receive several decorations for bravery. He was thrown out of politics shortly after undertaking it as a career.

An effective résumé
gives an applicant
a competitive edge

analyze their accomplishments and to include in their résumé only those related to the position they are seeking. According to Brown, though all previous work experience is pertinent, recruiters are particularly interested in a prospect's abilities and past achievements that set him apart from other job candidates. Because it is difficult to objectively judge one's own strengths and weaknesses, it is useful to ask a friend or a relative to help in such assessments. Since Roger Kerin is seeking a career in sales and management, employers will be especially interested in him if he can show that he (1) enjoys people and can motivate and lead them; (2) is flexible and adaptable to changing job requirements; and (3) has a high level of motivation. The personal qualifications listed in Roger's résumé seem to achieve this purpose.

✔ **Selecting needed personnel.** A generation ago hiring decisions for many jobs were often based on very scanty information. Frequently, the data were not even as complete as that given for the four "job applicants" on page 113 (inventor Thomas A. Edison, U.S. President Theodore Roosevelt, convicted killer John Dillinger, and British Prime

5-2   Example of a concise, effective personal résumé.

PERSONAL RESUME OF ROGER A. KERIN

Personal Information

Home address:
    5713 State Street
    Gainesville, Florida   32601

Telephone:
    370-2870

Birthdate:
    September 2, 1953

Physical characteristics:
    5'10", 165 pounds

Marital status:
    Single, available for
    position involving travel

Military status:
    4-A classification,
    inactive reserves

Interests: Golf, water
    skiing, local theater group

Immediate and Long-Range Career Objectives

My immediate goal is to obtain a position that will utilize my education and work experience in selling office or technical equipment to retail, commercial, or industrial accounts. My long-range goal is to utilize this sales experience to obtain a position in sales or marketing management in a manufacturing firm.

Personal Qualifications Illustrating My Potential

Three positions over the past six years have given me an opportunity to supervise others and to improve job procedures. At Burger Queen I managed the counter and was responsible for drawing up the weekly work schedule. While in the Army I supervised four men in repairing office equipment. During my final two years in college I served as the buyer for a newly formed cooperative eating unit; my duties included developing the necessary planning, ordering, and inventory procedures.

Education

Attended the University of Florida at Gainesville from 1971 to 1972 and then from 1974 to the present. Will receive a Bachelor of Science degree this spring with a major in marketing (B average) and a minor in journalism (B average). Course work emphasized marketing (21 credits) and journalism (15 credits).

Work Experience

June 1971 to August 1972. Peg's Burger Queen, 5119 Elm Street, Gainesville, Florida. Counter manager reporting to Peg L. Tonneson, restaurant owner.

September 1972 to July 1974. U.S. Army. Following basic training, my tour was spent in the Fourth Maintenance Service Unit, Fort Jackson, South Carolina. Specialist 5 supervising equipment repair reporting to Lieutenant M. M. Leary.

September 1975 to present. Chateau Co-op, 1321 University Avenue, Gainesville, Florida. Work as a buyer approximately 20 hours per week in cooperation with C. M. Spreigl, co-op president.

References

Professor John Faricy
Department of Marketing
College of Business Administration
University of Florida
Gainesville, Florida   32601
(Adviser)

Professor Louise Nesselhof
Department of Journalism
College of Liberal Arts
University of Florida
Gainesville, Florida   32601
(Independent study supervisor)

Dennis Leslie, Director
University Student Services
University of Florida
Gainesville, Florida   32601
(Co-op counselor)

Philip Rinehart, President
Rinehart Design Services, Inc.
3100 East River Drive
Tallahassee, Florida   32304
(Friend of family)

C. PETER McCOLOUGH OF XEROX: A FOCUS ON "SENSITIVE DECISIONS"— PEOPLE AND STAFFING

"A company's reputation," says C. Peter McColough, "good or bad, is made not only by the quality of its products and services but also by its people. . . ." McColough is the current chairman of the board of the Xerox Corporation. He believes the ceremonial role of the head of a corporation is important and has decentralized Xerox's decision-making processes to allow himself time for this role.

Yet, McColough finds time to get deeply involved in what he calls "sensitive decisions." He puts how the company treats its employees in this category. As an example, he reserves the right to veto the dismissal of any employee who has worked for Xerox for eight years or more. "The case for dismissal must come to my office and obtain my written concurrence," McColough says emphatically. "I have a lot of opposition in the company on that procedure, but I don't care whether they like it or not. I believe in democracy—up to a point."

Snap hiring decisions can be costly

Minister Winston Churchill, respectively). Their biographical sketches illustrate the need to obtain information about job applicants. Employers have found that shot-in-the-dark hiring decisions are very costly. For example, money spent in training employees is lost if they quit right after they are trained, and inefficient employees who are retained may cost the company more than they are worth. Thus, in today's business firms, selecting personnel usually involves the systematic screening of candidates through application forms, interviews, and tests. These devices help prospective employers identify qualified job applicants and reduce the chances of hiring unsatisfactory personnel. The screening process generally entails:

1. *Application blank:* The application blank provides information about an applicant in a clear, concise form that facilitates his or her evaluation. An application should be filled out neatly and carefully, since it indicates to interviewers the degree to which the applicant follows directions. The application form serves as a guide in the initial interviews; if no immediate openings exist, it may be filed and referred to at a later date when jobs become available. If the candidate is hired, the application becomes part of the permanent personnel record.

2. *Interview by personnel department:* A personal interview is conducted by a member of the personnel department to determine an

Personnel
departments
obtain and screen
many applicants
for a job

applicant's chance of successfully filling a position. Because the ability to meet people is an important part of a salesperson's job, the ABC interviewer will probably allow Roger Kerin to carry on a large part of the conversation to determine if he is articulate and if he answers questions directly. In addition, part of the interview may be devoted to answering Roger's questions about the job and to emphasizing the firm's assets. If Roger takes the initiative, the interview site may be at ABC; if ABC is actively recruiting for the position, the interview may be held in the placement office on Roger's college campus. Whatever the location, Roger should be familiar enough with the company to ask pertinent questions. This will not only provide him with useful information but it will also indicate his genuine interest.

3. *Psychological tests:* Many firms ask applicants to take one or more psychological tests. These include interest, aptitude (or potential ability), achievement (or knowledge), mental ability (or intelligence), and personality tests. Such tests serve as a further source of information about the applicant's probable future performance. Although the weight given to psychological tests varies with the firm, most personnel specialists and psychologists agree that test results should supplement other information on the applicant, not replace it. Any tests given Roger Kerin will probably be administered by a personnel specialist and interpreted by a trained psychologist—both members of ABC's personnel department.

4. *Interview by prospective manager:* Until now, the personnel department has been in charge of the selection process. At this point, the potential manager or the department in which the prospective employee will work enters the interviewing process. For example, 30 candidates for ABC's 15 available sales positions may be invited to the home office to be interviewed by the firm's sales manager; those eventually accepted may be assigned to field managers they have yet to meet. If the recruitment process is not highly centralized, the field sales manager may interview prospects directly. In either case, an executive from the department involved—not a member of the personnel department—normally interviews each prospect and makes the final decision on whether to extend a job offer.

The final decision
to extend a job offer
is made by the
prospective manager

5. *Physical examination:* An examination conducted by a physician serves two purposes. First, it identifies an applicant who may be prone to injury or illness and hence may be costly to the firm because of extensive absenteeism. Second, it identifies physical limitations so that an applicant is not given a job that may be too physically demanding. For example, a salesperson with chronic back problems should probably not be given a job selling office equipment which requires repeated lifting of the machines for demonstration purposes.

6. *Reference checks:* The references cited in a prospect's résumé and application blank are checked to be sure that the applicant has not exaggerated or misrepresented qualifications. The checks, normally made by mail or telephone, serve two purposes: they verify the information already provided by the applicant, and they serve as sources of additional information. Reference checks often focus on previous employers rather than on personal or academic references, since applicants tend to select personal or academic references who are likely to react favorably.

The steps in the selection sequence vary with the company and with the kind of job involved. Sometimes, one or more steps may be eliminated. For example, some companies prefer to give psychological tests before rather than after the first interview; other firms may not use psychological tests at all. A firm may conduct more or less than two interviews. Generally, the higher the position to be filled, the greater the number of interviews held.

Employment discussions should stop whenever one side is not genuinely interested

Three points about the selection process deserve emphasis. First, as each party learns more about the other, negotiations can be terminated. If, for example, Roger Kerin finds out during the first interview that the job requires him to be away from home more than he wishes, he may not wish to continue the discussions. The same situation applies to the employer. In fact, ethics and common sense dictate that one party should stop negotiations when no longer interested; this saves both parties time and effort.

Second, in recent years, serious questions have been raised about the effectiveness of psychological tests as predictive devices. Some divisions of IBM and of Procter & Gamble give prospective management candidates the psychological tests that recruiters use to assist them in making job-offer decisions. However, some firms that formerly used psychological tests have abandoned them, feeling that the tests did not accurately indicate on-the-job performance. For one thing, no one has been able to develop a valid test to predict motivation—an essential characteristic for prospective salespeople like Roger Kerin, who must be prepared to make repeated calls on clients without becoming discouraged. In addition, critics of psychological testing argue that the language and the data in such tests discriminate against recent immigrants and American minorities.

Tests cannot predict motivation

Some firms are concerned that their recruiters may rely so rigidly on these six general steps in the screening process that they will hire carbon copies of people already on the company payroll. For example, a firm that traditionally avoids hiring nonconformists for executive positions may establish standards that recognize only conservative characteristics. A truly creative person who deviates from these standards may be rejected, even though that person's potential contribution to the firm may be far greater than an acceptable prospect's. The individuals already discussed in this chapter provide startling examples. It is unlikely that Thomas Edison, Theodore Roosevelt, or Winston Churchill—even though each had managed large numbers of people—would have survived the general screen-

Thomas Edison

Theodore Roosevelt

Winston Churchill

ing process. In Edison's case, his résumé would be hopeless: he had no formal education, having left school at the age of seven. Reference checks with his only school teacher and first employer would have been disastrous. The teacher had expelled him, calling him "retarded"; the employer had fired him for accidentally starting a fire with some chemicals in the baggage car of a train. Yet, Edison's 1093 patents make him one of the outstanding technical geniuses in all of history. Had the brashness of both Theodore Roosevelt and Winston Churchill not caused them to flunk a prospective employer's personality test, such behavior would certainly have screened them out during their personal interviews. Yet, while they would be considered "strange" by today's traditional standards, each of these three men have altered history.

Many critics feel that of all the factors in the screening process, personality tests are most likely to lead to hiring carbon-copy employees. William H. Whyte, Jr., author of *The Organization Man,* was so distraught over the misuse of personality tests that he appended a section to his book titled "How to Cheat on Personality Tests." His principal recommendation to job applicants: "When asked for . . . comments about the world, give the most conventional, run-of-the-mill, pedestrian answer possible." Perhaps partly in response to Whyte's criticisms, many business firms now give less weight to personality tests than they did in the past.

The third point to be emphasized is the controversy about some aspects of the recruiting process. An example is a technique known as the *stress interview,* which simulates the unpleasant situations an applicant is likely to encounter on the job. For example, Admiral Hyman Rickover, who was instrumental in developing and staffing the Navy's early nuclear submarine fleet, insisted on personally interviewing all officers being considered for nuclear submarine service. He frequently kept officers scheduled for interviews waiting for hours—or even a day or two—in a small, stuffy anteroom, allegedly to simulate the close quarters and stress situations they might face on submarine duty. In the stress interview itself, the applicant may suddenly be on the defensive. For example, since Roger Kerin is being interviewed for a sales position in which he is likely to encounter irate customers, the interviewer might begin with: "I see you went to the state university; couldn't you get into one of the good private colleges?" and follow up with: "Your record shows you had only a B average; why did certain courses give you so much trouble?" The ability to remain composed and to give reasonable answers under unpleasant conditions is regarded as an indication of how the applicant will respond to similar situations on the job.

Postemployment Staffing Activities

Let us assume that Roger Kerin receives a job offer from ABC and begins to work for the company. We can now identify the ways in which Roger is affected by postemployment activities in the staffing function.

✔ Training employed personnel. Training—providing employees with the skills and knowledge they need to do their jobs effectively—can be divided into two types: on-the-job and off-the-job training. *On-the-job training* includes all instruction that might be given to an employee in the course of day-to-day work. For Roger Kerin, this will probably be limited to making sales calls for two to six months with an experienced ABC salesperson. During the first half of the training period, Roger will do virtually no personal selling; his on-the-job training will consist of watching an experienced salesperson make sales presentations and answer customers' questions. In the last half of the training period, Roger will probably make most of the sales presentations and answer questions himself; the experienced salesperson will answer only special questions and will offer constructive suggestions in private.

Off-the-job training may involve attending courses, seminars, or workshops developed either by the firm or by an outside organization or educational institution. For example, ABC sales management would probably develop an initial program of five to fifteen weeks to give new salespeople intensive instruction about the company's line of office equipment; thereafter, week-long sessions might be held annually to inform salespeople of additions to the line. The ABC personnel department might also develop programs that cut across several departments in the firm. As examples, employees might participate in workshops or courses on effective speaking or improving written communications. In addition, many institutes and colleges provide special continuing education programs to improve employees' skills and knowledge. An employee's attendance at these courses is often prompted by a supervisor's evaluation of that employee's performance. Thus, Roger Kerin's supervisor might suggest that Roger's written reports are not as clear or concise as they should be and, therefore, recommend that Roger take a course on written communications to make him a more valuable employee and to increase his chances for future promotion. Generally, courses that are specifically tailored to the needs of individual employees are more effective than blanket instruction programs attended by employees at every level in the firm.

Training may occur both on and off the job

✔ Appraising personnel. Most firms periodically review employee performance and provide constructive suggestions to improve that performance. Charles Schwab, a former president of Bethlehem Steel, continually evaluated his own performance, even though he was one of the few American executives who earned $1 million a year. Finding that minor details were crowding out time he should have been devoting to more urgent matters, Schwab asked management consultant Ivy Lee for help. Lee handed Schwab a blank sheet of paper and said: "Before you leave work tonight, list the six most important things you have to do tomorrow. Tomorrow morning start on item one, and work on it until it's finished. Then go on to the second item, and do the same."

Schwab asked Lee what the fee was for the consulting advice. Lee replied: "Try this method and pay me what you feel it's worth." Schwab tried the idea and was so pleased with the results that he reportedly sent Lee a check for $25,000. This story illustrates two important points. The first is the need for open-mindedness on the part of management—the willingness to try an idea that other people might consider too elementary or insignificant. The second is the importance of helpful appraisal and counsel by another interested person.

$25,000 for
five minutes
of advice

Appraising personnel involves a periodic (usually annual) written evaluation of the employees' performance to provide counseling to increase their effectiveness (perhaps suggesting training programs) and to provide them with equitable monetary compensation. In some firms, appraisal and compensation activities are part of the controlling function (discussed later in this chapter); in others, great pains are taken to divorce these two activities from management control.

Whatever method or combination of methods a firm uses, the appraisal process is usually performed by the subordinate's immediate supervisor. Some firms employ group appraisal, which includes evaluation by the employee's boss, his boss's boss, and a third person. In newly designed appraisal systems, the third person is usually a representative of the personnel department; in well-established systems, this person is usually a supervisor from a related unit. The goal of group appraisal is to develop consistent ratings across individuals and departments. In the case of Roger Kerin, a salesman who operates outside the firm, an individual appraisal will probably be made only by his supervisor, since few ABC people know Roger well enough to participate in a group appraisal.

✔ **Compensating personnel.** Employee compensations include both immediate monetary payments and fringe benefits such as vacations, holidays, and income paid for sickness, disability, and retirement. The goal of a compensation plan is to attract and to retain qualified, productive employees. The following discussion focuses on three topics related to cash payments for work: (1) factors determining the level of compensation; (2) the main elements of compensation plans; and (3) promotion, which may be viewed as a special reward for good performance.

To attract and to retain productive employees, a company must insure a fair and equitable compensation system. Several factors determine the level of job compensation:

1. *Importance of the job in terms of company objectives:* The firm must determine the relative worth of its various jobs and must design a compensation plan accordingly. The level of compensation assigned to a particular position reflects its relative importance in achieving the organization's objectives: presumably the president of a firm is paid more than any of the vice presidents because his work is more important in achieving the firm's goals.
2. *Wages and salaries in comparable firms:* A firm may make a survey of local competitors to determine their pay scales for comparable

jobs. Large firms may subscribe to national surveys conducted by such groups as the American Management Association, the Conference Board, and the U.S. Bureau of Labor Statistics. A firm that fails to meet industry standards in employee compensation runs two risks: a deterioration in employee morale and motivation, and a high turnover rate as employees leave the company for higher-paying jobs in competitive firms.

Factors affecting the level of job compensation

3. *Federal and state laws:* The federal government has established minimum wage laws for employees of firms engaged in interstate commerce; in addition, over 80 percent of the states have their own minimum wage laws. As we saw in Chapter 3, federal law also prohibits both employment and wage discrimination on the basis of race, color, religion, sex, or national origin.

4. *Collective bargaining by unions:* A union may negotiate with management for the employees it represents on such issues as the employment contract (wages, hours, and working conditions) and its administration (procedures for handling worker grievances). The level of compensation in unionized firms is directly affected by this collective bargaining. In addition, union negotiations have an indirect effect on wage structures in nonunionized firms, since these companies must compete with unionized firms for employees.

Factors such as the cost of living and conditions in the local labor market also affect wage and salary payments.

Compensation includes basic wages or salaries plus incentives

Compensation plans consist of two main elements, each of which has several variations. The *basic element* is generally called "wages" for blue-collar or hourly workers and "salary" for white-collar workers. Most wages are paid on an hourly basis and only for the time worked; thus, a machinist earning $5 per hour who works 40 hours in a week is paid $200 for the week. Salaried personnel are paid on a weekly, monthly, or annual basis. An office clerk might receive an initial salary of $100 per week; a new accountant might earn an annual salary of $12,000, paid in $1,000 monthly installments. The *incentive element* in a compensation plan refers to the extra money paid to employees who produce beyond a standard. In general, an incentive plan should include both a standard of performance and an easily measured output of work. Business firms use a variety of incentive plans, such as profit sharing, bonuses, and commissions, to reward employees for good performance. The major methods of employee compensation in American business will be discussed in Chapter 19.

Promotion gives special recognition to good performance

Another form of employee compensation and a means of improving an individual's morale and prestige is *promotion*—rewarding good performance by elevating an employee to a more responsible, higher-paying position. The appraisal methods discussed earlier for evaluating an individual's performance should also provide a basis for comparing employees fairly to identify those ready for promotion. Assessing employee performance is a difficult task. In *Up the Organization,* Robert Townsend, former president of Avis Rent-a-Car, stresses the need for avoiding snap judgments in making promotion decisions. He notes: "Keep in mind that first impressions of performance are often wrong. There are slow starters who become stars, and flashes in the pan who sputter out."

Professor Lawrence J. Peter of the University of Southern California, after examining a variety of organizations, has humorously concluded that good people in the right jobs are hard to find. Peter cites many examples of people whose outstanding performance on one job earned them promotions to positions for which they were unqualified: brilliant automobile mechanics who became inept garage repair supervisors; outstanding salespeople who became ineffectual sales managers; and spellbinding teachers who proved to be incompetent academic administrators. We can derive some satisfaction from knowing that this principle has held true throughout history. As evidence, Professor Peter cites the Duke of Wellington's comment on examining the roster of officers assigned to him for his 1810 campaign in Portugal: "I only hope that when the enemy reads the list of their names, he trembles as I do." Peter concludes that most people in an organization eventually achieve a position one level higher than where they belong. To describe this phenomenon, he has formulated the Peter principle: "In a hierarchy, every employee tends to rise to his level of incompetence."

The Peter principle

✔ **Providing miscellaneous services.** The personnel department of a firm provides a variety of auxiliary services to employees to improve their welfare and morale. One such service is the company credit union, which accepts and pays interest on employee savings and extends low-interest loans to members. In addition, the personnel department usually operates group insurance programs to protect employees against risks of sickness, injury, or death, as well as pension plans to provide employees with income after they retire. In manufacturing firms, the personnel department may hire a safety director to operate in-plant educational programs on safety and to make sure that workers are given protective equipment, such as goggles, safety glasses, and metal-tipped shoes. Finally, some firms offer recreational programs, legal aid, company-subsidized cafeterias, and personal counseling—all of which are usually managed by the personnel department.

Personnel departments may manage credit unions, insurance programs, and recreational activities

Communicating

Communicating is the process by which ideas are transmitted to others for the purpose of effecting a desired result. George S. Odiorne, author of *How Managers Make Things Happen*, estimates that managers and line supervisors spend from 55 to 80 percent of their time—about 1200 to 1500 hours annually—communicating directly with people. Perhaps three-fourths of this time is devoted to listening and one-fourth to talking. In addition, countless hours are spent reading and writing letters, memos, and

Communicating involves both sending and receiving messages

CATHERINE CLEARY OF FIRST WISCONSIN TRUST COMPANY: COMMUNICATING BY EXAMPLE—NOT BY CONFRONTATION

"I hope someone hasn't told you she thinks like a man, because Catherine just *thinks*." The speaker is a long-time business associate of Catherine Cleary—described by *Fortune* magazine as "an outgoing woman with a keen sense of humor."

"I've never had a plan," Cleary says. And without one plan—but with great capability—she has risen steadily in the ranks of trust administration. After graduating from the University of Chicago, Cleary taught before deciding to become a lawyer. After graduating from the University of Wisconsin Law School—first in her class—Cleary practiced law for a few years before joining First Wisconsin Trust, where she was named President and chief executive officer in 1970. There has been a marked increase in company profits since Cleary's takeover. Her comment: "If I had any sense, I'd quit right now."

But Cleary isn't quitting. As an administrator and in the capacity of President, she has been responsible for numerous improvements in her organization. Cleary has her own prescription for communicating with people to gain cooperation in effecting change: "I think you have to do this by kidding people along. I don't believe in confrontation—or not for myself, anyway. The greatest thing is example."

Her management style has gained Cleary widespread respect: she is currently serving as a member on five boards of directors—including those of two corporate giants, General Motors and A. T. & T.

reports. The importance of the communicating process lies in its role as a link among the remaining management functions.

Bases of Effective Communication

Communication in an organization can take innumerable forms. It may be formal organizational communication or informal scuttlebutt by way of the grapevine. If formal, it may be written or verbal. In face-to-face communication, nonverbal facial expressions, gestures, and body movements are an important part of the message and often conflict with the spoken word. The manager who says to a harried employee "Yes, tell me about your problem" while continuing to open and read the morning mail is guilty of transmitting conflicting messages. The employee is probably correct in weighing the indifference of the manager's nonverbal behavior more heavily than the manager's spoken message. When communications conflict, nonverbal behavior is usually more believable than verbal behavior.

Assuming that a communication is timely and relevant, it can have real value only if it is (1) received (heard or seen), (2) understood, (3) accepted, and (4) acted on. Thus, managers who wish to determine whether they have communicated effectively with an employee must ask: Did the employee hear the message? Does that employee really know what it means; accept the responsibility; take the desired action?

To be sure that a communication attains these four goals, the communicator must verify the action through feedback, by either watching or listening. In one communications study, people in college and in the business world were asked to summarize one or two key points from a short, simple spoken message. Results showed that the typical listener understood less than half the message content. This poor showing is attributable to the fact that few people are trained as well in listening as they are in reading, writing, and speaking. Recognizing this deficiency, many firms are asking employees to attend courses on effective listening.

Barriers to Effective Communication

There are a variety of barriers to effective communication between people in an organization. Some arise from personal differences. Others relate to the mechanics of transmitting messages. We will identify these barriers and then examine several ways to overcome them.

✔ **Different frames of reference.** Because of differences in background and experiences, each individual in an organization will have a personal *frame of reference* or a unique way of looking at things which determines how that individual interprets what is seen and heard. In general, an employee who has had good relationships with previous supervisors will accept requests without question; an employee who in the past was deceived by supervisors will react to even simple, straightforward requests with suspicion and skepticism.

The motivational and emotional states of the individual and the nature of the situation may also determine how a message is received. Psychologist Mason Haire cites a striking example:

Two people see
the same situation
somewhat differently

> During World War II, an aerial gunnery student was taking a training flight over the Gulf of Mexico. The pilot, enjoying the ride and the scenery, pointed over the side of the plane, in a friendly spirit, to call the student's attention to a speedboat below. The gesture was clear to him, but the student referred it to his own acute terror of being in the air, and interpreting it to mean that his worst fears were realized, he parachuted over the side.

Managers attempt to handle the problems posed by different frames of reference by recognizing that even individuals on the same level in a firm may feel threatened in business discussions. When people feel threatened, they become more defensive and less able to perceive the motives and values of the communicator. Even simple steps, such as talking to coworkers in their work locations rather than in the manager's office may reduce threat and a subsequent defensive attitude.

✔ **Status differences.** If two people on the same organizational level face communication barriers, it should not be surprising that communication problems worsen with employees at different status levels in the organization. A manager is not free to communicate everything to a subordinate because of conflicting responsibilities to other subordinates and to superiors. The result is a decline in the quantity and quality of downward communication in an organization. Studies have shown that only about 20 percent of the information moving down through management channels reaches the worker. This downward communication loss, sometimes termed *dilution,* can be reduced by a conscious effort on the part of managers to provide subordinates with enough information to obtain effective and enthusiastic job performances.

Downward communication suffers from dilution

Incomplete information is also likely to flow up the organization's communication channels. No one likes to admit his mistakes, especially to his boss. As a result, communications from subordinate to supervisor frequently encounter *filtering*—an intentional sifting of the information transmitted to place the sender and the message in a more favorable light. If managers are not careful, they may encourage a free flow of highly filtered messages that provide little genuine information. Remedies for filtering are (1) developing a well-designed control system to insure that realistic assessments of the situation are reaching higher management levels, and (2) establishing trust, confidence, and a rapport with subordinates so that they can discuss their problems with their supervisors.

Upward communication suffers from filtering

✔ **Clarity of messages.** The mechanical aspects of transmitting messages can also present communications barriers. A major problem resulting from poor mechanical transmission is lack of clarity. Consider the case of a plumber who attempted to correspond with a federal agency in Washington:

> A New York plumber wrote the Bureau that he had found hydrochloric acid fine for cleaning drains, and was it harmless? Washington replied: "The efficacy of hydrochloric acid is indisputable, but the chlorine residue is incompatible with metallic permanence."
> The plumber wrote back that he was mighty glad the Bureau agreed with him. The Bureau replied with a note of alarm: "We cannot assume responsibility for the production of toxic and noxious residues with hydrochloric acid, and suggest that you use an alternate procedure." The plumber was happy to learn that the Bureau still agreed with him.
> Whereupon Washington exploded: "Don't use hydrochloric acid; it eats hell out of the pipes!"

A SAMPLE OF GOBBLEDYGOOK

Poor writing often complicates simple messages. The passage below is an example of such writing, which is sometimes called gobbledygook. After you have read the passage, identify two characteristics of the writing style that make the message so complex. Knowing these two characteristics can help each of us improve our own written communications. Here is the passage:

In order to eliminate the possibility of errors occurring in time distribution relating to construction jobs through transposition of numbers or typing errors, each of the Division Planning Offices should set up a file of the yellow tickets showing all authorized unit-code and item-code numbers on each appropriation and make a daily check of the construction charges on all time distribution sheets forwarded to the Accounting Department to be sure that only authorized numbers are used.

To find out how a writing expert, Robert Gunning, simplified this passage and what two key writing factors he used to do it, see the text.

Gobbledygook versus plain talk

Experience and training in talking and writing plainly can eliminate such messages, often called *gobbledygook*. Whatever the educational or intellectual level of the listener, a written or verbal communication will be better understood if the message is simple and direct. Robert Gunning, a writing expert, has suggested how another example of gobbledygook (see the sample page above) can be simplified by (1) using fewer words containing more than two syllables, and (2) shortening sentence length:

Typing errors are easy to make in transposing code numbers of appropriations. We suggest each Division Planning Office set up a file of yellow tickets showing all authorized unit and item numbers. Then they [all divisional offices] can make a daily check of construction charges before sending time distribution sheets to the Accounting Department.

The original sentence contained 78 words, 11 of which were longer than two syllables. Gunning clarified the passage by using three sentences containing only 51 words, 5 of which were longer than two syllables. Lincoln's Gettysburg Address contains 266 words, but a government order to reduce the price of cabbage during World War II required 26,911 words. A person who knows what to say can say it in a few well-chosen words.

✔ **Poor listening.** For most people, the biggest single barrier to communication is poor listening. Because listening is basically a passive activity, people sometimes daydream while reading or hearing messages. Or they become so involved in formulating a response to the speaker that they do not really hear what is said. Even more serious than missing a message is receiving the wrong message—possibly through selective perception, a process in which listeners remember only the portion of a message that they want to hear and believe. The best way to become a more effective listener is to stop talking and to listen to the speaker with an open mind, in a genuine attempt to understand the other person's point of view. Active listening is also stimulated by taking notes and by asking pertinent questions. According to communications experts, the best way to test effective listening is to repeat the gist of the message to yourself. This procedure (1) checks your listening ability; (2) reinforces your knowledge of the message; and (3) tests your ability to separate the relevant from the irrelevant information.

Directing

Directing is the process by which management guides the performance of subordinates toward common goals. To understand this important management function, we will examine (1) factors that motivate people to behave as they do, and (2) leadership styles that may be used to direct people.

Motivation

✔ **The Hawthorne studies.** During the first third of this century, management's efforts to direct workers and to stimulate productivity were largely focused on improving work methods. Studies carried out at the Hawthorne plant of Western Electric in Chicago from 1927 to 1932—initiated to determine the effects of changes in environment and salary on worker productivity—are a milestone in management study. In a series of experiments and interviews with thousands of workers, the Hawthorne plant examined the effects of lighting, temperature, humidity, fatigue, layout, work groups, rest time, and pay scales on worker productivity.

In the first Hawthorne experiment, which examined the effect of lighting on worker efficiency, a sample of workers was divided into two groups: (1) an experimental group that was subjected to different intensities of illumination at its work site, and (2) a control group in a different location that worked under a constant intensity of illumination. When the lighting intensity for the experimental group was increased from 24 to 46 and then to 70 foot candles, production increased. However, it also increased in the control group by about the same amount. The lighting intensity for the experimental group was then reduced. Researchers expected the poor light to decrease worker production, but to their astonishment, production in the experimental group actually increased until the lighting intensity fell to .06 of a foot candle—that of ordinary moonlight.

The experimental group was then returned to the original lighting conditions. Again, productivity increased. The other Hawthorne studies revealed similar results.

These experimenters had discovered what was later to be called the *Hawthorne effect:* special treatment of workers—even abuse—can produce favorable results because of the human factor. In other words, employee attitudes significantly influence productivity. The attention paid to the workers in the experimental group gave them a feeling of importance; this produced a better attitude toward work which more than offset a physical factor like bad lighting. Subsequent studies indicated that even higher pay did not increase production until workers became involved in the decision-making process itself. In summary, the Hawthorne studies showed that employees are important in management planning, that a work group influences an individual's output, and that social and psychological needs motivate people as much as money does.

The Hawthorne studies recognized the significance of human relations and motivation

The result of the Hawthorne studies was an increased recognition of human relations on the job and of the importance of motivational factors in dealing with workers. During the 1930s and 1940s, this resulted in a trend away from Frederick Taylor's preoccupation with efficiency and toward emphasis on good morale, in the belief that a happy worker was automatically an efficient, productive worker. But experience has shown that this is not necessarily true. Today, most astute managers do not pursue either efficiency or good morale exclusively, but rather seek a balance that combines the best features of both by creating favorable working conditions that motivate employees to achieve both personal and organizational goals.

✔ **Maslow's hierarchy of human needs.** The Hawthorne studies provided the spark that prompted many psychologists to analyze human motivation in greater depth. Psychologist A.H. Maslow developed a theory of human motivation that classifies human needs into five groups (see Figure 5-3). These sets of needs exist in a hierarchy, so that as one set is largely satisfied, people are motivated by the needs on the next level. Thus, once a person has satisfied the physiological needs associated with staying healthy, the concern turns to the needs on the next higher level—protection from both physical and psychological danger. This may explain why many people seek employment in safe positions that provide security. Moving up Maslow's priority scale, people are motivated by the need for attention and to belong to groups, then by the need to attain self-

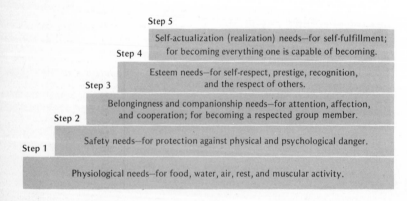

Step 5

Self-actualization (realization) needs—for self-fulfillment; for becoming everything one is capable of becoming.

Step 4

Esteem needs—for self-respect, prestige, recognition, and the respect of others.

Step 3

Belongingness and companionship needs—for attention, affection, and cooperation; for becoming a respected group member.

Step 2

Safety needs—for protection against physical and psychological danger.

Step 1

Physiological needs—for food, water, air, rest, and muscular activity.

5-3

Maslow's hierarchy of human needs.

Source: A.H. Maslow, *Motivation and Personality,* Second Edition (New York: Harper & Row, 1954), Chapters 4 and 5.

respect and the respect of others, and finally by the need for self-fulfill-ment—to become what one is capable of becoming.

Generally, as lower needs are satisfied, higher needs become domi-nant. One study of middle-management and first-line supervisors re-vealed that both groups perceived their greatest deficiencies to be at the top step of self-realization, and both to an equal degree. Thus, a manager should attempt to recognize the differing needs of subordinates and provide a job environment that will satisfy them. Employees whose jobs do not satisfy their needs may seek satisfaction from outside sources—perhaps by spending an increasing amount of time trying to reduce a golf handicap—to the detriment of their work.

✔ **Theory X and Theory Y.** In 1960, in *The Human Side of Enterprise*, psychologist Douglas McGregor presented one of the most widely dis-cussed and controversial theories of what motivates workers in an organi-zation. McGregor labeled the traditional managerial view of workers Theory *X*; the assumptions that describe Theory *X* are shown in the left-hand side of Figure 5-4. This pessimistic view suggests that a manager must protect workers from their own errors by close supervision and, if

HENRY R. ROBERTS OF CONNECTICUT GENERAL INSURANCE: DIRECTING BY USING AN "INFORM-FOR-HOLLERING DEVICE"

In 1974, after 12 years as chief executive officer of the Connecticut General Insurance Corporation, Henry R. Roberts reorganized the company. He decentralized Connecticut General into smaller units, each responsible for making its own profits. The company was decentralized not because of fi-nancial trouble, but rather because Roberts felt the old organization was too stifling.

The reorganization of Connecticut General also changed Roberts' own job. He now concentrates on decisions made at higher management levels and delegates more authority and decision-making re-sponsibility to his subordinates.

But, in terms of actual management, Roberts does direct his senior officers. When there is a decision to be made and it is not clear whose decision it is, Rob-erts has his officers use what he calls the "inform-for-hollering device." Roberts explains, "The officer in-volved informs me about what he's going to do—unless I holler. That's his way of testing me as to where my sense of that line is and making sure he's in order." Roberts accepts over half the decisions made at lower management levels without hollering. The whole method, he feels, "makes it easier for me to do that because people have told me what they propose to do. They're not asking. That's important. If people ask me what to do, it's going to be done my way."

Close interaction with subordinates is an impor-tant part of Roberts' personal style of management: "I spend an awful lot of time talking to people about their roles." And he stresses interrelations among Connecticut General employees. Roberts' goal: "finding a . . . congruence between individual and corporate purpose."

Assumptions underlying Theory *X*	Assumptions underlying Theory *Y*
1. The average human being has an inherent dislike of work and will avoid it if possible.	1. The expenditure of physical and mental effort in work is as natural as it is in play or in rest. The average human being does not inherently dislike work. Depending upon controllable conditions, work may be a source of satisfaction (and will be voluntarily performed) or a source of punishment (and will be avoided if possible).
2. Because they dislike work, most people must be coerced, controlled, directed, and threatened with punishment before they will put forth adequate effort toward the achievement of organizational objectives.	2. External control and the threat of punishment are not the only means for directing effort toward organizational objectives. People will exercise self-control to attain the objectives to which they are committed.
3. The average person prefers to be directed, wishes to avoid responsibility, has relatively little ambition, and wants security above all.	3. Commitment to objectives depends on the rewards associated with their achievement. The most significant of such rewards is self-actualization.
	4. The average human being learns, under proper conditions, not only to accept but to seek responsibility. Avoidance of responsibility, lack of ambition, and emphasis on security are generally consequences of experience, not inherent human characteristics.
	5. The capacity to exercise a relatively high degree of creativity in solving organizational problems is widely, not narrowly, distributed in the population.
	6. Under the conditions of modern industrial life, the intellectual potential of the average human being is only partially utilized.

Source: From *The Human Side of Enterprise* by Douglas McGregor, pp. 33-35 and 45-49. Copyright 1960 by McGraw-Hill Book Company. Used with permission of McGraw-Hill Book Company.

necessary, must goad them into action. The opposing view, which McGregor called Theory *Y*, is outlined in the right-hand side of Figure 5-4. Theory *Y* stresses the opportunity for managers to motivate subordinates by allowing them to obtain fulfillment through participation in goal setting. Clearly, McGregor's Theory *Y* assumptions are both optimistic and humanistic. The source of control under both theories is of central importance: Theory *X* stresses external control by management; Theory *Y* focuses primarily on self-control.

Theory *X* stresses external control; Theory *Y* stresses self-control

Leadership

The leadership pattern or style managers adopt largely depends on how they believe their employees are motivated. The following discussion focuses on two opposing views of leadership whose origins are four centuries apart.

✔ **Machiavellianism.** In *The Prince,* written in 1532, Niccolò Machiavelli advanced the idea that a ruler need not be concerned about the means used to accomplish necessary ends. A leader is justified in using any technique, no matter how deceitful, to manipulate and to control people and to strike down enemies. This leadership style has been termed *Machiavellianism.* Researchers have devised various tests to determine the degree to which individuals are "High Machs" (manipulators of other people) or "Low Machs" (not manipulators of other people). The short test in Figure 5-5 should give you some insight into your own managerial style. To find your Mach score, add up the numbers you circled on questions 1, 3, 4, 5, 9, and 10. For the other four questions reverse the num-

5-5

A test: Are you a high Mach or a low Mach?

Instructions: For each statement, circle the number that most closely resembles your attitude. The way to calculate your "Mach" score is given in the text.

Statement	Disagree			Agree	
	A lot	A little	Neutral	A little	A lot
1. The best way to handle people is to tell them what they want to hear.	1	2	3	4	5
2. When you ask someone to do something for you, it is best to give the real reasons for wanting it done rather than the reasons which might carry more weight.	1	2	3	4	5
3. Anyone who completely trusts anyone else is asking for trouble.	1	2	3	4	5
4. It is hard to get ahead without cutting corners here and there.	1	2	3	4	5
5. It is safest to assume that all people have a vicious streak and that it will come out when given a chance.	1	2	3	4	5
6. One should take action only when sure it is morally right.	1	2	3	4	5
7. Most people are basically good and kind.	1	2	3	4	5
8. There is no excuse for lying to someone else.	1	2	3	4	5
9. Most people forget more easily the death of their father than the loss of their property.	1	2	3	4	5
10. Generally speaking, people won't work hard unless they're forced to do so.	1	2	3	4	5

Source: Adapted from *Studies in Machiavellianism* by Richard Christie and Florence Geis, Copyright © 1970 by Academic Press. Reprinted by permission of the publisher.

bers you circled (5 becomes 1, 4 is 2, and so on). Your Mach score is the total of the ten numbers. A large sample of Americans had an average score of 25 on this test. The higher you score above 25 points, the greater your tendency to be a High Mach—a manipulator. (If you score above 40 points, you should probably conceal your High Mach status from your friends!) Most studies show that High Machs appraise a situation and other people in a logical and detached fashion rather than emotionally. Their trademark is "cool aloofness." Apparently this insensitivity permits them to manipulate others while pursuing their own goals. The Low Mach is often the typical "nice guy" who trusts people; empathy prevents Low Machs from being detached enough to exploit others.

Machiavellians are cool and detached

✔ **A flexible leadership pattern.** Theory *X* implies a boss-centered leadership style; Theory *Y* implies a subordinate-centered one. These positions are at opposite ends of a spectrum that runs from a manager making a decision and merely announcing it to a manager permitting subordinates to operate within set limits. In striking a balance between stressing either productive efficiency or morale almost exclusively, today's managers have generally discovered two important things. First, successful leaders are keenly aware of (1) their own strengths and limitations; (2) their employees, both as individuals and as members of work groups; (3) the company and the social environment; and (4) the specific problem situations they face as managers. Second, managers do not apply one particular pattern of leadership to all circumstances. Rather, they assess the four sets of factors just enumerated and select the most appropriate leadership or management pattern for each situation.

The best leadership pattern varies with conditions

Leadership styles vary dramatically. As battalion commander in France during World War I, Winston Churchill greeted his officers with: "Gentlemen, I am your new commanding officer. Those who support me, I will look after. Those who are against me, I will break. Good afternoon, gentlemen." Churchill did not appear to be encouraging group participation or minority opinions. In 1770, Ben Franklin offered the following low-key approach:

> The way to convince another is to state your case moderately and accurately. Then scratch your head and say, "at least that's what it seems to you, but of course you may be wrong." This causes your listener to receive what you have to say, and, like as not, come about and try to convince you of it, since you are in doubt. But if you go to him in a tone of positiveness or arrogance, you only make an opponent of him.

Although this is slightly manipulative, at least Franklin gave his listener the opportunity to be heard! To support the idea that the same leadership style does not work for everyone, management expert Robert Townsend draws this conclusion on leadership: "How do you spot a leader? They come in all ages, shapes, sizes, and conditions. Some are poor administrators; some are not overly bright. One clue: . . . the true leader can be recognized because, somehow or other, his people consistently turn in superior performances.''

↙ **Factors affecting group participation.**   Management experts note that a leader has at least three choices in the amount of participation to allow subordinates in the decision-making process: (1) none (the leader makes the decision without the group); (2) some (the group's opinions are heard, but the manager makes the decision); and (3) complete (the group makes the decision without the leader). The choice depends on assessing trade-offs between three key factors:

1. *Quality of the decision:* Consider the likelihood and the need for the "right" decision and who is in the best position to make it.
2. *Acceptance of the decision by the group:* In general, a group is more likely to accept and to execute decisions that it has helped to make.
3. *Timeliness:* If speed is crucial, the leader can probably make a quicker decision than the group.

Factors influencing a group's part in a decision

Often some aspects of one factor must be sacrificed to gain advantages offered by the other two factors. Thus, as noted above, the specific situation often affects the amount of participation in decision making that a manager allows subordinates.

TO WHAT DEGREE SHOULD SUBORDINATES PARTICIPATE IN A DECISION?

Suppose you are a manager or a supervisor in charge of a small group of people. You often face the dilemma of deciding how much the group should be allowed to participate in the decision making. You have at least three alternatives: (1) make the decision yourself without involving the group; (2) obtain the group's opinions and then make the decision; or (3) let the group make the decision. Choose the alternative you would select for each of the three short cases below:

Case A: As office manager, six clerks report to you. Every day, you close the office from noon to 1:00 PM while everyone goes out to lunch. However, the president has just announced that effective next week at least one person must remain in every office throughout the lunch hour to answer incoming telephone calls. How do you insure that at least one person will be in your office throughout the lunch hour in the future?

Case B: You are a highway department supervisor in Montana. The season's worst blizzard has been raging for eight hours, and your four snowplow truck crews—all with widely different levels of experience—have just completed an exhausting day and are ready to go home. A call arrives that a snowplow must be sent to free a school bus snowbound on a treacherous mountain road. How do you decide which crew to send?

Case C: As supervisor of an engineering design unit, you must select one of two design concepts for a complex new piece of equipment. The design incorporates mechanical, electrical, and hydraulic features. Your group consists of two mechanical engineers, three electrical engineers, and one hydraulics engineer. How do you choose the design you will use?

Now that you have your decisions, what two or three key elements seem to affect the amount of participation you allowed your group members in each case? For some possible solutions to these three cases and the factors affecting the amount of group participation, see the text.

In the three cases cited on the previous page, an experienced manager would probably take the following actions:

1. *Case A:* Let the clerks make the decision. They know who wants to go to lunch with whom, so the quality of the decision will be as good or better than a decision made by the boss. The clerks will also accept it better, making timing no problem.
2. *Case B:* You — the highway department supervisor — make the decision alone after establishing which crew is physically capable of handling the job. You will make the best decision because you can determine more quickly and objectively which is the most experienced crew. Acceptance is not a problem because the chosen crew will recognize the urgency of the situation.
3. *Case C:* You — the engineering supervisor — decide, after assessing all the technical opinions of the group. You will have to weigh the "expertness" of each engineer's opinion, but you should be the best person to make a key decision in which high technical quality is essential. Acceptance by the group and timeliness are secondary.

In summary, managers are in a better position to make decisions, when they know that their employees are willing to execute the decision, and can face an imminent deadline; then, they may manage subordinates through direct orders. Otherwise, managers may allow the group to become involved with or to actually make the decision.

Controlling

Controlling is the process by which management compares actual and planned performance and initiates corrective action when necessary. This section identifies the basic elements of controlling and describes a management method for achieving effective control that builds on the concepts just described.

Essentials of Control

Elements of control: goals, measurement, and feedback

Effective management control typically requires: (1) a measurable goal established in advance that serves as a performance target; (2) a measure of actual performance that can be compared with the target goal; and (3) a feedback mechanism to initiate corrective action so that actual performance is brought into accord with the target performance. Employees best achieve self-realization if they participate in the decisions that establish their performance goals. This participation must be genuine, not

JAMES P. McFARLAND OF GENERAL MILLS: ACCENT ON CONTROLS

In 1968, James P. McFarland became chairman of the board of General Mills. At that time, the firm primarily produced flour, cake mixes, and breakfast foods. McFarland immediately initiated a two-phase program that more than doubled General Mills' sales in six years. The first phase generated tremendous growth through a diversification of the Betty Crocker empire into clothing manufacturing, hobby stores, sporting goods shops, children's games, and restaurants. The second phase, begun in 1972, slowed diversification activities to concentrate on operating the new businesses.

An important part of McFarland's management style is direct, on-site communication with each division of General Mills. "I try getting out to each operating unit at least once a year," he says, and his travel schedule often finds him on the road three days a week. "You can't run this company from this office." But a key to McFarland's success is his management control system. To control General Mills' newly acquired operations, McFarland tracks his managers' progress through an elaborate performance-monitoring system that he expanded and refined himself. It is basically a computerized management-by-objectives system that allows operating heads to measure their financial achievements against the goals they helped to establish.

illusory. In fact, in McGregor's view, open coercion is preferable to the Machiavellian concept of giving employees "a sense of participation," for both ethical and practical reasons. Ethically, the Machiavellian practice reflects a lack of integrity. Practically, manipulation that is perceived by employees may backfire severely; that is, employees may be encouraged to use ingenuity to defeat the manager's purposes. Only when organizational objectives merge with personal objectives, through genuine employee participation in goal setting, will subordinates feel committed to company goals.

Management by Objectives

Objectives under MBO focus on specific, job-related activities

In recent years, increasing managerial effort has been devoted to operationalizing corporate objectives—translating them into specific objectives to be met by each unit, subunit, and individual in an organization. The most widely used method to achieve this is *management by objectives* (MBO), which seeks to define each person's area of responsibility in terms of expected results, using observable and measurable job-related criteria (for example, reducing costs by a specified amount in a given time) rather than vague, general criteria (honesty, initiative). Thus, MBO seeks to involve subordinates in setting their own goals, which in turn helps subordinates (1) to better understand what is expected of them; (2) to relate their goals to those of the organization; (3) to communicate more effectively with managers; and (4) to increase motivation to achieve their goals.

MBO is a cyclical process

The procedure used to implement management by objectives is illustrated in Figure 5-6. The supervisor clarifies to the subordinate both the goals of the entire organization and those of all levels above the subordinate's position. The subordinate then develops a list of objectives, which is supplemented by the supervisor's ideas, and a set of goals or objectives is worked out jointly. Supervisor and subordinate then meet occasionally to review progress and to assess how the subordinate may improve performance in achieving the set objectives; these meetings usually occur when a *milestone*—an important task or activity—is scheduled to be completed. A formal review is held periodically (usually annually), where actual results are compared with established objectives. Both the supervisor and the subordinate identify problems and suggest resolutions. Objectives are modified when necessary, and the cycle is repeated.

The major impediment to MBO is defining objectives precisely so that results are measurable. John B. Lasagna, who has helped to imple-

5-6 The cycle of management by objectives.

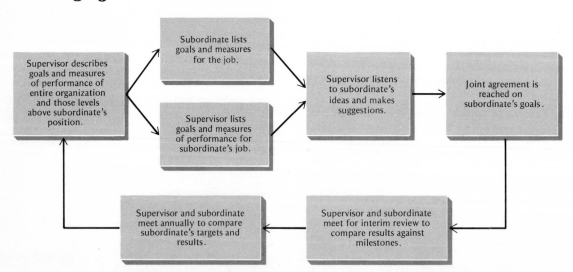

Source: Adapted from George S. Odiorne, *Management by Objectives* (New York: Pitman, 1965), p. 78.

PROBLEMS OF ORGANIZATIONAL GROWTH

People in business are often plagued by the problem of the continual addition of personnel without an increase in output. One cause: lack of control. In 1957, in his book, *Parkinson's Law,* British author and historian C. Northcote Parkinson formulated his own immutable law on this subject: "Work expands so as to fill the time available for its completion." The wisdom of this observation is startling. For example, a student who is given two weeks to complete a term project generally works on it (or perhaps worries about it) for two weeks and then stays up all night the day before it is due to finish it. The same student, given four weeks to complete the project, works on it (or worries about it) for four weeks and then stays up all night the day before it is due to finish it.

Applying his concept to organizations, Parkinson regards himself as a true prophet. In 1914, for example, the British navy—then the most powerful in the world—needed 4,366 officials to stay afloat. By 1967, when Parkinson judged the British navy "practically powerless," he noted that over 33,000 civil servants were barely sufficient to manage "the navy we no longer possess."

ment MBO at San Francisco's Wells Fargo Bank, suggests the following guidelines for writing down objectives:

Helpful rules in developing specific objectives

1. Begin with an action verb.
2. Identify a single key result for each of the objectives.
3. Give the day, month, and year of estimated completion.
4. Identify costs (dollars, time, materials, and equipment).
5. State verifiable criteria which signal when the objective has been reached.
6. Be sure the objective is controllable by the person setting the objective. If it is not totally controllable, at least isolate the part of the objective that is.

Lasagna further points out that good statements of objectives should concentrate on what is to be accomplished and when—not on why and how.

Companies using the MBO method believe that the program has been successful in translating company objectives into personal, individual objectives and in convincing employees that their supervisors are genuinely interested in helping them to do their jobs better. This is due in part to better planning and in part to an emphasis on self-control rather than on control imposed from above. Equally important are the corrective, constructive suggestions the employee receives that help to improve his or her future performance.

Control in MBO is largely self-control

KEY POINTS TO REMEMBER

1. Both the personnel department and individual managers share the responsibility for staffing, which involves selecting, training, promoting, and retiring subordinates.

2. Preemployment aspects of staffing include identifying manpower needs, finding and interviewing prospective candidates, and offering jobs to applicants who are deemed satisfactory.

3. Candidates applying for jobs must "sell" themselves — do something to demonstrate their unique abilities in comparison to those of competing candidates. A concise, effective personal résumé helps to achieve this.

4. To select new employees systematically, employers use a combination of various screening devices. But screening may accidentally eliminate some people who are well-motivated and creative.

5. Postemployment activities include training, evaluating, and compensating employees, as well as providing various auxiliary employee services.

6. Communicating involves transmitting messages to achieve a desired result.

7. To be of value, a communication must be received, understood, accepted, and acted on. In addition, management must verify that the message achieves the desired result through watching or listening.

8. Directing involves guiding employee performance toward common goals.

9. The Hawthorne studies, Maslow's hierarchy of human needs, and McGregor's Theory X and Theory Y concepts provide insights as to what motivates employees. An understanding of employee motivation helps a manager to select an appropriate leadership pattern.

10. Three factors present in a specific problem situation affect the amount of participation a manager allows employees in the decision-making process: (a) quality of the decision; (b) acceptance of the decision by the group; and (c) timeliness.

11. Controlling is the process by which management compares actual and planned performances and initiates corrective action when necessary.

12. Management by objectives (MBO) is a method of putting corporate objectives into practice that enables employees to improve their performance, mainly through self-control.

QUESTIONS FOR DISCUSSION

1. Cite the advantages and disadvantages of following a company policy of promotion from within.

2. How might the normal screening process used by a firm eliminate potentially talented employees?

3. How might the different personal frames of reference and the status of two people in an organization lead to ineffective communication?

4. As people communicate, filtering and dilution result in a sifting or a screening process. Explain each process and the difference between the two.

5. What did experimenters in the Hawthorne studies expect to find? What did they actually find?

6. What three key factors affect the amount of participation a manager might allow subordinates in a specific situation?

7. In what ways does management by objectives relate more closely to McGregor's Theory *Y* than to his Theory *X*?

SHORT CASES AND PROBLEMS

1. Suppose you are a college recruiter for the ABC Office Equipment Corporation, and Roger Kerin's résumé (Figure 5-2) is one of several in a stack on your desk. Roger is scheduled for an interview in ten minutes.

   (a) What information in the résumé particularly interests you?

   (b) What important information does not appear that you would want to hear more about?

   (c) How would you obtain the information in (b) during the interview?

2. Assume that you are the manufacturing manager of a plant that produces pajamas. Competitors have succeeded in producing pajamas of a quality equal to yours but at substantially lower cost. You have concluded that it is necessary to change the work methods and piece rates in your plant in order to remain competitive. Your task is to find a way to make these necessary changes while minimizing employee resistance and antagonism to the change. Analyze this problem in the following way:

   (a) Divide the class into groups of four or five students.

   (b) Have each group take 15 minutes to arrive at a solution, and write it down on paper in less than 75 words.

   (c) Have one student from each group read its solution to the class.

   (d) Have the class vote on which group's solution is best. How much employee participation does the class prefer to have in the decision?

   This problem is based on the results of two methods actually used in a pajama factory.

3. As sales manager, you supervise four salespeople who are located in different cities. Each salesperson calls on industrial customers in two or three different states. At the annual sales meeting, you point out that more information is needed about each sales call (a write-up of the results of a call on each customer) so that a new form of sales-call report can be designed. The new sales-call report will record topics discussed, sales attempts made, customer reactions to the firm's products, and actual sales. How would you go about developing the new form?

CAREERS IN PERSONNEL WORK

The primary function of **personnel workers** is to fill vacant positions in their organization with competent individuals. In addition, they counsel employees and develop pay scales, two responsibilities that require a general business background and interview skills. Both private industry and government employ personnel workers, but for somewhat different applications. Personnel people in private business firms usually interview and screen job applicants and try to place them in positions where their interests and their skills will be most useful. Government workers devote more time to classifying jobs and to scoring competitive examinations. A bachelor's degree in business or in personnel administration is preferred, but many personnel workers have been promoted to their jobs after competent execution of lower-level duties. Experienced personnel workers earn about $15,000 a year. With the increasing emphasis on worker needs, the demand for personnel workers is expected to expand rapidly. (*Additional information:* American Society for Personnel Administration; 19 Church Street; Berea, Ohio 44017.)

CAREERS IN CLERICAL WORK

File clerks function to increase office efficiency by locating, updating, and retrieving business information. Periodically, they also check their files for the correct placement of items and transfer outdated data to inactive files. Generally clerks are high-school graduates who receive on-the-job training until they are familiar with the firm's filing system. Accurate writing and spelling skills are essential. The yearly income for experienced file clerks is approximately $6700. Employment opportunities are expected to expand moderately, but at a slower pace than in past years due to the increasing automation of clerical duties. (*Additional information:* State Supervisor of Office Occupations Education; State Department of Education; your state capital.)

Receptionists greet customers and refer them to the appropriate company official. Their other duties include monitoring callers, opening and sorting mail, and, on occasion, operating a switchboard. Receptionists must be diplomatic and should enjoy meeting people. A high-school diploma and general secretarial skills are necessary requirements. Annual income is in the vicinity of $5800. Employment opportunities are expected to rapidly increase as management continues to place emphasis on public relations. (*Additional information:* American Society for Personnel Administration; 19 Church Street; Berea, Ohio 44017; and State Supervisor of Office Occupations Education; State Department of Education; your state capital.)

Stenographers and **secretaries** are responsible for the efficient transmission of business information. Although some of their duties may overlap, stenographers primarily take dictation, type, and file, whereas secretaries often handle more demanding tasks such as answering customer letters, writing reports, and doing statistical research. Basic shorthand skills are helpful; applicants without shorthand sometimes receive on-the-job training. Most employers require a high-school diploma, and an adequate knowledge of grammar and vocabulary is necessary. Yearly income averages are $6700 for stenographers and $8500 for secretaries. Occupational opportunities are expected to continue to increase rapidly despite a greater use of automatic equipment in offices. (*Addition information:* American Society for Personnel Administration; 19 Church Street; Berea, Ohio 44017; and State Supervisor of Office Occupations Education; State Department of Education; your state capital.)

The rapid and efficient processing of business data requires qualified **office-machine operators.** A number of positions are available, including **bookkeeping-machine operators,** who record financial transactions on bookkeeping forms, and **tabulating-machine operators,** who sort and quantify accounting data. Manual dexterity and an understanding of basic mathematics are mandatory. Most office-machine operators are high-school graduates who may have had some college and on-the-job help in the use of office-machine equipment. Yearly salaries vary: bookkeeping-machine operators earn about $6500; tabulating-machine operators, about $8500. The number of available jobs is expected to increase slowly due to a growing reliance on automated data-processing systems. (*Additional information:* State Supervisor of Office Occupations Education; State Department of Education; your state capital.)

CAREERS IN TECHNICAL WRITING

Technical writers are responsible for communicating a knowledge of scientific developments and new products in a manner that is understandable to both a professional and a consumer audience. Technical writers perform a variety of tasks, ranging from writing publicity releases to composing instructions for the use of new products. Aside from writing skills, technical writers must possess an adequate up-to-date knowledge of the technological developments in their field. Most technical writers have bachelor's degrees, often in technical journalism. Experienced writers earn from $8500 to $16,000 annually. Employment opportunities are expected to expand moderately and will be based largely on management's need for understandable information about the increasing production of complex goods. (*Additional information:* Society for Technical Communications, Inc.; Suite 421; 1010 Vermont Avenue, N.W.; Washington, D.C. 20005.)

A CRITICAL BUSINESS DECISION

—made by Robert F. Six

THE SITUATION In 1975, Robert F. Six had been President of Continental Air Lines for 37 years. A high-school dropout, in 1936 Six borrowed money to become part owner of a tiny mail-plane business. Today, Bob Six's business, Continental Air Lines, flies 22,657 miles daily from Chicago and Miami to the West Coast and Hawaii.

Six's flamboyant personality has left its imprint on Continental. From the first, he envisioned Continental as the little company battling big impersonal competitors (United Air Lines is five time as large) just as David battled Goliath. The result: a remarkable cohesive company spirit among Continental employees. Many know and most see Six personally, since he insists that company officers rub elbows with pilots, secretaries, and mechanics in employee cafeterias. And Six has an instinct for what customers want: for example, Continental was the first airline to offer hot meals and wide seats on coach flights. With his eye for detail, Continental Air Lines has realized a profit in 36 of the 37 years Six has been its President.

THE DECISION That is a hard act to follow. And no one knows it better than Bob Six who, by 1975, had spent eight years seeking his own replacement. The search was thoughtful, deep, and deliberate, because Six knows that no decision is more critical to the future of any firm than choosing a successor to its chief executive officer.

In 1967, with the aid of a management consultant, Six searched for qualified candidates within Continental who were capable of running the airline. The search identified four men, each of whom was described in a separate bound report that delved into background, character, education, management experience, personal aspirations, and private life. *Fortune* magazine observes: "By both their positions in the company and the initials of their last names, the four candidates composed the A, B, C, and D of Continental Air Lines." In 1975, *Fortune* summarized the records of Bob Six's four potential successors:

● **Richard M. Adams,** 56, Senior Vice President, Operating and Technical Services, is a quiet engineer who enjoys good music and photography. A patent attorney's son, Adams has a warmth and an air of ability that have won him a staunch following among his subordinates. He moved over from Pan American Airways in 1962 to head Continental's maintenance division and soon was put in charge of flight operations as well. Under him, Continental has achieved the best records in the industry for aircraft utilization and jet safety.

● **Charles A. Bucks,** 47, Senior Vice President, Marketing, quit college after World War II to become baggage handler in his home town of Lubbock, Texas, at an airline that was later acquired by Continental. Showing a natural talent for salesmanship, he rapidly moved up through the marketing division until, at 34, he became the air-transport industry's youngest vice president. One of his gimmicks: in 1959, to promote flights from Chicago, he dropped a helicopter into Wrigley Field in the middle of a game and had a crew of midgets "kidnap" the Chicago Cubs' centerfielder. Bucks is second only to Six in popularity among Continental's rank and file.

● **G. Edward Cotter,** 57, is Senior Vice President, Legal and Diversification, and the company Secretary. Disarmingly frank and ambitious, cool and well ordered, Cotter is the son of American missionaries in China. He worked for a New York law firm and was secretary of the Freeman Sulphur Company before taking over Continental's legal division in 1965. Cotter has an extraordinary conceptual grasp of such broad issues as the airline's needs for long-term growth. And he articulates these ideas with the self-confidence and the orderly flow of a seasoned lawyer. Yet, most Continental employees are unaware of his achievements. But everyone is aware of another fact of Cotter's life: his sister, actress Audrey Meadows, is Six's wife.

● **Alexander Damm,** 59, Senior Vice President and General Manager, is Continental's moneyman. Damm came from Trans World Airlines in 1959 to bolster the company's lackluster financial division. He installed tight budget controls and a monthly head count that allows Six to veto the most minute addition to the payroll. The son of a railroad roundhouse foreman, Damm is a serious, no-nonsense taskmaster. He lives by the memo, often to Six's exasperation, and insists that written communication is the best way for an executive to keep informed. Nevertheless, Damm's rigid system of controls has kept Continental profitable. He is not well liked by employees, largely because over the years he has had to execute the austerity programs that have laid off hundreds of men and women.

In 1975, Six organized a selection committee, comprised of three members of the Board of Directors and himself, to choose his replacement. Six and the selection committee were also concerned that in choosing Six's successor, Continental might lose the other three men—valuable employees who would be equally valuable to competing airlines.

QUESTIONS

1. If you were Bob Six, on what criteria would you base your selection of a new President?
2. Which man would you select? Why?
3. What action would you take to keep from losing the other three capable men who were not chosen to succeed you as President of Continental?

Collecting data is much like collecting garbage. You must know in advance what you are going to do with the stuff before you collect it.

Mark Twain

6

MANAGEMENT: MAKING EFFECTIVE DECISIONS

The four men suspected that the water in the river was too shallow for their heavily loaded flatboat. Their suspicions proved correct. The boat became lodged on a dam—its bow extending over the dam and its stern slowly sinking from the inrushing water.

If there's water in your boat . . .

The youngest man aboard—tall and with angular features— suggested a solution. The men moved the heaviest cargo to the riverbank, allowing the boat to level itself and the water in the boat to flow forward. Then the young man bored a hole in the bow of the boat to let the water drain out and whittled a wooden plug to fit into the hole. The lightened boat could then be poled over the dam.

The year was 1831; the dam was at New Salem, Illinois; and the young man who solved the problem was Abraham Lincoln. One of the other men—the boat's owner, Denton Offutt—was impressed with Lincoln's creative solution. After Lincoln maneuvered the boat down the Mississippi to New Orleans, Offutt persuaded Lincoln to work in his new store in New Salem. (*Warning:* Lincoln drilled the hole in the part of the boat that was *not* resting on the water. Experience indicates that the procedure presents problems when the entire bottom of the boat is floating on the water!)

. . . bore a hole!(?)

As this example illustrates, it is a mistake to assume that only in business are important decisions made or special problem-solving methods used. *Decision making* is the process of seeking to achieve some objective by consciously choosing a course of action from available alternatives. Thus, each day in a variety of situations—at home, at school, at work—we are called on to make decisions and to solve problems. No one can deny that making good decisions is hard work.

In Chapters 5 and 6 we will describe a systematic approach to decision making that can be applied to both individual and business problems. This approach, called the DECIDE process, is useful in analyzing and understanding the business problems that will be described in the remainder of the book. Business information will also be discussed. As we noted earlier in Chapter 4, decision making and business information underlie all six functions of management, in fact, all areas of business.

Everyone must make decisions

An Overview of the DECIDE Process

No magic formula exists that assures a good solution to all problems all the time. Even Lincoln made his share of poor decisions. For example, Lincoln's business venture with Offutt failed within a few months. But business managers often improve their decisions by using a formal, systematic series of steps to solve problems. This chapter emphasizes how decisions *should be* made, not how they often *are* made.

Using a
formal series of steps
can improve decisions

The systematic approach to decision making (or problem solving) described in this book involves six steps. The six letters in the acronym DECIDE represent the first word for each step and thus provide a checklist for the entire decision process. The six-step DECIDE approach applies to all problems—both personal and business. Let us consider the six steps in turn.

✔ D—**Define the problem precisely.** This step includes identifying the objectives to be achieved, the constraints placed on solving the problem (for example, its importance and the time and money available), and the measure of success to be used initially in choosing the best alternative and later in judging whether the chosen solution was a good one.

✔ E—**Enumerate two groups of decision factors.** First, all the realistic alternatives that the decision maker can control in solving the problem must be identified. Second, those factors that might influence the success of an alternative solution but that are beyond the decision maker's control must be considered.

The six steps
in the DECIDE
checklist

✔ C—**Collect relevant information that will assist in solving the problem.** Sometimes relevant information may be found quickly and easily, perhaps by making a telephone call or by examining existing reports. At other times, obtaining the information may be expensive and time-consuming (for example, surveying hundreds of consumers about their reactions to a product).

✔ I—**Identify the best alternative.** To select the best alternative, first summarize and condense the collected information, and then apply a simple structure in analyzing the problem. The best or preferred alternative is the *solution* to the problem.

✔ D—**Develop and implement a detailed plan to put the chosen alternative into effect.** Implementing the preferred alternative may require obtaining approval for the plan. Also, when the plan is complex, controls must be established to insure that the plan is implemented and carried to completion. Too many solutions halt in the planning stage.

✔ E—**Evaluate the decision and the decision process after the plan is implemented.** This final step helps to determine if the results of the plan actually achieve the initial objectives set forth in the problem-definition step. Such an evaluation may reveal that modifications should be made in (1) the solution that was developed, and/or (2) the decision process used to reach that solution.

Step 1 in DECIDE: Define the Problem

Philosopher John Dewey once observed: "A problem well defined is half solved." To learn how to define problems better, we will consider three important parts of the problem-definition step and then apply these parts to a simple problem.

The Three Parts to Defining a Problem

Defining
a problem
involves . . .

As shown in Figure 6-1, three parts of a problem must be specified: (1) the objectives to be achieved; (2) the constraints that restrict the available number of solutions; and (3) the measure of success to be used in judging whether a good decision was made.

objectives,

The *objectives* in a problem situation are the goals that the decision maker seeks to achieve. Examples of objectives in business problems are increasing revenue, reducing employee turnover, and introducing a line of new products. The *constraints* in a decision-making situation are the restrictions placed on potential solutions by the nature and importance of the problem. Common constraints in business problems are limitations on the time and money available to solve the problem; in addition, undesir-

constraints,

able side effects on other parts of a business often eliminate particularly promising solutions. For example, the marketing department of a paint manufacturer may conclude that the least expensive way to increase sales is to increase the number of colors the company produces; to do this, however, the production department must stock so many different colors that its inventory costs will become excessive. Thus, an attractive solution to increasing sales may eventually have to be discarded.

. . . and a
measure
of success

Successful decision makers also stress the importance of developing adequate *measures of success* (sometimes called criteria) at the problem-definition stage; in the confusion of discussion, it becomes difficult to choose among alternative solutions and easy to lose sight of the goal, that is, solving the particular problem. The measures of success in many, but

6-1 Step 1 in the DECIDE process.

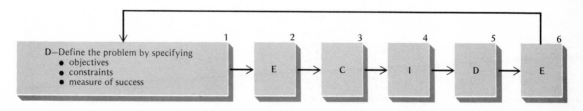

not all, business problems is profit which is expressed in dollars. In personal decisions, measures of success are more likely to be intangible factors, such as satisfaction, happiness, and good health.

Defining a Simple Problem

In many true-to-life situations, the six steps in the DECIDE process can be carried out informally and quickly. Consider the following circumstances:

Suppose that you are bitten by a dog while walking near your home one day. The dog disappears and is not found in the ensuing frantic 24-hour search. You face the problem of deciding whether to have rabies shots because the dog might be rabid.

This example illustrates step 1 in the DECIDE process. The three aspects of the problem-definition step in this example are:

Problem definition in terms of the dog-bite problem

Objective: Decide whether to get rabies shots.

Constraint: You have 24 hours after being bitten to begin rabies shots. Otherwise they will be of no value.

Measure of success: Do you avoid getting rabies and live?

Note that the measure of success is closely linked to the objective; without the use of a precise measure of success, a statement of objectives often becomes vague and fuzzy.

Step 2 in DECIDE: Enumerate the Decision Factors

We now turn to the two sets of factors that in combination affect the outcome of a decision: alternatives and uncertainties. Effective problem solving requires creativity both in defining a problem and in identifying

6-2   Step 2 in the DECIDE process.

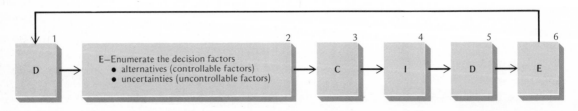

The results
of a decision
depend on two
decision factors . . .

these two sets of factors. In this section, we will examine several riddles, puzzles, and problem situations which are intended to provide insights into the ways you approach a problem and to suggest how you can improve your own decision making ability.

Two Kinds of Decision Factors

The term *decision factors* refers to two sets of variables that in combination determine the outcome of a decision. As shown in Figure 6-2, these two sets differ in the degree that they can be controlled by the decision maker. *Alternatives* are controllable factors over which the decision maker has complete command when making a decision. *Uncertainties* are uncontrollable factors that the decision maker cannot influence. In step 2 of DECIDE, the decision maker faces the problem of identifying in detail (1) the principal alternatives that can be considered reasonable approaches to solving the problems, and (2) the principal uncertainties that can affect a particular alternative and produce a good or a poor solution to the problem.

. . . alternatives . . .

. . . and uncertainties

↙ **Alternatives: the controllable decision factors.** The task of enumerating the alternatives in the dog-bite problem is straightforward: there are only two choices—get the shots or do not get them. Yet in some problems, dozens of alternatives may deserve consideration. This is especially true of the problems many people in business face when they look for ways to reduce costs, to increase worker productivity, to find new users or customers for existing products, and to develop new products.

It is important, then, to generate a group of reasonable alternative solutions to a problem. Many experienced decision makers do this by transforming a problem statement into an informal question. This method appears to produce good results, especially when the problem does not involve ethical or factual issues. The problem statement begins with ''In what ways can?'' Examples abound:

What the
decision maker
controls:
alternatives

> In what ways can we reduce overtime costs?
> In what ways can we use our draftsmen more effectively?
> In what ways can we use product X to new advantage?
> In what ways can we modify product X to increase its sales?

The decision maker then generates a larger number of reasonable alternatives. At this stage, he or she avoids final evaluation of any ideas (this will come later, in step 4 of DECIDE) and uses one idea to trigger others.

↙ **Uncertainties: the uncontrollable decision factors.** Scottish poet Robert Burns wrote: ''The best-laid schemes of mice an' men gang aft agley.'' A well-chosen alternative sometimes goes astray due to uncon-

How best-laid plans
often go astray:
uncertainties

trollable factors—uncertainties over which the decision maker has no control. In the dog-bite problem, the uncertainty is whether or not the dog is rabid. This uncontrollable factor combines with whatever alternative you choose about getting rabies shots to determine the outcome of the decision.

In business, a variety of uncertainties can affect the outcome of a decision. These uncertainties can result from factors within the firm or can involve consumers, competitors, national or international affairs, and even the weather. For example, in the late 1950s the Ford Motor Company introduced the Edsel only to discover that consumer tastes had changed from powerful chromium-plated cars to simpler compact cars. Also, the Edsel appeared on the market during the 1958 recession, when many families were reconsidering car-buying decisions. From Ford's viewpoint, changes in consumer tastes and deterioration in the U.S. economy were uncontrollable. Thus, the quality of Ford's decision to market the Edsel ultimately depended to some degree on factors over which it had no control.

Barriers and Aids to Problem Solving

Each person approaches a problem in his or her own way. This often implicitly structures the problem in a way that increases or decreases its difficulty.

✔ **Some sample problems.** We will examine some of the blocks to problem solving through a series of examples and then, through introspection, determine why we may have difficulty arriving at solutions.

Four riddles and puzzles are listed below. Without looking at the solutions, which are discussed later in the text, spend 15 or 20 minutes trying to solve the problems. (*Note:* Few people will be able to solve all four problems in that time.) As you study and attempt to solve these problems, remember your thoughts, for they will be useful later when you evaluate your own blocks to problem solving. The problems are:

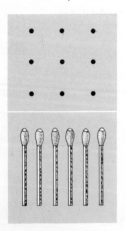

6-3

How do you
solve problems?

1. *The injured-boy problem:* A father and his son are riding on a train that crashes. The father is unhurt but is pinned in the train wreck. His son is knocked unconscious and is taken to a hospital, in need of an examination—and perhaps surgery. The doctor, upon seeing the boy, is visibly shaken and says, "I'm afraid I can't examine him or operate. The boy is my son!" *Problem:* What is the relationship between the doctor and the boy?
2. *The dot problem:* Nine dots are arranged in a square, as shown at the left. *Problem:* Connect the nine dots by drawing four continuous straight lines without lifting your pencil from the paper.
3. *The match problem:* Six matches are provided, as shown at the left.

Problem: Assemble the matches so that they form four congruent equilateral triangles, each side of which is equal to the length of one of the matches.

4. *The river-crossing problem:* Eight soldiers have to cross a river. The only means of crossing the river is a small boat in which two little boys are playing. At most, the boat can carry two boys or one soldier. *Problem:* How do the eight soldiers cross the river?

When experience
plays tricks

✔ **Problem solutions.** Let us examine the solutions to each of the four problems listed above and the typical errors made or "wrong tracks" taken by people who have trouble solving these problems.

In the injured-boy problem, the doctor is the boy's mother. The underlying difficulty in solving this problem is the stereotyped role of the doctor as a man in American society. This riddle probably would not be difficult to solve if most doctors in this country were women or if the riddle were recast with the mother at the scene of the accident. As it is, many people automatically start thinking of men's roles—stepfathers, grandfathers, adopted fathers—and do not arrive at the solution. If you step away from the problem, the solution becomes obvious—especially if the problem is redefined as: "Who might call a boy 'son'?" When the problem is stated this way, "mother" and "father" come to mind immediately!

The solutions to the dot and the match problems appear in Figure 6-4. In both instances, the potential problem solver usually makes implicit assumptions that are important barriers to solving the problem. In the dot problem most people assume that they cannot extend the lines beyond the square of dots. In the match problem, people usually assume that the problem must be solved with the matches lying on a flat surface. Psychologists call this tendency to cling misguidedly to a false premise or assumption a *fixation*. It is a major barrier to problem solving.

Fixations are
false assumptions

The river-crossing problem is difficult. Both small boys must cross the river together at the start. One boy stays there while the other boy takes the boat back. A soldier then crosses in the boat, and the boy returns the boat to the other side. This whole cycle is then repeated seven times. The essence of the solution to this problem is having the two boys go across the river first—a step that seems useless to most people, since the primary goal is to get the soldiers across the river. Solving the problem requires an implicit recognition that two different roles are played by the people riding in the boat: loads to be moved (the soldiers) and the means of moving the loads across the river (the boat rowers). Many people facing this problem violate its constraints by trying to put (1) two soldiers or (2) one soldier and one boy in the boat simultaneously. They repeatedly return to this approach.

The most direct route
isn't always the best

Here, an early enumeration of the alternative loads that the boat can carry is one way to obtain a solution: the boat can carry either one soldier, one boy, or two boys. Starting out with either one soldier or one boy in the

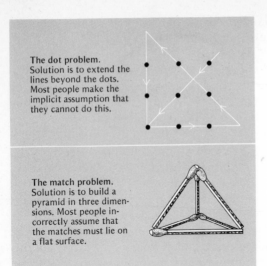

The dot problem. Solution is to extend the lines beyond the dots. Most people make the implicit assumption that they cannot do this.

The match problem. Solution is to build a pyramid in three dimensions. Most people incorrectly assume that the matches must lie on a flat surface.

6-4

Solutions to the dot and match problems.

boat provides no way of returning the boat to pick up more soldiers. Thus, the two boys must row the boat across the river first—a step most people assume is unnecessary.

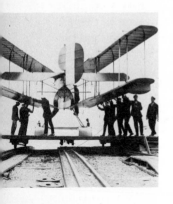

✔ **Ways to improve problem solving.** To learn to be better problem solvers, we must break away from fixations that either (1) make implicit assumptions or (2) rely on traditional associations as the source of alternatives. Standard, known solutions can be traps that hinder problem solving. Prior to the airplane, many brilliant inventors tried to fly in contraptions patterned after kites or birds. The Wright brothers only succeeded when they broke with tradition and invented the flaps on fixed wings. People tend to believe things that perform similar functions should look alike: early automobiles resembled buggies and early water skis were modeled after snow skis. Thus, recognizing some of the mistakes we made in attempting to solve the problems just discussed should help us in solving future problems.

Step 3 in DECIDE: Collect Relevant Information

There are two kinds of relevant information

As shown in Figure 6-5, *business information* is comprised of the methods and the data that are used to solve a business problem. *Methods* are the approaches used to analyze the problem under study; *data* are the facts and figures pertinent to the problem. In analyzing a business problem, methods and data combine to suggest possible solutions.

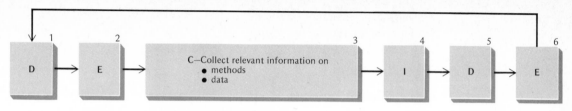

6-5 Step 3 in the DECIDE process.

Methods for Analyzing Business Problems

The search for appropriate methods to use in analyzing business problems has a simple goal: "to avoid reinventing the wheel." The rationale for the *methods search* (often called the library or literature search) is that it saves time and money by investigating other decision makers' solutions to substantially the same problems. A decision maker will probably obtain a better solution by applying, modifying, or tailoring known

6-6 Sources of business information.

General class of information	Kind of information		Examples of information	Examples of information sources
Methods	General methods for a variety of problems.		Statistical methods to analyze or to collect data.	Statistics textbooks and journals.
	Specific methods for specialized problems.		Ways to organize a firm.	Management texts and journals.
			Ways to handle plant depreciation.	Accounting texts and journals.
Data	Secondary data	Internal	Who buys the firm's products.	Firm's accounting records.
		External	U.S. population; family incomes; number of retailers.	Census reports compiled by the U.S. Bureau of the Census.
	Primary data	Observation	Effectiveness of personnel interviews.	Personal or mechanical recording of practice interviews.
		Survey	Employee dissatisfaction with personnel practices.	Employee surveys on ways to improve personnel practices.
		Experiment	Consumer preferences for new soft drink.	Consumer taste tests.

methods to a particular problem, than by starting from scratch. Figure 6-6 shows that analytical techniques may be divided somewhat arbitrarily into general methods and specific methods, according to a problem's degree of specialization.

✔ **General methods.** General methods apply to a variety of problems in a wide array of business fields, including management, finance, and manufacturing. Statistical methods are an example.

Statistical methods provide a way to summarize numbers

In many business problems, hundreds or thousands of figures must be summarized in order to be interpreted easily. *Statistical methods* can provide meaningful summaries of these numbers. One statistical technique often employed by business is the development of a *measure of central value*—a figure that in some way condenses a whole set of numbers into a single value. Statisticians define three such measures—the mean, median, and mode:

Mean: The number found by dividing the sum of a set of numbers by the total number of items in that set. The mean is also called the *arithmetic mean* and is what we think of as the *average.*

Median: The number located in the exact middle of an entire set of numbers when they are arranged from lowest to highest. When an even number of items comprises a set, the median is found by taking the mean of the two middle values. The median is the most typical of all the numbers in a set in the sense that half the numbers lie above the median and half lie below it.

Mode: The number that occurs most often in a set of numbers.

We will illustrate these three measures by examining the scores in the 1960 New York Yankee–Pittsburgh Pirate World Series. This will enable us (1) to calculate actual values for the three measures of central value defined above, and (2) to examine potential pitfalls in the careless use of these measures.

Analyzing World Series results

The number of runs scored by each team in each of the seven World Series games, from lowest to highest, were:

Runs scored by New York Yankees	Runs scored by Pittsburgh Pirates
2	0
2	0
4	3
9	3
10	5
12	6
16	10
Total 55	27

From these numbers, we can calculate the three measures of central value for each team:

	New York Yankees	Pittsburgh Pirates
Mean	$\frac{55}{7} = 7.9$	$\frac{27}{7} = 3.9$
Median	9	3
Mode	2	0,3

Recall that the median is the middle number in each set of numbers arranged from lowest to highest, or 9 for the Yankees and 3 for the Pirates. The mode is the number that occurs most often. The Yankees scored 2 runs twice, and all other numbers of runs only once; thus, 2 is their modal value of runs scored. The Pirates have two modes (0 and 3), because they scored each of these numbers twice and all other numbers once.

Many of us who have played in a series of games and lost have no doubt felt: "If our team could just rearrange its runs—winning most of the games by just one run and letting our opponents clobber us in the rest—our record would be great!" As you may have guessed, during the 1960 World Series this was a dream come true for the Pirates. The game scores were:

Game	Runs scored by New York Yankees	Runs scored by Pittsburgh Pirates
1	4	6
2	16	3
3	10	0
4	2	3
5	2	5
6	12	0
7	9	10

When the Yankees scored twice their opponent's runs —and lost!

The Pirates won the series, even though their four victories were by margins of 2, 1, 3, and 1 runs, respectively, and the Yankees outscored them by 13, 10, and 12 runs in the other three games. In fact, the Yankees scored more than twice as many runs as the Pirates and still lost the Series.

The question of what statistical measure to use for a specific problem has prompted a number of anecdotes. Consider, for example, the story of the statistician who drowned in a lake whose mean depth was two feet. Or the inspector who saw four 3-inch and four 5-inch diameter holes in the engine block of one automobile and approved it anyway, because the blueprint called for eight 4-inch diameter holes and he decided the holes were 4 inches in diameter "on the average!"

The moral should be clear. Although measures of central value are extremely useful in summarizing a large group of numbers, great care must be taken in selecting and interpreting the measure used. The ultimate test of which measure of central value is better for a particular problem is the relevant measure of success—part of Step 1 in DECIDE. Thus, in a World Series, the measure of success is not the most runs scored in the entire Series but the most runs scored in four of the games.

✔ **Specific methods.** In many business firms, there is a high degree of specialization—often even within a single functional area such as finance, accounting, manufacturing, or marketing. It is natural, then, that functional areas have developed specific methods directed at solving specialized problems in their respective fields. Examples of specific methods which we will examine later in this book are the market-product grid used to identify potential markets for a new product and accounting ratios used to interpret accounting statements. Figure 6-6 gives two other examples of specific methods used to solve specialized problems within functional areas.

Textbooks and journals are important sources of information about such methods. A journal is a periodical published by a university or a professional society. Journal articles inform readers about the latest research findings or developments in a particular field of study. The *Harvard Business Review,* the *Journal of Marketing,* and the *Journal of Finance* are three prominent and widely used business journals. A decision maker may seek help from a business librarian or may refer to four important indexes of business-related periodicals available in most business libraries: *Business Periodicals Index, Industrial Arts Index, Public Affairs Information Service,* and *Reader's Guide to Periodical Literature.*

Data for Business Problems

Business data, the facts and figures pertinent to a business problem, are of two types: primary data and secondary data. *Primary data* are new data collected by or for the decision maker for the immediate purpose or project at hand. *Secondary data* are data previously collected by another individual or group for some other purpose or project.

In most business studies, analysts first determine the nature and the extent of the available secondary data. They may then be more selective in collecting whatever primary data are required to close data gaps. Since business analysts initially seek out secondary data, we will examine various sources for such data first.

✔ **Secondary data.** As we saw in Figure 6-6, secondary data are of two types: internal data and external data. *Internal secondary data* are found within the organization in which the decision is being made. The individual firm is a source of innumerable bits of important business data. Accounting records, customer service complaints, quality control reports, sales call reports, and personnel histories are all examples of a firm's internal secondary data.

External secondary data are facts and figures obtained from outside the firm. The main sources of such data are U.S. government census reports. The U.S. census is really many different reports covering topics of direct interest to business. Three of the reports most relevant to business problems are:

1. *Census of Population and Housing:* Numbers and characteristics of the population and its housing.
2. *Census of Business:* Numbers of establishments, employment, and sales of retail, wholesale, and service trades.
3. *Census of Manufactures:* Numbers of establishments, employment, and value of shipments of manufacturers.

Census reports are compiled and updated periodically in other government publications, such as the *Statistical Abstract of the United States* (published annually) and the *County and City Data Book* (published every four to six years and containing data collected on both a county- and a citywide basis). The *Monthly Catalog of U.S. Government Publications,* available in most libraries, provides a guide to nearly all information sources published by the federal government and contains an index arranged by topic.

U.S. census
information:
a major source
of secondary data

Most federal reports are for public use and are available at a small cost. In addition, data published by state and local governments and by many colleges and universities are available free of charge or for a small fee. And trade associations — organizations supported by groups of firms usually within the same industry — make data available to their members.

Secondary business data should be (1) timely and (2) not slanted to reflect the bias of the data presenter. Secondary data that are satisfactory on these two counts often save the researcher significant amounts of time and money.

✔ **Primary data.** There are three basic ways to collect primary data: by observation, by survey, and by experiment. *Observational data* are collected either by mechanically recording or personally observing the behavior of machines or people. A familiar example of collecting observational data by mechanical means is the Nielsen Television Rating Index. The A.C. Nielsen Company connects an "audimeter" to the TV sets of 1200 families scattered throughout the United States. The audimeter is a

mechanical recorder that collects two kinds of information: the number of television sets turned on at any given time and the channels to which the sets are tuned. Through this procedure, Nielsen television ratings such as those shown in Figure 6-7 are developed. The figures in the right-hand column of Figure 6-7 indicate the percentage of the 1200 families whose

6-7 Nielsen ratings of the top ten national television programs, 1974–1975.

Rank	Program and network	Rating
1	All In The Family (CBS)	30.2
2	Sanford and Son (NBC)	29.8
3	Chico and The Man (NBC)	28.6
4	The Jeffersons (CBS)	27.6
5	M*A*S*H (CBS)	27.2
6	Rhoda (CBS)	25.9
7	The Waltons (CBS)	25.7
8	Good Times (CBS)	25.6
9	Maude (CBS)	24.9
10	Hawaii Five-O (CBS)	24.6

Source: A.C. Nielsen Company.

television sets were tuned to specific shows during the 1974–1975 program year. For example, 30.2 percent (or 362 families) in the Nielsen sample watched "All in the Family" that week. The Nielsen Index is not foolproof, however. In the 1960s, congressional investigations revealed that the Nielsen ratings for one week included a childless couple who left their television set on all day in order to entertain their dog while they were at work! Thus, these Nielsen ratings included the viewing habits of one all-American dog. Discussion question 2 at the end of the chapter asks you to consider your own television viewing habits and identify some potential strengths and weaknesses inherent in the Nielsen Index.

When mechanical means are impractical, the researcher must rely on personal observations. Suppose that a college is faced with the problem of providing adequate parking space for its students and faculty. If the college wishes to measure only the number of cars using its parking area, it can install a mechanical device to record the number of cars entering the lot. But, if the college is considering a program to assign preferential parking spots to students and faculty members who form car pools, it may wish to measure the number of people *in* each car that enters the lot. Direct personal observation is the most practical way to obtain such data.

Obtaining primary data by asking questions

Survey data are obtained by asking people questions in either personal or telephone interviews or in questionnaires. The most common form of self-administered questionnaire is the direct-mail survey, although other types of surveys are widely used (for example, in-store surveys, in which consumers are given a form and asked to complete and return it at their convenience). Business firms, colleges, and government agencies use surveys extensively to collect information. Answer the questions that appeared in one survey by a state legislator (shown in Figure 6-8), and see if you encounter any problems using this method of data collection.

Survey methods of data collection have two major advantages over observational methods: surveys provide greater flexibility, and they allow the actual participants to tell what they have done and why, thus avoiding the costly and time-consuming procedure of making direct observations. Personal and telephone interviews allow a great deal of flexibility in that the interviewer can pursue topics in greater depth whenever an unusual response is obtained.

Survey methods also have limitations, however. If questions are confusing, trivial, too personal, or highly controversial, respondents may not give useful answers; the family in a consumer survey who typically consumes four cases of beer a week may be unwilling to admit it. Care must also be taken to avoid asking *leading questions* that suggest or contain an answer in their wording. All five of the questions in Figure 6-8 are leading questions, biased by the legislator to obtain the following answers: no, yes, no, yes, yes. (Discussion question 6 at the end of the chapter asks you

6-8 How would you answer these questions from your state legislator?

Many state and federal legislators periodically use a mail questionnaire to obtain information on how their constituents feel about major issues. The following questions are taken from one state legislator's survey of the people he represented. Answer each of the questions "yes" or "no" by checking the appropriate space. What answers do you think the legislator wanted to hear to each question? To learn the answers as well as the survey problems these questions present, see the text.

Question	Yes	No
Consumer Protection:		
1. Would you favor a further infringement upon free enterprise by permitting the law to require all retail products to be priced per unit (that is, by the pound, ounce, quart, etc.) instead of by the package or as preferred by the packer?	____	____
2. Should we leave the free market system to the free enterpriser and let the best and the thriftiest come out on top, as was intended by our Constitution?	____	____
Environment:		
3. Do you think that our state should enact Gestapo-type laws that would reward citizens for spying on and reporting on other citizens for such offenses as air or water pollution?	____	____
University Autonomy:		
4. Would you agree that administrators of state-supported educational institutions should be discharged for pampering revolutionaries?	____	____
Drug Abuse:		
5. Recent research indicates marijuana may be more harmful than many medical authorities previously believed. Considering these facts, do you think the selling of marijuana should be regarded as a crime, and punishment administered accordingly?	____	____

to rephrase each of these questions to avoid this problem.) To insure that meaningful answers are obtained, survey questions must be developed and interpreted carefully.

Experimental data are frequently used when business problems require particularly careful analysis. In experimental studies, two essentially similar groups are identified and each group is exposed to a somewhat different business situation. Observational or survey methods are then used to collect the data, but the groups are still carefully separated. Fisher-Price Toys, the nation's largest toy maker for children under six, uses experimental situations to test their ideas for new toys. One control group of children is allowed to play in a nursery with a number of toys including the old design of the toy to be studied, and the number of minutes of playtime with the old toy is measured. An experimental group of children is placed in a similar environment in which the new toy design has been substituted for the old one, and the same measurement of playtime with the new toy is made. Fisher-Price then produces whichever design generates the most involvement in the children, as measured by minutes of playtime.

An overriding advantage of such experiments is that they enable the business firm to evaluate products on the basis of actual consumer use. The children, in Fisher-Price's nursery schools, for example, have found handles that are too small and cranks that don't work; moreover, they have demonstrated that dolls should be made to be sat on as well as loved. Identifying these problems has resulted in genuine product improvements in Fisher-Price toys.

Step 4 in DECIDE: Identify the Best Alternative

Choice Selection: Organizing the Information for Interpretation

Business analysts and educators who have examined the decision-making process have developed what we will call the *choice-selection method* to organize data pertinent to problems and to assist in identifying the best alternative — that is, the solution.

The choice-selection method: a framework for relating alternatives and uncertainties

Choice selection provides a framework that relates the alternatives available to decision makers to the uncertainties they face. This framework, often called the *payoff table,* is structured so that the alternatives are listed in rows and the uncertainties appear as column heads. The principal uncertainties over which the decision maker lacks control, enumerated in step 2 of DECIDE (Figure 6-2), are designated as *outcome states*. The number of alternatives and outcome states varies with the problem.

Relating alternatives to outcome states, the decision maker assesses the consequences for each box in the payoff table. Each box is the result of

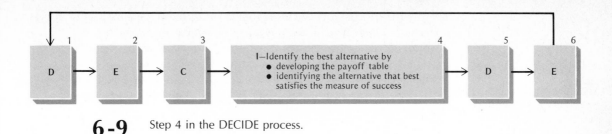

6-9 Step 4 in the DECIDE process.

The problem determines the number of alternatives and outcome states

the interaction of one alternative and one outcome state. Using the payoff table, the decision maker identifies the alternative that best satisfies the measure of success (Figure 6-9) developed in step 1 of DECIDE.

Applying the Choice-Selection Method

Two examples will explain the choice-selection method. The first pertains to a personal problem; the second to a business problem.

✔ **A personal decision: the dog-bite problem.** As we noted earlier, dollars often serve as a common denominator to measure both the benefits and the costs of alternatives in business problems, although many factors cannot be measured in terms of dollars. In personal problems, it is extremely difficult to measure such intangible factors as joy or sorrow, anxiety or relief, and especially life or death. But even here, the choice-selection method provides a framework for study.

Using the choice-selection method to study the dog-bite problem

Referring again to our earlier dog-bite problem as an example, there are two principal alternatives available: to get or not to get rabies shots. For simplicity, we will label these two alternatives A_1 and A_2 respectively in the payoff table in Figure 6-10. The outcome states (uncertainties) are very straightforward: either the dog is rabid or the dog is not rabid. Again,

6-10 Payoff table for the dog-bite problem.

	Outcome state	
Alternative	O : Dog is rabid	O_2: Dog is not rabid
A_1: Get rabies shots.	Many painful shots; ① live.	Many painful shots; ② live.
A_2: Do not get rabies shots.	Much worry; much ③ pain; possible death.	Much worry; live. ④

to simply the discussion, we will label these two outcome states O_1 and O_2 respectively. Each box in the payoff table is also numbered.

Now, look at the outcome of selecting alternative A_1, getting the rabies shots, in Figure 6-10. For outcome states O_1 and O_2, a rabid dog or a nonrabid dog, the consequences are the same. In both box 1 and box 2, you take the series of painful shots and live, never knowing whether the dog is rabid or not.

Selecting alternative A_2, refusing to get the rabies shots, produces a completely different situation. Box 3 shows the combined results of choosing alternative A_2, no shots, and encountering outcome state O_1, a rabid dog. Here you spend a great deal of time worrying over the possibility of getting rabies, ultimately contract rabies, experience a great deal of pain, and face the possibility of death. (In 1971, seven-year-old Matthew Winkler of Lima, Ohio, made medical history by being the first person on record who contracted rabies and lived without treatment. Suppose you are bitten by a rabid dog, are an optimist, and do not weigh the possibility of death very heavily. Then you may elect not to have the rabies shots, yet contract rabies, and be the second person in medical history to live. Good judgment, however, would dictate that you leave the honor of being number two to someone else.)

On skipping
rabies shots:
let someone else
be number two!

Finally, box 4 shows the consequence of alternative A_2 and outcome state O_2. Here, you elect not to get the rabies shots, and fortunately the dog is not rabid. You spend a great deal of time worrying but you live to tell about it.

Note that organizing the alternatives and outcome states in a payoff table like the one in Figure 6-10 provides you—the decision maker—with a concise summary of the problem. It enables you to understand the principal implications of each alternative when it is combined with each possible outcome state.

Hopefully, none of us will ever be faced with the dog-bite problem, but this example does show that the DECIDE process can be used in solving personal problems—particularly when the consequences in the payoff table are words and not numbers. In business situations, there is a greater effort to *quantify* results—to assign dollar or other numerical values to the benefits and to the costs reflected in the payoff table. In addition, business analysts are often asked to assess the likelihood of each outcome state that might occur in the future. In the business example that follows, we will extend the choice-selection method to include (1) numbers rather than words in the payoff table, and (2) the likelihood that a particular outcome state will occur.

When the
payoff table
contains words,
not numbers

✔ **A business decision: the soft-drink problem.** Suppose that a man owns a truck from which he sells soft drinks and sandwiches. One of his major business locations is the local manufacturing plant, where he sells to workers during their regular coffee and lunch breaks. After subtracting all

6-11   Payoff table for the soft-drink problem.

Alternative	Outcome state	
	O_1: Sunny weather (probability = 0.80)	O_2: Rainy weather (probability = 0.20)
A_1: Stay in city.	$40 ①	$30 ②
A_2: Go to beach.	$80 ③	$10 ④

Using the
choice-selection method
to sell soft drinks

costs, the vendor normally makes a profit of $40 on a sunny day. When the weather is rainy and many of the workers remain inside, business is poor and he makes only a $30 profit. These values appear in the top row of the payoff table in Figure 6-11.

Another prime place for the vendors is the public beach about 50 miles away. Even after subtracting the costs of traveling to the beach, the vendor makes a profit of $80 on a nice day; but on a rainy day, he makes only a $10 profit. These values appear in the bottom row of the payoff table in Figure 6-11.

Stated simply, the problem becomes one of deciding whether to stay in the city or to drive to the beach—a decision that hinges on the kind of weather the vendor expects to encounter. Since his sandwiches must be prepared the night before, the vendor's decision to stay or to go must be made in advance on the basis of the local weather prediction. Assume that a 20 percent chance of rain (or an 80 percent chance of sunny weather) is predicted for the following day. These probabilities of rainy and sunny weather appear in parentheses in the column headings in Figure 6-11.

As a measure of success, the vendor may calculate the *expected values* of going to the beach and of staying in the city. The expected value is obtained by multiplying the box value for each consequence of an alternative by its probability of occurrence and then totaling all of the consequences for each given alternative. Thus, the expected value of an alternative is the value obtained if the decision maker selects the same alternative many times under the same conditions. The expected values for the two alternatives in the payoff table in Figure 6-11 are:

Expected value of staying in the city consistently (probability that the weather will be nice multiplied by the profit anticipated from selling at the plant if the weather is nice *plus* the probability that it will rain *multiplied* by the profit made at the plant in rainy weather):

(0.8)($40) + (0.2)($30) = $32 + $6 = $38 average per daily trip

Expected value of going to the beach consistently:

(0.8)($80) + (0.2)($10) = $64 + $2 = $66 average per daily trip

Expected value:
finding the best choice
in the long run,
when the payoff table
contains numbers

Therefore, if the vendor decides to go to the beach each time there is a 20 percent chance of rain, he will average $66 in daily profits in the long run. If, under the same conditions, the vendor decides to stay in town, his profits will average only $38. But he will make only $10 at the beach on those few days when, given a 20-percent chance of rain, it actually rains. Although the choice-selection method will not yield the most profitable answer for each day, it will help the vendor raise overall profits. Question 2 in "Short Cases and Problems" at the end of this chapter asks you to re-evaluate the vendor's decision when the chances of rain are greater or less than 20 percent.

Usefulness of the Choice-Selection Method

Choice selection, which has become popular only in the last decade, is one of the most powerful analytical techniques currently available. Because of its flexibility, this technique can be applied to many types of problems: personal or business, simple or complex, qualitative or quantitative.

Step 5 in DECIDE: Develop and Implement a Detailed Plan to Put the Chosen Alternative into Effect

Developing and implementing a detailed plan

During his first few months in office, President Eisenhower was often astounded that he could agonize for hours over a problem and reach a decision, only to find that nothing ever happened. The decision was not implemented because no one was really sure whose job it was to follow through. Experienced business managers consider the failure to take the necessary steps to put a decision into effect one of the most important barriers to problem solving. This breakdown in step 5 of DECIDE is reflected in the weekend post-mortem analyses of football coaches and players: "Our game plan was fine; we just didn't execute it." Thus, step 5 in DECIDE involves developing a plan to put the chosen alternative—the solution—into action and then following this plan through to its completion.

In personal decisions, step 5 of DECIDE (Figure 6-12) presents few problems because the same person defines the problem, enumerates the alternatives and uncertainties, collects the pertinent information, and identifies and implements the best alternative. In the dog-bite problem, for example, you are the decider, the approver, and the implementer. However, important business decisions may involve a large number of people. In a complex business situation, an assistant may follow the DECIDE process from step 1 through step 4, a manager may make the actual decision, and a third person may be authorized to implement the decision.

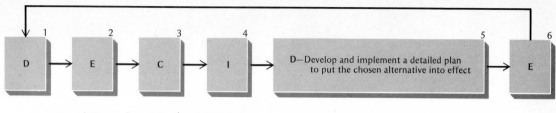

6-12   Step 5 in the DECIDE process.

In Chapter 4, we learned that effective planning is a key element in management. But the effective planner must recognize that events change and that when they do, it may be necessary to revise the initial plan. Flexibility is as essential in a business situation as it is on the football field.

Step 6 in DECIDE: Evaluate the Decision and the Decision Process

The final step in DECIDE is an evaluation of both the decision and the entire decision process. Figure 6-13 shows step 6 feeding back into step 1—a reminder that the decision maker should continually apply lessons learned in making past decisions to future decisions.

With respect to the decision itself, two questions should be raised once a decision has been implemented:

Evaluating the decision itself . . .

1. Based on the information available at the time the decision was made, was the decision correct?
2. Are conditions the same now as they were when the decision was made?

If the answer to either question is "no," the decision should be reviewed

6-13   Step 6 in the DECIDE process.

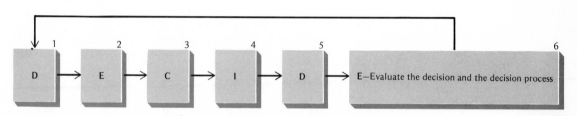

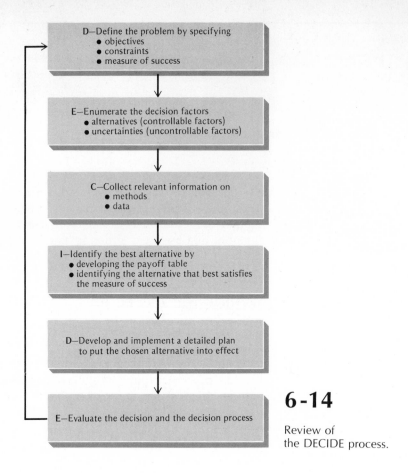

6-14

Review of
the DECIDE process.

and possibly revised, provided this is not too costly or inconvenient. In some cases, of course, implementation of a preferred alternative is irreversible, and any extended review or revision of the decision is impossible. The dog-bite problem is a case in point: once you have the painful series of rabies shots, if the dog is captured and is not rabid, your decision to have the shots cannot be altered. The wise decision maker, then, is especially careful in situations where a decision is irreversible once it is implemented.

Even more important in the long run is reviewing the decision process to see how it can be improved in the future. Such a review raises the following questions about the use of the DECIDE process:

1. Was the problem really defined adequately in terms of objectives, constraints, and measures of success?

2. Were pertinent alternatives and uncertainties identified?
3. Was relevant information obtained? Was enough time spent defining the problem and collecting the information?
4. Was the available information analyzed and interpreted logically?
5. Was the preferred alternative—the solution—implemented properly?

Honest answers to these questions will improve the chances of making effective decisions in similar situations in the future.

KEY POINTS TO REMEMBER

1. Decision making is the process of seeking to achieve some objective by consciously choosing a course of action from available alternatives.
2. A systematic method often helps an individual to make effective decisions, both in personal and in business situations. The DECIDE process described in this chapter is such a method. The six steps in the DECIDE process are summarized in Figure 6-14.
3. By attempting to solve some riddles and puzzles, we can gain insights into some of our own barriers to problem solving.
4. Information that is of value in solving a business problem falls into two categories: methods (approaches used to analyze the problem) and data (facts and figures pertinent to the problem). Numerous sources and kinds of methods and data are used in making business decisions.

QUESTIONS FOR DISCUSSION

1. The two brainteasers provided below will illustrate some of the barriers to problem solving. After you have solved each puzzle or your instructor has given you the answer, try (1) to remember the alternatives you considered in seeking an answer; (2) to identify where you ran into problems; and (3) to discover lessons you can apply to future problem-solving or decision-making situations.
   (a) Thomas A. Edison was approached by a young scientist with a perplexing problem: for several days, he had been trying to develop a mathematical equation to determine the volume of air inside an incandescent light bulb so that he would know how much air to pump out of it to form an adequate vacuum. Edison looked at the young man in shocked disbelief. In 30 seconds, Edison had an answer. How did he solve the problem?
   (b) What is the next number in the following sequence: 8, 5, 4, 9, 1, 7, 6? (*Hint:* Sometimes numbers can be viewed in nonmathematical terms.)

2. Based on your own television-viewing habits, what strengths and weaknesses do you see in estimating American television audiences by using the Nielsen audimeter to collect observational data?

3. Assume that you own a clothing store and are searching for ways to improve your store's operations. How could you use (a) observation methods and (b) survey methods to help you?

4. Step 2 of DECIDE may involve an individual search for alternative solutions. For example, Ephrem Gelfman invented a bottle cutter after seeing glasses being made from wine bottles in Santa Fe, New Mexico. To promote the sale of his invention, Gelfman identified many ways to cut and reassemble glass bottles. Think about the glass bottles you might find in a supermarket. What useful glass objects could you construct from them. (*Hint:* Start with soft-drink bottles.)

5. Step 2 of DECIDE may also involve several people searching together for alternative solutions.
   (a) As a class, brainstorm the following problem without evaluating suggested alternatives: In what ways could student registration and record keeping be simplified at your college without increasing costs?
   (b) What advantages and disadvantages do you see in collecting data by (1) direct-mail survey; (2) telephone survey; and (3) personal interviews to solve the problem you brainstormed in (a)?

6. Restate the questions in Figures 6-8 (page 157) so that they are no longer leading questions.

7. What do you consider the strengths and the limitations of the choice-selection method discussed in step 4 of DECIDE?

SHORT CASES AND PROBLEMS

1. Step 3 in DECIDE often involves the use of a measure of central value to condense or to summarize a large group of numbers into a single meaningful figure. Assume that a restaurant owner is trying to determine how many pounds of hamburger to order for the months of July, August, and September—a period of 13 weeks. Her records show that in the same period a year ago she used the following pounds of hamburger per week:

July	August	September
100	90	100
90	100	110
120	100	80
110	80	100
90		

The restaurant owner receives hamburger from her supplier once a week. Her business is about as good this year as it was last year.
   (a) Calculate the mean, median, and mode for hamburger usage last summer.
   (b) What problems may the owner encounter if she orders the mean usage from last summer each week during the coming three months?

(c) What problems may arise if she orders 120 pounds (the highest weekly usage rate during the same period last year) each week during the coming three months?

2. The choice-selection method may require an assessment of the probabilities of occurrence of various outcome states. As these probabilities change, the resultant changes in the expected values of alternatives may force the decision maker to select a different alternative.

(a) Referring to the payoff table for the soft-drink problem (Figure 6-11), determine which alternative (staying in the city or going to the beach) the vendor should select for each of the following probabilities of rainy weather: 10 percent; 30 percent; 50 percent; 70 percent; 90 percent.

(b) Do you see any pattern reflected in the answers you gave in part (a)?

3. Data collection is an important part of step 3 of the DECIDE process. As we noted in Chapter 6, primary data can often be obtained by conducting a simple experiment. Suppose that an appliance store owner has experienced problems in delivering major appliances (such as refrigerators, washers, and dryers) to customers. When a customer buys an appliance on a given day, the store agrees to deliver it from the warehouse within a week — on a day the customer selects. Frequently, the truck driver finds no one at home on the day of delivery, necessitating one or more costly return trips. The owner feels the problem can be alleviated if a reminder telephone call is made to the customer the day before the agreed-on delivery date and would like to conduct a simple experiment to determine if this step would reduce the number of return trips. How should the owner design and run this experiment?

CAREERS IN STATISTICAL ANALYSIS

Statistics clerks compile the numerical reports on which management decisions are based. Statistical tasks include recording transactions, as well as compiling, coding, and tabulating data, and work scheduling. Jobs exist within each statistical category: for example, **actuary clerks** tabulate numerical data for insurance purposes, and **demurrage clerks** are employed by railroads to tabulate data for transportation purposes. Most of the nation's 300,000 statistics clerks are high-school graduates and many also have college or vocational training in business arithmetic and bookkeeping. On-the-job training in the use of calculators and tabulating machines is provided. Clerks are generally promoted to their jobs and, with experience, may advance to the ranks of statistician or supervisor. Yearly salaries average $7500. Since many statistical duties cannot be computerized, employment opportunities are expected to continue to expand moderately. (*Additional information:* State Supervisor of Office Occupations Education; State Department of Education; your state capital.)

Statisticians collect, analyze, and interpret numerical data. This task requires expertise in statistical techniques as well as a knowledge of the subject matter under investigation. Thus, **market-research statisticians** have educational backgrounds in calculus and probability as well as in economics and business administration. A bachelor's degree either in statistics or in a functional area of business with a minor in statistics is the minimum requirement for a job in private industry. Advancement to upper-level management positions is possible. Annual income for beginning statisticians is about $10,000. Employment opportunities are expected to expand moderately, especially in the areas of market research and product quality control. (*Additional information:* American Statistical Association; 806 15th Street, N.W.; Washington, D.C. 20005.)

CAREERS IN MATHEMATICAL ANALYSIS

Applied mathematicians provide solutions for practical problems. An applied mathematician might perform such business functions as assessing the risk of an investment or developing quality-control tests for a manufacturing process. Communication skills are mandatory, since many of the people with whom mathematicians work have little knowledge of the technical aspects of the mathematical tools of probability, calculus, or computer programming. The minimal business career requirement is a bachelor's degree either in mathematics or in business administration with a minor in mathematics; advanced research positions require graduate degrees. Yearly earnings range from $10,000 to $30,000. Job competition will be keen because of the surplus of college graduates in mathematics. Opportunities will be more favorable, however, for holders of advanced degrees who are competent in research and development activities. (*Additional information:* Mathematical Association of America; 1225 Connecticut Avenue, N.W.; Washington, D.C. 20036.)

CAREERS IN INFORMATION COLLECTION AND LIBRARY SCIENCE

Medical-record administrators are employed by health-care facilities to organize and to maintain files on patients and the hospital treatments they receive. These files are used by hospital administrators and their staffs to prepare reports for a variety of purposes: research, treatment evaluation, insurance claims, and statistical reports required by government health agencies. Qualified applicants have a bachelor's degree in medical-record administration, with a solid background in medical science and terminology, health law, and statistics. Experienced medical-record administrators may advance to higher-level, hospital-management positions. Yearly income is about $12,000. Employment opportunities are expected to increase rapidly given the growing number of health-care facilities and health-insurance programs. (*Additional information:* The American Medical Record Association, Suite 1850; John Hancock Center; 875 North Michigan Avenue; Chicago, Illinois 60611.)

Although an assortment of library occupations exist, private industry provides three primary career alternatives: *special librarian, information-science specialist,* and *library technical assistant.* **Special librarians** are often employed by advertising agencies and research laboratories to accumulate and to arrange an organization's information resources. Special librarians also find information or compile bibliographies upon request. **Information-science specialists** perform many of the same functions as special librarians and an additional number of more responsible jobs, including summarizing technical data, preparing computer-programming techniques, and improving microfilm technology. **Library technical assistants** are instructed by professional librarians in functional matters such as operating data-processing and audio-visual equipment and purchasing and cataloging new books. Special librarians and information-science specialists generally have master's degrees in library science; doctoral degrees in library science provide a competitive advantage and facilitate promotion to administrative positions. Library technical assistants are either high-school graduates who have acquired necessary on-the-job training or community-college graduates who have Associate of Arts degrees in library technology. Yearly income varies: professional librarians average $14,000 annually; library technical assistants, about $8000. A growing need for the efficient storing, retrieving, and analyzing of technological information should create a moderately expanding job market for librarians and library assistants. (*Additional information:* American Library Association; 50 East Huron Street; Chicago, Illinois 60611; and Council of Library Technical Assistants; 6800 South Wentworth Avenue; Chicago, Illinois 60621.)

A CRITICAL BUSINESS DECISION

—made by Herbert and Belva Gibson

THE SITUATION It is 1970. The Gibson Products Company has just achieved the distinction of becoming the nation's seventh-largest nonfood retailer and its second-largest discounter (trailing only S.S. Kresge's K marts). The company's headquarters is in Seagoville, Texas, 20 miles south of Dallas; its chain of 583 discount stores boasts annual sales of $1.6 billion. The Gibson family owns 53 of these stores; the rest are franchises.

The fortunes of Gibson Products Company are directed by Herbert R. Gibson, Sr., chairman and chief executive officer, and his wife Belva Gibson, secretary-treasurer. In an interview with *Business Week*, Herbert Gibson describes how he got his start in business: "When I was 11 years old, back in Carroll County [Arkansas], my father gave me some hogs and cattle and told me, 'I want to learn you to make your own living.' " A year later, a man offered young Herbert $100 for a mule that he had bought for $60. "If he had offered me $70, I would have sold it to him," Gibson explains. "But when he offered me $100, I said 'Mister, what do you wanta do? Steal my mule?' " The man paid Gibson $125 for the mule.

Herb Gibson later embarked on a wholesale business in Little Rock, but lost 85 percent of his investment when the banks closed during the depression. Herb and Belva Gibson left for northern Arkansas, where they didn't have to rely on banks. By 1958, the Gibsons owned a chain of 34 wholesale houses in ten states. Then, as they saw more and more retailers buying directly from manufacturers, the Gibsons concluded that if they didn't change they'd go broke. So they began to convert their wholesale houses into discount stores.

THE DECISION From the outset, the Gibsons gained a reputation for selling directly from the carton. "The reason," they explain, "was that all we could do was open a carton before the customers were grabbing. We never had a chance to display anything." The Gibson stores have not changed since 1958. According to *Business Week*, they "still look like Army surplus stores and thrive on the old discount formula: stack it high and sell it low." The stores are small: more than half of them are under 28,000 square feet in floor space. Herb Gibson explains the success of the Gibson stores simply: "We sell quality merchandise without frills. If I could find a better way, I'd do it."

However, the Gibsons are aware of the change in discount strategy during the 1960s. Most major discount chains have increased their store sizes to 100,000 square feet or more and have changed their appearances to resemble conventional department stores.

Herbert and Belva Gibson face an important decision: Should they enlarge and upgrade the appearance of their stores to make them look more like department stores?

QUESTIONS

1. If you were the Gibsons, what kind of information would you consider in making this decision?
2. How would you go about collecting this information?

PART THREE

MARKETING AND PRODUCTION

People, business firms, and government agencies buy and use an almost infinite variety of products. Part Three of this book covers marketing and production—the two business functions most closely involved in supplying these products to the individuals and organizations that need them. Marketing entails two key steps: (1) identifying potential customers—what we call the "target market," and (2) finding ways to reach these customers using the four element in the marketing mix. Chapter 8 discusses the place element (whole-sale and retail firms used in marketing a product) and the price element. The tions through which the product will reach customers; the price charged for the product; and the promotion to inform potential customers about the product. Chapter 7 first describes American consumers and then examines the product element in the marketing mix. Chapter 8 discusses the place element (whole-sale and retail firms used in marketing a product) and the price element. The two major components of the promotional element—advertising and personal selling—are covered in Chapter 9. Both marketing and production personnel share the responsibility for creating new-product ideas. But production, which is examined in Chapter 10, must convert these ideas into designs that can be fabricated. Thus, in addition to product development, Chapter 10 discusses the other production activities of purchasing, manufacturing, and transportation.

If a man . . . make a better mousetrap, . . . the world will beat a path to his door.

Ralph Waldo Emerson

CHAPTER 7

MARKETING: CONSUMERS AND THE PRODUCT ELEMENT

D ick Woolworth, president of the Woodstream Corporation of Lititz, Pennsylvania, took Emerson's adage to heart. In the 1960s, Woodstream literally built a technically "better" moustrap—a plastic device that sold for a quarter, was easy to set, and caught mice with awesome efficiency. Woolworth distributed samples of the mousetrap to hardware stores across the United States and waited for the deluge of new orders. But new orders did not pour in; the sample traps remained on the shelves of all those hardware stores. Dick Woolworth felt that Woodstream had manufactured the ideal mousetrap. But the following essential marketing considerations may have been overlooked in the process:

The consumer decides what a "better" mousetrap is

1. Is the "better product" not only "better" to the manufacturer but also "better" to the consumers who purchase and use it?
2. Is the product adequately distributed so that it reaches all potential customers?
3. Is the price of the product low enough that potential buyers will receive a good value for their money and high enough that the producer will make a profit?
4. Is the word-of-mouth advertising implied in Emerson's adage adequate to inform potential buyers about the product? Or should the manufacturer inform potential customers through advertising and employ a sales force to sell the product?

The company had researched the sleeping, crawling, and eating habits of mice (Woolworth recommends peanut butter for bait), but not the preferences of the large percentage of homemakers who would use the mousetrap. And, the 25-cent price was high compared with the competing price of 15 cents for two wooden traps. A business expert summarized Dick Woolworth's marketing dilemma, noting that the people "who usually had to contend with the dead mouse, thought nothing of throwing away the old wooden snaptrap, mouse and all. But the new 25-cent trap was a different story—they didn't care for extracting the dead mouse and cleaning the trap." Fortunately, this story has a happy ending: Woolworth went back to making the standard wooden trap, and Woodstream is a prospering business again.

Homemakers prefer disposable mousetraps

The marketing considerations that Dick Woolworth overlooked illustrate the four areas in which marketing makes a potential contribution to business success. In Chapters 7, 8, and 9, we will discuss the nature of marketing, some important characteristics of American consumers, and the four elements in the marketing mix—marketing factors that business can control.

Why a Special Interest in Marketing?

In an American business firm, no one functional area—marketing, accounting, finance, or production—is necessarily more important than another. All areas must work together to assure a firm's success. Yet, marketing is one area of business that holds a special interest for many people, perhaps because of the following factors:

1. *Public exposure to marketing actions.* For example, consumers quickly become aware of most of the price changes on the items they purchase.
2. *The importance of marketing activities to consumers and employees.* Marketing experts estimate that half of every dollar spent by consumers is used to meet business marketing expenses. The marketing industry is also an important employer: today, more than 15 million Americans hold retailing and wholesaling jobs, and millions more are engaged in marketing activities in the manufacturing and service industries.

Reasons for public interest in marketing

3. *The belief held by many consumers that they are marketing experts.* As consumers, most of us are more familiar with the marketing activities of American business than we are with the production, accounting, or financial efforts. For example, homemakers spend thousands of hours becoming marketing experts—one reason that their opinions are often sought by product analysts.
4. *The controversy surrounding misleading or deceptive marketing practices.* As we saw in Chapter 3, the consumer movement gained its momentum from poor business practices, many of which involve marketing deficiencies. Studying the marketing function can help us to assess the underlying reasons for deficiencies and possibly to suggest effective remedies.

What Is Marketing?

Marketing involves that broad area of business activity that directs the flow of goods and services from producer to customer in order to satisfy customers and to achieve company objectives. Two parts of the marketing function deserve special attention: (1) the development of the marketing concept, and (2) the steps required in a successful marketing program.

The meaning of marketing

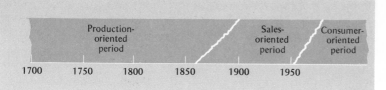

		Production- oriented period		Sales- oriented period	Consumer- oriented period
1700	1750	1800	1850	1900	1950

7-1

Three different buyer orientations in American business history.

The Development of the Marketing Concept

American business history: from production . . .

Compared with the America we know today, the United States in its early years was a land of scarcity. Then, emphasis was placed on the production of goods, since the market demand was great enough to absorb all of the items produced. This era can be termed the *production-oriented period* in American business history—a time when goods were so scarce that consumers accepted whatever was available (Figure 7-1).

WHY DO NEW PRODUCTS FAIL?

Products like Dick Woolworth's plastic mousetrap have a lot of company every year in the American marketplace. Thousands of products fail, costing American businesses billions of dollars annually. Product analysts have discovered three important reasons for such failures:

1. The product is not directed to a large enough market.
2. The difference between the new product and the competing products already being marketed is insignificant in the eyes of the consumer.
3. The quality of the product is not high enough (or is not as good as its advertisement implies).

Evaluate each of the following products against these three criteria:

Revlon's Super-Natural Hair Spray.
Pillsbury's Gorilla Milk (an instant breakfast; package shown at right).
Menley and James' Duractin (a sustained-release analgesic that relieves pain for eight hours).
General Foods' Post Cereals with Freeze-Dried Fruit.
Del Monte's Barbecue Ketchup (a catsup with finely chopped onions).

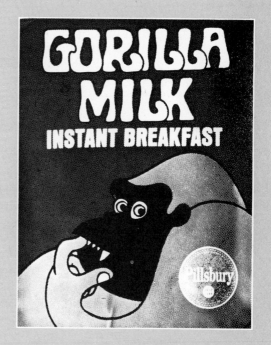

For the answers to what happened to each of these new products, see page 177.

As America's productive capacity increased, many firms assumed much more active roles in convincing consumers to purchase the vast number of new products on the market. At this point, America entered its *sales-oriented period.* In its ascendancy, some American businesses became known for their *caveat emptor* attitude toward marketing. For example, when asked if the public might not be hurt by one of his nineteenth-century stock manipulations, business tycoon William H. Vanderbilt reportedly replied: "The public be damned!" This tough, sales-oriented approach often produced goods that reflected the manufacturing and selling talents of the company—and not the needs of the consumer. Surpluses developed, and to counter them, marketers adopted the hard-sell approach, with techniques ranging from high-pressure personal selling to the allegedly subtle psychological manipulation of consumers—what Vance Packard has called the "hidden persuaders."

. . . to sales . . .

In the past decade, many firms have focused on the *marketing concept,* which stresses shaping products to meet consumer needs rather than molding consumer needs to fit the available products. This concept has played an important part in the emergence of the *consumer-oriented period* in American business, with its many tests and new product surveys designed to discover what consumers really want. Critics argue, sometimes justly, that business all too often depends on the consumer-oriented approach and the marketing concept to disguise sales-oriented, hard-sell tactics. Whether or not this is true is a matter of current controversy. Whatever the case, today's public is far better educated. As we noted in Chapter 3, it is probably fair to say that business in the 1970s, in its own enlightened self-interest, will display a higher degree of responsiveness to consumers than ever before.

. . . to consumer orientation

The Steps in a Successful Marketing Program

Two steps are essential to a successful marketing program: (1) identifying the *target market,* the specific groups of customers to whom the company wishes to appeal with its products or services, and (2) selecting the appropriate blend of marketing activities, the kind and amount of activities necessary to reach the target market.

Two steps are essential to a marketing program

✔ **Market-product grids: a way to identify the target market.** Suppose that a businesswoman living in a large metropolitan area observes the need for a fast-food restaurant near the local college campus. The restaurant would provide both booth and takeout service. The businesswoman's first task is to identify the *target market*—the specific customers to whom she wishes to appeal. This poses several questions:

1. Who would patronize the restaurant? Just college students? What about the dormitory residents who have meal contracts? What

WHY NEW PRODUCTS FAIL

All five of the new products listed on page 175 failed, mainly for one of the three reasons cited there:

Revlon's Super-Natural Hair Spray: Revlon lost millions of dollars on this product in the early 1960s because customers were confused by the meaning of "Super-Natural". To them, "Super" implied more holding power and "Natural" suggested less holding power. Confusion about what they thought they should expect from the product naturally produced consumer dissatisfaction with product quality.

Pillsbury's Gorilla Milk: The target market was high-school and college consumers—students who notoriously skip regular breakfasts. But Carnation was already marketing its Instant Breakfast, and buyers didn't feel that Pillsbury's new product was significantly better. Also customers in the target market considered the name "Gorilla Milk" to be too childish. The product failed in the test market.

Menley and James' Duractin: Here, the target market was simply insubstantial. The consumers' first concern was immediate pain relief. The long-term relief promised by the product was of secondary concern to the sufferer. This cost the firm several million dollars.

General Foods' Post Cereals with Freeze-Dried Fruit: A substantial number of consumers eat dry breakfast cereal with fruit on top (the target market). Here, the problem was poor product quality: by the time the fruit reconstituted, the cereal was soggy. The soggy cereal cost General Foods about $5 million.

Del Monte's Barbecue Ketchup: Here, again, the target market was not large enough. The product's point of difference actually worked against sales in an important target segment: the primary users of catsup are children, and most children dislike onions. The product failed in the test market, but variations of it are now reentering the market.

Identifying the target market for a prospective restaurant

about students who commute? Would noncollege residents in the area be likely to eat there?

2. Would most people be inclined to eat breakfast, lunch, or dinner at the restaurant? Should between-meal snacks be served? What about late-evening meals after school events or study dates?

3. Is there any relationship between the types or groups of people likely to eat at the restaurant and the meals these people would prefer?

The businesswoman's problem is to find a framework in which to organize the answers to these questions.

Such a framework is the *market-product grid,* a checkerboard used to study a market by relating the characteristics of potential consumers to the products they want. Each rectangle of the checkerboard relates a portion of the larger market—a group of potential consumers with similar characteristics—to the products wanted by that group of potential customers. The market-product grid in Figure 7-2 relates the potential customers for the proposed fast-food restaurant. Note that the grid emphasizes two important market dimensions: the type of meal which would be served and the group of people who would be patrons.

The × in each rectangle in the market-product grid represents a potential market for a particular meal and group of people. For example,

Market characteristics	Product characteristics				
	Breakfast	Lunch	Between-meal snacks	Dinner	Late-evening meals
College students: residents in contract dorms			X		X
College students: apartment residents	X	X	X	X	X
College students: commuters		X	X		
College faculty and clerical staff		X			
Noncollege area residents				X	X
Noncollege area workers		X			

7-2 Market-product grid of potential customers for a restaurant adjacent to a college campus.

× marks the potential customers on a market-product grid

dormitory students who hold meal contracts with the college would probably patronize the restaurant only for late-evening meals and between-meal snacks; commuting students would only eat lunch and between-meal snacks there. The size of the × is a crude measure of the dollar volume of each potential market. Similar relationships may be developed for the other customer groups shown in Figure 7-2.

Once the businesswomen has selected one or more groups of potential customers from the market-product grid, the selected customer groups collectively become the target market. In determining which groups are to be included in the target market, the businesswoman is interested in both the number of customers in each group and their potential spending power.

As valuable an aid as the grid is in identifying the target market, the market-product grid is still a simplification. It provides a framework for structuring the identity of the target market, but it must be supplemented with more detailed information before meaningful conclusions can be reached. It is important to emphasize that the market-product grid can also identify customer groups that a business may not want to attract. For example, the owner may conclude that her restaurant should have a college decor, which would appeal to students but perhaps would not appeal to noncollege residents, rather than a neutral decor which would not appeal to college or to noncollege customers. Or she may conclude that the breakfast market is negligible and may decide not to open the restaurant until 11 A.M.

✔ **Stressing the right elements in the marketing mix.** Having identified the target market, possibly with the aid of a market-product grid, the firm must then develop a strategy to reach that market effectively. As we noted in Chapter 6, it is important in systematic decision making to distinguish the controllable factors from the uncontrollable factors. Some important uncontrollable factors a firm must contend with include (1) the firm's objectives and available resources; (2) actions of competitors; and (3) environmental conditions such as energy shortages, inflation, and legal restrictions.

Marketing-department actions focus on the controllable elements in the marketing mix, which Professor E. Jerome McCarthy has popularized as *the four Ps:*

Product: The right product (or service) must be developed for the target market.

Place: Appropriate channels of distribution, including retailing and wholesaling institutions, must be found to insure that the product reaches the target market at the right time and in the right place.

Price: A price that gives good value to the customer and adequate revenue to the producer must be set for the product.

Promotion: Personal selling and advertising must be used both to communicate information about the product to the consumer and to facilitate sales.

These four elements are the controllable marketing factors that should be used to reach the target market. Hence, any discussion of marketing activities that direct the flow of goods and services to consumers must stress product, place, price, and promotion—the four Ps. Since all four elements are present to some degree in any marketing situation, the marketer's task is not to decide whether to use a particular element but rather is to determine the relative emphasis to place on each element in the final marketing program.

After a brief discussion of American consumers—the group that most American firms seek to reach—this chapter will focus on the first element in the marketing mix: the product sold by the firm. Two other elements—place and price—will be discussed in Chapter 8 and promotion will be examined in Chapter 9.

Who Is the American Consumer?

To be influential in the marketplace consumers must be (1) people, (2) with income, and (3) with a desire to buy. This section concentrates on the dramatic changes in population, income and consumer attitudes and values that have occurred in recent years. The consumer's impact on American business was touched on earlier in the discussion of consumerism in Chapter 3.

Consumer Population

On April 1, 1970, the U.S. Bureau of the Census counted 203,235,298 Americans living in the United States — about 24,000,000 (or 13 percent) more people than there were in 1960. This growth implies that more consumers will be buying goods and services now and that more workers will be seeking jobs in the decades to come. Let's consider the distribution of this new population among sex, age, and geographic groups and what this distribution implies for American business.

More consumers and workers

✔ **Sex distribution.** In 1970, women in the United States outnumbered men by about 5.5 million, an increase of 3 million over the margin in 1960. Striking changes in the ratio of males to females have occurred since 1900. The ratio has fallen almost continuously throughout the century — from about 105 males to every 100 females in 1900 to 95 males to every 100 females in 1970. More and more women are becoming career-oriented, necessitating a reevaluation of business opportunities available to women.

95 men for every 100 women

✔ **Age distribution.** Figure 7-3 highlights changes in the age distribution of the American population from 1960 to 1970. Three groups increased by more than 30 percent during this period: Americans over 75 increased by 2 million; those from 20 to 24 grew by 5.6 million; and those from 15 to 19 by 5.9 million. The business implications of these changes are tremendous. Most Americans who are over 75 are retired and have unique demands for special foods, housing, and health care. Americans 15 to 19 and 20 to 24, born in the decade after World War II, are both important new consumers and additional members of the labor force who need jobs.

Some age groups jumped in size . . .

Three age groups declined in total numbers from 1960 to 1970. Two of these, Americans from 30 to 34 and from 35 to 39, were the "depression babies" born in the years before World War II. Of particular interest, however, is the sharp decrease in the number of children under four years of

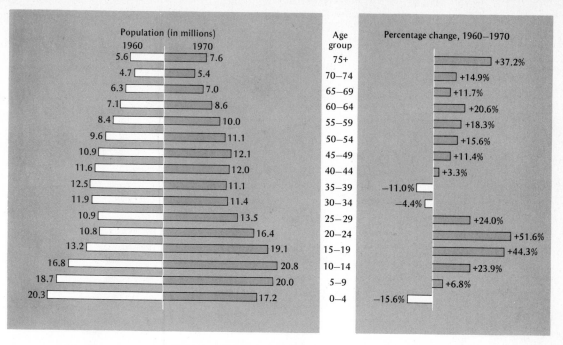

Population (in millions)		Age group	Percentage change, 1960—1970
1960	**1970**		
5.6	7.6	75+	+37.2%
4.7	5.4	70—74	+14.9%
6.3	7.0	65—69	+11.7%
7.1	8.6	60—64	+20.6%
8.4	10.0	55—59	+18.3%
9.6	11.1	50—54	+15.6%
10.9	12.1	45—49	+11.4%
11.6	12.0	40—44	+3.3%
12.5	11.1	35—39	−11.0%
11.9	11.4	30—34	−4.4%
10.9	13.5	25—29	+24.0%
10.8	16.4	20—24	+51.6%
13.2	19.1	15—19	+44.3%
16.8	20.8	10—14	+23.9%
18.7	20.0	5—9	+6.8%
20.3	17.2	0—4	−15.6%

7-3 U.S. population by age group and percentage change, 1960-1970.

Source: U.S. Bureau of the Census.

. . . and others fell

age—from 20.3 million in 1960 to 17.2 million in 1970—the largest decline in this age group since detailed statistical record keeping began in 1850. This decline has been felt not only by toy and baby-food manufacturers but also by schools. In the 1970s thousands of elementary school teachers throughout the United States are losing their jobs, and thousands of young graduates with bachelor's degrees in education cannot find teaching positions.

✔ **Geographic distribution.**   To detect important geographic population trends, business analysts often consider the populations of states in terms of (1) total size, and (2) changes over time. Figure 7-4 shows the population of each state in 1970 and the percentage change in state populations in each state from 1960 to 1970. The importance of consumer markets in California and New York is immediately apparent; in contrast, Alaska— the largest state geographically—contains a minor percentage of U.S. consumers. From 1960 to 1970, California gained about 4.2 million people and moved ahead of New York to become the nation's most populous state. Six other states recorded population increases exceeding 1 million during the decade: Florida, Texas, New York, New Jersey, Illinois, and Michigan. Growth-rate leaders were Nevada (71 percent), Florida (37 percent), and Arizona (36 percent). Three states—West Virginia, North

California, here we . . . came!

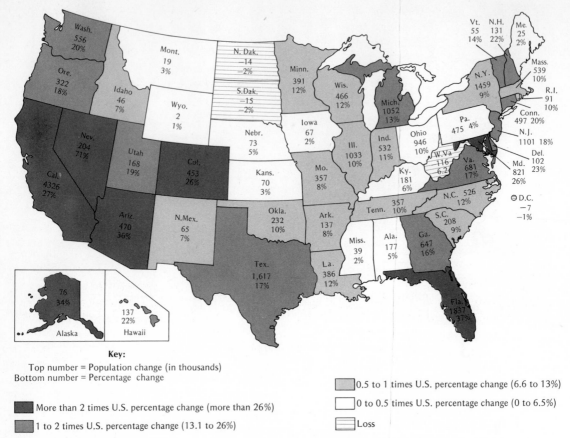

Key:

Top number = Population change (in thousands)
Bottom number = Percentage change

■ More than 2 times U.S. percentage change (more than 26%)

▨ 1 to 2 times U.S. percentage change (13.1 to 26%)

▨ 0.5 to 1 times U.S. percentage change (6.6 to 13%)

□ 0 to 0.5 times U.S. percentage change (0 to 6.5%)

▤ Loss

7-4 Changes in U.S. population by state in absolute and percentage terms, 1960-1970. The entire United States grew by 13 percent during the decade.

Source: *Statistical Abstract of the United States.*

Dakota, and South Dakota—and the District of Columbia declined in population during the decade.

Consumer Income

Two dimensions of consumer income are of special importance: the key aspects of consumer income and its distribution among Americans.

✔ **Personal, disposable, and discretionary income.** Three different aspects of consumer income merit precise definition:

Personal income: Total income from wages, salaries, business, professional, and agricultural receipts, dividends, rent, interest, and all government payments to individuals.

Disposable personal income: Amount of personal income available for personal consumption expenditures and savings. This is equal to total personal income *less* all personal tax and nontax payments to federal, state, and local governments.

Discretionary purchasing power: Amount of disposable personal income available for nonessential expenditures. This is equal to total disposable personal income *less* essential expenditures (for example, food, clothing, household utilities, local transportation) *and* fixed commitments (rent, mortgage payments, insurance, installment debt payments).

These three measures of consumer income have each grown dramatically since 1950. Of crucial importance in recent years has been the rapid increase in discretionary purchasing power, a concept developed by the researchers of the Conference Board. Discretionary purchasing power—an indication of dollars available to spend on nonessentials—is followed closely by business forecasters because it represents buying power that consumers can elect to exercise immediately or to postpone indefinitely. Since 1950, discretionary purchasing power has more than tripled and has allowed consumers "the freedom to be unstable." This has given added importance to consumer-mood surveys like those conducted by the Survey Research Center of the University of Michigan, which attempt to anticipate consumer purchasing preferences. From 1972 to 1974, failure to predict rapid changes in consumer moods caused the government to err in its domestic economic policies, producing first inflation and then recession.

Discretionary purchasing power: the freedom to be unstable

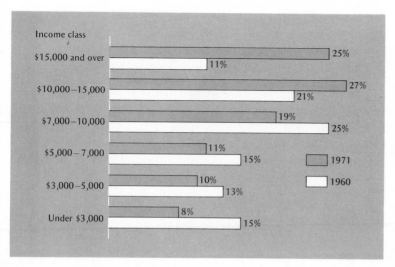

7-5

The percentage of U.S. families having annual personal incomes in six different income classes in both 1960 and 1971 (based on 1971 dollars). Note that family income distribution changed during this period: the percentage of families with annual incomes above $10,000 increased dramatically.

Source: U.S. Department of Commerce, reproduced in *A Guide to Consumer Markets: 1973-1974* (New York: The Conference Board, 1973), p. 129.

✔ **Income distribution.** Figure 7-5 shows the personal income distribution among U.S. families in both 1960 and 1971, using 1971 dollars to provide comparable data. The income distribution in this figure indicates the dramatic increase between 1960 and 1971 in the percentage of families with annual incomes above $10,000. And families with annual incomes above $15,000 jumped from 11 percent in 1960 to 25 percent in 1971. In that period, families in the $10,000-$15,000 annual income range increased from 21 percent to 27 percent. Since the percentage of U.S. families with annual incomes below $10,000 fell from 1960 to 1971, Figure 7-5 shows that the personal incomes of most American families increased during the 1960s.

Consumer Attitudes and Values

Attitudes and values are shaped by both cultural and social factors. *Cultural factors* are standards instilled in an individual by family, institutions, and society; *social factors* are norms established by an individual's current reference groups. A *reference group* consists of people who collectively influence a person's behavior because the person is or aspires to be a member of that group.

In the United States, people do their own thing to a startling degree. The result has been a growing consumer independence that permits consumers to move in opposing directions without apparent conflict. An example is the consumer's recurring complaint about "lack of time" in a period when Americans have never had so much leisure. Sales of time-saving convenience products—such as Polariod cameras, electric carving knives, and TV dinners have soared in recent years.

More leisure but less free time

An increased consumer independence has also been reflected in other changes in American attitudes and values in the 1970s:

1. *Women's movement:* The increased number of women in the labor force reflects a reevaluation of woman's role in American society. Women no longer must limit their adult roles to mother and wife.
2. *A change in moral standards:* This is reflected in the 1973 Supreme Court decision on abortion and in liberalized state laws on pornography and divorce.
3. *Changing attitudes toward debt:* For decades, Americans were hesitant about installment buying because of the Puritan injunction against debt. Now, following a period of massive installment buying, this hesitancy appears to be returning for some consumer groups.
4. *Accent on youth and vitality:* Sales of sports cars, youthful clothes, and health-club memberships have zoomed. All age groups are represented in this surge.

5. *A more relaxed way of living, which has led to a shift in consumer-spending priorities:* When lower-income people move into middle-income levels, they buy traditional goods and services. But many young, well-educated, middle-income consumers put their dollars into travel and education—even when it means a furnitureless home. This decreased concern for material goods and for conforming to past social norms has been dubbed "keeping down with the Joneses."

6. *Impatience with low-quality products and with the lack of product information:* This is the essence of consumerism. It is reflected in the federal laws, prompted by public pressure, that provide better and safer cars, toys, and food products and better information on products, interest charges on credit, and status of credit ratings.

The consumer
of the 1970s
cannot be
pigeonholed

To summarize, as *Business Week* magazine notes, "the consumer is harder and harder to pigeonhole." Yet, marketers must be aware of such key trends in order to provide consumers with the products and services that will satisfy them.

The Product Element in the Marketing Mix

To the average American consumer, a product is just a physical item with certain uses and a particular appearance. In terms of the marketing mix, it is much more than this. A product purchased by consumers encompasses functional, psychological, and aesthetic features as well as accessories, instructions on use, packaging, brand name, endurance, warranties, and the quality of repair service available if the product fails. All of these characteristics are simply called the product.

In some instances, the product may not be a physical item at all but a service that consumers find useful. Accommodations at a Holiday Inn, a professional football game, and a dry-cleaning operation are all examples of services. In general, we can define a *product* as a physical item or service that satisfies certain customer needs. This definition has the advantage of being consistent with the marketing concept, which stresses the importance of consumer needs and of including intangible items (services) as well as tangible items (products).

**A product
may or may not
be a tangible item**

The word "good" may be used interchangeably with "product." A traditional breakdown of products is based on whether the buyers are consumers or industrial firms. Thus, *consumer goods* are goods destined for use by ultimate consumers (individuals or households) and available in a form that can be used without commercial processing. *Industrial goods* (sometimes called *producer goods*) are goods sold to industrial firms for incorporation in a final product, for producing other goods, or for use in the administrative activities of the firm.

7-6 Types of marketable goods.

General category	Class	Explanation (definition)	Examples
Consumer goods	Convenience goods	Goods that the customer characteristically purchases frequently, immediately, and with a minimum of comparison shopping.	Cigarettes, soap, newspapers, chewing gum, many food products.
	Shopping goods	Goods that the customer, in the process of selection and purchase, characteristically compares on such bases as suitability, quality, price, and style.	Millinery, furniture, dress goods, ready-to-wear clothing, shoes. (These goods are frequently unbranded or, if branded, the names are not very important to the consumer.)
	Specialty goods	Goods with unique characteristics and/or brand identification for which a significant group of buyers is habitually willing to make a special purchasing effort.	Specific types and brands of fancy goods, hi-fi components, photographic equipment, custom-made suits. (Such goods are generally branded, and the brands are important to the consumer making a buying decision.)
Industrial goods	End-product goods	Goods incorporated by manufacturers in their final products and ultimately destined to be consumer or industrial goods.	Raw materials, fabricated components (such as a radio in a new car or an electric motor on a drill press).
	Production goods	Goods used by manufacturers in the production of other goods.	Machine tools, lathes, drill presses, fractionating towers in the petrochemical industry.
	Commercial goods	Goods used by business and manufacturing firms in the administrative activities required for their continuing operation.	Cash registers, filing cabinets, adding machines, office furniture, stationery, and supplies.

Source: AMA Committee on Definitions, Ralph S. Alexander, Chairman, *Marketing Definitions: A Glossary of Marketing Terms* (Chicago: American Marketing Association, 1960) pp. 289–93.

Products include consumer and industrial goods

Consumer and industrial goods in turn may be divided into several classes, as shown in Figure 7-6. Often, the lines between these classes tend to blur. It is difficult to see how candy bars could be anything but a consumer good or iron ore anything but an industrial good. Automobile tires, however, can be a consumer good if purchased by a car owner to replace worn tires or an industrial good if sold to General Motors to be used on a new car. The same is true of pencils, paper, and many other products. The important point is that industrial buyers may differ significantly from individual consumers in terms of their buying motives, skills, and the channels through which they purchase. The tactics used to sell 50,000 pencils to General Motors may be considerably different from those used to sell a box of pencils to a high-school student.

Matching Markets and Products

Stated simply, the basic problem in marketing is to identify the prospective customers (the target market), to shape a product to their needs, and then to bring the two together. In economic terms, this is a problem of matching demand (customers) and supply (products).

✔ **Market segmentation.** Market segmentation is the process of dividing potential customers for a product into meaningful consumer groups or *market segments* in order to identify a target market. This process involves three steps: (1) finding relevant characteristics that divide a market into smaller consumer groups (market segments); (2) using these newly found characteristics to identify all significant market segments and to relate them systematically to the products each segment might buy (the latter often with the aid of a market-product grid); and (3) selecting the target market—the collection of market segments most consistent with the firm's objectives and capabilities.

In the market-product grid for the fast-food restaurant (Figure 7-2), the characteristics used to identify individual market segments are the type of customer (student, faculty and staff, local resident) and the meal served (breakfast, lunch, between-meal snack, dinner, late-evening meal). When a market-product grid is used to display all market segments, the labels attached to the rows and columns represent the characteristics that are useful in analyzing the market. The three steps in market segmentation appear in Figure 7-7, using the fast-food restaurant as an example.

Sometimes the target market turns out to be too small to warrant developing a new product or engaging in other marketing efforts. In such cases, the business resources are invested elsewhere. At other times, it may be more important to concentrate on only a portion of the potential market segments in a target market rather than to dilute promotional efforts by trying to reach all of the market segments simultaneously. For example, in Figure 7-7, the breakfast segment and the noncollege area resident and worker segments have been eliminated from the target market (although some area residents and workers may still be attracted to the restaurant).

A key market-segmentation problem is to find useful ways to classify potential customers. Two common breakdowns are (1) demographic descriptions of the purchasers (sex, age, income, occupation, and so on), and

The three steps in market segmentation

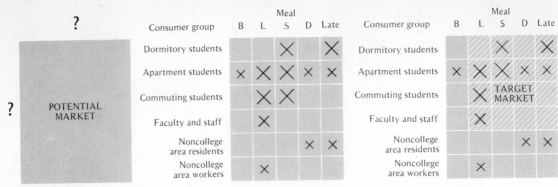

?	Consumer group	Meal					Consumer group	Meal				
		B	L	S	D	Late		B	L	S	D	Late
	Dormitory students			X		X	Dormitory students			X		X
	Apartment students	X	X	X	X	X	Apartment students	X	X	X	X	X
POTENTIAL MARKET	Commuting students		X	X			Commuting students		X	X TARGET MARKET		
	Faculty and staff		X				Faculty and staff		X			
	Noncollege area residents				X	X	Noncollege area residents				X	X
	Noncollege area workers		X				Noncollege area workers		X			

Step 1: Find relevant characteristics that divide a market into smaller consumer groups (market segments).

Step 2: Use these characteristics to identify and to display individual market segments (often with the aid of a market-product grid).

Step 3: Select the target market—the collection of market segments deemed most appropriate in view of the firm's objectives and capabilities.

7-7   Using market segmentation to identify the target market for a restaurant near a college campus. Note that the rows represent market characteristics and the columns represent product characteristics.

Ways to classify potential customers

(2) geographic location of the purchasers (region of the country, urban or rural, and so on). The proper basis for market segmentation depends, of course, on the product to be marketed. In our restaurant example, the market is segmented by combining occupation (college student, clerical staff, faculty) with place of residence (dormitory, on-campus apartment, off-campus residence). An age variable might be an appropriate basis of market segmentation for items as diverse as bubble gum and retirement homes. A geographic variable might be useful for snowblowers or for surfboards.

Two other ways to classify customers in a market are by (1) rate of product use, and (2) benefits that the user derives from the product.

✔ **Segments based on rate of product use.**   Market analyses are sometimes based on three categories of rate of individual or family product use:

Nonusers: Those who do not use the product at all.

The importance of heavy product users

Light-half users: Of the users, the half that uses the product less.

Heavy-half users: Of the users, the half that uses the product more.

Taking beverages as an example, a study showed that 22 percent of American families did not buy cola drinks at all. Of the 78 percent who drank cola, 39 percent were heavy-half users who consumed 90 percent of all cola drinks—or nine times as much cola as the 39 percent who were light-half users. Similarly, 67 percent of the families in the study did not buy beer. Among the 33 percent who did, the heavy-half users consumed about seven times as much beer as the light-half users. Research has indicated that the heavy-half users consumed roughly three to nine times as much as the light-half users of a variety of food and beverage products.

In view of its high consumption volume, the heavy-half market segment deserves—and gets—special attention. For example, since adult males are the largest market segment for beer, it is common for beer companies to advertise heavily on televised broadcasts of professional sports that appeal to men. In the 1970s, Hamm's, a Midwestern beer, was a sponsor of professional telecasts in several cities. One Hamm's commercial that many viewers found entertaining starred a bear who was continually getting into comical situations. Research showed that the viewers who were most entertained by the bear were grandmothers and children—groups that could hardly be included among the heavy-half beer users. As a result, the advertising was altered and a new theme was developed to appeal to the heavy-half users:

Man: (he-man type, carrying four cases of Hamm's beer and talking to his buddy.) Well, that does it for the party—thirty-two cases of Hamm's beer and a bag of beer nuts.

Buddy: What are we going to do with all the beer nuts?

✔ **Segments based on benefits to the user.** It may also be useful to analyze a market by the types of benefits that users derive from the product. The toothpaste market provides a case in point. Toothpaste preferences do not seem to depend too much on factors like age, sex, or income (demographic characteristics) or on factors like region of the country or whether the consumer lives in a city or on a farm (geographic characteristics). Rather, the market is best segmented by the different benefits that toothpaste users seek. Think about what these might be. What do you and some of your friends or relatives look for in a toothpaste? For three toothpaste producers' answers to this question and the way they were applied to market-segmentation strategy (see "How Toothpaste Producers Segment Their Market").

✔ **Strategies to use with market segmentation.** After a firm has identified the market-product segments, it must devise a strategy to attract the consumers who comprise them. Three different strategies can be followed: differentiated marketing, undifferentiated marketing, or concentrated marketing.

In *undifferentiated marketing,* the firm manufactures a single product and attempts to attract all buyers with a single marketing program. An example of this strategy is Henry Ford's statement about color selection for the Model T: "They can have any color they want as long as it's black." Ford believed that all consumers could and should be treated alike, and he

Grandmothers aren't the heavy-half beer users

Undifferentiated marketing: the same model for everyone

HOW TOOTHPASTE PRODUCERS SEGMENT THEIR MARKET

Since 1960, toothpaste producers have undertaken extensive marketing research to determine what consumers want in a toothpaste. The researchers found conventional demographic or economic characteristics of little use in segmenting the market. But they were able to divide consumers into three main groups, based on what they expected from a toothpaste:

● *Decay prevention:* People who wanted a toothpaste that would reduce cavities.

● *Clearer, prettier teeth:* People who wanted a toothpaste that would make their teeth whiter.

● *Fresher breath and a cleaner mouth:* People who wanted a toothpaste that would rinse their mouth and help to fight "bad breath."

From this research, competing firms developed and introduced three types of toothpastes, one aimed at each of these three target màrkets. The market-product grid and some typical ads for the three toothpastes are shown below.

Note that the leading brand in each of these three market segments is a product of a different company: Crest is produced by Procter & Gamble, Ultra Brite by Colgate-Palmolive, and Close-up by Lever Brothers. Since these toothpastes were first introduced, at least one of the brands has been "repositioned" slightly. Close-up now seeks to benefit consumers in two ways—by whitening teeth and freshening breath.

Market characteristic	Product characteristic		
	Cavity fighter	Tooth whitener	Breath freshener
Decay prevention	✔ Crest		
Cleaner, prettier teeth		✔ Ultra Brite	
Fresher breath, cleaner mouth			✔ Close-up

Crest

Ultra Brite

Close-up

developed a single product and marketing program. Significant production economies resulted because automobile parts did not have to be produced and inventoried for a variety of models and colors.

In *differentiated marketing,* separate products and marketing programs are designed for each market segment. This is the strategy that Ford, General Motors, and Chrysler now follow in offering wide selections of stan-

Differentiated
marketing:
a different model
for each segment

dard sedans, compacts, station wagons, and sports cars at a variety of prices. Procter & Gamble has made a similar shift to differentiated marketing. Fifty years ago, its dominant soap was Ivory; today, it produces a number of soaps intended for different market segments. But designing separate products and marketing programs can prove very costly for a firm.

Concentrated
marketing:
stressing only one
or a few segments

A compromise strategy is *concentrated marketing,* in which the firm concentrates on one or a few profitable market segments. There are many examples in both consumer and industrial markets of firms that have chosen this strategy. The Checker Cab Manufacturing Company produces automobiles that are used solely as taxi cabs and avoids competing with General Motors, Ford, or Chrysler for the remainder of the market. Economics Laboratory restricts its manufacturing to special washing compounds for use in dishwashers, thereby avoiding direct competition with soap and detergent giants like Procter & Gamble and Lever Brothers.

Figure 7-8 illustrates these three different marketing strategies, using the computer industry as an example. The relevant customer characteristics are assumed to be volume of data processing needed by the buyer (small, medium, or large) and application (clerical, such as payroll and inventory records, versus scientific). In the 1950s, computer manufacturers used an undifferentiated marketing strategy, selling the same type of computer to all buyers (Figure 7-8(a)). At the present time, IBM follows a differentiated marketing strategy, selling different computer models for different applications (Figure 7-8(b)). Despite the fact that IBM has cornered 70 percent of the computer market, Control Data Corporation has been able to compete successfully because its concentrated marketing strategy emphasizes large-size, scientific computers—only one segment of the total computer market (Figure 7-8(c)).

7-8 Three different marketing strategies based on market segments, using the computer industry as an example.

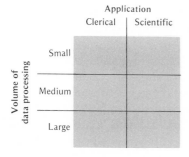

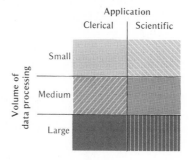

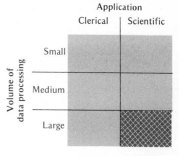

(a) Market for the computer industry in the 1950s.

Undifferentiated marketing—one product for all prospective buyers. The target market is all market segments or the entire market itself.

(b) Market for IBM today.

Differentiated marketing—a different product for each major segment of prospective buyers. Thus, each product is directed at a different target market. The total market segments of all these separate target markets often equal the entire market itself.

(c) Market for Control Data Corporation

Concentrated marketing—one product for one or a few market segments that constitute the target market. The firm competes only for the cross-hatched section and lets other firms compete for the remainder of the market.

Influence of Uncontrollable Factors on Product Sales

Product sales are sometimes influenced by factors that are largely beyond a firm's control, such as the use or disuse of a product by political or stage personalities. Men's fashions provide many examples. In the early 1960s, President John F. Kennedy's reluctance to wear hats had a damaging effect on the hat industry. Perry Como's "casual look" on television contributed to an increase in the sales of cardigan sweaters in the mid-1960s. When this casual trend continued, sales of men's suits in 1970 fell to 16 million, about 4 million fewer suits than were sold in the worst year of the depression. The barber business also declined significantly in the 1970s. Men began wearing their hair longer and making less frequent trips to the barber shop—a trend traceable in part to the Beatles.

Other Product Considerations

Three other important product considerations are related to the marketing mix: (1) the product line of a retailer or manufacturer; (2) the package in which the product is sold; and (3) the brand name given to the product.

The product line. It is obvious that most successful retailers and manufacturers deal with a variety of items rather than with an individual product. The *product line* is the array of products offered for sale by a business. The assortment of products that a retail firm offers is crucial to its success. A retailer with limited financial resources, may adopt a *breadth strategy*—selling a wide variety of products but stocking only a few of each type. Alternatively, the retailer may follow a *depth strategy*—offering only a few different products but stocking many of each type.

Most retail and manufacturing firms sell a line of products

Manufacturers face similar product-line decisions. Unless they are large in size, they usually choose to manufacture products that are related in some way. Such a product line offers (1) production advantages, (2) selling advantages (the sales force calls on the same customers but offers them a wider product line), and (3) a favorable consumer image. After World War II, General Mills sought to utilize the electromechanical capabilities it had built up during the war by offering a line of small home appliances. But the new product group proved unsuccessful, possibly because it was so dissimilar to the company's breakfast and flour line, which, due to production and sales expertise, had gained wider consumer acceptance.

The products offered in a given line may be *substitutes*—that is, one product may be used instead of another to perform substantially the same function. An example is the wide line of copiers offered by the Xerox Corporation. Alternatively, the products in a line may be *complements*—that is, one product may help to sell one or more related products. General

Electric allegedly began manufacturing appliances to develop a demand for the power-generating equipment it produces. Gillette not only produces the safety razor but the blades and shaving cream as well. Mattel's success with its Barbie doll is due as much if not more to the complementary wardrobe sold for Barbie and her friends as to the dolls themselves.

✔ **Packaging.** Packaging both protects and promotes a product. If the product is easily damaged, it may require some kind of vacuum-sealed container, as is the case with many grocery items. If the product is small and likely to be stolen (such as many items in drug or variety stores), it is often attached to a large card and shrink wrapped in plastic. The clear plastic packaging used on cuts of meats in many supermarkets protects the meat and also allows people to see what they are buying. An attractive package on a supermarket shelf may catch the consumer's attention and lead directly to a purchase. But if all competing products are similarly packaged, the package may lose its promotional effectiveness. For years, menthol cigarettes were sold in white and light blue or light green packages. Recently, some menthol cigarettes have been marketed in red packages to make them more distinctive at cigarette counters.

Packaging both protects and promotes

✔ **Branding.** Many business firms use a name, term, symbol, design, or some combination of these to identify their goods or services and to distinguish them from competitors' products. This procedure, known as *branding,* facilitates shopping because it reassures the buyer that the quality of the product will be similar to the quality experienced the last time that brand was purchased. Among grocery products, there are an estimated 38,000 brands, of which 6500 are stocked by a typical supermarket. The grocery shopper undoubtedly saves time by buying the brand-name frozen foods, toothpastes, and detergents that are familiar and that have produced favorable results in the past.

Because a well-known brand name is a valuable asset, companies invest huge sums of money in the quality control and advertising of their branded items. Sometimes they are so successful that an entire product class becomes known by its leading brand name—such as aspirin, adhesive tape, or shredded wheat—rather than by its more common descriptive name. When this occurs, the brand name is no longer protected and competitors can also use it. The manufacturers of Kleenex, Scotch tape, Xerox, and Frigidaire have taken great pains to prevent this from happening to their products. For example, Kimberly-Clark Corporation, the manufacturer of Kleenex, expects druggists to hand customers its brand and not any other pop-up tissue in a box when they ask for Kleenex at the counter.

Will Scotch tape go the way of adhesive tape?

In summary, the product element in the marketing mix involves (1) identifying the target market (often by means of market segmentation using the market-product grid), and (2) developing a product or a product line that meets the needs of this target market.

KEY POINTS TO REMEMBER

1. Marketing involves the broad area of business activity that directs the flow of goods and services from producer to consumer in order to satisfy customers and to achieve company objectives.
2. In recent years, increasing attention has been given to the marketing concept, which stresses shaping products to meet consumer needs.
3. Marketing-department actions focus on the four controllable factors in the marketing mix: product, place, price, and promotion.
4. Two steps are essential to a successful marketing program: (a) identifying the target market, and (b) selecting an appropriate blend of the four marketing-mix elements to reach the target market.
5. The market-product grid is a particularly useful framework for identifying customers in the target market.
6. Three key factors often account for the failure of a new product: (a) an insubstantial target market; (b) insignificant difference when compared to existing products; and (c) inadequate quality.
7. To be influential in the marketplace, consumers must be (a) people, (b) with income, and (c) with a desire to buy. Important trends in each of these areas are watched by firms to meet consumer needs better.
8. The product element in the marketing mix refers to a physical item or service that satisfies certain customer needs. The word "good" may be used interchangeably with "product." All goods or products may be classified as consumer goods or industrial goods, depending on to whom they are sold.
9. An important concept is market segmentation—the process of dividing potential customers into meaningful consumer groups (or market segments) in order to identify a product's target market.
10. Depending on the nature of the product, markets may be segmented in a number of ways, including by demographic or geographic characteristics, rate of product use, and product benefits derived by users.
11. Three market-segment strategies are undifferentiated, differentiated, and concentrated marketing.
12. The product element also includes product-line, packaging, and branding considerations.

QUESTIONS FOR DISCUSSION

1. If the marketing concept is effectively shaping products and services to consumer needs, manufacturers and retailers should be seeking feedback from consumers. In what ways have you and your family or your friends ever been surveyed to obtain such information?
2. Compare the different customer satisfactions provided in the following pairs of products: (a) a brand-name suit purchased at a department store versus an "all sales final" suit purchased at a discount store; (b) dinner at

the best restaurant in town versus a hamburger and a shake in the car at the local drive-in; and (c) a TV dinner versus a home-cooked meal.

3. Give several examples of products whose market demand would be affected by the following population factors: (a) sex, (b) age, (c) regional distribution. What about income factors? Changes in consumer attitudes and values?

4. Some marketing experts can intuitively measure the consumption characteristics of users of various products. For each of the following products, try to estimate the percentage of Americans who are users and the consumption of the typical heavy-half user as opposed to that of the light-half user: (a) lemon-lime soft drinks, (b) concentrated frozen orange juice, (c) bourbon whiskey, (d) dog food, (e) cake mixes, (f) bacon, (g) shampoo, (h) soaps and detergents.

5. In the discussion of the fast-food restaurant near a college campus, we made the point that the market-product grid approach was still a simplification. Referring to the grid in Figure 7–2, answer the following questions. (Cite examples whenever possible to support your position.)
   (a) Is each rectangle in the grid an equally important part of the total market?
   (b) Can the grid dimensions be in even greater detail than they appear in Figure 7–2?
   (c) What other dimensions might be added to the market-product grid?
   (d) What other factors which might not be easy to add to the grid should be considered in making the final decision about opening the restaurant?

SHORT CASES AND PROBLEMS

1. Josten's, Inc., produces and sells class rings and yearbooks for high schools and colleges. What effects might the changes in U.S. population, income, and consumer attitudes and values discussed in this chapter have on Josten's future sales? (*Hint:* First, check the age distribution of the U.S. population, shown in Figure 7–3.)

2. The market-product grid is a method used to analyze a specific business problem—in this case, identifying the target market for a new product. As the marketing manager of a firm that manufactures denim jeans (or "blue jeans," although they are not always blue), you must analyze the market segments to which you may sell.
   (a) What are the characteristics of potential purchasers that you might use to segment the market?
   (b) Develop a market-product grid incorporating the most useful characteristics you identified in part (a) for the denim-jean market at the present time.
   (c) Develop a market-product grid for the denim-jean market ten years ago.

3. Assume that you have decided to go into business for yourself. You are trying to decide whether to open (a) a sporting goods store, (b) a grocery store, (c) a drug store, or (d) a radio-television-stereo store. What effects might the changes in population, income, and consumer attitudes and values cited in this chapter have on each of these stores?

CAREER SELECTION: POSITIONS IN MARKETING RESEARCH AND PRODUCT MANAGEMENT

CAREERS IN MARKETING RESEARCH

Marketing research workers analyze existing data, construct surveys, and conduct interviews to determine the feasibility of a new product. They also forecast the future profitability of a new product, and, on the basis of their consumer studies, suggest advertising strategies and modify product designs. Most marketing research workers have bachelor's degrees; graduate degrees are usually essential for high-level research jobs. Applicants who have solid backgrounds in statistics, psychology, and economics begin as research trainees and may advance to supervisory or to management positions. Annual salaries range from $10,000 to $35,000. The demand for market research workers — especially those with graduate degrees — will increase rapidly as business firms continue to base more of their marketing policies on sophisticated research data. (*Additional information:* American Marketing Association; 230 North Michigan Avenue; Chicago, Illinois 60601.)

Home economists are employed by educational institutions, private businesses, and government agencies to study and to improve products and services for home consumption. Home economists communicate product information to consumers and assist in developing products to meet consumer needs. These responsibilities require communication skills as well as a specialized knowledge of the field in which the home economist is working. Entry positions require a bachelor's degree in home economics; teaching, supervisory, and research jobs often require graduate degrees. Annual salaries range from $8000 to $22,000. Job competition is keen for home economists with bachelor's degrees; there are considerably more job opportunities for home economists with graduate degrees. (*Additional information:* American Home Economics Association; 2010 Massachusetts Avenue, N.W.; Washington, D.C. 20036.)

Consumer psychologists analyze human behavior and motivation in relation to consumer buying patterns. They devise and administer surveys and psychological tests for a variety of purposes: to generate new product ideas; to gauge consumer reactions to new products; and to help to develop more effective advertising appeals. Most employers require a master's degree in psychology; doctoral degrees lead to more advanced research and administrative positions. Annual income ranges from $11,000 to $22,000. Private industry's growing reliance on sound technical research and development and on market-research programs is expected to create an expanding job market for consumer psychologists. (*Additional information:* American Psychological Association; 1200 17th Street, N.W.; Washington, D.C. 20036.)

CAREERS IN PRODUCT MANAGEMENT

Product management personnel are responsible for developing specific programs to market one brand or one product line effectively. They work for both consumer-goods firms like Procter & Gamble and the Pillsbury Company and industrial-goods firms like the 3M company and the Honeywell Corporation. For example, product management (sometimes called *brand management*) personnel working for the Pillsbury Company could be responsible for that firm's line of cake mixes. In this capacity, they would decide how to reach consumers most effectively in the four marketing-mix areas — product, price, place, and promotion. Product management personnel utilize marketing research information developed by marketing research workers, consumer psychologists, and home economists.

Although the job titles vary from firm to firm, careers in product management usually involve a sequence of three related jobs: *marketing* (or *brand*) *assistant; assistant product* (or *brand*) *manager;* and *product* (or *brand*) *manager.* The entry-level job is **marketing assistant,** for which a master's degree in business administration is normally required. The marketing assistant usually analyzes past sales trends, projects these trends into the future, and then devises possible pricing or advertising strategies. Annual starting salary is approximately $15,000 to $17,000. Length of work as a marketing assistant is about one year.

Men and women who demonstrated their capabilities as marketing assistants are promoted to the position of **assistant product manager.** In this capacity, they may be responsible for one or two specific items within the firm's product line. In addition, assistant product managers often search for new product ideas to broaden the product line. Length of work as an assistant product manager is one to three years; annual salary range is $18,000 to $21,000.

Successful assistant product managers are promoted to the position of **product manager.** In this capacity, they are responsible for marketing decisions that concern the entire product line, beginning with the development of an annual marketing plan intended to market the firm's present and potential product lines effectively. With three to five years experience as a marketing assistant and as an assistant product manager, product managers can expect to earn about $25,000 annually. In many firms, successful product managers can attain positions of increased responsibility and may become marketing manager (supervisor of several product managers), vice president of marketing, and perhaps eventually president of the company. (*Additional information:* contact the marketing departments of specific employers.)

A CRITICAL BUSINESS DECISION

—made by Jane Evans

THE SITUATION According to a company history, I. Miller is "the most widely recognized name in the footwear industry, specializing in the retailing of fine quality ladies' shoes and accessories." On May 26, 1970, the company makes history for itself by selecting a woman as president of its retail operations.

In 1893, Israel Miller started I. Miller with $500 and a dream of creating and selling the finest women's shoes in the world. For 25 years, the firm produced almost totally hand-crafted shoes for a select clientele. In 1919, I. Miller was incorporated in New York and won fame in the early 1920s by introducing its "heartbeat red calf" shoes—a landmark in an industry that had never before produced shoes in colors other than black, brown, blue, and white. In 1952, I. Miller merged with the Genesco Corporation—the world's largest manufacturer and seller of footwear and apparel. Today, the I. Miller Salons retail chain consists of 16 stores and 23 leased operations. Despite its growth, the company faces financial problems: in the last five years, it has realized a profit only twice.

The new president is Jane Evans, a 25-year-old graduate of Vanderbilt University and a native of Hannibal, Missouri. Fluent in four languages, Evans begins her career translating letters for the Genesco Corporation. Moving from the parent company to I. Miller, she is successively promoted to assistant shoe buyer, to handbag and hosiery buyer, and to the fashion coordinator in charge of the design and manufacture of women's shoes sold by Genesco to Sears Roebuck and Company. Largely due to her varied experience in manufacturing, wholesaling, and retailing, Jane Evans is named President of I. Miller in May 1970.

THE DECISION Stepping into the new job, Evans observes: "I see myself as a referee among product development, manufacturing, and retailing." She immediately dismisses "deadwood" personnel, curtails executive business trips, and solves inventory and quality-control problems. Her cost reductions include giving up the presidential limousine for the subway and insisting that company personnel —including herself—fly tourist rather than first class.

But it is in the marketing area that Evans focuses her major efforts. I. Miller stresses quality as well as fashion, and its shoes sell from $25 to $52 a pair. Evans believes that I. Miller's ability to become profitable rests largely on its becoming more "consumer-oriented." To achieve this goal, she realizes, the company must recognize that its customers are not all the same—that different "segments" of women buyers merit different marketing programs. This might mean different styles, brands, and prices—possibly even different retail outlets. After studying both present and potential I. Miller customers, Evans identifies three specific segments to which separate marketing efforts should be directed: (1) the well-established, well-to-do, conservative shopper; (2) the woman who adapts current fashion trends to her own tastes and who Evans sees as the target market of the future; and (3) the young, impulsive shopper—the "spirit of life in a store"—who is willing to experiment and who may turn a temporary fad into an accepted fashion.

QUESTIONS

1. What consumer characteristics did Jane Evans use to identify the three market segments that might become important target markets for I. Miller?
2. What different marketing programs might be used to reach each of these three segments? (*Hint:* Consider a different program of action for each of the four marketing-mix elements.)

If a nickel phone call now costs a dime, why does a penny postcard cost eight cents?

The Wall Street Journal
(November 1974)

CHAPTER

8

MARKETING: THE PLACE AND PRICE ELEMENTS

In spite of the nostalgia craze of the 1970s, most Americans accept reality and recognize that some things are probably gone forever: good five-cent cigars, nickel phone calls, and penny postcards, among them.

But at the beginning of this decade, a five-stick pack of chewing gum, bucking the trend of price increases, remained a nickel. A five-stick pack of gum retailed at 5 cents in the 1920s. Although inflation virtually eliminated the 5-cent candy bar from the market after World War II, a pack of gum still cost only 5 cents until 1970. In June of that year, gum producers, with the exception of the William Wrigley Company of Chicago (producer of Juicy Fruit, Spearmint, Doublemint, and P.K. gums), increased their wholesale price by a third, from 60 to 80 cents for a box of 20 five-stick packs. Most retailers responded by raising retail prices on all brands, including Wrigley's, to 7, 8, or 10 cents.

Thus, retailers made an unusually handsome profit on Wrigley's brands—at the consumer's expense. In August 1970, the Wrigley Company took the unusual step of running an anti-inflation ad in 560 newspapers across the country, warning gum chewers that "you should not be paying more for these packages than you have in the past." Unfortunately for consumers, the advertising attempt to arouse consumers to pressure retailers into setting a lower price on Wrigley brands was unsuccessful. In February 1971, the company raised its wholesale price to 72 cents for a box of 20 five-stick packs because Wrigley's costs had risen and retail prices had remained firm. Finally, in January 1972, Wrigley introduced the "dime pack"—a package of seven sticks for 10 cents—an innovation that cost the company $30 million for new gum-wrapping machines. Other companies followed suit, and by early 1972 you probably paid a dime for seven sticks of gum. When sugar costs soared in 1974, Wrigley was forced to increase its wholesale prices again, and you are now probably paying 15 cents for a seven-stick pack of gum.

Such public exposure of a conflict between manufacturer and retailer is unusual. The significant point is that a manufacturer as large as Wrigley lost control of its retail price by using a marketing channel that involved independent middlemen. This example also serves to introduce the two main topics we will discuss in Chapter 8: the place and the price elements in the marketing mix.

The Place Element in the Marketing Mix

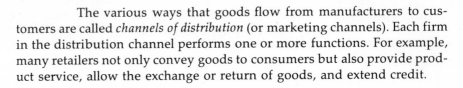

For a product to be of value to consumers, it must be available when and where they want it. The *place* element in the marketing mix refers to all institutions and activities that contribute to delivering goods at the times and to the places consumers desire. The major marketing institutions involved in this process are manufacturers, wholesalers, and retailers. *Middlemen* is the term given to wholesalers and retailers—two institutions used by manufacturers to distribute finished products to customers.

Place: the right time and location

Channels of Distribution

The various ways that goods flow from manufacturers to customers are called *channels of distribution* (or marketing channels). Each firm in the distribution channel performs one or more functions. For example, many retailers not only convey goods to consumers but also provide product service, allow the exchange or return of goods, and extend credit.

✔ **Important channel dimensions: title and physical possession.** Two important characteristics of a distribution channel are (1) the institutions that take title to (actually own) the goods, and (2) the institutions that take physical possession of the goods. Although many institutions in a channel do both, this is not a necessity. A wholesaler may arrange for a manufacturer to ship a large order directly to a retail customer; in this case, the wholesaler takes title to the goods and bills the retailer without ever possessing the goods. In contrast, General Electric normally retains ownership of its light bulbs, even though the hardware stores in which the bulbs are sold have physical possession of the product.

✔ **Typical channels of distribution.** Four common marketing channels are shown in Figure 8-1. The first channel in the figure is the *manufacturer–consumer channel* (also called *direct marketing*). This is the distribution of goods by a manufacturer directly to its customers without the help of any middlemen. Since numbers of customers are usually limited, the direct marketing of specialized industrial goods (large generators sold to electric utilities, for example) is very common. Some firms (Fuller Brush is one) market their products directly to consumers using door-to-door sales representatives. If a manufacturer also owns its retail outlets, it is involved in direct marketing because title to the goods remains in the manufacturer's hands until the products are purchased by consumers. Examples are Thom McAn shoes (the retail outlet of the Melville Shoe Corporation), Sherwin-Williams Paint, and Goodyear Tires.

Direct marketing: no middlemen at all

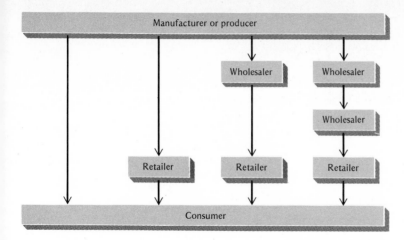

8-1

Four common channels of distribution for consumer goods.

The *manufacturer–retailer channel* is most applicable when large retailers purchase a significant volume of goods directly from the manufacturer. Large department stores, discount houses, and supermarket chains often deal directly with manufacturers.

Other channels are more complex

As purchase volume declines, it is less feasible for a manufacturer to have its own sales force call on retailers. A wholesaler then enters the picture, resulting in the *manufacturer–wholesaler–retailer channel*. Patented drugs and sundries, hardware, and convenience foods with a low-profit margin utilize this channel. Sometimes one or more wholesalers enter the distribution process, creating the *manufacturer–multiple wholesaler–retailer channel*. In the meat-packing industry, large wholesalers often find it convenient to sell to smaller wholesalers who in turn service individual supermarkets or food chains. In fact, the average meat product goes through more than ten middlemen.

✔ **Why middlemen exist.** A manufacturer chooses to use intermediaries because the value of the functions they perform outweighs the money they are paid for their services. In using one or more independent middlemen, however, the manufacturer gives up some control over the way its products will be sold. Our earlier example of Wrigley's problems with its retailers over the retail price of its gum illustrates this point. Generally, the more middlemen in the channel, the less control the manufacturer has.

It is a principle of marketing that "you can do away with a middleman but not his functions." Some other institution in the channel or the ultimate consumer must perform the functions formerly executed by the wholesaler or retailer middleman.

Figure 8-2 illustrates the valuable functions a middleman performs when one industry composed of three individual manufacturers chooses to sell to a wholesaler. By using a wholesaler, an individual manufacturer

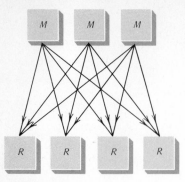

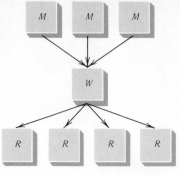

8-2

Effect of a wholesaler middleman (W) on the number of contacts required between manufacturers (M) and retailers (R).

(a) Number of individual contacts without a wholesaler middleman:
$M \times R = 3 \times 4 = 12$

(b) Number of individual contacts with a wholesaler middleman:
$M + R = 3 + 4 = 7$

Middlemen reduce the number of required contacts

reduces the number of contacts required to market its product from four to one (or by 75 percent), while the contacts for the entire industry are reduced from twelve to seven. Without the use of such middlemen, the manufacturer would have to increase the size of its sales force (because of the increased number of contacts), or to pay for the inventory and personnel required to operate its own warehouses and retail outlets.

Marketing Middlemen

Marketing middlemen are broadly classified into wholesalers and retailers. Now that we have seen how middlemen fit into a marketing channel, we can examine their functions in more detail.

Wholesaling: selling to almost anyone but the ultimate consumer

✔ **Wholesalers.** Establishments that sell to retailers, other wholesalers, or industrial users but do not sell in significant amounts to ultimate consumers are called *wholesalers.* They exist because they perform services for suppliers or customers more efficiently than the manufacturing firms themselves can. Among the services a wholesaler usually provides for its suppliers are finding customers, storing inventories, and furnishing market information (because of the wholesaler's proximity to sources of demand). For its customers, a wholesaler may forecast needs, regroup goods into required quantities, carry stock, transport goods, grant temporary credit, and provide specialized sales information.

A distinction can be made between two kinds of wholesalers: merchant wholesalers and merchandise agents (or brokers). *Merchant wholesalers* take title to the goods they sell and perform some or all of the wholesaler functions just specified. *Merchandise agents* do not take title to the goods they sell but represent buyers or sellers in marketing transactions; agents generally perform fewer services than merchant wholesalers do. An example is a manufacturers' representative—an agent for manufacturers of several different complementary product lines (for example, nuts and bolts, springs, and bearings) who takes orders from prospective customers and relays them to the manufacturers without physically handling the goods.

✔ **Retailers.** Institutions that purchase only consumer goods from manufacturers or wholesalers and sell them only to ultimate consumers are known as *retailers*. They are not involved with the sale of industrial goods or with the sale of consumer goods to other marketing institutions.

Retailing: selling only to the ultimate consumer

A retailer performs functions for its suppliers (producers or wholesalers) and for its customers (ultimate consumers) that are similar to those provided by a wholesaler but that are at a closer level in the marketing channel to the ultimate consumer. Most retailers forecast customer needs

WHERE THE MONEY GOES: THE COSTS OF PRODUCING AND MARKETING A $6.98 RECORD

Consumers often complain that excessive marketing costs are added to the final selling price. Marketing middlemen — the wholesalers and the retailers — are often singled out for special criticism. Here is where the money typically goes when a consumer pays $6.98 for a popular record at a retail store:

Vinyl and pressing	$ .40	
Record jacket	.85	
American Federation of Musicians	.07	
Songwriter's royalties	.20	
Recording artist's royalties	.70	
Freight to wholesaler	.05	
Manufacturer's advertising and selling expense	.60	
Manufacturer's administrative expenses	.58	
Manufacturer's cost	$3.45	
Manufacturer's profit	.50	
Manufacturer's price to wholesaler		$3.95
Freight to retailer		.02
Wholesaler's advertising, selling and administrative expense		.12
Wholesaler's cost		$4.09
Wholesaler's profit		.25
Wholesaler's price to retailer		$4.34
Retailer's advertising, selling and administrative expense		.70
Retailer's profit		1.94
Retailer's price to consumer		$6.98

Do the profits of the wholesaler and the retailer seem too large? Perhaps. But hundreds of record companies go out of business every year. In fact, many retailers who sell their records at "discount prices" make less than $1.00 profit per record. For example, low-overhead stores may buy directly from the manufacturer, add a slight markup, and sell a record with a list price of $6.98 for $4.69–$4.99. At such a low price and profit level, a few bad decisions as to which records to stock can cause a retailer to fail. The profits of the middlemen look high to some manufacturers, too. In an effort to increase profits and to find out what consumers want, some record manufacturers, such as Columbia Records and ABC, Inc., have opened chains of retail stores. So before you make your decision to open a retail record shop, look at the opportunities and the problems of a small business described in Chapters 16 and 17.

(by choosing the right goods to put on the shelf), regroup large purchases into smaller required quantities, deliver goods to the consumer's home, grant credit, and provide specialized sales information. Many retailers, however, do not extend all of these services; some, for example, require cash-and-carry terms.

The Evolution of Today's Retailing Institutions

Figure 8-3 shows the development of many of our most vital retailing institutions from 1850 to the present. These institutions grew or declined in response to the needs of each era, and those that persist today have been able to adapt to changing needs.

Prior to the Civil War, *general stores* (or trading posts) were the sole retail outlets for most villages. These stores carried everything that local consumers demanded, from flour, sugar, and cloth to animal feed, nails, and farm implements. General stores still exist in a few sparsely populated areas today.

After the Civil War, cities grew, transportation improved, and commerce and industry expanded. As a result, family income increased and workers became more specialized instead of remaining jacks-of-all-trades. These trends prompted two nearly concurrent developments in retailing: the single-line store and the department store. The *single-line store,* as the

The 1800s: general, single-line department, mail-order, and five-and-ten-cent stores

8-3 The evolution of American retailing institutions.

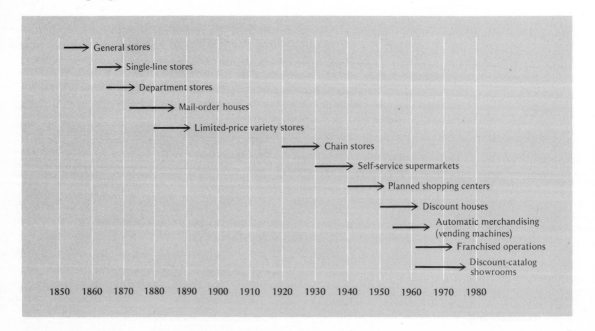

name implies, carries only one line of merchandise, such as furniture, hardware, groceries, or apparel. The distinguishing characteristics of *department stores* are that they are large and that they bring together under one roof a variety of separate lines — such as apparel, furniture, rugs, toys, and cosmetics — each of which corresponds roughly to a single-line store. Well-known department stores include Macy's, Gimbel's, Filene's, Wanamaker's, Nieman-Marcus, Dayton-Hudson, Marshall Field, and Bullock's.

In the years following the Civil War, rural areas did not benefit to any great extent from the retail services that were available in most urban areas. Toward the end of the nineteenth century, improved rail and postal services facilitated the introduction of *mail-order houses* — business enterprises that accepted and filled merchandise orders by mail. Because of their low prices and breadth of selection, these firms were able to compete successfully with the general stores operating in rural areas. The best-known mail-order houses are Montgomery Ward and Sears Roebuck, begun in 1872 and 1886, respectively. Today, these firms have broadened their operations; while continuing their mail-order business, they also operate large department stores and suburban *catalog stores* — outlets containing items advertised in their catalogs that customers can order and then pick up within a few hours or days.

Inflation has caused what our grandparents knew as five-and-ten-cent stores to be renamed *limited-price variety stores*. Originally, these stores restricted their merchandise to low-priced items; today, the upper price range is about $25 to $50. The F.W. Woolworth Company, begun in 1879, was the first of many competing stores, including S.S. Kresge and Company, W.T. Grant and Company, and J.C. Penny Company, and the Ben Franklin Stores.

During the twentieth century, there has been a continued evolution and diversification in retailing. The 1920s witnessed the emergence of *chain stores* — retail outlets under common ownership that sold similar merchandise. Prior to that time, most stores had been independently owned. As urbanization increased, chain organizations achieved many economies in buying, warehousing, delivery, and advertising that were not available to the smaller independent stores. *Supermarkets* became popular in the depression years of the 1930s. These stores operated on a self-service, cash-and-carry basis and were able to reduce personnel costs, increase volume, and offer lower prices. The 1940s saw the development of *planned shopping centers,* as families moved to the suburbs and found it increasingly inconvenient to shop downtown. These centers, which are often enclosed to protect shoppers from inclement weather, include many of the types of stores just discussed — supermarkets, single-line, department, catalog, and limited-price variety stores.

Discount houses were the major retailing development of the 1950s. Many services offered by department and single-line stores cost the customer money in terms of higher markups due to charge accounts, free delivery, and the breadth and depth of merchandise offered. Discount

houses merchandise nationally branded durable goods (those in which customers have confidence) at lower prices by reducing services (that is, making each transaction cash and carry), increasing volume, and frequently offering a narrower selection.

Automatic merchandising — the marketing of such convenience goods as candy, cigarettes, soft drinks, and newspapers through vending machines — grew rapidly during the late 1950s and 1960s. The development of coin and bill changers contributed to this growth. Industrial and college cafeterias, for example, rely increasingly on vending machines for food and drink sales.

The 1960s have become known as the decade of the *franchised operation*. A franchise is a binding contractual arrangement between a manufacturer and a local retailer or distributor which gives the latter the exclusive right to sell the manufacturer's products in a given territory. The corporation sponsoring the franchise specifies the common name of the enterprise, operating procedures, store layout, and type of promotion; the local retailer manages the operation and contributes part of the capital. Although the best-known franchises are in the fast-food business, such as McDonald's restaurants and Colonel Sanders' Kentucky Fried Chicken establishments, franchises now operate in virtually every area of consumer goods and services — including bowling alleys, miniature golf courses and driving ranges, motels, dry cleaners, and apparel shops. The U.S. Department of Commerce estimated that in 1975 sales of goods and services by the nation's half million franchise establishments totaled about $200 billion. (Franchises will be discussed in more detail in Chapter 17.)

The fastest growing retailing institution of the 1970s is the *discount-catalog showroom* — an institution begun about 20 years earlier in some rural areas and in the back streets of downtown wholesale districts. As the name implies, the discount-catalog showroom is a "hybrid" retail operation that combines the elements of (1) mail-order and catalog stores, (2) department stores with elaborate merchandise showrooms, and (3) discount stores. A showroom mails thousands of catalogs to prospective customers, often listing two prices — a so-called "regular" retail price and the showroom's price. Mail-order stores send most merchandise by mail, and their suburban catalog stores do not usually stock merchandise. But the average discount-catalog showroom will deliver 95 percent of the items on its showroom floor. This gives customers the opportunity to study a variety of catalog items in the convenience of their own homes and then to examine these items in the store — often in a relatively elegant department-store atmosphere — and still to pay discount prices. In 1971, these showrooms rang up $1 billion in sales and surpassed a $3-billion sales figure for 1975. Their catalogs feature national brands and often concentrate on profitable lines like jewelry, gift items, luggage, and small appliances. With little or no advertising, low pilferage, and a large sales volume, discount-catalog showrooms have often been able to undercut even those prices set by traditional discount stores.

The evolution of retailing in the United States from 1900 to the

present has also given rise to a system known as *scrambled merchandising*, in which certain goods are carried by many different types of outlets rather than by just one or two. For example, furniture wax is often sold not only in department stores but also in supermarkets, hardware stores, limited-price variety stores, drugstores, and discount stores. The goods carried by mail-order houses and discount stores often cannot be distinguished from department-store products. Large sales volumes of some items can appear in unexpected outlets; for example, supermarkets account for a fourth of all panty-hose sales.

The Price Element in the Marketing Mix

Price: perhaps more than dollars paid

Price, the third element in the marketing mix, is familiar to everyone but is difficult to define precisely because it also includes allowances, discounts, and services. For example, the $5,000 "price" paid for a new sports car may not be its actual price if a $500 allowance is made on the customer's trade-in. Moreover, the $5,000 payment (plus the trade-in) may buy not only a new sports car but a service warranty on defective parts. We will therefore define *price* as the money and the goods exchanged for the ownership or the use of some assortment of goods and services.

Factors Affecting Price

Two general sets of factors—demand and supply—determine the level of every price in the economy. *Demand factors* refer to the intensities with which customers desire and are able to pay for goods or services. *Supply factors* involve the quantities of goods or services that producers will place on the market. The two main components of supply are the total cost of producing and marketing a good and the number of producers of a good. Thus, we will consider three major sets of factors that determine price levels: (1) demand; (2) production and marketing costs; and (3) competition.

✔ **Demand.** The quantity of a good that customers will buy depends on the price that is charged for it. Few customers would be willing to pay $200 for a man's shirt, no matter what its quality or style was. Yet, if the shirt were of satisfactory quality and style and if it were priced at $10, the quantity sold annually would probably be large. This illustrates a fundamental principle of economics regarding the demand for a good: as the price of an item falls, the quantity of that item purchased by customers normally rises.

The demand curve relates quantity sold to price charged

This principle can also be shown by a *demand curve*, which indicates graphically the maximum quantity of a good that customers will buy for each price. Suppose, for example, that manufacturers in the shirt industry

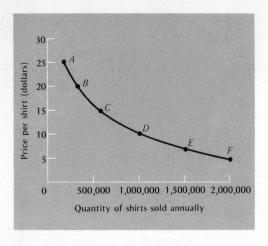

8-4

Demand curve for shirts, relating the maximum number of shirts sold to six possible prices.

collect information on the maximum demand for shirts at six different prices. The six combinations appear below:

Point on demand curve (Figure 8-4)	If the price charged per shirt is . . .	The annual number of shirts sold will be . . .
A	$25	200,000
B	20	300,000
C	15	600,000
D	10	1,000,000
E	7	1,500,000
F	5	2,000,000

The corresponding points on a demand curve are shown in Figure 8-4. Note that the demand curve in this figure conforms to the basic principle of demand: as prices fall, the number of shirts sold rises.

Demand depends on price, . . .

Because demand is very difficult to measure, marketers must often make intuitive guesses about its present and future levels and are therefore interested in the factors that determine demand. In addition to the price of the good itself, demand factors include (1) customer taste; (2) the price and the availability of other products, particularly close substitutes; and (3) customer income. The first two factors indicate what customers want to purchase; the third, what customers are able to purchase.

customer taste,

Customer taste refers to the preferences of consumers for particular goods or services. These preferences may reflect physical needs (sustenance, comfort) or psychological needs (status, acceptance). Customer taste, which forms the fundamental basis of the demand for a good, can be difficult to predict. In 1971, many retail stores and boutiques were left with large stocks of women's midi and maxi dresses; no matter what price the stores charged and despite the dictates of Paris fashion designers, American women didn't want them!

price and
availability
of substitutes,

The price and availability of other products, particularly close substitutes, influence the intensity of customer desires. *Substitute products* are products that perform the same or similar functions. Steel and aluminum are examples of substitutes used in many goods, such as beverage cans and car bumpers. During the East Coast power blackout in November 1965, some New York City retailers started charging angry consumers $5 or $10 for a single candle. Here, the temporary unavailability of one product—electricity—caused the demand and the price of a substitute product—candles—to rise dramatically. But this is an unusual illustration of the potential influence of this factor on demand.

. . . and
customer income

Customer income is another important determinant of demand. A customer may have a deep desire for a product that has no reasonably priced substitutes and yet be unable to buy it because of its high price. A ghetto family may want to move to the suburbs or the country but may not be able to afford a decent home at prevailing prices.

Changes in customer income often explain variations in demand. In 1974, many restaurants closed their doors for the last time because of decreased family incomes during the economic slowdown that year. Families with an unemployed breadwinner simply could not afford to eat out. Especially hard hit were restaurants in Midwestern cities where massive layoffs in the automobile industry dramatically reduced family incomes.

✔ **Production and marketing costs.** Production and marketing costs also have a bearing on the prices a marketer sets. Consider the story of the businessman who set his price so low that he lost a dollar on each sale but wasn't worried because he was "getting volume." Of course, unless somehow his costs decreased, he was moving one step closer to bankruptcy with each unit sold.

Understanding costs is crucial to business success. Henry Ford, who made millions "getting volume," illustrated this. Each year, Ford deliberately priced the Model T below the last year's costs, and each year his profits increased. When asked how he managed this, Ford pointed out that low prices made it possible for many more consumers to buy cars for the

---

WHY THE ECONOMIC PRINCIPLE OF "DEMAND" ISN'T QUITE A LAW

The economic principle regarding the demand for an item states that as the price of an item falls, the quantity of that item purchased by customers *normally* rises. We say "normally" because exceptions can occur. For example:
● In the early 1970s, the Whirlpool Corporation manufactured 18,000 too many vacuum cleaners on one production run.
● K-Mart bought a few of these surplus—but good quality—vacuum cleaners and test marketed them in two stores at $29 apiece. Consumers wouldn't buy.

● Western Auto Stores bought all the vacuum cleaners they could from Whirlpool, priced them at $49 each, and sold them all.

Apparently, consumers felt the low $29 price at K-Mart indicated poor product quality. But when Western Auto Stores raised the price to what consumers thought was a reasonable—but a bargain—price, they bought the vacuum cleaners. This explains an unusual phenomenon—a situation in which the quantity sold increases as the price increases.

first time; with this added sales volume, Ford's costs per car went down. Besides, he added with a grin, pricing below cost gave employees a maximum incentive to be efficient: if costs were not kept down, Ford would go bankrupt and all his employees would lose their jobs!

Costs put on floor or under a set price

In more normal instances, the costs of producing and marketing a good put a floor under a set price which it cannot fall below, except temporarily. If a price is set below the cost of producing and marketing each unit of a good, the business will sustain losses and will soon fail.

Now, consider the situation of all of the potential manufacturers in the shirt industry. A few manufacturers may be very efficient and may be able to cover all their production and marketing costs and still make a profit if their shirts are priced at $5. At higher prices such as $10, or $15, or $20, additional firms will be willing to produce shirts. This is because the price set for the shirts will be greater than their production and marketing costs, so that more potential shirt producers will be able to make a profit.

The supply curve: what manufacturers are willing to produce

Suppose that all potential shirt manufacturers were asked how many shirts they would be willing to produce at various prices. This hypothetical description of the maximum number of units offered for sale at various prices by all firms in the shirt industry is called a *supply curve*. A hypothetical set of six prices and the corresponding volume of shirts that would be produced at each of these prices appear below. The corresponding points on the supply curve in Figure 8-5 are given in the left-hand column:

Point on supply curve (Figure 8-5)	If the price charged per shirt is . . .	The annual number of shirts produced will be . . .
U	$25	1,800,000
V	20	1,700,000
W	15	1,400,000
X	10	1,000,000
Y	7	700,000
Z	5	400,000

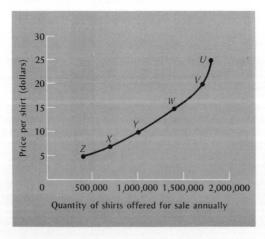

8-5

Supply curve for shirts, relating the maximum number of shirts offered for sale to six possible prices.

Figure 8-5 shows that as the market price for shirts increases, the number of shirts offered for sale by all the shirt-manufacturing firms also increases.

In Figure 8-6, both the demand curve for shirts and the supply curve for shirts are plotted on the same graph. The figure illustrates two key points. One is the differing impacts of changes in price on demand and supply. Figure 8-6 shows that as the market price of shirts decreases, the quantity of shirts demanded by consumers increases; thus, the demand curve slopes down and to the right. But the reverse is true for the supply curve: as the market price of shirts decreases, the quantity of shirts offered for sale by shirt manufacturers decreases; thus, the supply curve slopes up and to the right.

The second key point illustrated in Figure 8-6 is that the demand and the supply curves intersect one another. The point at which these two curves intersect establishes (1) the size of the market (in units), and (2) the market price (in dollars) at which the market is said to be in *equilibrium*. In Figure 8-6, the market equilibrium where demand and supply are equal occurs at a market size of 1,000,000 shirts and a market price of $10. In other words, the market equilibrium occurs at the price at which the number of shirts demanded by consumers is exactly equal to the number of shirts offered for sale by shirt manufacturers. This discussion and the demand and supply curves shown in Figure 8-6 emphasize that both demand and supply factors influence the price of a product.

This analysis has focused on the demand and supply factors for the entire shirt industry—not for just one shirt-manufacturing firm. Similar demand and supply curves could be drawn for each shirt manufacturer in the industry. The shirt manufacturer's choice is clear. Whatever price the manufacturer sets for a good, customer demand determines the maximum quantity of the good that can be sold. That price establishes the quantity of shirts the manufacturer is willing to offer for sale. For the manufacturer to remain in business, the price must cover production and marketing costs

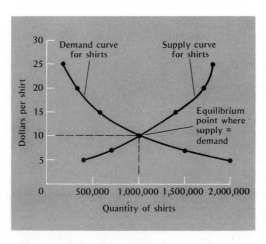

8-6

Equilibrium point for shirts, which is the market price at which the quantity of shirts demanded by consumers is exactly equal to the quantity of shirts offered for sale by shirt manufacturers. In this case, the market is in equilibrium at a market price of $10 per shirt and at a quantity of 1,000,000 shirts.

HOW XEROX FOUND A PRICING STRATEGY

In the early days of photocopying in the 1950s, many manufacturers set lower prices for their machines in order to charge more for the profitable photocopying paper that the customer had to purchase with the copier. For example, 3M's Thermofax copiers had to be fed 3M's Thermofax paper to work. The strategy of setting a low price on one item so that higher prices could be set on related high-volume items was not new. Gillette sets a low price on its razors to help sell its blades; Mattel sets lower prices on its Barbie dolls to help sell Barbie's clothes.

Xerox's problem, however, was different. It was developing a "plain paper copier"—a photocopier that would print on any kind of paper and not just on a special paper produced by Xerox.

Because of the high price of a Xerox machine, the company decided to rent rather than to sell the machines to users. But one big pricing problem still remained. John H. Dessauer, a Xerox Vice-President, describes how it arose at one meeting of top-level executives:

Could a small business office that made perhaps 1000 copies a month be expected to pay the same rental fee as a huge corporation that made 500,000 copies? Was it fair to expect both to pay equal amounts?

The problem was explored in depth at a number of executive sessions.

One day, an executive walking by the mailroom saw a clerk stamping letters with a Pitney-Bowes machine. This machine allows the user to pay for the actual amount of stamps dispensed. The executive's observation produced a whole new pricing and business concept: What Xerox would sell was copies!

Eventually, the idea was refined to include: (1) a meter on each machine; (2) a low rental fee that would allow a stipulated number of free copies; and (3) a low price—4 or 5 cents per page—for each additional copy.

This simple—but brilliant—strategy produced a single pricing policy for all Xerox customers that was equitable to large and small firms alike.

---

and provide some profit. Thus, the shirt manufacturer must choose the combination of price and quantity that produces a profit. When costs rise, the selling price normally must be increased to cover the extra costs. However, a manufacturer may elect to hold the price stable and reduce the quantity (or quality) of a product. For example, as cocoa prices rose between 1947 and 1969, Hershey chose to retain the nickel price and the high quality of its all-chocolate candy bar. But during this period, the size of the bar changed a dozen times, shrinking from 1⅓ ounces in 1947 to ¾ ounce in 1969.

If costs rise, price, quality, or quantity must change

✔ **Competition.** A final factor that must be considered in setting prices is competition—or the number of firms in the same industry that produce substantially the same product and the prices these firms charge. For example, given the demand for shirts and production and marketing costs, the shirt manufacturer might like to set a price of $15 per shirt. But if several competitors produce the same or a similar shirt for only $8, our shirt manufacturer will not be able to sell many shirts at $15. Most consumers will buy the competitors' lower-priced shirts.

The American steel industry provides an example of the influence of competition on price. In the 1960s and early 1970s, both large and small steel producers experienced losses or low profits and wanted to raise prices. They believed that their customers would be forced to pay the

Competition also influences price

higher prices because steel was an essential product. Yet, repeatedly, proposed price increases were wholly or partially rescinded, primarily because of the stiff competition from European and Japanese steel producers.

Even if our shirt manufacturer faced no competition, it still might not decide to set its price at $15 per shirt because a $15 price might be high enough to increase the competition: other firms, convinced that they could make good profits at such a high price, might decide to start manufacturing shirts themselves. Perhaps the most famous example of the influence of potential competition on prices occurred in the aluminum industry. For many years, one firm—the Aluminum Company of America (ALCOA)—controlled more than 90 percent of U.S. aluminum production. Yet, according to a federal court, ALCOA deliberately set aluminum prices below the most profitable levels, mainly to discourage potential competition.

How Prices Are Set

The three determinants of price—demand, costs, and competition—are summarized in Figure 8-7. Although marketing executives try to take all these factors into account in achieving the pricing objectives just listed, in practice this is not always feasible. Actual price-setting methods may be classified as: (1) demand-oriented pricing; (2) cost-oriented pricing; or (3) competition-oriented pricing.

Businesses set prices . . .

✔ **Demand-oriented pricing.** The pricing of new products is often demand-oriented, for the initial price a manufacturer sets can influence

8-7 Factors affecting the price set by the seller on the goods and services to be sold.

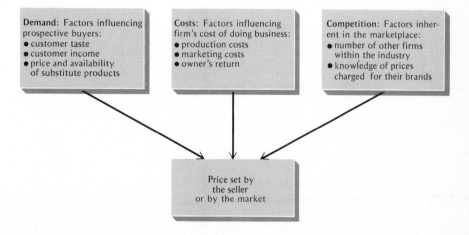

how rapidly the target market is penetrated. A high initial price tends to slow down the rate at which consumers buy a new product; a low initial price may attract new customers by broadening the product's appeal to include customers with lower incomes or with weaker desires for the product.

Skim-the-cream pricing and penetration pricing represent the opposite strategies manufacturers use in pricing new products. *Skim-the-cream pricing* involves setting a high initial price to obtain high immediate profits. This strategy relies on the fact that some buyers—for reasons as various as status or quality—may be willing to pay a significantly higher price than other segments of the market. The initial price may be reduced gradually, so that the manufacturer continues to obtain a higher price from consumer groups that are willing to pay a premium for the product. This strategy is particularly appropriate in introducing new products for which (1) some consumers are willing to pay the higher initial price; (2) the higher price does not produce such exorbitant profits that competitors are encouraged to enter the market (that is, a firm can reap its profits quickly and get out of the market before competitors enter); and (3) a high production volume is not required to maintain production costs at a reasonable level. An example of skim-the-cream pricing is the initial $15 to $20 price of Reynolds ballpoint pens—the first ballpoints on the market.

This type of pricing is also widely used for products that are not genuinely new—especially products that appeal to customers' fashion or status needs. When a "Paris original" or a new model car is purchased immediately after it appears on the market, a high skim-the-cream price is paid. Consumers willing to wait a bit can buy the same or a similar item at a much lower price.

Penetration pricing involves setting a low initial price on a product to attract as many buyers as possible. It is used when (1) few consumers are willing to pay a high initial price; (2) competitors are likely to offer a substitute product; and (3) high production volume is required to offer the product at a reasonable price. An example is the home trash compactor. The first manufacturers of this product set prices low enough to discourage many competitors from offering substitute products immediately.

Odd pricing is setting a price of 98 cents rather than $1 for a pad of paper or $495 rather than $500 for a living-room sofa. This strategy presumes that consumers will focus their attention on the lower price denoted by the first digit in the number and be more inclined to buy the product. Odd pricing was originally intended for low-priced items because it forced retail clerks to ring up the sales on their cash registers in order to make the necessary change; this prevented them from pocketing the money themselves when waiting on customers who were in a hurry, paid the exact amount, and did not bother to wait for their sales receipt. Many retail prices are odd prices. Probably the most common example is gasoline prices, which are almost always odd prices like 65.9 cents or 68.9 cents rather than whole numbers like 66 or 69 cents.

✔ **Cost-oriented pricing.** When a marketing executive deals with a large number of products, it is often too expensive and too time consuming to price each item separately. Or, if the products are technically complex, the research costs spent in developing the product may indicate the price to be charged. Such circumstances usually produce cost-oriented prices.

Most retail businesses in the United States employ *standard-markup pricing,* which involves adding a fixed percentage to the unit cost on all items in the same product class. The percentage added varies with the type of retail store (furniture, clothing, or grocery store) and with the type of product sold within a single store. In general, smaller markups are made on high-volume goods than on low-volume items.

For example, a supermarket might have a standard markup of 10 percent on a dairy product—a rapidly moving item. If it paid its supplier 70 cents per dozen eggs, the supermarket's selling price would be 77 cents (70 cents for cost *plus* 10 percent of 70 cents, or 7 cents, for markup). On spices —a slow-moving item—the markup might be 20 percent or more. Most retailers mark up direct costs (costs from suppliers); thus, markups must both cover overhead costs (store rent, manager's salary, and so on) and produce a profit margin for the store. Setting retail prices on the basis of costs will be discussed in Chapter 17.

Cost-plus-percentage-of-cost pricing is used by manufacturers when only one- or few-of-a-kind items are produced. This method was prevalent in World War I when private manufacturers sold ships to the U.S. Navy. If a firm agreed to build a cruiser for the Navy at an estimated cost of $10 million it would add a fixed percentage—say, 10 percent—to the price to produce a profit of $1 million. This encouraged government contractors to increase rather than to reduce their costs. The U.S. General Accounting Office (a watchdog for federal expenditures) described the cost-plus-percentage-of-cost pricing method as "the greatest device ever invented to pump money out of the U.S. Treasury." This pricing method has since been outlawed in federal contracts, but is still widely used in private industry on one- or a few-of-a-kind purchases. For example, an architect who designs a house may charge a fee of 13 percent of the construction costs. Thus, whether the house costs $20,000 or $40,000, the architect's fee remains a fixed 13 percent.

In government purchases of high-technology research items (an Apollo spacecraft or a supersonic transport, for example) so many technical or political problems may arise that no one can estimate the final costs or even be sure if the contract will be completed. This was the case with Boeing and the supersonic transport, which was canceled. In such instances, the government often uses *cost-plus-fixed-fee pricing* in which the fee is a fixed dollar value based on some percentage of the initial estimate of costs. The contracting firm is then paid for all its costs, even if they increase as difficult technical problems arise and are overcome, but its profits remain unchanged. For example, suppose that the North American

Adding a fixed percentage to costs . . .

sets the price in standard-markup pricing . . .

and in cost-plus-percentage-of-cost pricing . . .

. . . but not in cost-plus-fixed-fee pricing

Rockwell Corporation contracted to build its part of the Apollo spacecraft for $4 billion and an assigned profit of $400 million yielding a price of $4.4 billion. If technical problems caused costs to increase to $5 billion, North American would receive payment for all these costs, but its fee would remain fixed at $400 million, yielding a final price of $5.4 billion. Cost-plus-fixed-fee pricing, or some variation of it, is used in virtually all high-technology purchases of aerospace defense systems that the federal government makes today (see "How to Price a Lunar Module").

✔ **Competition-oriented pricing.** Sometimes prices must be set based on what all competitors (the market) or one or a few competitors charge. In such a situation, the pricing methods are said to be competition-oriented.

When a farmer sells wheat or an investor buys or sells shares of a well-known stock, the prices paid or received are determined by the market, and the competition box in Figure 8-7 is dominant. This is called market-determined pricing. In these instances, it is often said that the businesswoman or man is a "price taker" rather than a "price maker," because the market sets the price. If the going market price is $3 for a bushel of wheat of some specific grade and a farmer's wheat is priced at $3.01, the farmer will not sell any wheat, since thousands of other farmers will be selling the same quality of wheat at $3. By the same token, since the individual farmer is such a small factor in the market and can sell all the wheat at $3, lowering the bushel price to $2.99 would be foolish.

Thus, farmers have no control over prices and cannot make pricing decisions. But they are still influenced by demand, cost, and competition. Agricultural publications repeatedly make demand and supply projections for various types of grains. Farmers are keenly concerned about the three determinants of price, for they must decide not only what crops to raise but when to market them.

The wheat our wheat farmer produced was identical to the wheat thousands of other farmers produced. But when manufacturers, wholesalers, and retailers sell products that differ somewhat from substitutes, they may set their own prices according to the prices of their competitors. A firm may set its price at, below, or above the going market price, in which case it is following a strategy of *going-rate pricing, below-market pricing, or above-market pricing,* respectively. Soap and detergent manufacturers often match competitor prices and follow a going-rate policy. As we noted earlier, when the going price is subject to traditional increase—as it was with the 5-cent candy bar of the 1960s—a manufacturer often adjusts the quantity or the quality of a product to retain its customary price. Discount stores and grocery chains traditionally follow a policy of below-market pricing, setting lower prices for their private brands to make them more competitive with national brands. Boutiques and specialty stores often follow a policy of above-market pricing, obtaining premium prices for goods because of the individual attention given to customers and the

HOW TO PRICE A LUNAR MODULE

In 1962, the Grumman Aircraft Corporation was awarded a contract from the National Aeronautics and Space Administration (NASA) to research, design, and build the Lunar Module — the portion of the Apollo spacecraft that would actually land on the moon. Because the design details were vague, Grumman's contract specified a cost-plus-fixed-fee price totaling $350 million.

Less than a year later Grumman informed NASA of severe technical problems and claimed that the original price was too low. A new price of $650 million was negotiated for the Lunar Module contract.

By 1965, it was apparent that the module's price was still too low. Grumman sought a price of $1.27 billion. NASA countered with an offer of $997 million.

Negotiations had reached a stalemate. In early December, the NASA Project Director met with the responsible Grumman vice president to discuss a new contract price. It is said that after much haggling, the NASA Project Director asked what the date was that day. The answer: 12/05/65. The NASA negotiator then said, "Let's add enough zeros to give a reasonable contract price." This was

$$\$1,205,650,000.$$

The Grumman vice president allegedly responded, "Let's not quibble about the thousands. Since Christmas is coming up, let's give each other a present and agree on the date of December 25th." So the proposed price was

$$\$1,225,000,000.$$

They shook hands, and this became the new Lunar Module contract price. Before the last Lunar Module had flown, the price was raised again to $1.6 billion — making the price of each unit about $100 million.

This pricing example illustrates the extreme difficulties that can occur when the U.S. government and its suppliers try to price highly complex technical items.

special services the store provides (for example, free alterations and return privileges). The H.J. Heinz Company traditionally raises prices on its grocery products sooner and higher than competitors. H.J. Heinz once asserted, "Unless you charge a grocer a fair price for quality, he will not appreciate the goods." Company executives take Heinz's advice to heart: in 1974, when Gerber raised its baby-food price by 20 cents per case, Heinz responded with a 23-cent per case increase. And the price held.

Loss-leader pricing, a strategy used by some retail stores, is a policy of advertising well-known goods at prices below the going-rate prices. These advertised goods are only a small fraction of the items carried by the retailer and are intended to attract customers in the hope that they will buy not only the loss leaders but the more conventionally priced goods as well. The weekly "meat specials" offered by supermarkets are a common example of loss-leader pricing.

Sealed-bid pricing, widely used in purchases by local, state, and federal governments, involves developing a precise, written specification of the quality and quantity of the good to be purchased and then requesting interested manufacturers to submit sealed bids. These bids are opened and read aloud, and the contract is awarded to the seller with the lowest bid. This method is intended to provide the government with the lowest price by insuring fair and open competition. The winning bidder must deliver the contracted items at the bid price — even if the contract price does not cover costs.

KEY POINTS TO REMEMBER

1. The place element in the marketing mix refers to all institutions and activities that contribute to delivering goods at the times and to the places consumers desire.

2. Channels of distribution (or marketing channels) are the paths through which goods flow from manufacturers to customers, who may be either business firms or ultimate consumers. Many different channels exist; the type of channel depends mainly on the product.

3. Wholesalers and retailers are the two major kinds of institutions in channels of distribution. These institutions exist because their benefits in terms of the valuable functions they perform for manufacturers outweigh their costs.

4. A wide variety of retailing institutions have developed in the United States to meet consumer needs. Since 1950, new varieties of these institutions include discount houses, vending machines (automatic merchandising), franchises, and discount-catalog showrooms.

5. The price element in the marketing mix is the money and the goods exchanged for the ownership or the use of some assortment of goods and services.

6. Two general sets of factors affect price: demand factors and supply factors. Supply factors include (1) production and marketing costs, and (2) the number of producers of a good.

7. An economic principle regarding customer demand for an item states that as the price of an item falls, the quantity of that item purchased by customers normally rises. This relationship can be shown as a demand curve, which indicates graphically the maximum quantity of a good that customers will buy at each hypothetical price.

8. In addition to the price of the good itself, the demand for a product depends on (1) customer taste; (2) the price and the availability of other products, particularly close substitutes; and (3) customer income.

9. The production and marketing costs of a firm represent the floor under the price set for the firm's products. As prices increase for products manufactured by the firms in an industry, more firms will want to offer products for sale. A supply curve for an industry is a hypothetical description of the maximum quantity of the product offered for sale at various prices by all firms in the industry.

10. Actual price-setting methods often stress one of three basic factors, so that prices are (1) demand-oriented, (2) cost-oriented, or (3) competition-oriented.

QUESTIONS FOR DISCUSSION

1. Retailers offer a variety of services to ultimate consumers. But not all retailers perform all functions for all customers on all purchases. List the functions that *are* and that *are not* performed for the customer by the retailer in each of the following transactions:
   - (a) A purchase at a hardware store of something (the customer isn't sure exactly what) to fasten a wood lath to a concrete wall.
   - (b) A purchase at a supermarket of a box of Screaming Yellow Zonkers, Junior's favorite snack.
   - (c) A purchase of a brand-name refrigerator at a department store.

2. Three general distribution strategies are available to manufacturers of consumer goods: *intensive:* use as many retail outlets to sell the product as possible; *selective:* use only a few retail outlets in one geographic area; and *exclusive:* use only one retail outlet in one geographic area.
   - (a) For each of the three types of consumer goods cited in Chapter 7—convenience, shopping, and specialty goods—which distribution strategy seems most appropriate?
   - (b) Cite specific products to illustrate your answer.

3. Looking at Figure 8-6, suppose that customer tastes changed dramatically and that people began to buy and to wear more shirts. What would (a) the impact be on the demand curve in Figure 8-6, and (b) the impact be on the market price?

4. Suppose a major invention permitted shirt manufacturers to dramatically reduce their production costs. What would (a) the impact be on the supply curve in Figure 8-6, and (b) the impact be on the market price?

5. In this chapter, we discussed two widely used methods of pricing items sold to government agencies: cost-plus-fixed-fee pricing and sealed-bid pricing.
   - (a) What pricing method would be used to buy 100,000 mess kits? To buy the new U.S. Air Force B-1 bomber?
   - (b) Under which pricing method are taxpayers likely to pay a higher price than is called for in the original contract? Why?

SHORT CASES AND PROBLEMS

1. As the president of Evans Products, a small lumber company, you are considering opening a chain of retail outlets to sell your lumber and other building products directly to ultimate consumers. List the advantages and the disadvantages of such a plan compared to continuing to sell to independent lumber retailers. Would you open your own retail outlets based on your assessments? Why?

2. One reason that the nickel telephone call is gone forever is the cost to telephone companies of providing free information to subscribers. Cincinnati Bell, Inc., conducted an experiment in 1974 in which subscribers were allowed to make three free information calls a month and then were charged 20 cents for every additional request for information. Is this pricing strategy a good idea? Justify your answer.

CAREER SELECTION: POSITIONS IN RETAILING AND WHOLESALING

CAREERS IN RETAIL SALES

Retail trade salesworkers interact with customers and assist in purchasing decisions. A thorough knowledge of the merchandise to be sold is essential, especially for such complex products as farm machinery and electrical appliances. Salesworkers must be able to communicate clearly and persuasively. Employers generally hire high-school graduates and provide them with on-the-job training. Promotional opportunities are excellent: many salesworkers advance to jobs as buyers, advertising or personnel administrators, or general managers. Annual salaries average about $7000. The job market is expected to increase moderately due to an increase in consumer income. (*Additional information:* The National Retail Merchants Association; 100 West 31st Street; New York, New York 10001.)

Automobile salesworkers sell new or used cars at automobile dealerships. They determine the kind of car a particular customer wants to buy by asking questions and by discussing automobile displays with the customer. Over 100,000 automobile salesworkers were employed in the mid-1970s — most of them trained on the job by sales managers or experienced salespeople. Normally, a high-school degree is the minimal job requirement. Automobile salesworkers must be tactful, self-confident, and able to express themselves well. Most are paid on a straight-commission basis. Those employed by new-car dealers average earnings of $12,000 annually. The future job outlook is unclear and depends to a major degree on consumer demand for new cars. (*Additional information:* contact local new-car dealers.)

CAREERS IN WHOLESALE SALES

Manufacturers employ **wholesale trade salesworkers to** distribute their products to retail establishments. Salesworkers also check client inventories, advise clients of pricing and advertising strategies, and provide technical assistance with complex products. Salesworkers are generally high-school graduates; to become familiar with the manufacturer's product line, they often work for several years in a selling capacity in the wholesaler's warehouse. Opportunities for advancement to supervisory or management positions are good. Annual salaries range from $9000 to over $15,000. The job market for wholesale trade salesworkers is expected to expand moderately due to increases in population and in consumer income. (*Additional information:* National Association of Wholesaler Distributors; 1725 K Street, N.W.; Washington, D.C. 20006.)

OTHER CAREERS IN RETAILING AND WHOLESALING

Displayers design and install window exhibits in retail stores. Applying their artistic and merchandising talents, displayers devise attractive, enticing showcases to encourage customer purchases. Applicants are usually high-school or college graduates with creative abilities and mechanical aptitude. most employers provide on-the-job training in woodworking, merchandising, and window dressing. An experienced displayer may be promoted to display director or even to general manager. Annual salaries vary from $6000 to $30,000; self-employed displayers may earn even more. Job opportunities are expected to expand moderately, given the increased construction of retail stores. (*Additional information:* contact large local retailers.)

CAREERS IN DEPARTMENT-STORE BUYING

Challenging careers in *department-store buying* exist for both women and men. In most large department-store chains, a sequence of four positions prepare employees for buying careers: (1) *management trainee;* (2) *suburban sales manager;* (3) *assistant buyer;* and (4) *buyer.*

Department stores normally recruit college graduates for the position of **management trainee.** Trainees often have a degree in business administration and a major in marketing or retailing, but students with liberal arts degrees or with degrees in home economics and majors in fasion merchandising are also considered. Management trainees earn about $8500 annually and work in a variety of departments within the store until they are familiar with all aspects of the retail business. Management trainees work as salespeople, learn merchandise display, and perform essential inventory and record-keeping duties.

After six to twelve months of training in a large metropolitan department store, a management trainee is promoted to **suburban sales manager.** In this position, the employee is responsible for promoting and selling — but *not* buying — the merchandise to be carried in a group of related departments in a store located within a suburban shopping center. (For example, related departments might be in the better women's ready-to-wear lines: misses' and women's dresses and suits; young sportswear; the bridal salon). This provides a suburban sales manager with on-the-job ideas about which styles and fashions sell well and which do not. Annual salary ranges from $9000 to $12,000.

After 12 to 18 months as a suburban sales manager, the employee is promoted to the position of **assistant buyer.** The assistant buyer helps the **buyer** to select and order merchandise that is expected to sell well, to negotiate prices and quantities of needed items with the manufacturers' salespeople, and to work with department-store salespeople in planning special sales and promotions. Thus, assistant buyers and buyers make the buying decisions for all or for most of the stores in a department-store chain. An assistant buyer earns $10,000 to $13,000 annually. If job performance is satisfactory, an assistant buyer is promoted to the position of *buyer* after approximately one year. A buyer's annual salary ranges from $14,000 to $30,000, depending on years of experience and on the sales volume of the department a particular buyer serves.

Job opportunities in department-store buying are expected to increase moderately and to be closely related to the growth in both population and disposable consumer income. (*Additional information:* contact the personnel manager of a large, local department store.)

A CRITICAL BUSINESS DECISION

—made by Shri Kumar Poddar

THE SITUATION It is 1963. Shri Kumar Poddar, an engineering student at Michigan State University, decides to start his own business selling magazine subscriptions to supplement his income while studying. No sooner is his new business launched than Poddar is forced to leave MSU's engineering school—only 11 credits short of a degree—partially as a result of failing a course in which he has a personality conflict with the instructor. He transfers to business administration and continues his studies in philosophy, politics, economics, and business.

The son of a Calcutta Shell Oil distributor, Poddar writes to major publishers asking to be their sales agent. *Time, Newsweek, McCall's, Look, Reader's Digest,* and *Mademoiselle* respond favorably. He begins selling subscriptions to MSU students personally. However, Poddar concludes that

STUDENT COURTESY RATES

MAIL YOUR ORDER TODAY. SAVE UP TO 50% ON 37 FINE MAGAZINES (NEW & RENEWAL) BECAUSE YOU ARE A STUDENT. These are the lowest rates available anywhere. (For gift subscriptions ask for special order form). Check magazines you wish to order. Mail today! For renewals, circle "R".

Because Courtesy Rates are so low many single-magazine orders do not cover all our costs. You can help us — and save more money yourself — by ordering at least two magazines at one time.

TIME	TV GUIDE	NEWSWEEK	PSYCH. TODAY	EBONY
1 yr $9 reg $18 R	1yr 7.70reg9.50 R	1yr9.75reg19.50 R	1 yr $6 reg $12 R	1 yr$7.95reg$10 R
27 wks $4.87 R	30 wks $4.44 R	34 wks $6.50 R	2 yr $12 reg $24 R	9 mo $6 reg $7.50 R

FORBES	GLAMOUR	ESSENCE	NEW YORKER	REDBOOK
1 yr $12 reg $15 R	1yr $5.50 reg $9 R	1 yr $5 reg $7 R	1 yr $9 reg $18 R	1yr$5.97reg7.95 R

| 1 yr $5.50 reg $9 R | 1yr$4.97reg5.94 R | 1yr$4.95reg6.95 R | 6 iss $6 reg $6 R | 1 yr $7.50 reg $15 R |

PLAYBOY*	NAT'L. LAMPOON	ESQUIRE	MOTOR TREND	MOTHER EARTH NEWS
1yr$8.50reg$10 R	1 yr $7.95	1 yr $5 reg $10 R	1yr$3.75reg7.50 R	1 yr $8 reg $10 R

STEREO REVIEW — 1 yr $3.99 reg $7.98
POPULAR PHOTO. — 1 yr $3.99 reg $7.98
MODERN PHOTO. — 1 yr $3.98 reg $7.95

ATLANTIC — 1 yr $5.75 reg $11.50
HARPER'S MAG. — 1 yr $4.49 reg $8.97
SATURDAY REV. — 1 yr $10 / 18 iss $6.95

TENNIS — 11 mo 12.77 R / 1 yr $7
BLACK SPORTS — 1 yr $7.20 / 9 mo $5.50
SKIING — 1 yr $10 reg $6.98

ROLLING STONE — 1 yr $12 reg $14
WRITER'S DIGEST — 1 yr $5.95 reg $7.95
WASH. WATCH — 50 iss $10 reg $15

\# mags ordered ___ Enclosed $ ___ Bill Sign Me, Here ___
Miss ☐ Mr ☐ / Mrs ☐ Ms ☐
Address _____ Apt _____
City _____ State _____ Zip _____
☐ Graduate ☐ Undergrad at _____ Yr of Grad _____

*Payment with order only. "When You Think of Magazines, Think of E.S.S." 33

Printed on Partially Recycled Paper.

personal selling restricts his potential revenues and profits. He is anxious to find a low-cost method of reaching college students on campuses across the country.

THE DECISION Poddar calls his new business Educational Subscription Service, Inc., and designs a special subscription card offering "courtesy rates" to students and educators. But Poddar puzzles over the question of how to distribute these cards to his target market—college students and faculty—inexpensively.

Poddar makes his decision and puts it into effect. In an interview with a *New York Times* reporter, Poddar describes the three-point philosophy he follows in running his business. First, he notes, "In my business, there is no personal contact with the customer whatsoever. I am totally opposed to the forced sale of subscriptions." Second, "The magazine-subscription business is not known for its honesty, so the recipe is: be honest." Finally, Poddar confides, "We guarantee the subscriber the lowest price—or he gets a refund."

Apparently Poddar's decision and his straightforward marketing strategy—a low-key sales presentation, honesty, and low prices—make sense. By 1968, Poddar's business is generating annual sales of more than $1 million. In 1971, he opens a 5000-square-foot office to house his ten employees in a business plaza in Lansing, Michigan, about four miles from the MSU campus.

QUESTIONS

1. Identify some of the methods Poddar could have used to distribute his subscription cards to hundreds of thousands of college students and faculty across the United States in 1963.
2. Select the method that you would have used and justify your choice.

221

> I know half of my advertising's wasted, but I don't know which half.
>
> *John Wanamaker*

CHAPTER 9

MARKETING: THE PROMOTIONAL ELEMENT

Charles Bird is a Los Angeles advertising consultant who specializes in reaching the youth market—people in their teens and early 20s. One of his major problems is selecting the appropriate advertising media—magazines, newspapers, television and radio programs—to reach the target market. This is a special problem because American young people do not have the established reading, watching, or listening habits that other Americans do.

Walking through a college campus on the way to give a speech in 1971, Bird noticed that Volkswagens dominated the student parking lot. The observation was eventually to solve his media problem: Bird could suddenly see VW's with national advertisements painted on their sides being driven around cities wherever students traveled. The result: Bird formed "Beetleboards of America" to reach the youth market.

By early 1975, about 1500 VW bugs covered with brightly colored advertising decals were racing around. Drivers are paid $20 per month. Bird's company charges advertisers using 200 cars or more $110 a month per car. Probably the most unusual VW ad is the one for Irish Spring, a deodorant soap. The driver of the car appears to be sitting in the bathtub painted on the side of the car.

So don't be too surprised if on the way to class one morning you stumble upon a Volkswagen masquerading as a billboard. Clearly, this is a creative way to transmit the advertiser's message to the youth market.

Bird's Beetleboards are just one small—but innovative—aspect of *promotion,* the fourth element of the marketing mix. In this chapter, we will turn our attention to the two major components of promotion: advertising and personal selling.

What Is Promotion?

The meaning and components of promotion

Stated very simply, *promotion* is communication between seller and buyer. This communication can be made in various ways, but the two most important forms of promotional communication are advertising (sometimes referred to as mass selling) and personal selling. Other promotional activities—free samples, trading stamps, sweepstakes, cents-off coupons, and trade-show exhibitions among them—represent more specialized methods that are beyond the scope of this book.

Objectives and Methods of Promotion

Promotion seeks to inform, persuade, and remind

The broad general goal of promotion is to increase a firm's sales and profits. To accomplish this, a firm must engage in activities that (1) inform, (2) persuade, and (3) remind customers in the target market about its product. The principal task in promoting a new item is often simply to *inform* prospective customers about the existence of the product, to demonstrate its superiority over potential substitutes, and then to encourage customers to try the product and to form their own opinions. The promotional objective when a product faces competition from close substitutes is generally to *persuade* customers to buy the firm's product rather than another firm's product. If more substitutes appear in the marketplace, the promotional effort is directed toward *reminding* customers of their favorable experience with the product and encouraging them to continue to use it or to return to it if they have switched to another brand.

In Chapter 3, we examined the successive steps that prospective buyers take in making a purchase decision. These steps involve a consumer's prepurchase, purchase, and postpurchase behavior. As shown in Figure 9-1, these three steps are related both to key promotional objectives and to specific forms of advertising. In today's complex world, no one questions the consumer's need for genuine product information. The controversy centers on excesses that have developed in the persuasive and the reminder aspects of promotion — among them high-pressure personal selling, extravagant advertising claims, and annoyingly repetitive radio or television jingles.

Selecting the Right Blend of Promotional Activities

Different promotional methods compete for budget dollars . . .

Various promotional methods compete with one another in a business budget. Given limited promotional funds, a manufacturer that expands its sales force in order to concentrate on personal selling will have to reduce its advertising expenditures. Eventually, however, increased personal selling may lead to greater profits and sales, which in turn may enable the manufacturer to expand both personal selling and advertising. For example, a supermarket that decides to offer trading stamps may be forced to reduce local newspaper advertising; however, if the stamps attract more customers and store revenues increase, the supermarket may then be able to resume newspaper advertising.

. . . but also blend together to support one another

A major goal of promotion is to let consumers in target markets know that a firm's products are available at the right time, place, and price. This calls for selecting the right blend of promotional activities — the combination that best suits the particular produce class and its foothold in the target market. Convenience items such as candy, gum and cigarettes are

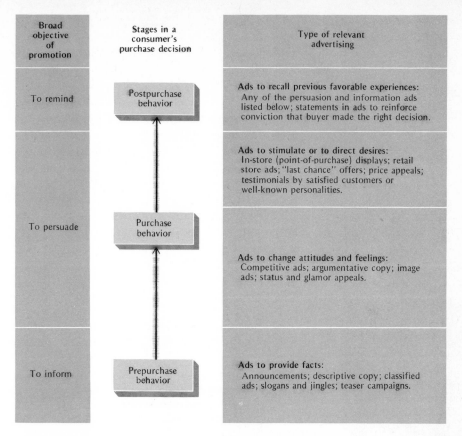

Broad objective of promotion	Stages in a consumer's purchase decision	Type of relevant advertising
To remind	Postpurchase behavior	**Ads to recall previous favorable experiences:** Any of the persuasion and information ads listed below; statements in ads to reinforce conviction that buyer made the right decision.
To persuade	Purchase behavior	**Ads to stimulate or to direct desires:** In-store (point-of-purchase) displays; retail store ads; "last chance" offers; price appeals; testimonials by satisfied customers or well-known personalities. **Ads to change attitudes and feelings:** Competitive ads; argumentative copy; image ads; status and glamor appeals.
To inform	Prepurchase behavior	**Ads to provide facts:** Announcements; descriptive copy; classified ads; slogans and jingles; teaser campaigns.

9-1 Relationship between the steps taken by a prospective buyer in making a purchase decision and key promotional objectives and types of advertising.

Source: Adapted from Robert J. Lavidge and Gary A. Steiner, "A Model for Predictive Measurements of Advertising Effectiveness," *Journal of Marketing* (October 1961), p. 61.

frequently sold by means of extensive advertising campaigns, with minimal personal selling. The opposite promotional blend is used by cosmetic houses and cleaning supply manufacturers that sell door to door. The Avon Products Company employs an interesting combination of advertising ("When your Avon lady calls, welcome her") and personal selling.

The promotion policies of the Hershey Chocolate Corporation, whose milk chocolate bars have dominated U.S. markets for decades, illustrate the influence of the product and its market foothold on the blend of promotional activities adopted. For 66 years, Hershey never advertised in the United States. Finally, faced with increased competition from other candy manufacturers, it ran its first ad in 1970. (In Canada, where Hershey bars are not well known, the company has advertised aggressively for years.)

Advertising

**The meaning
of advertising**

Advertising is any nonpersonal communication between seller and buyer that is conducted through paid media under clear sponsorship. The fact that the communication is nonpersonal distinguishes advertising from personal selling. The use of paid media under clear sponsorship distinguishes advertising from *publicity,* which is favorable news coverage obtained without overt initiation or payment by the firm.

A famous example of the use of publicity in American business was the Ford Motor Company's introduction of the Model A car in the late 1920s. Whenever the Model A was transported from the factory to its testing grounds, it was carefully covered. When public curiosity reached a fever pitch, a few Model A's were uncovered — supposedly for the purpose of being tested on the River Rouge Proving Grounds — and some "enterprising" reporters were naturally on hand to snap a few hazy pictures. The free publicity that resulted was equivalent to millions of dollars of advertising and thousands of orders were placed for the Model A — sight unseen. Apparently, Malcolm Bricklin learned a publicity lesson from Ford. In 1974, when his company introduced the first new mass-produced car in North America in 30 years (named the "Bricklin," of course), the car was so freely publicized by the press that Bricklin canceled all his advertising plans. Publicity is a relatively minor factor in the promotional budget of most firms.

Kinds of Advertising

Although advertising seeks to increase sales and profits, precisely how it does this is not really clear. Martin Mayer observes in his book *Madison Avenue, U.S.A.:* "Only the very brave or the very ignorant . . . can say exactly what advertising does in the marketplace." However, advertising can be classified according to how quickly its effects are felt. The two extremes are direct-action advertising and delayed-action advertising, but many gradations lie between these endpoints.

**Some advertising
seeks immediate sales**

Direct-action advertising, the most common form of retail advertising, seeks an immediate purchase by the potential buyer. Examples are a department store ad announcing a special sale starting at 9:30 A.M. Wednesday morning; a direct-mail ad offering reduced subscription prices on magazines; and radio ads sponsored by car dealers proclaiming a "last chance" to buy a car today at a bargain price. In each case, the advertiser's goal is an immediate sale. The only significant impact of the advertising is on prospective buyers who respond a few hours or days after the ad appears.

In contrast, *delayed-action advertising,* the approach commonly used by manufacturers, seeks not immediate sales but long-range effects such as improved brand awareness, increased product preference, and a more favorable company image. This type of advertising is designed to influence the attitudes of potential buyers, gradually encouraging them to take a more positive view of the company and its product so that eventually they become brand-loyal, repeat customers. Competitive products and short memories tend to reduce customer loyalty to a product. Examples of delayed-action advertising are beer commercials during timeouts in professional football games and magazine advertisements sponsored by automobile manufacturers. Sponsors generally do not expect immediate sales from their ads; instead, they try to create a favorable image for prospective customers so that the next time they purchase the advertised product class—whether it is in a month (beer) or in five years (an automobile)—they will remember the specific brand and buy it.

Other advertising seeks long-run changes in awareness, preference, or company image

Steps in Developing an Advertising Campaign

In contrast to the single advertisement (the nonpersonal communication itself), an *advertising campaign* represents the entire process involved in directing one or more advertisements at the target market. Whatever the size of the advertiser or the nature of the product, in order to develop an effective campaign, a firm must follow the systematic series of steps outlined in Figure 9-2. To make this discussion more meaningful, we will apply these steps to the advertising decisions made by two different-sized operations: a small shoe store and the Ford Motor Company's Pinto division.

9-2 Steps in developing an advertising campaign.

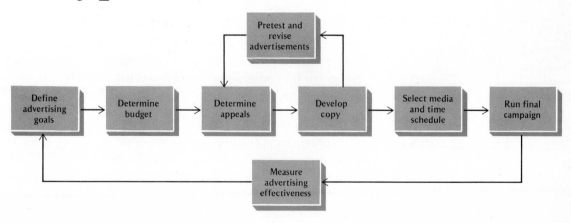

✔ **Defining advertising goals.** The first step in an effective advertising campaign is to define its goals or objectives as precisely as possible. There are two reasons for this. First, unless the marketing manager has a specific goal in mind, the money earmarked for advertising might be better spent on other elements of the marketing mix. Second, precise goals serve as meaningful benchmarks for measuring the effectiveness of the campaign after it has been conducted.

What are precisely defined goals? The shoe retailer might decide to conduct a direct-action advertising campaign aimed at selling an additional 100 pairs of shoes in a given week. In contrast, Ford might focus on a delayed-action campaign directed at long-run changes in consumer awareness. Suppose that in 1975 only 60 percent of American males over 18 (the target market) knew about Ford's small car, the Pinto. Ford's goal for the delayed-action campaign might be to raise this prospective buyer awareness to 70 percent.

✔ **Determining the budget.** The second step in developing an effective advertising campaign is to allocate an annual advertising budget among individual advertising efforts. This is a recurring problem for most firms. Advertising authorities identify four widely used methods for determining expenditures on annual advertising budgets or individual campaigns:

Affordable method: Set the budget at a "reasonable" level that the firm can afford after meeting other expenses.

Percentage-of-sales method: Set the budget at a specific percentage of sales occurring in a particular period (last year, last month, or as estimated for the coming year or month).

Competitive-parity method: Set the budget at the level that competitors spend for similar time periods or campaigns.

Objective-and-task method: Set specific advertising goals, define the tasks required to achieve them, and estimate the cost of performing these tasks. This cost is the estimated advertising budget.

All of the first three approaches have the advantage of simplicity, but each fails to recognize the important contribution that effective advertising can make to sales. As applied, these methods look backward rather than forward. For example, suppose that a firm using the competitive-parity method knows that other firms in the industry usually spend $1 million a year on advertising. If this firm plans to introduce a completely new line of products next year, past levels of advertising may be largely irrelevant. In contrast, the objective-and-task method forces the business-owner to look ahead and to assess the benefits and the costs of advertising.

Thus, our shoe store owner may find that in order to sell 100 extra pairs of shoes he has to be willing to spend $100 for advertising. He therefore sets $100 as his budget.

To understand how Ford arrives at a budget for Pinto, we should first examine Figure 9-3, which gives the national media expenditures of the ten leading U.S. advertisers in 1974. The figure illustrates the sizable amounts of money that some American firms spend on advertising as well as the wide variation in these expenditures as a percentage of a firm's sales. In particular, note that a number of firms in the drug and cosmetic industry (Bristol-Myers, American Home Products, Sterling Drug) and in the soap cleanser and allied products industry (Procter & Gamble, Colgate-Palmolive) have advertising expenditures exceeding 3 and in some cases 7 percent of sales. Critics argue that firms in these industries should reduce advertising expenditures in order to lower prices or to raise quality.

Some advertising
budgets exceed
10 percent of sales

Automobile manufacturers usually set their annual advertising budget for each car model in relationship to a fixed percentage of that model's selling price (a variation of the percentage-of-sales method). Figure 9-3 indicates that Ford spends about .4 percent of its sales on national advertising. For simplicity, we will assume that Ford's average selling price for a Pinto is $3000 and that expected annual sales are 100,000 cars. Thus, Ford's projected national advertising budget for the Pinto would be $1.2 million annually ($3000 per car x 100,000 cars x .004). An individual campaign budget is then set at some proportion of this total annual budget.

9-3   The ten leading U.S. advertisers in national media, 1974.

Rank	Firm	1974 advertising expenditures*	1974 sales	Advertising expenditures as a percentage of sales
1	Procter & Gamble Company	$246,433,800	$ 4,912,279,000	5.0
2	General Motors Corporation	173,885,100	31,549,546,000	.6
3	General Foods Corporation	146,465,000	2,986,692,000	4.9
4	Bristol-Myers Company	125,844,800	1,590,949,000	7.9
5	American Home Products Corporation	123,424,400	2,048,741,000	6.0
6	Sears Roebuck and Company	106,031,600	13,101,210,000	.8
7	R.J. Reynolds Industries	100,883,800	3,229,668,000	3.1
8	Ford Motor Company	97,755,400	23,620,600,000	.4
9	Colgate-Palmolive Company	92,467,300	2,615,448,000	3.5
10	Sterling Drug, Inc.	83,388,600	870,491,000	9.6

Sources: 1974 advertising expenditures reprinted by permission of *Advertising Age* (June 30, 1975), p. 56; copyright 1975 by Crain Communications Inc. 1974 sales from list of 500 largest manufacturing firms published by *Fortune* (May 1975).

✔ **Determining appeals.** Once an advertiser has defined advertising goals and set a budget, the right advertising appeals for the campaign must be determined. An *advertising appeal* is a theme intended to trigger buying decisions or to project a better company image in the target market. A given campaign may appeal to a consumer's reason (for example, emphasizing high quality at a low price) or to a consumer's emotions (promising a certain brand will give a radiant new smile). Since the shoe store owner's goal is immediate sales, let us assume that he decides to issue a straightforward price appeal: "In the next week, all shoe prices will be reduced $2."

Automobile companies have stressed virtually every type of appeal at one time or another: appeals to status (a Rolls Royce ad that uses the F. Scott Fitzgerald quotation "Let me tell you about the very rich; they are different from you and me"); appeals to economy (the Volkswagen series of "Think Small" ads); and appeals to a better life (the Edsel campaign pointed toward "the young executive on the way up"). Automobile firms have also stressed a wide variety of product features, including chromium-plated fins and other fittings (Detroit cars in the 1950s), power (Detroit cars in the 1960s), and lack of styling changes (Volkswagen throughout its history). Let us assume that Ford decides to focus its delayed-action campaign on how easy the Pinto is to repair, with an emphasis on do-it-yourself maintenance.

✔ **Developing copy.** The next step in an effective advertising campaign is to translate the selected appeals into *advertising copy*—the communication that the prospective buyer actually sees or hears (on billboards, on television or radio, in magazines or newspapers, and so on). Copy development involves answering the following kinds of questions:

1. Would a testimonial by a well-known personality or by a testing agency best present the appeal?
2. Should the copy stress pictures rather than words?
3. What specific pictures and words should be used?
4. What layout is most pleasing aesthetically?
5. Is the message clear and understandable to the target market audience?
6. Will the copy accomplish the goals set for it?

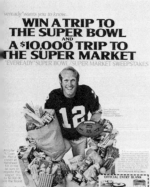

These are the tasks that creative advertising personnel attempt to perform.

For the shoe store, the copy may be a simple, straightforward ad written by a copywriter at a local newspaper. For the Ford Pinto, the task of copy development is far more complex, since it involves advertising that will be seen by tens of millions of people. The copy will probably be developed by an advertising agency hired by Ford. Let us say that the agency develops advertising copy that shows how a young woman can change a damaged Pinto grill in 30 minutes.

As indicated in Figure 9-2, advertising appeals and copy should be pretested before they are incorporated in a final, full-blown campaign. In the case of the shoe store ad, this may merely mean showing a draft of the ad to the owner to verify that it is clear and factually accurate. In the case of the Pinto ad, pretesting may involve showing alternate versions of the ad to several hundred consumers to determine which ad is most likely to achieve the goals set for it.

Good copy is
hard to write

What makes good advertising copy? Although opinions differ, many advertising copywriters suggest the following set of criteria: an ad should be attention-getting, easy to read and to understand, believable, and informative. Of course, there are other important factors. An ad could score well on each of these counts and yet fail to gain attention and interest in the target market because these aspects are imperfectly blended.

We can illustrate the difficulties of writing effective advertising copy with an example. Figure 9-4 shows two Honda motorbike advertisements that appeared in national magazines in the mid-1960s, at a time when Honda sought to make its motorbike an inexpensive form of transportation for "respectable" people. Each was a full-page advertisement in four colors. Subsequent interviews with magazine subscribers indicated that one advertisement generated more reader interest than the other. Study the two ads and their copy in Figure 9-4. Overall, which of the two ads do you think is better? Why? (Note that discussion question 1 at the end of the chapter asks you to evaluate both ads on the basis of each of the four criteria mentioned above. You may be surprised to find that the ad you rated highly in one or two areas—such as attention-getting or believability —may not be the better one overall!)

The Starch Advertisement Readership Service evaluated the two Honda ads and found that ad A was better: more readers "noted" this ad and read at least half of its copy. Philip Ward Burton notes that ad B was the last ad in which Honda used art instead of photography. This is an important point: photographs show product details much more clearly—a major advantage in attracting the attention and interest of consumers in the target market. Another important difference: putting Santa and the other fanciful characters in ad B apparently made it less believable. Burton also observes that these were two of the first ads in Honda's all-out effort to change motorcycling's bad image. Note that the word "motorcycle" is never used. Instead, the reader sees a Honda "motorbike" that is utilitarian, fun, and used by "nice" people.

✔ **Selecting media and time schedule.** The next task in developing an effective advertising campaign is to select (1) the media in which the advertisements will appear, and (2) their timing. *Advertising media* are the vehicles through which an ad is communicated to the target market. Possible advertising media include magazines, newspapers, radio, television, billboards, novelties (calendars, key chains), direct mail (brochures, letters), bus and train posters, and catalogs.

You meet the nicest people on a Honda

A bit of social climbing is in order. Hondas are definitely fashionable.

They never gulp gas. Just sip it: 200 miles to the gallon. They are soft-spoken even at 45 mph.

The 4-stroke, 50cc engine is a model of self-reliance. Practically looks after itself.

Other rewarding qualities include: 3-speed transmission, automatic clutch, cam-type brakes on both wheels. Even an optional pushbutton starter.

The price is a reasonable $245, plus a modest set-up charge. A Honda 50 might help you skip a few rungs on the ladder.

For the address of your nearest dealer or other information, write: American Honda Motor Co., Inc., Dept. AV, 100 West Alondra, Gardena, California.

HONDA world's biggest seller!

A   B

9-4 Two advertisements for Honda motorbikes. Did the single photograph or the several drawings attract more reader interest? For the answer, see the text.

Source: Philip Ward Burton, *Which Ad Pulled Best?* Marketing/Communications College Workbook Series (New York: Decker Communications, 1969), p. 69.

A   Text of advertisement

A bit of social climbing is in order. Look around. Hondas are definitely fashionable.

They never gulp gas. Just sip it: 200 miles to the gallon. Soft spoken even at 45 mph.

The 4-stroke, 50cc engine is a model of self-reliance. Practically looks after itself.

Other rewarding qualities include: 3-speed transmission, automatic clutch, cam-type brakes on both wheels. Even an optional pushbutton starter.

The price is a reasonable $245, plus a modest set-up charge. A Honda 50 might help you skip a few rungs on the ladder.

For address of your nearest dealer or other information, write: American Honda Motor Co., Inc., Dept. BZ, 100 West Alondra, Gardena, Calif.

B   Text of advertisement

Maybe it's the incredibly low price ($245 plus a modest set-up charge). Or the fact it doesn't gulp gas. Just sips it — 200 miles to the gallon. Or the way the masterful 4-stroke 50cc OHV engine carries you along at 45 mph without a murmur.

Or it could be the ease of 3-speed transmission, automatic clutch, and the extra safety of Honda's cam-type brakes on both wheels. The optional pushbutton starter makes you feel right at home, too.

But most likely it's the fun. Evidently nothing catches on like the fun of owning a Honda. You see so many around these days. And the nicest people riding them. Merry Christmas. For address of your nearest dealer or other information, write: Dept. AA, American Honda Motor Co., Inc., 100 West Alondra, Gardena, Calif.

The shoe store owner with a campaign budget of $100 has a limited number of media choices. If his store is in a small town, he may consider having handbills delivered directly to homes in the store's trading area or taking an ad in the local daily newspaper. If the store is in a suburb of a major metropolitan area, the owner may decide to run an ad in the weekly suburban newspaper. Since most metropolitan newspapers publish separate editions for different geographic areas, the shoe store owner can place ads in whatever regions he desires. Depending upon cost, he may select one or more of these media.

The selection of media for the Pinto campaign is much more complex. Since potential buyers of the Pinto are geographically dispersed, national as well as local media may be needed to reach the target market. Competing manufacturers differ in their opinions as to what media most effectively reach their target markets. For example, while Ford, General Motors, and Volkswagen all compete for the American small-car market, they allocate their media expenditures somewhat differently. Ford devotes the largest share of its total budget to network television; General Motors allocates a significant portion of its budget to television but also advertises heavily on radio. Volkswagen stresses general magazine and outdoor advertising much more than either Ford or General Motors; these two media, which sometimes use similar copy, are areas in which Volkswagen has had unparalleled success.

How should Ford select the proper media for advertising the Pinto? There are two aspects to this question. First, how does Ford choose among various media (for example, television versus radio versus magazines)? Second, within one medium, how does Ford select a specific vehicle for its message (for example, in choosing among magazines, should Ford select *Time, TV Guide,* or *Reader's Digest*)? A simplified answer to both questions is that Ford must consider (1) which medium presents its particular message best, and (2) which medium delivers the greatest target-market audience for the least cost. In determining the most effective medium, Ford must take into account the appeal of the advertising campaign. For example, if new colors and new styling are to be stressed, a four-color magazine ad would certainly be preferable to a radio ad and probably even a television ad. However, if cornering and smooth-riding features are to be emphasized, a television ad would probably demonstrate this better than a magazine ad. Let us assume that the feature Ford has chosen to highlight — the Pinto's do-it-yourself maintenance — can be displayed with equal effectiveness in a magazine or a television ad.

In regard to cost, Ford must weigh the cost of advertising in each medium against the number of consumers reached by that medium. Figure 9-5 shows the actual costs of advertising on some network television spots and in three magazines with large circulations. As high as these prices appear, special situations can prompt even higher advertising costs: one minute on the Superbowl Game costs over $200,000. Before reaching a

TRENDS IN MAGAZINE ADS IN THE 1970s

Advertising Age, the weekly news magazine serving the advertising industry, asked William Tyler to identify trends in creative strategy in magazine advertising during the first half of the 1970s. First, he cited some types of magazine ads that appeared less frequently:

● Fewer wacky and humorous ads. Radio and television continued on their merry, unconventional, funny ways. Magazines did not.

● Not many "informative ads" — ones with a lot of written copy loaded with product detail. This is surprising, because the Federal Trade Commission encourages advertisements that make more information available to consumers. When informative ads (such as the Mercedes ad shown below) were used, Tyler observed that "the sales response was immediate and all but overwhelming."

Then Tyler identified some of the types of magazine ads that appeared more frequently:

● Ads that did a better job of presenting a clear, concise product benefit or point of difference in graphic terms. Tyler's vote for possibly the best ad of the period was the Volkswagen ad (shown below)

that appeared right after man's first moon landing but didn't even show a Volkswagen: it didn't have to because the copy ("It's ugly, but it gets you there.") hit the main target point — reliability. Another example: American Tourister's ad of a car running over its suitcase without damaging the contents (not shown). And a third example: General Electric's dishwasher that was guaranteed to remove the remains of a burnt-on omelet from a frying pan — along with GE's promise to take the dishwasher back if it didn't (ad not shown).

● More ads devoted to the public interest. Examples: Allstate took off after the drunk driver (opposite page) and Continental Insurance ran a "shocker ad" pointing out the loopholes in state driving requirements (ad not shown).

● More use of "supportive" ads designed to reinforce recollection of effective television commercials. Two examples based on dramatic scenes from commercials: Volvo's "Are you in the market for a hardtop?" (opposite page), and Volkswagen's ad showing a car floating on a lake (ad not shown).

These ads illustrate the diverse creative strategies available to effective advertising copywriters.

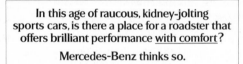

In this age of raucous, kidney-jolting sports cars, is there a place for a roadster that offers brilliant performance <u>with comfort</u>?

Mercedes-Benz thinks so.

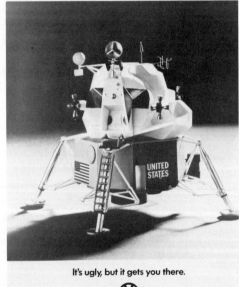

It's ugly, but it gets you there.

decision, Ford will also consider recent Nielsen data (discussed in Chapter 6), which provide an estimate of the number of sets tuned to each television program, and magazine circulation data. The next step is to arrive at some common denominator to compare the potential results of television and magazine advertising. Two widely used measures are cost per thousand households viewing a particular TV program and cost per thousand household circulation of a magazine. For simplicity, we will assume that there is one member of Ford's target market (males over 18) watching each television set or reading each magazine. On the basis of the information given in the right-hand column in Figure 9-5, Ford's best television buy on a cost-per-thousand basis would be "Chico and the Man" (at $3.95 per thousand television households apiece); for magazine advertising, Ford's best choice would be a full-page black and white ad in *TV Guide* (at $2.23 per thousand circulation).

TV Guide: a good buy at $43,300 per page

From this starting point, advertisers must rely on their own judgments (sometimes assisted by computers). Problems exist because no one can be exactly sure how many members of the target market see a particular television show or magazine ad. For example, the audience for "The Mary Tyler Moore Show" might consist primarily of women and children and contain few adult men (the target market). Another consideration in choosing between television and magazine advertising is that exposure to a television ad once run is lost forever (unless the ad is run again). In contrast, an ad in *TV Guide* may be seen several times as readers refer to the magazine during the week. For practical purposes, Ford will undoubtedly hedge its bets, selecting several different media and vehicles within each

9-5   Cost of advertising on selected network television programs and in selected general-interest magazines, 1975.

Advertising medium		Advertising vehicle	Cost per minute or per issue	Number of viewing households or total circulation	Cost per thousand households or per thousand circulation
Network television	Sports	NFL Football, Monday evening (ABC)	$100,000	12,950,000	$ 7.72
		NBA Basketball, Sunday afternoon (CBS)	16,000	3,290,000	4.86
		NFL Football, Sunday afternoon (NBC)	49,200	11,510,000	4.27
	Comedies	Chico and the Man, Friday evening (NBC)	78,000	19,730,000	3.95
		Sanford and Son, Thursday evening (NBC)	100,000	21,240,000	4.70
		Mary Tyler Moore Show, Saturday evening (CBS)	93,600	14,930,000	6.26
General magazines	Full-page, four-color	*Reader's Digest*	63,620	18,000,677	3.53
		TV Guide	55,000	19,382,471	2.84
		Time	46,460	4,307,638	10.79
	Full-page, black and white	*Reader's Digest*	52,915	18,000,677	2.94
		TV Guide	43,300	19,382,471	2.23
		Time	29,975	4,307,638	6.96

Source: The A.C. Nielsen Company.

medium. In 1975–76, Ford actually purchased network time on the three sports shows and in all three of the magazines listed in Figure 9-5.

Once the media have been selected, the advertiser must determine the frequency with which a specific ad should be run. Television ads are often run dozens of times; magazine ads are occasionally run in subsequent issues of the same magazine, but more often they are run in different magazines. The goal of this repetition is to reinforce the consumer's desire to buy the product or their awareness or image of the product or sponsor.

The final campaign

✔ **Running the final campaign.** After identifying the target market, determining the right advertising appeals, arranging for the ad copy to be written, selecting the media, and choosing the times to run the ad, the advertiser must await results. Depending on the preliminary results of the ad and on the goal of the campaign, the sponsor may take special action to terminate or to extend the campaign. Suppose, for example, that the owner of the shoe store plans to run a direct-action advertisement in three issues of the local newspaper; if he experiences no significant sales increase after the first two ads have appeared, he may decide to cancel the third ad. On the other hand, Ford may plan to run its delayed-action campaign on the Pinto for three months; if at the end of six weeks consumer awareness of the Pinto has increased to a greater degree than originally anticipated, Ford may decide to extend the campaign to four months. In general, however, when the immediate results correspond to the initial predictions, the advertising campaign continues to run according to the predetermined plan.

✔ **Measuring advertising effectiveness.** The final step in a well-organized advertising campaign is measuring the effectiveness of the advertising. As the feedback loop in Figure 9-2 indicates, this step is intended to assist the advertiser in assessing the value of the campaign, eliminating wasted effort, and applying past experience to future campaigns.

To judge advertising effectiveness, a comparison of actual results and intended goals must be made. The shoe store owner's original advertising goal was to sell 100 additional pairs of shoes during the following week. He actually sells 120 more pairs and judges the campaign to be a success. In this direct-action campaign, the owner may carry the analysis beyond sales to actual profits. Actual advertising cost was $100. Assume that the owner normally sells 40 pairs of shoes a week at an average profit of $5 per pair; thus, the average profit on each pair of shoes sold in the sale week is $3 ($5 less the $2 price reduction). To determine his profit margin, the owner multiplies 120 pairs of shoes by $3 and subtracts the $100 advertising cost and the $80 lost in profits on the 40 pairs of shoes that would nor-

HOW XEROX DEFENDED AN ADVERTISING CLAIM

In 1960, Xerox prepared to promote its first copier (the 914) with an advertising budget that was completely inadequate compared to larger competitors. So Xerox sought advertising appeals and copy "having the unique and fresh approach" characteristic of the product and limited its media choices to business magazines.

The first ad, run in *Fortune* and *Business Week*, was spectacular: a six-page, four-color gatefold with a hole that permitted the reader "to look in at the working deck" of the Xerox 914 copier. The advertising campaign was a tremendous success. It generated not only many product inquiries but also a lot of free publicity in editorials in business and advertising periodicals that complimented the ad's originality.

An important "point of difference" featured in this early ad was the 914's unique ability to make copies on any kind of paper. This prompted a Washington official to write a severe letter demanding proof of Xerox's advertising claim. Because such a letter from a high government official implied that some federal agency might take action to contest the advertising claim, the letter was shown to Xerox's legal counsel, Sol Linowitz.

Linowitz asked a technician, "Our machine *can* copy on any kind of paper, can't it?"
"Of course," the technician assured him.
"If you fed the machine a paper bag, could it make a copy on that?"
"No reason it shouldn't"
"Fine," Linowitz said. "Copy this letter on an ordinary bag and mail it back without comment to the man who wrote it."

And that's what Xerox did. They heard nothing more from Washington.

mally have been sold during the week without the price reduction of $2. Conclusion: the advertising campaign contributed $180 to profits.

Evaluating the success of Ford's delayed-action campaign is more difficult, since a relatively tangible measure like sales or profits is not available. Instead, Ford conducts a consumer survey and finds that consumer awareness of the Pinto in the target market has increased by 15 percent. The campaign is therefore judged a success, since Ford's goal was an increase of 10 percent or more. In light of the advertising appeal chosen (do-it-yourself maintenance), Ford might have selected as a goal "increased awareness of the ease of maintenance" and used this as a measure of effectiveness. The principal problem with intangible measures of advertising effectiveness — such as changes in consumer awareness, consumer attitudes, and product image — is that their link to sales and profits, the ultimate goal of advertising, is uncertain.

Advertising is alive with stories about the success of particular campaigns. The hard-sell television campaigns of Rosser Reeves, chairman of the board of the Ted Bates Advertising Company, during the late 1950s and 1960s are legendary. Reeves devised a one-minute commercial that illustrated the effectiveness of Anacin in relieving headaches, which were depicted as pounding hammers, coiled springs, and lightning bolts. This ad, which cost $8400 to produce, raised Anacin sales from $18 million to $54 million in a single year. Over the years, Anacin spent more than $86 million running the commercial on television. Rolaids replaced Tums as the number-one antacid tablet when a Reeves ad showed hydrochloric acid burning holes in cloth, accompanied by an offstage voice saying: "Rolaids absorbs 47 times its weight in stomach acid." Sales of Bic ballpoint pens soared after a Reeves commercial demonstrated that the pens could still write after being shot from crossbows through a two-inch-thick wooden board.

These examples are intended to emphasize one point. Using the systematic procedure illustrated in Figure 9-2 to develop an advertising campaign reduces uncertainty and increases the chances of a successful campaign. However, because of unpredictable reactions by customers in the target market, specific campaigns often succeed or fail beyond an advertiser's wildest dreams.

How good was the campaign? Measuring advertising effectiveness

Personal Selling

Personal selling is any personal communication between seller and buyer that is performed by a person who represents the seller. Thus, the personal selling may be conducted by an employee of a firm or by an agent representing a firm. For example, a customer might go to the United Airlines ticket counter at an airport to buy a flight ticket from a sales representative employed by the airline. Or the customer might purchase the ticket from a travel agent who represents United Airlines but who is not a direct employee. In either case, personal selling is involved.

Kinds of Sales Jobs

Sales jobs can be divided into four main categories, which we will discuss below.

✔ **Manufacturer's sales representatives.** This category covers a diverse group of salespeople that represents both industrial and consumer goods producers. For example, it includes technical sales representatives who are engineers employed by industrial goods manufacturers to call on other manufacturers and help them solve technical problems. It also includes salespeople employed by consumer goods manufacturers to call on wholesalers, retailers, and — occasionally — consumers.

✔ **Wholesaler's sales representatives.** A wholesaler stocks many items from different manufacturers. Thus, a wholesaler's salespeople serve retailers and other customers who find it more convenient to place one consolidated order for small quantities of many items rather than to send separate small orders to each manufacturer.

Salespeople operate at all levels in a marketing channel

✔ **Retail sales representatives.** This category represents the largest portion of sales occupations. It includes all salespeople who sell consumer goods to customers in retail stores.

✔ **Direct sales representatives.** These salespeople usually sell a single product or product line directly to consumers either in person or by phone. Examples are insurance salespeople, stock-and-bond brokers, and door-to-door sales representatives like those employed by the Fuller Brush Company and Avon Products, Inc.

From these job descriptions, we can see that sales representatives perform marketing and communications functions throughout every stage of a channel of distribution. Several selling occupations will be explored in more detail in the "Career Selection" section at the end of this and later chapters.

The Professional Salesperson

For many people, personal selling has a bad connotation. Yet, professionalism in personal selling is crucial to American business for one key reason: the salesperson is the customer's problem solver.

Objectives of the professional salesperson. Through hard work and integrity, many salespeople have attained the reputation of professional people. The professional salesperson generally follows these guidelines:

1. Focus on the customer's needs.
2. Provide personal service.
3. Solve the customer's product, economic, or personal (style, aesthetic, etc.) problems.
4. Sell only the items that you feel are *good* for the customer.
5. Recommend a competitor's product if you believe it will satisfy the customer's needs better than your own product.
6. Establish a long-term relationship with the customer that will result in repeat business.

A key to effective selling: the customer's needs

Note that these professional objectives apply to all of the sales jobs cited earlier, and they apply at all levels in a channel of distribution.

The salesperson's role in marketing. We have already identified one key role of the salesperson: to act as problem solver for the customer. But a number of other important factors are related to the salesperson's role. For example, salespeople are especially vital because to most customers they are "the company"—the only contact customers ever have with the firm. Also, salespeople form communications links up and down the marketing channel. Thus, a technical salesperson not only demonstrates how a product can solve a customer's problems but at the same time transmits customers' suggestions for new products back to the firm. Depending on the type of selling job, a salesperson may perform a number of other important functions for customers, such as transporting goods, checking on delayed orders, and finding lenders to finance a purchase. Generally, the greater the number and the complexity of the functions a salesperson provides for customers, the higher the salesperson's compensation.

Steps in the Selling Process

As shown in Figure 9-6, the selling process involves four main steps: prospecting, presale preparation, sales presentation, and postsale follow-up. However, not all salespeople are involved with all four selling phases; retail salespeople, in particular, are usually concerned only with sales preparation.

Prospecting. *Prospecting* consists of searching for and identifying potential buyers—individuals or firms that have the need for and the ability and authority to buy the product or service sold by the salesperson. More precisely, prospecting means identifying the target market in specific terms — by name and address or telephone number — so that an eventual sales presentation can be made. In practice, this is a difficult task. Insurance salespeople must research the names of prospects who are likely to need additional insurance. Technical salespeople handling machine tools must develop lists of factories that could use their equipment. Depending on the kind of selling involved, salespeople may find prospects by researching in libraries, studying published corporate data, reviewing lists of old customers in company files, obtaining referrals from satisfied customers, following up on advertising inquiries, and so on.

✔ **Presale preparation.** Salespeople seldom encounter customers who have just been waiting to be called so that they can buy a product. Thus, *presale preparation* involves two main steps. The first step is to find out everything possible about the specific prospect's potential needs and how these needs may be met by the sales products. The salesperson must understand the potential customer's unique requirements well enough to anticipate how the proposed product can help to solve the prospect's problems. The second step is to arrange a specific interview, either with or without a prior appointment.

✔ **Sales presentation.** The *sales presentation* is a direct communication between salesperson and prospective customer that is intended to complete a sale. Allan L. Reid, a professional salesman, divides the sales presentation into the following five steps (also summarized in Figure 9-6):

9-6   Steps in the selling process.

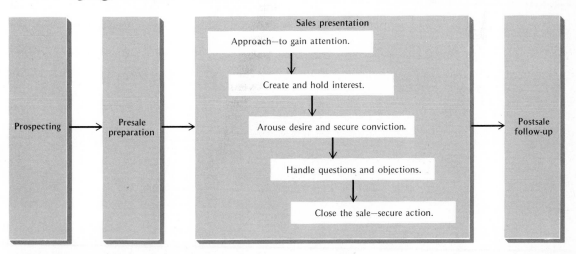

Source: Adapted from Allan L. Reid, *Modern Applied Salesmanship* (Pacific Palisades, Calif.: Goodyear Publishing Company, Inc., 1970), pp. 159-213.

HOW SUCCESSFUL SALESPEOPLE SELL

Successful salespeople tailor the four-step selling process shown in Figure 9-6 to meet their own unique selling abilities and situations. Thus, their creative talents are often focused on very specific elements of one selling step. Each of the following case examples illustrates an individual approach to one step in the selling process.

✔ **Prospecting.** Benjamin Feldman is an agent for the New York Life Insurance Company. He lives in East Liverpool, a city of 20,000 in southeastern Ohio. *Fortune* magazine describes him as "a stocky, amiable man, with a deceptively sleepy appearance" who "by almost everybody's reckoning, . . . is the greatest life insurance salesman in history." In 32 years, Feldman has personally sold more life insurance than most of the country's insurance firms have on their books! In recent years, he has been averaging $50 million in annual sales; his best year was 1971 when he sold $65,000,000.

Feldman left a $10 a week delivery job in 1939 to take an insurance firm's aptitude test. He flunked! And then proceeded to demonstrate his selling abilities by convincing the firm to hire him anyway.

One secret to Feldman's success is his approach to prospecting: he focuses almost exclusively on a very specific target market—the principal owners of private businesses. His reasons: because these owners have personal businesses representing substantial assets that cannot be easily converted to cash, they have the greatest need for large amounts of life insur-

Kenneth Dayton

ance. Feldman explains that an executor for a deceased person who owned an uninsured business might have to sell the business to pay estate taxes; with insurance the business can be passed on to heirs.

✔ **Presale preparation.** Kenneth Dayton is Chairman of the Board of the Dayton-Hudson Corporation, a nationwide retail chain of department, discount, and specialty stores. Early in his career, Dayton was a tie salesman in a department store in downtown Minneapolis.

He credits his success in selling to the lessons he learned from observing customers as they made their buying decisions. Dayton studied his customers' needs and observed that they really wanted help and recommendations in selecting ties. Yet the customers often remained indecisive, even when they felt the purchase of a tie was suitable. Based on these observations, Dayton planned a presale preparation strategy that could be planned before a prospective buyer walked up to the counter. His objective: "Get customers narrowed down to two ties—not one. This way they choose between two and buy one. Otherwise, the choice is between one and none at all."

This technique can also be used in scheduling sales appointments. The response to "Would you have time to see me tomorrow?" is likely to be "no." But "Which would be a better time to meet—9:15 Monday morning or 3:30 Wednesday afternoon?" will probably result in a scheduled appointment.

Benjamin Feldman

Joan Thomas

✔ **Sales presentation.** Real-estate agent Joan Thomas drove a young couple past several houses in Westfield, New Jersey—a New York City suburb. When they found a house they liked, the husband spent 15 minutes looking through it; the wife took 25 minutes. The result: the sale of an $80,000 home.

But all sales aren't that easy—even for Joan Thomas, who sold more than $1 million worth of real estate in 1973. "A lot of luck is involved," she says. "You have to have the right house at the right time." For example, one family needed a basement at least 40 feet by 23½ feet because they were building their own airplane.

Thomas credits her success in selling to working hard, being systematic, and listening to what customers say—a vital part of the sales presentation. She works an average of 50 hours per week and knows the houses in her area well. She keeps a record of the few sales she loses "so I don't make the same mistake again." And Thomas is a good listener. She stresses the importance of "understanding what people are looking for. You can almost get vibrations from them after seeing several houses." She is also quick to spot the signals that indicate serious interest in a house. "When customers start finding fault with a house, that's when you know they are ready to buy," Thomas says. "When they say a house is 'so nice,' that means they aren't interested."

✔ **Postsale follow-up.** Mehdi Fakharzadeh, a 52-year-old Iranian, was the top salesman for the giant Metropolitan Life Insurance Company in 1973. His office is in New York City. *Fortune* magazine observes that "of all the big-time insurance salesmen,

Mehdi must surely qualify on the most improbable. For although he has lived half his life in the U.S., he still struggles with the English language . . . and his accent renders some of his comments nearly unfathomable." Since hardly anyone can handle his last name, he is known to almost everyone simply as "Mehdi."

Mehdi's success lies in his extraordinary instinct for serving his clients personally. In the process of postsale follow-up, they grow to trust him, buy more insurance themselves, and eagerly provide the names of friends and relatives who might be insurance prospects. Such personal follow-up also pays Mehdi rich rewards. Several years ago a Metropolitan client had a heart attack. While recovering, he inquired about a provision in his insurance contract that allowed him to waive premium payments for the period that he was bedridden. The agent who had sold the client the contract was too busy to see him, so Mehdi paid the man a visit. Mehdi handled all the paperwork—not only for the Metropolitan policy but for policies with several other companies as well. The man was so grateful, he offered Mehdi some 20-dollar bills and five cases of whiskey. Mehdi refused. The client insisted that he be allowed to do something, so Mehdi suggested that the man introduce him to several friends and relatives whose insurance he might review. Two days later, Mehdi received a letter listing 21 names of prospects—complete with addresses, telephone numbers, and names and approximate ages of dependents. And the grateful client promised to introduce Mehdi to everyone on the list personally. So his post sale follow-up led him back to prospecting—where he could start the four-step selling process all over again!

Mehdi Fakharzadeh

1. *Approach:* The introduction must effectively gain and hold the prospect's attention and encourage the prospect to provide information about real needs, wants, and problems. The salesperson then emphasizes the product's appeal in terms of its benefits and values to the prospect.

2. *Create and hold interest:* Retaining interest is essential if the salesperson is to discover and to clarify the prospect's needs, wants, and problems. The prospect must admit to having problems and then be willing to consider the salesperson's proposal as a solution to those problems.

The test: the sales presentation

3. *Arouse desire and secure conviction:* The salesperson must generate a desire in the prospect to enjoy the benefits of the product and assure the prospect that these benefits fulfill real needs and wants.

4. *Handle questions and objections:* At this stage, the salesperson's job is to present the advantages and the disadvantages of each product, to answer the prospect's questions and objections, and to help the customer to make the best choice. This may involve an actual demonstration of the product. Sometimes customers may be insecure about purchasing unfamiliar products or products that involve fashion and style considerations. Recognizing this, the effective salesperson again describes the merits of the various alternatives, reassures the indecisive buyer about the desirability of the preliminary choice, and actually helps the buyer to make a decision.

5. *Close the sale:* Inexperienced salespeople often fail because they hesitate to "close the sale"—that is, to secure action by asking for the order. Alternatively, salespeople who are poor listeners may talk themselves out of an order: they may be so busy making their sales presentation that they fail to realize when the customer is ready to buy. With time to reconsider, the prospect may elect not to buy, and the sale is lost.

Salespeople must cope with frustration

At this point, several warnings are in order. Successful salespeople are usually highly motivated and are able to overcome the frustration of hearing a prospect's "No, thank you—I'm not interested." In fact, a typical industrial salesperson calls on a prospect six times before making a sale. This is one reason why the average cost of an industrial sales call now exceeds $60 per call. Astute salespeople also recognize that some prospects simply do not want or need their products; when this happens, the salesperson does not waste time and stops calling on the prospect. Or some prospects in changeable situations may not have an immediate need for a product but may be potential buyers at a later date. Again, the effective salesperson must have the good judgment to discern the "no-need-ever" prospects from the "may-need-in-six-months" prospects. The uniqueness of each selling situation is one reason the sales profession represents a challenge to many individuals.

✔ **Postsale follow-up.** The salesperson's job does not end with the actual sale. *Postsale follow-up* refers to all activities undertaken by a salesperson to insure future business with the same customer. These activities vary tremendously according to the kind of selling involved. Both retail and industrial salespeople may suggest the purchase of additional or complementary items (a shirt and a tie to go with a new suit, or a set of carbide-tipped drills for a new drill press). When the purchased item is of substantial value, a good salesperson checks several weeks after the sale to make sure that the customer is satisfied, that the item was delivered on time, and that it is working properly. On a made-to-order purchase like a computer system or a new kitchen, the salesperson must retain close customer contact to assure that specifications are met and that last-minute changes are incorporated in the design.

Selling may not stop with writing the order

Postsale follow-up is essential for salespeople who wish to obtain repeat sales from satisfied customers or to attract new customers through favorable word-of-mouth advertising. Such salespeople have a genuine incentive to serve customer needs. The most blatant problems of high-pressure selling and misrepresentation usually arise in one-shot sales presentations, when a salesperson is selling high-cost items and repeat or referred sales are not expected (for example, when selling a set of encyclopedia).

Managing the Sales Force

A salesperson's effectiveness bears a significant relationship to the quality of his or her preparation for selling. Adequate preparation, which is the job of sales management, involves (1) selecting and training salespeople; (2) designing appropriate sales territories; and (3) providing salespeople with adequate compensation and motivation.

✔ **Selecting and training salespeople.** Successful salespeople communicate effectively about the products they sell. Thus, retail clerks who sell dresses must have a knowledge of style, color, and fabric; people who sell aerospace systems must be technically proficient. In selecting salespeople, a manager uses a variety of techniques, such as personal interviews, personality tests, and aptitude tests. Salespeople must be continually trained and retrained in response to changes in company policy (such as a modification in company rules on returned goods), changes in products sold (the addition of a new product or a style change in an old one), and variations in selling techniques (stressing an entire computer system rather than a piece of computer equipment). This training often involves accompanying salespeople in the field and attending periodic training sessions on such topics as improving schedules (to reduce travel time and to increase time with prospects), identifying prospects, and handling questions about new items in the product line.

✔ **Designing appropriate sales territories.** A crucial consideration for the salesperson who makes personal calls on customers is whether the assigned sales territory can potentially provide reasonable income for reasonable work. Obviously, the sales potential of a given territory bears little relation to its geographic size; New York City, for example, has a greater potential for computer sales than most states do. This presents sales management with the difficult task of designing equitable sales territories for its salespeople. To solve this problem, management usually makes a tradeoff between two sometimes conflicting goals: (1) equalizing sales potentials among territories, and (2) equalizing workloads among territories (which necessarily involves the size of the geographic area to be covered). When a large metropolitan area is involved, a partial solution is to place a portion of the city in each sales territory. Every salesperson is then assigned a wedge-shaped territory that includes both high-potential urban areas (near the point of the wedge) and low-potential rural areas (near the wide part of the wedge).

Wedge-shaped territories may resolve sales inequities

✔ **Providing salespeople with adequate compensation and motivation.** In compensating and motivating their salespeople, sales managers seek to answer two interrelated questions: "What is an appropriate level of compensation?" and "What is the best method of payment?"

In determining adequate compensation, sales management uses two standards: (1) the compensation of salespeople performing similar jobs in other companies, and (2) the pay scale of other employees within the firm. As a general rule, salespeople who must seek out customers to obtain orders work harder and receive greater compensation than salespeople who take orders from customers who come to them. For example, some experienced salespeople who are paid on commission, such as insurance salespeople, can earn more than $50,000 a year. These jobs require great initiative and "stick-to-it-iveness," which explains in part why about three-fourths of all insurance salespeople do not last a year. In contrast, more routine order-taking sales jobs (like those in some retail stores) pay no more than the federal minimum wage.

MEHDI'S FIVE ESSENTIALS OF SELLING

Mehdi Fakharzadeh ("How Successful Salespeople Sell") is such a successful life-insurance salesman that he is frequently asked to speak to audiences about his selling technique. In Mehdi's own words, these are the five essentials of his sales method:

"*Number One:* You have to be honest.
"*Number Two:* When making a proposal to somebody, put yourself in the shoes of that person.
"*Number Three:* You've got to know your business. Constantly increase your knowledge.

"*Number Four:* You must work. If you have all the knowledge in the world and are the most honest man, if you're going to stay home, can you make any business?
"*Number Five:* Never, ever get discouraged and disappointed. No matter what business you're in will have ups and downs. Don't think this is the end of the world."

Mehdi modestly insists that anyone who follows these principles can sell as well as he does.

Straight salary:
security and
management control

Straight commission:
incentive and little
management control

After the approximate level of compensation has been set, the method of payment must be determined. The most common methods of sales compensation are straight salary, straight commission, and salary plus commision. *Straight salary* is a fixed monthly or annual compensation that does not vary with a salesperson's actual sales volume. Conversely, salespeople on *straight commission* receive a fixed percentage (say 5 percent) of the sales volume. Straight salary provides maximum security for salespeople and greatest control by management; straight commission provides maximum incentive for salespeople and sometimes too little control by management (for example, a salesperson may focus all efforts on immediate sales rather than on developing new accounts). To provide a balance between security and incentive, many firms offer *salary plus commission*—a plan that includes some salary and some commission. In addition to taking into account the factors of security, management control, and individual incentive, compensation plans should be flexible enough to adapt to changing conditions or different territories and simple enough for both salespeople and management to understand them thoroughly.

KEY POINTS TO REMEMBER

1. The promotion element in the marketing mix refers to communication between seller and buyer. Its two most important components are advertising and personal selling; but promotion also includes free samples, trading stamps, sweepstakes, cents-off coupons, trade-show exhibitions, and publicity.
2. The overall goal of promotion is to increase a firm's sales and profits. A firm's promotional activities accomplish this by (a) informing, (b) persuading, and (c) reminding target market customers about its products.
3. Advertising is any nonpersonal communication between seller and buyer that is conducted through paid media under clear sponsorship.
4. Based on how quickly its effects are felt, advertising can be divided into two categories: direct-action and delayed-action advertising.
5. Regardless of the size of a firm, an effective advertising campaign normally involves the same series of key steps. These steps are summarized in Figure 9-2.
6. Personal selling is any personal communication between seller and buyer that is performed by a person who represents the seller. That person may either be an employee of the company or an agent representing that company.
7. Four main categories of sales jobs can be identified: manufacturer's sales representatives, wholesaler's sales representatives, retail sales representatives, and direct sales representatives.

8. The salesperson has a key marketing and business role: to act as the customer's problem solver. Doing this effectively can establish a long-term relationship with the customer that will result in repeat business for the salesperson's company.

9. There are four main steps in the selling process: prospecting, presale preparation, sales presentation, and postsale follow-up.

10. Sales management involves preparing salespeople adequately for the job of selling. Thus, a sales manager must select and train salespeople, design appropriate sales territories, and provide salespeople with adequate compensation and motivation.

QUESTIONS FOR DISCUSSION

1. As we saw in this chapter, effective advertising copy must be attention-getting, easy to read and to understand, believable, and informative. Using a five-point scale (1 = very poor; 2 = moderately poor; 3 = average; 4 = moderately good; 5 = very good), evaluate the two Honda advertisements in Figure 9-4 on each of these four criteria. Then total the points for each ad. Overall, which ad is better? Was this your initial reaction when you first looked at both ads?

2. Is the appeal of each of the two Honda ads in Figure 9-4 primarily rational or emotional? Describe the specific appeal used in each ad (examples: price, quality, status, vanity).

3. What are some of the problems that must be faced in selecting the appropriate advertising media to use?

4. Are the advertising expenditures of the ten firms shown in Figure 9-3 too high? Why or why not?

5. During what months or seasons of the year would a retailer be likely to increase advertising expenditures for (a) toys; (b) cake mixes; (c) soft drinks; (d) automobiles; (e) school supplies; (f) shoes?

6. What is your impression of personal selling as a vocation?

7. Which of the sales steps shown in Figure 9-6 are important in selling (a) women's clothing in a store near a college campus; (b) a computer used for data processing by large business firms?

8. What kind of sales compensation would you provide for salespeople handling the following products: (a) Avon cosmetics; (b) life insurance; (c) office equipment; (d) men's suits; (e) groceries; (f) advertisements for a college paper? Give your reasons for each choice.

9. Some marketing experts stress a four-step approach to promotion that applies to both advertising and personal selling. The approach is AIDA—an acronym that spells the name of Verdi's well-known opera. The four steps are: Attention, Interest, Desire, and Action. Explain how the steps of AIDA apply to (a) advertising, and (b) personal selling.

SHORT CASES AND PROBLEMS

1. Assume that you own a bicycle store near a college campus and that you have an annual advertising budget of $500. Using Figure 9-2 as a guide, select goals, appeals, media, and timing for your advertising. How would you prepare to measure the effectiveness of the campaign?

2. The choice-selection method discussed in Chapter 6 can be applied to many types of business problems. Suppose that a firm is trying to decide whether to add five or ten additional salespeople to its sales force. Analysis of profits at three levels of market potential yields the following payoff table:

| | Outcome state | | |
Alternative	O_1: Low market potential	O_2: Medium market potential	O_3: High market potential
A_1: Hire five more salespeople	$20,000	$40,000	$60,000
A_2: Hire ten more salespeople	−$30,000	$30,000	$100,000

The sales manager assesses the probability of the occurrence of low-, medium-, and high-market potentials to be 0.4, 0.3, and 0.3, respectively. How many salespeople should the firm add?

CAREER SELECTION: POSITIONS IN ADVERTISING, PUBLIC RELATIONS, AND MANUFACTURERS' SALES

CAREERS IN ADVERTISING

Advertising account executives plan and direct advertising programs for the client firms of advertising agencies. Account executives plan these programs in accordance with client objectives and budgets and coordinate agency activities in developing the advertising copy and in selecting the proper media and timing. A college degree and 5 to 15 years' agency experience in copy layout, media buying, or campaign planning are normally required. Annual salary varies from $20,000 to $80,000.

Advertising copywriters consult with account executives and with clients to obtain information about the products or services to be advertised. Given budget limitations and the type of media to be used, copywriters develop original, written material for newspaper and magazine advertising and scripts for radio and television commercials. Some college is desirable; creativity is essential. Annual salaries range from $10,000 to $50,000.

Job opportunities for both advertising account executives and copywriters are expected to expand moderately as the U.S. economy expands. (*Additional information:* contact large, local advertising agencies.)

Commercial artists transform promotional ideas into appealing, effective advertisements by developing the artistic concept of an advertising campaign and then working with copywriters to design the actual advertising layouts and the final advertising copy. Commercial artists often specialize in a particular medium, such as direct-mail, catalog, window-display, film, or television advertising. Employers generally require occupational training or a bachelor's degree in commercial art. Promotion to the level of art director is usually more rapid if the artist has taken some general business courses. Experienced artists often become freelancers to achieve greater earnings. Annual income ranges from $6000 to more than $30,000. Career opportunities are expected to expand moderately due to the increasing use of visual media for product promotion. (*Additional information:* National Art Education Association; National Education Association; 1201 16th Street, N.W.; Washington, D.C. 20036.)

CAREERS IN PUBLIC RELATIONS

The public image of a business is maintained and enhanced by **public relations workers,** who are responsible for promoting the firm's business projects and accomplishments in newspapers and magazines and through personal contact with the public. Applicants must be socially and psychologically adept. Employers generally require a bachelor's degree in public relations, journalism, or English; journalism or advertising experience is helpful. Seasoned public-relations workers may advance to supervisory jobs and eventually to top-management positions. Annual salaries can range from $9000 to $50,000 depending on the level of job responsibilities and on the size of the business. Job opportunities are expected to increase moderately as business places more and more emphasis on good consumer relations. (*Additional information:* Service Department; *Public Relations News;* 127 East 80th Street; New York, New York 10021.)

Manufacturers' salesworkers sell products for virtually all manufacturers—from computers to cake mixers to can openers. Manufacturers' salesworkers sell to business firms and to institutions such as schools and hospitals. They typically visit prospective customers in their work locations. Manufacturers' salesworkers must be completely familiar with their products and must be able to answer customer questions, transact sales, and handle the paperwork involved. Although high-school graduates can be successful salespeople, more and more manufacturers are hiring sales trainees with some college background—even applicants with engineering degrees for technical sales positions. Most salesworkers receive formal training programs; the length of a program depends on the technical complexity of the product to be sold. An ability to get along well with diverse customers is necessary. Most manufacturers' salesworkers are paid on a salary-plus-commission basis. Beginning salesworkers now average about $9000 a year; experienced sales personnel earn $16,000 to $32,000 or more annually. Sales opportunities are expected to expand or to contract in the 1970s, with changes in manufacturing output.

Manufacturers' agents perform a similar selling function. But unlike manufacturers' salesworkers, manufacturers' agents are not employees of producing firms but merely act as their sales representatives. They usually sell lines of complimentary, noncompeting products for several manufacturers (for example, springs for one firm, nuts and bolts for a second firm, and small bearings for a third). Agents receive a straight commission based on the revenues or profits from their sales. Some manufacturers' agents earn $50,000 to $100,000 annually, but the average salary is about $20,000.

Sales managers supervise the activities of sales personnel at the district, regional, or national level of a firm. Salesworkers with good sales records who display managerial abilities are often promoted to sales-management positions. Sales managers may earn $20,000 to $60,000 annually.

Future job opportunities in personal selling and in sales management for manufacturing firms will vary depending on the industry involved. (*Additional information:* contact your local chapter of the Professional Sales Executives, a national organization for salespeople.)

A CRITICAL BUSINESS DECISION

—made by Matthew E. McCarthy

THE SITUATION At a meeting of his board of directors, Matthew E. McCarthy, board chairman and president of Pacific Air Lines, listens carefully to a presentation outlining a new advertising campaign. The speaker, Los Angeles entertainer and copywriter Stan Freberg, has based his promotional appeal on the recognition of airline passengers' fear of flying—a topic that has always been taboo in airline advertisements. McCarthy studies the advertisement's headline: "Hey there! You with the sweat in your palms." His eyes catch other parts of the copy:

> Do you wish the pilot would knock off that jazz about "That's Crater Lake coming up on the left down there, ladies and gentlemen," and tell you instead what the devil that funny noise was you just heard? . . . It's about time an airline faced up to something: MOST PEOPLE ARE SCARED WITLESS OF FLYING.
> DEEP DOWN INSIDE, every time that big plane lifts off the runway, you wonder if this is it; right? You want to know something, fella? So does the pilot, deep down inside. On Pacific Air Lines and on any other airline. And if he doesn't, that means he's letting his guard down and he should turn in his wings and his Smilin' Jack cap.

The advertisement attempts to calm passengers' fears with these closing words:

> WILL THIS AERONAUTICAL HONESTY on our part make passengers even more nervous about flying? Possibly. But we think that just talking about the existence of those sweaty palms should help you to relax a little more. Psychiatrists say that it helps to get things out in the open.

THE DECISION Pacific Air Lines serves West Coast cities. In recent years, it has made a concerted effort to improve both its service and its image. McCarthy, feeling that the airline is suffering because potential customers are unaware of Pacific's attributes, has asked Freberg to attract some attention to the airline. In 11 days, Pacific will inaugurate a new nonstop route between San Francisco and Hollywood–Burbank and will introduce jet service on two other nonstop routes.

For maximum impact, Freberg proposes to initiate the promotional campaign, featuring radio spots and full-page advertisements in San Francisco and New York newspapers, two days prior to these new Pacific Air Lines flights. To carry the theme to completion, Freberg suggests distributing "security kits" to first-time or nervous passengers. Each kit will contain a rabbit's foot, a fortune cookie, and a paperback copy of Norman Vincent Peale's *The Power of Positive Thinking*. Freberg's other plans include painting one of Pacific's Boeing 727s to resemble a railroad locomotive and projecting pictures of passing telephone poles on the cabin window shades.

While interested in Freberg's follow-up ideas, McCarthy is faced with an immediate decision: Should he approve the newspaper–radio campaign?

QUESTIONS

1. Assess the reactions of potential passengers to the proposed advertising campaign.
2. If you were McCarthy, would you approve the campaign?

A guy can make a fortune in this fast-paced age of change if he can just come up with some new, modern product that catches the fancy. Some guys did it with computers. Others did it with the mini-skirt.

The Wall Street Journal

CHAPTER 10

PRODUCTION: PRODUCT DEVELOPMENT, PURCHASING, AND MANUFACTURING

G ene O'Neill of Fostoria, Iowa, made a fortune in buggy whips—the proverbial out-of-date product. In the 1970s, O'Neill's plants in Fostoria (population: 200) and in Winnipeg, Canada, produced more than 100,000 whips, ranging from buggy and show whips to stockyard and hog whips. Business is booming: O'Neill has already captured more than a third of the U.S. whip market, and he expects annual increases of at least 10 percent in the foreseeable future.

The success of Gene O'Neill's business is due largely to careful and ingenious product development. O'Neill spent hours at the stockyards analyzing the construction of standard leather whips. Retreating to his basement, O'Neill developed four new ideas for improving the performance and the durability of whips: (1) substituting fiberglass rods for the traditional reed and rawhide core, so that whips wouldn't wilt in summer or snap in winter; (2) replacing the standard braided linen covering with plastic strips that wouldn't shrink in the rain; (3) providing handles of rubberlike plastic that lasted longer than leather; and (4) developing a replaceable popper (tail), so that whips wouldn't have to be discarded when the poppers broke off.

The Wonder Whip: the first new idea in whips in centuries

O'Neill bought an abandoned bank in Fostoria for $800 and converted it into a factory. After purchasing the necessary materials from suppliers, he began to manufacture the new product, which he called the Wonder Whip. Today, the nine employees in O'Neill's Fostoria plant can turn out a finished whip in less than five minutes—a far cry from the three or four days needed to braid and repeatedly varnish a standard whip.

The development of Gene O'Neill's Wonder Whip illustrates the main business activities involved in *production:* the use of people and machines to design new products, to buy and convert materials into finished products, and to supply these products to customers.

What Is Production?

Production is comprised of three interrelated activities: product development, purchasing, and manufacturing. *Product development* involves generating the designs, models, and prototypes (working models of products planned for full-scale manufacture) of all items to be produced. *Purchasing* involves buying the right item in the right quantity at the right price and making it available to the firm at the right time and place. This function is described by a variety of names: In manufacturing, finance,

Production includes product development, purchasing, and manufacturing and most service firms, it is purchasing; in retailing, it is buying; in many government agencies, it is procurement. *Manufacturing* involves converting purchased materials into useful products according to specifications developed by the firm and transporting these products to buyers.

Organization of Production Activities

The organization of production-related activities in a medium-sized business is shown in Figure 10-1. Each major department—product development, purchasing, and manufacturing—is headed by a manager or vice president who reports directly to the president. Departments are divided into various sections, according to the major function each performs.

The product development department (often called the engineering department) is usually managed by an engineer or a physical scientist. Its function is to provide detailed designs of products that the firm expects to manufacture and sell. The product-development department is sometimes divided into sections according to the kind of product manufactured or the physical process involved. For example, an appliance manufacturer that produces refrigerators, washers, and dryers may have a separate product-development section for each type of appliance. Or a manufacturer may establish separate product-development sections for the various physical characteristics of a product: mechanical design, electrical design, and external design (the outside appearance of the product).

Buyers report to the purchasing manager

The purchasing department is headed by the purchasing manager (or purchasing agent), who supervises a number of buyers. Each buyer is in charge of a purchasing section responsible for a group of items that are similar in some important respect. Purchasing sections in most manufacturing firms are subsectioned according to stage of manufacture—raw materials, semifinished parts, and finished parts—as shown in Figure 10-1. Firms that manufacture a number of different products may have purchasing sections responsible for each product line (refrigerators, washers, and dryers for an appliance manufacturer). When purchased items represent a relatively small portion of a firm's total sales, the purchasing function may be a part of the manufacturing department.

The manufacturing department has many subdivisions

The manufacturing department, headed by the manufacturing manager, is often divided into five major sections: production control, fabrication, final assembly, quality control, and transportation (again, see Figure 10-1). Depending on the product manufactured, each of these sections is in turn divided into specialized groups. For example, the fabrication section may consist of subsections responsible for particular types of machines, such as drill presses, lathes, and milling machines. Each section and subsection is headed by a separate supervisor or manager. Firms that manufacture several product lines may also have final-assembly subsections for each major product. The transportation (or traffic) section is generally

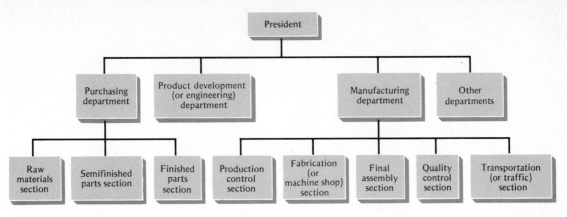

10-1 Organization chart showing the three production-related departments in a medium-sized manufacturing firm: product development, manufacturing, and purchasing.

responsible for the inbound movement of purchased items and for the shipment of final products to buyers. Because of this dual responsibility, the transportation section in some firms is in the marketing department rather than in the manufacturing department.

Interrelationship of Production Activities

Figure 10-2 shows the interrelationships between the three principal production activities. In the development stage, the product-development department provides designs and blueprints for the finished

10-2 Activities involved in providing a finished manufactured product. Note that manufacturing-department activities are shown in more detail than for the product-development and the purchasing departments.

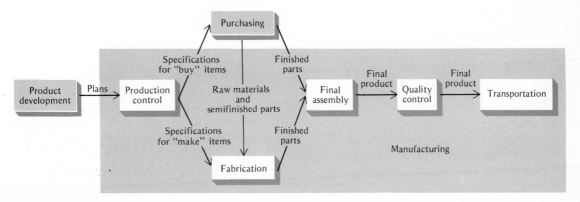

SERENDIPITY: AN ANGEL IN PRODUCT DEVELOPMENT

John H. Dessauer was the Haloid scientist who first saw the 25-line abstract describing Chet Carlson's invention that resulted in Xerox's photocopying process (see Chapter 1). Dessauer has strong feelings about the importance of "serendipity" (accidentally discovering one thing while seeking another) in business. Dessauer believes that his firm made so many accidental discoveries only because Haloid was "on the right road in the first place." He cites the following example.

In 1948, Haloid developed its first Model A copier. Although the machine required more than a dozen manual operations before it produced a finished copy, Haloid officials gloated over it. They asked four large companies to test the Model A copier and waited for the answers. The answers came quickly. All four firms reported that the copier was too difficult and too complicated to operate, that it sometimes produced illegible copies, and that it was of no value to them.

The company officers wondered if they had invested every available Haloid dollar in a useless gadget. The badly shaken officials regrouped and decided they must produce a better machine that would overcome the shortcomings of the Model A

copier. But this required money, and who would invest in another copier after this fiasco?

Just then a Haloid consultant called to ask, "Say, do you know what you've got there?"

"What have we got?" President Joseph C. Wilson responded into the phone.

The answer: "That flat plate Model A copier may not do for office copying. But a number of people have told us . . . that it's perfect for making paper printing plates for offset duplicating, especially with the equipment being marketed by Addressograph-Multigraph. I'm sure you can sell this copier to many offset users."

Again, Model A copiers were distributed—but this time to test their value in making offset-masters to use as printing plates. For this application, the Model A copier was a fantastic success. The Ford Motor Company reported that the cost of the first runoff copy was reduced from $3.12 to 37 cents and that the last of 20,000 copies was of as high a quality as the first copy.

If this were serendipity, in John H. Dessauer's words: "It saved the day. It saved the company. It saved Chet Carlson. And it produced a foundation for all our future activities."

The make-buy decision affects both purchasing and fabrication operations

product. These plans are then sent to the manufacturing department, where the production control section identifies and schedules the detailed steps necessary to produce the finished product. Before drawing up schedules, production control consults with other departments to determine the critical *make-buy decision*—an evaluation of which of the finished parts in the final product will be purchased from outside vendors and which will be fabricated by the firm itself. The production control section also develops the necessary *specifications*—detailed descriptions of materials, dimensions, and performance requirements—for all the items that comprise the finished product.

Specifications for the items to be bought from outside vendors are sent to the purchasing department, which buys the required raw materials, semifinished parts, and finished parts. Raw materials and semifinished parts are sent to the fabrication section, where they are converted into finished parts in accordance with the specifications drawn up by production control. Finished parts from both the purchasing department and the fabrication section are sent to final assembly.

Completed products coming off the final assembly line are inspected by the quality control section. Satisfactory final products are shipped to customers by the transportation section; unsatisfactory products are returned for corrections and repairs. All of the sections within the large gray area in Figure 10-2 are in the manufacturing departments of most business firms.

Product Development

Not all new products succeed

The objective of product development is to generate profitable new products and to improve existing products. The successful development and marketing of new products is one of the firm's most difficult tasks. The spectacular failure of many new products attests to this difficulty. In the early 1960s, Ford lost about $250 million in its ill-fated Edsel venture; in the 1970s, DuPont announced it was withdrawing Corfam (the "breathable," synthetic leather) from the market after losing almost $100 million on that product in eight years. Thousands of lesser-known products are quietly removed from the marketplace every year. To minimize the chances of failure, the product-development department must carefully evaluate and analyze a new product at each stage of its design.

Stages in Product Development

Figure 10-3 summarizes the steps in the development of new products and indicates the likely success rate of new ideas at each stage of development. As the figure shows, an average of one out of 58 ideas for new products becomes a commercial success. The horizontal space representing each step is a rough indication of the relative time necessary to complete that stage. Thus, during the development of a new product, the screening step generally takes the least amount of time; the development step takes the most time. The six steps in developing new products are:

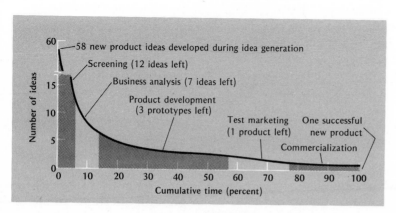

10-3

Steps in the development of a new product.

Source: From *Management of New Products* (Chicago: Booz, Allen, & Hamilton, Inc., 1968), p. 9.

1. *Idea generation:* Ideas for new products are collected from customers, employees (scientists, engineers, top management, salespeople, and so on), and competitors.

2. *Screening:* New product ideas are evaluated against company objectives and available resources. Ideas that do not satisfy these conditions are discarded.

3. *Business analysis:* A detailed analysis is conducted to estimate the profitability of manufacturing and marketing proposed products. The analysis includes estimates of market size, production and distribution of costs, and financial requirements. Up to this point, each product is only an idea, a blueprint, or a crude, nonworking model.

4. *Product development:* Prototypes of commercially promising products are produced in the laboratory in limited quantities to see if their features are practicable and if the products can be produced at reasonable cost. An example of a working prototype is a new detergent with a unique cleaning capability. Packaging and brand-name decisions are also made at this time, and surveys are conducted to determine initial customer reactions.

5. *Test marketing:* If the prototypes prove workable, the products are introduced into a limited number of cities to see if consumers will buy them in volume. Products that receive completely unfavorable consumer reactions are dropped immediately. If problems are uncovered that would result in favorable consumer reactions to a product when corrected, the product is returned to the development department for improvement. An example is the millions of dollars a major food processor recently spent to develop a catsup that captured the natural flavor of tomatoes. The product's impact in supermarkets was immediate: consumers avoided it like the plague. The reason: customers missed the overcooked, scorched flavor that they associated with the taste of a high-quality catsup. So the firm adjusted its equipment to overcook and scorch; sales of the "improved" catsup soared.

6. *Commercialization:* Products that achieve successful test market results are offered for sale, normally on a nationwide basis. This involves selecting a channel of distribution to transport the product to prospective buyers. Products that generate adequate profits are judged a commercial success. Unsuccessful products are withdrawn by the manufacturer.

Although the product-development department performs the central function in developing new products, all major departments in a firm share in the responsibilities that this task entails. For example, new product ideas often originate in the marketing department from customer surveys or from the suggestions of salespeople. In major product decisions, especially in small- and medium-sized companies, the president of the firm may take an active part in the first three stages of the product-

Six hurdles for a new product

development sequence. The finance department must assess in detail both the volume and the timing of financial needs. The manufacturing and the purchasing departments must evaluate proposed designs to determine if new products can be produced at reasonable cost.

The Varying Importance of Development Stages

In general, the time a product remains in each stage of the development sequence depends on its product class (whether it is a consumer good or an industrial good) and on its characteristics and complex-

WHERE DO PRODUCT IDEAS START—THE MARKET OR THE LAB?

A much-debated topic is whether a need for new products prompts technical innovation or whether scientific discovery generates practical application. In other words, do new products start in the market or in the laboratory? Countless examples of each point of view could be cited.

Need prompted a new product when a little girl asked her father why she had to wait so long to see the pictures he took with his camera. This father, Edwin H. Land, not only answered the question; he did something about it. The result was the Polaroid Land camera. The search for more portable food is another example of need prompting a new product. In 1846, a party of 87 settlers on their way from Illinois to California were trapped by deep snow; those who survived stayed alive by eating the flesh of those who died. The event not only posed a difficult moral question; it also prompted a Texas surveyor, Gail Borden, to search for ways to make various foods more portable and storable. Borden tried heating milk in a vacuum pan, but the milk stuck to the sides of the pan and then foamed and boiled over. Experts told him to give up the idea. In response, Borden merely greased the pan and, in that remarkably simple way, perfected the technology of condensing milk.

Technical developments also lead to new products. In the 1960s, a DuPont scientist formulated a new chemical compound, but the substance would not adhere to anything. So the scientist sought market applications that might exist for such a chemical compound. The result: DuPont named the compound Teflon and used it for griddle surfaces and in other cookware. Another example is Clarence Birdseye's experience in Labrador. While ice-fishing at −20°F, Birdseye placed his catch beside the hole. The fish quickly froze solid. Later, Birdseye dropped the frozen fish in a pail of water. To his shock, it

began to swim again. Birdseye was to discover that the cells of the fish had frozen so quickly that the large crystals that would have broken the cell walls and killed the fish had had no time to form. Birdseye first applied this quick-freezing process to seafood and later to many other frozen-food products, one brand of which bears his name.

In searching for new products, some technical people have an unusual ability to consider both market and laboratory factors. In an effort to find new sources of income for cotton farmers, George Washington Carver discovered 75 products made from the pecan, 118 from the sweet potato, and over 300 from the peanut. His untiring efforts prompted The New York Times to hail Carver as "the man who has done more than any other man for agriculture in the South." Thomas A. Edison's first patent in 1868 was for a machine that recorded the votes of legislators on a big board. When Edison showed the vote-recording device to a congressional committee, the chairman told Edison it was the last thing Congress wanted. "It takes 45 minutes to call the roll," the chairman explained to Edison. "In that time, we can trade votes. Your machine would make that impossible." Annoyed, Edison vowed never again to invent something that nobody wanted. And he kept his word. Edison maintained he was not a scientist but a "commercial inventor" who "worked for the silver dollar" and who was devoted to what he called the "desperate needs of the world."

In summary, perhaps these examples support the conclusion that the sources of new product ideas are most often creative people. These people, in turn, may have various orientations: toward the marketplace, toward technical ideas, or—as in the cases of Carver and Edison—toward having the rare genius to recognize both market and technical factors.

ity. For example, product development generally takes much longer for complex industrial goods than for consumer goods; commercial considerations such as branding and channels of distribution are usually more important for consumer items than for industrial goods. Within each product class, there is also a great deal of variation. A new clothes dryer may take years in the product-development stage; a new toy may be developed in a few days or weeks.

With new products, one or more development stages may be omitted entirely. For example, formal test marketing is rarely conducted for industrial products or for expensive consumer items like cars and major home appliances; a manufacturer of such goods normally designs customer suggestions into the item before or early in the product-development stage. Even lower-priced consumer goods may not be test marketed if the manufacturer believes that a market is clearly established. Revlon introduces many of its new cosmetics without test marketing. General Mills chose not to test-market its Wondra flour for fear that competitors would attempt to quickly introduce similar products.

Purchasing

As we noted earlier, the objective of the purchasing department is to buy the right product in the right quantity at the right price and to make it available to the firm at the right time and place. The following discussion focuses on purchasing activities in a manufacturing firm; retail buying will be covered in Chapter 17.

Steps in the Purchasing Process

Figure 10-4 outlines the sequence of steps a purchasing department follows when buying items for a firm. Purchased items are normally classified as direct material or indirect material. *Direct material* (also called *end-product goods*) includes the purchased raw materials, semifinished parts, and finished parts that are incorporated in the final product. *Indirect material* includes both *production goods* (equipment used to fabricate the firm's final product) and *commercial goods* (equipment and supplies needed to manage and operate the firm but not incorporated in the final product.

Two kinds of
purchased material:
direct and indirect

✔ **Need recognition.** Recognition of the need for an indirect material generally arises within the group that maintains an inventory of the item. When supplies must be restocked, the appropriate group sends a *purchase requisition*—an authorization to buy material from a supplier—to the purchasing department describing the item needed, the required

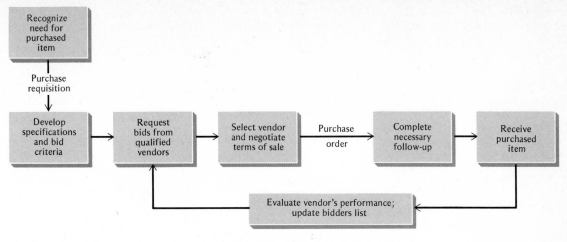

10-4 Steps in the purchasing process.

quantity, and the urgency of the need. The same procedure applies to direct materials that are used in standard items produced by the firm.

Need recognition can arise in two ways

When direct materials are required for the first time, need recognition usually arises within the product-development department. For example, an appliance manufacturer might develop a new window fan containing several new components that product-development engineers specified in the fan design. After make-buy decisions have been determined for these components, the production-control section sends the specifications for all new items to be bought from outside sources (for example, electric motors) to the purchasing department on purchase requisitions. These sources are called vendors or suppliers.

✔ **Specifications and bid criteria.** Specifications on interfirm purchase requisitions may be either rigid and precise or somewhat flexible, depending on the needed item. When some flexibility exists, members of the purchasing and the manufacturing departments perform a *value analysis*—a systematic appraisal of the design, quality, and performance requirements of an item in order to reduce purchasing costs. For example, if the product-development engineers for the the appliance manufacturer conclude that at least a $3/16$ horsepower motor is needed to power the window fan, the purchasing department would recommend buying a $1/4$ horsepower motor, which is available as a standard item from many vendors, rather than a $3/16$ horsepower motor, which must be made to order at a higher cost. The purchasing department may also rely on the technical expertise of vendors in developing appropriate design specifications. Specifications are generally given in terms of material, dimensions, and performance characteristics rather than in terms of brand name to maximize the number of qualified vendors available to the purchasing department and to insure genuine competition among bidders.

Value analysis reduces the cost of an item

WHAT BID CRITERIA ARE IMPORTANT IN AN INDUSTRIAL BUYING DECISION?

It seems reasonable to assume that in selecting a vendor for a specific purchase, an industrial buyer's bid criteria depends on the type and use of the item to be bought and the speed with which it is needed. Among important criteria to be considered are: (1) price; (2) ability to meet standard quality specifications; (3) ability to meet delivery schedules; (4) technical capability; (5) warranties and claim policies; (6) past performance on previous contracts; and (7) production facilities and capacity of the vendor.

Assume that you are the purchasing agent responsible for buying each of the items described below:

● *Case A — Paint:* An industrial chemical producer must repaint the interior walls of its manufacturing plant. All of the surfaces to be painted are cement and are exposed to severe chemical fumes, which cause paint to deteriorate. It is estimated that the project will require 10 barrels of paint.

● *Case B — Desks:* A large university requires 200 new desks. The desks are to be used by a large department in a soon-to-be completed university building. The university's policy is to furnish all new offices with metal desks.

● *Case C — Computers:* A large aerospace firm has received a government contract to build two satellites for astronomical research. Each satellite is to have an on-board computer that must stabilize the orbit precisely. The two computers are to be subcontracted, since their electronics and manufacturing tolerances are so complex that only firms with prior experience could guarantee satisfactory performance. The satellites are scheduled to be launched in two years.

Review the seven criteria listed above. For each of the three cases, select the five criteria you consider most critical and rank them from most to least important. To discover what criteria actual purchasing agents felt were important, see the text.

Before sending out bid requests, the purchasing department must weigh the relative importance of various criteria in evaluating the qualifications of vendors and their products. Four bid criteria often used in purchasing are price, quality, delivery, and service. Frequently, the purchasing department must tradeoff among these four criteria. Thus, a bidder's low price may be weighed against its ability to provide important supplementary services, such as ideas for improvements in later designs. Price also must be compared with necessary quality; for example, in purchasing wood for crating, low price can be given greater consideration than quality or appearance.

Purchasing criteria: price, quality, delivery, and service

"What Bid Criteria Are Important is an Industrial Buying Decision?" cites three buying situations that illustrate the use of different bid criteria. Professor Gary W. Dickson of the University of Minnesota presented these three buying situations to 170 purchasing agents, who identified the five most important bid criteria for each case as follows:

Rank	Case A: Paint	Case B: Desks	Case C: Computers
1	Quality	Price	Quality
2	Warranties	Quality	Technical capability
3	Delivery	Delivery	Delivery
4	Past performance	Warranties	Production facilities
5	Price	Past performance	Past performance

Dickson observes that despite the diverse nature of the purchases, three factors in each case were crucial in the choice of a vendor: (1) ability to meet quality standards; (2) ability to deliver the product on time; and (3) the buyer's past performance on previous contracts. Dickson also concludes that in buying standard items, such as the desks in Case B, price is generally the key factor. Conversely, when buying more technically complex products, such as the computers in Case C, more criteria are likely to influence the decision and the price becomes less important.

✔ **Bid solicitation.** The next step in purchasing is the solicitation of bids from potential suppliers. This involves selecting the names of vendors from a *bidders list* — a list of firms believed to be qualified to supply a given item — and sending each vendor a quotation request form describing the desired quantity, delivery date, and specifications of the product. Most purchasing departments maintain a separate bidders list for each general class of items they order. These lists are updated continuously, by adding the names of potential new vendors and deleting the names of unsatisfactory vendors. To further insure competition, many firms require that at least three bids be solicited for purchases exceeding a specified dollar amount.

✔ **Vendor selection.** When interested suppliers have returned quotation request forms, the purchasing department evaluates each quotation on the basis of its bid criteria and also considers the factors unique to each vendor. For example, a supplier's ability to deliver may be affected by recent or expected future changes in its operations, such as labor and financial problems or major commitments that may overshadow the contemplated order. On large or important orders, the purchasing department may choose to divide the final contract between two or more bidders to assure continual supply of the product in case a strike or an extended shutdown occurs at one supplier's plant. Thus, an appliance manufacturer might buy its paper supplies from a single vendor and its one-quarter horsepower motors from two different vendors.

Vendors may be selected immediately or after negotiations

Sometimes contracts are awarded directly to vendors based on the data they provide in the quotation request forms and on the background information provided by the purchasing department. At other times, the purchasing department may wish to negotiate with one or more bidders, particularly on high-dollar, high-volume items, when a part of the bidder's proposal is not entirely satisfactory. For example, a buyer who feels that all bidders are quoting excessive prices or offering unsatisfactory delivery terms may elect to negotiate some of the contract details rather than to accept a bid as submitted. However, both legal and ethical considerations require that unfair demands should not be made on suppliers and that all firms bidding on a contract should be given genuine consideration. Eventually, the buyer selects one or more vendors and awards the contract in the form of a *purchase order* — an authorization for the vendor or vendors to provide the items in accordance with the prearranged terms and to bill the purchasing firm.

Buyers follow through on problematic or important purchases

✔ **Vendor follow-up.** If the purchased item is of minor value and if no changes are made in the order after it is issued, the purchasing department rarely follows-up on the order. Vendor follow-up is essential, however, if an item is of high value, in short supply, or of crucial importance to the firm. If an item requires major design changes after the initial purchase order has been issued, the purchasing department must verify the status of the order, see that the required changes are made, negotiate new terms of sale if necessary, and expedite the order so that it does not hold up the firm's production.

Inspection: checking to see that the firm got what it ordered

✔ **Receiving purchased items.** A clerk at the receiving dock of the buyer's plant identifies the incoming material and checks it against the purchase order to make sure that quantities or weights are correct. The inspection department then performs tests to determine whether the material meets the stated specifications. For example, the motor for a window fan might be tested to see that it delivers the required torque at the three speeds at which the fan operates. If the material is not satisfactory, the purchasing department negotiates with the supplier to rework the items according to specifications or arranges for an entirely new shipment.

✔ **Vendor evaluation.** Experienced buyers realize that evaluation of purchasing decisions is essential. The vendor's performance is evaluated after final delivery of the purchased items. As shown in Figure 10-4, this information is often noted on a vendor rating sheet and used to update the bidders lists kept by the purchasing department. Thus, performance on past contracts determines a vendor's chances of being asked to bid on future purchases. A very poor performance can result in a vendor's name being dropped from the list.

Problem Areas in Purchasing

Among the important problems purchasing departments face are (1) the conflicting goals present in purchasing decisions, and (2) the purchase of highly technical research items that have never before been produced.

✔ **Conflicting goals in purchasing decisions.** A purchasing department seeks six major goals: low prices, high quality, no out-of-stock problems, a small investment in inventory, continuing sources of supplies, and good vendor relations. In practice, however, it is often impossible to attain all six objectives simultaneously, since several of these goals directly conflict with one another. A buyer can reduce the likelihood of encountering out-of-stock problems by increasing the quantity of the item in stock, but this will necessitate a larger dollar investment in inventory. Low prices may be achieved by buying in large volume to obtain quantity discounts, but again the buyer must face higher inventory costs. Awarding a contract to an unknown vendor who offers the lowest price may jeopardize a continuing source of supply (since the buyer cannot be sure that the new source will deliver) and may endanger good relations with higher-priced vendors who have performed well in the past. The purchasing department must take great care to recognize these conflicts and to balance both potential benefits and risks in making purchasing decisions.

The lowest bid isn't always the best bid

↙ **Purchasing highly technical research items.** The purchase of highly technical research equipment poses special problems. Uncertainties about such factors as technological problems and inflation may significantly affect the price, design, and delivery of the item, even after the initial contract is awarded. This is especially true in U.S. government-procurements of defense and space systems. For example, the first Polaris submarines had to be cut in half for the insertion of missile silos—a design element that was added when construction was almost completed. The tragic Apollo fire in 1967 that killed three astronauts necessitated redesign of the spacecraft to eliminate most of the flammable plastics. In fact, four- or five-fold price increases have been encountered on purchases of Air Force planes, such as the F-111 fighter and the C-5A cargo transport. Even technically complex items that never leave the ground are not immune to fantastic price increases: the cost of building New Orleans' "Super Dome" stadium jumped from an estimated $35 million to an actual price of $165 million.

In summary, it is significantly more difficult to purchase or to procure technically complex items that have never been built before than it is to purchase or to procure standard items with well-established specifications that have been previously produced in volume.

Manufacturing

The objective of manufacturing is to convert purchased items into finished products and to supply these products to customers. To understand the operations of a manufacturing department, we will examine (1) important characteristics of modern manufacturing; (2) classifications of manufacturing operations; (3) the direction of manufacturing activities; and (4) the means by which goods are transported to customers.

Important Characteristics of Modern Manufacturing

Two characteristics of present-day manufacturing should be singled out for detailed study: mass production and automation.

✔ **Mass production.** Mass production is far more than the production of goods in quantity. It is a method of organizing manufacturing activities in order to multiply the output of standardized articles. As we noted in Chapter 1, Eli Whitney's concept of interchangeable parts laid the foundation for mass production, which was brought to today's level of efficiency largely by Henry Ford. Ford's contributions highlight the five principles underlying modern mass production techniques:

1. *Standardization of parts:* Each part in a final product is standardized and interchangeable: it is basically the same as all other parts of the same type. In the production of television sets, for example, all the picture tubes manufactured for a given TV model must be interchangeable so that any picture tube, with the other components, can be assembled into a final set.

2. *Use of machine tools:* The standardization of parts is achieved through the use of machine tools such as drill presses and lathes. These precision tools enable almost identical parts to be produced. The use of machine tools often leads to fast, high-volume production of parts at a low per unit cost.

3. *Specialization of people and machines:* Each part of a finished product is produced by trained workers who operate machines designed to perform specific operations on that part. For example, a machine operator drills all the holes on the chassis of a television set. Specialization has greatly expanded worker output, as operators become skilled at a single task, and has led to the development of highly efficient machines that have replaced more costly human labor.

4. *Grouping of parts into subassemblies:* Items produced by specialized labor and machines are grouped into *subassemblies*—collections of parts that can be put together and stocked for use when needed. Subassemblies are then combined to make a complete unit on the final assembly line. In a television set, the tuner, the picture tube, and the channel selector are three subassemblies that are incorporated in the finished unit at final assembly.

5. *Use of moveable assembly lines:* Components of the final product pass by people and machines on a moveable assembly line, a system that capitalizes on each of the four preceding principles. In the production of a television set, for example, the chassis of the set is placed on a conveyor belt and subassemblies are added to it in a series of carefully planned operations.

Two techniques have been developed in recent years to improve the design of subassemblies: modularization and miniaturization. *Modularization* is the designing of subassemblies as self-contained units or *modules,* so that defective units may be replaced without readjusting adjacent subassemblies; on many television sets, the entire channel selector

Mass production
is more than
mere quantity

module can be replaced easily if it breaks down. *Miniaturization* is a significant reduction in the size of subassemblies and completed units; in television sets, miniaturized printed circuits have replaced wiring harnesses and vacuum tubes. The hand-held electronic calculator dramatically illustrates the efficiencies of mass production, modularization, and miniaturization. For example, in 1970, a scientist with pull and $400 could buy a hand-held electronic calculator that would add, subtract, multiply, and divide. By 1974, anyone could walk into a department store and buy a smaller, better packaged device that performed the same calculations for less than $20.

THE IMPOSSIBLE TAKES A LITTLE LONGER: AMERICAN PRODUCTION IN WORLD WAR II

In the United States, we are so accustomed to countless kinds of mass-produced goods—cars, refrigerators, clothes, TV dinners—that we take their manufacture for granted. Yet the American genius for mass production is the envy of the world. Several examples from World War II indicate this country's awesome ability to mobilize its production resources in times of need.

In 1940, Allied forces were disastrously routed from their toehold on the European continent at Dunkirk, France. Shortly afterward, Britain asked the United States to increase its military plane production from 200 to 3000 a month. The idea seemed ludicrous. But when the United States entered World War II in December 1941, President Franklin D. Roosevelt set even more ambitious production targets for the next year: 8,000,000 tons of new merchant ships, 45,000 tanks, and 60,000 planes.

Most production experts believed these goals were unattainable dreams. But U.S. manufacturers, government agencies, labor unions, and the American public cooperated to achieve these production targets. In fact, manufacturers unselfishly invited former competitors into their plants to share production ideas. Two striking examples of mass production during World War II follow.

- *Merchant ships:* Henry J. Kaiser was a bold and reckless paving and construction contractor before the war, but he managed to convince the U.S. government that he could produce the British-designed "Liberty ship." Kaiser introduced prefabrication, assembly-line techniques, and welding (to replace riveting), and built almost 1500 ships at his two California shipyards. The average construction time for one Liberty ship was 41 days, but at peak efficiency Kaiser's plant turned one out in 8 days!
- *Aircraft production:* When President Roosevelt called on the nation to produce 60,000 planes in 1942, he knew that the United States had produced only half that many planes in its entire history. Not only was the production volume staggering, but airplanes were among the most complex items to manufacture. Earlier, in 1940, the federal government had held a meeting in Detroit. There, aircraft parts were displayed and American carmakers were asked whether they could produce them. Automobile personnel were soon swarming through aircraft plants, answering "Yes." And car manufacturers began producing subcontracted parts for the aircraft industry. But Ford dissented. It wanted to make the whole plane—airframe, engines, and all—not just the parts. Ford management, visiting one aircraft plant, saw what it considered to be chaos: workers were climbing on fuselages scattered all over the plant. Ford management's recommendation: use moveable assembly lines. In one year, Ford had converted a flat pastureland outside Detroit into the world's largest aircraft plant—one mile long, a quarter of a mile wide, with a gigantic overhead conveyor system. Ultimately, this Willow Run plant produced 8760 B-24 bombers a year.

And what about Roosevelt's 1942 target of 60,000 planes—a goal that Charles Lindbergh had dismissed as "hysterical chatter"? By the end of 1942, the nation had missed its goal by only 12,000 planes. But the following year American factories turned out 86,000!

Such experiences led one production manager to give this now famous description of his firm's approach to these seemingly unreasonable goals set by the government: "The difficult we do immediately, the impossible takes a little longer."

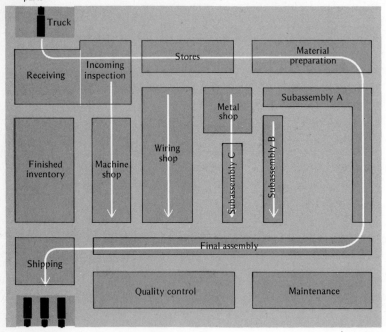

Raw
material
and
purchased
parts

Truck

Receiving

Incoming
inspection

Stores

Material
preparation

Finished
inventory

Machine
shop

Wiring
shop

Metal
shop

Subassembly C

Subassembly B

Subassembly A

Final assembly

Shipping

Quality control

Maintenance

Finished
product

10-5

Plant layout used in appliance production.

Source: Adapted from William Voris, *Production Control,* 3rd ed. (Homewood, Ill.: Richard D. Irwin, 1966), p. 41.

In the United States, mass production is probably most sophisticated in automobile and appliance manufacturing. Figure 10-5 shows an assembly line for an appliance such as a washer or a dryer and indicates how subassembly lines feed into the final assembly to achieve continuous, high-volume production.

Automation:
self-regulation
of machines
achieved by
feedback

✔ **Automation.** The term *automation* is used to describe both the production of goods by self-regulating machines and the process of making machines automatic. The distinguishing feature of a self-regulating machine is continuous *feedback* (or *feedback control*) — a process by which information about the output of the machine is repeatedly transmitted (fed back) by an automatic control device, so that discrepancies between the machine's actual performance and its desired performance can be corrected. Just as the machinery of mass production has freed humans from much of the physical labor in manufacturing operations, so the machinery of automation has freed workers from the mental labor involved in controlling machines.

Levi Strauss' Servo-Sewer is an example of the impact of automation.

After a pocket of denim is cut, the edge is sewn to prevent unraveling—one of the first of 37 sewing operations in making Levi's. A computer-contolled device called the Servo-Sewer feeds the sewn denim pocket facing and the pocket material under the sewing needle. In less than one second, the two pieces of material are sewn together, the thread is cut, and the end product—a denim pocket—is dumped into a collection basket. Automation doubles the sewer's output, reduces production costs, and improves product quality in the process.

Classifications of Manufacturing Operations

Manufacturing methods are determined by one of three characteristics: (1) the nature of the manufacturing process involved; (2) the length of the manufacturing run; or (3) the means by which the final product is obtained. These characteristics define the three major classifications of manufacturing operations, which we will now discuss.

Producing goods to your own specifications or to a customer's

✔ **Standard versus custom manufacture.** A firm that produces items in accordance with its own specifications performs *standard manufacture;* items so produced generally carry the firm's brand name. In contrast, a firm that produces items according to a customer's specifications performs *custom manufacture;* these finished items are often given the buyer's brand name. Most consumer goods are of standard manufacture: examples include breakfast cereals, appliances, and automobiles. Custom-manufactured items are produced by customer order; examples include specialized machine tools and made-to-order clothing.

Manufacturing products in extended runs or in short runs

✔ **Continuous versus batch process.** In a *continuous process,* the manufacturing operation remains essentially unchanged for extended periods of time—perhaps for months or years. Examples can be found in manufacturing industries that produce such diverse products as steel, petroleum, and automobiles. An unforeseen shutdown or a significant change in the sequence of continuous processing can be extremely costly. In contrast, in a *batch process* (or an *intermittent process*), the manufacturing time for an item is short enough that the tasks people and machines perform can be changed often so that different products can be manufactured.

Making products by assembly or by disassembly

✔ **Analytic versus synthetic process.** In an *analytic process,* final products are obtained by breaking materials down into their components. In this type of operation, the normal sequence of manufacturing activities changes. In meat packing, for example, disassembly comes first, followed by fabrication—from T-bone steaks to sandwich meats. In petroleum refining, crude oil is broken down to yield such final products as methane, gasoline, motor oil, and asphalt. In a *synthetic process,* final products are

All the people
involved in the production
of a Ford Falcon.

built or assembled from basic parts. Although the term is often restricted to processes involving chemical changes, we will use it to refer to any manufacturing operation that produces final products in this way. Thus, metal and wood items like appliances and chairs exemplify the synthetic process, as do chemical items like nylon and rayon.

Directing Manufacturing Activities

Two major functions are involved in directing manufacturing activities: production control and quality control. In contrast to fabrication and assembly, which vary significantly with the manufacturing operation involved, these two directional functions are essentially the same in all types of manufacturing firms.

Routing
and scheduling
manufacturing
operations

✔ **Production control.** Once the marketing department approves an order for a finished product, the production control section assumes responsibility for the timely delivery of the right quantity and the specified quality of that product. To accomplish this the sequence of activities necessary to complete the order must first be identified. For new products, this usually includes evaluating make-buy decisions. Next, the production-control section routes the job through the various fabrication steps, scheduling each step in light of the backlog of other work. Production control then monitors the progress of the job through the plant, making any changes in routing or scheduling needed to meet the order date.

Insuring that
the product meets
specifications

✔ **Quality control.** The function of the quality control (or inspection) section is to insure that the final product meets original specifications. The quality control section is generally responsible for the inspection of incoming purchased parts and materials, for testing the product at intervals during its fabrication, and for inspecting the final product.

Lives of customers often depend on adequate quality control. In August 1971, the Campbell Soup Company learned that botulism had been detected in some of its cans of chicken vegetable soup. Campbell's shut down the plant to which the cans were traced. After more than 300 controlled tests, Campbell's finally traced the problem to a combination of circumstances leading to slightly overstuffed cans that did not contain enough water and corrected it.

Transportation

Transportation involves the inbound movement of raw materials and parts and the shipment of finished products to buyers. In the United States, about $200 billion is spent annually on the movement of raw materials and consumer goods. Transportation contributes up to 50 percent of the selling price of many consumer products.

Moving products is an expensive job

✔ **The role of the transportation section.** The transportation (or traffic) section of the manufacturing department is responsible for seeing that the firm's final products reach buyers on time and in good condition. This section is also responsible for selecting the best *mode of transportation* (the method by which goods are moved to customers) and for making necessary storage and warehousing arrangements for the goods. In addition, the transportation section must arrange for the inbound transportation of some purchased raw materials and parts.

✔ **Selecting the best mode of transportation.** There are five basic modes of transportation: highway, rail, air, water, and pipeline. The transportation manager must select one or a combination of these modes on the basis of cost and ability to transport the firm's products to their destination in good condition and on time. When goods are perishable or needed urgently, cost considerations often become secondary. Thus, Hawaiian orchids or turbine generators needed to keep an important power plant in operation are flown to their destinations by air, even though this is generally the most costly mode of transportation.

Factors affecting the choice of transportation mode

The transportation manager chooses among transportation modes on the basis of cost and five major *operating characteristics:* speed, frequency, dependability, capability, and availability. The first two columns in Figure 10-6 identify these characteristics and explain how each is measured. The right-hand column in the figure ranks the five transportation modes from best to worst for each of the operating characteristics. For example, if speed is important in moving goods, air transportation is best, followed by highway, rail, water, and pipeline. Figure 10-6 can also be used to evaluate a given mode; thus, pipeline transportation is frequent and dependable, but it is also slow, inflexible in terms of the goods it can move, and relatively unavailable.

The transportation manager's selection of the mode of shipment varies with the product, location of customer, urgency, and changes in the relative cost of different modes. Products that have a high weight in relation to their value are moved by water when possible; examples are iron ore, coal, and grain. When customers are not accessible by air, water, rail, or pipeline, there is little choice but to use highway transportation. If a machine breakdown holds up a production line, the high cost of flying the

10-6 Comparison of operating characteristics
of the five modes of transportation.

Operating characteristic	How characteristic is measured	Ranking (best to worst)				
		1	2	3	4	5
Speed	Time from origin to destination.	Air	Highway	Rail	Water	Pipeline
Frequency	Number of movements between end points per time period.	Pipeline	Highway	Air	Rail	Water
Dependability	Performance compared with published or promised schedule.	Pipeline	Highway	Rail	Water	Air
Capability	Flexibility in moving a variety of goods.	Water	Rail	Highway	Air	Pipeline
Availability	Number of end points connected by the service.	Highway	Rail	Air	Water	Pipeline

Source: Adapted from J.L. Heskett, Robert J. Ivie, and Nicholas A. Glaskowsky, Jr., *Business Logistics*, pp. 70–71. Copyright © 1964 The Ronald Press Company, New York.

replacement part from a distant city may be inconsequential. Finally, if the relative cost of one mode of transportation decreases, that mode will probably be used more frequently. For example, as air-freight rates decline, many firms are switching from highway or rail to air transportation. The knowledgeable transporation manager keeps abreast of changes in such factors.

✔ Intermodal operations and containerization. Often, a manufacturing firm's transportation manager finds that using only one mode of transportation, such as highway motor truck, is slower or more costly that combining two or more modes of transportation. The best-known transportation combination is *piggyback* or trailer-on-flatcar service, which allows truckers to place their highway trailers on railroad flat cars. Thus, a refrigerator manufacturer can load its finished product into highway trailers sitting on a railroad flatcar at the firm's shipping dock. The refrigerators will be moved by rail to the city nearest the point of delivery. Then the piggyback trailer will be unloaded from the flatcar and hooked to the tractor cab that pulls the trailer. Deliveries of the refrigerators to wholesalers or retailers will then be made by highway. Other, less well known intermodal combinations include highway trailers on ships or barges (appropriately called "fishyback" service), highway trailers on airplanes, and railroad freight cars on ships or barges.

As intermodal transportation increases, both shippers and carriers are attempting to simplify the shift from one mode to the next. One result produced by this effort is an increasing stress on *containerization* — packing

Using several transportation modes on one shipment

like or unlike goods in enclosed boxes to eliminate rehandling these goods during shipment. Normally, containers are fitted with fixtures that allow them to be transferred easily from one mode of transportation to another. Containers are now used by all major modes of transportation except pipeline. Containerization generally (1) lowers handling costs and freight rates; (2) lessens product damage in transit; (3) reduces or eliminates pilferage during shipment; and (4) lowers in-transit insurance costs. Partially offsetting these advantages are the cost of the containers and the problem of returning empty containers to a point of reuse.

✔ **Transportation issues in the 1970s.** A growing nation requires a healthy transportation system to move both its goods and its people. Yet, many firms in the transportation business have gone bankrupt or have suffered severe losses. Examples are the Penn Central Railroad, the Rock Island Railroad, and Pan American World Airways. This poses a vital question: should competition be allowed or encouraged among different modes of transportation? For example, can the public allow railroads to shut down when they are essential to some small towns, when their competitors (highways and airports) are subsidized by taxes, and when railroads use less energy to deliver a ton of goods than either trucks or airplanes? Should American commuters be permitted to continue to drive private cars into the central cities, in spite of the tremendous pollution and energy costs involved? Even transportation experts do not agree on the answers to such questions. Because the public interest is heavily involved, government agencies such as the Interstate Commerce Commission and the Federal Aviation Administration regulate the operations of railroads and airlines. Such regulations will be discussed in Chapter 18.

KEY POINTS TO REMEMBER

1. Production is the use of people and machines to convert materials into finished products and to supply these products to customers. Production includes product development, purchasing, and manufacturing.
2. The development of a new product involves six steps: idea generation, screening, business analysis, product development, test marketing, and commercialization. Roughly one in every 58 new product ideas becomes a commercial success.
3. When the product-development department designs a new product, a make-buy decision determines which components will be purchased from outside suppliers and which will be fabricated by the firm itself.
4. The purchasing department obtains the necessary materials and parts from outside suppliers by soliciting bids from qualified vendors and then selecting the best bid—normally on the basis of price, quality,

delivery, and service. Which of these or some other bid criteria the firm considers most important depends on the type and use of the item to be purchased and the speed with which it is needed.

5. Mass production and automation have revolutionized manufacturing methods and have made higher quality products available at lower prices.

6. There are three broad classifications of manufacturing operations: standard versus custom manufacture, continuous versus batch process, and analytic versus synthetic process.

7. The functions of the manufacturing department vary significantly according to type of manufacturing operations and nature of product.

8. When final products have been assembled, the transportation section must ship them to customers on time and in good condition using one or a combination of the five available modes of transportation: highway, rail, air, water, pipeline. Developments such as piggyback service and containerization allow a business to use two or more transportation modes to move one shipment.

QUESTIONS FOR DISCUSSION

1. What are the six steps in the development of a new product? How does each step help a firm to minimize its chances of introducing an unprofitable product?

2. What factors might influence a firm in determining which components in a final product it will buy and which it will make?

3. Describe how each of the following pairs of purchasing objectives might conflict: (a) low inventory investment and few out-of-stock problems, (b) good vendor relations and low purchase prices; (c) low inventory investment and low purchase prices.

4. How does the moveable assembly line use each of the following mass production principles: (a) standardization; (b) use of machine tools, (c) specialization, (d) grouping parts into subassemblies?

5. Explain how the manufacturing functions of production control, fabrication, assembly (or disassembly), and quality control might differ in (a) the job-shop production of made-to-order kitchen cabinets; (b) meat packing.

6. What factors should a firm consider in selecting a mode of transportation for moving its finished products to customers? Describe the transportation mode or modes that you would be likely to use for each of the following products: (a) coal; (b) petroleum; (c) computers; (d) urgently needed parts.

7. How are some transportation modes—such as highway, air, and water (barge) transportation—directly or indirectly supported by tax dollars? In what ways has this put railroads at a disadvantage?

SHORT CASE

In purchasing decisions, identifying the best alternative may involve the use of the choice-selection method. Assume that on June 15, the steel buyer for a small manufacturing firm is trying to decide what purchasing policy to follow for the last half of the year. In buying steel—the firm's crucial raw material—the buyer has generally followed one of two policies: a *forward-buying* policy, in which enough steel is purchased at one time to cover production requirements for six months, or a *hand-to-mouth* policy, in which steel is purchased one month at a time.

The buyer knows that wage contracts in the steel industry lapse on September 1. Further, from past experiences, the buyer knows that there is a distinct possibility a strike may occur September 1 that will produce some price increase in steel. After considering the problem, the buyer identifies three principal outcome states:

O_1: No steel strike, but a small price increase in steel starting September 1.

O_2: A three-month steel strike starting on September 1, followed by a small price increase in steel.

O_3: A three-month steel strike starting on September 1, followed by a large price increase in steel.

Based on past experience, the buyer assesses that the probability of no strike and a small price increase is about 40 percent (or that the likelihood of a strike is about 60 percent). If a strike occurs, the buyer believes that the chances of a small or a large price increase are about equal. Thus, the probability of occurrence of each of these two final outcome states is 30 percent.

The alternatives and uncertainties and the estimated consequences (company profits for the coming six months) for each outcome state are summarized below:

	Outcome State		
Alternative	O_1: No strike; small price increase	O_2: Strike; small price increase	O_3: Strike; large price increase
A_1: Follow forward-buying policy	$40,000	$40,000	$40,000
A_2: Follow hand-to-mouth policy	$60,000	−$10,000	−$20,000

As the payoff table shows, the buyer faces a severe penalty if hand-to-mouth buying policy is followed and a steel strike occurs: if the firm has no steel inventory on hand, it will be forced to shut down temporarily.

(a) From the descriptions of forward buying and hand-to-mouth buying, explain the variations in the cell values in the above payoff table.
(b) Calculate the expected value for each alternative.
(c) Which alternative do you recommend? Why?

CAREER SELECTION: POSITIONS IN PRODUCT DEVELOPMENT, PURCHASING, MANUFACTURING, AND TRANSPORTATION

CAREERS IN PRODUCT DEVELOPMENT

Drafters prepare detailed drawings of manufactured goods and their component parts. In addition to determining an item's exact dimensions and specifications, drafters also calculate the strength, quality, quantity, and cost of the product materials. Technical training is mandatory, and may be acquired in technical institutes, in community colleges, or in apprenticeship on-the-job training programs. Yearly income averages $11,000. Future job opportunities are promising due to the increased production of technically complex items. (*Additional information:* American Institute for Design and Drafting; 3119 Price Road; Bartlesville, Oklahoma 74003.)

Industrial designers use their artistic talents to develop attractive and functional products. Applying their creative abilities as well as their knowledge of marketing and materials, designers create product models to successfully compete with similar goods already on the market. Large firms generally require a bachelor's degree in industrial design or fine arts. Annual salary ranges from $8000 to $20,000. Employment opportunities are expected to expand slowly as a dual consequence of increasing consumer population and rising incomes. (*Additional information:* Industrial Designers Society of America; 1750 Old Meadow Road; McLean, Virginia 22101.)

CAREERS IN PURCHASING

Uninterrupted manufacturing operations require **purchasing agents** to obtain adequate supplies of high-quality items (machinery, raw materials, and component parts) at the lowest possible cost to the firm. Purchasing agents also insure the timely delivery of requisitioned items and authorize payments once these items have arrived. An ability to analyze numbers and technical data is essential, and large firms often require a bachelor's degree in business administration or liberal arts. Annual salary ranges from $9000 to $45,000, depending on experience. The demand for purchasing agents who are knowledgeable in specific areas is expected to increase moderately as business functions and products become more and more specialized. (*Additional information:* National Association of Purchasing Management; 11 Park Place; New York, New York 10007.)

CAREERS IN MANUFACTURING

Manufacturing inspectors determine if raw materials, parts, and finished products conform to previously established specifications. Manufacturing inspectors are trained on the job, then assume limited responsibilities under close supervision (unskilled inspectors), and later advance to more specialized positions (skilled inspectors or quality-control technicians). An aptitude for numbers and measurement is indispensable in all quality-control activities. Annual earnings vary from $7000 to $14,000. Employment opportunities are expected to increase moderately despite a growing reliance on automatic inspection equipment. (*Additional information:* American Society for Quality Control; 161 West Wisconsin Avenue; Milwaukee, Wisconsin 53203.)

Shipping clerks must correctly fill and address a firm's outgoing orders and must record the weight and the cost of each shipment. *Receiving clerks* verify incoming goods against original orders and record the condition of each shipment. Clerks are usually high-school graduates who receive necessary on-the-job training. Some duties necessitate physical stamina. Annual earnings average $9000. The number of available clerical positions are expected to increase, although the rate of growth will be reduced due to automation. (*Additional information:* State Supervisor of Office Occupation Education; State Department of Education; your state Capital.)

Department supervisors communicate company policies to blue-collar workers. Specific duties include training new workers, scheduling work assignments, and maintaining production and employee records. Department supervisors are experienced, skilled, and possess leadership abilities — qualities that have facilitated their promotion through the ranks of blue-collar workers. A college education is not mandatory but increases the likelihood of advancement to higher management positions. Annual income is approximately $12,000. Employment opportunities are expected to increase moderately as our economy relies more heavily on complex production processes that require skilled supervision. (*Additional information:* American Management Association; 135 West 50th Street; New York, New York 10020.)

CAREERS IN TRANSPORTATION

Traffic managers oversee the transportation of materials and finished goods — a responsibility that entails selecting the most efficient mode of transportation as well as particular routes and carriers. Traffic managers must keep informed of changing transportation technology and government transportation regulations. College graduates comprise a growing proportion of the nation's 20,000 traffic managers. Yearly salary ranges from $10,000 to more than $40,000. Employment opportunities are expected to increase slowly due to widening distribution markets. (*Additional information:* American Society of Traffic and Transportation, Inc.; 547 West Jackson Boulevard; Chicago, Illinois 60606.)

A CRITICAL BUSINESS DECISION

—made by Edwin H. Land

THE SITUATION The date is April 25, 1972. Three thousand shareholders of the Polaroid Corporation sit in a cavernous warehouse and watch the man who has literally invented the $540 million-a-year instant photography market. He withdraws a box-shaped object from his jacket, unfolds it to reveal a camera, and focuses it on his meershaum pipe. He pushes the shutter button five times in quick succession. About a second after each touch, a 3×3 inch piece of dry plastic emerges from the front of the camera. The shareholders watch in amazement as color pictures of the meershaum pipe form on the five plastic squares in less than a minute.

The man is Edwin H. Land, inventor-scientist and board chairman of Polaroid, who dropped out of Harvard University in 1928 to pursue experiments in light polarization. Although he never graduated from college, he is called Dr. Land by nearly everyone: Land holds 14 honorary degrees, including an honorary doctor of science degree from Harvard in 1957, and hundreds of patents.

The camera is the SX-70, a revolutionary device requiring 260 transistors that Land plans to introduce for sale by Christmas of 1972. Boxes of blank film packages are already sitting in warehouses awaiting Land's decision on a name for the camera. The SX-70 is the culmination of Land's conviction as early as 1963 that consumers would be eager to buy a Polaroid camera that was easy to operate, portable, and litter-free. Land is so convinced of his theory that he never spends a dollar on market research to verify it.

THE DECISION As Land begins to research the SX-70 in 1963, he faces tremendous problems in product development, purchasing, and manufacturing. Land divides the development of the SX-70 into two parallel research efforts on film and camera. Land himself shuffles between the two projects, occasionally unnerving some associates. One project member recalls: "When we seemed to be putting all our efforts into camera design, someone would say, 'Damn it, Dr. Land, how about making the film?' And he would reply, 'Oh, that's all been taken care of; don't worry about that.' Actually, the film people couldn't believe their ears."

Failures litter the route of the SX-70 camera, but so do flashes of brilliance. Land originally wants a camera that doesn't need to be unfolded; two years are lost proving that this idea is impracticable. Searching for a powerful motor to run the camera, a Polaroid engineer wonders if the motor on his son's toy racing car might work; a variation of this toy motor eventually powers the SX-70. To avoid poor pictures from weak batteries, Land has an inspiration: put the battery in the film pack. Perhaps the most revolutionary concept is the film. Land wants to avoid wasting a photographer's time waiting for the film to develop inside the camera, so he seeks a way to develop the film outside the camera instead. Chemists work four years to accomplish this near miracle.

Land must make major decisions as to which components of the SX-70 to make and which to buy. In the past, Polaroid has manufactured only the camera shutter mechanism and portions of its film pack and has relied on other firms to produce and assemble the camera frames and the remaining parts of the film pack. In particular, Land faces make-buy decisions on three components of the new SX-70 camera: the camera frame, a special ten-light flashbulb assembly, and the film pack.

QUESTIONS

1. Identify the factors affecting the make-buy decision for each of the camera components.
2. If you were Edwin Land, which items of the SX-70 would you make and which would you buy?

PART FOUR

ACCOUNTING, FINANCE, AND DATA PROCESSING

Business can be viewed either in real or in financial terms. In real terms, business utilizes inputs of raw materials, labor, technology, and managerial talent to provide the outputs of goods and services that customers purchase. But each real business input or output has a financial counterpart. Raw materials must be purchased, labor must be hired and paid, technology must be developed or acquired from others for a fee, and management must be compensated. To be able to gain the real inputs essential to produce its goods and services, a business must obtain sufficient resources from the sale of its outputs. Moreover, if a business is to continue to operate, it must make a profit—revenues from selling its outputs must exceed the cost of its inputs.

The financial aspects of business discussed in Part Four are equally as important as the marketing and the production aspects presented in Part Three. Chapter 11 describes the accounting and budgeting process, which involves the recording and the classification of financial data. Chapter 12 probes the ways in which funds for operating and expanding a business are obtained throughout American industry. Chapter 13 deals with the effective use of the financial resources of a business—a key aspect of success or failure for most firms. Chapter 14 introduces the banking system and security markets, which represent major business sectors in their own right and which are the main sources of outside funding for American business. Finally, Chapter 15 deals with electronic data processing and computers. While computers are frequently used in physical production and marketing of goods and services, their widest application is in processing the financial data utilized by business.

Never ask of money spent
Where the spender thinks it went.
Nobody was ever meant
To remember or invent
What he did with every cent.

Robert Frost

CHAPTER **11**

ACCOUNTING AND BUDGETING

ix months after landing penniless in New York City, 29-year-old Thomas Edison sold his first invention, an improved stock ticker, and promptly established his own business to manufacture it. Edison used a very simple accounting system in his new shop: he put the bills he owed in one book and the accounts due him in another. When financial problems mounted because of his inability to identify and collect amounts due, Edison stubbornly refused to seek help, exclaiming: "I can always hire some mathematicians, but they can't hire me!"

Eventually, Edison was persuaded to hire an accountant to try to unravel his tangled financial affairs. Two weeks later, the accountant reported that the business had made a $3,000 profit, and Edison gave a party for his employees. Several days later, a downcast accountant approached the great inventor to announce that he had found some bills in a pigeonhole that converted the $3,000 profit to a $500 loss. The accountant continued to find financial records in the most unexpected places. Finally, he approached Edison with a smile and said: "Mr. Edison, I think I have found the last of your missing records, and I find you have been operating at a profit of $7,000."

This incident illustrates the critical importance of accurate accounting information in business. Edison was a genius at production as well as invention, yet his failure to collect amounts owed by customers on a regular basis nearly forced him into bankruptcy. The effective use of accurate and timely financial information is a prerequisite for business success.

In this chapter we will explore the nature of accounting and the three main aspects of the accounting process: (1) recording and classifying accounting transactions; (2) constructing accounting statements; and (3) verifying and evaluating accounting information. The chapter concludes with an examination of budgets—projected financial statements that guide a firm in conducting and assessing its business activities.

Accurate and timely financial information is essential in business

What Is Accounting?

Accounting is the functional area of business that deals with the collection, organization, analysis, and presentation of financial data.

Users of Accounting Information

Users of accounting data on the operations of a business firm can be divided into two types: those inside and those outside the firm. *Insiders* include management and employees who use the accounting data to make decisions on allocating the firm's financial resources. *Outsiders* include potential investors or creditors, the government, and the general public.

Users of accounting data are located both inside . . .

✔ **Management.** Managers make extensive use of accounting data as a vehicle for financial communication. The most important functions of accounting are to provide information on the financial status of a business and to aid in managerial decision making. Accounting data also assist management in its planning and control functions, aid in the detection of theft or fraud by employees, and provide useful information for evaluating the performance of the business.

✔ **Creditors, investors, and owners.** Most businesses experience a continuing need for new financial resources. These funds can be borrowed from creditors such as commercial banks, solicited from potential investors, or contributed by existing owners. Creditors and many investors rely on accurate, up-to-date financial information when deciding whether to lend or to supply money to a business. Stockbrokers, security analysts, and individual investors examine accounting data very closely when they purchase or sell securities. Business owners use accounting data to evaluate management decisions; in rare cases, owners may even replace management because of its poor performance as measured by accounting data.

. . . and outside the firm

✔ **Government.** Both large and small businesses interact with government at the federal, state, and local levels. Businesses are required by law to collect social security contributions, adhere to wage and hour standards, pay taxes, and meet a host of other requirements. Accurate accounting records are essential if a business is to fulfill its legal obligations. Accurate accounting data can also be helpful in planning business activities that will minimize future tax burdens.

✔ **The public.** Requests for wage increases are sometimes based on the purported ability of a business to absorb higher labor costs from profits. Consumers occasionally blame high prices on what they believe to be unfair markups by retailers. Newspapers frequently report the financial status of local businesses. Responsible citizens are often concerned with the financial well-being of businesses within their community. In all these cases, the release of timely and accurate accounting data can help to keep the general public informed.

Types of Accountants

Both profit-making businesses and nonprofit organizations employ accountants

As a result of the increasing demand for accurate accounting data, the number of accountants has grown steadily during the 1970s. Qualified accountants find a ready market for their skills, and the accounting profession has become a major source of talent for promotion to top management. A variety of accounting specialists serve both business and nonprofit organizations.

✔ **Industrial accountants.** Business firms employ *industrial accountants* (also called *commercial accountants*) to draw up important financial statements and to solve a variety of managerial accounting problems. Most large companies maintain an accounting department headed by a controller, a vice president, or a chief accountant. Since accounting practices and procedures differ among industries, most businesses attempt to hire some accountants with previous experience in their industry. Small businesses frequently employ accountants on a part-time basis or purchase financial recordkeeping services from specialized outside firms.

✔ **Government accountants.** Federal, state, and local governments also require the services of thousands of accountants. *Government accountants* typically handle financial data for organizations that do not seek profit as a primary goal.

✔ **Certified public accountants.** *Certified public accountants* (CPAs) are the guardians of accounting principles and procedures. CPAs are employed primarily in public accounting firms and specialize in verifying the financial records of businesses and nonprofit organizations. The most important tasks performed by certified public accountants are:

1. Verifying that a business or other organization has used proper accounting procedures and that reported financial data are accurate.
2. Certifying that records have been kept consistently and accurately. This certification is indicated in a firm's annual report by the statement that the financial data conform to "generally accepted accounting principles."
3. Assisting organizations with accounting procedures, budgets, internal review procedures, credit policies, and other financial matters.

Tasks performed by public accountants

Recently, public accounting firms have expanded into the management consulting field, where they assist other organizations with problems ranging from tax-saving programs to the marketing of new products.

THE INCOME TAX PEOPLE

The television camera stared unblinking at Henry Bloch, president of H&R Block, Inc., "the income tax people." Firmly and effectively, Henry Bloch began to discuss one of the 17 reasons why taxpayers should let H&R Block prepare their tax returns.

H&R Block, Inc., was formed by two brothers, Henry and Richard Bloch (who substituted the "k" in their company's name for the "h" in their last name to avoid confusing the general public). In 1955, H&R Block was a small Kansas City, Missouri, accounting firm with annual sales amounting to only $20,000. Then the Bloch brothers recognized a potential market: with tax laws becoming more and more complicated, wouldn't the public agree to pay professional accountants to prepare its federal income tax returns? Fast tax-preparation service would be easy to finance. Offices could be rented from December to mid-April, and employees could be hired only for that four-month period. And as Henry Bloch recalls those early days, "the company's greatest competition was the individual doing his taxes."

Today, H&R Block's 6500 storefront offices prepare 10 percent of all the U.S. tax returns submitted annually. The Bloch brothers' profits have risen dramatically, too. Although each receives a salary of only $36,000 the brothers have accumulated a fortune in H&R Block stock that is estimated at $150 million.

But the company does face some problems. Recent changes in tax laws have taken millions of Americans off the federal tax rolls and reduced H&R Block's market. And new competitors have entered the field, including banks that offer computer-based, tax-preparation services.

"Our company is maturing," warns Henry Bloch. "If we stay exclusively in tax preparation in the next ten years, we will show a drastically lower rate of increase. Being a public company, it's not profits that count, it's the increase in profits. I want the growth to keep going up."

H&R Block is far from resting on its laurels. Richard Bloch is investigating the possibility of opening foreign offices. And Block offers tax-preparation courses at cost to potential employees. In 1973, the company met with great success when it opened 147 income-tax centers in Sears, Roebuck & Company stores—a program both companies plan to expand. H&R Block has also opened several centers for the preparation of executives' tax returns on an appointment-only, year-round basis.

H&R Block is indeed an outstanding example of a small accounting firm that "made good" by recognizing a market for accounting expertise that no other business controlled.

Henry Bloch

Richard Bloch

The CPA is a highly trained professional certified by state law, who must pass a stiff examination administered by the state, complete designated educational requirements, have several years of accounting experience, and meet residency and character qualifications. Exact procedures for obtaining the CPA certificate vary from state to state. The CPA's stock in trade is a reputation for integrity. All CPAs are obligated to honor the accounting standards established by the Financial Accounting Standards Board of the American Institute of Certified Public Accountants. Some CPAs are self-employed or develop careers as professional executives. But most CPAs are engaged in public acounting, where the CPA certificate is essential for advancement.

CPAs must have a reputation for integrity

✔ **Tax accountants.** *Tax accountants* are familiar with the intricacies of both federal and state tax laws and aid businesses and individuals in their tax-planning programs and in the preparation of tax returns. Some tax accountants also assist individuals in planning estates and trusts.

The Role of Accounting in Business

In the past decade, accounting has changed in two important ways. First, computers have revolutionized the scope and the effectiveness of accounting procedures, eliminating many of the routine, time-consuming tasks formerly performed by accounting personnel. By recording their financial data on computer input media (punched cards, magnetic tapes, and so on), businesses can utilize computers to develop accounting statements more quickly and accurately and in greater detail than ever before.

Computers now perform many routine accounting tasks

Second, accounting is increasingly oriented toward providing financial data relevant to a firm's daily business decisions. Accountants formerly considered their primary function to be to report accurately on the overall financial position of a business and to detect any theft or embezzlement by employees. In a sense, accounting looked backward and concentrated on precisely reporting the firm's past operations. Today, the accounting function in business firms, often called *managerial acounting,* extends deeply into the area of managerial decision making. Managerial accounting is forward-looking and involves generating information that enables managers to anticipate potential problems and to identify both the past and the future profitabilities of various products, divisions, and courses of action. Using traditional accounting data as a base but interpreting the data in new ways, managerial accountants answer such questions as: "In which operations are costs too high in comparison with typical production and distribution costs in the past?" "In terms of estimated output and cost, is it better to purchase a new machine or to keep the old one?" Today, accountants in many large businesses devote a considerable portion of their time to dealing with managerial issues.

Managerial accounting provides information for decision making

Recording and Classifying Accounting Transactions

A basic objective of accounting is to present all of a firm's relevant financial information in a form that can be easily understood by potential users. The first step toward achieving this goal is recording and classifying accounting transactions.

The Accounting Transaction: The Basic Unit of Accounting

Accounting transactions: activities that affect the financial position of the firm

An *accounting transaction* is any activity that has an immediate and measurable financial impact on a firm, such as a decrease in its physical or financial capital or an increase in its financial obligations to outsiders. The sale or purchase of a product or service, wages paid to employees, tax payments, and the issuance of corporate stock are typical accounting transactions.

Recording Accounting Transactions

Transactions may be recorded by computers . . .

Operations in a modern department store illustrate how a contemporary accounting system works. When the customer makes a purchase (say, a pair of shoes) the salesclerk records the transaction on a point-of-purchase computer terminal. The numbers the clerk types indicate the date of the sale, the department in which the sale is made, the dollar value of the sale, the specific item sold (the style and size of shoes), and whether payment is made by cash or credit. The computer terminal prints both a salescheck and a receipt. Simultaneously, information about the customer's purchase is transferred to a computer, which maintains a continuous record of the department store's day-to-day sales.

Few businesses maintain accounting operations as elaborate as a point-of-purchase computer system. Nevertheless, most large companies use computers to record and to process financial data. Employees record financial data by typing them onto computer cards or tapes (as we will see in Chapter 15). In some small businesses, accounting transactions are recorded by hand in *journals* and *ledgers,* large volumes containing multi-columned ruled sheets. Increasingly, however, small businesses are taking advantage of the computerized recordkeeping services offered by public accounting firms.

Because businesses conduct many types of accounting transactions each day, accounting systems include separate classifications for the sales a firm makes, its cash holdings, its buildings, and so on. The *register* (or ledger) is a listing of all accounting transactions in a given category, and the *account* is the title given to the entire register or ledger.

Proper recording of financial data requires that hundreds or thousands of accounting transactions be organized into several dozen accounts. Computers automatically place accounting transactions into the proper categories by "reading" the number keyed to individual accounts. Both computer-based and manual accounting systems can provide reliable financial information only if accounting transactions are completely and accurately recorded.

Accountants must rely on their own judgment when recording certain accounting transactions. For example, suppose that a business purchases a new truck for $3000 that is expected to be useful for five years, at which time it will be worth only $500. Clearly, an accounting transaction occurs as the truck *depreciates* or loses value each year. But how should this acounting transaction be recorded?

Straight-line depreciation is one method accountants use to record depreciation. Annual straight-line depreciation can be found by subtracting the *salvage value* of an asset — the price it can be sold for at the end of its useful life — from its purchase price and then dividing by the number of years of its expected life. Thus, straight-line depreciation indicates that the $3000 truck loses $500 in value each year ($3000 *minus* $500, or $2500, *divided by* 5). So at the end of the first year, the accountant might record a loss of $500 as the proper amount for this transaction.

However, a motor vehicle depreciates more rapidly the first year after purchase than it does in subsequent years, as a motorist who attempts to sell a year-old car quickly discovers. Should the accountant accept the $500 figure or recognize that the truck will actually be worth $1000 less if it is sold after the first year? Similar questions of judgment arise in handling the depreciation of land, buildings, and equipment — assets whose useful lives and salvage values can at best only be estimated. Decisions like recording depreciation require that top management and the firm's accountants jointly agree on the acceptable recording procedures to be followed consistently over time.

Classifying Accounting Transactions

Accountants organize financial data by classifying every accounting transaction into an appropriate category (or account) and recording it in the firm's register. For example, the cash sale of a $150 bicycle by Century Cycle, Inc., a small bicycle retail and repair shop, is recorded as a $150 increase in Century Cycle's "sales" account and a $150 increase in its "cash" account.

A key principle of accounting is the *double-entry system,* in which each accounting transaction is recorded at least twice. This is why the $150 bicycle sale affects both Century Cycle's sales and cash accounts. By recording transactions more than once, the double-entry system sharply reduces the number of errors that are made when thousands of accounting transactions are recorded and classified. A separate register is usually kept for each category (account) shown on the income statement and the balance sheet, both of which will be discussed in the following section. In addition to recording the proper financial amounts involved in each transaction, accountants must master the principles used to place each transaction in its appropriate accounts.

Constructing Accounting Statements

Masses of financial data are of little value unless they are summarized in an organized form and presented in *accounting statements*. The most important accounting statements are the *income statement*, which indicates the revenues, costs, and profits of a business in a selected period, and the *balance sheet*, which shows the financial position of a firm on a given date.

The normal accounting period is one year

Any financial summary is based on a given length of time, called the *accounting period*. The normal accounting period for submitting comprehensive financial data to outsiders is one year; in addition, management frequently asks its accounting staff to prepare monthly or quarterly reports for internal use. In the United States, individual businesses are permitted to select their own accounting (or fiscal) year, which need not correspond to the calendar year. Since the preparation of year-end accounting statements is time-consuming, most businesses prepare such statements during periods of slack activity.

Accountants also summarize financial data in *supplemental accounting statements*. The most important of these is the statement of changes in financial position, which shows how a business acquired and used funds during a given period (usually one year). Supplemental accounting statements, which are discussed in detail in accounting textbooks, utilize the financial data developed for a firm's income statement and balance sheet and yield additional insights into the financial operations of a business.

The Income Statement

The income statement shows the profitability of a business

The income statement indicates the profits or losses sustained by a business during an accounting period (again, usually one year). Income statements are often prepared on a monthly basis for internal use by the firm. Provisional and usually incomplele quarterly income statements are often sent to stockholders, and a complete income statement is made available to the public at the end of the firm's fiscal year.

Profits and losses on an income statement are arrived at by calculating the difference between a firm's *revenues* (monies earned by a business) and its *expenses* (costs incurred by the firm in earning revenues). If revenues exceed expenses, the business earns a *profit,* which in accounting is defined as the difference between revenues and expenses. Conversely, if expenses are greater than revenues, the business suffers a *loss.* A business that experiences continuing losses will eventually be forced into bankruptcy.

Figure 11-1 shows the income statement of Century Cycle, Inc. for its fiscal year ending March 31, 19X1. The income statement reflects the company's *net income* (or profit) of $11,500 after taxes for the year. Century Cycle's income statement is divided into three basic categories: revenues, expenses, and net income.

11-1 Income statement for Century Cycle, Inc., for the fiscal year ending March 31, 19X1. Income statements indicate whether a business has made a profit or suffered a loss during a designated accounting period.

CENTURY CYCLE, INC.
Income Statement
For the Year Ended March 31, 19X1

Revenues			
Gross sales	$152,000		
Adjustments for bad debts	−2,000		
Net sales			$150,000
Cost of goods sold			
Inventory expenses	70,000		
Depreciation (repair shop and equipment)	3,000		
Labor (repair shop)	7,000		
Total cost of goods sold			80,000
Gross profit			70,000
Operating expenses			
Selling expenses			
Sales salaries	30,000		
Advertising expenses	4,000		
Total selling expenses		$34,000	
General expenses			
Office salaries	12,000		
Telephone and utilities	2,000		
Total general expenses		14,000	
Total operating expenses			48,000
Net operating income			22,000
Interest expenses			7,000
Net income before taxes			15,000
Income taxes			3,500
Net income for year			11,500
Net income per share			
(11,000 shares outstanding)			$1.05

✔ **Revenues.** The most important source of revenue for most businesses is sales to customers, which may be in the form of cash or accounts receivable (cash due the firm that will be collected later). Other common sources of revenue include income from a firm's financial investments, rent on property it owns, and royalties from its patents.

Adjustments to a firm's revenue are generally divided into three categories. *Discounts and allowances* include reductions in the prices offered to customers for prompt payment or for buying in large quantities. *Returned merchandise* represents refunds made to customers for defective or unsatisfactory merchandise. *Bad debts* are uncollectable accounts receivable, which usually arise because of the financial weakness or bankruptcy of customers. Discounts and allowances, returned merchandise, and bad debts represent reductions in a firm's revenue.

The revenue portion of the income statement is usually divided into the following accounts or categories:

Accounts in
the revenues portion of
an income statement

1. *Revenues:* The total financial receipts associated with all of a firm's commercial activities.
2. *Gross sales:* The total dollar value of all sales completed during the accounting period.
3. *Adjustments to sales:* Discounts and allowances, returned merchandise, and estimates of bad debts resulting from credit extended to customers.
4. *Net sales:* Gross sales *minus* adjustments to sales, or the net dollar amount a business can realistically expect to receive from its sales.
5. *Other income:* Income from equipment or building rentals, interest income on securities held by the business, the patent fees collected from other organizations.
6. *Net revenue or net sales:* The total receipts a business can realistically expect to earn during the accounting period (equal to net sales *plus* other income).

Because Century Cycle is a comparatively simple business, Figure 11-1 includes accounts only for revenues, gross and net sales, and adjustments. Specific dollar figures shown beside each account on the statement reflect Century Cycle's business operations for the fiscal year ending March 31, 19X1, as well as that company's methods of recording and classifying accounting transactions.

✔ **Expenses.** The expenses shown on an income statement are often divided into two categories: costs of goods sold and operating expenses. *Cost of goods sold* include materials purchased and inventory used, direct costs of the necessary labor to secure the firm's output, and plant and equipment depreciation. *Gross profit* is found by subtracting the cost of goods sold from net revenues. *Operating expenses* include the salaries of the sales force and top management, advertising costs, office supplies purchased, depreciation on office equipment, and the like. *Net operating income* is found by subtracting operating expenses from gross profit.

Expense accounts appearing on income statements include:

1. *Cost of goods sold:* The direct costs of manufacturing or obtaining the products sold by a business. Cost of goods sold may appear as a single account on the income statement or may be divided into inventory, labor, and depreciation expenses.
2. *Inventory expenses:* Beginning inventories (raw materials, goods in process, and finished goods owned by the firm) *plus* materials purchased during the year *less* ending inventories. Inventory expenses represent the costs of materials used to produce the firm's final products.
3. *Labor expenses:* Wages and salaries paid to production workers.
4. *Depreciation expenses:* Costs associated with the deterioration in plant and equipment as production continues. Depreciation expenses must be estimated by accountants and by top management.
5. *Gross profit:* Revenues *minus* cost of goods sold.
6. *Operating expenses:* These are comprised of *selling expenses* (sales salaries, advertising expenses, etc.) and *general expenses* (office salaries, utilities, insurance expenses, etc.). Some firms list each selling and general expense separately on their income statement.
7. *Net operating income:* Gross profit *minus* operating expenses or the profit a firm earns from its business operations.

Accounts in the expenses portion of an income statement

Because Century Cycle is a retail business, Figure 11-1 gives a detailed breakdown of its operating expenses. Many manufacturing businesses, on the other hand, combine all operating expenses as one total on the income statement.

**Net income:
profits of a business**

✔ **Net income.** The net income or profits section of the income statement shows a firm's net income for one business year after financial expenses and taxes have been deducted from net operating income. Accounts related to net income include:

1. *Interest expenses:* Interest costs associated with a firm's use of borrowed money.
2. *Net income before taxes:* Net operating income *less* interest expenses (and property or sales taxes, if applicable).
3. *Income taxes:* Federal and state corporate income taxes paid or owed on the gross income (net income before taxes) earned by the business.
4. *Net income:* Business profits after all expenses and taxes have been paid.

Accounts in the net-income portion of an income statement

5. *Net income per share:* Net income *divided by* the number of shares of outstanding company stock.

Net income and net income per share are the most closely watched pieces of financial data in American business. Management, creditors, investors, labor unions, and the general public frequently base decisions solely or mainly on "the bottom line," or the profit performance of a business.

✔ **Other uses of income statements.** The income statement is a key tool in business decision making. It indicates the profits or losses sustained by a business and can forewarn management of potential financial difficulties. The financial data shown on an income statement are a major measure of a firm's performance; for this reason, separate income statements are often developed for each product a firm sells. Comparisons of the growth of expenses in each category from year to year and of the relationships between expenses and revenues over time often enable management to identify areas in which the firm is operating inefficiently. Most management decisions involving financial matters are based on the data included in a firm's income statement.

The Balance Sheet

While the income statement shows flows of revenues, expenses, and profits during an accounting period, the *balance sheet* is a financial summary of the firm at a given date—the end of the accounting period. But before we can understand a balance sheet, we must examine a fundamental concept in accounting, *the accounting equation.*

The resources that a business utilizes in earning a profit are called *assets.* To acquire assets, businesses typically obtain funds from both owners and creditors. The financial obligations a business incurs in acquiring assets are called *liabilities.* The portion of assets that is owned outright by a firm is designated *owner equity.* The fundamental accounting equation expresses the relationship between assets, liabilities, and owner equity as:

The accounting equation

$$\text{Assets} = \text{Liabilities} + \text{Owner Equity}$$

This equation always holds, for the total assets of a business must be paid for either by creditors or by owners. The accounting equation of Century Cycle on March 31, 19X1, might be:

$$\text{Assets} = \text{Liabilities} + \text{Owner Equity}$$
$$\$151,500 = \$107,000 + \$44,500$$

CENTURY CYCLE, INC.
Balance Sheet
March 31, 19X1

Assets		Liabilities	
Current Assets:		*Current Liabilities:*	
Cash	$ 44,500	Notes payable	$30,000
Accounts receivable	10,000	Accounts payable	20,000
Cycle inventory	15,000	Total current liabilities	$50,000
Parts inventory	15,000		
Total current assets	$84,500	*Long-Term Liabilities:*	
		Mortgages payable	57,000
		Total long-term liabilities	$57,000
		Total liabilities	$107,000
Fixed Assets:		**Owner Equity**	
Furniture and fixtures	5,000	Common stock ($3 par	
Office equipment	2,000	value, 11,000 shares)	33,000
Building	50,000	Retained earnings	11,500
Land	10,000	Total owner equity	$44,500
Total fixed assets	$67,000		
		Total liabilities	
Total assets	$151,500	and owner equity	$151,500

11-2 Century Cycle's year-end balance sheet. The balance sheet indicates the financial soundness of a business on a given date.

Assets, liabilities, and owner equity are always expressed in monetary terms. Thus, accounting transactions are restricted to items on which a monetary value can be placed. Figure 11-2, Century Cycle's balance sheet on March, 31 19X1, illustrates the accounting equation and the monetary character of accounting transactions.

Now we will examine the basic categories or accounts in which the three elements of the accounting equation belong.

✔ **Assets.** The *assets* used by a firm to earn profits range from monetary resources such as cash to physical assets such as machinery and buildings. Examples of asset accounts include:

Assets: resources
a business uses

1. *Cash:* Cash and currency, checking and savings deposits in commercial banks, cashier's checks, bank and postal money orders, and bank drafts.
2. *Notes receivable:* Promissory notes on monies owed the firm by other individuals or businesses.

Accounts in
the assets portion
of a balance sheet

3. *Accounts receivable:* Obligations owed the firm, usually arising from its sales. Accounts receivable are due within one year.
4. *Merchandise inventory:* Inventory of goods purchased for resale or produced by the firm.
5. *Supplies inventory:* Inventory of supplies purchased for use in production.
6. *Machinery and equipment:* Machinery and equipment used in the business.
7. *Buildings:* Buildings housing the firm's business activities.
8. *Land:* Land employed in the business.
9. *Intangibles:* Assets deriving value from the rights they accord the holder. Patents, copyrights, trademarks, and franchises fall into this category. Separate accounts are used for each type of intangible asset.

Liabilities:
financial obligations
of a firm

✔ **Liabilities.** *Liabilities* are financial obligations of a firm indicating the business or the individual to whom money is owed and the date that each obligation becomes due. Examples include:

1. *Notes payable:* Promissory notes or monies owed to creditors.
2. *Accounts payable:* Obligations owed to creditors arising from purchases of goods and services on credit. Accounts payable are due in less than one year.
3. *Accrued liabilities:* Salaries, taxes, insurance premiums, and other expenses owed but not yet paid by the business.
4. *Long-term debts:* Mortgages, bonds, and notes payable with maturities of one year or more.

Accounts in the
liabilities portion
of a balance sheet

Owner equity:
contributions of owners
plus retained earnings

✔ **Owner equity.** From the fundamental accounting equation, the difference between assets and liabilities represents *owner equity*. Owner equity includes financial contributions made directly by the owners and earnings of the business retained by the firm.

OWNER-EQUITY ACCOUNTS FOR SOLE PROPRIETORSHIPS AND PARTNERSHIPS

Because sole proprietorships and partnerships do not issue public stock, their owner-equity accounts differ somewhat from those of corporations. For sole proprietorships, a proprietor's capital account is shown (the owner's name is listed, followed by the word "capital"). For partnerships, the partners' capital account is shown (each partner's name is listed, followed by the word "capital").

Sole proprietorships, partnerships, and corporations whose stock is not publicly traded are usually not legally obligated to have their accounting records publicly audited. This can result in a considerable savings in accountant fees. Small businesses organized as proprietorships or partnerships normally maintain accounting records for managerial purposes and for the detection of employee fraud rather than as a means of informing shareholders and the general public about their financial transactions.

The typical owner-equity accounts for a corporation are:

Accounts in the
owner-equity portion
of a balance sheet

1. *Capital stock:* Funds contributed by stockholders, measured by multiplying the number of shares outstanding in each category of stock issued by the stated value of each type of stock.
2. *Paid-in surplus:* Funds contributed by stockholders beyond the value that was stated for each category of stock when the stock was originally issued.
3. *Retained earnings:* Corporate profits *less* all dividends paid to stockholders in the past.

✔ **The year-end balance sheet.** The balance sheet that is developed at the end of a business's accounting year should be detailed and well organized (see "How to Organize a Balance Sheet" on the following page). A series of notes usually accompanies the income statement, the year-end balance sheet, and specialized accounting statements provided by accountants. These notes are designed to indicate the basis on which the income statements and balance sheets have been prepared, any changes in accounting procedures from the previous year, and all known long-term business commitments that might affect the firm's future earning power or financial stability.

Like the income statement, the reliability of the balance sheet depends on the accuracy with which accounting transactions are recorded and classified, as well as on judgments made by accountants handling the pertinent financial data.

✔ **Uses of the balance sheet.** Examination of a firm's balance sheet provides an excellent indication of the financial stability of the business. A firm that shows a profit on its income statement can still fail if its current liabilities exceed its current assets when creditors demand that company debts be paid. Unusually high inventories or accounts receivable are signals of potential danger since inventories cannot always be sold quickly and since customers are not always able to maintain their payments on merchandise purchased. Balance sheets also provide meaningful managerial decisions. For example, excessive accumulations in the "cash" account indicates that financial resources are being used poorly. Excessive cash could be more profitably used to purchase new plants and equipment or to buy government bonds, which would earn interest for the firm.

Relationship Between the Income Statement and the Balance Sheet

It is important to understand the close connection between the income statement of a firm and its balance sheet. When a firm earns a profit or sustains a loss, as indicated by the income statement, an increase or a decrease occurs in the owner-equity segment of the year-end balance

HOW TO ORGANIZE A BALANCE SHEET

In constructing balance sheets, acountants usually group similar asset and liability accounts into a few main categories. Asset accounts are usually combined into four main categories:

1. *Current assets:* Cash or highly liquid assets converted into cash within one accounting period.
2. *Long-term investments:* Assets held exclusively for investment (not resale) longer than one accounting period.
3. *Fixed assets:* Property, buildings, and equipment — the tools of the business.
4. *Intangibles:* Assets that derive their value from the rights they accord the holder.

Liabilities are grouped into two general categories:

1. *Current liabilities:* Obligations that must be met within one accounting period.

2. *Long-term liabilities:* Obligations that need not be satisfied in a single accounting period.

By examining these six main asset and liability categories, an accountant can quickly assess the general financial position of a business. Referring to Figure 11-2, how many of these six basic accounting categories can you find on Century Cycle's balance sheet? Which categories are missing from Century Cycle's balance sheet and why?

Answers: Four of the categories are found in the balance sheet in Figure 11-2: current assets, fixed assets, current liabilities, and long-term liabilities. Long-term investments do not appear because apparently Century Cycle does not plan to hold any investments such as U.S. treasury bonds longer than one year. Similarly, intangibles do not appear because Century Cycle has no patents, copyrights, or trademarks of value.

Income statements and balance sheets are closely connected

sheet. If a profit is made, owner equity increases by the amount of the net income *less* any dividends paid to shareholders. If a loss is sustained, owner equity decreases by the net loss *plus* any dividends paid.

The relationship between net income and owner equity can be illustrated by examining Century Cycle's financial statements. According to Century Cycle's income statement (Figure 11-1), net income for 19X1 was $11,500. If Century Cycle had no retained earnings at the beginning of its fiscal year and paid no dividends to stockholders during that year, then its retained earnings on its March 31, 19X1 balance sheet should be $11,500, as shown in Figure 11-2. Because of the double-entry system, some other asset or liability account would also be affected by Century Cycle's decision to retain its entire net income in the business. For example, if Century Cycle chose to keep its $11,500 profit in cash and made no other accounting transactions that affected its cash account during the fiscal

EFFECT OF NET INCOME (PROFIT) ON THE BALANCE SHEET

The Have a Happy Day Corporation earned an after-tax profit of $50,000 in 1976. Dividends to stockholders are $1.00 per share, and Happy Day has 10,000 shares of outstanding stock. The company retains half of its profits in cash and purchases a new building (also in cash) with the other half of its profits. The accounts on Happy Day's 1976 balance sheet are identical to those on its 1975 balance sheet, except the accounts that are affected by these

accounting transactions. Referring to the text, can you show what accounts on Have a Happy Day's 1976 balance sheet changed from its 1975 balance sheet? By what amounts did these accounts change?

Answers: Retained earnings rose $40,000 ($50,000 in profits *less* the $10,000 paid in dividends). The buildings account rose $20,000; the cash account increased $20,000.

year, Century Cycle would show an $11,500 increase in cash between its 19X1 balance sheet and the balance sheet sent to stockholders the previous year.

Verifying Accounting Statements

Auditing: Have the accounting data been reported accurately?

Auditing is the process of verifying that an organization has properly recorded and reported its financial data. In verifying that accounting statements are accurate, auditors sometimes make a detailed examination of every asset and liability associated with a business, physically counting its cash or inventories and contacting its debtors. Auditors also examine individual accounting transactions and frequently question the procedures and judgments used in processing accounting data. Auditors who uncover questionable accounting practices may refuse to certify the results or may insist that a discussion of a disputed practice be appended to a firm's accounting statements.

An organization may order a *complete audit* (or a *special audit*) when it suspects employee theft or fraud or when it cannot solve its own accounting errors. In addition, most large businesses order an occasional and usually unannounced *internal audit,* conducted by accountants who are employed by the firm but who are not specifically responsible for the accounts being audited. Large- and moderate-sized businesses often open their accounts to an *outside audit* by auditors hired for this purpose. In most cases, outside audits are made by public accounting firms. The Internal Revenue Service may conduct a *government audit* to determine whether a business has computed and paid its taxes properly. Banks, defense contractors, and a few other businesses are legally obligated to open their books to audits by government representatives.

"First, sort your checks by date or number and check them off against the stubs in your checkbook. Next, total up all the outstanding checks and add this to your current checkbook balance. Now subtract from this figure any service charges or other deductions shown on your statement . . ."

Drawing by Weber
© 1973 The New Yorker Magazine, Inc.

Evaluating Accounting Data

We have already noted that the evaluation of the financial information shown on accounting statements can yield valuable insights into the financial health of a business. A key technique in the evaluation of financial information is the use of *financial* (or accounting) *ratios*—mathematical comparisons of selected data on a firm's accounting statements. Financial ratios of a business are used to compare: (1) this year's results with those of previous years; (2) this year's results with the results of other firms in the same industry or of the industry as a whole; and (3) this year's results with target ratios acceptable to the individual conducting the analysis.

Where to find
financial data
Financial information on individual competitors and industries can be found from company annual reports or from general references like Moody's *Manual of Investments* and Standard and Poor's *Corporate Records*, which provide financial data on most businesses with publicly traded stock. In addition, Standard and Poor's, Moody's, Dun and Bradstreet, Robert Morris Associates, and most trade associations publish accounting data by industry.

Types of Financial Ratios

Financial ratios help both management and outside analysts to evaluate the data presented in accounting statements. In the following section, we will examine some of the ratios most frequently used in financial analysis: the current ratio, return on investment, return on sales, and earnings per share.

✔ **Current ratio.** The *current ratio* expresses the relationship between current assets and current liabilities and demonstrates the ability of the firm to meet its short-term obligations. As we saw earlier, current assets are highly liquid assets that are converted into cash within one year. From these assets, businessmen expect to obtain most of the funds needed to meet their short-term obligations (current liabilities). Century Cycle's current ratio for March 31, 19X1 is

Measuring
the firm's ability
to meet short-term
obligations
$$\frac{\text{Current assets}}{\text{Current liabilities}} = \frac{\$84,500}{\$50,000} = 1.69$$

This ratio indicates that Century Cycle has the potential to cover each dollar in short-term obligations with $1.69 in current assets. Accountants discourage the use of predetermined standards in the current ratio, but when they are used, a figure of 2.0 or more is considered desirable.

✔ **Return on investment.** *Return on investment* is a percentage figure that compares the after-tax profits of a firm with the assets employed in its operations. Return on investment may be calculated for a firm's total assets or for the portion of total assets represented by owner equity. In terms of equity, Century Cycle's return on investment is

Profit can be expressed
as a percentage
of investment . . .

$$\frac{\text{Net income after taxes}}{\text{Owner equity}} = \frac{\$11,500}{\$44,500} = 25.8\%$$

Return on equity in American business has averaged 12 percent annually since World War II. Return-on-investment comparisons based on a firm's total assets will be described in Chapter 13.

↙ **Return on sales.** *Return on sales* is a percentage figure that expresses the relationship between the net income of a business and its sales revenues. For Century Cycle, return on sales for the year ending March 31, 19X1, is

. . . or sales

$$\frac{\text{Net income}}{\text{Sales}} = \frac{\$11,500}{\$150,000} = 7.7\%$$

HOW TOUCHE ROSS SPOTS FRAUD

"Like Avis, we can try harder," says Robert S. Kay, the director of accounting and professional standards for Touche Ross & Company, one of the largest public accounting firms in the United States. Kay is referring to a set of specific guidelines Touche Ross developed to spot fraud or financial mismanagement among the organizations the firm audits.

Even a careful audit is not a complete guarantee against fraud or mismanagement, especially if the top management of an organization is actively involved in misrepresenting its company's position. Yet, many courts, government regulators, and investors believe a public accounting firm should be financially liable for any loss resulting from the bankruptcy of a business that one of its public accountants has certified.

"It's not a cookbook," Touche Ross' partner W. Donald George comments about the guidelines the firm has established for its auditors. "We're not coming in like Pinkerton's or trying to peel every grape. But we will be looking at all material transactions in greater depth." The following areas are subject to intensive scrutiny under Touche Ross' newly adopted guidelines:

● Accounting transactions that involve more than 5 percent of the income of a division or a business.

● Major accounting transactions that are bunched at the end of a quarter or at the end of a fiscal year.
● Key financial figures and ratios that deviate from trends over the past five years.
● Insufficient working capital or credit.
● The urgent need for high profits to support the firm's stock price.
● Dependence on a few products or customers.
● A declining industry with a history of many business failures.
● A great number of lawsuits, especially stockholder lawsuits.
● Rapid expansion or numerous acquisitions in the past few years.
● Difficulty collecting fees from key customers.
● A management dominated by a few key persons.
● Inadequate internal auditing staff and controls; separate accounting divisions using different systems; a large number of separate auditors for each accounting division; rapid turnovers of key financial personnel.

In most cases financial mismanagement—not fraud—is the culprit. But the one percent of cases that Touche Ross estimates involve outright fraud can rock the financial world and can undermine the public's faith in accounting firms in general.

Return-on-sales figures are widely used to evaluate the performance of various product lines in a firm or to compare the overall performance of the business with that of other firms in the same industry. While return-on-sales figures average around 4 percent for American business as a whole, percentage returns on sales differ widely among industries. Return-on-sales figures below the industry average may indicate excessive costs and inefficiencies within a business.

✔ **Earnings per share.** *Earnings or income per share* (EPS) — shown in Figure 11-1 as net income per share — indicate profits a corporation earns for each share of common stock outstanding at the end of its fiscal year. Income taxes, interest paid to bondholders, and dividends distributed to preferred stockholders are deducted from total corporate profits before earnings-per-share calculations are made. For Century Cycle, earnings per share for the fiscal year ending March 31, 19X1 are

Measuring
the financial health
of a business

$$\frac{\text{Net income after taxes}}{\text{Number of shares outstanding}} = \frac{\$11,500}{11,000} = \$1.05 \text{ per share}$$

Earnings per share is the most closely watched financial ratio in business. Persistent lack of growth in earnings per share usually indicates a business is in decline. Owners and investors regard earnings per share as an important indication of the financial soundness of their investments.

Uses of Financial Ratios

Financial ratios are used to evaluate the profitability and the financial stability of a business, the quality of its management in comparison to similar enterprises, and the performance of specific divisions within the business. Managers may be hired, fired, given bonuses, or reprimanded depending on how well the part of the enterprise in which they work performs in terms of key financial ratios. Projected financial ratios are also used in planning the future activities of a business, as we will see in Chapter 13. Advanced accounting and finance text books discuss many other important financial ratios.

Budgeting

Budgeting is a form of planning; hence, a budget may be viewed as a plan expressed in financial terms. The *master budget* shows projected revenues and expenses for the entire firm. *Specialized budgets* provide individual departments with guidelines for various types of business activities. Specialized budgets for a large corporation like General Motors include:

The budget:
a plan expressed
in financial form

1. Projected receipts and disbursements by division (Chevrolet, Buick, Frigidaire, and so on) and by administrative unit within a division (Chevrolet's sales department).
2. Projected receipts and disbursements by activity (Chevrolet's advertising budget, combining the projected advertising expenditures of several departments).
3. Projected levels of assets, liabilities, cash inflows, cash outflows, investments, purchases, inventories, and types of personnel for the business as a whole or for individual divisions.

By providing detailed financial projections on individual administrative units or activities, specialized budgets assist management in planning, control, and evaluation.

The master and specialized budgets of a business merely specify dollar targets for each type of commercial activity. For example, according to its 19X1 income statement in Figure 11-1, Century Cycle spent exactly $4000 on advertising. For its next fiscal year, ending March 31, 19X2, Century Cycle might decide that advertising expenditures of $5000 are justifiable because of projected increases in bicycle sales and repairs. Thus, Century Cycle's advertising budget for the year 19X2 would show total projected advertising expenditures of $5000, with expected advertising costs broken down in further detail by media (the expected costs of newspaper ads, radio plugs, direct-mail leaflets, and so on).

A budget directs the future activities of a firm

Because planning has an important effect on the financial performance of a firm, budget preparation is the responsibility of top management. In most firms, the president has the final authority to modify the complete budget, which is usually submitted to the owners or to the board or directors for approval.

The budget committee assists the president in preparing a detailed budget. In large corporations, the budget committee often includes several vice presidents, the heads of various operating departments, and the controller. The committee's basic task is to combine the various budgets proposed by administrative subunits into a master budget that is consistent and realistic. This process entails negotiating with administrative subunits, assessing the goals and resources of the business, and utilizing past financial data assembled by the accounting department. Quite often, the accounting staff is responsible for preparing final copies of the budget after it has been approved by the president and by the board of directors.

The Budget Cycle

Three important phases in the budget cycle

Budgeting is a cyclical process with three identifiable phases: (1) preparation and approval of the budget; (2) execution of the budget; and (3) accounting and auditing of the results. The completion of one phase in the budget cycle automatically initiates the next phase.

✔ Budget preparation. Budget preparation involves the development of a new budget and begins when the budget committee requests estimates from the operating departments. The requests are assigned by department heads to managers or assistants, who must prepare estimates within guidelines established by the committee for their particular activities in each department. The estimates are then reviewed by the department head. Initially, faulty estimates are reevaluated and revised. Eventually, the department head combines all of the estimates into a departmental budget that is sent to the budget committee. The committee then compiles all the departmental budgets and prepares the master budget for the entire firm. Budget preparation concludes when the president and the board of directors approve the master budget. In small businesses, budget preparation is a much less elaborate process.

Developing a new budget

✔ Budget execution. Budget execution—carrying out the planned budget—begins on the first day of the budget year. In many large businesses, the controller—a member of top management—is formally responsible for budget execution. The controller reports any serious deviations in a departmental budget directly to top management, which in turn may require the department to obtain permission for additional expenditures until its budgeted goals are realized.

Carrying out the planned budget

✔ Accounting and auditing. The controller utilizes acounting information and internal auditing procedures to determine whether or not individual administrative units are remaining within the guidelines projected in the budget and to prepare interim progress reports for management. The controller also relies on accounting data when unexpected revisions in the budget must be made.

Verifying budgeted expenditures

Uses of Budgets

Budgets are utilized by every major business in the United States as well as by most nonprofit organizations. Their widespread adoption by business reflects the many functions budgets serve.

✔ Planning. Budgeting is a way of expressing financial plans in concrete, quantitative terms. Since a firm's resource demands invariably exhaust its projected revenues, the budget guides the firm in allocating resources and in making periodic reassessments of its priorities and activities.

✔ Controlling. As a budget is implemented, actual performance should be compared with original projections. Because management controls the allocation of funds, departmental divisions cannot exceed specified budgetary limits without management's knowledge and approval. Indeed, organizational units must exercise internal control to remain within budgeted limits. For these reasons, budgets foster managerial control within an organization.

Comparisons of actual and budgeted performance also improve managerial decision making by warning management of potential trouble spots so that it can take action before serious problems arise. If, for example, actual sales do not keep pace with projected revenues in the sales budget, a firm may initiate remedial action by expanding its advertising program to generate new sales or by cutting production costs. By focusing on exceptions to or deviations from a firm's plans, management is able to conserve its energies and to function more effectively.

✔ **Measuring performance.** Carefully developed budgets permit management to set reasonable goals for individual employees or divisions and to measure their performances more accurately. Employees benefit from the preparation of a detailed budget because it indicates what specific goals management expects and what resources are available to attain those goals.

Variable Budgets

Budgets can become straitjackets if they are applied too rigidly. A decline in consumer demand, high prices, a strike, new competitive tactics, and a host of other changes can make business budgets obsolete. Thus, budgets should be viewed as guidelines that can be adapted to changing conditions—and not as hard and fast targets to be met in all circumstances.

Variable budgets
help a business
to respond to change

Variable budgets (also called *flexible budgets*) attempt to account for the many possible changes in business conditions by specifying several different sales levels and by providing alternative expense and operating budgets for each sales level. If the business does not generate expected sales volumes, rapid adjustments can be made in operating budgets.

KEY POINTS TO REMEMBER

1. Accounting is the functional area of business that deals with recording, classifying, and summarizing financial information. Accounting information is used by management, employees, creditors, and investors in business as well as by many other groups including government and the general public.
2. The basic unit of accounting is the accounting transaction—any event that has a measurable financial impact on a business.

3. A firm's accounting transactions are recorded in registers (or ledgers) and are summarized in income statements and balance sheets.
4. The basic objective of the income statement is to show the net income of a business for an accounting period (usually one year).
5. The basic objectives of the balance sheet are to show the financial position of a business at a given point in time and to indicate the basic categories in which its assets, liabilities, and owner equity are held.
6. "The bottom line" of the income statement indicates a firm's profits or losses and is the most important piece of a firm's financial information.
7. Budgets are accounting statements prepared in advance to help management plan future activities, recognize emerging problems by contrasting actual performance against budgeted performance, and control subunits of the organization by means of established budget targets.

QUESTIONS FOR DISCUSSION

1. What is accounting?
2. What groups make wide use of accounting data?
3. Describe the roles of industrial, government, and tax accountants. What functions do CPAs perform?
4. How does managerial accounting differ from the preparation of income statements and balance sheets by accountants?
5. What is an accounting transaction?
6. What is a register (or ledger)? What function does it perform?
7. What is the double-entry system, and what function does it perform in a business?
8. What is the income statement of a business? What items appear on it? In what ways are income statements useful?
9. How does the accounting equation relate to the balance sheet?
10. What items appear on the balance sheet? Of what use is this accounting statement?
11. Describe the major financial ratios and indicate how they can be used.
12. Define the master budget and the specialized budget. What uses does business make of budgets?
13. What is the budget cycle? Describe each step in the budget cycle.
14. Which of the following activities are accounting transactions?
    (a) The Johnson Corporation closes its books on December 31, pays its employees on November 15 for the week of November 1 to November 7.
    (b) The president of General Motors urges employees to participate actively in community affairs.
    (c) The owner of a gas station places an order for 10,000 gallons of gas with the Sun Oil Company.

(d) Engineers at the Port Huron Paper Company conclude that their second papermaking machine, which has unexpectedly broken down, is not repairable.

SHORT CASES AND PROBLEMS

1. Construct an income statement and a balance sheet from the following year-end totals in the accounts of Century Cycle, Inc., based on the following data for the fiscal year ending March 31, 1977:

Cash	$12,000	Depreciation (store	
Cost of goods sold	60,000	and equipment)	$ 5,000
Accounts receivable	30,000	Mortgages payable	50,000
Telephone expenses	6,000	Sales	200,000
Utilities expenses	5,000	Building	40,000
Accounts payable	20,000	Advertising expenses	20,000
Furniture and fixtures	8,000	Land	10,000
Common stock*	12,500	Parts inventory	17,000
Sales salaries	40,000	Insurance expenses	5,000
Store supplies	10,000	Income taxes	14,000
Cycle inventory	25,000	Retained earnings	24,500
Notes payable	35,000	Interest expenses	8,000

* 10,000 shares outstanding

2. Using the above year-end data for Century Cycle, calculate the following ratios: (a) current ratio; (b) return on investment; (c) return on sales; and (d) earnings per share.

3. As we saw in this chapter, financial ratio analysis pinpoints the strengths and weaknesses of a firm's operations. Interpret the ratios listed in Problem 2—excluding earnings per share—assuming that the relevant industry data are as follows:

	Ratio	Industry average	Century Cycle, Inc.
(a)	Current ratio	1.67	1.53
(b)	Return on investment	18%	73%
(c)	Return on sales	8%	18%

CAREER SELECTION: POSITIONS IN ACCOUNTING, CREDIT, AND RELATED FIELDS

CAREERS IN ACCOUNTING

Many important management decisions are based on financial reports that are prepared and analyzed by **accountants.** As we noted in Chapter 11, several subdivisions exist within the accounting field: public accountants are self-employed or work for public accounting firms; industrial accountants are responsible for the financial records of the firms that employ them; government accountants analyze the financial data of government agencies and private businesses that are subject to government regulations. Some accountants secure positions on the basis of experience or specialized training at correspondence or business schools. Generally, however, successful applicants have earned bachelor's degrees in accounting; a master's degree provides a competitive advantage. About 20 percent of all accountants are **certified public accountants** (CPAs). Accountants who obtain CPA certificates have successfully passed standardized examinations administered on a state-by-state basis; they are usually college graduates with at least two years of accounting experience. Qualified accountants are promoted to higher-level management and supervisory positions. Annual salary ranges from $9000 to $26,000, but partners in large CPA firms may earn over $100,000 annually. Because of the growth of business organizations and their constant need for sound financial data, the job market for accountants is expected to remain excellent. (*Additional information:* National Association of Accountants; 919 Third Avenue; New York, New York 10022.)

CREDIT CAREERS

Credit officials accept or reject customer credit applications. To evaluate the firm's risk in extending credit to a customer, credit officials interview applicants and review their financial statements and previous credit experience. Developing a credit policy which increases sales and reduces risks requires sound decision-making abilities. A college degree in liberal arts or in business administration is becoming increasingly important, although many employers provide on-the-job training for high-school and community college graduates. Credit officials begin in a trainee capacity and may advance to credit manager or to other top management positions. Annual salaries range from $7000 to more than $40,000. The growing reliance on business and consumer credit is expected to rapidly expand occupational opportunities for credit officials. (*Additional information:* The National Consumer Finance Association, 1000 16th Street, N.W.; Washington, D.C. 20036.)

Credit managers evaluate customers in terms of their credit worthiness and deal with delinquent accounts. Credit managers also frequently establish discount levels on open-credit transactions. Either a bachelor's degree or a master's degree in accounting or in finance is becoming an essential requirement. Credit managers' salaries range from $10,000 to $25,000 or more. Employment as assistant to a credit manager is frequently an entry-level position in the corporate finance area. (*Additional information:* The National Consumer Finance Association; 1000 16th Street, N.W.; Washington, D.C. 20036.)

CAREERS IN FIELDS RELATED TO ACCOUNTING

Bookkeepers record a firm's financial transactions. In addition to balancing incoming funds with funds paid out, bookkeepers calculate the firm's payroll and prepare customer invoices. In large firms, an entire department may be composed of bookkeepers, each of whom performs a specialized duty, such as preparing daily sales records or operating reports. Most bookkeepers are high-school graduates with backgrounds in arithmetic and bookkeeping; however, some employers only hire applicants who have taken bookkeeping courses in business schools or community colleges. Competent bookkeepers may be promoted to supervisory positions and, with the completion of college accounting courses, may advance to accounting positions. Annual salary averages $6600. Employment opportunities are expected to expand slowly due to the increasing computerization of bookkeeping tasks. (*Additional information:* State Supervisor of Office Occupations Education; State Department of Education; your state capital.)

Cashiers primarily receive customer payments, although they may also prepare bank deposits and requisition funds for company supplies. Manual dexterity and an ability to deal with people are essential. Applicants are usually high-school graduates with backgrounds in bookkeeping, arithmetic, and typing. Specific skills are acquired in on-the-job training programs. Annual income may reach $8300. Due to expanding business activities, the job market for cashiers is expected to expand rapidly. (*Additional information:* United Business Schools Association; 1730 M Street, N.W.; Washington, D.C. 20036.)

Banks employ **bank clerks** to record and tabulate financial transactions. Bank clerks perform general clerical duties in addition to specific tasks related to banking activities. Small banks often hire one clerk to handle a variety of duties, including the compilation of debit and credit slips and the preparation of monthly statements for depositors. Large banks hire a number of clerks who specialize in certain applications, such as bookkeeping machine operators, trust bookkeepers, and loan clerks. Because many clerical bank jobs involve the computer processing of financial transactions, employers often hire applicants who have had data-processing experience. Bank clerks must be able to work rapidly and accurately. Most clerks are high-school graduates with backgrounds in bookkeeping, arithmetic, and typing. Annual income averages $6500. Competent bank clerks may be promoted to teller, credit analyst, or a supervisory position. The growing number of banks and the services they provide are expected to afford a rapidly expanding job market for bank clerks. (*Additional information:* American Bankers Association; Bank Personnel Division; 1120 Connecticut Avenue, N.W., Washington, D.C. 20036.)

A CRITICAL BUSINESS DECISION

—made by W.R. Persons

THE SITUATION   The engineers at the Emerson Electric Company (known locally as Frugality, Inc.) of St. Louis, Missouri, were busy. During the recession of 1974 and 1975, the costs of manufacturing an important small electric motor had skyrocketed, and its selling price could not be increased due to stiff competition in the industry. Was Emerson about to lose its reputation as one of the most profitable electrical manufacturers in the United States? Could Emerson continue to achieve an after-tax return on sales of twice the national average for the industry as a whole?

Emerson's response was characteristic—to do what it does best: cut costs. Cost cutting became a way of life at Emerson when W.R. Persons became its chief executive officer in 1964. Since then, Persons' cost-cutting efforts have affected every corner of company activity from requiring company executives to fly tourist class to redesigning motors. "Limiting phone calls and picking up paper clips help keep costs in line," Persons explains, "but the real dollars and cents are saved in manufacturing products." The application of Persons' cost-cutting philosophy worked in the case of the small electric motor; the engineers came up with a new design that required 20 percent less wire and 11 percent less steel but that delivered the same amount of power as the old motor. The result: a $1.7-million cost saving.

Emerson boasts that the company has never missed a cost-reduction target. The acid test occurred in 1974 when Emerson sought to pare $35.4 million from its expenses. Despite the soaring inflationary costs of both raw materials and labor, actual cost savings were $43.6 million in that year. Richard Singer, a Chicago security analyst, observes of Emerson's cost-cutting performance, "If you watch what you eat, you don't have to diet. If you watch your costs, you don't have to initiate crash cost-reduction programs overnight."

THE DECISION   When W.R. Persons became chief executive officer of Emerson Electric in 1964, he was alarmed at what he found. The multimillion-dollar firm's profits were only $1 million that year. Costs were expected to rise by at least $1 million in 1965, and revenues were expected to fall by more than $1 million dollars in the next fiscal year due to stiff price competition from other firms. Moreover, Persons found one line of motors that produced $3.1 million in sales was losing $600,000. Because no correlation existed between factory costs and total costs—particularly if total costs included the costs of selling Emerson's outputs—Persons suspected and later confirmed that, in his own words, "we were actually selling a bushelful of products for a loss and didn't know it."

QUESTIONS

1. What specific types of accounting information did the Emerson Electric Company require to initiate and to continue its highly successful cost-reduction programs?
2. The Emerson Electric Company normally hires industrial and certified public accountants. Placing yourself in W.R. Persons' shoes, in what specialized fields of accounting would you prefer your accounting personnel to be trained if they are to assist in generating the necessary data to implement your cost-cutting programs?

"Money isn't everything — is it, Mr. Sage?"
"No, Mr. Simmons, the work of collecting it is important."

Conversation between
two bank directors

CHAPTER

12

OBTAINING FINANCIAL RESOURCES

O n January 1, 1947, James J. Ling formed the Ling Electric Company with a $2000 mortgage on his home. A Navy electronic technician during World War II, Ling first sold surplus government equipment to the construction industry. In 1954, Ling Electronics was so successful that Ling sold nearly half the company to the public for $800,000, personally hawking public shares at $2.25 apiece from a booth at the Texas State Fair. After his initial success selling stock to the public, James Ling made a daring decision: to turn over the management of the business he controlled to others and to devote all his attention to building a financial empire!

A corporate empire was built on a knowledge of finance

What followed was one of the most spectacular business careers in American history. From 1954 to 1967, Ling purchased dozens of businesses, ranging from Braniff Airways to Jones and Laughlin Steel, and financed his acquisitions with a bewildering variety of common stock issues, loans from banks and insurance companies, and corporate bonds. By 1968, LTV Corporation, as Ling Electric Company was eventually renamed, had become the fourteenth largest business in the United States with annual sales of $3.75 billion.

James Ling's success can be attributed to his genius for *finance* — the functional area of business that deals with the acquisition and the dispersement of funds. Ironically, in the 1970s, the LTV Corporation suffered financial hardships and James Ling was forced to retire because of his financial mismanagement.

Finance: obtaining and using funds effectively

The Importance of Finance

Financial policies may determine a firm's success or failure

While the LTV Corporation was affected to an extraordinary degree by James Ling's financial efforts, the survival of the typical business depends on sound financial management. As Irwin Friend, a specialist in finance, observes: "A firm's success and even its survival, its ability and willingness to maintain production and to invest in fixed working capital, are to a very considerable extent determined by its financial policies, both past and present."

Because gathering and dispensing funds is a central function in all businesses, financial managers normally occupy positions of considerable authority, often with titles like financial vice president, treasurer, controller, secretary-treasurer, and treasurer-controller. The financial manager is responsible for making important financial decisions such as whether or not to build a new plant or how to obtain several million dollars to finance a new venture. Day-to-day financial matters such as handling cash receipts and disbursements, making regular borrowings and payments, and formulating budgets are carried out by the manager's assistants. In small businesses, financial decisions are usually made directly by the owners.

Three reasons can be cited for the increasing importance of finance: the central role of financial decisions, an expanded role for finance in the 1970s, and higher capital costs.

The Central Role of Financial Decisions

Nearly all business activities have a financial impact

A business manager's ability to obtain and use funds is a key to the success or failure of a firm. Almost every business action has a financial effect on the firm, whether it is hiring a new employee, opening a new plant, selling additional stock, or acquiring a new customer. Money is the common denominator by which nearly all business activities are conducted and assessed.

Thus, good financial management is good business. But it is more than that. A financially well-managed firm uses its funds to purchase and to apply resources effectively in order to produce goods and services that consumers will buy. Good financial management contributes both to business profits and to an effective economy.

An Expanded Role for Finance

Investment decisions have become increasingly important

Prior to 1950, financial experts were concerned primarily with helping business to accumulate financial resources rapidly. Today, financial managers devote a large portion of their energies to the ways in which financial resources are used by business. This involves the proper allocation of a firm's financial resources — the making of investment decisions — and is of crucial importance to a business firm. Because of this new orientation, financial managers increasingly interact with top management.

Higher Capital Costs

Spiraling interest rates affect financial decisions

Interest rates on various types of loans have increased significantly in the last decade. Between 1965 and 1970, average interest rates on short-term loans from banks ranged from 5 percent to 9 percent. By the mid-1970s, rates on bank loans due within one year averaged as high as 14 percent. In addition, the United States experienced several credit crunches — periods when many businesses found credit unobtainable or in limited supply, no matter how much interest they were willing to pay. Because of

CAN YOU AFFORD A NEW HOME?

Atlanta builder William Porbet constructs homes that contain 1200 square feet of living space. Kaufman & Broad of Los Angeles eliminates dishwashers, refrigerators, and full basements from many of the new homes it sells. Miami's Deltona Corporation offers residences without garages, carpets, or screened porches. The basic, no-frills home is making a comeback.

The reasons are obvious: the high prices of new homes and the high interest costs of home mortgages. In 1975, according to a study conducted by the congressional Joint Economic Committee, an average new home in the United States cost $41,200—a price beyond the reach of 85 percent of all American families. Ten years ago, the average new U.S. home cost less than $25,000.

The escalation of interest rates has also decreased the number of purchasers of new homes. High general interest rates encourage investors to place their funds in assets other than mortgages. When mortgage money is scarce, it may be unavailable at any interest rate or lenders may require that a down payment of at least 20 percent of the purchase price

of the home be made in cash. Even if the prospective purchaser can secure sufficient cash, the mortgage that is obtained will be subject to extremely high interest rates. The mortgage interest rate dramatically affects the eventual cost of the home. Suppose that you pay $1200 in cash for a new house and obtain a 25-year, 5-percent mortgage for $40,000. Your monthly mortgage payments (both principal and interest) will be $233.84. At the end of the 25-year period, you will own your own house, but you will have paid a total of $71,352 for it: $40,000 in principal that returns to the holder of the mortgage (and you); $30,152 in interest payments on that mortgage; and $1200 in your initial cash outlay.

Can you estimate the monthly mortgage payment, the cost (principal and interest) of the home at the end of 25 years, and the total interest paid if the same mortgage was obtained at: (a) 6-percent interest, (b) 8-percent interest, and (c) 10-percent interest? In recent years, interest rates on mortgages have been as high as 8 or 10 percent. Do you think it would be wiser to purchase an older house or a new home? Why? (For the answers, see page 312.)

higher interest rates, the effective use of funds is becoming more and more important.

Modern finance provides guidelines for obtaining funds (discussed in this chapter) and for effectively using funds (described in Chapter 13). To obtain funds, the financial manager must: (1) determine a desired financial structure for the business; (2) identify alternate sources of funds; and (3) obtain the desired funding. Figure 12-1 provides an overview of the financial process.

12-1 An overview of the process of financial management. First, financial needs are determined; then alternative sources of funds are identified. The financial manager must subsequently secure the necessary funds. The three steps associated with obtaining funds are discussed in Chapter 12. The fourth step—the use of funds—will be covered in Chapter 13.

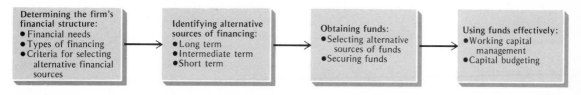

CAN YOU AFFORD A NEW HOME? *(ANSWERS)*

On the 6-percent mortgage, the monthly payment is $257.74, and the total paid for the house is $77,322 ($37,322 of which is interest). The 8-percent mortgage requires monthly payments of $308.62, or a total of $92,586 ($52,586 of which is interest). At 10-percent interest, monthly mortgage payments are $363.50, and the total paid for the house is $109,050 ($69,000 of which is interest).

A change in mortgage interest rates from 6 to 10 percent raises monthly payments from $257.74 to $363.50, and the total cost of the house (principal and interest) from $77,322 to $109,050. Thus, many persons who cannot afford to build a new "dream home" prefer to buy older residences. Picking up the established mortgage on an older home can result in a savings of thousands of dollars in interest, since the mortgage was probably issued a number of years ago when interest rates were much lower. When millions of potential purchasers of new homes choose to buy older homes instead, the housing industry and hundreds of other industries dependent on the construction of new homes suffer severe damage.

Financial Structure of the Firm

As Figure 12-1 indicates, a firm's *financial structure* reflects its assessment of financial needs, its various types of financing, and its criteria for choosing alternative sources of financing.

Assessing Financial Needs

Determining an appropriate financial structure

The financial manager must select a financial structure that is appropriate both to present and to future business needs by applying a knowledge of (1) the future investment opportunities that are available to the business; (2) the firm's basic objectives (such as its profit goals and the amount of risk it is willing to assume); and (3) the internal funds generated from retained earnings and other sources that will probably be available for future investments. Only in light of these considerations can a financial manager accurately estimate the amount of funds that must be obtained from sources outside the business.

Types of Financing

From the financial manager's viewpoint, the firm can obtain funds to conduct daily operations and to make long-term investments from inside or from outside the business. If outside financing is required, the firm can issue new stock or new bonds. If it issues new bonds or some other type of debt security, the debt may be repayable on a long-, an intermediate-, or a short-term basis. We will now examine possible sources of funds in more detail.

Funds can come from inside or from outside the firm

✔ **Internal and external financing.** Business managers can secure funds from inside the firm itself or from outside sources. The two main sources of *internal financing* are monies made available through depreciation and earnings retained in the business after taxes and dividends are paid (see Chapter 11). In the United States, these two categories generate nearly 60 percent of total corporate financing, with depreciation alone contributing about 50 percent. *External financing* is secured through contributions to the firm by existing or new owners or through borrowing from banks and other financial institutions. Various types of internal and external financing for the typical American business are shown in Figure 12-2.

Equity involves owning . . .

. . . and debt involves borrowing

✔ **Equity and debt financing.** External financing can take the form of either equity or debt. *Equity* represents all financial resources supplied by owners at any point in time. Equity includes ownership interests in sole proprietorships and partnerships, proceeds from the sale of corporate stock, and past retained earnings. The return on investment that equity owners receive depends on the profitability of the firm and on its policy of dispensing profits to owners. In the United States, the most typical financial transaction involving equity is the sale of new stock by a corporation. *Debt* includes any legally binding obligation of a firm to pay a fixed amount of principal or interest for a specified period. Sources of debt financing include bonds, notes, mortgages, drafts, and trade acceptances.

12-2 Where business obtains funds. Each dollar a business uses for working capital or expansion is obtained from . . .

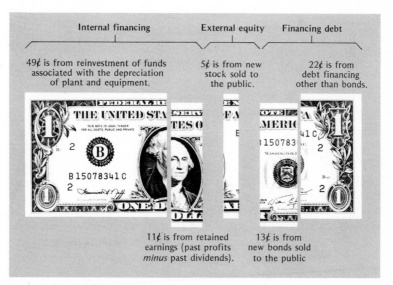

Internal financing   External equity   Financing debt

49¢ is from reinvestment of funds associated with the depreciation of plant and equipment.

5¢ is from new stock sold to the public.

22¢ is from debt financing other than bonds.

11¢ is from retained earnings (past profits *minus* past dividends).

13¢ is from new bonds sold to the public

Source: Adopted from Salomon Brothers, *Supply and Demand for Credit.*

Unlike equity owners in a business, holders of debt are promised a fixed return on their investments.

Maturity of debts. Several lenders offer a variety of maturities to firms that elect to borrow some of their funds. Funds secured through borrowing are generally divided into three categories according to the maturity of the debt: long-term loans, which mature in ten years or more; intermediate-term loans, which extend from one to ten years; and short-term loans, which must be repaid in a year or less. The maturity dates of loans are very important because the borrowing firm must make plans in advance to have cash on hand when debts become due.

The length of time that funds are borrowed is important

Criteria for Selecting Sources of Funds

Once a business has agreed on a satisfactory financial structure, the financial manager must evaluate each potential source of funds in terms of specific criteria important to the success of the business. These criteria include:

1. The costs of obtaining funds.
2. The timing of principal and interest payments.
3. The future restrictions involved, especially the possibility that obtaining funds from one source may restrict future borrowing.
4. Any effect on control of the business implicit in the terms demanded by potential financial sources. For example, a company that obtains new funds by selling a large block of stock to a single private investor runs the risk of an outsider taking over management.
5. The risks involved, especially the possibility that a financial contributor may someday try to withdraw an investment or to extract a higher interest rate.

Criteria for evaluating potential sources of funds

For many businesses, the costs of obtaining funds and the timing of principal and interest payments are the dominant financial considerations.

Alternate Sources of Funds

We noted earlier that the financial manager must identify the alternative sources of funds that are available. We already know that financing can be divided into three categories according to the length of time the funds are required: long-term (more than ten years), intermediate-term (one to ten years), and short-term (less than one year).

Long-Term Financing

The major sources of long-term financing include funds obtained by equity financing through the issuance of common and preferred stocks and funds obtained by debt financing through the sale of bonds.

Common stock:
an important
source of funds
for corporations

✔ **Common stock.** The sale of *common stock* to owners or investors is the most important source of long-term equity financing for corporations. Nearly all incorporated businesses obtain initial funds in this manner. Any public offering of new stock must be made through a *prospectus* —a brochure that describes the company, its financial condition, and the terms of the stock issue. Figure 12-3 shows a page from a prospectus issued for Playboy Enterprises, Inc., for a new offering of common stock.

The corporate charter specifies the maximum number of shares of stock the company can issue. The number of *authorized shares* can be increased by amending the charter. The stock actually outstanding, which is normally less than the number of authorized shares, is called *issued stock* (see Figure 12-4). Occasionally, common stock is divided into two classes:

12-3 New stock issues are a major source of equity financing.

PROSPECTUS

1,158,812 Shares

PLAYBOY ENTERPRISES, INC.
COMMON STOCK

Of the 1,158,812 shares being offered hereby, the Underwriters are purchasing 545,000 shares from the Company and 526,567 shares from certain Selling Stockholders as set forth under "Principal Stockholder and Selling Stockholders Participating in the Underwritten Offering." Of the remaining shares, 55,000 are being offered by the Company to employees as set forth under "Offering to Employees," and 32,245 shares may be offered as set forth under "Selling Stockholders Not Participating in the Underwritten Offering."

Prior to this offering there has been no market for the Common Stock of the Company. The public offering price for shares being offered by the Underwriters has been established arbitrarily by negotiations among the Company, certain Selling Stockholders and the Underwriters.

The Company intends to apply for the listing of its Common Stock on the New York Stock Exchange. Such listing will be conditioned, among other things, upon completion of distribution of the Common Stock in a manner satisfactory to such Exchange.

THESE SECURITIES HAVE NOT BEEN APPROVED OR DISAPPROVED BY THE SECURITIES AND EXCHANGE COMMISSION NOR HAS THE COMMISSION PASSED UPON THE ACCURACY OR ADEQUACY OF THIS PROSPECTUS. ANY REPRESENTATION TO THE CONTRARY IS A CRIMINAL OFFENSE.

1,071,567 Shares Offered By Underwriters	Price to Public	Underwriting Discounts and Commissions(1)	Proceeds to Company(2)	Proceeds to Selling Stockholders(2)
Per Share	$23.50	$1.35	$22.15	$22.15
Total	$25,181,824	$1,446,615	$12,071,750	$11,663,459

(1) For a description of provisions relating to the indemnification of the Underwriters, see "Underwriting."

(2) Before deducting expenses estimated at $285,908 payable by the Company and $112,010 payable by certain Selling Stockholders participating in the underwritten offering.

Source: Playboy and rabbit head symbol are marks of Playboy, Reg. U.S. Patent Office © 1972 Playboy.

12-4 Corporate ownership is indicated by a stock certificate.

Source: General Motors Corporation.

shares carrying no voting privileges (non-voting stock) and shares that entitle stockholders to vote for members of the board of directors (voting stock).

Warrants and options allow stockholders to purchase newly issued corporate stock on favorable terms. A warrant might permit the stockholder to purchase one share of American Telephone and Telegraph at a price of $60 until January 1, 1980. The market value of the warrant will depend on the $60 *striking price* (the permitted purchase price), on the current price of American Telephone and Telegraph stock, and on investor expectations about the future price of AT&T. Warrants and options are often given to stockholders in place of dividends or to corporate managers as bonuses.

Reasons for holding common stock

From the investor's viewpoint, there are two basic reasons for holding common stock. First, the investor may receive dividend payments from profits earned by the firm. Dividends are normally paid quarterly by company check; some firms also make end-of-the-year payments. Some companies issue dividends in the form of additional stock. For example, a

5 percent *stock dividend* entitles the stockholder to five additional shares of stock for each hundred shares held. Because dividends ultimately depend on company earnings, the investor in an expanding economy can expect dividends on common stock holdings to rise with corporate earnings. A second advantage to holding common stock is that the investor can realize a profit by selling shares if the market price of a stock advances. An investor who buys a stock at a low price and sells it at a higher price is said to realize a *capital gain* — a source of income that is taxed at a favorable rate. Stock market studies reveal that capital gains increase the incomes of common stockholders more than dividends do.

These two major advantages to holding common stock must be weighed against two major risks. First, if a firm is unprofitable, shareholders receive no dividends and may be forced to sell their holdings at a *capital loss* — a price lower than the original cost of the stock. For example, during the late 1960s, Minnie Pearl Fried Chicken (now Performance Systems, Inc.) sold at a peak price of $23 per share and then fell to 12.5 cents per share. Thus, investors who purchased 100 shares at the peak stock price saw the value of their investments fall from $2300 to $12.50! Second, in the event that a firm goes bankrupt, holders of common stock are legally entitled to share in corporate assets only after the firm has made financial restitution to its other creditors.

Watching $2300 turn to $12.50

✔ **Preferred stock.** Another important source of equity financing for corporations is the sale of *preferred stock.* Holders of preferred stock normally receive a fixed dollar dividend for each share of stock they own, and they enjoy priority over common stockholders in claiming corporate assets if a firm dissolves. Holders of a company's 6-percent $20 preferred stock, for example, receive $1.20 per share on dividends each year. If a firm is unprofitable, however, the board of directors may elect to omit dividends on preferred stock. Directors also enjoy the legal right to omit preferred dividends in years when earnings are favorable, although this right has rarely been exercised by American corporations.

Preferred stocks provide a fixed dividend to holders

Owners of *convertible preferred stock* can exchange their preferred shares for common stock on the basis of the terms specified on the stock certificate. The 6-percent $20 preferred issue described above, for example, might include a conversion privilege allowing holders to exchange one preferred share for two common shares. If the firm's common stock is selling at $10 per share, holders of the convertible issue will receive the exact market value of their investment if they decide to convert. Below this price, the preferred stock normally will not vary with fluctuations in the price of the common stock. However, owners of the preferred issue may find it to their advantage to convert when the market value of the common stock rises above $10.

Preferred stock can be divided into several classes: cumulative or noncumulative, participating or nonparticipating, voting or nonvoting, par or nonpar, and callable or noncallable. Definitions of these terms ap-

12-5 Characteristics of stocks and bonds.

Characteristic	Stocks	Bonds
Type of financial instrument	Equity	Debt
Order of claim	Dividends can be issued only after interest on all debts (including bonds) is fully paid.	Interest must be paid before any dividends on stock are issued.
Legal obligations to holders	Dividends may be varied or omitted at the discretion of the board of directors; no principal or maturity dates are involved.	Interest must be paid regularly to avoid insolvency; principal must be repaid at stated maturity date.
Rights of holders	Voting stockholders can influence management by electing members of the board of directors.	Bondholders have no voice in management as long as they receive interest payments.
Tax status	Dividends are not tax-deductible.	Interest as an expense of doing business is tax-deductible.

pear in the glossary at the end of this book. In the past 50 years, preferred stock has become a less important method of financing. It appeals mainly to conservative investors who prefer the relative safety of a fixed return.

✔ **Bonds.** The most important source of long-term debt financing for business is the sale of *bonds*. Bonds represent a fixed obligation in which a business agrees to pay interest plus a specified sum, called the *principal*, to investors. Suppose, for example, that on January 1, 1975, the Tampa Electric Company issues a 7-percent $5000 bond due January 1, 1995. According to the provisions of the issue, Tampa Electric is legally committed to pay each bondholder $350 in annual interest from 1975 through 1994 and to return the $5000 principal to each bondholder on January 1, 1995. The interest rates to be paid and the other terms concerning the bank issue are described in a document called an *indenture*, which is prepared by the firm prior to the sale of the bond. The characteristics of stocks and bonds are compared in Figure 12-5.

Unlike holders of common and preferred stock, bondholders do not

Bondholders do not share in earnings . . .

enjoy voting rights, do not participate in the earnings of the business beyond the stipulated interest payments and return of principal, and do not share in any growth of the firm's earnings. When prices rise, the purchasing power of the interest and principal payments made to bondholders steadily diminishes. Bondholders are creditors of the business and have priority over holders of common and preferred stock in changing corporate assets if the firm dissolves. A variety of bonds—including deben-

... but have priority
over stockholders
in claiming assets

tures, subordinated debentures, and income, mortgage, and municipal bonds—are available to investors and are defined in the glossary at the end of this book.

Bondholder rights are represented by a *trustee* (usually a bank or financial institution) that serves as a liaison between bondholders and the issuer of the bonds. The trustee sees that the terms of the indenture are observed by the issuing firm, certifies that the bonds issued are genuine and not forged, and represents bondholders in case of default on bond agreements or termination of the business. The trustee's sole legal obligation is to protect and to promote bondholder interests.

The safety and
high yields of bonds
appeal to people
with fixed incomes

The safety and high yields of bonds attract investors with fixed incomes who prefer a stated return on their investments. In recent years, yields on corporate bonds have been 3 to 5 percent higher than dividends on common stocks. The largest purchasers of corporate bonds include pension funds and insurance companies, which must meet the fixed claims of their policyholders.

The market price of a bond often differs from its *face value* (or *nominal value*)—the principal indicated on the bond certificate (see Figure 12-6). Suppose, for example, that after an investor purchases the 7-percent, $5000 Tampa Electric issue, a subsequent shortage of investment funds arises,

12-6   Corporate bonds pay a fixed return.

Source: General Motors Corporation.

and interest rates on bonds of comparable quality issued by other companies reach 8 percent. If the holder of the Tampa Electric issue wishes to sell, the investor will have to conclude the transaction at a *discount*—a price below the initial $5000 paid for the bond—since potential buyers will prefer the 8 percent yields on other issues. But if general interest rates fall, the Tampa Electric bondholder will realize a *premium* on the $5000 bond. Although bond prices fluctuate, they tend to be less volatile than common stock prices.

The market yield of a bond is also affected by the financial soundness of the issuing firm. Bonds of financially strong businesses are backed by solid assets and therefore represent less risky investments; such bonds offer substantially lower yields than issues of poorer quality. Standard and Poor's and Moody's bond-rating services offer investors impartial, professional judgments on the quality of most corporate bonds.

Long-term borrowing: financing assets with long lives

✔ **When long-term financing is used.** Businesses normally confine long-term financing to acquisitions of long-lived assets such as land, buildings, and machinery. Only rarely is long-term borrowing used to finance current operating expenses, since it is a very costly method of meeting temporary funding needs. People who are willing to invest their savings in a firm's stocks or bonds seek a high return on their contributions, for they often expect to risk their savings for ten years or more. In addition, a firm that uses long-term financing to meet temporary financial requirements during ordinary periods will build up idle capital which earns little or no interest. However, long-term financing can provide businesses with urgently needed resources to meet financial crises. It also permits businesses to negotiate for intermediate- and short-term funds from a sound financial base.

Intermediate-Term Financing

The major sources of intermediate-term financing include term loans, equipment loans, and government loans from the U.S. Small Business Administration (SBA).

✔ **Term loans.** A *term loan* is an extension of credit by a bank or by an insurance company for a period of more than one year. Typically, the business pays from .25 to .50 percent more for a term loan than it does for a loan with a shorter maturity from the same source. The exact provisions of a term loan are negotiated between the borrowing business and the lender and are incorporated in a formal document called a *loan agreement*. The loan agreement describes the interest rates, maturities, and other terms of the loan and outlines certain conditions designed to protect the lender, such as clauses allowing the lender to inspect the firm's books or provisions requiring that the business maintain specified levels of working capital.

Collateral: assets pledged to support a loan

✔ **Equipment loans.** An *equipment loan* is an extension of credit for which a firm's machinery or equipment is pledged as collateral. Equipment loans are available from commercial banks, insurance companies, suppliers from whom the equipment was purchased, and finance companies (the most expensive source of funds). Normally, the amount of credit extended in an equipment loan is less than the market value of the equipment or other assets pledged as collateral. Equipment loans decrease in proportion to the depreciation of the assets.

✔ **Government loans.** Loans from the U.S. Small Business Administration are a major source of intermediate-term financing for small businesses. Government-licensed small business investment companies (SBICs) make both equity and debt capital available, and some states sponsor state development authorities that lend funds on favorable terms to businesses agreeing to operate in specific regions in the state. The federal government has also established programs to aid minority businesses in obtaining capital. In most cases, a business loan from the federal government can be obtained only after a business can prove that it has exhausted all other likely funding sources. Although most government-sponsored loans are intermediate-term loans, government loans with longer or shorter maturities can be obtained.

Immediate-term credit: financing assets with lives of one to ten years

✔ **When intermediate-term financing is used.** Businesses normally use intermediate-term financing to purchase assets with useful lives of from one to ten years (for example, cars and trucks owned by the business and rapidly depreciating machinery and tools). In the case of equipment loans, the amount of credit extended diminishes as the market value of the assets declines over time. Short-term financing is rarely used to finance major asset purchases, since it is difficult for a business to support repayments of large principals in a short time period.

Intermediate-term borrowing benefits businesses in three major ways. First, it guarantees access to financial resources without involving a firm in long-term or permanent financial commitments. Second, it is usually inexpensive to administer. In contrast, the continuous renewal of short-term loans can be costly and time-consuming, and floating a long-term bond or stock issue to finance each major asset is prohibitively expensive. Third, intermediate-term financing does not affect a firm's short-term financial position. Excessive dependence on short-term borrowing causes current liabilities to rise relative to current assets—a situation that can lead to financial crisis or to loss of investor confidence in the firm.

Short-Term Financing

Three major sources of short-term funds are available to businesses: trade credit, commercial paper, and short-term loans. Short-term financing is an important source of funds for small businesses.

12-7 Major types of financial arrangements between purchasers and suppliers.

Type of trade arrangement	Description	Trade credit extended to customer?
Progress payments	The purchaser pays the supplier while the goods are being manufactured; progress payments are often made in installments, with each payment becoming due as the supplier completes a given stage of manufacture.	No
Cash before delivery (CBD)	The supplier asks for payment before delivery of the goods; this arrangement is often used when the financial status of the purchaser is unknown or questionable.	No
Cash on delivery (COD)	The supplier asks for payment when the goods are delivered; COD is used in the same circumstances as CBD, except that the supplier takes the risk that the purchaser will accept delivery.	No
Open-account credit	The purchaser pays the supplier according to the terms indicated on the invoice, which usually allow the purchaser a grace period during which it can owe suppliers money without paying interest.	Yes
Notes payable	The purchaser signs a promissory note agreeing to pay the supplier at a specified date after the goods are delivered; under this arrangement, the supplier can sell the promissory note to a banker.	Yes
Trade acceptance	The supplier sends the goods to the purchaser with a draft—a promissory note payable to the supplier. The transporting agency is instructed to give up physical possession of the goods only when the purchaser signs the draft and designates at what bank the draft will be paid. When the draft is accepted and signed by the purchaser, it becomes a trade acceptance.	Yes

✔ **Trade credit.** When a business purchases goods or services from a supplier, it must make some arrangements for compensating that supplier. Because of their desire to sell products, most suppliers are willing to extend *trade credit* to purchasers. The various trade credit arrangements between suppliers and purchasers in the United States are described in Figure 12-7.

Open-account credit is the most common type of trade agreement between suppliers and purchasers. In this arrangement, the buyer sends the supplier a *purchase order*—a document describing the types of goods the purchaser wishes to buy. When the supplier ships the goods, it sends the purchaser an *invoice*—a document detailing the items shipped, their destination, and the selling price, which has been previously negotiated. The supplier retains the original purchase order and a copy of the invoice—the only evidence of the transaction that remains in the supplier's possession. In an open-account arrangement, the purchaser is allowed a grace period before it must pay for the items ordered. The most common form of open-account credit combines a grace period and a cash discount for prompt payment. For example, 2/10 net 30—terms found in many American in-

Open accounts: the most common form of business credit

dustries—means that the purchaser must pay the total price of the goods within 30 days after the invoice is received but that it will be granted a 2 percent discount if payment is made within 10 days.

Businesses can use open-account credit as a costless source of short-term financing by delaying payment on the purchased goods until the last day before the discount is lost. A business can also delay payment for the full grace period. In this case, however, it forfeits discount privileges and must pay a high price for the short-term funds. For example, when terms are 2/10 net 30, the purchaser who delays payment for the full grace period is in effect borrowing money from the supplier at an interest rate of 2 percent for 20 days. (This is equivalent to an annual interest rate of 36.5 percent.) Thus, it is usually wiser to borrow funds from banks to pay suppliers than to forego discounts on open-account credit.

Commercial paper:
short-term
promissory notes

✔ **Commercial paper.** *Commercial paper* is comprised of short-term promissory notes issued by a business, usually in multiples of $25,000. Interest rates on commercial paper are generally 1 to 2 percent lower than the interest rates bankers charge for short-term business loans. Commercial paper is *unsecured*—that is, it is issued without the pledge of collateral by the borrower. As a result, only financially strong, established businesses are able to take advantage of this form of short-term financing. Purchasers of commercial paper are protected only by the ability of the issuing business to meet its financial obligations.

Commercial paper is generally sold to dealers, who charge a fixed commission (usually .125 percent of the face value of the note) for their services. An issuing firm may also place commercial paper directly with bankers and with other businesses that have temporary cash surpluses.

✔ **Short-term loans.** A survey taken in 1970 revealed that short-term loans accounted for about 5 percent of the total financing of American manufacturers. Short-term loans, which are available from banks and other financial institutions, can be unsecured or secured.

Short-term loans
can be unsecured
or secured

Unsecured short-term loans involve no pledge of collateral and are generally issued only to businesses with high credit ratings. *Secured short-term loans* require the pledge of some asset (such as inventories) to guarantee repayment of the debt. If a borrowing firm is new or if its ability to repay a loan is doubtful, the firm is generally required to provide collateral

HOW BUSINESSES BORROW MONEY FROM BANKS

Banks are a prominent source of credit, especially for small- and medium-sized businesses. Bank loans to businesses often involve lines of credit extended over several years. When a business establishes a *line of credit* with a bank, the bank informally agrees to make a designated amount of credit available when requested by the business involved. For example, a small flour mill and Bank of America might agree to a line of credit of $500,000. Although the bank is not legally obligated to provide specific amounts of credit, its Board of Directors seldom violates such an agreement. A bank that fails to meet its borrowers' lines of credit soon earns an undesirable business reputation.

Terms	Type of loan	Description
Unsecured (no collateral)	Transaction	A firm borrows funds for a particular transaction and repays the loan when the transaction is finished. For example, a developer draws unsecured short-term funds to pay subcontractors for their assistance in constructing an office building.
	Line of credit	The firm establishes a line of credit—the maximum amount it can borrow on a short-term basis—with a bank. Although bankers are not legally obligated to provide the designated funds, they almost always do so. The maximum amount of credit allowed is renegotiated each year.
	Revolving credit	Revolving credit resembles a line of credit, except that the banker is legally obligated on demand of the lender to make the designated funds available.
Secured (specific assets pledged as collateral)	Accounts receivable	Accounts receivable from a firm's customers are used as collateral. In a nonnotification arrangement, the firm's customers are not involved in settling the loan; in a notification arrangement, customers send their checks for purchased items directly to the borrower's bank.
	Inventory	The borrower's inventories serve as security. If a mortgage on the borrower's inventories is obtained by the lender, inventories are identified specifically and cannot be sold without the lender's permission.
	Other assets	Stocks and bonds held by a firm, the cash value of a firm's paid-up life insurance, and other assets are often used as collateral.

for its short-term borrowings. The major types of unsecured and secured short-term loans are described in Figure 12-8.

Most secured short-term loans involve the use of a *security agreement* (or *security type device*)—a contract signed by the borrower and the lender that describes the assets pledged as collateral for the loan. If the borrower defaults, the lender may seize these assets, irrespective of any other debts

ESTABLISHING YOUR OWN LINE OF CREDIT

Having a line-of-credit agreement with a bank can save service charges on individual checking accounts, since commercial banks typically collect a fee when account balances fall below a designated level or when checks are returned for insufficient funds. Interest rates on line-of-credit loans from banks are generally lower than equivalent installment or charge-account borrowing rates. Line-of-credit loans from banks are generally lower than equivalent installment or charge-account borrowing rates. Line-of-credit arrangements also enable customers to keep low balances in their checking accounts and still have available funds.

When a bank offers its line-of-credit facilities to a business and the extended credit is not used, the bank normally charges an annual interest rate of ½ or ¾ of one percent of the maximum amount that the firm could have borrowed. Consumers who open personal lines of credit at banks, however, are able to write checks without having equivalent deposits up to an agreed credit limit. If no funds are borrowed, no interest charge is made by the bank.

of the borrowing firm. Security agreements are a matter of public record and are filed with a state official, in most cases, the secretary of state. Before making a loan, a lender will investigate the secretary of state's files to make sure that no other claims are outstanding on the collateral offered by the borrowing firm.

Short-term credit is used to meet temporary financial needs

↙ **When short-term financing is used.** Businesses normally use short-term credit to meet seasonal or unexpected demands for funds caused by fluctuations in their sales. The major advantage of short-term financing is its low real cost, especially when commercial paper is issued. Because short-term borrowing can be adjusted to meet temporary financial needs, it permits businesses to borrow only when funds are needed.

Obtaining Funds

Once a firm's financial objectives are developed and its available sources of funding have been identified, the business manager must obtain the actual financial resources. This task involves (1) selecting preferred sources of funds, and (2) arranging financing from these sources.

Selecting Preferred Sources of Funds

Factors affecting sources of funding

The financial manager ultimately selects funding sources on the basis of the interest rates, maturities, and other financing conditions quoted by potential investors or lenders. A business will deviate from a desired financial structure—and even revise it—whenever funds become available from an unexpected source at favorable terms. For example, when stock prices approach record highs, many firms turn to equity financing, and the market in new stock issues becomes exceptionally active. A business may also deviate from its desired financial structure when circumstances facing the firm unexpectedly change. For example, an addition to a firm's product line may increase the company's need for machinery and equipment, necessitating more intermediate-term financing than the firm had originally anticipated.

Thus, sensible financial managers pay close attention to developments in security markets. In addition, managers who lack extensive knowledge or experience in finance often seek financial advice from bankers or from *underwriters,* firms specializing in the sale of new securities to the public. For rapidly growing businesses experiencing chronic shortages of capital, a key consideration in acquiring financial resources is finding external funding sources willing to invest in the firm on reasonable terms.

Arranging Financing

Once the preferred sources of funds have been selected, the business manager faces an important question: what is the best way to acquire funds? Should discussions be initiated with several competing financial organizations, or should negotiations be made directly with a single lender or underwriter? Both large and small businesses can benefit from negotiating with several lenders or underwriters, since one source may be able to offer a larger amount of capital or more favorable terms. On the other hand, a well-established financial connection with a single lender can result in considerable savings in time and effort and may entitle the business to preferential treatment when shortages of funds develop throughout the economy.

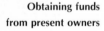

Conducting negotiations with one lender or with competing lenders

If the business elects to obtain financing through the sale of stocks and bonds, it may acquire funds from existing owners of the firm (pre-emptive placement), from the public (public offerings), or from a few selected investors (private placement).

✔ **Preemptive placement.** When new stock is issued through *preemptive placement,* the owners of a business are sent a form, called a *stock right,* entitling them to subscribe to the new issue. In most cases, rights offerings are made on a proportional basis (that is, one stock right for each share of common stock held), so that the ownership structure of the firm remains essentially unchanged. The market value of the rights is roughly equal to the current selling price of the common stock *minus* the discount price of the new issue. For example, a company whose common stock is currently selling for $20 may offer owners the opportunity to purchase an additional share of common stock for $12 plus four rights. In this case, the rights to purchase each new share are worth about $8 to owners, or each right is worth about $2.

Obtaining funds from present owners

Owners are notified of a rights offering through the mail, and those who wish to subscribe must respond within a stated period (usually 30 days). If all owners subscribe to the offering, the company ends up with more outstanding stock and added equity funds in its treasury. If owners do not wish to purchase additional stock, they may sell their rights to other owners or to outside investors interested in the company. Owners who fail to exercise or to sell their rights suffer a direct financial loss.

✔ **Public offering.** In a *public offering,* stocks are sold to the public rather than to a firm's existing owners exclusively. Occasionally, a small business operating within a single state will sell its stock directly to the public. In most cases, however, a firm hires an investment banker or underwriter to place its stock or bond issues with the public. When the issue

WHAT HAPPENED AT TEXAS GULF SULPHUR

The exploration for sulphides—chemical combinations of sulphur and other useful minerals such as copper and zinc—had been going on for two years in Eastern Canada. It was November 10, 1963. A young geologist, Kenneth Davis, was examining a hole 150 feet deep that had just been drilled at Kidd-55, a one-square-mile marshy piece of land 350 miles northwest of Toronto, Canada. The core from deep in the earth looked so promising that Davis rushed to the nearest telephone (17 miles to the south in Tinnins, Canada) to call his boss at the Texas Gulf Sulphur Company.

Texas Gulf Sulphur moved quickly. Several top executives examined the site and ordered the drill rig removed and the test hole returned to its natural state. Drilling then began at a test spot several miles away, where no ore was expected or found. Quietly, Texas Gulf Sulphur began to purchase the mineral rights to the land at Kidd-55. Only after these mineral rights had been secured, did the company drill two more holes to confirm the samples taken from the first drillings.

In late March and early April of 1964, the test results were complete. Kidd-55 contained an immense block of ore with an average copper content of 1.1 percent and a zinc content of 8.4 percent—figures which one mining expert characterized as "just beyond your wildest imagination." The mine was eventually to produce 10 percent of Canada's total output of copper and zinc.

On April 16, 1964, Texas Gulf Sulphur announced "a major discovery of zinc, copper, and silver. . . . Preliminary data indicate a reserve of more than 25 million tons of ore." From November 10 to April 16,

top executives at Texas Gulf Sulphur had been purchasing more than 15,000 shares of its common stock, paying between $20 and $25 per share. On April 16, 1964, Texas Gulf's stock closed at 36⅜, up $7 from its closing price the previous day. By the end of 1964, the price of a common share of Texas Gulf stock had reached $70.

As a result of these activities, the federal government filed a suit alleging that 13 of the top executives at Texas Gulf Sulphur had used their favored positions as corporate insiders to earn excessive profits and to damage the shareholders from whom they purchased Texas Gulf stock. In a now famous ruling, the Circuit Court of Appeals held that: (1) a business has a legal obligation to disclose all "material" information to the general public on a timely basis—to promptly inform the public of all events that are likely to have a significant impact on the market price of company stock, and (2) to make this information available to all persons and organizations on an equal basis. Thus, a business cannot legally provide material information to one brokerage firm nor can a financial manager give material information to personal friends without informing the public as a whole.

The Texas Gulf Sulphur decision has made the relationship between a financial manager and an underwriter or a financial adviser much more difficult. The financial manager must be extremely careful not to make material information exclusively available to an underwriter. Under the Texas Gulf decision, an underwriter or a financial advisor who receives material information on an exclusive basis can be liable along with the firm itself for any damages that result.

Obtaining funds from the public is large, several investment banking firms may combine as an underwriting syndicate, sharing both in the responsibility for placing issues and in the commission charged for the service. The major investment banking houses include Goldman Sachs and Company, First Boston Corporation, and Merrill Lynch.

To market a new issue, the underwriter places it with individual investors or with financial institutions, who agree to purchase or to sell the issue at prices quoted by the underwriter. In this way, a market is generated for the securities. In most instances, the investment banker agrees to purchase any unsold portions of the new issue, which are retained in an inventory to be sold later. In some instances, new issues are handled by investment bankers on a "best-efforts" basis, in which case any unsold securities are returned by the underwriter to the issuing business. In a "best-efforts" offering, the underwriter is not financially responsible for any unsold securities.

Selling securities
to a few investors

✔ **Private placement.** *Private placement* (also called *direct placement*) involves selling securities to a single investor or to a small group of investors. Terms of the placement are negotiated by the issuing firm and by the potential investors, often under the advisement of an investment banker. This type of placement is popular with small- or medium-sized businesses that lack sufficient recognition to make a successful public offering. Private placement is a very costly method of obtaining funds, since few organizations or individual investors are able or are willing to risk large sums of money in a single investment. As a result, private investors can demand attractive terms from businesses.

KEY POINTS TO REMEMBER

1. Finance is the functional area of business that deals with the acquisition and the dispersement of funds.
2. The financial structure of a business reflects the proportions in which a firm acquires various types of funds.
3. Common stock is a form of equity financing in which stock is sold to existing or to new owners of the corporation. Stockholders are entitled to receive dividends—payments which vary with the profits of the company and which are made at the discretion of the board of directors. Preferred stock represents equity financing in which dividends are fixed.
4. Bonds are a form of long-term debt financing in which the firm assumes a fixed obligation to pay interest and principal on designated dates.
5. Forms of intermediate-term debt financing include term loans, equipment loans, and government loans.
6. Forms of short-term financing include trade credit, commercial paper, and short-term loans.
7. Long-, intermediate-, and short-term financing typically support purchases of assets with useful lives of ten, from one to ten, and less than one year, respectively.
8. Preemptive placement involves selling securities to existing stockholders; a public offering involves sales of securities to the general public; and private placement involves selling securities to a private group of investors.

QUESTIONS FOR DISCUSSION

1. How does present-day finance differ from finance during the early 1950s?

2. What are the major sources of funds for American corporations?

3. Distinguish between internal and external finance, equity and debt finance, and the maturities available on debt financing.

4. What factors should a financial manager consider in establishing a desirable financial structure for a business?

5. Discuss the advantages and the disadvantages of investing in common stocks. In preferred stocks. In corporate bonds.

6. What is a term loan? An equipment loan? A government loan? Trade credit? Commercial paper? A short-term loan?

7. What are the various types of unsecured short-term loans? Of secured short-term loans?

8. Discuss the advantages and the disadvantages of long-term, intermediate-term, and short-term financing.

9. Differentiate between preemptive placement, public offering, and private placement.

10. A warrant entitles its holder to purchase Ford Motor Company stock at $40 until January 1, 1982. Although the stock's current price is $25, an investor pays $10 for the warrant. Why would the investor follow this course of action?

SHORT CASES AND PROBLEMS

1. Two students are arguing. Martha observes, "If I were in business, I would insist on cash on delivery. There are far too many untrustworthy people around these days who don't pay their bills." "No," Linda comments, "I think most people are honest, and a business should extend the courtesy of open-account credit." As a business manager, what are the advantages and disadvantages of insisting on cash on delivery? Of extending open-account credit?

2. Spare-a-Part Auto Stores owes a bill of $10,000 to a supplier on terms 2/10 net 30. Spare-a-Part can borrow money at its bank at an interest rate of 10 percent. How much money would Spare-a-Part save by borrowing at the bank and taking advantage of the trade discount?

3. The Hasselrig Corporation plans to purchase two $200,000 machines, each with an expected life of eight years. Each machine should save the firm $100,000 (after taxes) in labor and other costs each year. What types of loans should Hasselrig consider? What factors would you consider in evaluating alternate sources of funds? If money can be borrowed at an interest rate of 10 percent and if the machines have no salvage value at the end of eight years, how much money would Hasselrig make each year if it bought the machines and borrowed the $400,000 to pay for them?

Because accounting and finance are closely related fields, specialists in accounting and in finance may be found within the same occupational category. In addition, titles in the occupational areas of finance vary widely from business to business. The careers discussed in this section are those that people interested in finance are most likely to hold in an industrial or in a service business. Specialized jobs in insurance, real estate, banking, and security markets are often held by finance specialists and will be described in the "Career Selection" sections at the end of Chapters 13 and 14. For additional information about each of the careers described in this Career Selection section, contact the financial manager of a business in your locality.

FINANCE SPECIALISTS

Cash budget analysts maintain weekly or daily records on the cash inflows and outflows of a business. Cash budget or cash flow analysts may also be responsible for a firm's short-term investments. Some accounting training is essential, and a bachelor's degree in accounting or in finance is becoming a common prerequisite for employment. Salaries typically range from $10,000 to $15,000.

Inventory control specialists try to balance the costs of inventory maintenance against the benefits of a large inventory of various items that will appeal to various customers. Inventory control specialists may also be responsible for maintaining accurate records of inventory levels and their locations. Training in production or in finance, often at the bachelor's or at the master's level, is becoming a common occupational requirement. A knowledge of quantitative methods and statistics is especially helpful. Salaries normally range from $10,000 to $20,000.

Project analysts (also known as financial analysts, capital budget analysts, capital expenditure analysts, and capital project analysts) participate at the decision-making level in determining the major investments a firm will make in new products, expensive plant and machinery purchases, and other long-term financial commitments. A keen analytical ability is vital, and maintaining effective working relationships with specialists in accounting, marketing, production, and management is essential. The project analyst projects revenues and costs for alternative uses of the firm's monies and decides in what areas the firm should pursue new investments. A bachelor's degree in finance or in accounting is the minimal training requirement for most newly employed project analysts. More advanced training at the Master's of Business Administration level or beyond is becoming an increasingly common requirement. Salaries normally range from $15,000 to $40,000. Opportunities for project analysts are expected to grow rapidly in the next decade because many firms are trying to develop common methods of analyzing financial information and are also trying to secure financial expertise at the divisional as well as at the corporate level.

TOP-MANAGEMENT CAREERS IN FINANCE

Financial vice presidents, controllers, and **treasurers** are the chief financial officers in a business. Responsibilities include the supervision of accounting and financial personnel, communication with top management, maintenance of relationships with investment bankers and with other organizations that provide funds, and communication of financial matters to stockholders (if a corporation is involved) and to the public. Financial vice presidents also participate in most key business decisions, since important business activities usually have a financial impact or cost. In consultation with top management, financial vice presidents decide what amount of the firm's profits will be returned to the owners and what amount will be retained in the business. In large firms, duties may be divided among several positions: for example, a large business may have a financial vice president and a treasurer. A keen analytical ability, a thorough knowledge of accounting and finance, a capacity for effective administration, and public relations skills are desirable. Financial vice presidents have normally received training in either accounting or finance, increasingly at the MBA level or beyond. Salaries range from $25,000 to $200,000, or more; salary level depends both on the size of the business and on the responsibilities assigned. Considerable work experience in the accounting or the finance area is usually essential. Many financial vice presidents are promoted to president or to chief executive officer of the business.

A CRITICAL BUSINESS DECISION

—made by Jack Simplot

THE SITUATION This decison maker describes himself as a "gol-durn potato farmer." *Fortune* magazine calls him a "private conglomerate," and his rags-to-riches story probably explains his unusual approach to business financing.

The man is Jack Simplot, a native of Declo, Idaho, who left the four-room schoolhouse in his hometown before finishing the eighth grade. Using the money he had earned sorting potatoes and working on the irrigation canals that sent water from the Snake River to Idaho farmlands, Simplot started his own hog farm a year after leaving school. Starting with a few sow hogs, he fattened his feeder pigs, as new litters arrived, at almost no cost using a mash of wild horse meat, cull (rejected) potatoes, and a little barley. Simplot's farm kept expanding, and when hog prices soared to 7.5 cents a pound, he sold his entire hog spread for $7500.

Simplot then went into the potato business, buying an old truck and a big supply of seed potatoes, renting farmland, and spending $254 on an electrically driven potato sorter. Simplot used this machine to sort his potato crop and—for a fee—his neighbors' crops as well. In the 1930s, the U.S. Bureau of Reclamation's work on the Snake River assured a permanent water supply for farmers. Simplot was one of the first Idaho farmers to recognize that this also meant a permanent change in the economics of potato growing.

Most of the diverse enterprises that make Simplot a one-man conglomerate can be traced to his original interest in potatoes. For example, as Simplot's operations grew, he found himself overwhelmed by a river of potato offal—the waste peelings, sprouts, eyes, and culls thrown off the processing lines. Simplot learned that the offal could be mixed with alfalfa, barley, and several chemical supplements to provide a nutritious feed for cattle. Since his first experiment in cattle feeding, he has increased the number of cattle moving through his feedlots to 150,000 annually.

By 1940, Jack Simplot was shipping 10,000 carloads of potatoes a year and had branched out into high-volume onion farming—shipping cull onions for half a cent a pound to California to be dried and made into onion powder. When he accidentally bumped into a man from Chicago who was buying the California dried onions for 21 cents a pound, Simplot agreed on the spot to supply the man with 500,000 pounds of dried onion powder and flakes by the following fall. "It looked like a real good deal," recalls Simplot, "just for squeezin' out the water." Applying this knowledge to the potato business, Simplot developed an inexpensive way to peel and then dehydrate potatoes. Between 1942 and 1945, he dehydrated 33 million pounds of potatoes annually—about a third of the potatoes consumed by the U.S. military during World War II.

Because Simplot needed to crate his potatoes, he also got

into the lumber business. Toward the end of the war, he found himself running short of the fertilizer that he supplied to the farmers who grew potatoes for him. With a government loan, Simplot built a million-dollar fertilizer plant at Pocatello—a railroad town on the Snake River—but then ran into difficulty finding a supplier for the phosphate he needed. By chance, he heard that there was some phosphate rock 27 miles north of Pocatello. "I drove up there one day and scratched around with a scraper," says Simplot. "Damned if I didn't latch onto the biggest phosphate deposit west of Florida." He was in fertilizers to stay.

In the late 1940s, Simplot developed a unique method for freezing French fried potatoes, and by 1960 his plants were processing and freezing about 12,000 carloads of potatoes a year—a sixth of Idaho's annual potato crop. In the 1970s, Simplot dreams of building a plant to combine fried chicken and French fries in one product—an idea that may cost as much as $50 million.

THE DECISION Despite this extensive cash requirement, Simplot has no intention of changing the approach to financing his business that made him Idaho's richest and most prominent industrialist. With an estimated personal wealth of $200 million, Jack Simplot is indebted to no one. Simplot cites the advantages of being his own man: "What I own, I built. It's mine. Nobody ever had to put a penny at risk in my rig. . . . I make the decisions and, believe me, I enjoy making 'em."

QUESTION

Assess the advantages and the disadvantages of Jack Simplot's approach to financing his business—that is, obtaining financial resources without selling corporate stock to the public.

A fool may make money but it takes a wise
man to spend it.

Charles Hoddon Spurgeon

T he key to financial success in business is the wise use of funds. Occasionally, good fortune or a spurt in product demand enables a poorly managed firm to earn temporary profits. Or, a financial genius like James Ling may be able to convince the financial community to invest in a firm. But if a business places its financial resources in unprofitable ventures, high profits and outside monies soon disappear. Skill in obtaining funds is of value to a business; skill in using funds is indispensable to its survival.

The wise use of funds is crucial to business success

Funds acquired by a business are used to purchase assets. Thus, the efficient use of funds is often described as the management of assets. There are two types of asset management: working capital management and capital budgeting. *Working capital management* refers to decisions about current assets and short-term debts. Current assets include cashlike items, accounts receivable, and inventories, all of which are normally converted to cash by a firm within a year of acquisition. *Capital budgeting* involves the use of financial resources to purchase assets that are usually not converted to cash in less than a year. These resources include fixed assets (land, buildings, and machinery) and long-term investments in research and development, new products, and new distribution systems. In Chapter 13, we will examine the management of working capital and capital budgeting and then describe a function closely associated with finance — risk management and insurance.

Working Capital Management

Working capital management: how to use short-term funds

The main categories of working capital are cash and near cash, accounts receivable, and inventories. We will examine the problems that the financial manager faces in handling each of these three types of assets.

Managing Cash and Near Cash

Businesses need to retain cash and *near cash* — interest-bearing assets that can easily be converted to cash — in order to conduct normal business transactions like paying employees and suppliers and meeting unexpected emergencies. The amount of cash and near cash a firm needs depends on the adequacy of its financial planning, the quantities of its other current assets, and the business fluctuations it normally experiences. Because cash provides no direct monetary return, to manage this asset

13-1 Near-cash financial instruments used by business.

Financial instrument	Description	Maturity
Treasury bill	Obligation of the U.S. government; weekly auctions determine yield.	91-day maturity 182-day maturity
Federal agency issue	Obligation of a federal agency such as the Federal Land Bank or the Federal Home Loan Bank.	6-month maturity (Federal Home Loan Bank)
Banker's acceptance	Business agreement to pay a given sum at a future date, guaranteed by a bank.	Highest quality, 1- to 180-day maturity
Certificate of deposit (CD)	Bank deposit on which a specified interest rate is paid. Most CDs can be resold to third parties in advance of indicated maturities.	90- to 149-day maturity (in $100,000 units or larger)
Commercial paper	Unsecured note issued by a firm.	Highest quality, 30- to 270-day maturity
Tax-exempt note	Short-term obligation of a local or state government.	Various maturities

effectively the financial manager must (1) accelerate the collection of monies due; (2) conserve funds; and (3) place idle cash in interest-bearing assets (near cash) until cash is needed.

✔ **Collecting monies due.** Since a firm must offer credit terms to customers in order to remain competitive, it usually cannot force customers to pay for purchases immediately. But several techniques can accelerate the collection of a firm's receipts:

1. *Collection centers:* Under this system, regional collection centers handle receipts from local customers. Invoices are sent to local customers directly from the collection center, rather than from the more distant head office, which saves a day or so in mailing time. Customers remit payments to the collection center, which immediately deposits the receipts in a local bank where the firm maintains an account.

2. *Lock-box system:* A local post office box is rented by the firm, and a regional banker is authorized to pick up all customer remittances from this box several times a day. The banker immediately deposits the receipts in the firm's received-funds account. The lock-box arrangement accelerates the collection process because it eliminates the handling time needed to transfer payments from collection centers to local banks.

3. *Large remittances:* Air mail, special delivery, or personal messenger services may be used to speed the collection of large remittances.

Methods of accelerating a firm's collections

The observation "time is money" applies particularly well to the collection of funds by business: a firm that is successful in accelerating its flow of remittances by several days often reduces its short-term borrowing requirements substantially.

✔ **Minimizing cash use.** The financial manager can conserve funds in several ways. First, amounts owed can be paid on the last possible day before discounts from suppliers are lost. This requires a carefully organized and efficient bill-paying procedure. Second, anticipated cash inflows from accounts receivable can be used to offset the cash outflows necessary to pay the firm's bills. This allows the firm to hold cash resources that at any given amount are a small fraction of the daily bills it must pay. Finally, careful control can be exercised over all the firm's bank accounts, and the excessive accumulation of idle cash in any one account can be prevented by transferring funds to accounts with low cash balances.

Delaying disbursements until just before discount privileges are lost

✔ **Converting cash to near cash.** A firm can also improve its management of working capital by converting cash, on which no interest is received, to interest-bearing investments. Figure 13-1 shows the major financial instruments American businesses use to convert cash to near cash. Note that intermediate- and long-term securities as well as short-term investments may serve as near cash. *Treasury notes*, for example, are U.S.

When possible, substitute near cash for cash

WHAT'S NEW IN CASH MANAGEMENT?

● Every weekday, an employee of the First National Bank of St. Louis boards a plane for Chicago carrying a suitcase that contains $15 million in checks. This operation is completely legal—it is a part of effective cash management.

By immediately depositing these checks in three Chicago banks, the First National Bank of St. Louis can use the money a day or two earlier than it could if the checks were cleared through normal banking channels. The result: a saving of $2 million in First National's normal requirements for short-term funds.

● Financial managers' seat-of-the-pants methods for locating lockboxes are no longer adequate. Most large companies now gather data about the locations and the amounts of their customer receipts. A computer then analyzes the information to determine how many lockboxes a company should have and where they should be located. The Phoenix-Hecht Cash Management Service of Chicago even compares mailing times from 105 Zip-Code localities to 47 receiving cities—information that helps the computer determine the best lockbox locations.

● The automated deposit-transfer system is used mainly in businesses like supermarket chains, which

have many separate outlets. In the past, the manager of an individual unit carried the checks and the cash received from customers directly to a local bank, sent a check for part of the deposit to the company headquarters, and used the remainder of the deposit for the unit's operating expenses.

In an automated transfer system, the manager makes the deposit and then reports the time and the amount of the deposit to an informational clearing house. In the meantime, the bank transfers portions of the deposit to the firm's various accounts, according to a formula the firm and the local bank have already agreed upon. After all of the unit managers have submitted their reports, a computer at the clearing house provides the financial manager with a daily summary of the amounts and the locations of all of the firm's cash receipts. The financial manager can then use the cash receipts immediately, rather than having to wait to receive confirmation of the daily deposits by mail. Robert C. Schmidt, who is in charge of cash management for the First National Bank of St. Louis, observes that speeding up collections by using couriers, lockboxes, and automated transfer systems, is "the white-hot part of cash management."

governments obligations with maturity dates ranging from one to seven years; *Treasury bonds* mature in more than seven years. The market for Treasury notes and bonds is very active. Business owners frequently purchase Treasury notes or bonds that have been held for several years by other owners, thus acquiring long-term financial bonds that will mature shortly after purchase. Thus, in effect, Treasury notes and bonds come to serve the same function as *Treasury bills,* obligations of the U.S. government with maturity dates of a year or less.

Managing Accounts Receivable

As we saw in Chapter 12, most firms extend open-account credit to customers to expand sales and to avoid the paperwork involved in preparing a formal agreement for each business transaction. Two dimensions of a firm's management of accounts receivable are its credit policy and its credit management.

A firm's *credit policy* determines the conditions under which it extends credit to its customers. If a business selects the open-account system, it can choose among a wide variety of credit terms. Uniform credit terms are normally established throughout an industry, but occasionally businesses compete for new customers by offering them more favorable credit terms.

A firm's standards for evaluating the credit-worthiness of its individual customers are central to credit policy. Under what conditions should a firm extend credit to a customer and under what circumstances should a firm require cash before delivery or cash on delivery? The answers to these questions depend on four key factors:

Credit policy: obtaining new business while avoiding bad debts

1. *The profitability of the transactions involved:* If a firm ordinarily obtains profits of, say, only 1 percent of sales, failure to collect 1 percent or more of its accounts receivable will automatically cancel all business profits. Credit would be extended to such a firm with caution.
2. *The influence of credit on additional sales:* If customers are not greatly influenced by credit policy, the firm can adopt a restrictive credit policy without reducing sales substantially.
3. *The firm's assessment of the probability of default:* If a large number of customers to whom credit is extended are expected to default on payments of accounts receivable or to delay payments for an extended period, a restrictive credit policy is indicated.
4. *The risk preferences of management:* A management that wishes to avoid risk is usually careful in extending credit.

Factors affecting a firm's credit policy

In a large firm, the financial manager and the *credit manager*—a specialist in handling accounts receivable—formulate the general policy of the

PLEASE NOTE WHETHER NAME, BUSINESS AND STREET ADDRESS CORRESPOND WITH YOUR INQUIRY.

Dun & Bradstreet® BUSINESS INFORMATION REPORT
RATING UNCHANGED

SIC	D-U-N-S	© DUN & BRADSTREET, INC.	STARTED	RATING
34 61	04-426-3226	CD 13 APR 21 19--	1957	D D I
	ARNOLD METAL PRODUCTS CO	METAL STAMPINGS		

53 S MAIN ST
DAWSON MICH 66666
TEL 215 999-0000

SUMMARY

SAMUEL B. ARNOLD)
GEORGE T. ARNOLD)   PARTNERS

PAYMENTS   DISC PPT
SALES $177,250
WORTH $42,961
EMPLOYS   10
RECORD   CLEAR
CONDITION STRONG
TREND   UP

PAYMENTS

HC	OWE	P DUE	TERMS	APR 19--		SOLD
3000	1500	1 10	30	Disc		Over 3 yrs
2500	1000	1 10	30	Disc		Over 3 yrs
2000	500	2 20	30	Disc		Old account
1000			30	Ppt		Over 3 yrs
500			30	Ppt		Over 3 yrs

FINANCE

On Apr 21 19-- S.B. Arnold, Partner, submitted statement Dec 31 19--

Cash	$ 4,870	Accts Pay	$ 6,121
Accts Rec	15,472	Notes Pay (Curr)	2,400
Mdse	14,619	Accruals	3,583
	------		------
Current	34,961	Current	12,104
Fixed Assets	22,840	Notes Pay (Def)	5,000
Other Assets	2,264	NET WORTH	42,961
	------		------
Total Assets	60,065	Total	60,065

19-- sales $177,250; gross profit $47,821; net profit $4,204. Fire
insurance mdse $15,000; fixed assets $20,000. Annual rent $3,000.
Signed Apr 21 19-- ARNOLD METAL PRODUCTS CO by Samuel B. Arnold, Partner
Johnson Singer, CPA, Dawson

-----0-----

Sales and profits increased last year due to increased sub-contract
work and this trend is reported continuing. New equipment was purchased
last Sept for $8,000 financed by a bank loan secured by a lien on the
equipment payable $200 per month. With increased capacity, the business
has been able to handle a larger volume. Arnold stated that for the first
two months of this year volume was $32,075 and operations continue profitable.

BANKING

Medium to high four figure balances are maintained locally. An equipment loan is outstanding and being retired as agreed.

HISTORY

Style registered Feb 1 1965 by partners. SAMUEL, born 1918, married.
1939 graduate of Lehigh University with B.S. degree in Mechanical Engineering. 1949-50 employed by Industrial Machine Corporation, Detroit, and
1950-56 production manager with Aerial Motors Inc., Detroit. Started this
business in 1957. GEORGE, born 1940, single, son of Samuel. Graduated in
1963 from Dawson Institute of Technology. Served U.S. Air Force 1963-64.
Admitted to partnership interest Feb 1965.

OPERATION

Manufactures light metal stampings for industrial concerns and also
does some work on a sub-contract basis for aircraft manufacturers. Terms
net 30. 12 accounts. Five production, two office employees, and one salesman. LOCATION: Rents one-story cinder block building with 5,000 square feet
located in industrial section in normal condition. Housekeeping is good.
4-21 (803 77) PRA

THIS REPORT MAY NOT BE REPRODUCED IN WHOLE OR IN PART IN ANY FORM OR MANNER WHATEVER.
It is furnished by DUN & BRADSTREET, Inc. in STRICT CONFIDENCE at your request under your subscription agreement for your exclusive use as a basis for credit, insurance, marketing
and other business decisions and for no other purpose. These prohibitions are for your own protection — your attorney will confirm the seriousness of this warning. Apprise DUN &
BRADSTREET promptly of any question about the accuracy of information. DUN & BRADSTREET, Inc. does not guarantee the correctness of this report and shall not be liable for any loss or
injury caused by the neglect or other act or failure to act on the part of said company and/or its agents in procuring, collecting or communicating any information. 9R2-216802021

13-2   A Dun & Bradstreet credit report.

Source: Dun & Bradstreet, Inc.

business. Implementation of credit policy, known as *credit management,* is carried out by the credit manager and the manager's assistants, who usually form one section of the firm's finance department.

Once the general credit policy of a firm is established, the credit manager (1) investigates individual credit applicants; (2) decides on the amount, if any, of credit to extend to each account; and (3) establishes collection policies when individual customers delay payments. Financial managers frequently rely on past experience with a customer or on accounting statements supplied by a new customer when making credit decisions. Most commercial banks maintain credit departments, which assist depositors in obtaining credit information on potential customers. Organizations like the National Association of Credit Men exchange information on the credit-worthiness of various businesses. For a fee, commercial credit-rating services also provide businesses with accounting information and credit reports on potential customers. A credit report prepared by Dun & Bradstreet, perhaps the most well-known and comprehensive credit-rating service, is shown in Figure 13-2.

Once the credit investigation of a customer has been completed, the credit manager or an assistant analyzes the customer's short-term liquidity, payment record, quality of management, and other factors. Financial ratios (already discussed in Chapter 11) are often utilized in this type of analysis. If a decision is made to extend credit, it often takes the form of a *line-of-credit arrangement,* in which the customer is permitted to make purchases on credit up to a fixed dollar limit. The amount of credit allowed is periodically reviewed, but a line-of-credit arrangement means that the credit-worthiness of a customer does not have to be reevaluated every time an order is placed.

The collection of delinquent or past-due accounts represents one of the credit manager's most delicate tasks. Usually a series of letters is sent to the customer. Phone calls and personal visits may also be made by the credit manager's assistants. If these fail, the credit manager may call in a collection agency, which charges a fee often equal to half the unpaid balance, or the firm may initiate direct legal action against the customer.

Managing Inventories

Inventories include stockpiles of raw materials used in manufacturing a product and quantities of partially or completely finished goods kept on hand by the firm. The major advantages and disadvantages of maintaining inventories are listed in Figure 13-3.

In large businesses, inventory control is normally the task of the manufacturing department, which estimates the levels of inventories to be maintained and indicates when inventories should be replenished. The manufacturing department must exercise careful control over the amount of inventories it holds. Large inventories may tie up capital, but they

Implementing the credit policy

Businesses limit the amount of credit extended to individual customers

13-3 Advantages and disadvantages of maintaining inventories.

Inventories allow businesses to . . .	But problems arise because inventories . . .
1. Meet sudden spurts in customer demand.	1. Tie up scarce and costly financial resources that could be used to purchase materials or to produce finished goods.
2. Provide adequate service from stocks of spare parts.	
3. Keep the production line operating by avoiding unexpected shortages of raw materials.	2. Cost money to count, control, protect, insure, and maintain.
4. Continue production when strikes or other problems interrupt the flow of supplies.	3. Depreciate in value if the prices of purchased materials or of finished products decline.
5. Obtain greater profits if suppliers subsequently raise their prices.	4. Become obsolete and possibly worthless if models, styles, or fashions change quickly.
6. Sell to customers for a time even if the firm's employees strike.	

Inventory management: enough but not too much

provide protection if costly out-of-stock problems arise. The reverse is true of small inventories. Thus, maintaining a proper inventory balance is essential.

The financial manager evaluates a firm's inventory policy to determine that a proper inventory balance is achieved; savings in inventories can then free financial resources for other uses.

Goals of Working Capital Management

Working capital—cash and near cash, accounts receivable, and inventories—yields little if any return on investment if it is held in excessive amounts. Ideally, financial managers seek just enough working capital to support their profitable long-term investments. This minimal level of working capital is financed by short-term borrowing, which can be terminated quickly when the funds are no longer needed. Temporarily idle working capital can be held as near cash.

In practice, however, it is rarely possible to maintain ideal cash balances. Firms occasionally misjudge working capital needs, experience sudden and unpredictable changes in working capital requirements, or discover that the conditions under which the financial community will lend short-term funds have altered. To overcome these difficulties, prudent businesses usually maintain some excess working capital as a marginal safety. Thus, financial managers face a fundamental choice between risk and return in the management of working capital: reductions in working capital increase the chances of financial crisis but add to business profits.

The finance manager's choice: less risk or greater return

TROUBLE AT SCHAAK ELECTRONICS

Schaak Electronics is hardly a household word. But in 15 years, its president, Dick Schaak, changed a small electronics store in Minneapolis, Minnesota, into a prosperous, 39-unit consumer electronics operation. It was 1974, and Dick Schaak was about to receive the "Entrepreneur-of-the-Year" award from Stanford University.

Suddenly, Schaak Electronics experienced a $772,000 loss in 1974 that caused the company to violate its credit agreements. Stockholder equity fell 1/3 to $1.5 million; the loan agreements were contingent upon Schaak maintaining stockholder equity of $2.0 million or more.

Dick Schaak's brilliant marketing and selling tactics had paid handsome dividends over the years. But Schaak's financial management had been intuitive and informal. Of particular concern:

● Company checking accounts were examined and reconciled at six- to nine-month intervals.

● The company's accounting system did not provide up-to-date information and did not follow-up on doubtful accounts due.

● Inventories were examined only at the end of the year.

● Schaak's accounting system failed to identify accounts payable quickly, and suppliers were not paid promptly.

● When suppliers raised prices, Schaak's accounting system did not inform the store manager, who kept retail prices at existing levels for weeks after the suppliers' prices had changed.

Dick Schaak has experienced many difficulties that a business owner who is an unskilled financial manager must face once the firm becomes successful. Using the methods of sound working capital management discussed in this section, describe and classify Schaak Electronic's specific problems. Can you suggest any corrective actions? (For the answers, see "How Schaak Took Corrective Action.")

Capital Budgeting

Capital budgeting: a key to business success

If working capital management is the financial staff's most time-consuming activity, capital budgeting is its most important function. *Capital budgeting* determines the long-range projects and activities that a firm will undertake. Proposals to build a new plant, terminate a division, extend a product line, replace worn-out machinery, or alter research and development expenditures represent capital budgeting decisions because they involve commitments of financial resources for one year or more. Capital budgeting also determines the proportion of funds that a business will devote to working capital management and the proportion of funds that a business must secure from external sources. Capital budgeting involves three key steps: (1) determining return on investment; (2) utilizing financial leverage; and (3) assessing risk.

Return on Investment

The financial manager's primary function is to seek profitable uses of business funds, whatever the size of the firm. *Return on investment* (ROI) is the common measure of the effective use of funds. Return on investment is usually expressed in percentage terms and is determined by *dividing* the estimated profits associated with a project by the dollar value of the assets used in the project. Suppose, for example, a small business owner is considering two alternative projects—opening a shoe store or buying an apartment building—each of which requires an investment of $50,000. If the business owner projects profits (the annual return after all expenses, including depreciation, have been paid) at $20,000 for the shoe store and at $15,000 for the apartment building, return on investment is:

ROI: profits divided by assets used

$$\text{ROI (shoe store)} = \frac{\text{Estimated annual profit}}{\text{Total assets used}} = \frac{\$20,000}{\$50,000} = 40\%$$

$$\text{ROI (apartment building)} = \frac{\text{Estimated annual profit}}{\text{Total assets used}} = \frac{\$15,000}{\$50,000} = 30\%$$

A central principle of sound financial management is that, in general, a business should use its funds to promote projects that promise the highest returns on investment. Thus, the small business owner with only $50,000 in capital available for investment should choose to open the shoe store rather than to purchase the apartment building.

ROI is used to evaluate business activities

The goal of systematically selecting projects that have the highest potential returns on investment possible applies to every activity a business undertakes, from the introduction of a new product whose failure could bankrupt the business to the purchase of a new typewriter for the steno pool. (The new typewriter should boost worker output sufficiently to yield an acceptable return on its investment cost.)

Financial Leverage

Rather than choose between two alternative investments, a knowledgeable small business owner may consider a third possibility: would it be even more profitable to borrow the remainder of the funds

---

HOW SCHAAK TOOK CORRECTIVE ACTION

Dick Schaak's first corrective action was to hire a professional financial manager, who quickly drafted a two-inch thick book of accounting instructions and sent one to each store manager. Cash balances for each store are now checked daily to avoid maintaining excess cash on hand. Schaak's credit management was drastically altered. The company no longer extends its own credit to customers, but it does accept credit cards like American Express and BankAmericard; the credit-card firms must then absorb their own losses if accounts default. Inventories, which had become unmanageable, had previously been checked annually but now are examined quarterly. The new accounting system makes time-

payments to suppliers in order to take maximum advantage of the trade discounts they extend to Schaak. Finally, a system of store-by-store financial planning was initiated and district managers were assigned. The district managers have been given such responsibilities as immediately notifying each store when Schaak's suppliers raise their prices.

By mutual agreement, Dick Schaak did not accept the "Entrepreneur-of-the-Year" award offered by Stanford University. But his prompt corrective actions did enable Schaak Electronics to recover to the point that it now has a good chance of surviving in the marketplace.

needed to purchase both the shoe store and the apartment building? Suppose a local banker agrees to lend the owner $25,000 for each project at 10-percent annual interest. The small business owner makes the following calculations:

Project	Total investment required	Total investment after borrowing $25,000 on each project	Estimated annual profit	Interest paid to bank ($25,000 × 10%)	Profit after interest payment
Shoe store	$50,000	$25,000	$20,000	$2500	$17,500
Apartment building	50,000	25,000	15,000	2500	12,500

Since only $50,000 is available for investment, if the business owner does not borrow funds, we already know that the owner will open the shoe store and realize a profit of $20,000. By borrowing $25,000 on each project, the business owner will be able to purchase the shoe store with an investment of $25,000 (the $50,000 total original cost *minus* the $25,000 in borrowed funds) and the new apartment with an investment of $25,000 (again, the $50,000 total original cost *minus* the $25,000 in borrowed funds). Each project's return on investment will diminish by the $2500 in interest payments that must be made on each $25,000 loan at 10-percent annual interest. Thus, the owner's net profit on the shoe store will be $17,500 ($20,000 in estimated profits *minus* $2500 in interest), and the net profit on the new apartment building will be $12,500 ($15,000 in estimated profits *minus* $2500 in interest). By borrowing $50,000 from the bank to purchase both the shoe store and the apartment building, however, the business owner's total profits are $30,000 ($17,500 from the shoe store and $12,500 from the apartment building)—far more than the $20,000 that would have been realized if the owner had not borrowed funds and had purchased only the shoe store.

Wise use of financial leverage is the reason for our small business owner's increased profits. *Financial leverage* (or the *leverage factor*) expresses the dollar value of a firm's debt as a percentage of the total investment in the business. The owner's combined financial leverage on the shoe store and on the new apartment building can be found by using the following formula:

$$\text{Combined financial leverage} = \frac{\text{Dollar value of business firm's debt}}{\text{Total investment in the business}}$$

$$= \frac{\text{Small business owner's debt}}{\text{Small business owner's debt} + \text{investment}}$$

$$= \frac{\$50,000}{\$50,000 = \$50,000} = 50\%$$

DOES FINANCIAL LEVERAGE AFFECT YOU?

Many people find that financial leverage is an important factor in their lives. Suppose, for example, that you have $1000 in savings and that you have the opportunity to make one of two alternative investments. The first investment is a $10,000 vacant lot in a growing part of town. Your local bank is willing to provide a $9000 mortgage on the land at an annual interest rate of 7 percent. You know that the values of comparable lots in this area have risen 10 percent each year.

The second investment is 100 shares of common stock in a local company at $20 per share. Because you have only $1000, your broker suggests that you invest $1000 in a margin account and borrow the remaining $1000 from the brokerage firm at an annual interest of 7 percent. You are positive that the stock will increase 15 percent in value each year.

Since you believe strongly in your estimates, risk is not a major factor in making your decision. And, after some study, you conclude that neither the upkeep and taxes on the land nor the commissions on the purchase of the stock are major considerations. Using the concept of financial leverage described in the text, which investment will you make? (For the answer, see "Putting Financial Leverage to Work for You.")

Financial leverage can apply either to the firm as a whole or to individual activities within the firm.

It is easy to see why financial leverage can be profitable for most businesses. The ROI on the shoe store and on the apartment building are 40 percent and 30 percent respectively. By borrowing funds at a 10-percent interest rate, the small business owner can purchase the apartment building in addition to opening the shoe store. By borrowing $50,000 at an annual interest of 10 percent to invest in a project that yields a 30-percent estimated return, the owner is able to pay the 10-percent interest and to pocket the "extra" 20 percent as profits.

Combining the concepts of the rate of return on investment and the interest costs of borrowing produces a second basic principle of finance: as long as rates of return on investment exceed the interest costs of borrowing and as long as borrowed funds can be obtained without additional contributions of capital, it is profitable for a business owner to borrow as much as possible to increase a firm's financial leverage. If a firm's rate of return on investment is greater than the interest rates it must pay, the business is said to be enjoying *favorable financial leverage*. For example, a bank's success depends on its ability to obtain favorable financial leverage. It does this, say, by paying depositors 5 percent on their savings and lending these dollars to borrowers at an interest rate of 7 or 10 percent. American businesses make wise use of favorable financial leverage: historically, U.S. firms have earned approximately 12 percent on business assets and have paid 7–10 percent for borrowed funds. For this reason, American firms utilize short-, intermediate-, and long-term borrowing (discussed extensively in Chapter 12).

Financial leverage can increase profits . . .

. . . and diminish them

Unfortunately, borrowing is not always profitable to business owners. *Unfavorable financial leverage* occurs whenever a firm's rate of return on investment drops below the interest rates it must pay. If our small business owner borrows $50,000 and ROI estimates on the shoe store and the new apartment building are far too high, unfavorable financial leverage can force the owner into bankruptcy. For example, if the ROI on both projects falls to 1 percent, total profits from the $100,000 investment will be $1000. By borrowing $50,000 at 10-percent annual interest, the owner must pay $5000 in annual interest expenses and realize a net loss of $4000. Thus, given unfavorable financial leverage, it is better for the owner not to borrow. Investing only in the shoe store would produce a one percent or a $500 profit on the $50,000 investment—hardly a satisfactory return, but far better than suffering a loss.

Assessing Risk

Risk is ever-present in business

Risk, when defined as variations in the outcome of a decision, is ever-present in business life. Estimates of potential returns on investments may not be accurate; uncontrollable natural factors such as earthquakes and floods may intervene; or *business risks* like recessions or new zoning ordinances may turn potentially profitable investments into financial disasters. When unfavorable business outcomes due to risk combine with extensive financial leverage, the effects can be catastrophic for a firm.

Most people prefer to avoid risk—especially when making financial decisions. For example, bonds issued by the largest and the most stable corporations pay lower interest rates than corporate bonds issued by smaller businesses. U.S. government bonds, which are viewed as very secure, carry an even lower interest rate than corporate bonds. The pricing of bonds as well as of most business investments reflects a key principle of finance: the *risk–return relationship.* According to this concept, the greater the risk associated with a business activity, the higher the anticipated return on investment.

Are risk and return inversely related?

"And so, extrapolating from the best figures available, we see that current trends, unless dramatically reversed, will inevitably lead to a situation in which the sky will fall."

Drawing by Lorenz;
© 1972, The New Yorker Magazine, Inc.

PUTTING FINANCIAL LEVERAGE TO WORK FOR YOU

If you purchase the lot and it appreciates by 10 percent the first year, the lot will be worth $11,000 ($10,000 *plus* the 10-percent appreciation). Thus, in the first year, you will make $1000 (if you choose to sell the lot). Your expenses will be the interest you must pay on the $9000 mortgage, which is equal to $9000 *times* the 7-percent interest, or $630. Your profit on the investment, if your estimate of a 10-percent appreciation is correct, will be $1000 *minus* $630, or $370. On a $1000 investment, the $370 potential profit represents a return of 37 percent.

If you invest in the stock and it appreciates by 15 percent, the value of the stock after one year will be $2300 ($2000 *plus* the 15-percent appreciation). Your profit (if you choose to sell the stock) will be $300 *minus* your interest expense, which is $70 ($1000 borrowed on the stock *times* the 7-percent interest). Thus, your investment gain is $230, or a 23-percent return on your original of $1000.

You will earn a greater return on your investment if you purchase the vacant lot. This example illustrates a very important principle of finance that applies to individuals and to businesses alike. When return-on-investment rates are higher than interest rates on borrowed funds, it often pays to undertake a project with a lower overall return-on-investment rate on which substantial amounts can be borrowed. This insight is crucial to an understanding of many investment situations and many business activities.

Every businessowner must make two key decisions concerning risks:

1. In view of the possible bad effects of leverage, how much financial leverage am I willing to assume in the hope of raising my profits?
2. How much additional risk am I willing to accept in order to raise my expected return on individual projects and activities?

How specific business owners answer these two key questions depends on their attitudes toward risk and on the financial strength of their firms. Some thrive on high risk; the oil wildcatter is a spectacular example. Others treat risk with caution; the stereotype of the conservative banker serves as an example. A firm's ability to assume risks depends on the soundness of its financial foundation. Thus, a real-estate developer with limited financial resources may prefer to avoid an alternative high-risk investment even though it yields a higher estimated return.

Arranging investments by their returns

✔ **Selecting projects.** In selecting the activities a firm will undertake, the financial manager must evaluate investment possibilities in terms of their projected returns. The financial manager will concentrate the firm's investments on projects with the highest potential returns on investment. In general, the alternative projects are ranked from highest to lowest, based on projected rates of return. But how far down the list of alternate investments should the financial manager go? The cutoff point between investing and not investing depends on the amount of investment funds available and on the average cost of acquiring funds.

To be included in a capital budget, a business activity must:

1. Have a higher potential return on investment than any project the firm elects not to undertake.
2. B art of a group of projects whose total investment does not exceed the firm's ability to obtain equity or debt financing.
3. Have a projected rate of return that exceeds the firm's cost of obtaining the necessary capital, especially the cost of borrowing funds.
4. Involve a level of risk that is acceptable to the business.

Deciding on specific investments

A business activity should be conducted only if it meets all four of these criteria.

An Overview of Financial Management

Sound financial management involves three main steps. First, the financial manager must obtain funds as cheaply and on as favorable terms as possible (Chapter 12). Second, the financial manager must provide a sound level of working capital for the firm by securing sufficient funds to prevent short-term bankruptcy and by avoiding excessive accumulations of working capital on which little or no return is earned. Working capital decisions are usually evaluated by applying financial ratios similar to those discussed in Chapter 11. The current ratio, for example, is used to evaluate a firm's ability to meet its short-term financial obligations.

Three steps to sound financial management

The third and most important stage of sound financial management involves capital budgeting. In evaluating capital budgeting decisions, the financial manager assesses the performance of each major business activity to determine whether it should be expanded, maintained at its existing level, reduced in scope, or dropped entirely. In evaluating the performance of both old and new business activities, ROI rates are compared with original projections and with actual results in other areas of the firm.

The ultimate measure of the financial health of a business is its ability to secure adequate profits as measured by return on investment, return on sales, and growth in earnings per share. The overall financial performance of a business largely reflects its ability to obtain funds, manage working capital, and plan capital budgets on a sound basis.

Risk Management

Financial decision making is closely linked with risk, for projections of future returns on investment at best only approximate actual results. Uncertainties like economic fluctuations, changes in customer tastes, ac-

13-4 Important activities of a risk manager.

Responsibility	Shared most commonly with . . .
Risk determination and evaluation	Financial manager
Insurance selection	Financial manager
Claims handling (property and liability insurance other than worker's compensation)	Not specified
Insurance accounting	Financial manager
Loss prevention	Safety engineer
Self-insurance administration	Financial manager
Claims handling (worker's compensation)	Personnel manager, safety engineer
Safety administration	Safety engineer
Design of group insurance plans and negotiations with carriers	Personnel manager

Source: Adapted from *American Society of Insurance Management Study of the Risk Manager and ASIM* (New York: Woodward and Fondiller, March 1969), Table 9.

tions of competitors, strikes, shortages of raw materials, fires, wars, and new government statutes disrupt even carefully managed businesses. The financial manager must reduce risk to the lowest possible level while maintaining a firm's desired rates of return and must minimize the adverse effects of risk in case an outcome is unfavorable to the firm. In most large businesses, the details of handling risk are assigned to a specialist called the *risk manager*. Figure 13-4 indicates the major responsibilities that a risk manager shares with other people in the firm.

Basically, businesses reduce risk by sound management, the reduction or avoidance of physical hazards, self-insurance, and transference of risk to another individual or organization through hedging, business insurance, and employee insurance.

Sound Management

Normal business risks can often be reduced by sound management. Effective forecasting and planning enable the financial manager to anticipate and to adjust to economic fluctuations or changes in customer tastes. An aggressive research and development program can help a business respond to vigorous competition. Well-conceived personnel programs sometimes help to reduce the number and the length of strikes.

Sound management can reduce risk

The financial manager plays a key role in reducing risks. A manager can reduce potential financial difficulties by directing long-term investments into profitable ventures and by channeling the firm's funds into combinations of high-risk and relatively safe investments. Above all, the financial manager can practice sound working capital management, making sure that adequate quantities of current assets will be available to meet unanticipated drains on the firm's financial resources.

Reduction or Avoidance of Physical Hazards

An important means of minimizing business risk is to reduce or to avoid physical hazards within the firm. This is usually undertaken by the risk manager in association with another specialist, the *safety engineer*. Major protective and preventive measures to avoid physical hazards include:

1. Designing or purchasing buildings and machinery that reduce the chances of fire and employee accidents.
2. Protecting a firm's property by hiring plant guards, screening employees carefully, and improving burglar alarms, locks, and safes.
3. Introducing safety education programs for employees and regularly inspecting and repairing safety devices.

The role of the safety officer has been expanded considerably as a result of the passage of the Occupational Safety and Health Act (OSHA), which sets federal job safety and health standards and guarantees periodic inspections of the standards maintained by individual businesses.

Self-Insurance

Self-insurance: absorbing losses yourself

A firm can meet risks by paying for its own losses through *self-insurance,* either by establishing a special contingency fund or by absorbing losses with current financial resources. Self-insurance is feasible whenever the values of the assets involved are small relative to the size of the business. For example, a large corporation need not carry fire insurance for the equipment it owns in a small suite of rented offices. Self-insurance is also desirable when the probability of loss is extremely low or when the firm owns a large number of similar assets. Thus, an international oil company that owns several hundred tankers will generally be self-insured. Even a loss as unlikely as one tanker per year may cost the company less than the insurance premiums it would have to pay to protect all the tankers it owns.

Hedging

Businesses that derive profits primarily from processing a major raw material (for example, grain, coffee, or copper) can protect their profits by transferring risk to another party through a process known as *hedging*. In the United States, raw materials are bought and sold on commodity markets, such as the Chicago Board of Trade and the New York Mercantile Exchange. For example, suppose in late September 1976 that the price quoted on commodity markets in Chicago for wheat to be delivered in September 1977 was $5 per bushel. By purchasing a September 1977 *futures contract* in that commodity, a baking company could guard (or hedge) against future crop failures or additional sales of wheat to foreign countries by guaranteeing itself access to a fixed amount of wheat at a specified price. The same logic applies to a wheat seller. A farmer, fearing that crops will be large or that foreign purchases of American wheat will decline, can guarantee a fixed price for the product by selling a futures contract in wheat. Under the terms of the contract, the farmer agrees to deliver wheat to the purchaser at a stated price at some later date.

**Hedging:
transferring risk
to another party**

The prices specified in futures contracts fluctuate, reflecting the supply and demand for future deliveries of a product. For example, by December 1976, the demand for September 1977 wheat may increase and buyers of futures contracts may pay $7 per bushel for delivery on that date. Such fluctuations in the prices of futures contracts encourage speculators to participate in commodity markets. Futures prices are quoted in most major newspapers and are watched closely by many businesses and individual investors.

Businesses may also hedge against price fluctuations by negotiating *requirements contracts*—long-term agreements between purchasers and suppliers indicating the quantities and the prices of goods or services that will be sold. Both seller and buyer benefit from the terms of a requirements contract. For example, a 20-year requirements contract between an electric utility and a coal producer guarantees an adequate supply of coal for the utility and a sizable market for the coal producer.

Insurance

The most widely used method of transferring risk in American business is the purchase of insurance. The underlying concept of insurance is simple: for a fee (an *insurance premium*), one party (the *insurer*) agrees to pay another party (the *insured*) a sum of money specified in advance if the second party sustains a loss under conditions indicated in a written contract (*insurance policy*). Insurance premiums are based on statistical probabilities recorded in *actuarial tables*, which represent insurers' past experience with potential benefit payments. Simplified actuarial statistics on the life expectancies of Americans at various ages appear in Figure 13-5.

**Insurance benefits
both the insured
and the insurer**

The purchase of an insurance policy offers advantages to both the insured and the insurer. For example, for an annual premium of $1000, a business might insure itself for $200,000 against the death or disability of a top executive, with the $200,000 payable to the company. The probability

13-5 A simplified actuarial table.

Age	Probability of survival to age 65	Average remaining lifetime (years)	Average remaining lifetime beyond age 65 (years)
0	.71	69.9	4.9
10	.74	62.2	7.2
20	.74	52.6	7.6
30	.75	43.2	8.2
35	.76	38.5	8.5
40	.76	33.9	8.9
45	.78	29.5	9.5
50	.80	25.3	10.3
55	.84	21.4	11.4
60	.90	17.7	12.7

Source: From *Risk Management,* 2nd ed., by C. Arthur Williams and Richard M. Heins, p. 158. Copyright 1971 by McGraw-Hill Book Company. Used with permission of McGraw-Hill Book Company.

of collecting the $200,000 is low. But the insured firm benefits by receiving $200,000 if it must survive the loss of the executive. The insurer benefits in two ways. First, it usually sets premiums at high enough levels to make money on the law of averages. For example, if 300 firms bought $200,000 policies from an insurance company at annual premiums of $1000, the total revenue of the insurance company would be $300,000 ($1000 × 300). If an average of one in 300 executives can be expected to die or become disabled each year, the insurance company would pay $200,000 in benefits. Thus its profit, before deducting other expenses, would be $100,000. Second, insurers have the use of insurance premiums from the time they are contributed by the insured party to the time the benefits are paid.

Insurable and Uninsurable Risks

Normally business risks like changes in demand, reactions of competitors, and strikes are not insurable. Noninsurable business risks cannot be transferred to an insurance company. To be insurable, a risk must be:

Types of insurable risks

1. *Predictable and measurable:* If an insurance company is unable to project the probability that an insured firm or individual will sustain a loss or if it is unable to measure the dollar value of a loss, the company will refuse to offer insurance.
2. *Geographically confined:* For example, no insurance company would be willing to insure an entire town against a hurricane unless the company was able to reinsure (sell individual policies at a discount to other insurance firms).

3. *Recoverable:* Utility companies can obtain insurance against explosions in nuclear power plants only from the federal government. A private insurance company would rarely — if ever — offer such insurance because of the enormous loss that an individual company could suffer.

Within broad limits, however, most risks are insurable. Lloyd's of London, the largest insurance underwriter in the world, has offered protection against such wide-ranging risks as injury to a concert pianist's hands and rain at a college football game.

The Role of the Risk Manager

The risk manager evaluates the firm's insurance activities

The risk manager is closely involved with a firm's insurance activities. A risk manager's responsibilities, which are often carried out under the supervision of the financial manager, include determining the types of tangible and intangible assets to be insured, the levels of coverage to be included, the specific insurers to be used, and the methods of benefit collection.

A very important part of the risk manager's job is *contract analysis* — evaluating the detailed coverages and costs of potential insurance policies. In many instances, a risk manager may elect to purchase a *comprehensive policy* (or a *package policy*) that combines several types of insurance coverage. Because comprehensive policies are less expensive to sell and involve less paperwork, insurance companies are usually able to offer lower rates to the business purchaser. When separate coverage is purchased, several types of business-related insurance are available from insurance companies.

Business Insurance

Each year, businesses lose several billions of dollars due to fire and other natural disasters, employee accidents, burglaries and thefts, and other misfortunes. The risks of such losses can be transferred to insurance companies through the purchase of fire, automobile, marine, worker compensation, burglary or theft, public liability, fidelity, business interruption and business life insurance policies.

✔ **Fire insurance.** *Fire* (or property) *insurance* protects a business against the destruction of its physical premises by fire. Usually a *rider* (a supplementary agreement with a higher premium) is attached to property insurance to protect the business against other natural disasters such as wind damage, earthquakes, and hailstorms. Separate coverage can be obtained for damage sustained from the explosion of a furnace or a boiler, the destruction of plate glass, an interruption in electric power, water leakage, or the failure of customers to pay their bills.

Most types of property insurance policies include a *coinsurance clause*. This provision typically states that the insurance company is liable for damages from an insured loss only in the proportion that the face value of the insurance (the value of the insurance purchased) is to 80 percent of the market value of the property being insured. Thus, a business owner who purchases $60,000 of insurance on a $100,000 building is insured for only three-fourths of any losses to the building (since 80 percent of $100,000 is $80,000, and the face value of the insurance, $60,000, is three-fourths of $80,000). Because of coinsurance clauses, full insurance protection up to the face value of an insurance policy can be obtained only by insuring property at 80 percent or more of its market value.

✔ **Automobile insurance.** Businesses and individuals usually insure the cars and trucks they operate. *Comprehensive fire and theft coverage* insures vehicles up to their current market value against fire, theft, and damage by flying objects. *Collision coverage* reimburses the owner of a vehicle for damage the car or truck suffers as a result of colliding with another vehicle or with a stationary object. Nondeductible collision coverage reimburses the entire loss; deductible collision coverage, which is purchased for a lower premium, requires that the vehicle owner pay an initial portion of any loss (usually $50–$200).

Public liability insurance protects a vehicle owner against damage inflicted on other persons or property. For example, a $50,000/ $100,000/$20,000 policy provides a maximum protection of $50,000 if one person is hurt in an accident, of $100,000 if more than one person is injured, and $20,000 protection against property damage. *Public liability coverage* protects victims or property owners who suffer damage from an accident; no payments are made to the owner or to the operator of the vehicle responsible for the accident. Public liability coverage is especially important to businesses and to wealthy individuals, since the driver or owner of a vehicle responsible for an accident can be sued by the accident victims or by owners of property damaged in the accident. Courts sometimes impose penalties of millions of dollars in accident cases. A *medical-payments endorsement* requires an insurance company to pay any doctor and hospital bills of the driver and the occupants of an insured vehicle. The *uninsured motorist's endorsement* insures a motorist and other people in the vehicle against a driver who is responsible for an accident but who has no public liability insurance.

Fire and theft, collision, public liability, medical payments, or uninsured motorist insurance may be purchased separately or as part of a comprehensive insurance policy. For example, businesses often insure an entire fleet of cars and trucks under a single group policy.

No-fault automobile insurance, which is becoming increasingly popular, specifies that the driver and the occupants of an insured vehicle collect from their own insurance company, regardless of who is at fault in an accident. Medical benefits and reimbursements for lost earnings are paid according to an established set of standards based on the type of injury sustained. The objective of no-fault insurance is to lower insurance costs by avoiding expensive automobile accident suits in court.

✔ **Marine insurance.** *Marine insurance* (or transportation insurance) derives its name from the ancient practice of insuring ship cargoes during hazardous voyages. *Ocean marine insurance* covers the shipment of goods across the seas. *Inland marine insurance* covers land shipments by truck, train, barge, or airplane.

✔ **Worker compensation.** *Worker compensation* protects employees from job-related accidents or ill health. Benefits include medical payments, partial compensation for lost wages, and a lump-sum death payment. Worker compensation benefits are established by state law, and the level of benefits varies from state to state. Private businesses normally obtain worker compensation coverage from an insurance company; in some states, voluntary participation in a state-administered fund is also possible. Worker compensation insurance premiums are normally paid by collecting a percentage of an employer's payroll. This percentage depends on the level of worker compensation benefits required in the state where the employer is located, on the types of jobs covered (it is less costly to insure clerical workers than people in more hazardous occupations, for example), and on the employer's *experience rating* — his or her past record with regard to accidents. In addition to protecting employees against occupational accidents and ill health, worker compensation programs encourage employers to provide safe and healthy working environments. Employers who manage unsafe and unhealthy plants usually must pay higher worker compensation premiums, placing them at a competitive disadvantage.

Protecting employees

✔ **Liability insurance.** Other than automobile insurance, *public liability insurance* protects businesses and individuals from damages resulting from negligence. For example, a customer who slips on a freshly waxed floor in a retail store, who is injured playing with an unsafe toy accidently produced by a manufacturer, or who walks through a plate-glass window in a hotel is often able to sue the business for the damages incurred. By purchasing public liability insurance, a business can wholly or partly transfer the risk of such suits to an insurance company.

Protection from negligence

✔ **Burglary insurance.** Burglary, robbery, and theft have varying definitions under state and local laws, but all involve the illegal seizure of property. Businesses and individuals can protect themselves from most or all of the cost of illegal property seizures by purchasing *burglary insurance.* However, most burglary insurance does not protect a business against its

Protection against theft

most serious problem—pilferage by employees and customers, which accounts for billions of dollars of lost business property annually.

✔ **Fidelity and surety bonds.** *Fidelity bonds* are issued by bonding companies to protect a business against employee dishonesty. Coverage is generally provided for individual employees or for groups of employees. The amount of the policy is based on the value of the money or goods to which the employees have access. *Surety bonds* protect a business against nonperformance by an employee or by a party with whom the firm has entered into a contract. For example, a business might purchase a surety bond on the construction of a new building. If the building contractor fails to meet commitments on time, the bonding company is liable for the amount designated in the policy.

Protection from dishonesty and nonperformance

✔ **Business interruptions insurance.** *Business interruptions insurance* protects a firm against any disruption in its activities arising from natural disasters like fire, storms, and even strikes. The amount of coverage is based on the normal profits and expenses the business could have expected during the period that its activities were interrupted.

Protection against interruption of the business

✔ **Business life insurance.** *Business life insurance* (also called key executive insurance) protects a firm against the loss of an executive who is vital to its operations. Benefits are paid to the business rather than to the insured person's estate. This type of insurance is also widely used in sole proprietorships to protect the owners who inherit a business upon the death of a proprietor against being forced to sell the firm to pay estate taxes. Partnerships often purchase key executive insurance that provides benefits payable to the heirs of a deceased partner. By agreement, if one partner dies, ownership of the business reverts to the remaining partners.

Protection against loss of key executives

Employee Insurance

Businesses also purchase insurance on behalf of their employees. As an insurance specialist, the risk manager works closely with the personnel manager in designing insurance and retirement programs that benefit workers. Such programs also help the firm attract and retain high-quality employees. In many industries, labor contracts and government statutes require businesses to participate in employee insurance and pension programs.

Typically, businesses purchase *employee insurance* on a group basis, where large numbers of employees are covered under a single *master agreement* or a general insurance policy. Because the costs of selling and administering *group insurance* are much lower than expenses on individual policies, employers can often purchase more insurance per premium dollar than individuals can. Insurance and retirement programs either are

Group insurance: more coverage for each premium dollar

contributory, with the employer and the employee sharing in premium expenses, or are paid completely by the employer. In the United States, employee insurance ranges from private health and accident coverage to social security, which is administered by the federal government.

Insuring the health of employees . . .

✔ **Health and accident insurance.** *Health and accident insurance* protects individuals against illness and accidents and generally covers all or part of hospital, medical, and surgical expenses. The most popular plans are Blue Cross, which provides hospital benefits, and Blue Shield, which pays doctor fees; both programs are issued by private nonprofit organizations. In addition, some companies have their own medical insurance programs. Health and accident insurance usually includes sick pay, which provides wage payments for up to 26 weeks if an employee is unable to work because of sickness or accident; a disability feature, which pays a percentage of wages as long as an employee is physically unable to work; and benefits for dismemberment (loss of an eye, hand, or foot) or death resulting from an accident. Many companies also offer employees *major medical insurance* to cover the costs of extended illnesses. Major medical insurance pays benefits only when medical expenses exceed a stated minimum, often $500.

. . . and their lives

✔ **Life insurance.** *Life insurance* provides financial protection for dependents or heirs upon the death of a family member. It is by far the most widely used and most important form of insurance: nearly $1.5 trillion of life insurance is in force today. In a *term-life policy,* protection is provided for a designated period of time (usually 20 years). After the policy has expired, the insurer can refuse to reinsure or can charge higher rates. In a *whole-life policy,* insurance premiums are paid throughout a person's lifetime and the full amount of the policy is payable upon death. The insurance company cannot terminate a whole-life policy as long as premiums are paid promptly. A *limited-life policy* is similar to a whole-life policy, except that all payments are made within a designated period (usually 20 or 30 years). An *endowment policy* provides insurance protection for a specified period of time, after which the face value of the policy is returned to the policyholder. Thus, the endowment policy is the only type of life insurance which pays benefits while the insured person is alive.

Life insurance premiums reflect the age, sex, and health of the insured, and the type of insurance purchased. As Figure 13-5 indicates, as a person's average remaining lifetime diminishes, the likelihood that the insurance company will pay death benefits increases. Hence, life insurance rates rise as a person's age increases. People in good health tend to live longer and therefore enjoy favorable insurance rates. A term-life policy is the least expensive insurance to purchase for a given level of coverage, since the insurer is obligated to pay benefits only if the insured dies within the designated time period. Limited-payment life insurance is

THE INSURANCE COMPANY YOU SELECT MAKES A DIFFERENCE

Insurance commissioners are usually political unknowns who seldom raise tempers to the boiling point. But the chairman of the board of a billion-dollar insurance company angrily mutters "Denenberg" whenever he misses a putt on the golf course. Herbert S. Denenberg was the insurance commissioner of Pennsylvania until 1974.

Under the direction of the controversial Commissioner Denenberg, the Pennsylvania commission has produced a series of shoppers' guides to various types of insurance. While quality of service and financial stability are important considerations when purchasing insurance, the cost of the policy is usually of greatest significance to the buyer. The ten lowest and the ten highest estimated annual premiums on a $10,000 straight-life policy issued by U.S. insurance companies, according to one of Denenberg's shoppers' guides, appear below:

Best buys	
Company	Premium cost*
1. The Bankers Life (Iowa)	$61.97
2. Home Life	64.03
3. National Life (Vt.)	66.80
4. Connecticut Mutual Life	67.27
5. Phoenix Mutual Life	67.63
6. The Northwestern Mutual Life	67.87
7. Central Life (Iowa)	68.33
8. State Mutual Life (Mass.)	70.17
9. Modern Woodmen of America	70.40
10. Lutheran Mutual Life	70.60

Worst buys	
Company	Premium cost*
1. Georgia International Life	$119.30
2. The State Life (Ind.)	114.67
3. Valley Forge Life	113.77
4. Old Republic Life	113.07
5. Pennsylvania Life	112.77
6. Puritan Life	111.13
7. Security Life	110.80
8. The Travelers	110.73
9. Monumental Life	110.53
10. Government Personnel Mutual Life	110.20

* Premium costs are averages of costs paid by persons in their early 20s, mid-30s, and early 50s. Premium costs are adjusted to include policy dividends, cash values of policies, and any interest that would have been earned if no insurance had been purchased.

normally more expensive than a whole-life policy because the insurance company must collect sufficient premiums to pay benefits, cover expenses, and profit during a short payment period. The endowment policy is the most costly form of life insurance, since benefits are either paid to the insured when the policy terminates or to the beneficiaries when the insured dies.

Life insurance may be purchased in virtually any amount, although policies are usually offered in multiples of $1000 or $5000. Most life insurance policies do not cover death by suicide, war or civil insurrection, or the crash of an unscheduled airplane. Individuals are often permitted to borrow against their whole-life, term-life, or endowment policies at very favorable interest rates (often 5 or 6 percent). The cash value of a policy determines the maximum amount the insured can borrow.

Many businesses now offer customers a rapidly expanding form of life insurance called the *credit-life policy*. Under a credit-life plan, decreasing term insurance is available to customers who obtain credit from a business. For example, bankers often require homeowners with bank mortgages to purchase credit-life insurance. As the monthly mortgage payments are made, the face value of the insurance decreases by the amount the mortgage is reduced. If the homeowner dies before the mortgage is completely paid, the insurance company pays the remaining amount to the bank and the mortgage is canceled.

Pension plans:
employee income
during retirement

✔ **Pension plans.** Although technically not insurance, many businesses sponsor pension plans to provide retirement incomes for their employees. In *trustee pension plans,* a bank or a trust company is appointed to administer pension payments. Labor unions also administer pension plans. In *profit-sharing pension plans,* a percentage of the firm's profits is placed in the employee's retirement fund each year. In some cases, employees also contribute to profit-sharing pension plans from their earnings. In 1974, federal legislation established guidelines for the administration of private pension plans designed to protect employee rights under such plans.

Social security:
federally administered
employee benefits

✔ **Social security.** The social security system provides disability incomes to employees who are unable to work, health and old age pensions to retired persons, and a variety of other benefits. The social security program is administered by the federal government. Both employers and employees contribute to the program.

KEY POINTS TO REMEMBER

1. The efficient use of funds, central to business success, requires prudent working capital management and capital budgeting.
2. Working capital, which refers to assets that are normally converted into cash within a year, consists of cash and near cash, accounts receivable, and inventories.
3. The central goals of working capital management are to invest the minimum amount of funds consistent with prudent levels of risk, to collect monies owed the business promptly, and to place as much cash or near cash in interest-bearing securities as possible.
4. Capital budgeting involves committing funds for more than one year

to major projects such as building a new plant, expanding existing capacity, purchasing a new machine, or introducing a new product.

5. Capital-budgeting decisions indicate the yield a business expects from its investments and therefore influence decisions on smaller projects and on allocations of working capital.

6. Capital-budgeting decisions typically involve estimating returns on investment (ROI). Efficient capital budgeting requires that a business systematically select projects that have the highest potential returns on investment.

7. To obtain financial leverage, a business borrows funds. Borrowing enables a firm to undertake more projects than its current available capital allows. Favorable financial leverage—when the ROI exceeds the interest cost of borrowing—increases earnings. Unfavorable financial leverage decreases earnings.

8. Business investments normally include an element of risk, since uncontrollable economic and market factors may make initial ROI estimates inaccurate. Risk also increases when financial leverage is used.

9. Risk can be reduced by successful risk management, which may consist of sound management, the reduction or avoidance or physical hazards, self-insurance, hedging, and insurance.

10. Insurance transfers certain types of risks, called *insurable risks,* from the business to an insurance company. For service, the business pays a fee or a premium. Arrangements between a business (or an individual) and an insurance company are described in a written document, the insurance policy.

11. Major forms of business insurance include fire, automobile, worker compensation, liability, burglary, fidelity, business interruption, and business life insurance.

12. A business also purchases insurance for its employees. Health insurance, life insurance, pension plans, and social security are all forms of insurance often paid for and administered wholly or in part by the employer.

QUESTIONS FOR DISCUSSION

1. Is it possible for a business to have too much cash?

2. Referring to Figure 13-2, would you, as credit manager of the United States Steel Corporation, favor a request from Arnold Metal Products Company for $30,000 to purchase steel shapes?

3. After taxes, the net profit of a large grocery store chain is $.01 on each dollar of sales; therefore, the supermarket has a low return on investment. Do you agree with this statement? Why or why not?

4. Risk should always be reduced to the lowest possible level. Why do you agree or disagree with this statement?

5. In what ways can risk be reduced?

6. The larger the business, the more it will self-insure. Do you agree with this statement? Why or why not?

7. In what ways can insurance benefit both the insurer and the insured?

8. It is impossible for a business or an individual to be over-insured. Is this observation correct? Why or why not?

SHORT CASES AND PROBLEMS

1. Suppose you are the risk manager in a firm that has assets of $1.5 million and no debts. Your firm has six plants, each worth $150,000 if sold on the open market. Because inflammable chemicals are used in your plants, you estimate that there is a five-percent chance of a plant fire and that the entire plant will be destroyed if a fire occurs. The insurance company sets a premium at $10,000 per plant. What are the advantages of purchasing this insurance? Of self-insuring? What type of insurance would you choose? Why?

2. Suppose that you purchased only $100,000 of insurance on each plant in Problem 1 and that the policy included a standard coinsurance clause. How much insurance would you collect if fire completely destroyed one of your plants? If the fire was contained and caused only $10,000 of actual damage?

3. Pfeifer Drilling wishes to insure 4000 employees under a $1000, 20-year term policy per employee. The Sun Insurance Company offers a rate of $3 per employee per year, which Pfeifer accepts. Sun Insurance finds that an average of ten Pfeifer employees die per year, that it makes a 10-percent return on the money it collects from Pfeifer at the beginning of each year, and that its expenses for administering the account are 15 percent of its premium income from Pfeifer. What is the total annual cost of Pfeifer's insurance? What can Sun Insurance expect its annual net profit from the Pfeifer policy to be? Why do you think Pfeifer purchases its insurance from Sun when Pfeifer could make a similar profit itself?

4. Margaret argues that it is easier for a large company to invest in risky ventures, since a large business can afford the loss if a project fails. Kevin maintains that large businesses are very conservative and refuse to take many risks. Managers in large firms, he claims, merely try to get by. If they encourage the firm to take a risk and the project fails, they may be fired or their careers may be jeopardized. It is safer to avoid risks and guarantee a modest profit by maintaining the status quo. Do you agree with Margaret or with Kevin? As a manager in a large firm, what would your policy be?

UNDERWRITING AND ACTUARIAL CAREERS

Insurance companies employ **underwriters** to evaluate the risk of extending coverage to new clients. If the company considers a client a reasonable risk, the underwriter draws up a preliminary insurance contract, suggesting appropriate premium rates. Appraising and selecting insurance risks require sound judgment and mathematical aptitude. Employers generally recruit applicants with bachelor's degrees in liberal arts or in business administration, but high-school graduates can begin as underwriting clerks. Qualified underwriters may advance to chief underwriter or to underwriting manager. Yearly salaries range from $8000 to $20,000. A rise in personal income and the increasing production of expensive consumer goods should create a moderately expanding demand for underwriters in the near future. (*Additional information:* Insurance Information Institute; 110 William Street; New York, New York 10038.)

Actuaries compile and analyze statistics to determine profitable yet competitive insurance premium rates. They assemble actuarial tables containing the expected insured losses for all types of insurance risks. The minimum credential is a bachelor's degree in mathematics, in statistics, or in a related field. Professional actuaries must also have completed a series of standardized examinations. (The series of tests may take up to ten years to complete, but most actuaries have successfully passed two or three of the tests upon graduation from college.) Advancement potential is good: many actuaries move into administrative and supervisory positions. Annual salaries range from $8000 to $35,000. Employment opportunities are expected to expand rapidly with the growing demand for insurance coverage both by private industry and by consumers. (*Additional information:* Society of Actuaries; 208 South LaSalle Street; Chicago, Illinois 60604.)

CAREERS IN SALES AND CLAIMS

Both businesses and individuals buy insurance protection from **insurance agents** and **brokers.** Agents and brokers develop insurance programs to fit specific clients' needs, assist with claim settlements, and interview insurance prospects. Good communications skills are essential. Brokers and agents function in the same capacity, except that brokers are not employed by a particular company while agents usually represent one or more insurance companies. A bachelor's degree in liberal arts or in business administration is helpful, but most employers also recruit high-school and community-college graduates who have had some practical experience. Agents and brokers must obtain licenses; the necessary background to pass the standardized examination is generally provided by on-the-job training. A competent agent can be promoted to sales manager or to another top-management position. Annual salaries range from $8000 to over $30,000. Some agents and brokers earn more than $50,000. The increase in insurance sales is expected to create a moderately expanding job market for both insurance agents and brokers. (*Additional information:* Life Insurance Agency Management Association; 170 Sigourney Street; Hartford, Connecticut 06105.)

Insurance companies employ **claim adjusters** to investigate and to negotiate insurance claims filed by policyholders. Claim adjusters determine the extent of insured losses and sometimes authorize payments to policyholders. Sound judgment is necessary to guarantee a fair, noninflated compensation. A bachelor's degree in business administration is becoming increasingly important, although many claim adjusters are hired on the basis of specialized experience and receive on-the-job training. (For example, automobile repairers are often recruited as auto adjusters.) Most states require that adjusters pass an examination before obtaining a license. Experienced adjusters can be promoted to supervisory or to managerial positions. Annual incomes range from $10,000 to $20,000. Despite the growing number of nofault insurance programs, the demand for adjusters is expected to continue to increase moderately. (*Additional information:* National Association of Public Adjusters; 1613 Munsey Building; Baltimore, Maryland 21202.)

Claim examiners verify the accuracy and honesty of insurance claim applications and authorize payments for insured losses. An examiner determines that the adjuster has followed proper investigative procedures and solves any problems that remain, often by interviewing medical specialists. Claim examiners also gather statistical information for the firm's computer-processing system. A bachelor's degree in business administration is a competitive advantage, although many insurance companies hire and train high-school and community-college graduates who have communications and clerical skills. After successfully completing on-the-job training and a series of standardized examinations, a claim examiner may advance from a trainee position to senior claim representative or to some other supervisory position. Annual salaries range from $8000 to $20,000. The job market for claim examiners is not expected to expand in the near future due to the increasing application of computer processing in this field. (*Additional information:* Institute of Life Insurance; 277 Park Avenue; New York, New York 10017.)

A CRITICAL BUSINESS DECISION

—made by Peter Haas

THE SITUATION   The tough old miner paraded through San Francisco singing the praises of his "Levis"—a pair of pants made by a small shopkeeper named Levi Strauss, a Bavarian immigrant who had come to the United States in 1850 to search for gold. An unsuccessful prospector, Strauss soon entered the retail business, selling dry goods and mining equipment to the prospectors who flocked to California during the Gold Rush in the early 1850s. One day, a miner asked Strauss if he sold any pants that could withstand the harsh punishment of the mines. Strauss made a pair of miner's pants from the only available material—the canvas used for tents and wagon covers. (Strauss later switched to the now familiar blue denim.) Cowboys discovered that Levi jeans were comfortable and serviceable under all weather conditions. They soon became part of western folklore.

By the 1950s, a century later, Levi Strauss and Company had grown considerably, its annual sales reaching $30 million. But in the late 1960s and in the early 1970s, the more casual and informal lifestyles of many people throughout the world made jeans an essential part of an increasing number of wardrobes. By 1974, Levi Strauss was enjoying annual sales in excess of $650 million.

THE DECISION   In the late 1960s, Peter Haas—President of Levi Strauss and great-grandnephew of the founder of the company—faced a fundamental decision. Historically, Levi Strauss had been cautious in its approach to the American market, building production facilities and introducing new products only when ample cash was available. A rigorous system of accounting and financial controls over costs and inventories was typical in all of the company's domestic markets.

But Haas felt that European sales could be regarded as a different matter. American jeans had suddenly become a high-fashion item among Europeans of all ages and income levels, and European customers were paying as much as $25 for a pair of used jeans. At this point, Peter Haas made a crucial decision: Levi Strauss should expand its European markets before its competitors became established, even at the cost of relaxing its customary financial controls.

As a result, by the early 1970s, Levi's European operations were humming. Its staff had grown from a handful of employees to 3000; it had acquired 13 subsidiaries; its manufacturing plants had expanded from one to nine, and its warehouses from one to 12. The demand for Levis seemed inexhaustible. "Trucks and cars were backed outside," one executive recalls of Levi's main warehouse near Antwerp, Belgium. "We had a table there and our customers would start fighting over the goods. Pretty soon they'd be sneaking around the table into the warehouse. They'd drive away with pants flopping out the back of the truck." But European tastes began to change in the early 1970s. First, it became fashionable to wear jeans in unusual colors made from fabrics like upholstery and velvet. Then patch-pockets caught on, and by the spring of 1972, Europeans wanted bell-bottom jeans. Levi Strauss responded by introducing a high-fashion line of its own, manufacturing its denim jeans in 27 colors and its bell-bottom jeans in 25 colors.

Because of poor financial controls, it took Levi more than a year to realize that it was accumulating massive inventories of unwanted jeans due to rapid changes in consumer tastes. Meanwhile, Levi's competitors, who had similar problems, had already started to sell their inventories of outdated jeans at sharply reduced prices. By the time Levi had discovered its excessive inventories, the retail price of unpopular styles of jeans had fallen as low as $2.50 per pair.

Levi's inventory was massive: eight million pairs of jeans—a normal six months in sales—mostly in odd sizes, styles, and colors. "All we had left," one executive moaned, "was cats and dogs." At a hastily called meeting in 1973, Levi's European managers spent from 8 A.M. to 9 P.M. identifying inventories at each of the firm's foreign operations. In the words of one participant, as the totals were reached, "a lot of young men began to look very old." Levi Strauss' European operations would eventually lose $14 million.

QUESTIONS

1. In what areas of financial management do you think Levi Strauss failed?
2. If you had been Peter Haas in 1973, what constructive steps would you have taken to counteract Levi Strauss' deteriorating market and outdated inventories?

The whole community derives benefit from the operations of the bank. It facilitates the commerce of the country. It quickens the means of purchasing and paying for the country's produce . . . .

Thomas Paine

CHAPTER 14

UNDERSTANDING FINANCIAL MARKETS AND FINANCIAL NEWS

FINANCIAL INSTITUTIONS
Commercial Banks
The Federal Reserve System
Investment Banks
Savings Banks
Savings and Loan Associations
Credit Unions
Insurance Companies
The Role of Financial Intermediaries

SECURITY MARKETS
Stock and Bond Markets
How to Read Stock and Bond Quotations
How to Buy Securities
Selecting Securities
Government Regulation of Security Markets

T he company's office locations were impressive: Park Avenue in New York City; Wilshire Boulevard in Los Angeles; comparable addresses in Chicago, Atlanta, San Francisco, and Philadelphia. A list of the company's clients, many of whom had invested hundreds of thousands of dollars, was even more impressive. From the business world: Walter Wriston, president of First National City Bank; investment analyst G.W. Godman, former Chairman of the Board of Directors of both General Electric and Pepsi Cola; the presidents of Time Incorporated and American Express. From the entertainment world: Alan Alda, Bob Dylan, Mia Farrow, Liza Minelli, Barbra Streisand, Barbara Walters, Andy Williams.

A total of more than 2000 of the elite in the entertainment, sports, and business worlds had invested more than $100,000,000 in the Home-Stake Production Company, promoted by a smooth-talking Oklahoma lawyer, Robert S. Trippet. The scheme was simple. Home-Stake would use its invested funds to drill oil wells. If the oil wells were successful the company would pay fabulous investment returns; if the wells were unsuccessful, the investment losses would be deductible under federal tax law and would cost the high-income investors little more than they would normally pay in taxes.

There are
sophisticated
and gullible
investors . . .

But instead of using the invested funds to drill dozens of oil wells, Trippet and his colleagues paid themselves handsome salaries and sold their personal property investments to Home-Stake at inflated prices. Some capital was returned to the investors. Russell W. McFall, president of Western Union, was pleased to receive a dividend of $6220 on his $60,000 investment in Home-Stake. He did not know that the dividend was paid from sums sent to the company by other investors attracted by the apparently high yields on Home-Stake stock. Trippet had already spent McFall's original $60,000 investment.

Home-Stake's marketing strategy was highly effective. Trippet would approach a potential investor and casually drop the names of the celebrities already involved in the venture. As one rueful client observed, "When investors of the caliber of the top executives at First National City Bank have a piece of the action, there is a tremendous psychological effect." To make the hoax more convincing, Home-Stake actually drilled five oil wells on a California vegetable farm and persuaded the farmer to paint his irrigation pipes orange and code them with oil-field markings. Potential investors could then be shown an "oil field" in full operation!

. . . but all were taken in by an "oil field"

The Home-Stake fraud should serve as a warning to potential investors. Fortunately, deceptions like the Home-Stake venture are rare, but they do tend to undermine public confidence in the American financial system.

The wise investor is wary

Financial Institutions

The financial system in the United States consists of financial institutions and security markets. Major *financial institutions* (or organizations) include commercial banks, savings and loan associations, credit unions, and insurance companies. Major *security markets* consist of stock and bond markets like the New York Stock Exchange. An understanding of the American financial system is vital to all of us because:

As citizens, we deal with the financial system on a daily basis (when we write a check or use a credit card, for example).

As investors, we channel most of our savings through the financial system.

Financial institutions
and security markets
are important

As potential employees, we are increasingly likely to consider positions with financial institutions. The financial system is becoming more and more important in the economy and is hiring large numbers of well-trained and well-educated persons.

As potential managers, we usually depend on the financial system for capital for daily commercial business transactions.

In Chapter 14, we will describe: (1) the major financial institutions in the United States, and (2) the key security markets in the American economy.

In 1974, commercial banks, savings and loan associations, insurance companies, and other financial institutions extended more than $1.7 trillion in loans to businesses, consumers, and governments.

Commercial Banks

Commercial banks are financial institutions that accept deposits and make loans. The distinguishing feature of a commercial bank is that it allows customers to make deposits upon which checks can be drawn. A *check* is a negotiable instrument that a depositor uses to direct the bank to pay a designated amount of money to a specific person or organization.

Banks are
key financial
institutions . . .

In 1974, the 14,348 commercial banks in the United States accounted for nearly half the annual credit extended by all U.S. financial institutions. The ten largest U.S. banks, shown in Figure 14-1, accounted for 30 percent of the $853 billion in assets held by the entire U.S. banking system.

✔ **Organizing a commercial bank.** A bank is a private business run for the profit of its owners. During the early history of the United States,

14-1 The ten largest bank holding companies in the United States. Because of their great financial power, these commercial banks have an important influence on American business and banking systems. (Assets as of December 31, 1974.)

Rank	Bank	Assets (millions of dollars)
1	BankAmerica (San Francisco)	$60,376
2	Citicorp (New York City)	58,304
3	Chase Manhattan (New York City)	42,352
4	J.P. Morgan (New York City)	25,963
5	Manufacturers Hanover (New York City)	25,754
6	Chemical New York (New York City)	22,175
7	Bankers Trust New York (New York City)	20,387
8	Continental Illinois (Chicago)	19,798
9	First Chicago (Chicago)	19,139
10	Western Bankcorp (Los Angeles)	18,727

Source: *Business Week.*

. . . run for profit

private banks issued their own currency, which was commonly used to make purchases and to pay debts. During the Great Depression of the 1930s, hundreds of banks failed and millions of depositors lost most or all of their savings.

Banks are no longer permitted to issue currency. This has become an exclusive function of the federal government. In addition, numerous federal and state regulations have been passed to protect commercial-bank depositors. These include:

1. *Federal and state chartering of banks:* Persons who intend to organize a bank must secure a *bank charter*—a legal document issued by the federal or a state government permitting the bank to operate. To obtain a charter, potential bank owners must usually prove that their community needs and can support a bank, that they can contribute sufficient capital to make the bank financially sound, and that they and the management they expect to hire have appropriate banking experience.

Protecting bank depositors

2. *Examination of banks: National banks* are chartered by the Controller of the Currency and are examined by officials from the U.S. Department of the Treasury. *State banks* obtain their charters from state governments and are examined by employees of state regulatory agencies. Examiners evaluate the honesty and the accuracy of a bank's accounting records. They also verify that a bank can meet minimum financial requirements, as specified in federal and state laws.

3. *Insuring bank deposits:* The Federal Deposit Insurance Corporation (FDIC) was initiated in 1933 to protect depositors against bank

failures. Each account in an FDIC member bank is insured up to a maximum of $40,000. For this service, the bank pays an annual fee equal to $1/12$ of one percent of its total deposits. Since the corporation's inception, depositors have not lost a single dollar in an FDIC-insured account. The FDIC also conducts periodic examinations of member banks.

Thus, although banks are private, profit-seeking businesses, they are closely regulated by federal and state governments, and the organization of a bank requires a thorough knowledge of banking regulations.

✔ **Services of commercial banks.** Banks offer many valuable services to businesses and to consumers. First, commercial banks provide facilities for *checking accounts,* so that a person or an organization can write checks against their deposited funds. The major advantages of paying by check rather than by cash are (1) safety (cash can be lost or stolen); (2) convenience (large amounts of bills and change need not be kept on hand); and (3) a permanent record of each transaction is automatically maintained (the bank returns the canceled checks to the account holder). An individual can open a checking account simply by filling out an application form and signing a signature card. To open a business checking account the Board of Directors (or the owners) of the company must authorize the account and must specify who can write company checks or borrow money from the account. Signature cards for each designated official are necessary.

Interest is not paid on checking accounts

Cashier's checks and certified checks are two specific forms of bank checks. A *cashier's check* (see Figure 14-2) is a check that is drawn on a bank itself. A cashier's check virtually alleviates the risk of default, since it is backed by the solvency of the bank upon which it is drawn. For this reason, cashier's checks are widely used in commercial transactions.

14-2   A cashier's check. A check drawn on an individual checking account may be returned because the account contains insufficient funds. Default on a cashier's check occurs only if the bank on which the check has been drawn fails.

OFFICIAL CHECK

The Merchants Bank of New York
757 THIRD AVENUE, NEW YORK, N. Y.

T16852

NEW YORK, N.Y.   June 17, 1975

1-679
260

PAY   - MERCHANTS - $I \; OO \; DOLS \; OO \; CTS$
BANK OF NEW YORK

$100.00

TO
THE
ORDER
OF   JESSICA KRASILOVSKY

⑆0260⑆0679⑆   ⑈ 990077⑉

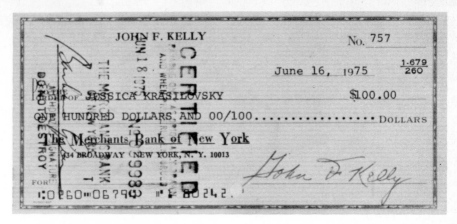

JOHN F. KELLY   No. 757

June 16, 1975   1-679/260

PAY TO THE ORDER OF JESSICA KRASILOVSKY $100.00

ONE HUNDRED DOLLARS AND 00/100 . . . . DOLLARS

The Merchants Bank of New York

34 BROADWAY (NEW YORK, N. Y. 10013

FOR

John F. Kelly

14-3   To minimize the risk of default, the bank withdraws certified check funds from an individual checking account before a certified check is prepared.

A *certified check* (Figure 14-3) is similar to an ordinary check, except that the bank guarantees payment by certifying that sufficient funds to cover the amount of the check have been withdrawn from the checking account in advance. Certified checks are widely used in real-estate and security transactions, where they function as cashier's checks.

A second valuable bank service is the provision of facilities for longer-term savings. If an individual or a business does not expect to use funds immediately, monies may be placed in a *savings account.* Checks cannot be written against savings-account deposits, and a commercial bank has a rarely used legal right to delay withdrawls from a savings account for a designated period of time (often 90 days). Unlike checking accounts, which earn no interest, savings-account holders receive interest on their deposits. Savings depositors generally receive higher interest rates if they deposit greater amounts of money for longer periods of time.

Banks pay interest on savings deposits

Like a savings account, a *time certificate of deposit* is a non-negotiable, nontransferable, interest-bearing instrument issued by a commercial bank. A five-year time certificate of deposit for $10,000 that is purchased January 1, 1976, is due December 31, 1980, and bears an interest rate of 8 percent, guarantees that an initial investment of $10,000 will earn $800 in annual interest and that the $10,000 principal will be returned to the investor on December 31, 1980. Unlike a savings account, funds invested in a time certificate cannot be withdrawn without penalty (see Figure 14-4).

The *negotiable certificate of deposit,* commonly called a CD, is a rapidly growing source of commercial-bank deposits. CDs, typically issued in amounts of $100,000 or more, often provide that interest and principal are payable to the *bearer*—the individual who has possession of the certificate. CDs are usually purchased by large organizations that collect interest on idle short-term funds and that resell the CDs to other organizations when

14-4 A time certificate of deposit.

they need funds. From the bank's viewpoint, CDs represent long-term investments that cannot be withdrawn until they mature. Thus, banks pay higher rates of interest on CDs than they pay on savings accounts.

A third commercial-bank service uses funds from depositors to make loans and investments. *Commercial loans* are made to large and small businesses. *Installment loans* are extended to investors who intend to purchase expensive items like automobiles or make minor home improvements. Commercial banks often provide funds to the construction industry by purchasing mortgages and other financial instruments issued by builders and property owners. Banks also invest funds, typically in U.S. government securities and in high-quality municipal bonds.

Banks loan or invest most of the deposits they receive . . .

Other commercial-bank services that are valuable to businesses and to consumers include:

1. *Safe-deposit boxes:* Safe-deposit boxes can be rented from commercial banks to protect valuables and important papers.
2. *Bond purchases:* Banks sell U.S. Savings Bonds and will usually act as brokers in the purchase of many industrial and municipal bonds.
3. *Foreign exchange:* For a fee, banks provide foreign currency for their customers at official exchange ratios. It is also common for banks to issue *letters of credit,* indicating a customer's financial status in domestic and foreign trade.

. . . and provide many other services

4. *Traveler's checks and credit cards:* Most banks sell traveler's checks and issue credit cards sponsored by larger commercial banks.
5. *Business services:* Commercial banks obtain credit information for their customers. For a fee, most banks provide financial counseling, handle business payrolls, and complete business tax returns.

6. *Trust services:* Trust departments at commercial banks manage funds for individuals and businesses according to the objectives and rules drawn up in a trust agreement. Many trusts involve estates, and commercial banks endeavor to fulfill the terms of estates and to manage their assets wisely. Trust departments also serve as trustees for common and preferred stockholders and pension-plan holders.

Recently, banks have begun to offer more comprehensive financial services to both business and individual clients. By meeting the financial needs of their clients in a more integrated manner, commercial banks hope to retain old customers and attract new ones.

✔ **Commercial banks and profits.** Like other businesses, banks must earn profits to survive. A commercial bank seeks profits in two basic ways. First, a bank endeavors to earn a higher return on loans and investments than it pays in interest on savings accounts and on CDs. Banks assume risks to earn profits, since some customers may default on their loan payments and some investments may produce poor returns. Thus, a bank must earn high enough returns on its loans and investments not only to meet its interest obligations but also to compensate for losses on its loans and investments and to cover its operating expenses.

Banks seek profits in two basic ways

A commercial bank also secures profits by charging fees for various services. Banks have recently begun to identify the actual costs of each type of service they provide and, to the extent competition permits, to charge users for these services. Thus, annual rentals for safe-deposit boxes should be sufficient to cover the cost of this service and to provide the bank with an acceptable profit on its investment in the bank vault and in the deposit boxes.

Although they receive lower interest rates on their savings deposits than they could earn by directly investing their funds, commercial-bank depositors avoid the risks of the long-term fund commitments, and the administrative costs of direct investment.

✔ **Bank holding companies.** Many commercial banks have close relations with other banks. Most banks in small communities, for example, are associated with correspondent banks often located in larger nearby cities. A *correspondent bank* receives deposits from and makes loans to smaller banks and provides customer services that are impossible or unprofitable for smaller banks to offer. Large banks frequently have correspondent relationships with banks located in other sections of the country or abroad. Correspondent banks enable a large bank to provide its customers with banking services on a worldwide basis.

The bank holding company: many banks operated by a single firm

Over time, larger banks have purchased many smaller banks, especially those the larger banks have served. As a result, bank holding companies have developed. A bank holding company may own and control

ARE BANK HOLDING COMPANIES TOO POWERFUL?

Americans have often been fearful of big business, particularly of large banking conglomerates. Because of their tremendous financial resources, large banks are often capable of buying most of the manufacturing and service enterprises in their localities. When the control of many banks is placed in a bank holding company (a "superbank"), the threat of a giant bank monopolizing a region's economy becomes doubly dangerous.

The Bank Holding Company Act of 1956 restricted the right of bank holding companies to enter financially unrelated businesses. But the Act included a loophole: a one-bank holding company could be involved in any type of business. (A one-bank holding company owns a single commercial bank, which, in turn, may own other banks and other nonbanking businesses.) Most large banks soon became part of one-bank holding companies and began to enter nonbanking businesses. The Bank Holding Company Act of 1970 authorized the Federal Reserve System to enforce the elimination of all nonbanking activities that concentrated too much economic power in the hands of one-bank holding companies.

But the role of the one-bank holding company is still undefined. Should banks be permitted to sell insurance, to operate computer business services, or to buy and lease equipment on which loans are made? These activities are somewhat related to many of the services banks already provide, and commercial banks may handle such services more efficiently than other businesses. On the other hand, should commercial banks be permitted to own and operate unrelated businesses: to produce manufactured goods, to operate mines, or to own railroads? Just how much economic power should one-bank holding companies — and, consequently, large commercial banks — be granted?

dozens of banks. The bulk of the banking activity in many states is controlled by a few giant bank holding companies.

The Federal Reserve System

As interpreted by the United States Supreme Court, Section 8 of the U.S. Constitution grants the federal government the right to control the amount of money in circulation. In 1913, the Federal Reserve Act in effect delegated this responsibility to the Federal Reserve System.

The Federal Reserve System is a regulatory agency of the federal government with a seven-member Board of Governors. Each Governor of the Federal Reserve System is appointed to a 14-year term by the President, with the advice and consent of the U.S. Senate.

The Federal Reserve System regulates the amount of money and credit . . .

The Federal Reserve System consists of approximately 5800 commercial banks that contain nearly 85 percent of all commercial-bank deposits. The Federal Reserve System is organized into 12 districts, with headquarters and branch banks (see Figure 14-5).

✔ **The Federal Reserve System and the economy.** The Federal Reserve System affects the economy by regulating the amount of credit (or money) that banks can extend to businesses and to consumers. If banks have adequate funds for commercial and consumer loans, borrowing is easily accomplished and the demand for goods and services tends to ex-

. . . and seeks to counteract business cycles

pand. If, on the other hand, banks have loaned most or all of their available funds, it is very difficult to increase the demand for goods and services.

Thus, during a recession, the Federal Reserve System makes funds available to commercial banks so that they, in turn, can make loans to their customers. Customers then use these funds to buy goods and services. Such "easy-money" policies are designed to expand the demand for goods and services and to reduce the unemployment caused by a recession. During an inflationary period, a "tight-money" policy is stressed. The Federal Reserve System makes less funds available to commercial banks and they, in turn, make fewer loans to their customers. Thus, businesses and consumers can purchase fewer goods and services, and some of the shortages that may have helped to cause the inflation can be reduced.

✔ **How the Federal Reserve System affects commercial-bank loans.** The Federal Reserve System uses three tools to influence the amount of money that commercial banks can lend to their customers:

1. *Variations in reserve requirements: Reserves* represent the amount of cash or cashlike funds that banks must retain to meet depositor withdrawls. By increasing the percentage of the deposits that banks must retain in cash, the Federal Reserve Bank reduces the amount of funds banks can lend. Decreasing reserve requirements produces the opposite effect.

2. *Regulation of the discount rate:* Banks may borrow funds by selling U.S. government bonds or other high-quality financial assets to the Federal Reserve Bank. A charge similar to interest is made for this service. By selling assets to the Federal Reserve Bank, a

How the
Federal Reserve
influences
the money supply

SHOULD THE FEDERAL RESERVE SYSTEM BE INDEPENDENT?

The room was tense. The Chairman of the Board of Governors of the Federal Reserve System was being closely questioned on "Meet the Press." He was adamant; even though there was a recession, the Federal Reserve System would be cautious in increasing the money supply to alleviate the fear of future long-run inflation. A Presidential election year was approaching and Republicans and Democrats alike were calling for a rapid expansion of the money supply to achieve full employment—a politically popular goal. Political leaders in both parties were cutting taxes and increasing government spending simultaneously. The deficit in the federal budget would be huge during the election year.

Unblinkingly, the Chairman fielded a barrage of questions. No, the Federal Reserve would not rapidly increase the money supply. The long-run economic effects had to be considered. No, he did not believe control of the money supply should be delegated to the Congress and the President. No, monetary and fiscal policies were not uncoordinated; he meets with the Secretary of the Treasury weekly.

But critics sharply disagreed. The independence of the Federal Reserve System should be curtailed. Monetary and fiscal policies should be coordinated to attack the recession.

Every person in the United States will be importantly affected by the outcome of this continuing debate over the Federal Reserve System's insulation from congressional and Presidential control.

commercial bank accumulates funds to loan to its customers. By raising or lowering the *discount rate,* the "interest" charge on such commercial-bank loans, the Federal Reserve System affects the amount of money banks can lend.

3. *Open-market operations:* Under the direction of the Board of Governors, a special group known as the Open Market Operations Committee can sell or purchase government bonds. When the Federal Reserve System sells government bonds directly, commercial banks have less money to lend. The reverse is true when the Federal Reserve System purchases bonds.

Changes in reserve requirements, in the discount rate, and in open-market operations are known collectively as *monetary policy,* since all of these factors influence the amount of money and credit in circulation. A tight-money policy is characterized by high reserve requirements, a high discount rate, and the sale of government bonds by the Federal Reserve System. An easy-money policy requires that reserve requirements and the discount rate be kept low and that the Federal Reserve System buy government bonds. Because it affects the economy, monetary policy is of vital importance to business.

✔ **Federal Reserve services to commercial banks.** The Federal Reserve System *clears checks* for member banks. A depositor's check drawn on an Atlanta bank to cover the cost of a purchase from a New York City coin dealer will normally be deposited in a New York City bank. The check

Key:
▬ Boundaries of Federal Reserve districts
— Boundaries of Federal Reserve branch territories
★ Board of Governors of the Federal Reserve System
⊙ Federal Reserve Bank cities
● Federal Reserve branch cities
▢ Federal Reserve Bank facilities

14-5

The Federal Reserve System. Federal Reserve districts are designated by number. Each district has a Federal Reserve Bank, and some districts have Federal Reserve branch banks. Alaska and Hawaii are included in district 12.

will then be cleared through Federal Reserve district 1 (New York), will be returned to district 6 (Atlanta), and will eventually reach the depositor's own bank. Examiners from the Federal Reserve Bank also periodically inspect commercial banks that are members of the System.

Investment Banks

Investment banks are financial intermediaries that do not accept deposits from the public. The investment bank markets securities — bonds, notes, preferred and common stocks — for businesses. Investment bankers charge a commission for their marketing services. On new common stock issues, for example, the investment bank's commission is often 10 percent of the stated price of the security.

As we saw in Chapter 13, firms normally employ investment bankers to publicly offer security issues. Investment bankers also frequently assist in the private placement of a security issue. Many commercial banks and brokerage firms maintain investment banking facilities.

Investment banks underwrite stock and bond issues

BLIPPING AND THE MONEY FACTORY

The tall glass and concrete building at 111 Wall Street is a money factory. Inside, 40-foot-long sorting machines roar and hiss; robot forklift trucks hurry from station to storage bin and back again. The factory handles 3 million checks worth $20 billion each day. First National City Bank's 6500 employees debit and credit accounts and send checks to clearing houses and to endorsers. The factory is one of the most efficient in the world. Its check-processing costs are low and its efficiency has contributed to the low cost of bank services to First National City customers.

Life in the Branch Channel of Checking Operations is the most hectic. Each evening, bags containing a total of 1.5-million checks from First National's 215 branch offices in the New York City area are dumped into the sorting room. On the right-hand bottom corner of each check, an encoder translates the amount of the check into a series of squarish numbers in magnetic ink that can be read by computers. Encoders are paid on an incentive basis. Their goal: to encode as many checks as possible. The record: 2400 an hour. "You really don't see a check," an encoder who earns about $15,000 a year observes. "You sense it. It doesn't really go through your brain. Your fingers feel it."

The encoded checks are placed into trays and the checks are fed into a climate-controlled computer at a speed of 40 mph. Each check is recorded on a tape, photographed on microfilm, and identified by an orange code the computer places directly on the check. Rejects are sent to the "reject repair" room, where "reconcilers" and "investigators" attempt to recode missing or improperly marked checks. They must work fast: every $1-million worth of checks that does not make the 11:30 PM delivery truck to the Federal Reserve Bank costs First National City $167 in lost interest. Each check must be accurately sorted and marked for delivery to the proper bank before it can be sent to the Federal Reserve Bank.

Managers at First National City Bank, according to a recruitment brochure, must be able to "flourish in a crisp quantitative environment." The best kind of manager, one employee observes, "is someone with the ability to think like a system, to think like the machine. They're very unique individuals; they're valuable to us." Slang and computer talk are rampant. "Marti" is Machine Readable Telegraphics; "ASR" refers to an employee's Annual Salary Rate; to "save" is to reduce costs; "rock" represents a tough problem; and to "blip" is to fall short of one's assigned goal.

Blipping is a serious matter. Each job involves a specific set of duties; each employee must meet an annual target or forecast developed by management, which includes an improvement factor. No excuses or rationalizations are accepted. "You sort of expect to meet the forecast or else," a young manager comments ruefully.

Savings Banks

Savings banks are located predominantly in the Northeast region of the United States. These banks solely maintain savings accounts for depositors and do not provide checking accounts. Investments are made in bonds, mortgages, real estate, and, where law permits, in corporate stock.

Savings banks handle savings deposits only

Savings banks earn profits to the extent that their investment income exceeds their operating expenses and the interest they pay to their depositors. Savings banks may be owned either by stockholders or by depositors. In the latter, called *mutual savings banks,* depositors' profits are apportioned according to the relative sizes of their savings deposits.

Savings and Loan Associations

With combined assets in 1975 of more than $300 billion, savings and loan associations represent America's second most important financial institution. Because of their aggressive advertising and promotional activities and their generally favorable suburban locations, the assets of savings and loan associations have grown rapidly in comparison to commercial-bank assets.

Savings and loan associations provide funds to the housing industry

Like savings banks, savings and loan associations offer no checking accounts. Savings deposits and accumulated interest are typically recorded in passbooks or on monthly statements that are sent to depositors. Savings accounts in a savings and loan association that is a member of the Federal Savings and Loan Insurance program are protected up to $40,000. Federal regulations traditionally permit savings and loan associations to pay slightly higher interest rates on deposits than those allowed to commercial banks.

Savings and loan associations invest more than 95 percent of their deposits in home mortgages. Their remaining assets are kept in cash or cashlike assets to meet customer withdrawals and to make new mortgage investments. Savings and loan associations invest heavily in single-family dwellings, while banks tend to invest in commercial real estate.

Credit Unions

A *credit union* is a financial institution formed by a group of people with a common interest (typically, employees in a single organization). Individuals who contribute savings to a credit union are called *shareholders* and are awarded shares in proportion to the amount of their deposits. Credit unions make small secured or unsecured loans (usually for less than $5000) often for purchases of automobiles or home appliances or for minor home repairs. The interest rates charged on credit-union loans normally vary from 8 to 12 percent annually and are lower than the rates most competing financial institutions offer for comparable loans.

Credit-union earnings are based on the interest paid by borrowers and the interest the credit union receives on its investments (usually in U.S. government obligations) *less* the cost of operating the credit union. Shareholders as a group are entitled to receive these earnings. An efficiently operated credit union simultaneously benefits borrowers by charging lower than conventional interest rates, and shareholders, by paying higher dividends than those available from other financial institutions where the owners must earn a profit. An important objective of the credit union is to involve its members in the organization; many credit unions have induced valuable voluntary efforts from their shareholders.

Insurance Companies

Insurance companies, with combined assets of more than $250 billion in 1975, represent the third most important type of financial institution in the United States. As we learned in Chapter 13, insurance companies receive premiums from their policyholders. The companies, in turn, invest these premiums to earn interest until policyholder claims are paid.

Insurance companies invest primarily in corporate bonds, commercial and home mortgages, corporate equities, and municipal bonds. Because many insurance companies are large, a business frequently sells most or all of a new debt or equity issue to an insurance firm, either by directly approaching a particular insurance company or by employing the services of an investment banker.

The Role of Financial Intermediaries

Commercial banks, investment banks, savings banks, savings and loan associations, credit unions, insurance companies, and the other financial institutions defined in Figure 14-6 are often described as *financial intermediaries*. These financial institutions protect investor deposits and spare savers the detailed and complex task of analyzing alternate investment opportunities. Monies can also be withdrawn with relative ease from most financial intermediaries. Businesses, comsumers, and governments, borrow large amounts of money directly from financial intermediaries instead of approaching individual savers. Financial institutions earn profits by placing themselves in an intermediate position between savers and borrowers of funds.

14-6 Operations of selected financial institutions. These specialized financial institutions are not discussed in the text, but they are important in some sectors of the American economy.

Type of Financial Institution	Description of Operations
Commercial-paper dealers	Commercial-paper dealers purchase *commercial paper*—the unsecured notes of businesses with good credit ratings—and resell it after adding a fixed fee.
Factors	Factoring companies purchase a firm's accounts receivable. The *factor* typically makes a cash payment which is less than the value of the accounts receivable and is then responsible for collecting the amounts due. Factors are widely employed in the furniture, textile, and glassware industries.
Finance companies	*Consumer finance companies,* such as Household Finance, make small loans to consumers. *Sales finance companies,* such as General Motors Acceptance Corporation, loan consumers money to purchase automobiles and other consumer durables.
Mutual funds	Mutual funds place the combined savings of many investors in bonds, equities, and other assets. Returns, from which a fee is often deducted, are paid directly to investors or are credited to their mutual-fund accounts for future use.
Pension funds	Pension or retirement funds consist of the savings of wage earners and are often administered by a bank or a business firm. Pension funds are invested in bonds, stocks, and other financial assets to provide additional income upon retirement.

Security Markets

Security markets provide for the exchange of financial assets

Although financial institutions like banks ultimately purchase most of the stocks and bonds issued by business, these stocks and bonds are exchanged in security markets. *Security markets,* such as the New York Stock Exchange and the New York Bond Exchange, are the central areas where financial assets are traded. Most of the securities that are exchanged have already been issued, but new stock or bond issues are also traded on security markets.

Security markets are important to a financial manager for two basic reasons. First, the performance of a company's stock in a security market is a measure of both the stockholders' and the general investment community's confidence in the firm. A rapid fall in the price of a company's stock is a warning of future stockholder discontent and potential trouble for management. The purchase of large amounts of a firm's stock by a small number of people may indicate that a company is being taken over. Since new owners often replace old management, most firms carefully analyze changes in their stockholder lists. Second, a firm's ability to attract new employees, to issue new stocks or bonds, and to raise money from other sources are affected by the prices of its stock.

Security markets are vitally important to most investors. Nearly 40-million Americans own corporate stock and, as indicated in Figure 14-7, wealthy Americans are particularly attracted to stock and bond investments.

Stock and Bond Markets

The major security markets in the United States are the New York Stock Exchange, the American Stock Exchange, and over-the-counter markets. The New York Stock Exchange is a large club: its 1366 members hold *seats* or exclusive rights to participate in the market. To become a member of the New York Stock Exchange, an individual or firm must be judged financially sound according to rules established by the Exchange's board of governors, who are elected by its members, and then must purchase a seat (which has cost less than $75,000 during the 1974 decline in

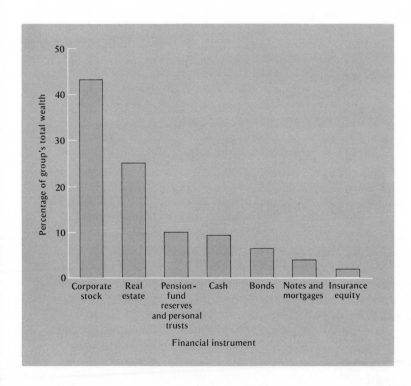

14-7

Where the wealthiest one percent of Americans put their money.

Source: Internal Revenue Service.

**Members of
security exchanges
represent both
buyers and sellers**

the stock market and more than $500,000 during periods of great market activity). Only exchange members or their designated representatives are permitted to buy and sell securities without charge. Members profit by acting as agents for nonmembers, charging them a commission for each purchase or sale of securities. The American Stock Exchange is organized in a similar manner.

Trading on a security exchange is conducted like a series of large auctions in which members, as agents for investors, bargain over the prices of securities. An exchange member is obligated to obtain a security for a buyer at the lowest possible price. A member who represents a seller of a security is obligated to secure the highest possible price. A sale is consummated only when two members can agree on a price.

Listed securities are traded on established exchanges like the New York Stock Exchange and the American Stock Exchange. To have its securities listed by an exchange, a firm must be approved by that exchange's board of governors and must meet the minimum financial qualifications established by the membership. These qualifications are designed to insure that there will be sufficient investor interest in the firm's securities.

Unlisted securities are traded in over-the-counter markets, which operate like security markets except that auctions are negotiated (usually by telephone) rather than conducted in a formal exchange, where buyers and sellers meet. Trading in unlisted securities is conducted by brokerage firms or dealers, most of whom are members of the National Association of Securities Dealers (NASD), a self-regulatory organization for broker-dealers in over-the-counter markets. A brokerage firm markets a security by announcing its willingness to purchase shares at a given price, the *bid price,* and to sell these shares at a slightly higher price, the *asked price.*

**Trading in
over-the-counter
markets**

When several brokerage firms handle a given security, each firm is guided by competing bid and asked prices in setting its own price. Brokers' negotiations to obtain the best available selling and buying prices for their customers limit the differential between the purchase price and the selling price of a security and establish a fair and orderly market for the issue. The *spread* (or difference) between bid and asked prices in over-the-counter transactions is a major source of profits for dealers in unlisted securities. The NASDAQ computer system (National Association of Securities Dealers Automated Quotations), introduced in 1971, instantly transmits bid and asked price quotations on most available unlisted securities to NASD members across the United States (see Figure 14-8).

The modern electronic computer may enable national, regional, and over-the-counter markets to be linked in an integrated securities system like the one that already exists in Great Britain. Bid and sales orders could be entered in a computer terminal (to be discussed in Chapter 15) and the computer could be programmed to set market prices. If this step is taken, national and regional stock exchanges would have far less influence on security trading.

14-8

An NASDAQ computer monitor, showing bid and asked quotations on over-the-counter securities. Courtesy of the OTC Information Bureau.

How to Read Stock and Bond Quotations

Figures 14-9 and 14-10 show you how to read stock and bond quotations.

Stock and bond quotations appear in daily newspapers

The results of securities trading are reported in detail in the financial pages of most newspapers. Figures 14-9 and 14-10 show you how to read stock and bond quotations. Newspapers also print stock-market averages or indexes that summarize daily trading activities. The best known listings are the Dow Jones average, Standard and Poor's average of 500 stocks, and the New York Stock Exchange index. These averages attempt to show, through a sampling of stocks, the general direction of price movements for all securities traded on the exchange.

How to Buy Securities

Individual investors or businesses purchase securities in the following manner:

1. *Opening an account with a brokerage firm:* To open an account, an investor must sign a few simple papers and, depending on credit rating, may have to make a small deposit.

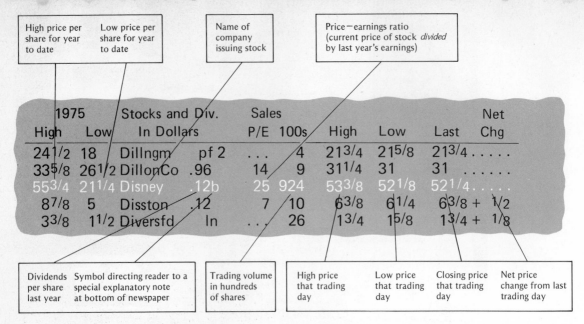

| High price per share for year to date | Low price per share for year to date | | Name of company issuing stock | | | Price—earnings ratio (current price of stock *divided* by last year's earnings) | | | |

1975		Stocks and Div.		Sales					Net
High	Low	In Dollars		P/E	100s	High	Low	Last	Chg
24 1/2	18	Dillngm	pf 2	. . .	4	21 3/4	21 5/8	21 3/4	. . . . .
33 5/8	26 1/2	DillonCo	.96	14	9	31 1/4	31	31	. . . . . .
55 3/4	21 1/4	Disney	.12b	25	924	53 3/8	52 1/8	52 1/4	. . . . .
8 7/8	5	Disston	.12	7	10	6 3/8	6 1/4	6 3/8	+ 1/2
3 3/8	1 1/2	Diversfd	In	. . .	26	1 3/4	1 5/8	1 3/4	+ 1/8

| Dividends per share last year | Symbol directing reader to a special explanatory note at bottom of newspaper | | Trading volume in hundreds of shares | | High price that trading day | Low price that trading day | Closing price that trading day | Net price change from last trading day |

14-9 Interpreting the stock quotations reported in daily newspaper.

Source: *The Wall Street Journal* (November 14, 1975).

2. *Selecting an account executive:* The investor is assigned or chooses an account executive (broker). The account executive will advise the customer, handle requests for information, and supervise the account.

3. *Ordering the security:* The investor must place an order with the account executive to purchase or sell a security. In most cases, the investor will place a *market order,* which means that the transaction will be carried out on the most favorable terms available when the order is received at the stock exchange or, in the case of over-the-counter stocks, at the brokerage house dealing with that security. Alternatively, the investor can place a special *buy order* or *sell order* instructing the broker to carry out the transaction when the security reaches a price specified by the investor.

Steps in buying securities

4. *Paying for the security:* Securities are usually paid for five trading days after an order is placed. Receipts from sales of securities normally reach an investor within a week of sale.

5. *Paying commissions:* For its services, the brokerage firm charges a commission, which generally ranges from 1 to 2 percent of the total value of the stock transaction. The lower the value of the transaction, the higher the percentage of commission that is normally charged. A commission must be paid when the security is

purchased and again when it is sold. A slightly higher commission is charged when stocks are traded in *odd lots* (blocks of less than a hundred shares). Since May 1975, the exchanges have permitted brokerage firms to set their own commissions. Hence, commission charges vary among the individual brokerage houses.

6. *Keeping the security:* Customers can either retain possession of stock and bond certificates themselves (in such cases, it is usually wise to keep them in safe-deposit boxes) or they can instruct the brokerage firm to hold their certificates.

Selecting Securities

Prospective investors must not only know how to purchase securities; they must also know which securities to buy. Many investors rely on "hot tips"—information from friends or acquaintances that a given security is a good buy. Personal investment tips or the unverified advice of an account executive, whose livelihood depends on promoting securities, can be disastrous. The careful investor: (1) examines investment objectives; (2) collects and analyzes information about securities; and (3) uses sensible investment techniques to make purchase and sale decisions.

14-10   Interpreting the bond quotations reported in daily newspapers.

Source: *The New York Times* (August 6, 1975).

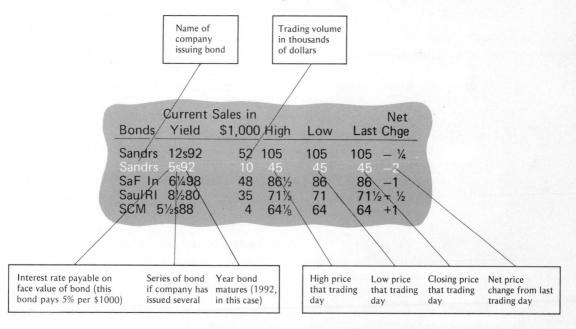

SHOULD YOU HAVE INVESTED IN BALLY?

In 1971, the comparatively tiny Bally Manufacturing Company, the nation's largest producer of slot machines and pinball games, offered a new issue of its stock to the public. At that time, the company's major product was banned in all but one state and company management was allegedly controlled by organized crime. Bally's president was under indictment by a federal grand jury.

Nonetheless, profits in 1971 had increased by more than 40 percent, and 17 states had introduced bills that, if passed, would ease restrictions on gambling. Investor interest in Bally's new issue was keen.

Based on the material discussed in this section, to what type of investors do you believe Bally's new issue would appeal? For the answer, see the explanation given in the text below.

Selecting securities requires a definition of investment objectives

✔ **Investment objectives.** *Investors* normally seek a reasonable rate of return on their assets that is consistent with a moderate degree of risk. *Speculators* seek a high rate of return and are usually willing to assume a high degree of risk. Most speculators are interested in making quick profits; most investors prefer to earn more modest and more stable profits over longer periods of time. Investors usually hold stock for six months or more; speculators may purchase and sell stock within a single day or a week. Because speculators retain securities for a very short time, they are less interested in the underlying value of a purchase than they are in the psychological reactions of buyers and sellers of the security within the next few days.

Investors normally fall into two categories. *Income-oriented investors* are concerned with the safety of their investments and with earning good returns on their assets. Income-oriented investors tend to buy bonds or preferred stock rather than common stock. When purchasing common stock, they invest in companies with long records of stable earnings and dividend payments. *Growth-oriented investors* emphasize *capital gains*— the potential appreciation of the market price of a stock. These investors choose to place their assets in common stock and tend to invest in companies that have records of growth in sales and earnings. Growth-oriented investors prefer to purchase stock in companies that pay little or no dividends, since these firms use their retained earnings to generate even higher future sales and earnings. For example, unless a purchaser expected state gambling laws to change within a month or so, a purchase of Bally stock would appeal to growth-oriented investors (see "Should You Have Invested in Bally?").

It is important that investors relate their investment objectives to their financial needs. It would rarely be sensible, for example, for a person near retirement to set growth-oriented objectives. Most financial experts also believe that potential investors should not consider purchasing stocks or bonds until the funds in their checking and savings accounts are approximately equal to six month's normal living expenses.

✔ **Obtaining and analyzing information.** Many sources provide financial information about individual companies. Both Moody's Investment Service and Standard and Poor's contain a variety of reports on individual firms and are available in most libraries and brokerage houses. Babson's Investment and Barometer Letter, United Business Service, Value Line Investment Service, and many other information services provide relevant information and investment advice concerning individual companies. Brokerage firms also employ security analysts who periodically issue reports and recommendations about individual securities.

Collect and analyze
relevant information . . .

Information on stock-market performance as a whole is provided by stock-market averages. The most widely known is the Dow Jones average of 65 stocks, which includes 30 industrial stocks, 20 transportation stocks, and 15 public-utility stocks. If the Dow Jones average rises from 800 to 810 on a given day, the price of a single share has not risen by $10. Rather the 65 stocks in the Dow Jones average have risen by 10/800, or 1.25 percent. A share of a given stock that sells for $100 would have risen in value by 1.25 percent to $101.25 if its performance was typical of the market as a whole on that day. The New York Stock Exchange (NYSE) Index differs in two respects from the Dow Jones average. The NYSE Index includes all (rather than 65) of the securities that are traded on the New York Stock Exchange. It is also a weighted average, for changes in the prices of stocks issued by such corporations as General Motors and American Telephone and Telegraph are weighed more heavily than changes in the prices of stocks issued by smaller companies. Stock-market averages are also available for the American Stock Exchange and for over-the-counter markets.

A knowledge of stock-market averages is an important tool in selecting securities, since the timing of purchases and sales is very important. When market averages indicate that the stock market has reached a peak, the prices of most securities are high. When stock-market averages are

---

FINANCIAL ADVICE ISN'T ALWAYS WHAT IT SEEMS

"I expect," said Irving Fisher, the most famous economist of the time, "to see the stock market a great deal higher than it is today within a few months." A few days later, the Great Crash of 1929 began on Wall Street. Within a few years, millions of investors found that they held worthless securities.

Identifying good buys in individual common stocks can be as difficult as predicting whether the stock market will go up or go down. In the 1950s, when Margaret Harris, a young employee in Haloid's advertising department, asked the Chairman of the Board of Directors about the prospects for xerography, he whispered, "Confidentially, Margaret, I think it's damn foolishness. But if Joe Wilson believes in it, I'm willing to go along." Joseph Wilson was then President of Haloid.

The young woman explained, "The reason I ask is that I'm thinking of buying some company stock on the prospects of the copying machine."

"Put your money into Kodak," the Chairman advised. "It's safer."

The Chairman of the Board was giving Margaret what he believed to be sound financial advice. She ignored it. Other potential investors received similar warnings: against the advice of friends, a Rochester cab driver bought 100 shares of Haloid stock for $1000.

Margaret's small investment in Haloid (now the Xerox Corporation) has left her free from financial worries for life. The cab driver has seen his original investment of $1000 grow to about $1,500,000.

low, most individual securities are available at bargain prices. An investor who anticipates market highs and lows by measuring stock-market averages can earn considerable profits. Unfortunately, as many investors have found, it is not easy to anticipate movements in general-security prices.

In analyzing information on individual securities, an investor may consider such factors as the price-earnings ratio of the stock involved, the past achievements and future prospects of the industry or industries with which the firm is associated, the firm's growth record in terms of profits and sales, new products that may become available to the firm, and the return that the firm normally earns on its equity investments. A major but intangible factor is the quality of the firm's management. Does it aggressively and imaginatively take advantage of new opportunities? Is it more efficient than its major competitors? Does it utilize talented employees?

✔ **Investment strategies.** Price trends in security markets are sometimes unpredictable, and even a thorough analysis of an individual security may yield inaccurate results. Investors may improve the performance of their holdings by considering several investment strategies. *Dollar averaging* requires that a designated sum be invested in a stock or in a group of stocks on a regular basis. By investing a fixed amount (say, $500 on a given stock every six months) the investor will purchase a larger number of shares when the stock's price is low: $500 will purchase ten shares when the price of the stock is $50; when the stock's price is high (say, $100 after six months), $500 will purchase only five shares. Over a period of time, the investor can buy a stock at a favorable average price. For example, over one year, an investor can purchase ten shares when the price is $50 per share and five shares when the price is $100 per share. Thus, the investor can buy 15 shares for a total of $1000 at an average cost of $66.67 per share. Unless the price of the stock remains low for a long time, dollar averaging should produce favorable results.

... and use sound investment strategies

Diversification involves purchasing a number of different securities, preferably from firms located in widely varied industries. Investing your total savings in a single stock raises the level of risk considerably. If the stock does well, profits can be large. But if the stock performs poorly, your entire investment can be lost. The process of diversification may be expanded even further; investors may purchase many different types of financial assets (stocks, bonds, land, buildings, mortgages, and so on) to reduce their dependence on a single type of investment.

Many investors pool their resources in *mutual funds* in order to purchase securities. An investor in mutual funds can:

1. Benefit from the expertise of professional security analysts the mutual fund employs to direct their investments.
2. Secure diversification with very limited initial investments. Since the mutual fund pools the savings of thousands of investors, it

normally purchases dozens of different types of securities. Investing $500 or less in a mutual fund can secure far greater diversification at reasonable cost than directly investing $500 on a securities market.

3. Utilize savings on brokerage fees. Because a mutual fund buys and sells thousands of shares in a single transaction, its commissions per share are lower than commissions on individual investor transactions.

Mutual funds are quoted in most daily newspapers. Extensive lists of mutual-fund quotations appear in both the *Wall Street Journal* and *The New York Times*.

Government Regulation of Security Markets

After the Civil War, security markets began to make important contributions to the financing of American manufacturing. However, some abuses soon developed. Swindlers operating "bucket shops" produced and sold fraudulent stock and bond certificates to an unsuspecting public. Promotors formed companies that were backed by nothing of value—by the "blue skies" of peoples' dreams. To prevent such abuses, state "blue-sky" laws were passed, requiring that both the securities sold and the brokers themselves be registered.

Federal legislation helps to protect investors

When securities markets collapsed during the Great Depression of the 1930s, popular support for federal regulation of the security industry grew. The Federal Securities Act of 1934 established the Securities and Exchange Commission (SEC), which to this day remains the most effective supervisory agency in the securities industry. Important activities of the SEC include:

1. Most publicly traded companies in interstate commerce must submit registration statements and periodic reports that fully disclose their financial status. A company subject to the jurisdiction of the SEC must also present investors with a prospectus or a summary of relevant financial information when issuing new securities.
2. Brokerage firms, mutual funds, and security exchanges are required to file periodic reports with the SEC.
3. Account executives dealing in listed and over-the-counter securities must pass a SEC-approved examination.

Because of its vast regulatory powers, the SEC influences almost every aspect of security-market operations.

The Securities Investor Protection Act of 1970 insures investor accounts up to $50,000 against losses resulting from the failure of a brokerage firm. Brokerage houses and exchanges contribute to a fund administered by the Securities Investor Protection Corporation, which, like the Federal Deposit Insurance Corporation, reimburses investors for such losses.

KEY POINTS TO REMEMBER

1. Financial institutions include commercial banks, investment banks, savings banks, savings and loan associations, credit unions, and insurance companies.
2. Commercial banks normally collect deposits in checking and savings accounts. With funds collected from savers, banks make direct loans to businesses, consumers, and governments and also invest in various types of securities.
3. A government agency, the Federal Reserve System, controls commercial-bank lending. By varying reserve requirements and discount rates or by utilizing open-market operations, the Federal Reserve System influences the demand for goods and services.
4. The major U.S. stock markets are the New York Stock Exchange, the American Stock Exchange, and over-the-counter markets. Corporate, government, and municipal bonds are traded on bond exchanges, the most important of which is the New York Bond Exchange.
5. Brokerage firms and exchanges act as financial agents, bringing buyers and sellers of securities together by establishing market prices for stocks and bonds.
6. Some individual investors purchase or sell securities by setting up appropriate accounts at brokerage firms.
7. In determining which securities to buy, individual investors should consider their investment objectives, collect and analyze information on the securities of individual companies, and investigate systematic investment strategies like dollar averaging and diversification.
8. Security markets are extensively regulated by federal and state governments.

QUESTIONS FOR DISCUSSION

1. Why is it important for you to understand the functions of financial institutions?
2. How are commercial-bank depositors protected by federal and state government regulations?
3. What services do commercial banks offer to businesses? To consumers?
4. In what two basic ways do banks earn profits?
5. What is the Federal Reserve System? Discuss its organization and administration.

6. As a member of the Board of Governors of the Federal Reserve system, what policies would you advocate during a recession? During inflation?

7. Describe the major services offered by: savings banks, savings and loan associations, credit unions, insurance companies, commercial-paper dealers, factors, finance companies, mutual funds, and pension funds.

8. Why is an understanding of security markets important to businesses? To individual investors?

9. Explain what each column signifies in newspaper listings of individual stock quotations. Of individual bond quotations.

10. List the steps a careful investor should follow when choosing a specific security.

SHORT CASES AND PROBLEMS

1. You are a manager who is considering the purchase of a new $10,000 truck. You check three financial institutions, which offer you the following terms:
   (a) A bank loan at 10-percent simple interest for one year.
   (b) A bank loan at a discounted 9-percent interest rate. In effect, you would borrow $9100 (the $10,000 note *minus* the $900 in interest) initially; at the end of the year, you would pay the entire $10,000 back.
   (c) A sales finance company offers to lend you $10,000 at 8-percent interest; the $10,800 (principal and interest) loan would be payable in 12 monthly installments of $900 each.

   Since simple-interest, discount, and installment credit are all common business practices, you will have to make this kind of choice often. If your only concern is obtaining the funds at the lowest cost in terms of real interest, which form of credit will you choose to finance the truck?

2. The stock of Company A is selling for $50 per share. Company A's earnings are $2, and it pays $1 per share in dividends. Stockholder equity per share is $40. From 1972 through 1976, Company A's sales have increased from $100 million to $200 million and its earnings have grown from $1 million to $3 million. Experts estimate that sales in Company A's industry will rise about 20 percent per year.
   (a) Compute the following statistics for Company A: its price–earnings ratio; its dividend-payout rate (its dividends as a percentage of the price of its stock); its return on equity; the estimated annual percentage rate of increase in its sales and earnings from 1972 through 1976.
   (b) Would Company A's stock appeal more to income-oriented or to growth-oriented investors?
   (c) Would Company A's stock be as attractive an investment as the other type of stocks that would appeal to the investors described in part (b)?

CAREER SELECTION: POSITIONS IN BANKING, REAL ESTATE, AND FINANCIAL SECURITIES

BANKING CAREERS

The management of a bank is composed of **bank officers,** who make policy and operational decisions within the general framework provided by the bank's board of directors. Bank officers may specialize in a variety of areas: **loan officers** evaluate financial data and make credit decisions; **trust officers** evaluate investment risks; and **operations officers** coordinate work schedules and maintain organizational efficiency. Employers generally hire management trainees with bachelor's degrees in business administration or in liberal arts. Occasionally, qualified bank tellers are promoted to officer status. Trainees receive one-half or one full year of on-the-job training, rotating among the various bank departments until they become familiar with the scope and basic functions of bank operations. Annual salaries range from $7800 for trainees to more than $24,000 for high-level officers. The increase in commercial banking services promises to provide a rapidly expanding job market. (*Additional information:* American Bankers Association; Bank Personnel Division; 1120 Connecticut Avenue, N.W.; Washington, D.C. 20036.)

Loan officers evaluate the quality of applicants who apply for credit from commercial banks. Commercial loan officers process business applications for bank loans and handle consumer loans. Loan officers may also evaluate potential bank investments, usually following guidelines established by top management and by the bank's board of directors. In larger banks, loan officers may specialize in treasury securities, commercial paper, corporate bonds, or other types of securities. More and more commercial banks are requiring that loan officers hold bachelor's or MBA degrees, preferably in finance or accounting. Annual salaries range from $7500 to $25,000, or more, depending on the complexities of the decisions to be made. Job opportunities for loan officers are expected to rise rapidly in the next decade.

Tellers receive bank deposits, process deposit withdrawals, and record these banking transactions. In large banks, tellers specialize in a particular service, such as savings, foreign exchange, or securities. Good clerical and mathematical skills are essential, since duties include counting cash on hand and balancing the day's deposits and withdrawals. Tellers must be personable and must communicate effectively with bank customers. Employers generally hire high-school graduates and provide them with on-the-job training. Experienced tellers may be promoted to head teller. Annual salaries average $5800. Job opportunities are expected to expand rapidly as more banks are established and as more financial services are provided.

REAL ESTATE CAREERS

Property owners who wish to sell or rent their homes, other buildings, or land contact **real-estate salesworkers** or **brokers.** Salesworkers and brokers show property to potential buyers and make the necessary financial arrangements when a buyer decides to purchase property. Brokers are self-employed businesspeople; salesworkers are hired by brokers to sell real estate, to compile listings (names of sellers who will use the firm's services), and to manage rental properties. Employers usually hire high-school and college graduates who have some knowledge of selling, psychology, and finance. On-the-job training programs are often provided. A bachelor's degree and an associate degree in real estate are competitive advantages. Both brokers and salesworkers must pass a comprehensive, standardized examination to obtain a license. Qualified salesworkers may advance to the position of sales manager or general manager. Commissions represent the largest portion of annual salaries; experienced salesworkers and brokers earn as much as $30,000 a year. The increased purchase and construction of residential property is expected to create a moderately expanding job market for real estate salesworkers and brokers. (*Additional information:* National Association of Realtors; Department of Education; 155 East Superior Street; Chicago, Illinois 60611.)

CAREERS IN FINANCIAL SECURITIES

Securities salesworkers represent investors who buy or sell stocks, bonds, or mutual-fund shares. Securities salesworkers relay buy or sell decisions to security exchanges and provide clients with investment advice. Salesworkers are employed by brokerage firms, investment banks, insurance companies, and mutual funds. Successful job applicants are generally high-school or college graduates who are self-motivated, outgoing, personable, and honest. Large firms often require college degrees in business administration or in finance. Short-term, on-the-job training programs prepare the salesworkers for the standardized examination that they must pass to obtain licenses. Salesworkers may advance to the position of office manager. Annual salaries are primarily based on commissions. Experienced salesworkers average $21,000 a year; some earn more than $50,000. Job opportunities are expected to expand moderately as a result of rising corporate profits and consumer discretionary income. (*Additional information:* Contact the personnel department of a local securities firm.)

Security analysts are usually employed by brokerage firms, banks, mutual finds, or pensions funds to evaluate individual common stocks. A bachelor's degree in business administration, with specialization in finance or economics, is usually the minimum educational requirement. An MBA or a master's degree in economics is frequently required. Security analysts must have high-level analytical abilities and must be able to skillfully present their recommendations in an understandable way. Annual salaries range from $15,000 to more than $25,000. Job opportunities are expected to increase moderately, if stock and bond markets continue to perform well and to attract public interest.

A CRITICAL BUSINESS DECISION

—made by Richard L. Kattel

THE SITUATION Miles Lane, retiring President of the Citizens & Southern National Bank of Atlanta, would be a hard act to follow. Lane, fond of wearing rumpled suits and neckties inscribed with "It's a Wonderful World!" would tell a visitor, "Sit down; can I sell you some money?"

But under Lane's guidance, Citizens & Southern had prospered. With over $2.5 billion in assets, the bank ranked 36th largest in the United States. Citizens & Southern also owned 5 percent or more of the stock in roughly 24 Georgia banks and in at least 40 other banks outside the state. Citizens & Southern was also noted in banking circles for its financial statements, issued with extraordinary frequency—usually at monthly intervals—and filled with unprecedented details about C & S's business operations.

After suffering two heart attacks, Miles Lane stepped down from his post as head of Citizens & Southern National Bank in June of 1973. A brash, 37-year old New Yorker, Richard L. Kattel, was selected to replace the best-known banker in the South. Of Finnish extraction, Kattel had attended Valley Forge Military Academy in Pennsylvania and subsequently Emory College. While at Emory, he had married Gay Mitchell from Orlando, Florida, described as "a daughter both of the Revolution and of the Confederacy."

As a colleague describes Kattel's career, "Kattel came in here right out of college, and with unabashed arrogance said he would be Executive Vice President in X number of years, and by God he was." Kattel's success was indeed meteoric: he began his career posting ledgers in the C & S bank in Decatur, Georgia; ten years later Kattel was Executive Vice President of C & S's Savannah bank.

THE DECISION Kattel awakens at 5:45 A.M. and tries to be in his high-ceilinged, dark-paneled office by 7 A.M., where he works steadily until 4:30 or 5 P.M. He pays regular visits to C & S's 600 offices and banks in the company's dark green helicopter and knows every bank manager by name. Kattel's activities are designed to achieve high objectives. "By 1980," the young President predicts, "we see C & S as a $7 billion bank employing 14,000 people and earning $91 million a year."

In his first year as President, Kattel confronted a severe problem. A booming economy radically increased the number of C & S customer loans during 1973 and the first nine months of 1974. Determined to expand C & S's loan position as rapidly as possible and attracted by the high interest rates borrowers were willing to pay, Kattel decided to gamble: C & S extended a large volume of long-term credit to its customers and hoped for a large, off-setting inflow of monies from depositors. But when deposits did not flow in as expected, C & S was forced to borrow short-term funds at high interest rates from other commercial banks and from the Federal Reserve System. The result was predictable: C & S's earnings declined for the first time in a decade during Kattel's initial tenure as President.

QUESTIONS

1. Why did C & S have to pay such high interest rates during 1973 and the first nine months of 1974 on the funds it borrowed, in view of the Federal Reserve System's desire to control the raging inflation then taking place?

2. The United States experienced a recession in late 1974 and in 1975. How do you think changing business conditions affected the monetary policy of the Federal Reserve System and the interest rates that C & S had to pay on its borrowed funds? Did Richard Kattel's decision benefit C & S in the long run? Explain your answer.

389

It would take 50 people working day and night for 200 years to make the same mistake that an electronic computer can make in only two seconds.

News and Views Junior, 1971

"Enter our contest as often as you like." read an instruction in a $50,000 West Coast contest sponsored by the McDonald's hamburger chain. In March 1975, students at the California Institute of Technology took the company at its word: they used their mathematical expertise to program an IBM computer to print 1.2 million entries from the Caltech student roster.

McDonald's lawyers ruled that the duplicate entries were legal, and the company decided to award matching prizes to each winner. The Caltech students and their friendly computer won about 20 percent of all the contest prizes. The biggest winner, Becky Hartsfield, received $3000 worth of groceries and a new station wagon. She gave the car to charity and the cash equivalent of the groceries to Caltech for housing improvements.

This example—although admittedly unusual—illustrates the magnitude of both the information a computer can process and numerous ways in which information processing can affect our everyday lives.

In a more practical sense, in less than three decades, *electronic data processing* (EDP)—the analysis and summarization of data by electronic computers—has revolutionized the operation of American business in two important ways: by increasing the speed and the accuracy of processing massive volumes of data and by providing people in business with timely information in a required form at a reasonable cost. (To appreciate both the speed and the expense of computers, try to answer the questions in "How Fast and How Cheaply Can Computers Calculate?".) Each year, electronic data processing and computers are used more and more in business decision making.

This chapter focuses on the development of the computer and its importance in collecting pertinent information and communicating these data in a meaningful form to business decision makers. Four main topics will be discussed: (1) the development of electronic data processing and the computer industry; (2) the nature of an electronic computer; (3) computer programming; and (4) how computers assist in making effective business decisions.

How EDP and computers have revolutionized business

Development of Computers and the EDP Industry

We have already seen that innovations can arise from two opposing directions: through a market need or through a technological breakthrough. Generally, electronic computers have evolved as a result of a market need: the increasing demand for processing and summarizing data quickly, accurately, and inexpensively.

Early calculators

The Growing Need for Information

Industrialization has dramatically increased the need for communication and information flow within a firm. Manually developed reports were often lacking in detail, too costly, somewhat inaccurate, and too untimely to serve management's information needs. In the nineteenth century, the use of mechanical devices (typewriters, adding machines, and calculators) greatly increased worker productivity and reduced error. These devices were the early ancestors of the modern computer.

Origin of Computers

First we will identify some of the important milestones in the evolution of today's electronic computer.

✔ **The analytical engine.** Charles Babbage, an English mathematician at Cambridge University, is generally regarded as the godfather of the modern computer. Born in 1792, Babbage spent much of his life working to build a machine he called the "analytical engine." Babbage's dream (to detractors, it was "Babbage's folly") embodied all the elements of a modern computer: an input device using punched cards, an arithmetic unit or "mill," a memory unit or "store," an automatic printout, and a sequential program control. In short, Babbage had designed but had not completed a prototype computer. He had only two problems: he underestimated development time and costs and he lacked the necessary mechanical and electronic technology to perfect his machine.

Charles Babbage

✔ **Punched cards.** The principle of punched cards was developed by French loom designer Joseph Jacquard in the late eighteenth century. Jacquard used cards with pattern-punched holes to control thread selection and thereby the design of a weave.

A century later, necessity prompted the use of punched cards in data tabulation. In 1885, the U.S. Bureau of the Census realized that the data collected in its 1880 census would not be completely tabulated until almost 1890—the year the next census was to begin. By then, of course, the information would be outdated. The Bureau of the Census asked statistician Herman Hollerith to serve as a special consultant to find a solution to its data tabulation problems. In 1887, Hollerith developed a punched card that could be "read" by a device he called the "census machine." Hollerith's new device took much less tabulating time than manual methods required: the 1890 census was compiled in less than three years! Hollerith

The "census machine": using punched cards to tabulate population

15-1 Standard 80-column punched card, showing numbers, letters, and other characters punched in Hollerith code.

left government service to form his own company, which eventually merged with other firms to become the International Business Machines Corporation (IBM).

Figure 15-1 shows a modern standard 80-column punched card in *Hollerith code* — the punching system Hollerith designed to represent both numbers and letters. The columns on the card are numbered consecutively; the bottom ten rows are numbered from 0 through 9, with two extra rows on top. Each number is represented on the card by a single punch in the row corresponding to that number. A letter or a special character requires two or more punches in a single column.

HOW FAST AND HOW CHEAPLY CAN COMPUTERS CALCULATE?

Most of us realize that computers can perform mathematical computations on data quickly and inexpensively. Yet, comprehending these two facts can be mind boggling. To appreciate this, try to answer the following questions:

1. William Shanks, a British mathematician, spent 20 years computing the mathematical ratio of π to 707 decimal places.
   (a) In 1949, ENIAC (Electronic Numerical Integrator and Calculator), the first truly electronic computer, calculated π to 2000 decimal places and revealed that Mr. Shanks had made an arithmetic error in the 528th

place. How long do you think it took ENIAC to calculate π to 2000 decimal places?
   (b) How much time do you think it would take the fastest computer available today to calculate π to 2000 places?

2. In 1952, it cost $1.26 to perform 100,000 multiplications on an IBM computer.
   (a) How much do you suppose 100,000 multiplications cost in 1964?
   (b) How much do you suppose 100,000 multiplications cost in 1975?

For the answers, see page 394.

HOW FAST AND HOW CHEAPLY CAN COMPUTERS CALCULATE? *(Answers)*

1. (a) The ENIAC took just over 70 hours to calculate π to 2000 places.
   (b) Today, the same calculation on Control Data Corporation's 7600 computer, among the largest and fastest computers in the world, can be made within eight seconds—without an error.

2. (a) In 1964, the cost of performing 100,000 multiplications on an IBM computer was 12 cents.
   (b) In 1975, the same 100,000 multiplications cost 1 cent.

These statistics illustrate the power of today's computer and why it has had such a revolutionary effect on American business.

✔ **Unit-record equipment.** From the end of World War I until 1954, all mechanized business data were processed on punched-card equipment, more commonly referred to as *unit-record equipment.* The latter term is derived from the use of *unit-record processing*—the consolidation of all information related to a particular system into a single (or unit) record that can be used again and again in the preparation of reports. Each time a report is prepared, only the pertinent items are extracted from the unit records. Provided these unit records are accurate, this system saves file storage space and eliminates the need to transcribe data manually—a process that often results in clerical errors.

Unit-record equipment: the backbone of the precomputer era

The punched card is the basis of unit-record processing. A punched card is normally divided into *fields*—single columns or groups of columns that collectively have a special meaning. Figure 15-2 shows a master payroll punched card for an individual employee; this is a unit record of the information obtained from the employee's personnel form. Note that

15-2   Master payroll punched card.

the card is divided into 14 fields. A specific number or letter placed in a field has a special or *positional meaning*. The same number or letter in another field has an entirely different meaning. For example, in Figure 15-2, the third field (columns 5 and 6) identifies the employee's department number, and the sixth field (columns 36-41) identifies the date the employee began working for the company. Clearly, great care must be taken to make sure that both card-punching equipment and computers read the columns correctly, or serious errors will occur.

Unit-record equipment includes *card sorters,* which place a series of punched cards in numerical or alphabetical order and sort out cards according to particular characteristics, and *tabulating machines* (also called *electrical accounting machines*), which add, subtract, multiply, and divide and print reports based on information fed to them on punched cards. Today, smaller firms still use unit-record equipment in such applications as payroll records and card sorting of survey data, but it has largely been replaced by electronic computers. Figure 15-3 is a photograph of a modern card sorter.

Although unit-record equipment is a great improvement over manual transcription methods, it still has two major drawbacks: (1) inflex-

15-3   A modern example of punched-card equipment: the card sorter.

Source: International Business Machines Corporation.

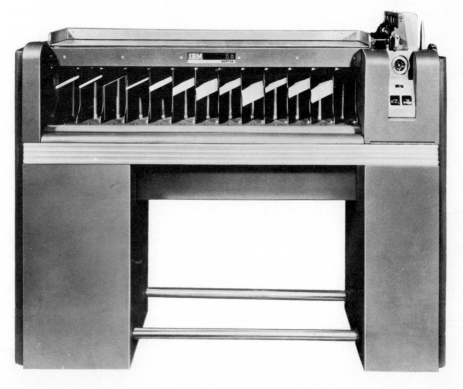

ibility, and (2) the need for manual intervention. The tabulating machine illustrates both of these problems. Wired control boards (called external plug boards) connected to the machine direct it to perform a particular operation. Thus, each punched card that passes through the tabulating machine receives exactly the same treatment. In order to change an operation to achieve flexibility, new control boards must be installed and the machine must be rerun—a time-consuming process. The tabulating machine also requires continual manual intervention: it must be fed cards, started and stopped, and trays of cards must be inserted and removed between each step. This intervention is necessary because of the inflexibility of the machine and the lack of integration between the various pieces of unit-record equipment.

**Drawbacks of
unit-record equipment**

✔ **Electromechanical computers.** The national security needs of the United States during World War II set the stage for the development of the modern computer. From 1937 to 1944, Howard Aiken of Harvard University utilized established technology and Hollerith's punched cards to build a machine that could compute ballistics tables for U.S. Army and Navy projectiles. The machine, called the Mark I, used electromechanical relays for arithmetic counting. The Mark I was the first electromechanical computer—the realization of Babbage's dream. A significant technical achievement of the Mark I was its use of a stored program—instructions kept within the machine that directed its operations and that could be altered to instruct the computer to perform successive steps automatically. Thus, the computer eliminated the need for manual intervention between data input and data output. The concept of internally stored instruction sets the computer apart from all other unit-record equipment.

**Internal storage
distinguishes
the computer
from unit-record
equipment**

✔ **Electronic computers.** The team of John W. Mauchly and J. Presper Eckert, Jr., built the first electronic computer at the University of Pennsylvania between 1939 and 1946. Dubbed the ENIAC (Electronic Numerical Integrator and Calculator) the computer replaced electromechanical relays with 19,000 vacuum tubes, which greatly increased its calculating ability. The ENIAC could perform 300 multiplications per second, making it 300 times faster than any other machine of its day.

In a technical paper prepared in 1946, mathematical genius John Von Neumann of the Institute for Advanced Studies paved the way for the modern electronic computer by suggesting that *binary arithmetic* be used both in the counting operations of the computer and in the instructions fed to the computer to direct its operations. Binary arithmetic is a system of counting with only two digits, 0 and 1, in which any unit (letter or number) can be represented in code by a unique sequence of binary digits (01,011,101, and so on). Binary arithmetic is particularly suited to computers, since all electronic components operate in binary fashion; that is, they can be either on (represented by the 1 symbol) or off (represented by the 0 symbol).

**Binary arithmetic:
computers count
. . . on one finger!**

Von Neumann's concepts have been incorporated in all subsequent electronic designs. In 1949, the Remington Rand Corporation acquired a small computer company founded by Mauchly and Eckert and developed the first mass-produced, general-purpose electronic computer, called the UNIVAC I (UNIVersal Automatic Computer). The first UNIVAC I was delivered to the U.S. Bureau of the Census in 1951. In 1954, a UNIVAC I purchased by General Electric's Appliance Park plant was installed to process business data. The computer era in business had begun.

Growth of Computer Usage

During the 1960s, computer shipments by American manufacturers grew at the astounding rate of 15 to 20 percent annually. In the early 1970s, U.S. businesses and government institutions spent from $20 to $25 billion per year on computers, related equipment, and operating staffs.

An index of the growth of electronic data processing is the number of computers that have been installed by American businesses and government institutions. Total computer installations in the United States increased tenfold from a handful of computers in use in 1955 to 100,000 computers in use in 1975. Today, approximately a half million Americans devote their creative talents to expanding and improving computer performance.

U.S. computer installations grew dramatically in 20 years

What Is a Computer?

Kinds of Computers

In its broadest sense, the term "computer" refers to any device that calculates, reckons, or computes. Thus, an abacus, a slide rule, and an adding machine are all computers. In today's narrower usage of the term, a *computer* is an electronic device that processes data, that is capable of receiving input and producing output, and that possesses the characteristics of high speed, accuracy, and the ability to store a set of instructions for solving a problem. Two main types of computers are in use today: digital and analog.

✔ **Digital computers.** A *digital computer* is a machine that processes discrete (as opposed to continuous) values by a sequence of internally stored instructions. This is in contrast to a calculator, on which the sequence of instructions is impressed manually by the operator. As we have already noted, the use of stored, alterable instructions is what distinguishes the computer from any other machine.

The nature of a digital computer can be illustrated by the workings of a digital clock, which shows the time in exact digits that change every minute and that can be read directly by an observer. Between minutes, the continuous time changes are not visible, as they are on a standard clock with a second hand. The digital clock is similar to a digital computer because it solves a problem (measuring time) and displays the results in discrete values. Electronic digital computers are widely used in business and are what we will generally refer to as computers in the remainder of this chapter.

✔ **Analog computers.** An *analog computer* is a device that solves a problem by translating physical variables (such as liquid flow or a change in temperature or angular position) into related electrical or mechanical quantities. These quantities are then presented in a continuous fashion on a scale from which the observer reads the correct value. The standard clock can be considered an analog computer of time. The hands of a standard clock move continuously from one number to the next, and the observer must judge the exact time by estimating the distance the hands have traveled between the numbers. Analog computers are widely used in scientific and engineering problems, but are seldom applied to business problems.

Computer Components and Functions

✔ **Principal components of a computer.** The electronic digital computer has five basic components:

Input device: The unit designed to bring processable data into a computer.

Storage or memory unit: The device in which data are stored and from which they are obtained when needed.

Arithmetic-logic unit: The device that performs addition, subtraction, multiplication, and division, compares the relative sizes of two values, and senses positive and negative values.

Control unit: The portion of the computer that directs the sequence of operations, interprets coded instructions, and initiates proper commands to the computer circuits.

Output device: The unit designed to translate electrical impulses into a usable form, such as printed copy or punched cards.

In addition, because modern computers must store enormous volumes of data, their capacities are often augmented by *secondary storage* or *secondary memory units.*

✔ **Central processor and peripheral equipment.** *Computer hardware* refers to all the physical equipment used in a computer system. This

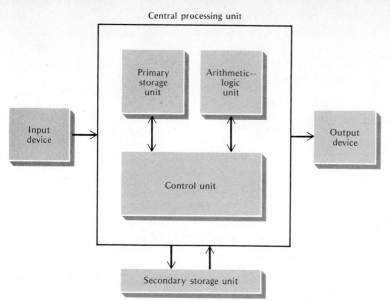

Central processing unit

Primary storage unit

Arithmetic-logic unit

Input device

Control unit

Output device

Secondary storage unit

15-4

The principal components of a computer. Note that the primary storage unit, the arithmetic-logic unit, and the control unit comprise the central processing unit or main frame of the computer. The input and the output devices and the secondary storage unit comprise the peripheral equipment.

Hardware includes the central processing unit and peripheral equipment

equipment is normally divided into two categories: the central processing unit and peripheral equipment.

The *central processing unit* (often called the central processor, or simply CPU) consists of three of the components mentioned earlier — the memory or storage unit, the arithmetic-logic unit, and the control unit — plus the operating console. The operating console is an extension of the control unit that resembles an electronic switch panel attached to an electric typewriter and desk. A computer operator uses the console to perform a number of activities: turning the computer on and off, finding errors in computer instructions, troubleshooting operational breakdowns, and operating and testing peripheral equipment. The CPU is also called the computer's *main frame.*

Peripheral equipment consists of all computer hardware that is not associated directly with the main frame. This hardware generally includes two remaining components — the input and output devices — plus the secondary storage or memory units. Figure 15-4 illustrates the relationships between the various computer components. Figure 15-5 contains photographs of these components in a modern computer installation. Because input and output devices are the two main points at which people interact with computers, these pieces of peripheral equipment deserve special study.

Input data must be understandable to computers

✔ **Input devices.** A supervisor directs business activities by talking to workers directly or by writing them memos. The same does not apply to computers. Just as humans cannot understand electrical impulses, a computer cannot understand the spoken or handwritten word. The compro-

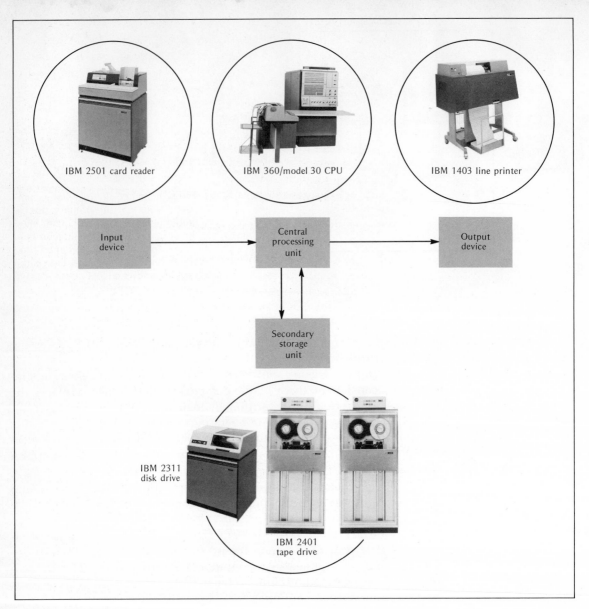

Input device → Central processing unit → Output device

IBM 2501 card reader

IBM 360/model 30 CPU

IBM 1403 line printer

Secondary storage unit

IBM 2311 disk drive

IBM 2401 tape drive

15-5   What components look like in a modern computer system.

mise is in favor of the computer. The user must translate the data to be processed into a form the computer can read, termed *machine-readable media*. Putting information into the computer, then, has two aspects: (1) selecting the machine-readable media to use, and (2) developing input devices to accept the chosen media.

The punched card, the dominant medium for computer inputs in the early 1950s, is still in wide use today. However, punched cards have two major drawbacks: they are bulky to store, and they bend and tear easily. In recent years, a variety of media have been developed to replace the punched card: punched paper tape, magnetic tape and disks, mark-sensed cards, teletype terminals, and cathode ray tubes (TV screens) combined with a typewriter keyboard or an electronic stylus. Input devices translate the information from these media into electronic impulses that the computer can understand. The magnetic ink characters identifying account numbers on bank checks represent a unique input medium used in the banking industry to sort and process checks electronically.

✔ **Output devices.**   Output devices translate the results of the computer's efforts. They receive data in the form of electrical impulses from the computer's storage unit, at the direction of the control unit. Some output devices function essentially as input devices—translating the data into other electrical impulses that are stored on magnetic tapes, disks, and drums or that are transmitted to cathode ray tubes and remote teletype terminals. Other output devices translate electrical impulses into mechanical action. These devices include the printer, which prints data results on paper (called hard-copy printouts), and the card punch, which punches the information on cards. Thus, computer outputs can be read by people or utilized by other machines.

Output data may be read by people or computers

Programming: Telling the Computer What to Do

A *computer program* is a sequence of instructions the computer uses to solve a problem. *Computer programming*—the task of writing the program—is undertaken by a computer programmer. Problem solving programs and other computer instructions that simplify the programming process are referred to as *computer software*. The program, which is stored in the computer's memory unit to instruct the control unit, is what makes the computer a unique and powerful machine.

Software includes programs and related aids for instructing the computer

Programming Languages and Steps

When computers were first produced, a different programming language was used for each kind of computer. Thus, a programmer who was familiar with one machine could not write instructions for another type of computer. To overcome this problem, researchers developed programming languages that could be used interchangeably on different computers. Two of the more frequently used multipurpose computer languages are FORTRAN (*FOR*mula *TRAN*slation) and COBOL (*CO*mmon *Business Oriented Language*). Although originally designed for engineering and scientific purposes, FORTRAN has been used in some business

applications. COBOL, designed primarily for business problems, is most widely used in administrative and accounting applications. Currently, even more simplified programming languages are being developed to enable programmers to learn the language faster and to simplify their job of restructuring computer programs they have not written.

Given a particular problem, a programmer normally prepares a precise sequence of instructions for the computer to follow. The programmer first analyzes the problem in terms of its elements, then outlines the sequence of operations and decisions required for its solution (usually in the form of a flow diagram, discussed in the next section) and writes the program instructions in a computer language such as COBOL. After the programmer has checked the instructions thoroughly for consistency and accuracy, the computer program is transcribed by a trained operator onto a machine-readable medium such as punched cards.

Programming:
writing and debugging
computer instructions

Before the program is considered operational, it must be "debugged"; that is, all potential errors or problems must be found and corrected. This is where programmers really earn their pay. Very few new programs are flawless. A programmer usually runs the new program through the computer with some test data which contain all of the possible variables and extremes that may be encountered when the program is actually used. If "bugs" are discovered, the program must be altered and modified until it runs without interruption or error. It is not unusual for programmers to spend as much time debugging programs as they spend writing them.

Programming has been called "the most problem-plagued component of the data-processing business." Major computer users like the federal government spend more on programmers' salaries and on preparing programs than they spend on buying or renting computers. While occasional hardware malfunctions do occur, it is generally agreed that about 90 percent of all computer errors are the result of incorrect programming.

The case of the
$18.5-million
hyphen

Computer programming requires the utmost accuracy, since even the slightest error can be disastrous. Several years ago, an Atlas-Agena rocket was launched from Cape Kennedy carrying the first U.S. spacecraft programmed to fly past Venus. After erratic wanderings, the rocket was blown up on command from the ground. Subsequent analysis showed that a computer programmer had accidentally left out a hyphen, which represented an entire formula. It was history's costliest hyphen, resulting in the destruction of an $18.5 million rocket and spacecraft. At the Vandevers department store in Tulsa, Oklahoma, accounts receivable amounting to $2 million were accidentally stored in the memory unit of a computer; fortunately, the programming error was found and corrected after 45 days. Gimbel's department store chain was not as lucky. As a result of a programming error, many of Gimbel's charge customers were not billed for two years or more. The $6 million in accounts receivable were equal to almost half the company's profits in 1970. And some of the debts were so old, they were uncollectable by the time the error was discovered.

15-6

Flow diagram of the steps required to find and check out books from a library.

Flow Diagram of a Problem

A *flow diagram* is a graphic representation of the sequence of steps required to solve a given problem. Programmers frequently use flow diagrams to outline the decisions and operations involved in instructing a computer. This process can be illustrated by a simple library research problem. Suppose you have a list of the approximate titles and authors of several reference books that you need. The flow diagram in Figure 15-6 outlines the sequence of steps you might follow to locate one or more of these books and check them out of the library.

Each rectangle or *operation box,* in a flow diagram represents an action that is to be taken; circles generally represent the beginning or the end of the program. The diamond-shaped *decision boxes* illustrate the detailed logic the programmer must apply to instruct the computer. Note that each decision box in Figure 15-6 (numbered 3,4,6,7, and 9) asks a question that can be answered yes or no. The required sequence of steps varies with the answer, as indicated by the two different paths leading out of each of these boxes. This division into alternative paths is called *branching.* When one of the paths returns the flow to an earlier stage in the sequence, the operation is termed *looping.* Path C in Figure 15-6 is an example of looping.

The power and flexibility of the computer lie in its ability to perform two operations: (1) selecting different paths through branching, and (2) repeating a particular sequence as many times as necessary through looping. In essence, programming a computer involves using binary arithmetic to translate flow-diagram questions and yes or no answers into an electronic circuit containing a series of components that are either on or off, as prescribed by the program. The components that are on or off establish the branches and loops that make up the electronic instructions of the program.

Suppose that there are four books on the list you take to the card catalog. You take path C in Figure 15-6 after trying to find the call number (but not necessarily finding it, as shown by path B) for each of the first three books on your list. For the fourth book, you note that the book is the last one on your list and answer "yes" to the question in decision box 6; in this case, you move on to box 7, rather than back through path C as you did for the first three books. At decision box 7, you go to the book stacks if you have found at least one call number; if not, you leave the library. If you find one or more books in the stacks, you check out the books and leave the library. If you find no books in the stacks, you leave the library empty-handed.

COMPUTERIZED THEFT: THE CASE OF THE SHORT-CHANGED PAYCHECKS

The company (which shall remain nameless to protect the guilty) had a genius in its payroll department. When asked to order the computer to pay each of its thousands of employees every two weeks, he also ordered everyone's paycheck to be rounded down to the nearest cent. For example, an employee who earns $10,400 per year should receive an average of $866.667 per month; but the computer was ordered to pay that employee only $866.66 in each monthly paycheck. No one in the company noticed that they were receiving a few tenths of a cent less in their paychecks each month, and the computer was ordered to pay the clever crook the remaining sum. A few tenths of a cent distributed over tens of thousands of employee checks added more than a thousand dollars each month to the computer expert's pay. Finally discovered, the company agreed not to prosecute if the employee would correct the computer program. As a final gesture of defiance, however, the genius wrote the new computer program in such a way that no company employee could be paid unless the expert continued to receive his salary. So subtly did he manipulate the computer program that it took the company's other computer experts nearly three weeks to find out how he did it.

How Computers Serve Business

As we have seen, computers can greatly increase the speed and accuracy of data processing if they are properly directed and controlled. Without this guidance, computers can wreak havoc. To understand how computers can serve business, we will examine (1) the characteristics of useful management information; (2) methods of utilizing computers; (3) present applications of computers in business; and (4) the future of electronic data processing and computers.

Characteristics of Useful Management Information

Figure 15-7 shows the typical sequence used in business electronic data-processing operations. Ideally, raw inputs (data, methods used to analyze the data, and details on the form of the output) are fed into the computer, which processes the information and provides useful output for management. In practice, however, this is not always the case. Data-processing specialists have coined the acronym GIGO to describe what happens on some occasions: Garbage In, Garbage Out. Many managers have learned to overcome the tendency to accept a computerized report without question when they would reject the report if it were typewritten.

Without proper guidance: GIGO

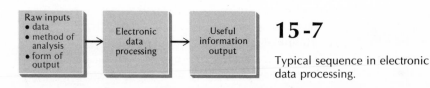

15-7

Typical sequence in electronic data processing.

The usefulness of business information is generally evaluated by five criteria: (1) accuracy, (2) timeliness, (3) completeness, (4) conciseness, and (5) relevancy. Since these five criteria often conflict, they must be balanced against one another. For example, the information may be so exhaustive that it overwhelms the user. This situation, often called *information overload,* can result in wasted time and money and in poorer management decisions. Thus, the user may elect to sacrifice completeness in the interest of conciseness. Or, the user may decide to collect more complete information and to pay a time penalty by having to wait to make a decision and to take action until the data are available. Users at all management levels should periodically reassess their information needs and balance these five criteria accordingly.

Methods of Utilizing Computers

The great flexibility of electronic digital computers is reflected in the diverse ways in which they assist businesses and government institutions. Methods of utilizing computers include general- and special-purpose processing, batch and online processing, and time sharing.

✔ **General- and special-purpose processing.** The digital computer can be programmed either to process data for a wide variety of applications or to solve one specific problem. The former is called a *general-purpose computer* and is often referred to as a *data computer* or a *white-collar computer* since it performs the functions of clerical and professional personnel. Examples of general-purpose data processing are the computers to assist businesses or government in handling scientific problems and in performing routine clerical jobs.

General-purpose computers solve many different problems

A computer tailored to a specific application is called a *special-purpose computer* and is also referred to as a *process computer* or a *blue-collar computer,* since it performs the functions of manufacturing shop personnel in many applications. Special-purpose computers measure changes in various work processes and then react to correct or control those processes. Many automated manufacturing operations employ machine tools controlled by special-purpose computers. The Chrysler Corporation uses a computer-controlled system to adjust a boring tool to compensate for heating and wearing effects. A Chrysler system is being developed to measure the exact diameters of finished pistons and to transmit the data to the machine boring cylinder blocks so that cylinder holes will match the pistons at final assembly. The dominant users of special-purpose computers are the continuous-process industries that refine petroleum and process metals and chemicals.

Special-purpose computers solve a single problem

In all its applications, the computer must be monitored by an operator. At Armco Steel's plate mill in Houston, a computer controls the steel-rolling process, but an operator must override the computer for an average

Westinghouse Electric Corporation's 2500 minicomputer.

of 18 minutes in every eight-hour shift. As the supervisor notes: "The computer and its sensors can handle the normal cases, but there's no computer big enough to handle all the abnormal cases."

In the 1970s, an increasing number of firms began to agree with this statement. Large computers such as Control Data Corporation's 7600 model rent for more than $100,000 per month and sell for more than $5 million (the exact price depends on the "extras" the user requests). Yet even at these astronomical prices, large computers are not ideally suited to the variety of detailed problems they must handle. The result has been a dramatic increase in the sales of *minicomputers,* a class of small stored-program computers that are suitable for general-purpose applications and that may also be used for special-purpose applications. Minicomputers are often small enough to fit on a desk top, are extremely versatile, and are available at lower costs (prices range from $3000 to $50,000; monthly rental prices, from $300 to $1000). As general-purpose machines, minicomputers can be applied to business data processing, as well as to engineering and to scientific computations. As special-purpose devices, they can be used to control machines, production lines, and traffic signals. In analyzing ways to help U.S. manufacturers reduce production costs and improve product quality, a Ford Motor Company executive observes that the minicomputer is the "most powerful single tool for productivity improvement that we will have during this decade."

Minicomputers: extremely flexible devices

✔ **Batch and online processing.** Most computer data processing can be categorized as batch or online processing. *Batch processing* involves accumulating a volume of work and then processing it at one time. This method is used for routine administrative and accounting jobs, such as payroll, personnel updates, and customer billing.

Batch: waiting to process a group of items

Online processing involves immediate input-output access to the computer whenever a user wishes to obtain information. When a query is sent to the computer, its current operations are stopped and the query is processed based on the information stored in the computer up to that point. After the query has been answered, normal computer operations are resumed. Online systems are used for specialized applications, such as processing airline and motel reservations. A *remote input-output device* (a terminal that is some distance away from the central computer but linked to it electrically) instantly shows the reservations clerk if an airline seat or a motel room is available and immediately records a new reservation. Many brokerage firms obtain the latest transaction prices of stocks from an online system. Online systems are playing an increasing role in managerial decision making. Today, an executive at a remote online terminal can obtain status reports or solve a problem using a computer many miles away.

Online: instant computer access

Online applications are expanding each day: inventory control, ticket sales, truck dispatching, and credit investigation are some examples. However, because online processing is much more expensive than batch processing, many business managers are reassessing the importance of the instant response online systems provide. One automotive executive changed from online to batch processing in areas such as labor timekeeping and inventory control after concluding that "Once-a-day processing is adequate and is much less expensive."

✔ **Time sharing.** An increasingly popular method of computer utilization is *time sharing*—a procedure that links many remote input-output terminals (usually teletypewriters) to a central computer with a large storage capacity. The links are ordinary telephone lines leased specifically for this purpose; thus users may be located miles from the data processing terminal. The computer is programmed for online operation, and the programs of the various users are stored within it. Users identify the programs they need, enter the data at their terminals, and receive output. Although many people are utilizing the computer simultaneously, the fractional-second time delay required to connect to the computer allows each user to communicate with the machine independently. Figure 15-8 is a photograph of a time-sharing system with a teletypewriter as the input-output device.

Time sharing: hooking your desk to a computer

Many colleges and universities use time-sharing systems. For a monthly charge, a school is given access to computer programs related to many academic subjects. A student or a faculty member may use this system for problem solving or for research, or simply to practice programming techniques. The advantage of time sharing in comparison to other

15-8

Time-sharing computer system using a teletypewriter as the input-output device.

Source: Teletype Corporation.

methods of computer utilization is cost. The user purchases a tremendous processing capacity for a fraction of what it would cost to buy or rent equivalent equipment. The disadvantage of a time-sharing system is its slow speed in feeding data in and out of the computer.

Present Computer Applications

To understand the importance of modern computers, we will explore the diverse computer applications in modern industry and the use of computers in business decision making.

What's here: computerized checkout counters

🡒 **Computer applications in industry.** New computer applications have increased dramatically during the past decade. Savings and loan associations use online systems to process customer savings accounts. The amount of a deposit or a withdrawal is keyed into a device at the teller's window that immediately posts the information to the central computer, which is often miles away. Publishing companies use computers in composing and editing manuscripts. Newspapers use computers to typeset and edit, as well as to process classified ads.

The computer-operated supermarket checkout system is an example of a computer application that may soon affect all of us. Before reading the next paragraph, study the description of the system on the opposite page. Then try to assess the potential advantages and disadvantages that such a system offers to (1) the supermarket, and (2) the consumer.

A computerized checkout system will eliminate the need for clerks to price-stamp every item and will reduce the number of checkout personnel —cutting a supermarket's costs by an estimated $40,000 annually. Other important advantages will be the elimination of checkout errors and an instantaneously up-to-date inventory control system. The disadvantage? The cost of installing this system in a supermarket with eight checkout counters will be about $125,000.

Clearly, consumers will also benefit from a reduction in checkout time (estimated at 45 percent) and from the elimination of checkout errors. But the possible disadvantage that worries supermarket owners is consumer reaction to the system: prices will not be marked directly on the packages, and consumers will have to refer to the price information displayed on the product shelves. How critical this problem proves to be in test situations will largely determine how soon you will see electronic scanners in your local supermarket.

HOW A WAVE OF THE WAND COMPUTERIZES GROCERY SHOPPING

One Saturday in June 1974, Jim and Sharon Roberts of Troy, Ohio, noticed something strange when they walked into March's Supermarket to do their weekly shopping: the checkers weren't punching cash register keys; instead, they were sliding each grocery item across a glass window built into some newly installed checkstands.

The Roberts discovered that the National Cash Register Company and March's Supermarkets, Inc., had chosen the Troy store to test a new computer checkout system. This system has two key elements. One element is the Universal Product Code: an inch-square symbol accompanied by ten digits that appears on each grocery item, telling who made the product and what it is. For example, on the label shown here, 20000 is the code for the Green Giant Company, and 11196 is the code for a 16-ounce can of *French Style* Green Beans. The lines above these ten digits are designed to be read by an electronic scanner, which either is built into the checkout counter—the system in the Roberts' store—or is contained in a fountain-pen sized wand the checker waves over the item.

The electronic scanner is part of the second key element in the system—a computer that operates both the electronic cash register and an elaborate inventory control system. A benefit of the system is that grocers will no longer need to mark prices on each of their items. Instead, all the prices will be kept in the store's computer and well be keyed to the Universal Product Code. The checkout register instantaneously looks up the price for each coded item and then rings it up with a short description of that item on a sales-slip tape. At the same time, the register displays the price on a screen for the customer to see. The computer also keeps track of items that are subject to sales tax, to cents-off promotions, and to Sunday sales bans. It can also issue trading stamps and maintain a memory bank of bad checks. This system eliminates the chance for human error at the keys of the traditional cash register. In addition, the computer keeps track of inventories, alerts management to possible shortages, and may even issue a purchase order for additional merchandise.

From this description of the computer checkout system, assess its potential advantages and disadvantages to (1) the supermarket, and (2) the consumer. To compare your answers with the assessments of the supermarkets that are considering buying this system, see the text.

Left: **what your "new" shopping receipt might look like after the computer computes it.** *Right:* **the Universal Product Code on a can of** *French Style* **Green Beans produced by the Green Giant Company.**

✔ **Using computers in business decision making.** In the physical sciences, laboratory experiments are conducted on small models of an operation or process to determine what will happen under certain controlled conditions. The computer has made a similar experimental situation, called *computer simulation,* possible in business. *Computer simulation* involves programming the computer to answer "what if" questions using a *business model*—a representation of some business situation.

For example, suppose an executive of a firm that manufactures a single grocery product wishes to know the impact of variations in three factors on a firm's annual income: (1) the number of cases of the product sold during a year; (2) the price per case; and (3) the dollars to be spent annually in advertising and selling the product. The various revenue and expense items in the income statement and their mathematical relationships (for example, cases sold annually *times* price per case *equals* annual revenue or dollar volume) are written in a computer program. The executive uses an online computer terminal to combine various numerical estimates of these factors and observes their differing impacts on annual profits. In this case, the computer is acting as a giant calculator, incorporating the executive's estimates in a stored program to obtain the projected income statement.

Computer simulation:
answering "what if"
questions

Figure 15-9 illustrates four outputs of a computer simulation in which the executive has allowed only one factor—number of cases sold—to change. In other simulations, the executive may vary another factor or possibly two or more factors at once. Such simulations clarify the profit implications of various factors and help in selecting a future course of action. More elaborate computer simulations can help business managers to assess the impact on profits of a 10 percent wage increase, a 5 percent price increase in raw materials, a change in taxes, and so on.

The Future of EDP and Computers

EDP's future promises to be as revolutionary as its past. In the next few years, computer manufacturers will produce larger and faster machines that are less expensive than current models, as well as computers that are compact enough to fit in a briefcase. Progress is also expected in the area of input media: optical character recognition of handwritten symbols will be perfected; voice recognition is already in the developmental stage. Imagine writing a letter to a computer or talking to a computer telephone operator! The perfection of word-processing techniques will enable an executive to dictate a letter directly to a computer which will address, type, and proofread it in a matter of seconds. Banks are predicting a cashless economy, with computers handling all personal bookkeeping. Consumers will use credit cards to conduct all business

Will computers
read handwriting
and take dictation?

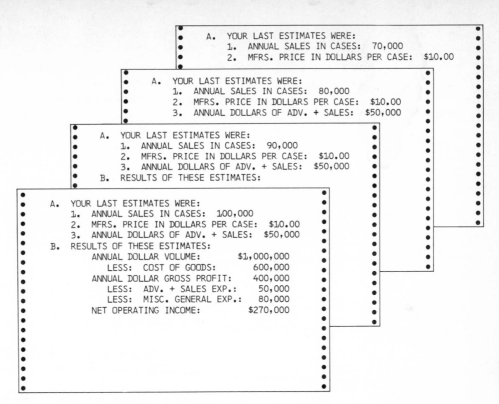

15-9 Computer simulation output obtained by a manager to assess the profitability of a grocery product.

transactions, and stores will use remote online terminals instead of cash registers. A credit card will be placed in the terminal, which will post the information to the customer's bank. The bank account will be updated and payment will be credited to the store's account—all in the same operation. Think of the implications such a system would have for credit investigation, check processing (which would nearly disappear), and mail volume.

We should note, however, that computers are not a panacea for all business problems. Their use must be controlled by the needs of people. Many individuals and groups have rebelled against the prospective "depersonalization" the widespread use of computers may produce. In many cases, too, people are more efficient than computers, especially in utilizing EDP to provide management information. California's Commission for Teacher Preparation and Licensing "fired" its computer on December 31, 1971, pared its staff from 240 to 160, and cut the average processing time for credentials from three months to ten days. *The Wall Street Journal* quotes an official as saying: "The computer was a good worker but just couldn't compete with people."

KEY POINTS TO REMEMBER

1. Industrialization has dramatically increased the need for improved information and communication flow in management decision making. As the scale of business operations grew, data processing using mechanical devices like adding machines, calculators, and typewriters proved time-consuming, inaccurate, and costly.

2. The development of unit-record equipment—processing business data on punched cards—after World War I represented a vast improvement over mechanical data-processing methods.

3. The modern computer has revolutionized data processing by handling the task electronically. The ability of the electronic computer to store a set of problem-solving instructions makes it a unique and powerful device.

4. The electronic digital computer has five main components: input device, memory or storage unit, arithmetic-logic unit, central unit, and output device.

5. In the past 20 years, the number of computer installations in the United States has increased about tenfold.

6. A computer's ability to process data depends on its hardware (its physical components) and on its software (the programs that supply problem-solving instructions to the computer).

7. Computer programming is the task of writing a sequence of instructions to be used by the computer in solving a problem. A flow diagram graphically depicts the sequence of instructions.

8. Today, every American industry utilizes computers—often in ways undreamed of when the first computer was purchased for business use in 1954. Computers are used as general- and special-purpose devices, in batch and online processing modes, and in time sharing.

9. Computer simulation is a technique that involves programming the computer to answer "what if" questions based on business models to assist executives in making business decisions.

10. Exciting opportunities exist for knowledgeable people to provide useful management information by utilizing electronic data processing more effectively.

QUESTIONS FOR DISCUSSION

1. Professor Donald H. Sanders of Texas Christian University identifies nine basic steps in all data processing, including EDP. These steps, in alphabetical order, are calculating, classifying, communicating, originating—recording, reproducing, retrieving, sorting, storing, and summarizing.

(a) Arrange these nine steps in a logical sequence based on how you process data when you solve a problem.

(b) What do you believe is involved in each step?

2. In this chapter, we identified the five principal components of an electronic computer. Match each of the following technical breakthroughs with one of these components or with the entire concept of a computer: (a) typewriter, (b) calculator, (c) analytical engine, (d) punched-card controlled loom, (e) Mark I, and (f) binary arithmetic.

3. What is the difference between the central processing unit and peripheral equipment? What computer conponents does each include?

4. What is the difference between computer hardware and computer software?

5. Referring to the flow diagram for the library problem in Figure 15-6, describe the complete sequence of steps you would follow in each of the following situations:

(a) You have one book on your list and do not find it in the card catalog.

(b) You have three books on your list, find only the second and third books in the author index, and find only the third book in the stacks.

(c) You have four books on your list, find all the call numbers by the most direct route possible, and find all the books in the stacks.

SHORT CASES AND PROBLEMS

1. In our discussion of effective decision making in Chapter 6, we stressed the need to set criteria before making a business decision. Suppose you are the purchasing agent for a small manufacturer that uses unit-record equipment in its administrative record keeping. Someone is trying to sell you a computer to replace your existing equipment. What criteria should you use in comparing the effectiveness of your present equipment to that of the proposed computer?

2. You are looking for information that you believe is in one of three books, and you have ranked these books from most to least likely to contain this information. You go to the library and try to find one of these three books. If a book appears in the card catalog, you immediately go to the stacks to find it and to determine if it contains the required information. You stop your search when you find the right book (which you check out) or when your list is exhausted. Develop a flow diagram to describe your search procedure.

CAREERS IN COMPUTER OPERATIONS

Electronic computer operating personnel execute duties related to the "input," the "operation," and the "output" stages of data processing. **Keypunch operators** transcribe data and programming instructions onto punched cards. **Console operators** feed the coded data into the computer, run the computer, and watch for programming errors or mechanical problems. **Auxiliary equipment operators** translate computer output into intelligible words and numbers. Electronic computer operating personnel are usually high-school graduates who receive on-the-job training. Competent keypunch and auxiliary equipment operators occasionally become console operators; console operators assume some supervisory duties. Annual salaries average $7000 for keypunch and auxiliary operators and $9400 for console operators. With the rapid increase in computer installations, employment opportunities for console and auxiliary operators are expected to be favorable. Demand for keypunch operators will not be as great, since card-punch equipment is becoming obsolete. (*Additional information:* Data Processing Management Association; 505 Busse Highway; Park Ridge, Illinois 60068.)

CAREERS IN PROGRAMMING AND SYSTEMS ANALYSIS

If computers appear to think, it is only because they are following step-by-step instructions that have been prepared by **programmers.** After determining the logical sequence of problem-solving steps in a flow diagram, computer programmers develop detailed instructions for both the computer and the computer operator. Programmers also "debug" instructions by running sample programs through the computer to correct any errors. Educational requirements vary: an engineering or a scientific programmer must have a college education; a business data programmer must usually have a high-school or a two-year college education and subsequent training. Annual salaries range from $8500 to $19,000. Positions in the programming field are expected to increase rapidly. (*Additional information:*

American Federation of Information Processing Societies; 210 Summit Avenue; Montvale, New Jersey 07645.)

Systems analysts plan and assign data processing activities. After precisely defining a data processing problem, an analyst identifies the data that must be obtained and specifies the procedures and equipment that will be used to process that data. Sophisticated techniques like cost accounting and mathematical model building are important tools analysts use to devise efficient data processing systems. Programmers receive their instructions from systems analysts. Employers generally require either a bachelor's degree or a graduate degree in the relevant functional area; occasionally, however, positions are filled by promoting experienced programmers or computer operators. Annual income ranges from $11,000 to $25,000. With the widespread application of data processing systems, employment opportunities for systems analysts are expected to increase rapidly. (*Additional information:* Data Processing Management Association; 505 Busse Highway; Park Ridge, Illinois 60068; and American Federation of Information Processing Societies; 210 Summit Avenue; Montvale, New Jersey 07645.)

CAREERS IN INSTALLATION AND MAINTENANCE

Computer service technicians install and maintain data processing equipment, periodically inspect computer systems, and make any necessary repairs in the event of equipment malfunction. A knowledge of specialized tools and testing devices is essential. Computer service technicians must also review the latest technical information and any revised maintenance procedures. Technician trainee jobs require a high-school education and one or two years of specialized training in electronics or in electrical engineering. Trainee programs consist of formal instruction in mathematics and electronics as well as on-the-job training. Annual salaries range from $7800 for trainees to $16,000 for experienced technicians. Demand for service technicians is expected to accelerate through the mid-1980s. (*Additional information:* Institute of Electrical and Electronic Engineers; 345 East 47th Street; New York, New York 10017.)

A CRITICAL BUSINESS DECISION

THE SITUATION The Hewlett-Packard Company began in a garage in Palo Alto, California. Named after its two founders, William H. Hewlett and David Packard, the company first produced a new audio oscillator. During World War II, Hewlett-Packard developed high-speed microwave instruments "because we didn't know any better," Packard recalls. By the 1950s, a half dozen new electronic products were created each year.

In 1972, William Hewlett conceived the possibility of producing a handheld scientific calculator. The results were spectacular. The HP-35, introduced in 1972 and priced at $395, was an immediate success. The HP-35 eventually generated revenues of $120 million and profits of at least $40 million.

By 1974, a new handheld calculator emerged: the HP-21, with a computational capacity that was approximately equivalent to the HP-35 but produced at such low cost that it could be profitably sold for $125. Simultaneously, Hewlett-Packard began research on a radically new concept—a handheld computer.

Introduced in 1974, the HP-80—a small computer that could be fully programmed—was initially priced at $795. User could either program the HP-80 directly using small punched cards or purchase sets of previously programmed cards from Hewlett-Packard.

THE DECISION It has always been difficult to price high-technology products like calculators and computers. A common pricing strategy popularized by such electronic industrial giants as Texas Instruments and the Digital Equipment Corporation is "experience curve pricing." This approach prices a new product on the basis of the costs the manufacturer expects to incur when the product is mature, when volume is high, and when cost is low. By pricing the product below initial production costs, the manufacturer expects to achieve market dominance before competitors can realize the cost advantages of large-scale production.

But Hewlett-Packard takes a different view. "If you have a new product that makes a contribution," claims Packard, "it's easy to sell all you can produce at a respectable price. Then as you actually achieve cost reductions, you can lower the price accordingly." The HP-35's unexpected success almost forced Hewlett-Packard from its basic philosophy of

David Packard and William R. Hewlett

building new products that were technologically superior and selling them to customers at premium prices. "Somehow we got the idea that market share was an objective," Packard recalls. "I hope that's straightened out. Anyone can build market share, and if you set your prices low enough, you can get the whole damn market. But it won't get you anything around here." To implement its price strategy, Hewlett-Packard actually raised prices while other calculator and minicomputer producers frantically cut their prices in 1973 and 1974. And while other electronics firms cut their research and development expenditures drastically to make ends meet, Hewlett-Packard increased its R&D spending by more than 60 percent.

QUESTIONS

1. Hewlett-Packard has chosen to stress technological innovation to produce premium products that can be sold at relatively high prices. What are some of the advantages and the disadvantages of this strategy?
2. An expert in the electronics field observes that in the industries in which Hewlett-Packard competes "the pioneer has very little lead time now." Do you think a reduction in the length of time that the company can expect to have a technically superior product will affect the success of Hewlett-Packard's strategy of technological innovation and premium prices?

PART FIVE

SMALL BUSINESS

Perhaps the closest many Americans come to doing their own thing is to own and operate a small business. No one doubts that running a small business is exciting and rewarding—or that it is hard work.

Because their fates depend largely on their own efforts, small business owners need a good working knowledge of the functional areas of business discussed earlier, such as management, marketing, accounting, and finance. And they must be willing to spend long hours applying this knowledge to concrete situations.

In Part Five, we will explore both sides of the small-business coin: its rewards and pitfalls; its challenges and demands. A person who is interested in owning a small business must assess the opportunities and the potential market for that business (Chapter 16) and must obtain the funds needed to open and to operate the business effectively (Chapter 17). If, after reading these chapters, you feel that the benefits of independent business ownership are worth its demands and outweigh its risks, then you may be suited to a career in small business.

The essence of the American economic system of private enterprise is free competition, ... [which] cannot be realized unless the actual and potential capacity of small business is encouraged and developed.

U.S. Small Business Act of 1953

CHAPTER **16**

ASSESSING THE OPPORTUNITIES FOR A SMALL BUSINESS

WHAT IS A SMALL BUSINESS?

SELECTING A SMALL BUSINESS
Is Small Business for You?
Choosing a Small Business
Other Factors to Consider in Starting
 a Business

ESTIMATING THE MARKET FOR THE BUSINESS
Finding a Reasonable Location
Judging the Size of the Trading Area
Estimating Sales Revenue

L
ate in 1974, Harry Marcowitz found himself with an impressive title—President of American Hydraulic Paper Cutter, Inc.—and not much else. The corporation consisted of one other employee and a 6000-pound industrial paper-cutting machine Marcowitz had built using $25,000 of his own money. As president of a small, self-owned business, Marcowitz had many attributes: (1) an amazing self-developed mechanical aptitude; (2) a successful 8-year record selling insurance; (3) a solid working knowledge of the new company's target market—the printing and binding industries—based on four years selling and servicing paper cutters; and (4) a good personal reputation.

The president of a firm with one employee

But do all these advantages offset the problems of starting a new business? Marcowitz has two immediate concerns: securing a bank loan to maintain business operations until more paper cutters are constructed, and selling the finished paper cutters to customers. A printing-machine distributor described Marcowitz's dilemma—one that faces many small business owners:

> The main thing will be for Harry to get some machines into commercial operation. That way customers can see how they do. It's kind of a vicious circle—you can't sell many machines unless you've proved they work, and you can't prove they work until you sell some.

It is too early to know whether Marcowitz's firm will prosper. But this example illustrates the challenges facing many small business owners.

Large corporations utilize specialists in each major functional area of business. In stark contrast, small business owners choose independently to manage self-owned businesses and therefore must have some degree of expertise and knowledge in all of these areas. Being a jack-of-all-trades can be challenging and rewarding as well as potentially risky to the small business owner.

The small-business challenge: the chance to be independent and a jack-of-all trades

To help you understand the challenges and pitfalls of small business ownership, in Chapters 16 and 17 we will ask you to assume that you are considering owning and operating your own small retail business. These chapters will provide you with a step by step outline of your activities as a small business owner. You will begin by deciding whether or not to go into business for yourself and will conclude with an evaluation of the performance of your business at the end of two years. For discussion purposes, we will divide the activities in developing and managing a small business into the four steps shown in Figure 16-1. The first two steps—selecting the business and estimating its market—will be covered in this chapter. Financing and operating the business will be discussed in Chapter 17.

You are a prospective small business owner

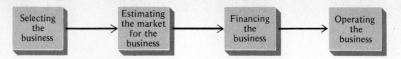

16-1 The four steps in developing and managing a small business.

What is a Small Business?

When people describe a concern as a small business, they generally mean three things: (1) the business is small in size, both in terms of sales dollars and employees; (2) the capital to operate the business is supplied by only one person or by a few people; and (3) the managers of the business (usually a sole proprietorship, a partnership, or a family-owned corporation) are its owners, who are responsible only to themselves and who are independent of a board of directors or a "corporate office."

The question of size deserves special attention here. The U.S. Small Business Administration (SBA), a federal agency created by Congress in 1953 to help small businesses grow and prosper, defines small businesses as:

SBA criteria for a "small business"

1. *Retail or service firms:* Annual sales or receipts of up to $1-5 million, depending on the industry.
2. *Wholesale firms:* Annual sales of up to $5-15 million, depending on the industry.
3. *Construction firms:* Annual sales or receipts of not more than $5 million, averaged over a three-year period.
4. *Manufacturing firms:* Up to 250-1500 employees, depending on the industry.

Firms that conform to these criteria are classified as small businesses and are eligible for loan and management assistance from the SBA.

Small business in the United States is important for two major economic reasons. First, small business is central to the American economy. In 1975, the nation's 5.5 million small businesses accounted for 95 percent of all U.S. businesses and 37 percent of the nation's gross national product. Second, many economists believe that small business has been a major contributor to American economic growth. In a real sense the small business entrepreneur represents the American dream. Sparked by the same innovativeness and competitiveness that inspired Colonel Harland Sanders (who founded the Kentucky Fried Chicken Corporation) or DeWitt and Lila Wallace (who founded *Reader's Digest* on a shoestring budget and who still own *all* of its voting stock), many small business

Why small business is important

owners strive to become giants in their field. In contrast, other small businesses have controlled their growth, deliberately remaining small or moderate in size.

Selecting a Small Business

Finding the right business to own
The first step in developing and managing a small business is choosing the business you wish to operate. To do this, you must answer three questions: (1) Is small business for you?; (2) What business should you choose?; and (3) What other factors should you consider in starting a business (for example, form of ownership, new versus existing businesses, and franchise versus independent operation)?

Is Small Business for You?

To evaluate honestly your interest in owning your own business, you must consider both the attractions and the drawbacks of small business management.

✔ **Attractions of small business.** The attractions of owning your own small business fall into five general categories:

1. *Sense of independence:* You are the person in charge. You report to no one, and you cannot be fired.
2. *Immediate chance for higher income:* You have the opportunity to collect a salary and to obtain a profit or a return on your investment. Profit sharing is generally not possible if you work for someone else.
3. *Long-run pride in and benefits of ownership:* You can build an investment in your firm which may be marketable if you wish to sell it in the future.
4. *Opportunity to be a jack-of-all-trades:* You are not pigeonholed as a salesperson or an accountant. If you choose, you can wear many hats—manager, personnel specialist, salesperson and accountant among them.

Weighing the attractions and . . .
5. *Operating advantages relative to large competitors:* You have the flexibility to react quickly to change and can adapt your operations to local conditions. In contrast, larger competitors are often restricted by procedures developed by a far-removed home office. A small business has definite advantages relative to large competitors when the market is small or highly seasonal, when personalized service is important, or when convenience is essential.

A COMMON SMALL BUSINESS MISERY: THE PLIGHT OF THE NATION'S SOBS
(Sons Of Bosses)

"Listen," declares Richard Pocker of New York, a self-proclaimed SOB who tells it like it is.

I love my dad. He's a terrific guy. But the business wasn't big enough for both of us. . . . So about a year ago, I sent him on a vacation to Europe. While he was there, I called him up on the phone and told him he was fired, that he was out of a job. Wham! That was it. There wasn't much he could do about it.

Sometimes for the sake of the business, its employees, and its customers, turnover in top management is essential. Still, if this seems to be a brutal attitude, remember that Richard Pocker is an SOB. *The Wall Street Journal* observes that Pocker is ". . . not just your average, run-of-the-mill SOB. He's an accomplished SOB. What's more, he wears the title with pride."

These days, the term "SOB" often stands for "son of a boss"—a member of Sons of Bosses International. An SOB is an heir who has taken over or who is likely to take over the control of a family business. Daughters of bosses (DOBs) and sons-in-law of bosses (SLOBs) also qualify for SOB membership.

Meetings of SOB International are held in chapters in 12 states, generally to discuss the common problems its members face. A key issue is to determine how much authority a relative is willing to yield to a family member who joins the business. If the answer is "none," a parting of the ways is inevitable—one way or the other.

Two fine points: Richard Pocker did not fire his father singlehandedly. He seized power with his sister Robin, who is now a full partner in the business. And their father accepted his plight better than most bosses. Why? Because in 1954, he had fired his own father, the founder of the firm.

. . . the drawbacks
of owning
your own business

✔ **Drawbacks of small business.** The attractions of owning a small business must be weighed against certain drawbacks. The more important of these include:

1. *Less independence than you think:* The independence of running a small business is partly illusion. After all, you must satisfy your employees, customers, and creditors, as well as government tax and wage laws. Moreover, your competitors largely dictate when you are open and the prices you charge. Sometimes you may be required to work closely with members of your own family who are also involved in the business; this often presents problems (see "A Common Small Business Misery" above). And, at least at the beginning, you can expect long hours of hard work and few vacations.

2. *Sole responsibility for the business:* Your bad judgment can result in losses to you and to your employees, customers, and creditors. Even if you are a capable business manager, uncontrollable business factors (an economic recession, more efficient competitors, a highway relocation, and so on) can force you into bankruptcy. Generally, you must face these adverse conditions alone.

3. *Continual need to meet financial obligations:* You must be prepared to meet your financial obligations to employees and creditors, to a landlord (if you rent your building) or to a bank (if it holds the mortgage on the building you have purchased), and to tax collectors.

4. *Lack of expertise:* You may be an excellent salesperson but a poor accountant, or vice versa. In either case, your weakness may bring about your downfall. For example, many highly skilled carpenters have started their own businesses after working years for other people. Somewhat dismayed, they find they must spend so much time selling, bidding on new jobs, and scheduling work crews that they have no chance to use their carpentry skills. Suddenly forced to devote most of their time to doing the very things they know the least about, their businesses fail.

5. *Operating disadvantages relative to large competitors:* Large competitors have several advantages over smaller firms: specialists in all business areas; the ability to attract better employees by offering higher wages and greater opportunities for advancement; economies due to large-scale production that may lead to lower prices; and financial resources to weather temporary economic setbacks that might force small businesses into bankruptcy.

After weighing these attractions and drawbacks, Americans establish almost 400,000 new firms every year (most of them small businesses). About 350,000 businesses are discontinued each year, voluntarily or involuntarily; about 10,000 fail due to bankruptcy or the demands of creditors.

Over 90 percent of business failures are the result of managerial inexperience or ineptitude

✔ **Why small businesses fail.** A 1974 survey of almost 10,000 unsuccessful businesses showed why they fail. To compare these reasons with your knowledge of small business operations, see "Why Do You Think Small Businesses Fail?" below. Over 90 percent of American business failures were directly traced to managerial inexperience or ineptitude, as indicated by the top four bars in Figure 16-2. These results followed the "usual pattern," according to the originators of the survey, Dun & Bradstreet, Inc., a firm that has analyzed American business failures for the past century. While managerial inexperience or ineptitude was the underlying cause of over 90 percent of the failures surveyed, immediate

---

WHY DO YOU THINK SMALL BUSINESSES FAIL?

All of us are familiar with retail stores or manufacturing plants that have gone out of business. In some cases, we may have even shopped or worked in businesses that have subsequently failed. Usually, we cannot identify the specific reasons for a particular business failing. Yet, studies identify the following key reasons for small-business failures, listed here in alphabetical order:

Disaster (fire, burglary, strike) _____
Fraud (false financial statement, irregular disposal of assets) _____
Incompetence _____

Lack of general managerial experience _____
Lack of specific experience in the line of business _____
Neglect (poor health, bad habits) _____
Unbalanced experience (lack of well-rounded experience in areas like sales, finance, purchasing) _____

From your experience, rank these causes of business failure from 1 (most important) to 7 (least important). For the actual ranking of these causes in order of importance, see Figure 16-2 and the text.

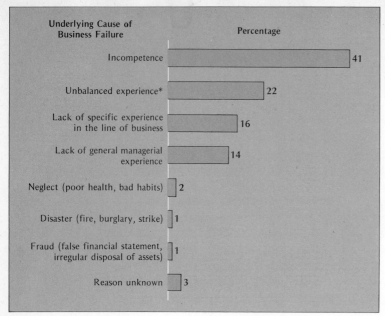

16-2

Underlying causes of failure in 9,915 American business firms in 1974.

Source: *The Business Failure Record: 1974* (New York: Dun & Bradstreet, Inc., 1975) pp. 12–13.

*Lack of well-rounded experience in sales, finance, purchasing, and production on the part of the individual (in the case of a proprietorship) or of two or more partners constituting a managerial unit.

causes among firms in all industries included inadequate sales (cited by 49 percent of the failing firms), competition (23 percent), and heavy operating expenses (16 percent). In addition, manufacturers and wholesalers cited difficulty in collecting accounts receivable as a primary reason for failure; retailers surveyed felt poor location and inventory difficulties were also important factors.

Figure 16-2 shows us that experience in business is not enough. A small-business owner may not have broad enough experience to be familiar with the specialized areas of sales, finance, purchasing, and production. "Typically, the person starting the business is a salesman who doesn't know much about production or an engineer who doesn't know much about sales," observes Rowena Wyatt, Vice President of the Business Economics Division of Dun & Bradstreet, Inc. Or the owner may have had little actual work experience in management in the firm's specific line of business.

The Dun & Bradstreet survey and other similar studies reveal some interesting points about a new business's chances of success. First, survival rates vary among industries. Wholesale firms have the best survival rate, followed by real estate, finance, construction, and manufacturing firms. Service trades (such as appliance repair, dry-cleaning, and beauty shops) have a below-average survival record, and retailers have the worst survival record.

Continued survival
varies with industry,
business area, and
length of operation

Second, rates vary among businesses within a specific industry. In 1974, the failure rates per thousand for six different types of retailing firms were:

Line of business	Failures per thousand
Men's ready-to-wear clothing	7.3
Women's ready-to-wear clothing	6.2
Sporting goods	5.7
Cameras and photographic supplies	4.9
Shoes	3.7
Groceries, meats and produce	1.2

Thus, a women's ready-to-wear retailer was five times as likely to fail as a grocery store.

Finally, a firm's chances of success improve as the business ages. Chances are about five in ten that a firm will be sold or liquidated before its second birthday and about nine in ten that it will change hands or cease to operate before its tenth birthday. Generally, firms that endure longer provide their owners with higher and more stable incomes than firms that change hands or are liquidated.

↙ **Could you be a small business owner?** To determine whether you are the type of person to own and operate a small business, you must assess your strong and weak points objectively. Be truthful: after all, you are going to be your most valuable employee.

The U.S. Small Business Administration has developed several checklists like the one in Figure 16-3 to help people decide whether they are suited to small business ownership. The rating chart in Figure 16-3 is in no sense a scientific or a psychological test. Its purpose is to encourage you to focus your attention on your own personality traits somewhat more vividly than you normally would.

Now, try rating yourself before you read further. You might also have a friend ask several people who know you well to rate you anonymously. You may be startled by the results. Of course, no appraisal by yourself or by anyone else is a guarantee that you will succeed or fail as a small business owner. But the evaluation in Figure 16-3 should give you a general idea of your *potential* for success or failure. Moving from left to right, assign values of 4, 3, 2, and 1 to the four columns in Figure 16-3 and to the respective boxes you checked in each column. Then total your score. A rough estimate of your potential for owning and operating your own successful small business are: excellent (25-28), very good (21-24), good (17-20), fair (13-16), or poor (12 or less).

In assessing
your personal traits,
don't kid yourself!

Be sure to answer the questions honestly. If you recognize your weaknesses, you can compensate for them by finding partners or employees who are strong in the areas in which you are not. However, if you have too many marks on the right-hand side of Figure 16-3, it is possible that you are not suited to small business ownership.

16-3 Evaluate yourself as a small business owner. For each trait listed below, check the box that you feel best describes your personality. Then see the text to find out how to rate your evaluation.

	☐	☐	☐	☐
Initiative	Seeks additional tasks; highly ingenious.	Resourceful; alert to opportunities.	Performs regular work without direction.	Routine worker; awaits direction.
Attitude toward others	Positive; friendly interest in people.	Pleasant, polite.	Sometimes difficult to work with.	Can be quarrelsome or uncooperative.
Leadership	Forceful; inspires confidence and loyalty.	Order giver.	Driver.	Follower.
Responsibility	Welcomes responsibility.	Accepts without protest.	Unwilling to assume without protest.	Avoids whenever possible.
Organizing ability	Highly capable of perceiving and arranging fundamentals in logical order.	Able organizer.	Fairly capable of organizing.	Poor organizer.
Decisiveness	Quick and accurate.	Good and careful.	Quick, but often unsound.	Hesitant and fearful.
Perseverance	Highly steadfast in purpose; not easily discouraged by obstacles.	Maintains steady effort.	Average determination and persistence.	Little or no persistence.

Source: Adapted from Wendell O. Metcalf, *Starting and Managing a Small Business of Your Own*, second edition (Washington, D.C.: U.S. Small Business Administration, 1962), p. 4.

Choosing a Small Business

We will assume that you have passed the checklist quiz to your own satisfaction and that you are convinced you want to own your own business. Now, what business should you choose? Three important factors should influence your decision:

1. *Your own background and experience:* Match what you like to do

with what you are able to do well, as indicated by your past education, part-time and full-time work experience, and hobbies.

Factors to consider in choosing a small business

2. *Present and future customer needs:* Will consumers want what you have to sell? Will they continue to buy your product in the future under different economic conditions?

3. *The degree of competition:* Are competing products so good or so firmly entrenched that customers won't purchase your product? Is the competition likely to change in the future?

Assume that your work experience included a part-time job in a small shoe store when you were in high school. Your duties were to wait on customers and to maintain a stock inventory. After high school, you worked in the same store for two years on a full-time basis to earn enough money to go to college. During that time, you kept inventory records and helped the owner decide what shoe styles to stock. You believe that you have a knack for buying shoes that meet customer needs. From your research, you discover that shoe purchases increase with population and income although not as dramatically as luxuries like sporting goods purchases. But the figures cited on page 425 show that recently sporting goods stores have been failing at a higher rate than shoe stores—a possible indication of degree of competition.

You're going into the shoe business

You have made your decision to open a retail store that carries shoes for the entire family.

Other Factors to Consider in Starting a Business

For simplicity, we will assume that you make three other important decisions before starting your business. First, you recognize that while you have experience in buying and selling, you know little about accounting and finance. You have a friend who is an able accountant and who is willing to work for you part time in return for a share of the profits. Thus, after considering the advantages of the various forms of business ownership (see Chapter 2) and consulting with a lawyer, you decide to operate as a corporation. Next, after checking available shoe stores to determine sales prices and after considering the pros and cons of starting a new business versus buying an existing one (see discussion question 2 at the end of this chapter), you decide to open your own store. Finally,

Other important decisions are necessary

rather than operate as a franchised shoe store, you elect to operate as an independent store. The potential advantages and disadvantages of a franchised operation will become more apparent later in this discussion; franchising will be covered in Chapter 17, both in the text and in the Critical Business Decision. The name you have chosen for your new business is Family Shoe Store, Inc.

Estimating the Market for the Business

Estimating the market (the annual sales revenue expected) for a business is the second major step toward managing your own business. This step involves answering three important questions:

1. How do you find a reasonable store location?
2. How do you judge the size of the store's trading area?
3. How do you estimate the store's annual sales revenue?

Finding a Reasonable Location

✔ Locational factors. For many retailers, the proper store location is the difference between success and failure. One of the most important locational factors to consider is the number of potential customers in the area to be served by your store. Do enough people live or work near the area who will pass by your store? Do they have enough income to buy what you sell? What has happened to population and income in the past, and what is likely to happen to these factors in the future?

Do enough customers want to buy what you're selling?

In a study of business failures for the Small Business Administration, Kurt B. Mayer and Sidney Goldstein cite two small restaurants in Rhode Island that went bankrupt because of a failure to recognize customer taste. Greco's Restaurant, which offered a variety of Italian dishes, was located in a solid, middle-income neighborhood; but its residents were primarily of Swedish ancestry. Neighborhood residents stopped eating at Greco's once the novelty of the Italian restaurant wore off because they preferred their own style of cooking. The venture failed in ten months. Mangia's Pizza House, located in the heart of a Jewish neighborhood, met disaster for the same reason. Despite such failures, some entrepreneurs have demonstrated their uncanny ability to broaden the ethnic food market. One small manufacturer, Jeno Palucci, became a millionaire selling Chinese food (under the Chun King brand name) to Americans across the country. Palucci has since sold Chun King and is now well on the way to making another million offering Italian pizza to Britons in English pubs.

Do competitive stores do an adequate job?

Another critical locational factor is competition. Are there nearby competitors? Do they service customers in the area adequately? Are more competitors expected in the future? An SBA case study of a small grocery illustrates a flagrant disregard of the competition. Within one and a half blocks of the new grocery, there were two small groceries, one medium-size grocery, and a supermarket. The new store failed in six weeks.

It is also important to consider the physical factors of the potential site for your store. Will the street or highway on which the store is to be located provide adequate access to the store? (Either too low or too high a traffic volume can present problems.) Are highways likely to be relocated in the future, thereby affecting access to the store? Do barriers such as freeways, lakes, or rivers limit the geographic market area? Will present or future changes in local zoning laws alter the residential or commercial composition of the area?

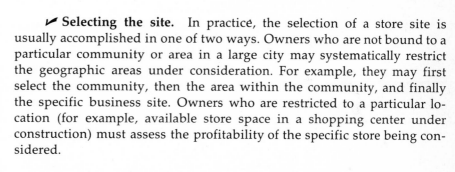

Are there physical or geographic factors that may affect sales?

In another SBA case study, Mayer and Goldstein cite the example of George Elm and Ed Burns, who purchased a service station located near a stoplight on a main street. George and Ed never achieved their goal of building a neighborhood clientele by offering high-quality service. Shortly before the purchase, an expressway was completed nearby. Heavy traffic passed down the main street only during rush hours, but people were reluctant to pull into the station then because it was too hard to get back into the oncoming traffic. The expressway diverted most of the traffic during the rest of the day. George and Ed's station closed after three months.

Answers to the questions posed above can be found by referring to U.S. census data, by consulting state and local agencies (such as highway departments, chambers of commerce, and planning commissions), and by talking with local residents throughout the area to be served by the store.

✔ **Selecting the site.** In practice, the selection of a store site is usually accomplished in one of two ways. Owners who are not bound to a particular community or area in a large city may systematically restrict the geographic areas under consideration. For example, they may first select the community, then the area within the community, and finally the specific business site. Owners who are restricted to a particular location (for example, available store space in a shopping center under construction) must assess the profitability of the specific store being considered.

✔ **Your own site decision.** Assume you live in an urban area that houses both low-income and middle-income families. The area has few existing retail outlets and is undergoing redevelopment. A vacant city block in the area is being considered as a possible site for a small shopping center that will contain 10-20 stores; a family shoe store has been suggested for the center. You must appraise the site as a potential location for your new business.

You're considering locating your store in a shopping center

Checking reveals that a location in a shopping center has some important advantages. In particular, a center generates more prospective customers because a broad range of stores serves more consumer needs. A shopping center also attracts customers from longer distances. Finally, stores in a center can coordinate advertising and promotional activities.

The disadvantages of a shopping-center location include the need to make your outside decor compatible with the motif of the entire center and the need to pay your share of common area costs (maintenance of parking and mall areas) and advertising activities.

On balance, you conclude that locating your store in a shopping center warrants serious consideration, and you decide to analyze the opportunity further.

Judging the Size of the Trading Area

The *trading area* of a retail store or of a shopping center is the geographic region from which the store or center draws most of its customers and obtains most of its sales revenue. The trading area varies with (1) the size of the store or center, and (2) the kinds of goods sold. For example, a regional shopping center that contains 100 stores may attract customers within a radius of 25 miles; a neighborhood grocery will probably obtain most of its sales from customers within a three-block radius. Similarly, stores selling shopping or specialty items such as dresses or sporting goods may attract customers for miles; stores selling convenience items such as bakery goods usually draw sales from a maximum distance of only a few blocks.

The trading area: from what distance can you attract customers?

✔ **Factors affecting the trading area of a store.** Given a particular type and size of store, what factors determine the size of its trading area? One factor is the natural barriers to customer travel (lakes, rivers, mountains) or the constructed boundaries (limited-access thruways, railroad tracks, parks). Another consideration is the mobility of potential customers: Do they travel primarily in private cars or on public transportation? In lower-income areas where mobility is generally restricted, the size of the trading area may be reduced. A final factor is the location of competitors who offer the same goods or services and whether they serve customer needs adequately.

Physical barriers, customer mobility, and competition affect the trading area

✔ **Your store's trading area.** You conclude that a shopping-center location should provide a larger trading area for your shoe store. Normally, a small neighborhood shopping center of 10 or 15 stores draws customers from a maximum distance of about a mile. Figure 16-4 locates your store's shopping center in the general area from which it expects to draw customers. The numbers on the map are census tracts established by the U.S. Bureau of the Census. Each tract encompasses an area of 30 to 50 city blocks that has six to eight blocks on each side.

A detailed analysis of these census tracts can determine the appropriate boundaries of your store's trading area. To the west, the trading area is bounded by a park and a golf course, barriers that will virtually eliminate customer access to the shopping center. To the north a shopping center comparable to the proposed neighborhood center is located along

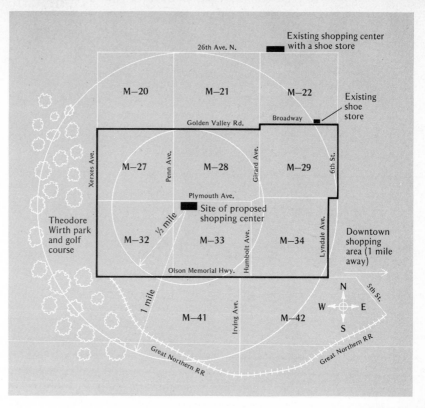

16-4 Census tracts surrounding the proposed shopping center that is being considered as a location for Family Shoe Store, Inc. The trading area to be served by the shopping center is outlined in black.

Specifics:
the trading area
for your shoe store

26th Avenue North, effectively eliminating census tracts M-20, M-21, and M-22 from your trading area. In addition, a small shoe store is located on Broadway on the northern boundary of census tract M-29, and this store will probably reduce sales to shoppers living in that tract. To the east lie competing stores in the downtown area about a mile away and few permanent residents in areas east of census tracts M-29 and M-34; this makes Lyndale Avenue and 6th Street the eastern boundary of your trading area. To the south, the heavily traveled Olson Memorial Highway is a significant travel barrier to residents in tracts M-41 and M-42. It is also possible that the highway may be upgraded to a limited-access thruway, which would make it even more difficult for your store to attract shoppers from these two census tracts. Even though there are no shoe stores in these tracts, it is safe to assume that the Olson Memorial Highway is the southern boundary of your trading area; sales may be generated south of the highway, but it will be unwise to depend on them.

In summary, the trading area for your shoe store is represented by the six census tracts outlined in black in Figure 16-4.

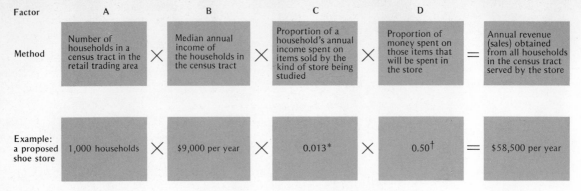

Factor	A		B		C		D		
Method	Number of households in a census tract in the retail trading area	×	Median annual income of the households in the census tract	×	Proportion of a household's annual income spent on items sold by the kind of store being studied	×	Proportion of money spent on those items that will be spent in the store	=	Annual revenue (sales) obtained from all households in the census tract served by the store
Example: a proposed shoe store	1,000 households	×	$9,000 per year	×	0.013*	×	0.50†	=	$58,500 per year

16-5 A method for estimating the annual sales revenue a retail store will obtain in a specific census tract.

Source: Adapted from William Rudelius et al., "Assessing Retail Opportunities in Low-Income Areas," *Journal of Retailing* (Fall 1972), pp. 96-114.

Estimating Sales Revenue

Market size: how much revenue can you expect?

In Chapter 7, we learned that consumer demand in the marketplace depends on (1) people, (2) income, and (3) a desire to buy. To estimate the market size in terms of annual dollars of sales revenue expected, we must find a systematic method to translate these concepts of consumer demand into meaningful numbers.

✔ **A practical method to estimate a retail store's sales revenue.** Figure 16-5 illustrates a method for estimating market size and defines the four factors necessary to estimate the sales revenue a new store will obtain from a specific census tract in its trading area. Note that three of the factors are based on secondary data and that one is based on primary data. The factors and sources of data are:

Factor A: Number of households in a census tract in the retail trading area (secondary data from the *U.S. Census of Population and Housing*).

Factor B: Median annual income of the households in the census tract (secondary data from the *U.S. Census of Population and Housing*).

Factors determining sales revenue

Factor C: Proportion of a household's annual income spent on items sold by the kind of store being studied (secondary data from sources such as the U.S. Bureau of Labor Statistics and the Conference Board).

Factor D: Proportion of factor C—money spent on items sold by the kind of store being studied—that will be spent in the proposed store (primary data from personal interviews with residents to determine the extent to which they intend to make purchases at the proposed store).

Multiplying the four factors together (see the lower part of Figure 16-5) yields the annual sales revenue your prospective shoe store can expect from all the households in a census tract in its retail trading area.

✔ **Your store's sales revenues.** Now we will apply the general method described in Figure 16-5 to estimating the annual revenue for your family shoe store. A worksheet for this estimate appears in Figure 16-6. The sources of secondary data for factors A, B, and C identified above are readily available.

The best way to obtain estimates of factor D (the proportion of annual personal expenditures on shoes that your store can expect) is to conduct interviews with residents in the area to be served by the store. Personal interviews can be costly and time-consuming, but they can also provide prospective store owners with valuable information on the general shipping problems of area residents and the likely expenditures of individual families in the proposed stores. In addition, neighborhood surveys can give store owners insights into the special circumstances of area residents, such as the availability of private versus public transportation for shopping trips.

Estimating the annual sales revenue for your store

16-6 Worksheet for estimating the annual sales revenue of Family Shoe Store, Inc.

Worksheet for Estimating The Annual Sales Revenue of Family Shoe Store, Inc.

(1) Census tract in the trading area	(2) Number of households in the census tract (factor A)	(3) Typical (median) annual household income (factor B)	(4) Total personal income (column 2 × column 3)	(5) Proportion of household's annual income spent in shoe stores (factor C)	(6) Personal consumption expenditures in shoe stores (column 4 × column 5)	(7) Proportion of column 6 captured by proposed shoe store (factor D)	(8) Estimated annual sales revenue of proposed shoe store (column 6 × column 7)
M-27	1,110	$6,569	$7,291,590	0.013	$94,791	0.35	$33,177
M-28	938	$5,155	$4,835,390	0.013	$62,860	0.40	$25,144
M-29	1,047	$2,822	$2,954,634	0.013	$38,410	0.30	$11,523
M-32	801	$8,443	$6,762,843	0.013	$87,917	0.45	$39,563
M-33	982	$4,660	$4,576,120	0.013	$59,490	0.45	$26,771
M-34	777	$1,936	$1,504,272	0.013	$19,556	0.40	$7,822
Total	5,655	—	$27,924,849	—	$363,024	—	$144,000

Source: Adapted from Robert F. Hoel et al., *A Neighborhood Shopping Center in North Minneapolis: An Economic Analysis* (Minneapolis: University of Minnesota, College of Business Administration, 1970), p. 171; and *Retail Location Manual: Small Businesses in Low-Income Areas*, Vol. I (Chicago: Retail Estate Research Corporation, 1967).

If it is too difficult or time-consuming to obtain personal estimates of factor D, Delphi estimates or individual judgments may be used. However, care must be taken to avoid overoptimistic estimates, particularly if a store must capture a large percentage of sales from a particular census tract to be successful. Customers are so mobile today that few stores can hope to penetrate more than 50 percent of the market in a particular census tract. Depending on too high a sales percentage may result in overestimating the actual revenues once a store is in operation.

As the worksheet in Figure 16-6 shows, the estimated annual sales revenue for your family shoe store will be about $144,000. But is this a large enough annual revenue to make your business profitable? To answer this question, you must estimate your store's operating costs — one of the topics we will discuss in Chapter 17.

KEY POINTS TO REMEMBER

1. The term "small business" generally implies that: (a) a concern is relatively small in size; (b) its capital is provided by only one or a few people; (c) its owner-managers are independent of a "corporate office."
2. There are 5.5-million small businesses in the United States. Small business is a major contributor to the nation's growth.
3. Owning and operating their own businesses gives many individuals the opportunity to be independent and to be jacks-of-all-trades. The drawbacks of small-business ownership include being totally responsible for the business and for meeting continuous financial obligations.
4. In the 1970s, more than 90 percent of American business failures were directly traceable to managerial inexperience or ineptitude.
5. The first step in developing and managing your own business is twofold: (a) determining if you are suited to small-business ownership, and (b) finding a small business that makes the best use of your talents and interests.
6. The second step involves estimating the market — the annual sales revenue — for your proposed store. To do this, you must (a) select a store site; (b) estimate the boundaries of your store's trading area; and (c) project your store's annual sales revenue.

QUESTIONS FOR DISCUSSION

1. We saw in this chapter that each year about 350,000 businesses in the United States cease operations, either voluntarily or involuntarily.
   (a) List some of the reasons that Dun & Bradstreet cites for business failure?

(b) How can prospective business owners reduce the chances of failure before they begin new business ventures?

2. What are (a) the potential advantages and (b) the potential disadvantages of buying an existing retail business?

3. What three factors should you consider in selecting a location for a retail store? What additional factors would you consider in selecting a location for a manufacturing plant? What is the relative importance of the factors you cited for a retail store as opposed to those you cited for a manufacturing plant.

4. In estimating the market for a small shoe store, we focused on sales to local residents and largely neglected sales to people employed in the area and to those driving past the store. What kinds and locations of stores would be important to people who are employed in the store area or who drive by the store?

5. In Figure 16-6 the proportions for factor D (dollar expenditures on shoes by families in the trading area that the proposed shoe store expects to capture) vary by census tract. Based on the information in this chapter and on the map in Figure 16-4, explain these proportional variations.

SHORT CASES AND PROBLEMS

1. Data collected from personal interviews are used in estimating a retail store's potential sales.
   (a) How would you phrase an interview question in order to obtain information about factor D from potential customers living in the trading area to be served by your shoe store?
   (b) What potential biases do you think will be present in the answers to your question?

2. The choice-selection method, discussed in Chapter 6, involves analyzing both the alternatives and the uncertainties related to a particular problem. Suppose you are trying to decide whether to own and operate a retail shoe store or a TV-appliance store for the next five years. You conclude that the profitability of the store depends significantly on whether the economy is mainly in a boom or in a recessionary period. Your five-year payoff table of profits is:

	Outcome State	
Alternative	O_1: Mainly a boom period	O_2: Mainly a recessionary period
A_1: Operate shoe store	$60,000	$50,000
A_2: Operate TV-appliance store	$90,000	$30,000

Economists project a 60-percent likelihood of a boom period and a 40-percent likelihood of a recessionary period during the next five years. Use the choice-selection method to decide which store you should own and operate to maximize your expected profits.

CAREER SELECTION: POSITIONS IN CONSTRUCTION AND DECORATING LEADING TO SMALL–BUSINESS OWNERSHIP

While some people in construction and in the construction-related trades are employed by builders or by large organizations, thousands are self-employed small businessmen and businesswomen.

CONSTRUCTION CAREERS

Carpenters perform a variety of tasks for contractors and homebuilders that range from erecting wood frameworks and scaffolding to installing windows and hardwood floors. A substantial number of carpenters are self-employed either on a permanent or on a temporary basis. Carpenters are generally high-school graduates who learn most of their skills on the job. Four-year apprenticeship programs provide the novice with practical experience and with formal instruction in mathematics and drafting. Annual salaries vary: apprentices average $7800; journeyman carpenters, about $15,600. The job market for carpenters is expected to expand moderately as construction activities continue to increase. (*Additional information:* Associated General Contractors of America, Inc.; 1957 E Street, N.W.; Washington, D.C. 20006.)

Electricians install electrical systems and electrical machinery. They are often hired by construction firms, although self-employed contractors represent a substantial minority. Electricians must be high-school graduates; a supplemental background in electronics from either a correspondence or a technical school is common. Successful applicants are placed in four-year apprenticeship programs, consisting of on-the-job training and formal instruction in mathematics, blueprint reading, and electrical theory. Most cities require electricians to pass a state examination to obtain a license. Annual income ranges from $8000 for an apprentice to $17,000 for a master electrician. Because of an increase in construction activities and a greater consumer and industrial reliance on electrical equipment, job opportunities are expected to expand rapidly. (*Additional information:* International Brotherhood of Electrical Workers; 1125 15th Street, N.W.; Washington, D.C. 20005.)

Plumbers install and repair pipe systems and plumbing appliances. Most plumbers are employed by plumbing contractors, although many are self-employed. Plumbers are usually high-school graduates who have backgrounds in mathematics, physics, and chemistry. Many employers provide five-year apprenticeship programs, combining on-the-job training and courses in drafting and applied physics and chemistry. Most cities require plumbers to pass a state examination to obtain a license. Mechanical aptitude and physical dexterity are mandatory. Annual income varies: trainees average $8000; master plumbers, about $17,000. Job opportunities are expected to expand moderately due to an increase in construction activities and to a greater consumer demand for household appliances. (*Additional information:* National Association of Plumbing-Heating-Cooling Contractors; 1016 20th Street, N.W.; Washington, D.C. 20036.)

Roofers install asphalt, metal, tile, and slate roofs and waterproof and dampproof walls, tanks, and swimming pools. Roofers must have physical stamina and good balance! Some roofers are self-employed, but most work for roofing contractors. Employers provide three-year apprenticeship programs, offering on-the-job training and instruction in both mathematics and blueprint reading. Yearly salaries average $10,000 for apprentices and $15,000 for journeymen. Employment opportunities are expected to expand moderately due to an increase in construction activities. (*Additional information:* National Roofing Contractors Association; 1515 North Harlem Avenue; Oak Park, Illinois 60302.)

Plasterers finish internal and external walls by applying cement, stucco, or fire-resistant coatings. They are also qualified to perform decorative and ornamental tasks. Most plasterers are high-school graduates who have acquired necessary experience either from formal apprenticeship programs or from informal on-the-job training programs. Self-employed plasterers benefit from general business courses as well as from specialized instruction in drafting and in mathematics. Physical stamina and manual dexterity are essential. Apprentices earn about $8000 a year; experienced plasterers, about $16,000. An increase in construction activities is expected to lead to a moderate expansion in the demand for plasterers. (*Additional information:* Bricklayers, Masons, and Plasters' International Union of America; 815 15th Street, N.W.; Washington, D.C. 20005.)

DECORATING CAREERS

Both **painters** and **paperhangers** apply finishes to walls, but they work with different materials: painters use varnishes and paints; paperhangers use wallpaper, vinyl, and other materials. Painters and paperhangers learn their craft by experience, either from formal, three-year apprenticeship programs or from informal on-the-job training programs. Apprenticeship programs provide courses in paint chemistry, color harmony, and cost estimating. Painters and paperhangers must be in good physical condition and must have good color vision. Annual salaries are approximately the same for both crafts: apprentices earn about $8000; experienced craftsmen, about $15,000. The job market for painters and paperhangers is expected to expand moderately with the anticipated increase in construction activities. (*Additional information:* International Brotherhood of Painters and Allied Trades; 1925 K Street, N.W.; Washington, D.C. 20006.)

A CRITICAL BUSINESS DECISION

—made by Berry Gordy, Jr.

THE SITUATION In August 1975, recording star Stevie Wonder signs a seven-year contract for $13 million with Motown, the largest black-owned U.S. recording company.

But such million-dollar contracts have not always been easy for Motown or for its board chairman, Berry Gordy, Jr., to land. In 1953, after an Army stint, Gordy opened a record shop in Detroit, using his personal savings and a loan from his father. Gordy featured jazz records, but consumer taste at that time was leaning toward the newly arrived rhythm-and-blues recording style. His business went bankrupt in two years, and Gordy worked for his father as a plasterer.

Unhappy as a plasterer, Gordy tried his hand at songwriting. A few of his tunes were produced by major recording companies, but their renditions often varied markedly from Gordy's original ideas. The next step? Tired of being a hungry songwriter, Gordy decided to become an independent producer.

In 1960, Gordy joined forces with another songwriter, William "Smokey" Robinson, to write "Shop Around." When that song was recorded in 1961, Motown was on its way to its first million-record seller. The ultimate result: Motown Record Corporation and its "Motown Sound."

By the 1970s, Motown had become a multimillion dollar corporation. The names of many of its recording artists—Stevie Wonder, Diana Ross, Smokey Robinson and the Miracles, the Supremes, the Temptations, and the Jackson 5, among them—were internationally known. The company was also producing television specials and films like "Lady Sings the Blues," for which Diana Ross won an Academy Award nomination for best actress.

THE DECISION Journalist Herschel Johnson notes that "these feats were largely accomplished through Gordy's firm business sense and his almost clairvoyant ability to spot talent in Detroit's inner city and to develop it." Being able to recognize which songs and which artists are likely to succeed is critical in the recording business. This is especially true for Motown, since, although extremely successful, it is still a small firm in a $3-billion record industry dominated by two giants: RCA Victor and Columbia. Yet, Motown has always been at or near the top of the industry in terms of the percentage of its releases that have become strong sellers. For example, in 1973, three-fourths of Motown's 75 singles and two-thirds of its 46 albums reached the national charts and were considered hits.

A key decision illustrates Gordy's and Motown's good business judgment. In the 1970s, the recording business thrives on album sales, which represent 78 percent of total industry sales. Yet, Motown enjoys the unique position of selling a greater number of single records than any other company—even giant competitors like RCA Victor and Columbia. Motown's goal is to maintain its leadership position in single-record sales while increasing its album sales.

Singer Diana Ross and Motown Chairman Berry Gordy, Jr. discuss an upcoming recording session.

QUESTION

If you were Berry Gordy, Jr., what strategy would you use to capitalize on Motown's strength in single-record sales in order to sell more albums?

Work don't hurt nobody — work is
wonderful for you. You'll rust out
quicker'n you'll wear out.

Colonel Harland Sanders
(at the age of 80)

FINANCING
AND OPERATING
A SMALL BUSINESS

Colonel Sanders often gives this piece of advice. It is probably just what the Colonel was thinking when he took the first $105-social security check he received after retirement to start a "little business" of his own. And before long, the Colonel had acquired substantially more than $105 to finance and operate the little business, which is known today as Kentucky Fried Chicken.

In Chapter 16, you chose a small business and analyzed the market for your store at a specific site. Now you must obtain adequate financing in order to open your store and to operate it effectively. In this chapter, we will focus on the major activities involved in financing and operating a small business. In a concluding section, we will identify the various sources of financial and management assistance that are available to small business owners.

Financing a Small Business

Financing—the third step in developing and managing a small business—involves answering two important questions:

1. How do you estimate the cash needs of your business?
2. After estimating your cash needs, how do you obtain funds?

A business must carefully estimate its cash needs before borrowing

A prospective small business owner who does not know how to estimate cash needs may try to borrow funds from a bank or from the U.S. Small Business Administration (SBA) before making any financial projections. In such cases, banking or SBA personnel will assist in estimating cash needs. However, business owners who develop careful estimates of their cash needs before attempting to secure their loans can greatly enhance their chances of receiving the necessary funds. Lending officers invariably require sound, formalized financial estimates before they consider loan requests, and detailed financial plans are convincing evidence that potential retailers have thoroughly investigated their business opportunities. Persons starting a new business as a franchisee of a national chain of stores receive special planning assistance from the chain. An example of what a McDonald's franchisee gets and gives appears on the next page.

WHAT A McDONALD'S FRANCHISEE GETS—AND GIVES

If you are thinking of going into your own business, you should probably consider the possibility of owning a franchised outlet. Some important appeals of being a franchisee lie in the two areas we will cover in this chapter: financing and operating the business. As an example, we can identify the key commitments a franchisee (1) *gets* from signing a franchise agreement to operate a restaurant for the McDonald's hamburger chain, and (2) *gives* to the corporation in return.

What a Franchisee Gets

A person franchised (or licensed) to operate a McDonald's restaurant gets the following assistance from the corporation:

1. A location selected by McDonald's real estate department, using scientific methods.
2. Supervision of the building of the restaurant by McDonald's construction department.
3. A 19-day course at McDonald's "Hamburger University" outside Chicago that provides training in every operational and managerial

phase of the business. This is supplemented with periodic regional seminars for existing owners, plus detailed operating manuals and training materials.
4. Assistance in finding qualified suppliers and in obtaining price savings through volume-buying contracts.
5. Visits by field consultants at regular intervals. Also, telephone assistance is available from regional offices, which are staffed by experts in purchasing, personnel, training, and advertising.
6. Advertising materials supplied at McDonald's printing costs.

What a Franchisee Gives

In return for the benefits received from McDonald's, a franchisee's obligations include:

1. To obtain at least $120,000 to start the business (the estimated total cost of a McDonald's License and Lease). At least $76,500 of this must be in cash to cover site selection and development ($2500), an exclusive license that includes assistance in obtaining supplies and opening the unit ($10,000), security deposit against the lease ($15,000), and a cash down payment for lighting, signs, food-service equipment, and landscaping ($49,000).
2. To obtain necessary financing on the franchisee's own credit rating.
3. To pay the McDonald's Corporation 3 percent of monthly net-gross sales as a service fee and 8.5 percent of monthly net-gross sales in rental. McDonald's defines net-gross sales as total sales *less* any local and state sales tax deductions.
4. To spend 4 percent of net-gross sales on advertising.
5. To spend at least 100 hours working in a McDonald's restaurant before taking the 19-day course at Hamburger University.

And what does all this mean to a McDonald's franchisee? Only about 1 percent of McDonald's licensees have had prior association with the food industry. Yet the pretax margins of well-run McDonald's stores run from 12 to 15 percent of sales. Licensees normally pay off their original investments in three to five years, and some older stores have gross sales in excess of $1,000,000 annually.

Estimating Cash Needs

Financial planning involves budgeted financial statements

As we saw in Chapter 12, one aspect of obtaining financial resources involves estimating the financial needs of the firm. For a small business, three financial statements that are used in financial planning require emphasis: (1) the budgeted income statement; (2) the budgeted balance sheet; and (3) the cash budget. Each of these plans should be prepared for at least the first two years of business operation to protect the original cash investment in the firm. In the following section we will examine the general methods and the sources of data used in developing budgeted financial statements, and we will analyze the three plans that you and your accounting partner might develop for Family Shoe Store, Inc.

✔ **Methods and data sources.** For the sake of simplicity, we will analyze each of the three budgeted financial statements in sequence. In practice, however, all three plans are prepared simultaneously in trial-and-error fashion and necessary tradeoffs are made to develop a satisfactory overall financial plan.

Financial ratios permit comparisons with similar firms

In developing a budgeted income statement and a balance sheet for a new firm, a business owner should first examine the achievements of firms of similar size in the same business. Established industry patterns are generally expressed in terms of standard income statements and balance sheets and their related financial ratios. Income statements provide some very useful financial ratios that designate various costs as percentages of net sales revenue. Other financial ratios, such as net profit on tangible net worth, are calculated by combining data from income statements and balance sheets. Both kinds of ratios can be used to relate the operations of one firm to those of similar businesses. Standard operating ratios are published by various trade associations, government agencies, banks, and research departments of industrial firms and universities. Among the best-known sources are Dun & Bradstreet, Robert Morris Associates, the Accounting Corporation of America, and the National Cash Register Company. Figure 17-1 summarizes some important financial ratios for shoe stores developed by Dun & Bradstreet. Individual firms may vary significantly from industry standards, but average financial ratios provide useful benchmarks for the potential small business owner.

✔ **Your store's budgeted income statement.** The budgeted or projected income statement measures the profitability of a business and its ability to continue as a going concern. A potential business owner should develop a budgeted income statement carefully. A plan that fails to indicate that a firm can operate profitably will either be rejected by a bank or

17-1 Financial ratios for a sample of retail shoe stores, 1972.

Description	Financial Ratio*		
	Bottom quarter of firms (lower quartile)	Most typical firms (median)	Top quarter of firms (upper quartile)
Current ratio: Current assets are *divided by* current liabilities	2.07	2.76	5.09
Net profits on net sales: Net earnings after taxes are *divided by* net sales (sales *less* returns, allowances, and cash discounts).	0.59%	1.68%	3.09%
Net profits on tangible net worth: Net profits are *divided by* tangible net worth (total assets, after deducting intangibles, *less* total liabilities). A ratio of at least 10 percent is often regarded as necessary to provide dividends and funds for future growth.	2.17%	6.32%	10.54%
Net profits on net working capital: Net working capital is equal to current assets *less* current liabilities and indicates the ready cash available to meet day-to-day business operations. This ratio is obtained by *dividing* net profits after taxes *by* net working capital.	2.30%	6.97%	13.42%
Net sales to tangible net worth: Net sales are *divided by* tangible net worth.	2.81	3.65	4.74
Net sales to net working capital: Net sales are *divided by* net working capital.	3.09	4.55	5.70

* Ratios were obtained from financial statements for a sample of shoe stores and were arrayed from lowest to highest. The median value is in the middle of the array; the lower quartile is halfway between the median and the lowest value; the upper quartile is halfway between the median and the highest value.
Source: *1972 Key Business Ratios: Retailing* (New York: Dun & Bradstreet, 1973).

SBA office or will be reassessed to see how the business might become profitable.

The first step in developing a budgeted income statement is to estimate your store's total sales revenue for the first two years of operation. In

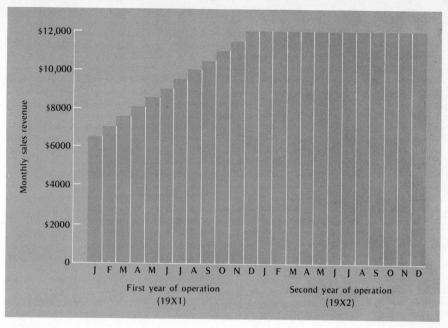

17-2 Estimated monthly sales revenue for the first two years
of operation of Family Shoe Store, Inc.

the market analysis worksheet in the last chapter (Figure 16-6), the projected annual revenue for your store was $144,000, or an average of $12,000 per month. However, your store will probably reach this income level gradually. We will assume that you can expect sales of $6500 during the first month the store is in operation (January 19X1), with regular monthly increments of $500 throughout the first year. By the last month of the year (December 19X1), sales will reach a plateau of $12,000 per month. These values are plotted in Figure 17-2. Your store's monthly growth during the first year represents the time necessary to develop a loyal group of new customers. Thus, your total sales for the first year will be $111,000, and your sales for the second year will be $144,000 — the income level we projected in Chapter 16.

Sales build slowly during the first year

A budgeted income statement for Family Shoe Store's first two years of operation appears in Figure 17-3. There are two sources for the expense estimates shown in this figure. The first is a study published by the National Cash Register Company giving operating ratios for family shoe stores with annual sales revenues of between $100,000 and $149,999. The second source is an assessment of each of the remaining expense items that you and your accounting partner make in accordance with your own store's unique situation and its proposed location. The basis for each of these estimates is given below with the letters keyed to items in Figure 17-3:

(a) *Rent:* Your past experience suggests that you will need about 1000 square feet of total floor space for your store. At $5 per square foot per year, a typical rental price, your annual rental will be $5000.

(b) *Depreciation:* Standard ratios suggest that $10,000 of furniture and fixtures will be required if a permanent annual sales volume of $144,000 is to be maintained. Assuming equal depreciation each year, a life of ten years, and no salvage value at the end of ten years, your yearly depreciation expense will be:

$$\frac{\$10,000 - 0}{10} = \$1000$$

(c) *Insurance:* You estimate that during the first two years of business operations the insurance premium will be $1500 annually, payable in installments of $750 every January and July.

17-3   Budgeted income statement for the first two years of operation of Family Shoe Store, Inc.

Family Shoe Store, Inc. Budgeted Income Statement
Years Ending December 31, 19X1, and December 31, 19X2

Income statement item	Year 19X1	Year 19X2	Basis of estimate Percentage of sales	Other
Annual sales	$111,000	$144,000	100.0	
Less: Cost of goods sold	68,000	88,300	61.3	
Gross profit	$43,000	$55,700		
Less: Operating expenses				
Owners' salary	$9,100	$11,800	8.2	
Employee wages	11,000	14,200	9.9	
Rent	5,000	5,000		(a)
Depreciation	1,000	1,000		(b)
Advertising	3,110	4,000	2.8	
Insurance	1,500	1,500		(c)
Interest	1,600	1,327		(d)
Utilities	1,200	1,200		(e)
Miscellaneous	2,160	2,800	1.95	
Total expenses	$35,670	$42,827		
Net profit (loss) before income taxes	$7,330	$12,873		
Less: Income taxes (22%)	1,613	2,832		(f)
Net profit (loss) after income taxes	$5,717	$10,041		

Source of information in the column headed "Percentage of Sales": *General Information: Expenses in Retail Business* (Dayton, Ohio: National Cash Register Company, n.d.), p. 38.

(d) *Interest:* After completing your projected balance sheet, you find that you will need to negotiate a five-year bank loan of $20,000 (which will probably have to be guaranteed by the SBA). Your interest cost will be 8 percent on the outstanding principal. The bank requires that loan payments be made in equal annual installments of $5009, an amount that will cover both the interest cost on the outstanding balance and the repayment of principal. Note that this is the same procedure used in a home-mortgage loan: each monthly payment is for the same amount, but successively larger portions of the monthly payments are applied to reducing the principal on the mortgage and successively smaller portions are applied to the interest payments. At the end of the first year, your $5009 payment to the bank will be composed of $1600 interest (.08 × $20,000) and $3409 repayment of principal. At the end of the second year, your $5009 payment will be composed of $1327 in interest ($20,000 − $3409 = $16,591, and .08 × $16,591 = $1327) and $3682 in principal.

(e) *Utilities:* You estimate that charges for items such as light, heat, and telephone service will be $100 per month, or $1200 annually.

(f) *Income tax:* Your store is incorporated and you pay 20 percent on your first $25,000 in profits in annual income taxes, 20 percent of which is federal corporate income tax and two percent of which is state tax.

Note that some of the expense items analyzed above, such as depreciation and interest, cannot be completed until the budgeted balance sheet is completed. This supports the point we made earlier about the importance of developing plans simultaneously rather than sequentially.

✔ **Your store's budgeted balance sheet.** The budgeted or projected balance sheet summarizes how much of various assets (such as cash, inventory, accounts receivable, land, buildings, and equipment) will be needed to operate the business. As we noted in Chapter 12, these assets are financed by owner contributions, trade credit (through accounts payable to suppliers), short-term bank loans, and long-term borrowing (either through the sale of bonds or through loans from banks, government finance agencies, or insurance companies). A business owner must make detailed estimates of the assets that will be needed and of the cash that will be required to provide these assets. Once cash needs have been projected, the amount to be borrowed from outside sources can be determined by subtracting owner contributions *plus* the earnings generated and retained in the business during the first year from this total.

Let us assume that you and your accounting partner have prepared the budgeted balance sheet that appears in Figure 17-4, and that the item-by-item breakdown is as follows:

Family Shoe Store, Inc., Budgeted Balance Sheet
December 31, 19X1, and December 31, 19X2

Balance sheet item	December 31, 19X1		December 31, 19X2	
Assets				
Current Assets				
Cash	$4,748		$5,387	
Accounts receivable	5,560		7,200	
Inventory	17,000		22,080	
Total current assets		$27,308		34,667
Fixed Assets				
Equipment (furniture and fixtures)	$10,000		$10,000	
Less: Accumulated depreciation	(1,000)		(2,000)	
Total fixed assets		9,000		8,000
Total Assets		$36,308		$42,667
Liabilities and Owner Equity				
Liabilities				
Short-term debt	$2,000		$2,000	
Intermediate-term loan (8%)	16,591		12,909	
Total liabilities		$18,591		$14,909
Owner equity				
Capital	$12,000		$12,000	
Retained earnings	5,717		15,758	
Total owner equity		17,717		27,758
Total liabilities and owner equity		$36,308		$42,667

The cash balance: the amount needed for day-to-day business operations

1. *Cash:* The cash balance on the worksheet in Figure 17-4 is not the total amount of cash you need to start your business. Rather, it is the amount of cash you need to run your business on a day-to-day basis and to pay your regular short-term obligations as they become due. Until the business begins to run smoothly, your cash on hand should serve as a buffer against erratic sales revenue and should be sufficient to cover all fixed operating costs and loan repayments. The average minimum amount of cash that a business should retain is generally figured as a multiple of the firm's monthly operating expenses. We will assume that one-and-a-half months' operating expenses is a safe cash balance for your store.

Therefore, your minimum cash balance at the end of each of the first two years your business is in operation will be:

$$\text{First year: } \frac{\$35,670}{12} \times 1.5 = \$4460$$

$$\text{Second year: } \frac{\$42,827}{12} \times 1.5 = \$5350$$

It is important to realize that these are *minimum* figures and that your cash balances do not have to correspond exactly to these amounts. Cash is used as a balancing item in the budgeted balance sheet and need only meet this minimum requirement. So we will not fill in the cash balance in Figure 17-4 yet.

2. *Accounts receivable:* The accounts-receivable balance depends on a store's annual sales volume and also upon the proportion of sales that represent charge-account business. For a retail shoe store, the

Other details needed
for your budgeted
balance sheet

volume of accounts receivable is generally quite small and may simply be approximated as a percentage of annual sales. We will assume that the accounts-receivable balance for your shoe store will be about 5 percent of annual sales, or $5560 for the first year and $7200 for the second year.

3. *Inventory:* Inventory consists of all items for sale that are purchased from suppliers. Let us assume that you will need to stock four distinct shoe styles for the four seasons. To provide an adequate depth and breadth of shoes for your customers, you should maintain a three-month inventory at all times; in other words, your stock should turn over four times per year (12 months *divided by* 3 months). Thus, your inventory balance should be one-fourth of the annual cost of shoes sold, or $17,000 ($68,000 *divided by* 4) at the close of the first year and $22,080 ($88,300 *divided by* 4) at the close of the second year.

4. *Equipment (furniture and fixtures):* Estimates of the total investment needed for fixed assets such as shelves, chairs, and sales counters can be obtained from store-layout specialists and from SBA studies. A good working figure for a family shoe store handling an annual sales volume of $144,000 is $10,000 for furniture and fixtures. Assuming a ten-year life with straight-line depreciation and zero salvage value, the annual depreciation expense on your store's equipment will be $1000. Thus, the net book value of fixed assets will be $9000 at the end of the first year and $8000 at the end of the second year.

5. *Total assets:* For the first year, your total assets will amount to an investment of $5560 for accounts receivable, $17,000 for inventory, and $9000 for fixed assets, plus a minimum cash balance of at least $4460, giving you a working figure of about $36,000 for total

assets. For the second year, the comparable working figure will be $42,000. Once you have determined the actual cash balances you will have on hand at the end of each year, you will be able to compute the exact totals.

Loans and owner equity cover the cost of financing assets

6. *Liabilities and owner equity:* Several sources can supply your store's capital needs. Owner contributions of $12,000 and business profits of $5717 can be reinvested as capital (retained earnings). So for the first year, the owners and the business can provide $17,717, leaving $18,591 to be borrowed to cover the cost of obtaining assets. Since loans are generally made in round numbers, you will attempt to secure a bank loan of $20,000 to open your shoe store. The balance remaining on the loan after repayment of principal and interest at the end of the first year will be $16,591 (see Figure 17-4). Finally, to meet your firm's day-to-day cash requirements (see the discussion of the cash budget below), you will need to negotiate several short-term loans, $2000 of which will be outstanding at the end of the first year. Thus, your liabilities and equity for the first year will total $36,308.

Determining the final cash balance

You can now determine the exact cash balance that your store will have on hand at the end of the first year. Subtracting total assets exclusive of the estimated cash balance ($31,550) from total liabilities and equity ($36,308) will leave a net cash balance of $4748 for the first year.

During the second year, an additional $10,041 in profits will increase your retained earnings to $15,758. To meet your capital requirements, you will also need to negotiate another short-term loan of $2000 at the end of the year. The balance on your intermediate-term bank loan for the second year will be $12,909. Using the procedure described above, you calculate that your actual cash balance at the end of the second year will be $5387.

This completes the budgeted balance sheet for the first two years that Family Shoe Store, Inc., is in operation.

✔ **Your store's cash budget.** The cash budget indicates a firm's ability to meet cash needs on time, regardless of sales revenue. Such cash needs include employee salaries, interest costs and repayment of principal, suppliers' fees, and taxes. Substantial default on any one of these payments can easily lead to bankruptcy.

The use or sale of any resource ultimately affects the cash balance of the firm. For example, suppose that a retailer must spend $5000 to buy fixtures before opening a store and that sales are expected to increase gradually during the first year or two that the business is in operation. In this case, the effect of the fixtures item on cash is immediate, while the effect of sales on cash is delayed. The net result is that the retailer must carefully reassess cash needs many different times during the year, particularly if the business has highly seasonal sales and a large volume of accounts receivable. A cash budget may be reassessed on a monthly or on a quarterly basis, depending on the type of business and on the variability of its cash inflows and outflows.

The significance of cash planning is emphasized by the fact that a profitable budgeted income statement does not guarantee that a firm will be solvent (that it will have sufficient cash to meet its short-term obligations) at all points within the accounting period covered by the income statement. Moreover, the net-profit figure on an income statement does not indicate an increase in the cash balance of the firm; there is no direct relationship between the two items. In fact, when a new business begins operation or when an established firm expands quickly, it frequently places severe strain on the firm's cash supply which can easily lead to business failure. This strain occurs because cash payments for such items as inventory and wages grow faster than cash receipts from sales. Thus new manufacturing firms must often have access to sizable cash resources so that they can continue operating for two or three years until new products are developed, produced, and sold. Although retail operations can realize immediate sales, a year or more is usually required to establish a large enough clientele to generate projected sales revenues.

The cash budget indicates when a business may be faced with ex-

Potentially profitable businesses may run out of cash and fail

Applicants for franchisee licenses must submit detailed reports to the franchising operation describing their educational background, job experience, and financial status.

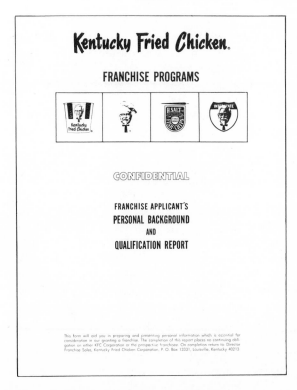

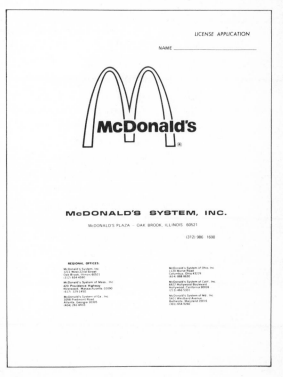

treme cash deficits or cash surpluses so that corrective action can be taken in advance. By anticipating a cash deficit, a retailer can calmly evaluate alternative solutions to the problem. In addition, if short-term loans are required, lending officers are much more receptive to well-planned requests than to urgent last-minute appeals. Anticipating a cash surplus gives the retailer time to arrange short-term investments.

Although the analysis is too detailed to present here, you have a key objective in developing a cash budget for Family Shoe Store, Inc.: to pinpoint cash inflows and outflows as they occur and to estimate the monthly cash balances for the first two years that your store is in operation. This will give you the advance warning necessary to take steps to insure that your business will always have sufficient cash on hand to meet its day-to-day obligations. For example, suppose that the high initial expenses required to open your shoe store cause you to run out of cash after six months. If you anticipate this cash deficit, you can choose one of two alternative solutions: (1) increasing your initial borrowing, or (2) obtaining short-term loans to cover expenses and paying the loans back when cash is available. Thus, your cash plan would enable your store to meet its necessary cash payments and would help you to avert bankruptcy in the early months of operation—the very reason many potentially successful small businesses fail.

Cash planning: analyzing cash needs throughout the year

Obtaining Funds

✔ **Sources of financing.**   There are three major sources of financing for most small businesses: (1) equity capital contributed by the firm's owners; (2) debt capital provided by loans from private financial institutions, such as banks and insurance companies; and (3) debt capital provided by loans from federal agencies, especially the U.S. Small Business Administration. Substantial equity capital contributed by the firm's owners is important for two reasons: (1) it represents a personal commitment to the business that encourages owners to redouble their efforts when problems arise, and (2) it provides protection for prospective lenders since the business could be liquidated (converted to cash) to pay creditors and lenders if it failed.

Commercial banks are an especially important source of small-business debt financing for two reasons. First, except for trade credit, banks are the major source of short-term funds. Second, commercial banks provide more than 80 percent of the intermediate- and long-term funds for small-business expansion. By federal law, the SBA may not loan a small business funds that it can obtain from a bank or another private income source. Traditionally, banks have always been more likely to grant loans to continue or to expand existing firms than to start new businesses. The U.S. Small Business Act of 1953 authorizes the SBA to make loans directly or jointly with banks "to assist small firms to finance construction,

Owner equity must often be supplemented by debt capital

conversion, or expansion; to purchase equipment, facilities, machinery, supplies or materials; and to acquire working capital." Thus, the SBA is an important source of financial assistance for retailers who intend to establish new businesses.

✔ **Financing your shoe store.** To obtain the necessary funds to open and operate your shoe store, you will probably need to investigate all three of the sources of financing we have just described. As indicated in the budgeted balance sheet in Figure 17-4, you and your partner have a limited amount of your own money ($12,000) to use to provide some equity financing for the business. All three of the plans we discussed earlier indicate that more financing will be required.

Your next step is to go to a bank to obtain the intermediate- and short-term funds that you need. There, a loan officer points out that banks normally finance the affairs of profitable existing businesses, which reduces your chances for a loan. In addition, the officer identifies the "three Cs" of credit that guide the bank's loan decisions:

Character: The borrower must be reliable and must conserve business assets to insure repayment of the loan.

The three Cs
of credit

Capacity: The inherent soundness of the business and the expertise of its owners must indicate that the firm is likely to succeed.

Collateral: The owners of the business must have substantial assets in an existing firm or must be willing to back up their credit standing with personal collateral such as a privately owned home, life-insurance policies with cash-surrender values, or marketable securities.

The loan officer concludes that your character appears sound, but that you have not demonstrated a capacity to operate your business successfully and that you have no collateral with which to support it. For these reasons the bank will not directly lend you the funds that you need.

Obtaining an SBA guaranteed loan

However, the loan officer is impressed by the details of your budgeted income statement, balance sheet, and cash plan and agrees to go with you to the local SBA office. There, you discuss your financial needs with SBA and banking officials, and they agree to provide you with an SBA guaranteed loan at 8-percent interest with a life of five years. Your bank will issue the loan, and the SBA will guarantee to repay 90 percent of the loan to the bank if your business fails and you are unable to meet the loan payments. The remaining 10 percent of the principal represents the bank's risk—the portion of the loan it will lose if your business fails. The bank also agrees to provide you with short-term loans to meet your cash needs during the first two years.

To summarize: your detailed financial plans for what appears to be a viable small business have enabled you to obtain the necessary intermediate- and short-term loans to open the doors of Family Shoe Store, Inc.

Operating a Small Business

The final step in becoming a small business owner is to begin store operations. The major aspects of operating a business have already been discussed in preceding chapters. In this section, we will focus on four considerations in operating a firm that are of special concern to the small business owner:

1. How do you buy and price products?
2. How do you advertise and sell products?
3. How do you select and train personnel?
4. How do you measure the performance of your business?

Buying and Pricing Products

Many small businesses fail because their owners lack the experience and judgment to buy the merchandise their customers want and to price it properly.

✔ **The right merchandise and prices.** To buy the right merchandise for resale to customers, a retailer must find out what type, brand, quality, color, size, and style of a product will sell best. This involves paying close attention to customers, salespersons, trade journals, and catalogs to identify purchasing trends in the coming months. In addition, suppliers must be selected who can provide the kind and quality of goods desired.

Finally, repeated decisions must be made regarding the quantity of merchandise to buy from suppliers. This is a difficult problem, since the retailer faces conflicting objectives. Buying in large quantities insures quantity discounts, reduces the likelihood of running out of stock and hence losing sales, and decreases the volume and cost of inventory paperwork. But buying in small quantities ties up much less money in inventory and minimizes the possibility of buying the wrong merchandise, which would eventually necessitate price reductions. Thus, each retailer must strike the right balance between these two extremes by relying on judgment, past experience, and financial guidelines like the rate of inventory turnover.

After considering general pricing factors related to cost, demand, and competitors' prices (discussed in Chapter 8), a retailer must determine the **Underpricing is a danger** prices of individual items or of groups of items. To avoid underpricing (an error inexperienced business owners frequently make) the retailer should examine standard operating ratios for similar businesses, available from such sources as Dun & Bradstreet and the National Cash Register Company. In addition, the retailer can examine a variety of SBA reports, such as *Ratio Analysis for Small Business,* which provide information on the sources and the uses of important financial ratios for small businesses. These ratios include estimates of the average percentage of gross profit each dollar of sales must generate to cover operating expenses and to contribute to profits.

Suppose that a retailer's income statement contains the following items:

Item	Amount	Percentage of sales
Annual sales	$500	100%
Less: Cost of goods sold	350	70
Gross profit	$150	30%
Less: Operating expenses	100	20
Net profit before taxes	$ 50	10%

The item termed *gross profit* (also called *gross margin* or *markup*) refers to the amount available to cover operating expenses and profit. As long as these terms are expressed in dollar amounts, their meaning is clear.

Markup as a percentage: Is the reference selling price or cost?

Confusion arises, however, when the terms above refer to percentages — especially the term "markup," which is commonly expressed in percentage terms. Suppose that the $500 of annual sales in the above example were obtained by selling 500 units at $1 apiece. The cost of goods sold for each item would be 70 cents, leaving a markup of 30 cents. Should the markup be expressed as a percentage of cost (30 cents *divided by* 70 cents, or 42.9 percent) or as a percentage of selling price (30 cents *divided by* 100 cents, or 30 percent)? It is especially convenient to use the term

---

WHAT MARKUPS DO RETAILERS REALLY USE?

An inexperienced person opening a small business often prices products too low. Thus, the markup is not high enough (1) to cover operating expenses, and (2) to provide an adequate level of profit that will enable business operations to continue. Pricing experts have developed the following generalizations about markups in retail stores:

● Within a given retail store, the slower an item sells, the higher its markup is likely to be.
● Among different kinds of retail stores, the more elaborate the store and its services — and the slower an item sells — the higher its markup is likely to be.

Applying these two guidelines to the following products, what would you expect their retail markups (or selling prices) to be? (To help you, some markups are given.)

Items	Markup
In a grocery store:	
Coffee	
Cereal	21%
Canned meat	
Spices	
Light bulbs	48%
Rug cleaner	
Average for all products	
In other retail stores (average for all products):	
Discount stores	
Department stores	40%
Shoe stores	

For the answers, as well as how "percent markup" relates to turnover, see p. 455. (*Hints:* Within a supermarket, markups range from 5 to 20 percent; among retail stores, they range from 15 to 50 percent.)

"markup" to refer to a percentage of selling price, since it makes markup equivalent to the gross-profit or gross-margin percentage. However, because there is not complete agreement on whether markup should be based on cost or on selling price, it is important to clarify the term in business conversations.

One important warning is in order: adding the percentage markup based on selling price to an item's cost will result in underpricing the product. In the above example, a 30-percent markup on an item costing 70 cents results in a selling price of 91 cents (70 cents *plus* 30 percent of 70 cents), not the intended price of $1.

To set prices accurately, a retailer must often convert from one markup to the other. Many suppliers provide retailers with conversion tables that express markup percentages in terms of both selling price and cost to assist them in setting appropriate prices. If conversion tables are not available, the retailer can use the following formulas:

Converting markup from cost to selling price and vice versa

Percentage markup on selling price
$$= \frac{\text{percentage markup on cost}}{100 + \text{percentage markup on cost}} \times 100$$

Percentage markup on cost
$$= \frac{\text{percentage markup on selling price}}{100 - \text{percentage markup on selling price}} \times 100$$

If all 500 units in the above example were sold at $1 apiece, the markup percentage on each item would be equal to the gross-profit or gross-margin percentage taken from the income statement. However, retail stores generally use different markup percentages for different items, so that the markup on a particular item will rarely equal the gross-profit percentage in the income statement. Finally, not all retail items are actually sold at their original selling prices, because of such factors as markdowns and shrinkage. *Markdowns* are reductions in original selling prices due to overstocking, sudden style changes, soiled and faded display goods, and odd sizes left at the end of the season. *Shrinkage* refers to losses due to theft, spoilage, or breakage. The final markup percentages used in pricing goods must be high enough to cover markdowns and shrinkage. To assess how some key factors affect markups of various items in different kinds of retail stores, see "What Markups Do Retailers Really Use?".

Markup must also allow for markdowns and shrinkage

✔ **Your buying and pricing actions.** Relying on your prior experience, you have chosen the brands and styles of shoes that you think your customers will like. After negotiating with several suppliers, you obtain the necessary inventory to stock your store. You have completed your initial buying.

Now you must make your pricing decisions. We will assume that the average pair of shoes you purchased from your supplier cost $15. Your budgeted income statement (Figure 17-3) shows that your cost of goods sold is 61.3 percent of annual sales, leaving you with a gross profit of 38.7 percent. Checking reveals that to allow for markdowns and shrinkage you should increase your gross-profit figure to 44 percent when establishing your selling price. This 44 percent will be your typical markup on selling price. Using the second equation above, you calculate:

Is a markup of 78.6 percent enough?

Percentage markup on cost

$$= \frac{\text{percentage markup on selling price}}{100 - \text{percentage markup on selling price}} \times 100$$

$$= \frac{44}{100 - 44} \times 100 = \frac{44}{56} \times 100 = 78.6\%$$

Thus, the retail selling price on an average pair of shoes is:

Retail selling price = cost + markup on cost
= \$15 + 78.6% of \$15
= \$15 + (.786 × \$15)
= \$15 + \$11.79 = \$26.79

WHAT MARKUPS DO RETAILERS REALLY USE? *(Answers)*

The markups (as a percentage of selling price) for the various grocery items and for products in other retail stores are listed below, accompanied by annual turnover rates:

Items	Markup	Turnover
In a grocery store:		
Coffee	11%	24
Cereal	21%	35
Canned meat	22%	12
Spices	31%	3
Light bulbs	48%	6
Rug cleaner	58%	1
Average for all products	24%	15
In other retail stores (average for all products):		
Discount stores	29%	8
Department stores	40%	5
Shoe stores	50%	4

Turnover is simply the annual dollars of sales *divided by* the average dollars of inventory. Thus, turnover is a measure of how quickly items in stock are sold. A turnover of 12 for canned meat, for example, indicates that the complete inventory of this item is exhausted on an average of once a month;

rug cleaner, a slow-moving item, turns over on an average of once a year.

The data for the grocery items shown above give an indication that fast-moving items (those with high turnovers) have lower markups than slow-moving items. The data also reveal that the higher the markup among different kinds of stores, the lower the stock turnover. In the case of grocery items, for example, the average markup is 24 percent and the average turnover is 15; for a shoe store, the average markup is 50 percent, but the average inventory turns over only 5 times per year.

The figures for the average shoe store carry a mild warning for Family Shoe Store, Inc. Your store's markup of 44 percent on its sample pair of shoes is less than a typical shoe store's markup (50 percent), and your first year's estimated turnover of 6.5 (annual sales *divided by* average inventory = \$111,000/\$17,000) is substantially greater than the turnover rate for a typical shoe store (4).

It is well to note that a large markup in itself does not insure a store's profits; the store must also maintain a good turnover to be profitable and to remain in business. And because markups cover operating expenses as well as profits, retailers do not generally obtain exorbitant profits at the expense of their consumers.

Since retailers often use *odd pricing* — pricing a few pennies below the exact dollar value — you might set your retail price at $26.95 for this pair of shoes. Although a markup on cost of 78.6 percent seems excessive, it is necessary to provide a markup on selling price of 44 percent for this pair of shoes. This pricing procedure will enable you to earn an average gross profit on all shoe sales of 38.7 percent, to meet your operating expenses, and to realize some profit. To see how this markup compares with that of a typical shoe store and with markups that various retailers actually use, see the answers given on page 455.

Advertising and Selling Products

Advertising media
for retailers

Advertising can build retail sales, especially the direct-action advertising most retailers use (see Chapter 9). The advertising media available to retail stores include newspapers, trade papers, the yellow pages of the telephone directory, radio, television, handbills, and direct mail. A retail store that is part of a shopping center is generally expected to participate in cooperative advertising and promotional campaigns sponsored by other stores in the center.

In setting your advertising budget, you will probably use the competitive-parity method; that is, you will devote the same percentage of your annual sales to advertising that comparable stores of your size do (2.8 percent, according to Figure 17-3). When possible, you should attempt to measure the effectiveness of your advertising efforts, using the method we have already outlined in Chapter 9.

In a retail store, selling includes both personal selling and merchandise display. Personal selling can build up a loyal customer following and can generate repeat sales. Thus, it is essential that you believe that your merchandise will satisfy your customers. The steps in personal selling presented in Chapter 9 apply to both you and your sales personnel.

Merchandise displays attract customers

Merchandise display should attract customers. Your store windows should generate enough interest to make people who are walking by stop, look, and enter. Inside the store, you should set up additional attractive displays to assist customers in making style selections. From your experience as a shoe store clerk in high school, you may be able to create attractive, interest-generating displays; if not, you may wish to hire a part-time display expert to do this.

Selecting and Training Personnel

Now, you and your partner must hire several employees to help run your store. Many inexperienced small business owners make the mistake of hiring personnel before they know exactly what they expect their employees to do. Will new employees sell, maintain inventories, perform bookkeeping, or what . . . ? Although it is important to have flexible employees who are willing to perform a variety of tasks, you should prepare a specific job description (discussed in Chapter 5) for each prospective employee. This not only clarifies your own thinking but also outlines the prospect's exact duties. Until your business grows, you will probably employ several part-time workers who have flexible schedules (homemakers, college students, and high-school distributive education students). Later, you may need to hire one or two employees on a full-time basis.

A written job description for each prospective employee

To be a real asset to your store, a new employee must be properly trained. Some guidelines for employee training are:

1. Allow sufficient time for training.
2. Do not expect too much from trainees in a short time.
3. Have employees learn by performing under actual working conditions, with close supervision.
4. Follow up on your training.

Once employees have received their initial training, you should review the key points of their jobs, keep them up to date on new developments, and encourage them to ask questions. Training is a continual process.

Measuring the Performance of a Business

In measuring the performance of a business, it is essential to keep adequate accounting records (Chapter 11). Various SBA reports, such as *Financial Recordkeeping for Small Stores,* offer valuable information about recordkeeping procedures for small retail firms. In addition, the SBA's *Management Audit for Small Retailers* provides retailers with a checklist, which they can use to appraise their performance in such areas as planning, budgeting, buying, pricing, and insurance.

Adequate records are essential for measuring business performance

Suppose that you have opened your shoe store and have operated it for two years. You now wish to make a detailed analysis of your business to identify problem areas and to take corrective action where necessary. From your records, you should be able to develop an income statement and a balance sheet to assess your store's performance. The "Short Case" at the end of this chapter asks you to appraise your sales revenue after two years.

Assistance Available to Small Businesses

Three major sources offer special assistance to small businesses: the Small Business Administration, colleges and universities, and franchising organizations. In addition to providing the information and financial assistance discussed earlier in this chapter, the SBA offers management counseling to small businesses, mainly through two volunteer programs: the Service Corps of Retired Executives (SCORE) and the Active Corps of Executives (ACE). The SBA also provides management training courses, one-day conferences, problem clinics, and workshops. Special SBA assistance is available to members of minority groups and to veterans. Some colleges and universities provide courses for small business owners and offer advisory assistance in business problems. Franchising organizations help franchisees to plan their operations prior to opening and to manage day-to-day business affairs. The Critical Business Decision at the end of this chapter assesses the advantages and the disadvantages of owning and operating a franchise.

KEY POINTS TO REMEMBER

1. Figure 17-5 summarizes the four main steps in developing and managing a small business. The first two steps—selecting the business and estimating its market—were discussed in Chapter 16. This chapter has focused on the final two steps—financing and operating the business.
2. Financial planning for a small business involves developing three types of plans: (a) the budgeted income statement, (b) the budgeted balance sheet, and (c) the cash budget.
3. Budgeted income statements and budgeted balance sheets are prepared using (a) financial information published by sources such as Dun & Bradstreet, Inc., and the National Cash Register Company, and (b)

17-5   Summary of the steps in developing and managing a small business.

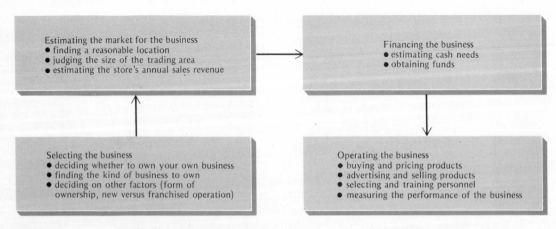

Estimating the market for the business
- finding a reasonable location
- judging the size of the trading area
- estimating the store's annual sales revenue

Financing the business
- estimating cash needs
- obtaining funds

Selecting the business
- deciding whether to own your own business
- finding the kind of business to own
- deciding on other factors (form of ownership, new versus franchised operation)

Operating the business
- buying and pricing products
- advertising and selling products
- selecting and training personnel
- measuring the performance of the business

personal estimates retailers need to make if they are going into their own business.

4. The cash budget is an important tool in business financing, since many small businesses project sizable profits in their budgeted income statements but go bankrupt because they are unable to meet day-to-day cash obligations.

5. Operating a business involves buying the merchandise that prospective customers want and pricing it correctly.

6. New small business owners often underprice their merchandise. The price generally must include a high enough markup to cover all operating expenses and to produce some profit.

7. Other important operational aspects of a business are advertising and selling products and selecting and training capable employees.

8. Adequate financial records must be maintained to assess business performance and to recognize when corrective action must be taken.

9. Special assistance is available to small businesses from the SBA, from colleges and universities, and from franchising organizations.

QUESTIONS FOR DISCUSSION

1. Many businesses, particularly retail stores, face ups and downs in sales revenues due to seasonal factors.
   (a) During which months do you think a family shoe store might have especially good sales? Especially poor sales? Why?
   (b) Suppose that the actual sales for Family Shoe Store, Inc., correspond exactly to the projected sales in your budgeted income statement ($111,000 for the first year and $144,000 for the second). What implications does the seasonal pattern you identified in part (a) have for your cash budget?

2. Two factors that should be considered before starting a new business are net profits on tangible net worth (defined in Figure 17-1) and the average hourly earnings of the owner(s) if plans materialize.
   (a) From the information given in Figure 17-3, determine the net profits on tangible net worth for each of the first two years that Family Shoe Store, Inc., is in operation, if projections prove accurate.
   (b) If you and your partner spend an average of 80 hours per week operating your store and keeping business records during its first two years, what average hourly salaries should you and your partner receive based on the information in Figure 17-3?
   (c) Would it be more profitable for you and your partner to work for someone else?

3. A retailer must be careful to note whether markup percentages are based on selling price or cost.
   (a) Convert the following markups on cost to markups on selling price: 10 percent; 20 percent; 30 percent; 40 percent.
   (b) Assume that the markups in part (a) are based on selling price and convert them to markups on cost.

Evaluation is crucial in any business decision, whether it is the assessment of a single business problem or the overall performance of the firm. Suppose that Family Shoe Store, Inc., operates for two years. The results of your efforts appear in the income statement and the balance sheet in Figure 17-6.

17-6 Income statement and balance sheet for the second year of operation of Family Shoe Store, Inc.

Family Shoe Store, Inc., Income Statement Year Ending December 31, 19X2

Annual sales	$150,000	
Less: Cost of goods sold	96,000	
Gross profit		$54,000
Less: Operating expenses		
Owners' salary	$12,300	
Employee wages	18,000	
Rent	5,000	
Depreciation	1,000	
Advertising	2,500	
Insurance	1,500	
Interest	1,327	
Utilities	1,200	
Miscellaneous	2,500	
Total expenses		$45,327
Net profit (loss) before income taxes		$8,673
Less: Income taxes (22%)		$1,908
Net profit (loss) after income taxes		$6,765

Family Shoe Store, Inc., Balance Sheet December 31, 19X2

Assets		
Current Assets		
Cash	$1,300	
Accounts receivable	2,300	
Inventory	26,400	
Total current assets		$30,000
Fixed assets		
Equipment (furniture and fixtures)	$10,000	
Less: Accumulated depreciation	(2,000)	
Total fixed assets		8,000
Total Assets		$38,000
Liabilities and Owner Equity		
Liabilities		
Short-term debt		
Intermediate-term loan (8%)	$12,909	
Total liabilities		$12,909
Owner equity		
Capital	$12,000	
Retained earnings	13,091	
Total owner equity		25,091
Total liabilities and owner equity		$38,000

(a) Using the operating ratios developed by the National Cash Register Company (cited in Figure 17-3) and the financial ratios for shoe stores developed by Dun & Bradstreet (cited in Figure 17-1), identify the apparent problems inherent in the business operations of Family Shoe Store, Inc.

(b) What corrective actions do you recommend?

(c) In general, the higher the values of the financial ratios shown in Figure 17-1, the better the financial condition of the firm. However, there are exceptions to this rule. For example, can you think of any reason why a high current ratio might be undesirable?

CAREER SELECTION: SERVICE AND RETAIL POSITIONS IN SMALL BUSINESSES

Small sole proprietorships, partnerships, and corporations are all rich sources of service and retail occupations. Several representative careers in each of these three types of businesses are discussed below.

POSITIONS IN SERVICE AND REPAIR

Appliance servicers repair and occasionally install consumer appliances. They often specialize in one category of household appliances, such as washers and dryers or refrigerators and freezers. Most servicers are high-school graduates who have a background in electronics, although many appliance servicers obtained further training in the use of tools and testing devices from technical schools or from community colleges. Employers generally hire trainees, who must complete several years of on-the-job training before they are considered fully qualified servicers. Experienced repairers frequently open their own service shops. Annual income ranges from $5200 for trainees to $12,000 for experienced servicers. Job opportunities for appliance servicers and repairers are expected to increase as the production of technically complex consumer goods increases. (*Additional information:* Association of Home Appliance Manufacturers; 20 North Wacker Drive; Chicago, Illinois 60606.)

Automobile-body repairers restore damaged vehicles. This highly skilled craft requires a substantial knowledge of automobile construction and repair techniques. Because many specialized tools are used in automobile repair work, employers usually hire high-school graduates and provide them with several years of apprenticeship training. Automobile repairers must be in good physical condition, since many of their tasks require the handling of heavy equipment. Annual income averages $13,000. Employment opportunities are expected to vary with the number of automobile accidents. (*Additional information:* Automotive Service Industry Association; 230 North Michigan Avenue; Chicago, Illinois 60601.)

Television and **radio service technicians,** often self-employed, repair many types of electronic equipment, including televisions, radios, tape recorders, and stereos. Employers generally select high-school graduates who have backgrounds in electronics, mathematics, and physics; technical-school training is a competitive advantage. Technicians begin as trainees and gradually acquire a sufficient knowledge of electronic components and circuits to be considered fully qualified to repair complex electrical equipment. Annual income ranges from $6200 to $13,500. Job opportunities are expected to expand moderately as consumer demand for highly technical products increases. (*Additional information:* National Alliance of Television and Electronic Service Associations; 5908 South Troy Street; Chicago, Illinois 60629.)

POSITIONS IN SMALL BUSINESSES

In their capacity as drug experts, **pharmacists** in retail drug stores dispense prescription and nonprescription medicines. Pharmacists also advise customers as to the proper selection and use of drugs. Self-employed pharmacists benefit from a basic business knowledge, since many of their responsibilities like accounting and staffing are not directly related to their pharmaceutical training. The minimum educational requirement is a bachelor's degree in pharmacy. Pharmacists must also pass a state board examination to obtain a license. Annual salary varies from $11,000 to $17,000. The employment outlook is promising due to both the growing number of pharmaceutical products and a rising consumer demand for these products. (*Additional information:* American Pharmaceutical Association; 2215 Constitution Avenue, N.W.; Washington, D.C. 20037.)

Jewelers make and repair precious jewelry, a craft that requires both dexterity and patience. Jewelers often specialize in one particular type of jewelry or in a specific skill, such as jewelry design, polishing, or stone setting. Private industries provide apprenticeship programs for applicants who have a high-school or a technical-school background in chemistry, mechanical drawing, or art. Training programs in small jewelry shops are also available and may be preferred by apprentice jewelers who want to supplement their specialized skills with a knowledge of general business. Industrial salaries average $10,400; self-employed jewelers have a much greater earning potential. Because of the continuing consumer preference for mass-produced costume jewelry, the job market for jewelers is not expected to increase appreciably in the near future. (*Additional information:* Retail Jewelers of America, Inc.; 1025 Vermont Avenue, N.W.; Washington, D.C. 20005.)

Locksmiths repair damaged locks, make duplicate keys, and may install electronic burglary alarm systems. They also assist people who are locked out of their homes, cars, or safes. Some specialized duties require a background in electronics, but most locksmiths are high-school graduates who have received on-the-job training. About half of all qualified locksmiths own their own businesses; self-employed locksmiths can benefit from community-college or correspondence courses in general business. Mechanical aptitude and manual dexterity are essential requirements to be a locksmith. Annual salaries average $5000 for trainees and $10,500 for experienced locksmiths. Job opportunities are expected to increase moderately, especially for locksmiths who are qualified to install and service security systems. (*Additional information:* Associated Locksmiths of America, Inc.; 11 Elmendorf Street; Kingston, New York 12401.)

A CRITICAL BUSINESS DECISION

—made by Brad Hubbart

THE SITUATION The scene is McDonald's "Hamburger U.," a modern concrete and tinted-glass building located in Elk Grove, Illinois. Old H.U. demonstrates what many people have suspected for years: McDonald's—the hamburger people—take hamburgers a little more seriously than anyone else. Other franchised restaurants hold seminars and training programs, but only McDonald's has a "university," where a 19-day course leads to a "Bachelor of Hamburgerology, with a minor in French fries." Each course at H.U. is divided into two sections: basic operations (for all new owner-operators) and advanced operations (for owners, managers, assistant managers, and occasional veteran owners who return for refresher courses).

THE DECISION Let's join a *New York Times* reporter in the back row as Basic Operations Class 120 begins at H.U. The instructor, Jerry Gorman, a genial and informal man, speaks firmly to his audience of new owners: "All classes do require your attendance. . . . Keep your manuals and notebooks with you at all times."

One of the topics of the first session is production control. Gorman explains that McDonald's is dedicated to speed—to turning out a hamburger, a shake, and French fries in 50 seconds. Since the company also stresses freshness, any cooked hamburger that is not sold in seven minutes must be thrown away. Gorman points out that a McDonald's hamburger is a machine-stamped, 1.6-ounce patty 3.875 inches wide and .221 inches thick before cooking; that it is garnished with a quarter-ounce of onion, a pickle slice, mustard, and ketchup after it is cooked; and that it rests on a 4.25-inch-diameter bun.

Gorman points out that the major problem is to regulate production so that customers do not have to wait more than a minute to be served and so that no hamburgers are thrown away. This critical job is handled by the production control manager, who operates near the middle of the counter yelling instructions to grillers, shakers, and fryers.

"Our basic run of burgers is 12," Gorman explains. "But to that the production man must add enough burgers for the doubles he thinks he'll need. So let's say he thinks he'll need six doubles. He yells, '12 and 6,' and the griller lays 18 burgers down. The next thing the griller needs to know is how many of these burgers should have cheese on them. So the griller will yell, 'cheese on 0 and 6,' which means, of the 6 doubles and 6 regulars I've got, how many do you want cheesed?"

"Now, let's say the production control manager wants two cheeseburgers and two double cheeseburgers. He'll yell back, '2 and 2,' which tells the griller what he needs to

know, unless you get some 'grills'—orders for burgers without some of our normal ingredients. The grills come in on slips from the counter, and the griller has to deduct the grills from the other total. Got that?"

Gorman surveys his class skeptically. Only one man in the front row appears to understand.

"O.K.," Gorman says. "Let's see. If the calls go this way—'12 and 4,' 'cheese on 4 and 8,' '2 and 2'—and you get two 'ketchup only' grills, what do you make?"

Most of the students still seem at a loss. But the big man in the front row calmly answers: "Two double cheeseburgers, two double hamburgers, two cheeseburgers, four hamburgers with ketchup only."

Gorman nods. "You got it."

After class, someone asks Gorman who the big guy is. "Oh, don't you know?" he replies. "That's Brad Hubbart, who used to play fullback for the San Diego Chargers."

Later, the reporter writes: "Suddenly it all fell into place. I realized what McDonald's operation reminded me of: pro football. All those signals. . . . The mathematical precision. The sheer technology of it all. . . . No wonder Brad Hubbart understood it all."

Hubbart is already back at work studying the McDonald's manuals, reflecting on his decision to enter the restaurant business as a member of a franchised operation rather than as an independent owner. Hubbart knows that this decision was an important one.

QUESTION

Considering Brad Hubbart's experience, can you assess some of the advantages and the disadvantages of being part of a franchised operation rather than an independent restaurant owner.

PART SIX

THE ENVIRONMENT
OF BUSINESS

In the mixed economy of the late 1970s and the 1980s, American business will interact with other organizations in major ways. How do environmental factors limit and shape business decisions? In what ways can business deal more effectively with government and labor? How will the emergence of an integrated world economy affect American business in the near future?

The governmental impact on business (described in Chapter 18) is so important that most key business decisions require a careful consideration of probable government reactions. Since the 1930s, the American labor movement (examined in Chapter 19) has exerted considerable influence on business. And as American firms "go international," fewer and fewer industries will remain isolated from the world market. Thus, international business (discussed in Chapter 20) becomes increasingly relevant to businesses and to consumers alike. Similarly, both businesses and individuals must face difficult future choices. One choice may be between continuing economic growth and an improved quality of life—the topic of the Epilogue.

The very essence of a free government consists in considering offices as public trusts, bestowed for the good of the country and not for the benefit of an individual or a party.

John C. Calhoun

CHAPTER

18

GOVERNMENT AND BUSINESS

O n May 9, 1959, Julian Granger, a 35-year-old reporter for the *Knoxville News-Sentinel,* spent a quiet morning reading his back mail. It was a steamy Saturday in Tennessee and there was no news to distract Granger except a routine news release from the Tennessee Valley Authority (TVA). The article stated that the TVA had just purchased a 500,000-kilowatt generator from the Babcock and Wilcox Company of Atlanta, Georgia, that the agency had leased six acres of park land to the city of Anab, Alabama, and that rainfall in the Tennessee Valley during April was 4.66 inches, a bit above average. Only a sense of duty prompted Granger to read further. Suddenly, a parenthetical statement about a $96,760 contract for transformers awarded to the Westinghouse Electric Company caught his eye. "On the bidding," the paragraph stated, "Allis-Chalmers, General Electric, and Pennsylvania Transformer quoted identical prices of $112,912."

A reporter's discovery in Tennessee

With mounting interest, Granger read on. Another parenthetical statement noted that the TVA had received identical bids of $198,438.24 on a contract for conductor cable from seven of the most prominent electrical equipment manufacturers in the United States. How, Granger wondered, could seven firms independently submit secret, sealed bids that were identical to the cent? He decided to pursue the story and called Roy Wagner, TVA's general manager. On that sleepy afternoon in Tennessee, Granger could not have known that he was about to uncover the most extensive bid-rigging conspiracy in American business history.

Government's increasing role in business

Government intervention in the American economy has increased steadily in recent years. Today, nearly 40 percent of the gross national product is devoted to government activities. Sometimes, government decisions seek to correct specific business abuses, as the U.S. Department of Justice did when it filed antitrust suits against General Electric, Westinghouse, and the other bid riggers Julian Granger exposed. On the other hand, government often acts to restrict business activities in an effort to achieve such objectives as full employment, price stability, and an internationally acceptable dollar.

How government interacts with business

Government interacts with business in three basic ways. First, governmental activities themselves affect business, as when a decision is made about the location of a new superhighway. In many communities, spending by government employees is a major source of retail sales. Second, as we noted in Chapter 1, government is a major direct purchaser of goods and services from private businesses. Third, government controls certain business practices through laws and regulations—legislation to which firms must conform or face penalties enforceable in court.

In this chapter, we will examine four major topics in the vital area of government-business relations: (1) the evolution of government policy toward business; (2) the antitrust laws; (3) government regulation of business; and (4) taxation of business.

The Evolution of Government–Business Relations

The Role of Government

The historical American commitment to a government "of the people, by the people, and for the people" is a very deep one. But how can Lincoln's famous phrase be translated into a viable system of government? Let's examine some divergent views Americans hold about the role of government in contemporary society.

Principles underlying American government

✔ **Limited government.** Fearful of the potential tyranny of highly centralized rule, the framers of the U.S. Constitution sought to grant the federal government only the minimum powers necessary for effective national leadership. At the same time, they knew that a strong federal government was essential to the survival of the fledgling nation. In a brilliant series of compromises, the delegates to the Constitutional Convention of 1787 organized American government according to three key principles:

1. *Division of functions:* The American government is organized at three basic levels: federal or national government, state governments, and local governments. Among the important functions assigned to the federal government under the Constitution are the power to wage war, to coin money, and to administer justice (shared with the states). Powers not specifically assigned to the federal government are delegated to the states; in turn, the states designate some of their powers to local governments.
2. *Separation of powers:* The federal government is divided into separate executive, legislative, and judicial branches. The legislative branch is further divided into two houses: the Senate and the House of Representatives.
3. *Restrictions on government:* The written Constitution, the Bill of Rights and 15 additional Constitutional amendments passed after 1789 place important restrictions on American government. Government may not abridge such basic human rights as freedom of speech, freedom of assembly, freedom to practice the religion of one's choice, and access to due process of law.

✔ **Government as mediator.** In the first half of the twentieth century, the rise of organized interest groups (giant businesses, powerful trade associations, strong unions, and others) propelled American government into a fundamental new role: that of mediator. When well-organized economic interests, regions, social classes, or ethnic groups clash, failure to resolve such disagreements can produce disastrous results: severe losses in production, riots, and even civil war.

Government can serve as a mediator, resolving disputes among powerful interests

As we will see in Chapter 19, the government plays its strongest role as mediator in labor-management relations. As organized labor achieved sufficient economic power to compete with business, the public became increasingly dependent on the government to mediate the economic conflicts between these two parties.

✔ **Government as a countervailing power.** The concept of *countervailing power,* articulated most forcefully by economist J.K. Galbraith, holds that economic power in one aspect of the production of a good or service usually produces economic power in other aspects of production. A prominent example is the tire industry, where a few dominant firms appear to have been successful in controlling price structures. Sears Roebuck, an important tire purchaser, has won significnat price discounts from B.F. Goodrich, Firestone, and other large tire manufacturers. In addition, a powerful union, the United Rubber Workers of America, has been able to obtain significant wage increases and fringe benefits for its members from tire manufacturers. In short, economic power among tire manufacturers is counteracted by the growth of offsetting economic power among purchasers (Sears) and suppliers (the union).

Countervailing power: when strong economic interests clash

Countervailing power affects government in two ways. First, government itself may become part of the countervailing power mechanism. For example, when railroads achieved domination of the American transportation system after the Civil War, a federal government agency, the Interstate Commerce Commission, was established to check railroad activities. When strong special interest groups develop powers that are unchecked by other interest groups, governments may be called on to control resulting abuses.

How countervailing power affects government

Second, government may seek to make countervailing power work more effectively by encouraging the formation of special interest groups or by protecting unorganized groups from the powerful interests. In the 1930s, the federal government passed legislation designed to increase the power of organized labor, so that unions could deal more effectively with business on even terms. In recent years, the federal government has focused increasing attention on two important but comparatively unorganized interest groups: consumers and farmers. Thus, many Americans have come to believe that in situations involving countervailing power, government should become an active partisan of the "little people," helping them to organize and protect themselves against powerful special interest groups.

✔ **An activist government.** Abraham Lincoln once observed that "government should do those things that the people cannot do as well for themselves." While the framers of the Constitution would not have

disagreed with this statement, contemporary Americans accept levels of government activity that would have been inconceivable to previous generations. Popular demand for an expanded, activist government reflects the American desire for:

1. Maintenance of a stable economy and avoidance of depressions, recessions, or excessive inflation.
2. Increased public goods—products or services like education, national parks, and scientific research that the private enterprise system may not adequately provide.
3. Protection from irresponsible behavior by special interest groups —false advertising, control of essential raw materials by a few businesses, and deliberate encouragement of low productivity by labor unions.
4. Added security—protection from natural disasters, unemployment, and old age.
5. Conservation of natural resources and protection of the environment—programs designed to reduce soil erosion and industrial pollution.
6. Equal opportunity—aid to ghetto schools and fair employment laws.
7. Reduction of social problems—crime, poverty, and public transportation in urban areas.
8. Development of products or services that require greater initial investments than private business groups can supply—atomic energy, space exploration, highways.

Many Americans believe that in order to promote these and other objectives, government has a right to oversee private business activities and to make sure that these activities conform to the best interests of society.

Business and the Federal Government

The executive, legislative, and judicial branches of the federal government encompass nearly three million employees and operate under a total budget of more than $400 billion. The size and complexity of contemporary government have important implications for American business.

The growing complexity of the federal government

✔ **Business and the executive branch.** The executive branch of the federal government is organized into separate Cabinet departments and dozens of independent agencies. Each Cabinet department is headed by a secretary, who is a political appointee of the President. Political appointees represent less than 1 percent of all government employees, but they are found at the policymaking levels of government. The government's daily work is carried out by the *civil service*—a permanent staff whose positions are based on merit as measured by entrance examinations or recommendations and periodic examinations for promotion.

Access to the executive branch is often extremely important to businesses, since most legislation grants the executive branch substantial descretion in carrying out established laws. Increased concentration of power in the Office of the President means that a business owner's influence with the presidential "inner circle" can be of great assistance to the firm. For example, a railroad company that has received what it believes to be an arbitrary order from the Interstate Commerce Commission can often seek redress of its grievance by appealing directly to the President or to presidential assistants. In addition, many business owners seek temporary employment in the executive branch for the experience and the opportunity for social service it affords.

Committees dominate the House and the Senate

✔ **Business and the legislative branch.** The legislative branch of the federal government is composed of 435 members of the House of Representatives and 100 members of the Senate. Most congressional work is accomplished by committees, which usually consist of 15 or fewer legislators. These committees in turn delegate portions of their work to various subcommittees. Committees and subcommittees collect information, hold investigations and hearings, issue reports, and make legislative recommendations.

Because federal legislation has a major impact on business activities, business owners have a vital interest in monitoring the actions of Congress. Most trade associations maintain representatives in Washington who research and report government activities of interest to their members. In addition, many businesses subscribe to publications that provide detailed, up-to-date information on government announcements and policies in such areas as antitrust, labor laws, and taxation. Finally, businesses seek to direct legislation and the execution of legislation by lobbying. Professional *lobbyists* attempt to influence government through the use of personal contacts, information-gathering techniques, political contributions, and letter-writing campaigns.

Businesses seek to influence legislation

✔ **Business and the judicial branch.** The judicial branch of the federal government consists of a Supreme Court of nine judges appointed by the President subject to Senate approval. Most judicial cases are decided in the lower courts, which include district courts in each state and several appeals courts. Litigation normally begins in district courts, may be processed through various appeals courts, and can eventually reach the Supreme Court. The judicial branch also includes a number of specialized courts, such as the U.S. Tax Court, which handles cases involving federal taxation.

When businesses become involved in litigation with other firms, individuals, labor unions, or government, important issues are often at stake. Hence, many business-related cases are appealed beyond district courts. A small business often retains an attorney or a legal firm to repre-

BLOWING THE WHISTLE ON GOVERNMENT WASTE

Ernest Fitzgerald, a Pentagon cost analyst, makes a dramatic revelation before a congressional investigating committee. Contrary to the public statements of the Pentagon, unanticipated increases in costs on the giant C-5A transport plane would require an extra $2 billion from American taxpayers. Fitzgerald's superiors in the Department of Defense, less than enthusiastic about his testimony, fire him from his $38,000 job.

At 8:30 PM in a French restaurant just outside Detroit, John Moffatt pounds the table as he shuffles documents purporting to show that the Internal Revenue Service is about to spend hundreds of thousands of dollars on office furniture it doesn't need. Mr. Moffatt, a $26,178-a-year IRS employee in Michigan with a master's degree in business administration, presents a convincing case to the press and to high Washington officials.

"Only the intervention of Washington," Moffatt argues in a letter to a Deputy Treasury Secretary, "can save me from the local 'lynch mob' and subsequent punitive reprisal to my person and position in the IRS." Finally, the Chairman of the Senate Subcommittee that approves IRS appropriations learns of John Moffatt's plight. In firm tones, he announces that the Subcommittee will investigate IRS furniture purchase plans and warns the agency to reduce its pressure on Moffatt.

IRS reaction is prompt. All charges against Moffatt

Ernest Fitzgerald

are dropped, he is granted a scheduled pay increase, and he is transferred to Washington.

Ernest Fitzgerald and John Moffatt have, in the words of the *Wall Street Journal*, added their names "to a lengthening list of civil servants willing to buck the federal establishment to disclose questionable governmental action or inaction they believe the public should know about."

The court system is important to business

sent it in litigation involving the firm; large businesses maintain their own *legal departments,* which handle routine legal matters and most of the firm's litigation. When a firm becomes involved with highly technical or important litigation, it normally hires *outside counsel* — individuals or firms specializing in the kind of trial work required. Thus, it is possible for persons interested both in law and in business to practice *corporate law* — the area of law that deals with business and its relationships to other organizations and to private individuals.

Business and Local Governments

The structure of state and local governments reflects the provisions of state constitutions and statutes, local charters, and practices that have evolved over time. Except for Nebraska, which has a unicameral (one-house) legislature, the organization of state governments closely parallels that of the federal government. County, city, and town governments, school districts, airport commissions, water and sewage districts, and dozens of other types of local government units consist of a board, council, or commission. There are more than 200,000 separate government units in the United States.

Among the most costly services provided by states are financial support for education, welfare and insurance programs, mental health facilities, and public roads. Local government units provide services ranging from the administration and financial support of education to the maintenance of parks and libraries.

Business owners must understand the functions of state and local governments, since these units make decisions vital to their firms. The most important areas of concern to businesses under the influence of state and local governments include:

The functions of local governments affect business

1. The level of police protection, fire protection, and sanitation services available to the community.
2. Ownership of water and electrical generating plants.
3. The right of eminent domain. *Eminent domain* is the right of government to confiscate private property (usually real estate) for just compensation, as determined by private negotiations or by the courts. State and local governments often exercise eminent domain to acquire land for roads and other public projects.
4. The amount of taxation. State and local taxes profoundly influence business because they can place local firms at an advantage or a disadvantage relative to competitors in other states or towns.

State and local governments influence the quality of life

The business community is usually more influential at the state and local levels than at the federal level. One reason is that business owners who consider themselves unfairly treated by state or local officials can move to other locations; escape from the decisions of federal officials is more difficult. In addition, since businesses contribute valuable employment opportunities and tax receipts to local communities, local governments tend to be responsive to business needs. Because of their potential influence on local governments and the importance of efficient local government to their firms, many business owners are making even greater contributions in these areas.

Government and Business Today

Growth in government power has been accomplished by several striking changes in government policies and procedures.

Government spending patterns are changing

✔ **Changing priorities.** The period following World War II saw an unprecedented expansion in peacetime expenditures on national defense.

In 1952, defense spending accounted for 61 percent of federal expenditures and 13 percent of GNP; by 1976, government defense spending represented less than 30 percent of total federal expenditures and 5 percent of GNP. This relative decline in defense spending was accompanied by a rapid expansion in government expenditures for social programs like manpower retraining, aid to minority communities, public housing, and welfare.

✔ **Cooperation among governments.** The divisional duties of federal, state, and local governments are steadily eroding as all levels of government attempt to deal with mounting economic and social problems. What has been called the "new federalism" contemplates cooperative relationships among all governmental units to achieve common objectives. The new federalism has been accompanied by a spectacular growth in federal grants-in-aid to state and local governments.

Grants-in-aid (also known as *revenue sharing*) are programs under which a central government transfers some of its revenues to local governments to help finance public projects. In fiscal 1965, federal grants-in-aid to local governments amounted to $11 billion; ten years later, the figure was $80 billion. Before 1972, revenue sharing by the federal government consisted entirely of grants-in-aid for specific projects like urban renewal. In September 1972, the federal government initiated *general revenue sharing,* in which funds are made available to state and local governments, largely for projects of their own choice.

✔ **Government transfer payments.** A government *transfer payment* is any expenditure for which the government does not receive goods or services in return. A common example is the issuance of government checks to veterans or persons on social security. The government uses transfer payments primarily to raise the incomes of the poor and the disadvantaged.

The rapid rise in transfer payments in recent years has created a number of new problems for the federal government. First, many types of transfer payments are administered by separate trust funds over which Congress has little control. For example, although Congress establishes general administrative criteria for the social security system in its legislation, the Social Security Administration has great latitude in dispensing the actual funds. Second, recipients of certain transfer payments have become dependent on receiving regular checks. As a result, government is currently involved in a number of programs that commit federal funds many years into the future. The long-term commitment of such funds, or *mandated expenditures* means that a large portion of the government budget is no longer under the effective control of public officials. Transfer payments and other mandated expenditures now constitute more than 70 percent of the federal budget. This has obvious implications for the flexibility of government.

Mandated expenditures affect government's control of funds

✔ A new era for government-business relationships? Many Americans believe that the future will usher in a new era of government-business relations. Historically, businesses have viewed government with hostility, regarding government regulation as a limitation on their economic freedom and their right to make a profit. Government itself has often contributed to this climate of distrust by blaming business for its own shortcomings.

The disappointing results of some government programs, such as agricultural subsidies, the postal service, and local sanitation services, have led many Americans to reexamine the role of government. In their view, government and business must become less antagonistic and more cooperative. While government should be obligated to correct specific abuses arising in the private sector, most government activities should be confined to establishing general guidelines, leaving the detailed implementation of policy to the marketplace. For example, the repair of city streets could be opened to competitive bidding by private firms rather than be carried out by city employees. Local governments would retain the responsibility for deciding how much money to spend on road repairs in comparison with other public needs. In short, the private sector should be asked to assume an increasing responsibility for many activities now carried out by government. In addition, businesses should provide expertise to the government, participate in government decision making, and faithfully carry out the policies developed by democratically elected officials.

Substituting private firms for government agencies

The Antitrust Laws

Forty years ago, in a landmark study, *The Modern Corporation and Private Property,* Professors A.P. Berle and Gardner C. Means noted that many key American industries were dominated by a few giant corporations. On the basis of calculations of the relative growth rates in large and small businesses, Berle and Means projected, only half in jest, that in 360 years the American economy would be dominated by a single giant business whose life expectancy would rival that of the Roman Empire!

One giant monopoly for America?

The problem of *economic concentration*—the control of an industry by one or a few businesses—first appeared in the United States after the Civil War, when a series of monopolies and oligopolies were created in many key industries, including lead, sugar, whiskey, and cordage. A *monopoly* exists when one firm dominates an industry to the extent that it controls prices and excludes potential competitors. An *oligopoly* is the domination of an industry by a few powerful firms. A public outcry soon arose over the high prices and the dubious commercial tactics of some of the newly created monopolists and oligopolists. Popular dissatisfaction led to the passage of a series of *antitrust laws* designed to prevent or to control economic concentration.

The Sherman Antitrust Act

In 1890, the Sherman Antitrust Act was passed to curb the growth of conspiracies and monopolies. The Sherman Act prohibits conspiracies in restraint of interstate commerce. Examples of illegal conspiracies include:

1. *Price fixing:* Bookstores near a college campus agree to price used books in good condition at 75 percent of the retail price for new books.
2. *Market division:* Soft drink bottlers divide up the market for their product. Each competitor agrees to sell to retailers only within an assigned area.
3. *Bid rigging:* Electrical equipment manufacturers meet to divide up contracts from public utilities. Each contract is assigned to a specific producer, who bids at a designated price. Competitors bid a specified higher price in exchange for the opportunity to be low bidder on other contracts.

Preventing conspiracies and monopolies

To prosecute firms for alleged conspiracy, the government must prove by direct or by circumstantial evidence that some formal or informal meeting has taken place among competitors. More than 60 percent of antitrust cases involve alleged violations of the Sherman Act.

The Sherman Act also makes the monopolization of an industry illegal. Monopolization occurs when a firm attempts to gain control over the price of a product or to exclude new competitors from the market it dominates. Firms with control over more than 60 percent of a market are often regarded as potential monopolists by the courts.

The Clayton Act

The Clayton Act of 1914 was passed to strengthen Section 2 of the Sherman Antitrust Act by preventing the formation of monopolies rather than by directly attacking well-entrenched monopolists. Section 2 of the Clayton Act, which was supplemented in 1936 by an amendment known as the Robinson–Patman Act, prohibits price discriminations that lessen competition or that tend to create a monopoly. *Price discrimination* occurs when a business charges customers different prices for products "of like grade and quality." Under the terms of Section 2 of the act, businesses are allowed to reduce prices to favored customers only if the

Restricting business practices that lead to economic concentration

discounts are intended to meet competition or are based on the costs of servicing the customers.

Section 3 of the Clayton Act condemns *tying contracts,* which force customers to purchase a firm's products only in combination. For example, Eastman Kodak originally sold its color film only with processing included in the retail price. As a result of a federal antitrust investigation in 1954, Kodak was forced to make its color film available separately as well as at a higher price that included processing.

The key provision of the Clayton Act is Section 7, which was strengthened in 1950 by an amendment known as the Celler–Kefauver Act. Section 7 prohibits a firm from acquiring the assets or stock of competitors "where in any line of commerce in any section of the country the effect of such acquisition may be to substantially lessen competition or to tend to create a monopoly." One of the most common business practices covered by this provision is the *merger*—a combination of one or more businesses into a single firm. A *horizontal merger* occurs when firms acquire competing businesses. The acquisition of the Chevrolet Motor Company by General Motors in 1919 is an example of a horizontal merger. A *vertical merger* involves a firm's acquisition of one of its suppliers or customers—for example, the purchase of the Fisher Body Corporation by

The rise of conglomerates

BLANKENHEIM ON PRICE FIXING

It was March 1975. The room was crowded with 130 business students from San Francisco State University. The speaker was Eugene Blankenheim, president of Diamond International, a label manufacturer based in New York City. "I am not the kind of man who is indifferent to his reputation," Blankenheim observed. "I have been married to the same girl for 36 years. I have four children and eight grandchildren. In 45 years, I have had only two minor traffic violations. I did not intentionally set out to violate any law."

Blankenheim and Diamond International were among eight executives and seven firms convicted of price fixing in federal district court several months earlier. "There are conventions, meetings . . . you get to know your competition. And you talk about your business and their business," Blankenheim tells the San Francisco audience. "I would not be here today had I known of the legal risks in casual conversation. Prices bid—and to be bid—were discussed, before and after meetings. I realized when the storm hit that some of these friendships were based on my position in my company."

When asked how to price in an inflationary environment without violating the antitrust laws, Blankenheim replied, "You just increase prices and hope that you don't lose the business. But you lose some.

You always lose some when you raise prices. It is not wrong to talk about your common problems . . . labor problems, marketing problems. But it is wrong to increase somebody's prices through collusion."

General Motors in 1919. A *conglomerate merger* unites firms that produce dissimilar products. The acquisition of Philco, an important producer of radio and television sets, by the Ford Motor Company in 1961 is an example of a conglomerate merger.

Four great waves of mergers—after the Civil War, in the 1920s, after World War II, and from 1965 to 1971—have characterized the American economy. Since the passage of the Clayton Act, the federal government has vigorously prosecuted horizontal and vertical mergers. As a result, recent mergers have been of the conglomerate variety, and *conglomerates*—firms that produce many types of goods and services—are enjoying remarkable growth. For example, International Telephone and Telegraph, which ranks among the nation's ten largest corporations, is comprised of over 40 separate companies, including the Grinnell Corporation, Hartford Fire Insurance, and the Sheraton Corporation of America.

The Federal Trade Commission Act

The Federal Trade Commission Act was passed in 1914 to deal with unfair methods of competition not covered by the Clayton Act. The 1914 act provides for the establishment of the five-member Federal Trade Commission (FTC), which has the power to enforce the act. In 1938, an

18-1 Typical complaints handled by the Federal Trade Commission. Activities prosecuted by the FTC involve alleged harm to competition or to consumers.

Unfair methods of competition and unfair or deceptive practices
1. Manufacturer of a liquid cleaning fluid falsely advertises that the cleanser will remove foreign matter from fabrics, will leave no ring, and will not injure material or color.
2. Manufacturer of aspirin falsely advertises that its product reduces toxicity and alleviates pain and fever more quickly than ordinary aspirin.
3. Printer uses the word "Engraving" in its corporate name, even though its process is merely printing in simulation of engraving.
4. Manufacturer of radios appropriates the trade names of certain well-known radio manufacturers and places their names on its radio sets.
5. Antiseptic-mouthwash manufacturer falsely claims that the U.S. government officially endorses its product.
6. Manufacturer misrepresents the composition of its "Method of Heatless Permanent Waving," which utilizes a physically harmful curling solution.
7. Distributor of vitamin concentrates misrepresents vitamin content to the extent that the concentrates could not have the therapeutic value claimed.
8. Clothing manufacturer and retailer falsely claims that its clothing is recommended by all consumer research bodies in the United States as the best in the low-priced field.
9. Manufacturer of baseball caps fails to disclose that its caps are not new but renovated.
10. Correspondence school falsely states that the tuition charge for a course will be raised soon to encourage students to enroll quickly.

Source: Federal Trade Commission.

amendment, the Wheeler–Lea Act, considerably strengthened the FTC's authority. The core of the Federal Trade Commission Act provides that "unfair methods of competition in commerce, and unfair or deceptive acts in commerce, are hereby declared unlawful." Typical unfair or deceptive practices prosecuted by the FTC are shown in Figure 18-1.

Restricting business activities that are harmful to competition or to consumers

The Federal Trade Commission is empowered to take action against any business practices that are deemed harmful either to competing firms or to consumers. Consumers and business owners who believe they have been harmed by unfair or deceptive practices may complain to the FTC, which carefully investigates such allegations. If the FTC believes that a violation has occurred, it issues a formal complaint, which must be answered by the alleged violator within 30 days. If, after additional investigation, the FTC is dissatisfied with the response to its complaint, it can issue a *cease-and-desist order* requiring that the offending act be discontinued. The business owner who is charged with a violation has three available options: to discontinue the practice as requested by the FTC; to appeal the case through the federal courts; or to continue the violation and risk a fine of up to $5000 a day. The Federal Trade Commission is also empowered to obtain data on the operations of a business, to issue periodic reports on business firms, to safeguard the public by preventing false advertising of such products as food, drugs, and cosmetics, and to administer most sections of the Sherman and Clayton acts in cooperation with the antitrust division of the U.S. Department of Justice.

Antitrust Enforcement

Objectives of antitrust laws

The basic objectives of antitrust enforcement are (1) the prevention of monopoly; (2) the elimination of conspiracies among ostensible competitors; (3) the control of unfair business practices that allow powerful firms in an industry to weaken their competitors; and (4) the protection of the public from deceptive advertising, false product labeling, and other misleading business practices.

Government agencies encounter a number of difficulties in attempting to realize these objectives. First, resources devoted to antitrust enforcement are meager in comparison with the huge U.S. gross national product. Total spending by all antitrust enforcement agencies—including state governments like New York and California, which vigorously enforce state antitrust laws—is less than $100 million annually. Second, court procedures to enforce antitrust laws are notoriously slow. It is common for an antitrust case to be processed through the court system for a decade or more. Third, antitrust penalties, shown in Figure 18-2, are small in comparison with the profits often obtained by violating the law. Finally, important industries like agricultural cooperatives, insurance, most public utilities, transportation, and labor unions enjoy partial or complete immunity from antitrust prosecution.

18-2   Important antitrust penalties. Antitrust penalties are varied but often less severe than the profits gained from violating antitrust laws.

Type of penalty	Who pays penalty	Description
Imprisonment and fine	Business executives	Executives who participate in antitrust violations can be jailed for a maximum of one year and can be fined up to $50,000 for each violation. Both penalties can be imposed simultaneously.
Fines	Business firms	Firms can be assessed a maximum fine of $500,000 for each violation.
Injunctions	Business firms	Businesses can be ordered by the courts to cease any practice that violates the law.
Dissolution	Business firms	The courts can order that a violating firm be divided into smaller units so the firm will not be powerful enough to reinstitute the violation.
Treble damages	Business firms	Private businesses as well as state and local governments that have been economically harmed by an antitrust violation can recover three times the amount of their damages. Recovery by the federal government is limited to the amount of the damages incurred.

The United States is the least concentrated industrialized economy

These and other difficulties in antitrust enforcement have allowed large businesses to grow still stronger and have permitted firms to engage in some practices that are not in the public interest. Despite these problems, economic concentration is lower in the United States than it is in any other industrialized nation; today, prudent American business owners weigh antitrust implications carefully when making important decisions.

Government Regulation of Business

Although the federal government encourages competition among American businesses, there are exceptions to this policy. In selected industries, which collectively represent 11 percent of the U.S. gross national product, monopoly is tolerated and even encouraged. These industries include:

1. *Transportation:* Railroads, trucking companies, bus lines, water carriers, airlines, and natural gas pipelines.

2. *Public utilities:* Firms providing electricity, gas, water, and sanitation services; radio and television stations; and telephone and telegraph companies.
3. *Financial business:* Banks, savings and loan associations, insurance companies, and security markets.

These firms are subjected to surveillance by federal and state *regulatory agencies,* which seek to control many of the activities in these industries.

Reasons for Government Regulation

Government regulation of private firms in the public utility, transportation, and finance sectors of the American economy has been justified on several grounds. First, monopoly may be inevitable and may even be desirable in certain industries. For example, if telephone companies competed for service within the same community, prices for telephone service would be prohibitively high, since each competitor would have to make a huge initial investment in lines and equipment. Through government regulation of *natural monopolies* like telephone service and other public utilities, prices charged to customers can be regulated as a result of the lower cost associated with having a single firm in the industry.

Second, some regulated industries provide services that are essential to the public. When an electric utility or a railroad abandons service to a community because of unprofitable operations, the welfare of the community may be threatened. In this case, public interest may take precedence over the economic well-being of the regulated business.

Third, some valuable activities may be undertaken only when investors are guaranteed the security of high monopolistic profits. For example, prospective investors might fear that competing cable television companies within a city would be unable to realize reasonable profits; in order to provide its residents with a cable television system, the city may have to accept a monopoly and endeavor to regulate it.

Finally, regulation may be essential when there is only a limited supply of a valuable resource. For example, allowing unrestricted competition among radio and television broadcasters would soon produce chaos on the airwaves. Here again, regulation may be necessary to prevent destructive competition.

*Acceptance
of monopoly
is essential in
some industries*

Functions of Regulatory Agencies

*Government agencies
supervise
regulated industries*

At the federal level, regulation is carried out by commissions whose members are appointed by the President subject to Senate approval. The most important federal regulatory agencies include the Federal

Communications Commission, the Interstate Commerce Commission, the Federal Aviation Administration, the Civil Aeronautics Board, the Atomic Energy Commission, the Federal Maritime Commission, the Federal Power Commission, and the Securities and Exchange Commission. Commission decisions are determined by a majority vote of commission members and can be reviewed by federal courts.

At the state level, business is regulated by a commission whose members are either elected by popular vote or are appointed by the state governor with the advice of the state senate. In some states, regulation is centralized in a single appointed or elected commissioner rather than in a board. Regulation by local government frequently involves the issuance of a *franchise*—a legal document permitting businesses to carry out activities over which the local government can exercise legal control. For example, cities often grant franchises to taxicab companies which allow them to sell their services within city limits. Franchisees must conform to the terms and conditions outlined in the franchise agreement.

What regulators do

The functions of government regulatory agencies include supervision of (1) the rates of prices charged by regulated businesses; (2) the quality and frequency of service provided by regulated firms; (3) the maximum profit permitted regulated businesses; and (4) the conditions under which new firms may enter the regulated industry. The content of regulation varies from industry to industry, reflecting the terms of the particular statute authorizing the regulation and the powers assigned to regulatory agencies.

State and Local Government Regulation

In the American federal system, state and local governments are responsible for protecting the health, safety, morals, and general welfare of their citizens. To promote these ends, state and local governments have established many regulations that affect businesses. Major areas of regulation include:

1. *Health and sanitation:* Laws and ordinances set safety and health standards and usually provide for the inspection of business premises.
2. *Business location and construction:* Local *zoning ordinances* allow businesses to operate only in designated areas within a community. *Building codes* set standards for the construction of residential housing and business offices or plants.
3. *Entry into professions and some businesses:* State and local governments often issue *licenses* permitting selected persons and businesses to engage in a given economic activity. Lawyers, accountants, doctors, dentists, and other professional groups frequently

must secure a public license before they are permitted to practice. Hotels, restaurants, bars, barbershops, theaters, and many other retailers must purchase licenses to legally operate a business. State and local governments issue licenses in an attempt to regulate the quality of the services offered, to collect revenues, and to control the number of people or businesses offering a particular service.

4. *Wages and working conditions:* Many state and local governments regulate the minimum wages an employer can pay, the hours a business can remain open, and the quality of the work environment. The amount of space allotted per worker, the available sanitation facilities, and the safety provisions in force are subject to state and local law to the extent that these matters are not covered by federal legislation.

5. *Usury laws:* State and local laws frequently specify the maximum interest rates various financial institutions can charge borrowers. Rates vary with the type of loan extended and with the credit worthiness of the borrower.

6. *Utility and insurance regulation:* Most state and local governments regulate the rates charged by public utilities like electric and gas producers and the premiums required by insurance companies. Typically, affected businesses must apply for a rate increase. A *public hearing* often takes place, at which the reasons for the application are reviewed. Opponents of the rate change are also allowed to voice their opinions. Eventually, the appropriate public officials must reach a decision. The new rate can be appealed through the state court system.

Reflecting a growing citizen concern over the quality of local neighborhoods, state and local governments have become much more active in the regulatory area. Some states and localities have even sought to use regulation to control or to halt local population growth. For example, the signs on some Oregon cars read "Please Visit Oregon But Don't Stay Here!"

SHOULD THE TRUCKING INDUSTRY BE REGULATED?

The application was intended as a joke. A midwestern trucker following due legal procedures requested that the Interstate Commerce Commission grant his firm permission to haul yak fat on an interstate basis. (When the application was filed, there were only a handful of yaks in the entire United States, and they were in zoos.) The railroad industry filed the standard reply: permitting additional trucker competition in the hauling of yak fat would undermine the American Railroad. Year after year, the ICC file on the yak-fat controversy continued to thicken.

Many experts believe that the trucking industry exemplifies the type of service that can best be sold in a competitive marketplace. Entry is inexpensive, and small trucking firms and self-employed truckers have demonstrated that they can compete effectively with larger firms. Yet the trucking industry is closely regulated by the ICC. Truckers must obtain ICC licenses to move goods from city to city (if interstate commerce is involved). And truckers frequently must backhaul — returning part or all of the way with an empty load because they lack appropriate ICC licenses. Truckers must also use ICC-required routes, most of which do not reflect post-World War II highway improvements.

Problems of Regulation

Like the government agencies that enforce the antitrust laws, regulatory agencies suffer from limited resources and from long delays while decisions are being made and implemented. Many regulation experts believe that regulatory commissions have been unsuccessful for two primary reasons.

Reasons that
regulation
has not been
entirely successful

✔ **Regulation protects the regulated.** While government regulation is intended to protect the public, regulatory agencies sometimes protect the businesses that they are supposed to be regulating. Small increases in prices for such regulated products as natural gas and telephone service generally go unnoticed by the public; consequently, most consumers are indifferent to the actions taken by regulatory bodies. But a few extra cents per month from thousands of customers can add up to substantial profits for gas or telephone companies. Thus, regulated industries have a powerful incentive to lobby for control over regulatory commissions. Since the contest for control is frequently between an involved, regulated industry and an indifferent public, it is hardly surprising that some regulated industries use the regulators to protect themselves from new competition.

✔ **Regulation promotes inefficiency.** Another deep-seated problem is that government regulation tends to foster inefficiency in business. In regulated industries, profits are determined according to a standard known as the fair rate of return. A *fair rate of return* is defined as the amount of profit that can reasonably be expected on investments of comparable risk in unregulated businesses. Historically, regulatory commissions have allowed profits to range from 5 to 8 percent annually; in recent years, annual rates of about 7 percent have been common.

The basic difficulty posed by this approach is the lack of incentive it provides. If a regulated business is inefficient, it will normally be allowed to raise its prices to cover its excessive costs. If the regulated business is efficient, any resulting profits will be removed through price reductions ordered by the regulatory commission. In the absence of meaningful incentives to reduce costs, regulated businesses can become highly inefficient.

Government Taxation of Business

Article 1, Section 8, of the U.S. Constitution allows the federal government "to collect revenues, to pay debts, and to provide for the common defense." Today, the taxing power of federal, state, and local governments is so extensive that a large corporation may be forced to file as many as 20,000 separate tax returns each year. The typical American corporation pays 44 percent of its net profits in federal income taxes alone. Few modern business decisions are made without a detailed examination of their potential tax consequences.

The Tax System

A *tax* is a sum levied by a governmental unit on an activity, usually for the purpose of raising revenue to support public expenditures. The four-cent federal tax on gasoline, collected on every gallon sold at every gas station, is a typical tax. Revenue from the federal gasoline tax is placed in a special Highway Trust Fund and is used to support highway construction and maintenance and to aid urban mass-transit systems.

The total dollar revenue produced by a tax is dependent on two factors; the tax base and the applicable tax rate. The *tax base* is the volume of economic activity that is taxed. Thus, the tax base for the federal gasoline tax is the number of gallons of gasoline consumed annually by American motorists. A four-cent tax per gallon on kerosene would produce far less revenue than the federal gasoline tax, since kerosene is in much less demand and therefore has a much lower tax base.

The *tax rate* represents the amount of tax collected for each unit in the tax base. A tax rate may be expressed as a given levy per physical unit of the tax base. For example, the federal gasoline tax is four cents per gallon, regardless of the selling prices of gasoline. Tax rates are often expressed as a given percentage of the tax base. For example, the federal tax on air travel is 8 percent of the selling price of each airline ticket purchased. It is important to observe that raising a tax rate may *reduce* government revenues by producing a decline in the tax base. For example, the very high federal and state taxes on hard liquor seem to have been one factor that encouraged consumers to shift to beverages with lower alcoholic content to the point that the high taxes eventually reduced revenue. An additional problem is that some producers and consumers try to evade paying excessively high taxes by "bootlegging," or selling liquor illegally to avoid paying the required taxes.

Taxes are commonly described as progressive, proportional, or regressive. Under a *progressive* tax, persons with high incomes are required to pay a larger percentage of their earnings to the government than are low-income families. The federal income tax, for example, requires individuals with very high incomes to pay as much as 50 percent of their annual earnings in taxes, while very poor families pay no tax at all. Despite numerous tax exemptions and "loopholes," studies indicate that the federal income tax is largely progressive in its impact.

Under a *proportional tax,* the same percentage of income is taxed, regardless of the level of earnings. Some state income taxes are proportional, requiring that income recipients pay a fixed proportion of their incomes to the state. Few, if any, exemptions are allowed.

Under a *regressive tax,* poor families are required to pay a higher portion of their income in taxes than the rich. A four-cent state sales tax, collected on all items purchased at retail, is considered a regressive tax. Normally poor families use all of their incomes to purchase basic necessities and therefore pay a sales tax on their total incomes. Wealthy families, on the other hand, are able to save a portion of their incomes and pay no sales tax on this saved income. Thus, a sales tax is typically regressive. Many states reduce or eliminate this regressiveness by exempting food and drugs from the sales tax.

Regressive taxes: the rich pay little or nothing

Goals of Taxation

Many taxpayers consider a "good" tax one that is imposed on someone else. In the public interest, however, an effective tax should meet the following criteria:

1. *The tax should be capable of raising meaningful amounts of revenue.* Frivolous or minor taxes should be avoided because they can be both confusing and costly. *Confiscatory taxes,* where the imposition of the tax destroys or seriously erodes the tax base, are also undesirable.

A good tax should meet several criteria

2. *The tax should cause minimum economic distortions.* Excessive taxes on particular industries or economic activities often disrupt the free enterprise system because the affected taxpayers are forced to raise the prices of the goods or services they offer in the marketplace. Customers then base their purchasing decisions on these artificially inflated prices instead of on the actual costs of producing the commodities. The result is a poor allocation of resources (already discussed in Chapter 2). Excessive income taxes on individuals and businesses may also reduce their incentive to work long and hard or to take risks, since much of their resultant gains may disappear in taxes. Excessive taxation of business can reduce aftertax profits to the point that business owners are unable or unwilling to invest in new plant and equipment. Reduction of future productive capacity lessens opportunities for new jobs and tends to be inflationary, since the quantity of goods and services that can be produced does not rise rapidly. Taxes are also altered to counter business cycles. By lowering tax rates during a recession, the government places added purchasing power in consumer hands. Increased consumer spending should produce an economic upturn and increased employment. The opposite action

is followed during inflation, when tax rates are adjusted upward in an attempt to reduce consumer spending.

3. *The tax should be equitable.* What constitutes a fair tax is a controversial question. Two contrasting views are widely accepted. Under the *benefit principle,* users of government services are required to pay a tax or a fee that is approximately equal to the cost of providing the service. The four-cent federal gasoline tax is an example of the use of the benefit principle, since the motorists who use government-financed highways the most pay the bulk of this tax. The *ability-to-pay principle* assumes that tax collections should be based largely on the taxpayer's economic status. According to this standard, taxpayers in superior financial positions—high-income families or highly profitable businesses—should pay a larger tax share than their proportionate usage of governmental services indicate. Most income taxes are based on the ability-to-pay principle.

4. *Taxes should be inexpensive to administer and to collect.* The cost and time involved in assessing and collecting a tax should be small in comparison with the revenue the tax produces. The costs to be considered include the expense and the time required of the taxpayer as well as of the government.

5. *Taxes should be simple and direct and should give the appearances of fairness.* Taxes should be simple and direct so that they will be understood by the taxpayer. Indirect or hidden taxes are undesirable because the taxpayer may be deceived about the costs of government services. Legal or illegal methods of nonpayment should be avoided because they erode citizen confidence in the fairness of the tax system.

Taxes are often designed to secure a variety of specific objectives other than those just described. For example, taxes on gambling are intended to discourage this activity. Tariffs on imports are designed to protect affected American industries from foreign competition.

All taxes are imperfect No tax is perfect. Sales taxes are easy to understand and raise large amounts of revenue, but their regressiveness is unfair to many people. Thus, a tax is considered "good" if it achieves minimum levels of acceptability in terms of each tax objective.

Types of Taxes

Differences in objectives and in the political powers of various special interest groups have resulted in a large variety of taxes. The major sources of federal funding are individual income taxes, social security taxes, corporate income taxes, and excise taxes (see Figure 18-3). State and

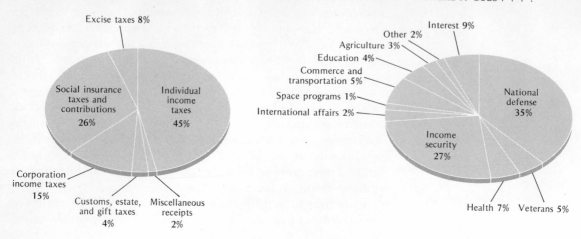

WHERE IT COMES FROM . . . .

Excise taxes 8%

Social insurance
taxes and
contributions
26%

Individual
income
taxes
45%

Corporation
income taxes
15%

Customs, estate,
and gift taxes
4%

Miscellaneous
receipts
2%

WHERE IT GOES . . . .

Interest 9%

Other 2%

Agriculture 3%

Education 4%

Commerce and
transportation 5%

Space programs 1%

International affairs 2%

National
defense
35%

Income
security
27%

Health 7%   Veterans 5%

18-3   The annual federal budget, 1970–1973 average. The major sources of federal revenue are income and social security taxes.

Source: *Statistical Abstract of the United States.*

Major types of taxes include . . .   local government finances are based on property and sales taxes (Figure 18-4). The most important taxes in the United States include income taxes, sales taxes, property taxes, payroll taxes, estate taxes, and customs duties.

✔ **Income taxes.** *Income taxes* are levied on all persons or family units who reach a level of income prescribed by the federal government

18-4   The state and local government dollar, 1971. The major sources of revenue for state and local governments are sales and property taxes.

WHERE IT COMES FROM . . . .

Utilities and
liquor stores
6¢

Insurance trusts 7¢

Federal
government
16¢

Property
taxes
22¢

Charges and
miscellaneous
14¢

Other
taxes
15¢

Sales and gross
receipts taxes
20¢

WHERE IT GOES . . . .

Utilities and
liquor stores
6¢

Insurance trusts
6¢

Other general
expenditures
27¢

Education
34¢

Public welfare,
hospitals, and health
16¢

Highways
11¢

Source: *Statistical Abstract of the United States.*

and by some state and local governments. The typical taxpayer is required to fill out a *tax return*—a document on which income received and certain expenditures are listed. We already know that the federal income tax is progressive and is intended to reflect the ability-to-pay principle. An important feature of most income taxes is *the withholding system,* in which the employer deducts a portion of an employee's wages from each paycheck. The withheld wages are sent to the appropriate government agency, which credits them against the tax liability indicated on the employee's tax return. Businesses must participate in the withholding system; a firm is legally responsible for making appropriate withholding adjustments in its employees' pay.

income taxes,

Corporate income taxes are taxes levied directly on businesses by the federal government and by most state and many local governments. At the federal level, corporations pay 22 percent of the first $25,000 of profits in corporate income taxes; 25 percent on the second $25,000 in profits; and 48 percent of profits beyond $50,000. Because most businesses are entitled to various tax deductions, the average effective corporate tax rate is 44 percent of net income.

The bulk of corporate income taxes are ultimately paid by the public, because businesses normally pass their tax burdens along to the consumer in the form of higher priced goods and services. Corporate income taxes are especially attractive to political leaders, because of their low visibility and the large revenues they produce.

✔ **Sales taxes.**   *Sales taxes* are levied on consumers by many state and local governments. A *general sales tax* is a tax on all commodities, with the possible exception of food and other basic necessities of life. The sales tax is a percentage of the selling price of the goods purchased. Businesses and other affected organizations are responsible for collecting sales taxes from consumers and distributing them to the appropriate government agencies. State sales tax rates usually vary between 3 and 5 percent of the selling price of the goods or services purchased.

sales taxes,

Excise taxes are sales taxes on particular commodities. The eight-cent federal tax on each pack of cigarettes is an example of an excise tax at the manufacturer's level. Retail excise taxes include the state and local taxes on stores that sell alcoholic beverages and cigarettes.

Although sales and excise taxes are usually regressive, they appeal to government officials. These taxes are sometimes less painful than income taxes, since the taxpayer is charged only a few pennies at any one time. Sales and excise taxes are readily understandable and are difficult to avoid.

✔ **Property taxes.**   *Property taxes* are the most important source of revenue for local governments, especially for primary and secondary education. Each local government unit (and a few state units) levy property taxes based on the *assessed valuation* of a person's property and on the applicable property tax rate. A local government official, the tax assessor, estimates the value of a family home or a business plant, usually at much

property taxes,

less than the property's market value. The assessed valuation is then multiplied by the applicable tax rate. For example, in a city where the property tax rate is $50 per $1000 of assessed valuation, the owner of a home assessed at $30,000 would pay $1500 in property taxes.

A major disadvantage of property taxes is the unfair tax burden that results from inaccurate assessments. It is hard to be completely objective about valuations of property, and a very real opportunity for corruption is present in the assessment process.

✔ **Payroll taxes.** Employers usually pay employee or *payroll taxes* by withholding a fixed percentage of a worker's wage. Major payroll taxes include social security taxes, which are administered by the federal government; worker compensation taxes, which are paid to state governments; and local payroll taxes, which are levied by some local governments. Unlike income taxes, payroll taxes are based solely on wage earnings and exclude income from rented property, interest on savings, and capital gains.

✔ **Estate taxes.** *Estate taxes* or *death duties* are on the wealth of an individual at death. Estate taxes payable to federal and state governments are assessed on the market value of all assets owned by the person at death. At the Federal level, estate taxes are progressive and the first $60,000 of the estate is not taxed.

Some state governments levy *inheritance taxes* on each heir, according to the size of the inheritance and to that heir's relationship to the deceased. Inheritance taxes are paid by recipients of a bequest and not by the estate of the deceased.

Persons who transfer money or property to other persons by donation must pay *gift taxes*. Federal gift tax rates provide each donor with a $3000 annual exemption and a $30,000 lifetime exemption. Gift taxes are progressive and are levied so that wealthy persons cannot avoid estate and inheritance taxes by transferring property before death.

Estate, inheritance, and gift taxes have an important impact on businesses. Many family-owned companies are sold in order to pay estate and inheritance taxes. In addition, providing a *trust fund* or *trust account*—a legal method of transferring wealth from one individual to another—can reduce estate and inheritance taxes. Banks, insurance companies, and other financial institutions manage hundreds of billions of dollars in trust accounts—a major source of business for this important sector of the U.S. economy.

The increased size of government has burdened everyone with higher tax bills. In 1977, the average American family is expected to pay 40 percent of its income in direct and indirect taxes to all levels of government. High taxes have produced a growing concern with tax reform. Most tax-reform proposals emphasize the following points. First, inequitable tax burdens should be removed. Because of high property and sales taxes, poor families often pay as large a portion of their income in taxes as the very rich do. Second, tax loopholes that conflict with the public interest should be removed. The very substantial tax advantages still enjoyed by the oil industry, for example, are difficult to justify in an era of high oil prices and oil company profits.

Taxes and Business Decisions

Taxes directly affect business in a number of ways. Business managers normally consider the *after-tax* profitabilities of alternative investments when making financial decisions. Plant-location decisions are often based on prevailing tax levels in various regions or nations. Business owners may base their decisions to expand or to contract production of a particular commodity on tax considerations. Businesses often prefer debt to equity financing, because interest is a tax-deductible expense while dividends are not. Business owners and managers frequently receive a portion of their pay in fringe benefits like health insurance and retirement programs, because fringe benefits are not subject to taxation within specified limits.

Taxation also burdens business with considerable paperwork. In addition to the physical job of filling in hundreds of thousands of tax returns, businesses must maintain accounting records in the manner that taxing agencies prescribe. Like individual taxpayers, business owners must be prepared to justify their tax returns since businesses are subject to government audits, usually once a year. Most important, the business owner serves as a tax collector. A business sends the sales taxes it collects from customers to the state treasury. Employee contributions to federal and state withholding income tax systems and to the social security system are collected by the business and are forwarded to the appropriate government agency. Such varied tax-related activities provide ample employment opportunities for specialists in tax law and tax accounting.

Taxes affect business decisions . . .

. . . and add to paperwork

KEY POINTS TO REMEMBER

1. Government influences business by (1) the types of services it offers; (2) its direct purchases from business; and (3) the laws and regulations it administers.
2. The influence of government, at first limited in scope, has steadily expanded. Today, government serves as a mediator between conflicting interest groups, as a creator of countervailing power, and as an active provider of services.

3. The federal government is divided into the executive, legislative, and judicial branches, as are many state and local governments.

4. Federal antitrust legislation seeks to promote competition and to prevent economic concentration. Antitrust laws prohibit price fixing and monopolization and regulate mergers.

5. Government regulation of business extends throughout much of the transportation, public utility, and financial industries. Rates, services, profits, and conditions under which new firms may enter the industry are the main areas regulated by commissions, whose members are appointed by government officials.

6. To finance their activities, federal, state, and local governments rely on taxes collected from consumers and businesses.

7. An effective tax raises revenue, causes minimum economic distortions, and is equitable, inexpensive to administer, and direct.

8. Businesses are legally responsible for collecting a number of federal and local taxes. Business owners pay several taxes; the most extensive are corporate income taxes and business property taxes.

9. Taxes affect financial business decisions, since the *after-tax* profitabilities of alternative decisions are frequently considered.

QUESTIONS FOR DISCUSSION

1. Discuss the main ways in which federal and local governments affect business.

2. Government has been viewed as playing a triple role, acting as a mediator, as a source of countervailing power, and as an active economic and social force. Define and contrast these roles. Which role or roles do you believe government should play?

3. In what ways have government activities been changing in the 1970s?

4. "The antitrust laws are designed to promote competition among businesses and to direct competition into economically desirable channels." In what specific ways do the antitrust laws attempt to accomplish the objectives outlined in this statement?

5. "Direct government regulation of business seeks to secure and to control monopoly." In what specific ways do regulatory government agencies illustrate this statement? Are other activities that are not related to the control of monopoly subject to direct government regulation? Explain and illustrate your answer.

6. Can tax rates be set too high? Explain your answer.

7. Contrast a progressive, a proportional, and a regressive tax. What type of tax do you believe to be fairest?

8. What criteria must a tax meet before it can be said to be in the best interests of the public?

9. Define individual income tax, corporate income tax, sales and excise taxes, and property, payroll, estate, inheritance, and gift taxes. Evaluate each tax in terms of the criteria you developed in response to Question 8.

SHORT CASES AND PROBLEMS

1. Evaluate the following business practices in terms of (1) their probable effect on the business proposing them; (2) their impact on competition in the industry; and (3) their legality. Which practices, if any, do you think are in the public interest?
   (a) Slope Ski Company sells skis and ski boots only in combination, charging $79.95 for both.
   (b) Gasoline stations in your hometown simultaneously raise prices from 62 cents per gallon to 68 cents per gallon.
   (c) Baking companies with national distribution charge 28 cents per loaf of bread in Nebraska and 40 cents or more per loaf elsewhere.
   (d) Slimline bread is advertised as containing fewer calories per slice. Investigation indicates that the claim is accurate only because Slimline bread slices are thinner than other brands.

2. Assume that you are an executive in charge of transformers. In the last two years, because of tough competition, prices have slipped below production costs. Your boss informs you that there will be a major shakeup in the company unless the transformer division's profits rise to an acceptable level. You know that price fixing is successfully restoring profits in other company divisions. With your job on the line, you are invited to meet with competitors at an isolated Canadian lodge. What is your response to the invitation?

3. Calculate the following taxes due:
   (a) On a state income tax, you have a total income of $20,000, deductions of $5000, and a flat income tax rate of 10 percent of your taxable income, defined by the state tax code as total income *minus* deductions.
   (b) Homes in a local community are assessed at 50 percent of their market value, with a tax rate of $25 per $1000 of assessed valuation. Your house has an estimated market value of $40,000.
   (c) A business corporation earns a profit of $1,050,000. What is its federal income tax? (*Hint:* Remember that *several* rates apply to the federal corporate income tax.)

Nearly 25 percent of the civilian labor force is employed at the federal, state, or local government level in thousands of varied occupations. Information concerning federal job opportunities is available either from the U.S. Civil Service Commission (see your local telephone book or contact your local post office) or from your state Civil Service Commission. The following job descriptions represent only a small sampling of the many government jobs that are available, but these occupations do indicate that the salaries of government employees have increased much more rapidly than the incomes of employees in private industries.

CAREERS IN URBAN PLANNING

Urban planners develop proposals to improve the quality of city life. Some of the specific urban planning problems that require an imaginative decision-making ability are the restoration of blighted residential and industrial districts, the development of recreation and transportation facilities, and the reduction of air and noise pollution. A bachelor's degree in city planning, architecture, or engineering is essential; many state and federal jobs also require a graduate degree. Advancement is limited, although exceptional planners may be promoted to planning director. Annual salary ranges from $7700 to $25,000 and depends upon the size of the city for which the planner works. The trend toward urbanization is expected to moderately expand the job market for urban planners in the immediate future. (*Additional information:* American Institute of Planners; 917 15th Street, N.W.; Washington, D.C. 20005.)

CAREERS AS GOVERNMENT INSPECTORS

Health inspectors enforce government regulations to protect the public welfare. Health inspectors are employed at all levels of government and generally specialize in one specific type of consumer protection: **food and drug inspectors,** the largest subcategory of health inspectors, insure that products are wholesome, safe, and honestly labeled; **meat and poultry inspectors** enforce proper sanitation practices and check the accuracy of product labeling; **foreign quarantine inspectors** guarantee that both immigrants and imported cargoes are free from contagious disease. The educational requirements for health inspectors vary: food and drug inspectors must have a bachelor of science degree; meat and poultry inspectors and quarantine inspectors are often high-school graduates who have had several years of work experience in a related field. All health inspectors begin as trainees and, after learning the specialized inspection procedures in their particular field, may advance to the position of supervisory inspector. Inspectors must also score satisfactorily on a civil service examination. Annual income averages $13,000. The growing emphasis on consumer protection is expected to create a rapidly expanding job market for health inspectors. (*Additional information:* Interagency Board of U.S. Civil Service Examiners for Washington, D.C.; 1900 E Street, N.W.; Washington, D.C. 20415.)

Like health inspectors, **regulatory inspectors** enforce government regulations to safeguard and protect the general public. An assortment of specialized positions exists: **customs inspectors** insure that imported and exported goods meet legal and health standards and that travelers comply with immigration laws; **aviation safety officers** inspect both aircraft equipment and aircraft personnel to see that they meet safety and quality regulations; **mine inspectors** enforce safe and healthy mining practices; **wage-hour compliance officers** verify that minimum-wage, overtime, and equal-employment procedures comply with federal law. Most regulatory inspectors must have three to five years previous experience in a related field; applicants with some education at the college level can qualify with less actual work experience. Only wage-hour compliance officers must have a bachelor's degree, usually in accounting, business administration, or economics. All regulatory inspectors must past a civil service examination. After the completion of a long training program, competent inspectors may advance to supervisor or district manager. Annual income averages $15,000. A growing recognition of the need for public protection should create a moderately expanding job market for regulatory inspectors. (*Additional information:* Interagency Board of U.S. Civil Service Examiners for Washington, D.C.; 1900 E Street, N.W.; Washington, D.C. 20415.)

Construction inspectors are primarily employed by municipal and county building departments to insure that the quality of construction activities meets standard safety regulations. Construction inspectors interpret and enforce building codes, zoning ordinances, and contract specifications, and—in the event of legal infractions—issue "stop-work" orders. High-school graduates who have several years of general construction, electrical, or plumbing experience are considered qualified job applicants. Community-college courses in blueprint reading and in technical mathematics are assets. Employers provide on-the-job training programs to acquaint new employees with building ordinances and inspection techniques. Advancement to a higher position generally requires an engineering degree. Annual salary ranges from $7000 to $18,000. The continuing expansion of construction activities is expected to foster a rapidly growing job market for construction inspectors. (*Additional information:* International Conference of Building Officials; 5360 Workman Mill Road; Whittier, California 90601.)

A CRITICAL BUSINESS DECISION

—made by Benjamin Franklin Bailar and the U.S. Postal Service

THE SITUATION   During July 1971, amid much fanfare, the U.S. Postal Service was created—a step President Nixon was subsequently to hail as "one of the major achievements of my administration." The Post Office, once widely regarded as a plaything for politicians, had been drastically reorganized. No longer directly affiliated with the federal government, headed by a politically appointed Postmaster General and supervised by Congress, the new U.S. Postal Service was an independently operated public corporation, much like the Tennessee Valley Authority.

The initial performance of the new Postal Service was impressive: its operating deficit narrowed from $175 million in fiscal 1971—the first year of full operation—to $13 million in fiscal 1973. The Service also began to make the huge capital investments in mail-handling equipment that most experts believed would increase the speed and lessen the expense of mail delivery. But then disaster struck. In 1974, the Service's deficit widened to $438 million; its deficit in 1975 was an estimated $869 million. The Postal Service was forced to cover its ominously mounting operating deficits by long-term borrowing. Service began to deteriorate. In 1969, it took 1.3 days to deliver an average first-class letter; by 1975, the equivalent figure was 1.6 days.

THE DECISION   "Our direction to a large extent is set by the law," explains J.T. Ellington, Jr., an Assistant Postmaster General. Postal charges are regulated by the Postal Rate Commission—an autonomous government-appointed body. The Postal Rate Commission has delayed Postal Service requests for rate increases for months and, in some cases, for several years. Nevertheless, in the first four years of operation, Postal Service charges increased by an average of 67 percent, in contrast with a 31-percent increase in consumer prices during the same period.

John Strachan, Postmaster of New York, describes the main cause of the Postal Service's problems: "The way it's going, this will always be a labor-intensive industry. The mail carrier still puts the sack on his back." Led by strong, politically active, public-service unions, postal employees have won substantial pay increases. The annual earnings of an average postal worker rose from $10,300 in 1971 to $15,461 in 1975—an average individual gain of 49 percent. Thus, the total payroll of the Postal Service ballooned from approximately $7 billion in 1971 to more than $11 billion in 1975.

Wages were rising dramatically, but gains in productivity remained slight. In 1974, the productivity of Postal Service employees actually fell one percent. Employee unions have also resisted changes in work standards designed to improve productivity, claiming that they would result in the elimina-tion of 15,000 to 20,000 jobs and that many of the new work standards were trivial and unproductive.

And increased postal rates have generated stiff competition. United Parcel Service—a highly respected private carrier—has captured more than half of the parcel-carrying market from the Postal Service. Even in areas where direct competition is legally prohibited, the Postal Service market may be eroding. Transmission of checks and data by telephone could substantially reduce first-class mailings, which currently account for 58 percent of all Postal Service revenues.

Finally, higher postal charges, compared with lower long-distance telephone rates, have caused the public to use the mails less both on an absolute and on a per-capita basis. Thus, as the population has grown, the number of delivery points has also risen—the Postal Service estimates that it currently costs an average of $48 annually to service a typical home mailbox—but without an equivalent gain in revenues from the public.

Thus, in 1975, Postmaster General Benjamin Franklin Bailar and the U.S. Postal Service confront several key decisions. Should the Postal Service seek renewed subsidies from the U.S. Treasury? Could the Postal Service survive as an independent business? Should the Postal Service once again be operated directly by the federal government?

QUESTION

In what major ways does the operation of the U.S. Postal Service—a publicly owned enterprise—differ from the operation of a private business firm?

When a great many people are unable to find work, unemployment results.

Calvin Coolidge

THE AMERICAN LABOR MOVEMENT

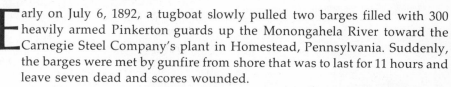

Early on July 6, 1892, a tugboat slowly pulled two barges filled with 300 heavily armed Pinkerton guards up the Monongahela River toward the Carnegie Steel Company's plant in Homestead, Pennsylvania. Suddenly, the barges were met by gunfire from shore that was to last for 11 hours and leave seven dead and scores wounded.

The Pinkerton detectives had been hired by Henry Clay Frick, Carnegie Steel's militantly antiunion general manager, to break a strike called by the Amalgamated Association of Iron, Steel, and Tin Workers. When a truce was finally called, the Pinkertons agreed never to return to Homestead.

This confrontation between the nation's most powerful union and one of its largest corporations received tremendous publicity. On July 7, the *Chicago Tribune* devoted its entire front page to "a battle which for bloodthirstiness and boldness was not exceeded in actual warfare."

The Homestead battle was just one of a series of confrontations between labor and management that occurred from the late 1800s to World War II. On occasion these confrontations were violent, but more often they were fought in the courts. With the advent of the New Deal in 1933, labor unions gradually became sanctioned and protected by federal statute. Today, unions no longer need to battle for their right to exist, but they retain some of the militancy born of their early struggle for recognition. Highlights of the development of the American labor movement appear in Figure 19-1.

American Labor Today

Types of unions

A *labor union* is a group of workers who band together to achieve common goals related to their employment. *Craft unions* like the Brotherhood of Machinists represent a single profession. *Industrial unions* encompass all workers in a plant, whatever their occupation. Thus, the United Auto Workers, a very influential industrial union, includes nearly all skilled and unskilled employees who earn hourly rates in the automotive industry. The ten largest labor unions and their memberships appear in Figure 19-2.

19-1 Milestones in the American labor movement. American unions have a long history of activity, internal controversy, and confrontation with business and government.

Year	Event	Significance
1636	Fishermen employed by Robert Trelawney of Richmond Island, Maine, mutiny when their wages are withheld.	First recorded American labor dispute.
1794	The Federal Society of Journeymen Cordwainers (shoemakers) is formed in Philadelphia.	First permanent continuing labor union.
1827	The Mechanics Union of Trade Associations is founded in Philadelphia.	First association of unions on a city-wide basis.
1830	Worker parties are formed in many localities; labor unions try to influence elections.	First attempt by unions to exert political power.
1834	The National Trade Union is organized.	First attempt to organize a labor federation on a national scale.
1869	The Knights of Labor is organized in Philadelphia by Uriah S. Stevens. Membership is open to all workers, except doctors, lawyers, bankers, liquor sellers, stockbrokers, and professional gamblers. The Knights oppose strikes and emphasize political reform, abolition of the wage system, and the development of cooperatives.	First effective national federation of labor unions.
1886	Samuel Gompers organizes the American Federation of Labor (AFL) around four principles: (1) internal independence of each affiliated union; (2) nonencroachment of affiliates on other members' jurisdictions; (3) assistance to friends, regardless of political party; and (4) achievement of wage increases and other employee benefits by direct negotiation rather than by legislation.	First strong national federation of craft unions.
1938	John L. Lewis organizes the Congress of Industrial Organizations (CIO), an association of industrial unions, after splitting with the AFL in 1935.	Independent organization of industrial unions.
1955	The American Federation of Labor and the Congress of Industrial Organizations merge to form the AFL–CIO, which represents about three-fourths of all unionized workers.	First merger of national labor organizations
1969	The United Auto Workers (UAW) leave the AFL–CIO, joining the teamsters and the chemical workers to form the Alliance for Labor Action. In 1972, the teamsters drop out of the alliance.	Organized labor once again divides into two rival national federations.

Organization of Unions

To understand the organization of today's labor unions, it is essential to examine union operations at the local, regional, and national levels.

🖊 **The local level.** The basic unit of a labor union is the *local* (or the *local union*), in which each member is enrolled directly. Locals hold periodic conventions to elect their officers and to select representatives to

19-2

Membership in the ten largest labor unions in the United States, 1973. Major labor unions enroll hundreds of thousands of members and possess considerable economic and political powers.

Rank	Union	Membership
1	Teamsters, Chauffeurs, Warehousers, and Helpers	1,855,000
2	Steelworkers	1,409,000
3	Automotive, Aircraft, and Agricultural Implement Workers	1,394,000
4	Electrical Workers	957,000
5	Carpenters and Joiners	829,000
6	Machinists	758,000
7	Retail Clerks	633,000
8	Hod Carriers, Building and Common Laborers	600,000
9	Meat Cutters and Butchers	529,000
10	State, County, and Municipal Employees	529,000

* Excludes professional groups like the American Medical Association and the National Education Association.

Source: *Directory of National Unions and Employee Associations: 1973* (Washington, D.C.: U.S. Bureau of Labor Statistics, 1974). p. 74.

higher-level union organizations. Locals also hold meetings to conduct union business, hear speakers, and sponsor social affairs. Each member is entitled to participate in union discussions and to vote on all matters that come before the membership. Unions also require members to pay *union dues,* which cover the cost of membership meetings, provide salaries for union officials, and help unions promote their legislative efforts.

At the local level, the most important union official is the *shop steward* (or the *business agent*), who collects union dues, handles worker grievances, and represents the union to the workers. Shop stewards are elected by the local as a whole or by the smaller worker group they represent.

The shop steward represents the work group

✔ **The regional level.** At the state or regional level, unions are represented by district offices, regional councils, and joint boards. State or regional officials are elected either by the entire union or by the combined vote of all locals within the region. These officials coordinate the activities of locals and represent their union before appropriate public bodies.

✔ **The national level.** National (or international) unions are composed of the elected representatives of the locals, who are required to convene at least once every five years. In most unions, the president and other officials are elected at the convention; in about a quarter of all unions, national officers are elected by direct referendum among the membership. The president, other union officials, and the permanent staff are expected to work full time for the national union and are paid accordingly.

Functions of the national union

When unions negotiate with large businesses, the most important bargaining usually takes place at the national level. Locals negotiate with

management only when a dispute involves a particular plant. The main functions of the national union are:

1. To negotiate with employers at the national level.
2. To represent union members before Congress and the executive branch.
3. To discipline corrupt or overly militant locals. Most national unions have the power to place locals in receivership and appoint their officers and delegates to other bodies.

Craft and industrial unions often join together at the local, state, and national levels to achieve joint goals. At the local level, federations of unions within a municipality, called *city centrals,* represent most local union members. At the state level, the state or regional council is often the most important official speaker for organized labor. The main purposes of such federations are to coordinate union political activities and to provide assistance to members through interunion loans and agreements to respect the picket lines of striking union workers. As Figure 19-3 indicates, the apex of union organization is the AFL–CIO, which represents more than 300 separate local, state, and national union bodies and a total of over 15 million workers.

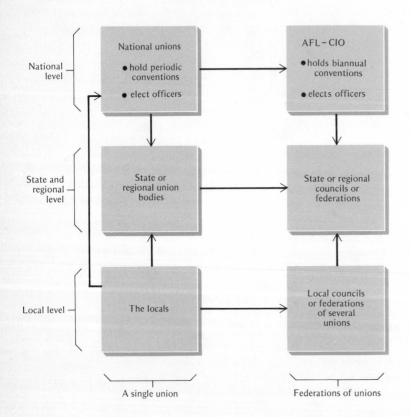

19-3

Union organization in the United States. Arrows indicate how each level of the organization normally elects or appoints representatives to the appropriate union.

Challenges to Organized Labor

Like other institutions in American society, organized labor faces a number of problems and challenges. The ability of unions to respond to these challenges will determine their influence in the future.

Union membership is lagging

✔ **Loss of vitality in organized labor.** Figure 19-4 shows union membership from 1930 to 1973 as a percentage of the civilian labor force. These data clearly indicate that the growth rate of union membership, which peaked in 1943, is beginning to decline. Some experts attribute this loss of vitality to an aging union leadership and to lagging drives to organize new workers, particularly white-collar workers and employees in service industries—the most rapidly growing segments of the labor force.

However, unions are enjoying spectacular success in organizing employees in the rapidly growing public sector of the economy. More and more firefighters, police officers, teachers, professors, and civil service personnel at all levels of government have joined unions in the 1970s. Although most states maintain laws that prohibit or restrict strikes by organized public employees, unions in the public sector often successfully defy the law, creating major dilemmas. Examples: Should Montreal police officers have been allowed to strike, producing a spectacular rise in crime? Can New York City afford to have garbage pile up in its streets while municipal sanitation unions engage in prolonged arbitration? To jail all public service employees who strike is clearly impossible. To capitulate to union demands is to force higher taxes or poorer government services on the public.

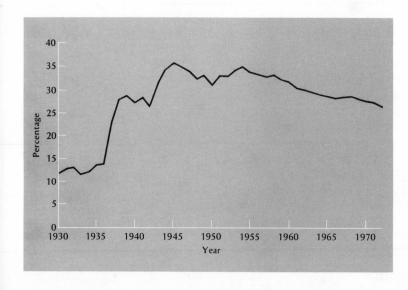

19-4

Union membership as a percentage of the civilian labor force has declined since World War II.

Source: *Statistical Abstract of the United States.*

The generation gap in labor. Nearly half of all union members are under 40 years of age and a third are less than 30; yet, the majority of union leaders are over 50. This generation gap is reflected in growing ideological differences among union members. Older workers tend to emphasize preservation of the *seniority system*, which assigns employees important work privileges (such as protection against layoffs) on the basis of their years of service. Older union members also favor increases in *fringe benefits*—employer contributions in addition to basic wages or salaries, such as paid holidays, free health and accident insurance, and pension plans. In contrast, younger workers resent the seniority system, prefer immediate wage increases, and seek more varied and interesting jobs.

Older union members and younger workers often differ

Foreign competition. In recent years, American labor has faced a stiff challenge from foreign industries in Western Europe and Japan, where lower labor costs and increasingly competitive productivity rates often enable manufacturers to undersell American-made products, both abroad and in the United States. According to public opinion polls, most Americans and most union members believe that costly wage settlement negotiations are pricing U.S. products out of world markets. The flood of foreign imports in heavily unionized industries like steel, automobiles, and machinery, and the subsequent loss of union jobs, may be the two most important long-term problems American labor will have to face in the near future.

Foreign competitors: a challenge to unions

Unions as a political force. In the 1930s the American Federation of Labor (AFL) began to aid workers by taking direct political actions, such as improving the legal status of organized labor and obtaining higher minimum wages. Since then, labor has become a powerful political force in American life, and the objectives of labor have inevitably clashed with the goals of other special interest groups. As one union official observed: "Now we step on everyone's toes, not just the employer's toes." Over 70 percent of the American people oppose the further growth of unions, and 55 percent believe that unions already are too powerful.

While American labor still confronts many challenges, it has emerged from its stormy beginnings into a major economic and social force. Like other powerful organizations, the actions of American labor are closely scrutinized by the public.

Sources of Labor–Management Conflicts

The American labor movement presents business with a stiff challenge, since the goals of employees and unions often conflict with the policies of management. Business managers incapable of understanding the sources of these differences are often confronted with severe labor problems.

A business challenge: understanding labor's goals

Basic Goals: The Employee View

We have already seen that there are significant differences in goals among individual workers. Moreover, unions do not always fully represent employee desires. In negotiating with employers, however, unions traditionally emphasized five basic goals.

✔ **Better wages and fringe benefits.** Improvements in wages, in other methods of employee payment (see Figure 19-5), and in fringe benefits have been a primary goal of organized labor. Unions have become so successful that the costs of such fringe benefits as pensions, free health care and insurance, and paid vacations have reached 50 percent of the total costs of wages and salaries.

19-5   Common methods of payment to employees in American business. Types of payment vary from industry to industry and from job to job within individual industries.

Method of payment	Description
Straight salary	Weekly, monthly, or annual payments are made for the period worked.
Hourly pay	Wages are paid on the basis of the number of hours worked multiplied by agreed-on pay rate per hour. Workers record the number of hours worked by punching in on a time-clock or by signing a time card.
Overtime pay	Overtime rates apply when an employee works beyond the stated minimum number of hours per week. Employees are often paid one and a half times the normal hourly rate for overtime during the work week and double the hourly rate for overtime on weekends.
Shift premiums	Employees often receive higher hourly wages for working evening or early morning shifts in plants that operate more than 8 hours per day.
Piecework	Workers are paid according to their output: for example, 5 cents for each rim placed on a tire in a tire factory.
Commissions	Often paid to sales personnel, commissions are a fixed percentage of an employee's total sales. The percentage may be increased if the employee performs especially well.
Bonuses	Employees receive extra pay when their work is outstanding or when the business has had a good year. The amount of the bonus varies with the employer.
Profit sharing	Workers receive periodic payments in addition to their regular wages or salary. The amount of the profit-sharing payment is related to the employee's base wage and to the firm's profitability.
Guaranteed annual wage	The firm agrees to pay each worker a stipulated minimum annual income, whether or not there is enough work to keep the employee busy throughout the year.
Cost-of-living escalator	Increases are made in hourly or other wage payments to keep the employee abreast of rising consumer prices.

CAN YOU PROTECT YOURSELF AGAINST INFLATION?

The French say "Salaries go up by the stairs; prices take the elevator." To compensate for inflation, many unions now include *cost-of-living escalators* in their contracts with management. A typical cost-of-living escalator provides that 80 percent of any increase in prices as measured by the Consumers Price Index (CPI) be reflected in higher hourly wages. Cost-of-living adjustments may be made quarterly, semiannually, or annually. Thus, if the CPI shows a 10-percent inflation rate in a given year, the annual cost-of-living adjustment will be 8 percent.

Suppose that you earn $7.50 per hour and that you are protected by a cost-of-living escalator equal to 80 percent of the rise in the CPI. The new union contract provides a 5-percent basic annual wage increase and the anticipated rate of inflation is 7.5 percent. What do you expect your earnings to be next year?

Many people naively believe that they are in a better financial condition during periods of inflation because their monetary wages increase. But they do not consider the steady rise in prices. *Money illusion* occurs when people feel financially comfortable even though prices are rising as fast or faster than their incomes. Even if you recognize that money illusion exists, it is still very difficult to protect your wages against inflation. Suppose your employer agrees to a 100-percent cost-of-living escalator. If the prices you pay and the wages you receive increase by the same amount, what *after-tax* purchasing power do you have?

Answers: Your hourly pay will be $8.32½. Your after-tax purchasing power actually decreases, since you must pay some of your additional wages in income tax. Because the Federal Income Tax is progressive, the more rapid the inflation, the higher your tax bracket and the worse off you are!

✔ **Improved working conditions.** Unions have been actively involved in obtaining better working conditions for their members. The most important improvements sought in this area include:

Employee goals: more income, a better working environment . . .

1. Amenities for workers: pleasant surroundings, adequate sanitary facilities, and opportunities for recreation.
2. Reasonable scheduling of shifts, work crews, working hours and rest periods, and overtime.
3. Acceptable assembly-line pace and job definitions.
4. Adequate safety precautions.

Many unions also demand shorter work weeks at the same wages, and the 35-hour work week is now common in many industries.

✔ **Job security.** Rapid technological changes and unemployment in certain industries make workers especially sensitive to the possibility of job loss. Employees who spend many years acquiring skills are naturally anxious when they find these skills are in danger of becoming economically or technologically obsolete. Job security becomes especially important during periods of high unemployment, when it is harder for displaced workers to find alternative jobs. Because of the high unemployment experienced in 1974–1976, American unions have become particularly sensitive to job-security issues. Figure 19-6 indicates some of the major issues in the conflict over job security between management and labor.

✔ More challenging jobs. Affluent workers tend to become interested in challenging work as well as in material rewards. High labor turnover, absenteeism, and growing worker dissatisfaction with assembly-line routines have prompted several companies to experiment with different approaches to mass production. One program, a joint effort of the United Auto Workers and Chrysler, allows workers to supervise their own assembly lines and to assemble complete subunits on separate tables designed especially for that purpose. Employees also like to feel that their work is worthwhile. Many workers seek more control over what they are doing—greater freedom to define their jobs, to vary what they do occasionally, and to use their own ingenuity.

. . . job security, more challenging work . . .

✔ Union security. About 80 percent of all union members are covered by *union security arrangements,* which typically involve (1) some form of compulsory union membership, and (2) checkoff procedures. Under the *closed shop,* a stringent form of compulsory union membership, employers agree to hire only union members. In a *union shop,* management is free to hire whomever it chooses, but all workers must join the established union within a designated period (usually 30 days). In both closed and union

19-6   Major issues in job-security conflict. The differing objectives of management and labor unions are reflected in their conflicting positions on those key aspects of job security.

Issue	Description
Seniority	Allocates jobs on the basis of years worked. During slack economic periods, employees with the highest seniority are laid off last.
Subcontracting	Permits employers to hire other firms to produce part or all of a product. To preserve members' jobs, unions often attempt to control the amount of subcontracting in a firm.
Introduction of new technology	Frequently allows business to reduce its work force. Unions often attempt to prevent the introduction of new technology by practices such as featherbedding—requiring an employer to retain workers even when they are no longer needed. For example, for many years, railroads were forced to retain firemen on diesel locomotives.
Promotion, hiring, dismissals, and transfers	Affect the job security of union members. Unions endeavor to restrict management decision making in these areas by obtaining veto powers or by requiring management to demonstrate legitimate reasons for any action it takes against union members.
Job reductions	Eliminate union jobs. Job reductions may occur because a plant is unprofitable or because demand is declining. To reduce job losses, unions try to force management to retain existing union employees.
Severance pay	Provides temporary financial protection against job loss. Unions are often successful in forcing employers to pay a year or more in wages to workers who are laid off permanently.
Apprenticeship programs	Protect skilled workers against competition. Some unions protect members' jobs by requiring long and arduous training programs that few new workers can complete. Apprenticeship programs may improve the skills of new workers, but they also keep professionals in short supply, safeguarding union members' jobs.

shops, remaining a union member is a condition of continued employment. In an *open shop,* employees may decide whether or not they wish to join the union. The main source of economic power for organized labor lies in union security arrangements, since unions are assured that workers will participate in whatever actions they undertake. Workers who oppose union tactics against employers risk losing union membership and their jobs.

. . . and union security

Checkoff procedures require that employers deduct union dues from employee paychecks and send these monies directly to the appropriate union. Procedures for the collection of dues are usually specified in the union contract. When compulsory union membership is combined with checkoff procedures, unions are placed in a powerful bargaining position.

To the extent that workers believe organized labor advances their goals, employees desire union security. But union security arrangements may also force individual workers to join and contribute to organizations in which they prefer not to participate.

Basic Goals: The Employer View

Employers view
labor as a resource
and wages as a
business cost

From management's viewpoint, labor is a resource essential to production, and employee wages are an ordinary cost of conducting business. Consequently, a primary goal of management is to obtain the highest possible output from labor at the lowest possible cost. Achieving this goal depends on the following three key factors.

✔ **Control of unit labor costs.** *Unit labor costs* represent the average cost of the labor necessary to produce one unit of a product. If the unit labor costs of producing a Ford Pinto amount to $600, for example, then the Ford Motor Company spends $600 on wages and fringe benefits to assemble the typical Pinto. When unit labor costs (as well as other production costs) are carefully controlled, a business can achieve adequate profits and effectively compete in the marketplace. If unit labor costs soar out of control, profits will decline and the firm may eventually be forced into bankruptcy.

To control unit labor costs, a business manager must (1) pay wages that are reasonable in terms of product prices and the wages and fringe benefits paid by competitors, and (2) obtain acceptable levels of productivity from employees. A firm that fails to meet either of these objectives is headed for disaster.

✔ **Management rights.** To operate a business efficiently, managers must employ, promote, and dismiss workers on the basis of their performances; introduce new technology; plan production schedules in relation to market demand; and terminate unprofitable facilities. To accomplish these goals, management must make business decisions flexibly and quickly, without union interference.

THE MAN IN THE MIDDLE

Ed Hendrix faced a crisis. Two workers had balked at some recently assigned tasks, claiming that they could not keep up with Ford's assembly line. As their supervisor, Hendrix threatened disciplinary action. The workers, supported by their union, argued that the work pace was too rapid. The company stood behind Hendrix, and in the face of possible disciplinary action, the workers backed down.

Ed Hendrix is one of 8000 supervisors in the Ford Motor Company. He must implement management decisions, battle the union, and keep new cars rolling off the assembly line. Ed Hendrix must also live with the bitterness that is the result of maintaining a high rate of production. "The foreman is the punching bag," says 29-year old Hendrix. "You get your ears beat off from both sides of the fence."

Management pressures supervisors to increase productivity and keep quality high. Hendrix is pressured by his own supervisor, who can promote or fire him, by other lower level supervisors whose performances are affected by the output of Hendrix's workers, and by two inspectors who oversee his 300-foot stretch of the assembly line and his 34 workers.

"I drift along the line," Hendrix says. "I check the installations. If there is a problem, I talk to the operator." If prodding fails, Hendrix calls in the shop steward. If necessary, Hendrix must try to apply enough discipline to accomplish the work but not enough to dissatisfy his workers or the union.

Ed Hendrix must be careful. He cannot fire or transfer workers. And as one worker put it, "It's easy to make a foreman look bad. Just screw up." Yet, hundreds of things can go wrong that may force Ed Hendrix to push the button that stops the assembly line and idles over 1500 workers who earn $5 per hour.

A better-than-average supervisor, Hendrix has an unlisted phone number to avoid having too much contact with his workers. "I don't drink with them very often," he says. "Sometimes it is hard to be a friend and a foreman." And . . . "I used to be scared of the men. But after a while you get a thick skin. When you come through the door, you say, 'I've got a job to do. They've got a job to do.' You get so you can look 'em straight in the eye."

A chain smoker, Ed Hendrix cannot get his job off his mind, even at home. He worries about whether enough workers will show up for the morning shift. He wonders whether he will be fired for mistakes made by his workers over which he has no control. Then why does he remain a supervisor? Hendrix receives $13,000 in regular pay and approximately $5,000 in overtime each year—considerably more than he could earn on the assembly line. And there is always hope for advancement: many positions in lower and middle management are held by former supervisors.

Management wants employees who are loyal to the business

✔ **Worker loyalty.** The management of a business is capable of controlling and supervising only a fraction of the daily activities of its employees. Highly motivated employees can make invaluable contributions to an efficient business. Thus, management seeks loyal workers who will identify strongly with the firm and act in its best interests.

Employee–Employer Conflict

Union and management objectives are not always compatible. Labor's demands for higher wages and fringe benefits, shorter hours, and better working conditions add to employers' unit labor costs. Management's efforts to retain authority in business decisions clash with employees' desires for job security and control of their working environment. Thus, conflict between labor and management is inevitable. To attain their objectives in employer–employee disputes, unions and management rely on several economic weapons (see Figure 19-7).

507   *Sources of Labor–Management Conflicts*

✔ The strike: labor's chief economic weapon. A union's most important economic weapon is the *strike*, in which union members collectively refuse to work until their demands are met by management. By disrupting business operations, unions seek concessions from employers who fear accumulated losses from their idle plants. In a *wildcat strike*, employees walk off their jobs without union authorization; in a *sitdown strike*, which is now illegal, employees remain in the plant but refuse to work. Strikes are usually supported by *picketing*, which involves posting union members at entrances to businesses that are being struck. The principal objectives of picketing are to publicize the strike, to develop a greater solidarity among striking union members, and to discourage nonstriking employees from entering the plant. To reduce economic pressure on workers, many unions set aside a portion of their collected dues as *strike funds* to compensate members during work stoppages. In addition, striking workers in some states can collect welfare benefits.

✔ The lockout: management's strongest economic weapon. When management–union conflicts develop, the major weapon available to business is the *lockout*, in which management discontinues all operations.

19-7 Methods of economic coercion available to labor and management. The tactics of both management and labor are designed to inflict as much damage as possible to the other side without sustaining injuries beyond an acceptable level to themselves.

Methods of coercion used by labor	Methods of coercion used by management
1. *Strikes:* All or most employees refuse to work.	1. *Lockouts:* Employer shuts down operations, forcing workers to lose wages.
2. *Picketing:* Workers march in front of employer's plant in order to (a) prevent nonstriking workers from entering the plant; (b) obtain publicity; and (c) discourage suppliers or other union-associated personnel from dealing with the firm.	2. *Strikebreaking:* Employer continues to operate during a strike with the assistance of nonunion personnel, either supervisors or strikebreakers (nonunion workers employed temporarily or permanently).
3. *Slowdowns:* Employees refuse to work at a normal pace until the labor dispute is settled.	3. *Court injunctions:* Employer obtains a court order outlawing strikes, picket lines, or slowdowns if violence is present or if the contract is violated by union activities during strike.
4. *Boycotts:* Workers attempt to stop the purchase of goods or services from an employer in order to gain union recognition from management or to support a strike.	4. *Blacklisting:* Employer attempts to destroy unions by refusing to hire new employees suspected of being union members.
5. *Strike funds:* A portion of union dues are set aside to help workers during long strikes when they receive no pay from employers.	5. *Yellow-dog contracts:* Employers require workers to pledge not to join a union as a condition of employment. In most circumstances, this tactic violates federal law.
6. *Selective strikes or negotiations:* Unions focus bargaining efforts on one employer in an industry. For example, the United Auto Workers might strike Ford Motor Company but continue to work at General Motors and Chrysler, putting greater pressure on Ford to settle.	6. *Strike insurance:* Firms in the same industry agree to share profits with any firm that is struck.
7. *Mutual-aid pacts:* Unions in different industries agree to aid one another financially whenever one union is participating in a strike.	7. *Joint bargaining or shutdown agreements:* Firms in the same industry negotiate union contracts together or jointly agree to close down if a single firm is struck.
8. *Lobbying:* Unions attempt to obtain assistance from Congress or from the executive branch in securing a settlement.	8. *Lobbying:* Employers attempt to obtain assistance from Congress or from the executive branch in securing a settlement.

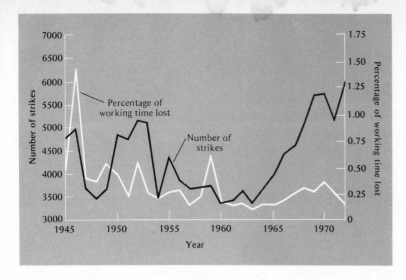

19-8

Number of work stoppages and percentage of working time lost due to strikes, 1945–1972. Strikes have a minor impact on business in terms of lost working time.

Source: *Statistical Abstract of the United States.*

<table>
<tr><td>The lockout:
a major
economic weapon
for management</td><td>By closing its plants, management places considerable economic pressure on union members, who receive no wages or salaries during the lockout. Management may also place economic pressure on unions at little cost to the business if it continues to operate using supervisory and other personnel despite a union strike.</td></tr>
</table>

✔ **Conflict and compromise.** Despite these sharply differing objectives, serious breakdowns in labor–management relations are rare. Because they are so spectacular, strikes are highly publicized by the media. Yet, in 1970, for example, strikes caused direct losses in working time of only .4 percent of total hours worked, or less than 16 minutes per worker per year (see Figure 19-8). The typical labor–management dispute is settled peacefully; if not, resultant work stoppages are usually brief.

Peaceful settlements are in the interest of both management and labor
The basic reason for this situation is clear. Although the short-term goals of labor and management often clash sharply, a prolonged economic confrontation results in lost wages for workers and in reduced profits for business. Even more important, continuous labor disputes mean higher profits for nonunionized and foreign competitors and for industries that manufacture substitute products. Since the number of union jobs available as well as the amount of union wages ultimately depend on the firm's receipt of adequate revenue, enlightened self-interest requires that labor and management resolve their differences peacefully and quickly.

Settling Labor Disputes: Collective Bargaining

Collective bargaining is the procedure by which disputes between unions and management are settled. Collective bargaining consists of continuous private negotiations between labor and management.

Prenegotiation Meetings

Management and labor set their objectives before they negotiate

Before formal negotiations are begun, management and labor determine their objectives for the period of time to be covered by the contract. Generally, objectives set by both sides are strongly influenced by current labor agreements in similar industries. For unions, determining a negotiating position can be a complex process that involves preparation of relevant data by a hired staff of accountants, attorneys, economists, and other experts as well as a series of meetings of elected union officials. The union then appoints a bargaining committee to conduct direct negotiations with management.

Management establishes its objectives in meetings between general managers and the personnel department, which normally represents management in the collective bargaining process. In large businesses, a specialist, often the vice president of labor relations or the vice president of personnel, handles labor–management negotiations. Since labor contracts involve matters vital to the welfare of the business, negotiators for management must maintain close contact with top executives.

Negtotiating the Contract

Formal negotiations between unions and management begin with expressions of goodwill and hope for a settlement on both sides. Normally, negotiations are conducted at a neutral site (not at the plant or union headquarters). Often they have the appearance of a summit meeting between two world powers, with labor and management negotiators supplemented by extensive technical staffs. The atmosphere at the first negotiating session is usually cool and businesslike, since both sides wish to appear uncompromising.

The agenda for subsequent meetings is established at the first collective bargaining session. During later negotiations, the basic goal of each side is to determine how far the other side is willing to compromise without revealing the degree to which it will make concessions. Less important differences are often settled in various smaller committee meetings prior to the main negotiations.

Negotiations are often tense and dramatic

The toughest stage of negotiations usually occurs shortly before or during the first few days of a possible strike, when both parties have the strongest incentive to settle. Tension is high, bargaining sessions are long, and tempers run short. It is at this eleventh hour that the skills of experienced negotiators are invaluable. Whether or not collective bargaining produces a satisfactory agreement depends on factors such as the relationships established between labor and management over the years, the seriousness of the disagreements dividing the parties, and the skill of the negotiators involved.

Mediation and Arbitration

The vast bulk of negotiations between unions and management are concluded successfully without outside intervention. When stalemates occur, however, labor and management often submit disputes to mediation or arbitration. *Mediation* is an attempt to settle labor–management conflicts through the intervention of a third party who is neutral to the dispute. Mediators may be political or social leaders in the community, distinguished national figures, professors, or other parties mutually acceptable to both sides. The Federal Mediation and Conciliation Service, a federal agency, and many state governments make lists of mediators available to unions and management.

Arbitration differs from mediation in that the arbitrator has the power to make binding decisions that affect both labor and management. Under *voluntary arbitration,* labor and management agree to refer any unresolved issues to an arbitrator or to an arbitration panel. Under *compulsory arbitration,* a third party (usually the government) forces labor and management to submit to arbitration.

Mediation and arbitration help to settle labor–management disputes

When mediation and arbitration fail, public officials often attempt to settle labor–management disputes by private arm twisting, or by appointing a fact-finding panel to outline a reasonable agreement, or by legally sanctioning "cooling-off" periods during which strikes and lockouts are suspended while negotiations continue.

The Union Contract

The eventual result of collective bargaining is the *union contract* —a written agreement between labor and management that specifies in detail the rules and the procedures to be followed by both parties during the contract period. Provisions of the union contract typically include:

1. Names of the parties.
2. Duration of the agreement and provisions for its renewal.
3. Wage rates and fringe benefits, job classifications, shift differentials, and overtime pay.
4. Working conditions: hours, timing of shifts, permissible breaks, severance pay, and so on.
5. Union security: hiring of new workers and checkoff procedures.
6. Job security: outside contracting of work, seniority, and so on.
7. Management rights.
8. Procedures for terminating and promoting employees.
9. Limitations on the rights of workers to engage in strikes or of employers to initiate lockouts while the contract is in effect.
10. Methods (including grievance procedures and the appointment

The union contract describes rules for labor and management

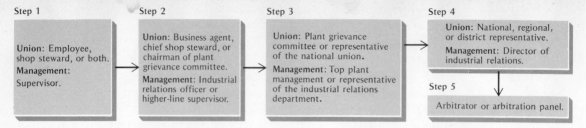

Step 1

Union: Employee, shop steward, or both.
Management: Supervisor.

Step 2

Union: Business agent, chief shop steward, or chairman of plant grievance committee.
Management: Industrial relations officer or higher-line supervisor.

Step 3

Union: Plant grievance committee or representative of the national union.
Management: Top plant management or representative of the industrial relations department.

Step 4

Union: National, regional, or district representative.
Management: Director of industrial relations.

Step 5

Arbitrator or arbitration panel.

19-9 A typical grievance procedure. If a mutually satisfactory resolution of the dispute is not reached at step 1, the union or management can renegotiate differences at as many of these subsequent levels as necessary.

of arbitrators) for resolving disputes over contract language and for dealing with alleged contract violations by either party.

11. Signatures of the parties.

In short, the union contract describes the rules that labor and management agree to follow for a specific period of time. Violations of a union contract either by management or by labor can result in court action.

Contract Enforcement

Grievance procedures prevent contract disputes from getting out of control

Labor–management strife does not terminate with the signing of a union contract. Subsequent disagreements arise over the interpretation of the contract and over whether each party is keeping its side of the bargain. More than 90 percent of all union contracts require that labor–management disputes concerning contract interpretation or adherence be submitted to a formal *grievance procedure* (see Figure 19-9).

Grievances may be initiated by an aggrieved employee, by the union, or by management. Most grievances are settled at the local level by direct negotiation between the affected parties. If a settlement cannot be reached by direct negotiation, the grievance is referred to plantwide or to national representatives of labor and management. If both sides still cannot resolve their differences, the dispute goes to the arbitrator or to the arbitration panel designated in the contract. The arbitrator may collect evidence by examining the transcripts of previous negotiations, holding hearings, and/or listening to presentations by parties in the dispute. Arbitration decisions are usually based on the language of the union contract, evidence in the specific case, established practices in the industry, past arbitration awards in the business, and relevant decisions of arbitrators in other industries.

Arbitration of grievances provides a carefully organized procedure for settling disputes between labor and management. Differences in opinion are resolved by direct negotiation between the parties involved or by a neutral third party and are not allowed to reach such serious proportions that they threaten labor–management relations. Arbitration of grievances is an outstanding example of judicial procedures voluntarily initiated, supported, and conducted entirely by labor and management.

Government Policy Toward Labor

Collective bargaining depends on a system of direct negotiation between labor and management as coequal partners who recognize and accept the legitimacy of each other's goals. Contemporary collective bargaining is strongly influenced by four major statutes that deal with labor.

The Norris–LaGuardia Act

Norris–LaGuardia Act:
protecting the right
to strike

Historically, labor unions were severely handicapped by the willingness of many courts to issue *injunctions* against labor's chief economic weapon, the strike. The first major piece of prolabor legislation, the Norris–LaGuardia Act of 1932, substantially strengthened labor's position

ARE STRIKES OBSOLETE?

In 1973, professional baseball players reached a highly publicized agreement with club owners. That same year, a much less publicized interim agreement was reached between the United Steelworkers of America (USW) and most of the large steel producers, which involved nearly 1.5 million workers and represented a landmark in American labor history. Both the baseball players and the steelworkers engaged in what is known as "future-terms" arbitration. More and more public employees are covered by future-terms labor contracts—a practice that is spreading into the private sector of the economy as well.

The future-terms arbitration illustrated by the 1973 interim agreement between the USW and the large steel producers contained three major provisions:

● In exchange for the USW's promise not to strike before August 1, 1977, the steel companies agreed to pay each worker a bonus of $150.
● Wages were to rise by a minimum of 3 percent on August 1, 1974, on August 1, 1975, and on August 1, 1976. The cost-of-living escalator already in effect was to be continued through August 1, 1977.

● Well in advance of August 1, 1974, when the original union contract was to expire, union and management would consult with one another to arrive at a mutually acceptable new union contract. If no contract agreement could be reached, all unresolved issues would be submitted to arbitration. Any decision the arbitration panel (to be established by mutual agreement between union and management) reached would be accepted by both negotiating parties (except for eliminating the minimum wage increase and the cost-of-living escalator already described).

Well before August 1, 1974, the USW and the steel industry reached an agreement that provided for an average wage increase of 28 cents per hour in 1974, 16 cents per hour after August 1, 1975, and 16 cents per hour after August 1, 1976.

Using the information in this section, determine how future-terms arbitration differs from arbitration of grievances. Why would future-terms arbitration tend to reduce strikes? What do you suppose motivated both the USW and the steel industry to reach their 1973 agreement? (For the answers, see page 514.)

ARE STRIKES OBSOLETE? (Answers)

Union leaders find that blue-collar workers are no longer eager to strike. Today, the earnings of unionized workers frequently fall into the middle-income bracket. Like everyone else, union members have to make mortgage payments, pay installment loans, and meet the costs of educating their children. A worker with an income of $200 or $300 a week will lose substantial income during a prolonged strike.

The USW and the steel companies both benefit from maintaining a strike-free record. In the past, shortly before contracts have reached expiration, steel buyers have accumulated large steel inventories in anticipation of a strike. Even if a strike is averted, the industry and its workers are prosperous prior to the end of the old contract and then enter a period of low output and low employment after the new contract is signed. Moreover, previous steel strikes have primarily benefited European and Japanese steel producers. The steel industry's troubled labor history has provided opportunities for foreign producers to attract steel industry-related sales and jobs.

Thus, steel workers and steel producers have a common interest in future-terms arbitration, since it reduces strikes by providing for the automatic arbitration of unresolved issues. Unlike the arbitration of grievances procedure, the last step in future-terms arbitration is negotiating the terms for a new contract. Grievance arbitration deals solely with the interpretation of the union contract currently in effect.

in contract disputes by preventing employers from utilizing court injunctions, except in cases of violence. The Norris–LaGuardia Act also prevented employers from making effective use of *yellow-dog contracts,* which require workers to pledge not to join a union as a condition of employment. The basic objective of the Norris–LaGuardia Act was to permit labor and management to engage in collective bargaining with a minimum of interference from the courts.

The Wagner Act

The National Labor Relations Act of 1935, popularly known as the Wagner Act, forced employers to bargain with unions, required that management abstain from a long list of antiunion practices (including dismissing union leaders unfairly, spying on unions, forming business-dominated unions, and refusing to bargain in good faith with employees), and created the National Labor Relations Board (NLRB), a government agency, to administer its provisions. The NLRB carries out two primary functions. First, on the petition of affected workers, the NLRB conducts *representation elections,* in which employees choose by secret ballot the union they wish to join or vote to remain unaffiliated with any labor group. Second, the NLRB investigates claims by management or by labor that the other side's activities have violated federal law. If the NLRB uncovers an unfair labor practice, it is legally bound to punish the offender. The basic objectives of the Wagner Act were to encourage free collective bargaining between the two equally powerful organizations of management and labor and to establish collective bargaining guidelines.

Wagner Act: insuring that management will bargain with unions

The Taft–Hartley Act

By the end of World War II, the American labor movement was well established, and the postwar era saw an unprecedented series of spectacular strikes. In 1947, despite bitter union opposition, Congress passed the Taft–Hartley Act. This amendment to the Wagner Act provided:

1. A list of unfair union practices such as secondary boycotts, in which unions induce outside parties to refuse to buy products of companies with which union workers are having a dispute.
2. A procedure under which the President is authorized to stop strikes for an 80-day cooling-off period if they adversely affect the national interest.
3. Limitations on undesirable union practices such as featherbedding.
4. A method by which individual states can pass right-to-work laws, under which employees cannot be forced to join unions as a condition of employment.

Taft–Hartley Act: equalizing the rights of management and labor

The Taft–Hartley Act attempted to reduce strikes by restoring what was felt to be a more equitable balance between labor and management.

The Landrum–Griffin Act

In the 1950s, a series of dramatic congressional investigations uncovered internal corruption and lack of genuine democracy in some unions. As a result, in 1959, Congress passed the Landrum–Griffin Act, which amended the Wagner Act to include provisions designed to protect the financial integrity of the administration of members' funds by union leaders and to insure that unions genuinely represented their memberships. The Act required that every union develop a constitution to be filed with the Secretary of Labor; ordered the fair implementation of union election procedures; established a bill of rights for union members; and defined additional unfair labor practices by unions. The Landrum–Griffin Act attempted to improve the internal operations of organized labor and to make unions responsive to the needs of their members.

Landrum-Griffin Act: protecting the interests of union members

Although the Taft–Hartley Act and the Landrum–Griffin Act sharply curtail some union practices, the basic principles laid down in the Wagner Act remain largely intact today. Contemporary labor law encourages the continuance of collective bargaining in private hands; government intervention is considered necessary only when intolerable abuses develop.

KEY POINTS TO REMEMBER

1. Unions attempt to represent the occupationally related interests of a collection of workers.
2. Employees seek better wages and fringe benefits, improved working conditions, job security, more challenging jobs, and union security. Employee objectives tend to raise production costs and to lessen management's control over the business.
3. To survive and prosper in a competitive environment, businesses must achieve acceptable levels of unit labor costs and product quality as well as sufficient flexibility to operate efficiently.
4. A union uses a strong economic weapon, the strike, to secure its objectives. To achieve its goals, management frequently employs the lockout or attempts to operate its plants without unionized workers.
5. Normally, labor–management disputes are settled by private negotiation between the affected parties. If private negotiations are unsuccessful, public officials may mediate, arbitrate, or intervene. Labor and management are strongly motivated to settle early: prolonged strikes decrease business profits, and wages are paid from the firm's revenue.
6. The union contract specifies the conditions under which employees and their employers will behave for a specific period of time. Disagreements arising over contract interpretation or adherence are settled by the grievance procedure, in which outside arbitrators resolve differences between labor and management.
7. Collective bargaining includes the entire process of negotiating and drawing up a union contract and implementing the grievance procedure. Government policy toward labor has been to encourage private collective bargaining, to equalize power between labor and management, to prevent strikes, and to insure that unions are governed honestly and fairly.

QUESTIONS FOR DISCUSSION

1. Describe the structure of a labor union. How are workers represented at each level in the structure?
2. Do contemporary unions accurately reflect the goals of their members? Explain your answer.
3. What are the main objectives of union members? Of management? Why do they clash?
4. "Wage increases are less important to workers than they used to be." Do you agree with this statement? Why or why not?

5. What are the steps in the normal grievance procedure?

6. Many Americans believe that labor unions have become too powerful. How, if at all, has this attitude been reflected in recent labor legislation? Do you agree with this view?

SHORT CASES AND PROBLEMS

1. Suppose that you represent the management of General Motors in negotiations with the United Auto Workers for a new two-year contract. What factors would you consider in establishing your collective bargaining position?

2. Assume that the language of the labor contract developed between General Motors and the UAW specifies that "employers may not order workers to undertake unsafe tasks," and that the contract also states that "employees are obligated to follow reasonable orders issued by their supervisors." A union welder has just refused to follow a supervisor's order, claiming that to do so would be hazardous to his safety. Union and management have been unable to agree on the interpretation of the contract. As the assigned arbitrator, what steps would you take to reach your decision?

3. Whirlpool's engineering department estimates that in 1976 it used an average of 20 hours of union labor to build a typical refrigerator. In the past, labor productivity at Whirlpool has risen 5 percent a year—a trend that is expected to continue into 1977. Whirlpool's union contract calls for a 10-percent increase in wages and fringe benefits, which averaged $6.00 per hour during 1976, on January 1, 1977. Determine Whirlpool's unit-labor costs in 1976 and 1977. Suppose that in view of these results, Whirlpool launches an efficiency program, cutting the labor necessary to assemble an average refrigerator by 10 percent. What would the increased productivity be? What would happen to Whirlpool's unit-labor costs in view of the efficiency program?

CAREER SELECTION: POSITIONS IN INDUSTRIAL RELATIONS AND SELECTED UNIONIZED OCCUPATIONS

Labor unions represent workers who are employed in hundreds of different types of jobs. A sampling of largely unionized occupations in private industries follows the two careers in industrial and labor relations described below.

CAREERS IN INDUSTRIAL AND LABOR RELATIONS

Industrial relations managers represent business interests in labor–management negotiations. This responsibility entails preparing briefs for negotiations, assuring that final contracts meet top management's specifications, interpreting contracts for management and union representatives, and resolving labor grievances. Five years of experience in a lower-level employee relations job is the normal prerequisite for promotion to industrial relations manager. A bachelor's degree or a master's degree in industrial relations, business administration, or labor economics is essential. Annual salaries range widely, beginning at $9000. Experienced industrial relations managers may earn more than $30,000. (*Additional information:* Contact a local industrial relations school or the industrial relations department of a local college or university.)

Labor-union business agents represent union interests in labor–management negotiations. In addition to these collective-bargaining responsibilities, business agents must handle their union's public relations: promote union membership, find jobs for union members, and arrange union meetings. Employee grievances are generally relayed to management by the **shop steward,** who is a company employee as well as a union representative. Competent shop stewards may be promoted to the rank of business agent. (*Additional information:* Contact local unions.)

CAREERS IN TRANSPORTATION

Pilots are responsible for the safe and timely transportation of airplane passengers and cargo. Airline pilots conduct preflight tests, supervise crew members, and maintain flight records. They must be in excellent physical condition and must be capable of making quick and accurate decisions. Employment standards are strict: airline pilots must be at least 23 and must have logged a minimum of 1500 hours of flight time before they are eligible to apply for an airline transport pilot's license. To obtain this license, applicants are required to pass an additional battery of Federal Aviation Administration examinations and psychological tests. Pilots must be high-school graduates; many airlines require two- or four-year college degrees. The sequence of promotion is generally from flight engineer to copilot to pilot. Yearly salaries range from $17,000 to $60,000. An increasing reliance on air travel should create an expanding job market for airline pilots. (*Additional information:* Airline Pilots' Association; 1625 Massachussetts Avenue, N.W.; Washington, D.C. 20036.)

Long-distance truck drivers transport raw materials and manufactured goods. Truck drivers must have sufficient mechanical aptitude to assess the operating condition of their trucks. Since truckers are sometimes required to load and unload the shipments they transport, they must be in good physical condition. Truckers must also maintain trip logs, following U.S. Department of Transportation requirements. Most employers require some high-school education; a vocational school course in truck driving is beneficial. Applicants must be 21 and must have a chauffeur's license. Truckers must also pass the written U.S. Transportation Department examination. Ironically, immediate promotion may lead to salary reductions, but some truckers prefer to advance to driver supervisor or to dispatcher. Annual income for truckers averages $15,800. Job opportunities for long-distance truck drivers are expected to expand moderately as the volume of highway freight increases. (*Additional information:* American Trucking Association; 1616 P Street, N.W.; Washington, D.C. 20036.)

OTHER LARGELY UNIONIZED CAREERS

Welders join, trim, and cut metal parts by applying gas or electric heat. Skilled welders must be able to read technical blueprints and must be familiar with the safety and strength qualities of various metals. Less knowledgeable, semiskilled welders perform more repetitive tasks, usually welding identical surfaces in one particular position. Good coordination and good eyesight are essential. Most employers require high-school or vocational-school training in welding, mathematics, and mechanical drawing. Necessary skills are learned either on the job or in formal apprenticeship programs. Welders may become inspectors or may advance to supervisory positions. Annual salary averages $9400. An increase in metalworking activities is expected to create a rapidly expanding job market for welders. (*Additional information:* The American Welding Society; 2501 Seventh Street, N.W.; Miami, Florida 33125.)

Printing press workers and **assistants** are employed by commercial printing shops and by book, magazine, and newspaper publishers to prepare type forms and pressplates for final printing. They operate the presses, control margins and ink flow, and cut and assemble printed pages. Most employers require that applicants have a high-school education; vocational courses in chemistry and in physics are assets. Press workers often begin as journeymen and are then placed in lengthy apprenticeship programs. Annual income averages $12,400. The rising demand for printed materials is expected to create a moderately expanding job market for printing press workers and assistants. (*Additional information:* Printing Industries of America, Inc.; 1730 North Lynn Street; Arlington, Virginia 22201.)

A CRITICAL BUSINESS DECISION

—made by Charlie Bragg

THE SITUATION   The woman at the Ford Motor plant in Wixon, Michigan, was upset. The paint in her spray gun was too thin and was squirting all over her apron. Previous complaints to her supervisor had produced no results.

Her solution: to call in Charlie Bragg, officially known as a District Committeeman and the local representative of the United Automobile Workers (UAW). As the union's shop steward at the Ford plant in Wixon, Charlie Bragg was popularly elected by the 237 union members in the plant's Thunderbird Trim department. Notified of the woman's problem, Bragg acts quickly. He confers with her supervisor and telephones the person responsible for the spray-gun repairs. Within minutes, the spray gun is fixed.

Charlie Bragg's typical work routine might seem easy to anyone who is unfamiliar with factory organization. Bragg roams around, chatting with union members and periodically poking his head into unfinished cars. Bragg's duties also include fighting disciplinary actions by Ford, arranging vacations and leaves of absence for union members, supervising the repair of supply racks, and even seeing that bathrooms are clean and that drinking fountains remain unclogged. For this work, Bragg is paid about $15,000 a year—approximately the same salary he would earn on an assembly line. (According to union contract, Ford is obligated to pay the salaries of shop stewards.)

Bragg believes that many of the problems on the shop floor are the result of poor supervision. "A bad foreman," Bragg feels, "is a guy who doesn't care about his people. All he cares about is just trying to get that dollar, and he lets his bosses or his employees run his area. He's inconsistent. He lets things run rampant for a while, then tries to crack down all at once without being fair. Nobody respects him."

Charlie Bragg is highly regarded by his coworkers. "He's an outstanding committeeman," observes one. "He comes around and talks to you, and when he is paged, he makes it there as quick as he can. . . . he'll win some and lose some, but the losses are always close." But Ed Hendrix, a foreman at Ford, views Bragg with grudging admiration: "He's one of the better committeemen," Hendrix comments, "even though he and I don't get along. He's on his side of the fence and I'm on mine."

THE DECISION   One of the major sources of conflict between UAW members and the Ford Motor Company is work standards. "Standards men are running our plant," Bragg asserts hotly. "In the old days, you had time to go to the bathroom if you wanted. Now, you need a relief man for that. You can't even breathe. These standards experts went to school, but they didn't take the human factor into account." To counter assembly-line speedups, UAW shop stewards use stopwatches to time every assembly line in the plant. When the speed is higher than that allotted in the union contract, they complain. (However, Bragg kept quiet recently when his stopwatch showed that one assembly line was moving too slowly.)

Committeeman Bragg also represents workers who believe their jobs are too involved to complete in the amount of time they are allowed. Firey disputes often arise over such standards. One veteran worker complained that he didn't have enough time to finish working on one car before another car rolled in on the assembly line. Bragg timed the worker and found that he was allowed only 1.2 seconds to correct any errors and to make any necessary tool changes between cars—a figure hotly disputed by Ford. Standards problems become particularly acute when models are changed to conform to market demand or to accommodate new model styles. "These are the times you wish you didn't have this job," Bragg reacts. "You wish you could just crawl in a hole and hide."

When dealing with disputes between labor and management, especially disputes concerning work standards, Charlie Bragg faces an important decision: How often should he rely on grievance procedures contained in Ford's union contract with the UAW to settle outstanding disputes between the workers he represents and Ford management?

QUESTIONS

1. As Charlie Bragg, what would be your general approach in dealing with Ford's management? Would you stress compromise settlements with supervisors and with other management personnel, or would you make extensive use of grievance procedures?
2. Charlie Bragg and Ed Hendrix (see "The Man in the Middle," page 507) are employed in the same Ford Motor plant. How do their attitudes toward what is important in the plant differ? Do you think that these differences accurately reflect the conflicting goals of labor and management, respectively, that are described in Chapter 19?

The benefit of international trade — a more efficient employment of the productive forces of the world.

John Stuart Mill

CHAPTER **20**

INTERNATIONAL BUSINESS

A remote Asian village and a sophisticated European capital like London or Paris have very little in common except their ever-present Coca-Cola signs. American producers base potential films largely on how foreign audiences are expected to react, since half of Hollywood's profits are derived from abroad. An Arab oil embargo, a grain sale to the Soviet Union, or a change in the value of the U.S. dollar can affect the well-being of the average American.

International business has long been a major American preoccupation. The War of 1812 was fought over the right of American ships to freedom of the open seas, and Yankee clipper ships dominated ocean transport for several decades in the early nineteenth century. Admiral Perry's visit to Japan was intended to open that nation to American commerce. Prior to the Second World War, American trade policy was primarily concerned with *international trade*—the exchange of goods and services across national boundaries. After World War II, however, many American businesses began to purchase and to build plants in foreign countries. As American and some foreign businesses developed more sophisticated international trade operations, they began to raise capital, to produce goods and services, and to market them in many nations. Eventually, these *multinational corporations*—companies with major operating facilities in six or more countries—began to consider themselves more responsible to their stockholders throughout the world than to the nations in which their firms had originated.

In this chapter, we will examine three key aspects of international business: (1) international trade; (2) American investment abroad and the rise of the multinational corporation; and (3) the United States' position in the international economic community.

World trade has always been an American concern

U.S. investments abroad are now equally important

International Trade

For centuries, civilization has clustered around international trade routes. In his search for the rare spices of China, Marco Polo established trade routes with the East. The discovery of America was a byproduct of the search for shorter trade routes to India. But the most rapid growth in international trade has been recent, as is shown in Figure 20-1, which depicts the dollar volume of world trade between 1900 and 1975. Although international trade declined by nearly 50 percent during the Great Depression, it rose to its 1929 level again by the end of World War II. From 1945 to

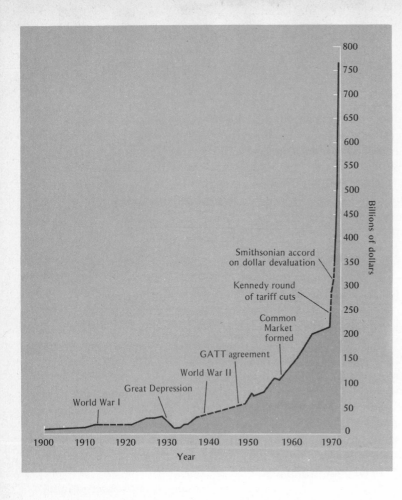

Smithsonian accord
on dollar devaluation

Kennedy round
of tariff cuts

Common
Market
formed

GATT agreement

World War II

Great Depression

World War I

Billions of dollars

Year

20-1

The growth of world trade since 1900. The expansion of world trade has accelerated rapidly since World War II.

Source: United Nations Statistical Office.

World trade is expanding

1975, international trade expanded nearly fifteenfold. In 1975, international trade amounted to over $750 billion—more money than the gross national product of any nation in the world except the United States.

Why Is There International Trade?

Since World War II, the United States and other industrialized nations have sought to expand world trade for both economic and political reasons. In the 1970s, the U.S. government began to encourage trade with the Soviet Union, Communist China, and other Communist nations. Such international trade agreements have proved mutually beneficial in a variety of respects.

Reasons for world trade include . . .

✔ **Unavailable goods.** Natural resources, favorable climates, and productive capabilities are scattered unevenly throughout the world. The

United States, for example, purchases tin from Malasia, coffee from Brazil, and industrial diamonds from South Africa; without world trade, these commodities would be unavailable or prohibitively expensive to Americans. Similarly, Japan is lacking in timber resources and purchases huge quantities of lumber from the U.S. Pacific Northwest.

The economic position of the United States has altered in recent years with respect to world resources. During most of its history, the United States was a major exporter of raw materials that were unavailable or unexploited abroad. As the American economy grew, however, foreign and domestic demands for raw materials increased and known U.S. reserves of many natural resources began to diminish. By the 1970s, the United States had become a net importer of natural resources, and studies indicate that the American economy of the 1980s and the 1990s will become increasingly dependent on raw materials that are produced abroad. Thus, the United States has a growing stake in world trade: without trade, the American economy will be deprived of essential natural resources.

ABSOLUTE AND COMPARATIVE ADVANTAGES OF INTERNATIONAL TRADE

International trade agreements are mutually beneficial because of international differences in costs. Let's suppose that the United States and the Soviet Union decide to trade wheat and gold and that the production costs are:

	U.S. (dollars)	USSR (rubles)
Gold (per ounce)	200	100
Wheat (per bushel)	4	8

If both countries were to remain self sufficient, the United States would mine some of its gold at $200 an ounce and the Soviet Union would produce some of its wheat at 8 rubles a bushel. Assuming an exchange rate of one dollar equals one ruble, if the Soviet Union used its additional resources to mine enough gold to meet American needs and if the United States produced enough wheat to meet Soviet needs, savings from trade between the two nations would be considerable. They would equal the saving per ounce on gold (200 U.S. dollars *minus* 100 rubles, or $100 in the Soviet Union) *multiplied by* the number of ounces of gold mined in the United States prior to trade and then *added to* the savings in wheat (8 rubles, or $8 *minus* $4) *multiplied by* the number of bushels of wheat produced in the Soviet Union prior to trade. The monetary savings resulting from international trade could be used to produce more of the two commodities or more of other goods desired by Russian and American consumers. Economists call

this *absolute advantage*, since, in this example, the Soviet Union and the United States are each most efficient in the production of one commodity.

But what would happen if one nation was most efficient in the production of *all* commodities? (Economists would call this *comparative advantage*.) The answer is surprising. Let's suppose that it cost the Soviet Union 300 rubles to produce an ounce of gold in the above example. To achieve comparative advantage, the USSR would specialize in gold mining and the United States would concentrate on wheat production. From the Soviet viewpoint, it costs the USSR 300 rubles or $300 to produce one ounce of gold which it then sells to the United States for $200. But with its $200 proceeds from this sale, the Soviet Union can buy approximately 50 bushels of U.S. wheat, since it costs American farmers $4 to produce a bushel of wheat. The 50 bushels of wheat are worth 400 rubles or $400 in the Soviet Union (50 bushels *multiplied by* 8 rubles production cost per bushel). Thus, the Soviet Union will sell gold that is worth 300 rubles but will purchase wheat that is worth 400 rubles, freeing 100 rubles to devote to additional Soviet production. By trading wheat for gold, the United States can benefit in the same manner.

Although both the Soviet Union and the United States benefit from mutual trading, the two nations at times have been reluctant to deal with one another. Read the text to learn why the United States and the USSR have found it difficult to agree on some world-trade matters.

✓ Lower-priced products. As national and regional economies become more developed, they begin to specialize in the commodities that they can produce most efficiently. A region may be able to produce a particular commodity because that country possesses a unique natural resource, a favorable location or climate, or the skills of a talented innovator. When a country or a region begins to specialize, it can produce greater quantities of a commodity at less than the product's original cost. Thus, if each nation specializes in the goods and services that it can produce most efficiently and trades its surplus commodities for products that it cannot produce domestically, total world production will be greater than it will be if every nation strives to remain self sufficient. Growing international production and trade also increase the living standards of every person in the world. (See "Absolute and Comparative Advantages of International Trade.")

. . . lower
prices . . .

Consumers receive direct benefits from international trade. By specializing in the commodities they can most efficiently produce, businesses in all countries can charge low prices throughout the world and still secure adequate profits. International trade also supplies consumers with a wide variety of goods and services.

✓ The political benefits of trade. An increase in international trade has produced some important political consequences. A stated goal of American foreign policy since World War II has been to encourage trade between the United States and underdeveloped countries. The objective has been to utilize the tendency for world trade to be mutually beneficial by promoting the economic development of poorer nations in order to improve human conditions and to block communist expansion. This position is often expressed as a preference for "trade not aid" in dealing with the underdeveloped countries.

. . . and possibly
a better chance
for world peace

International trade inevitably generates many commercial ties among nations and a corresponding growth in the knowledge of foreign needs and cultures. Close commercial relationships also increase interdependence among economies. Advocates of expanded world trade argue that its byproducts—greater international understanding and increased economic cooperation—are a major force for world peace.

Barriers to Trade

Despite the benefits of international trade, most governments have established restrictions on the free flow of commerce across national boundaries. Major barriers to trade include tariffs, quotas, and exchange controls.

✓ Tariffs. A *tariff* or a *customs duty* is a charge levied by a government on its country's imports or, less commonly, on its country's exports. A *specific duty* is a tariff levied on each physical unit of a good. For example, the United States has placed a specific customs duty of 1 cent on each pound of imported butter. An *ad valorem duty* is a tariff expressed as a fixed percentage of the market value of a good. The ad valorem duty on an imported car, for instance, is 3 percent of the new car's retail selling price.

Tariffs:
taxes or trade

The main objective of most modern tariffs is to reduce competition between foreign and domestic producers of a commodity. *Protective tariffs* tend to insulate domestic industry from foreign competition by raising the cost of imported goods, forcing the foreign manufacturer or importer to raise retail selling prices in order to pay the customs duty. *Revenue tariffs* are designed to raise monies for governments. Unlike protective tariffs, revenue tariffs remain at modest levels to encourage a large volume of trade.

✔ **Quotas.** A *quota* is a government-imposed restriction on the physical quantity of a commodity that can be imported from a specific nation during a designated period (usually one year). For example, for many years, there has been a U.S. quota on the amount of cane sugar that can be imported into the United States. An importer of cane sugar from Cuba or the Philippines must secure an import license from the U.S. government before shipping sugar into a U.S. port. The annual allotments a government specifies when issuing import licenses reflect that country's yearly quota.

Quotas:
physical limits
on trade

Quotas normally reduce competition between domestic and foreign producers far more effectively than tariffs do. Under a system of quotas, imports can never exceed a prescribed amount; customs duties permit efficient foreign producers to penetrate as much of the domestic market as they can, provided they can still undercut domestic prices after paying the customs duties. Quotas are also a rich source of political corruption, since those who are fortunate enough to secure import licenses can normally expect to realize high profits. Despite these drawbacks, many experts believe quotas now play a quantitatively more important role in reducing international trade than tariffs do.

✔ **Exchange controls.** In order to purchase commodities abroad, an importer must obtain *foreign exchange*—currency of the foreign nation from whom the goods are to be purchased. For example, an importer of Japanese cameras must purchase the cameras with Japanese yen before reselling them at a profit in another currency. Foreign exchange may be purchased directly from foreign nationals but more frequently, it is secured indirectly through a banking system.

Exchange controls:
financial limits
on trade

Exchange controls are government restrictions on the amounts and the types of goods that foreign exchange can be used to purchase. A country that is striving to industralize may restrict its foreign exchange to the importation of tools and machinery. A nation that lacks adequate foreign exchange may restrict its use to essential purchases of food and raw materials from abroad.

✔ Other trade restrictions. *Export controls* limit the quantity of goods that can be sold to a specific nation. For example, the federal government has the legal power to restrict U.S. sales of agricultural products to foreign nations. In this case, controls are employed in order to prevent excessive exports of food, which could result in higher food prices to the American consumer. *Embargoes* represent government restrictions on the flow of commodities in international commerce. For many years, the United States has maintained an embargo on most trade with Cuba and has also restricted the export of military and other highly technological goods to Communist nations. *Nationalistic buying policies* also restrict trade by encouraging government agencies or business firms in a country to use only the goods or services that are produced within that country. For example, as part of the "Buy America" campaign, foreign steel may not be used in the construction of U.S. interstate highways.

Why Restrict Trade?

If international trade is beneficial, then why are tariffs, quotas, and exchange controls used to restrict the free flow of international commerce? *Protectionists*—advocates of increased barriers to trade—cite several reasons for their position.

Reasons for limiting world trade include . . .

✔ National defense. Nations strive to be self sufficient in the production of many defense-related products. For example, historically, the United States has imposed protective tariffs on high-quality watches because skilled watchmakers can be valuable in the production of bomb sights during wartime. Thus, some barriers to trade can be justified on the grounds of national defense, even though they may also perpetuate inefficient industry and lower national living standards.

. . . encouraging self-sufficiency . . .

✔ Protect wages. In the 1970s, U.S. labor unions, led by the AFL–CIO, supported protectionist measures like high tariffs on some products. The reasoning behind this view is that, industries paying high wages often cannot compete successfully with foreign firms paying generally lower wages. Unions feel that to maintain high wages and full employment, U.S. industries require protection from foreign competition.

. . . protecting jobs and wages . . .

This type of protectionism is gained at the expense of the consumer, who pays higher prices for protected goods, and at the expense of U.S. exports, which decrease because foreigners have fewer dollars to spend on American-made goods. Nevertheless, the U.S. Congress has rarely been able to resist the combined political pressures to issue protectionist laws when they are advanced by such powerful producers as the American steel industry and such powerful unions as the United Steelworkers of America.

526 *International Business*

✔ **Infant industries.** Young, struggling domestic industries that face powerful competition from abroad may require temporary protection in order to mature. Once an industry has become large enough to achieve mass production and financial stability, protection can be withdrawn and that industry can be allowed to compete freely in international markets. A basic difficulty in protecting infant industries is that the typical industry becomes so large and powerful that it is then politically impossible to remove the trade restrictions.

While needs for national defense, higher wages, and support for infant industries are all arguments for trade restrictions, the real struggle is frequently a political one. Most industries—and often their employees—have an obvious stake in obtaining protection for themselves as producers. As purchasers of the products of other industries and as exporters, however, industries strive to reduce the amount of protection accorded their competitors. Hence, political struggles over trade restrictions can become unusually ferocious, typically pitting industry against industry, union against union, and region against region.

Trade and the Individual Business

The growth in international trade has been accompanied by an ever-increasing involvement in exporting and importing on the part of ordinary businesses.

✔ **Advantages of international trade: a business perspective.** Exports are attractive to businesses for four major reasons. First, the profits in foreign markets are often very attractive, either because selling prices are high or because the market is growing rapidly. Prices may be high in foreign markets because local production is inefficient, because there is a lack of competition in local markets, or because foreign consumers prefer American-made goods. The potential for export growth may be large

---

EXPORTING ICE TO ICELAND?

Ever since the end of World War II, Great Britain has had to cope with chronic international trade problems. Usually, receipts from Britain's exports have not been sufficient to pay for the food and the other raw materials that the nation must import to survive. In 1975, as a public service designed to encourage desperately needed exports, a distilling firm in Warrington, England, awarded prizes for the most unusual items sold to foreign customers by British firms. Prizes went to firms exporting:

1. Tom-toms throughout the world, including Nigeria.

2. Cigarette-lighter fuel to the Arab countries, including Saudi Arabia, one of the largest oil producers in the world.
3. Bistro restaurants to Europe, including one to Paris.
4. Whole-meat spaghetti to Europe, including Italy.

Other exports in the competition included popsicles to Iceland, artificial snow for a ski slope in Finland, and sand for the filtration unit of a sheik's swimming pool in the Persian Gulf!

because of a rapid rate of economic growth abroad (as in Japan) or because foreign consumers are just beginning to acquire a product with which the American market is already saturated (for example, color television sets in western Europe).

Second, exports can help to reduce the costs of manufacturing and distributing a product. In industries with economies of scale, adding export to domestic sales can increase production volumes and can reduce unit costs. Thus, even if profit margins on exports are low, a savings in both domestic and foreign sales can justify exportation. A dramatic example of this is *dumping*, where surplus products manufactured in one country are sold in other countries below cost. By dumping surplus production abroad, a business is able to recover some of its costs without disrupting its domestic markets. In 1975, the large U.S. automobile manufacturers and the United Auto Workers Union accused Volkswagen of deliberately selling its Beetle models in the United States at substantially lower prices than in Europe.

Third, a firm may find that it is less expensive to export its products than to enter a new domestic market. Once a firm has achieved as large a share of the domestic market as it can realistically expect given its current product lines, that firm can either export its current products or initiate new products. Since new products can be costly and risky ventures, a sensible business may elect to begin international operations. As an example, see "Xerox and British Doors."

Finally, exports can help a business stabilize the demand for its products. Stablization of demand is possible because national economies are seldom perfectly synchronized. Thus, a business may find that its export sales have remained satisfactory but that its domestic sales have declined because of a recession in its home nation. Seasonal patterns may also help to stabilize demand, especially in nations south of the equator that have opposite seasonal patterns to those in the United States and Europe.

International trade can be profitable for business . . .

XEROX AND BRITISH DOORS

The 914 Xerox copier was such an immediate commercial success in the United States that Xerox soon began to consider marketing the 914 copier abroad. To accomplish this, Xerox formed a joint subsidiary, Rank–Xerox, half owned by the Rank Organization and half owned by the Xerox Corporation. (This is the same Rank Organization whose early British comedies still delight moviegoers and devotees of late-night television.) John H. Dessauer, a Xerox executive, describes what ensued:

. . . But we were not supermen, and we were subject to making some mistakes that could be called downright silly. In the main, they were the fault of simple oversight. To illustrate: we sent five early models of the 914 to Rank–Xerox. We dispatched them with a feeling of pride and accomplishment. Our British associates received them with equal admiration. They decided to test them in their own offices. And then they made an appalling discovery. Our best engineering brains, and theirs, too, had overlooked the fact that British doors are narrower than American doors! The 914 could not be moved into the typical British office! . . .

The situation was finally resolved by flying British engineers to Rochester, New York, where they and their American colleagues finally managed to reduce the 914's cabinet just enough so that it could squeeze its way into British offices. The risks involved in marketing products abroad, one of which is illustrated by Xerox's experience with British doors, are discussed in the text.

Thus, Rossignol Skis sell well in the United States in January and February, but peak sales in Chile are in July and August—the prime skiing season in that country.

American businesses import goods and services from abroad for three basic reasons: (1) the commodities are unavailable or are in short supply in the United States; (2) the prices of imported goods are lower than domestic prices; and (3) foreign goods are more prestigious in the eyes of American consumers. American businesses also purchase commodities from foreign firms with whom they have close commercial ties so that they can market their products to these foreign businesses. The Boeing corporation, for example, has made effective use of a variation of this practice. Purchasing many aircraft-engine components abroad has enabled Boeing to secure huge orders from foreign governments for the Boeing 747 aircraft, which dominates such government-owned airlines as British Airways and Air France.

✔ **Barriers to trade: a business perspective.** In addition to such government-imposed restraints on trade as tariffs and quotas, several practical barriers to trade must be overcome by the successful exporter:

1. *Language differences:* While English is becoming a fairly common second language, misunderstandings can still arise easily. Even the translation of brand names can present difficulties. For example, the Chevrolet Nova in Spanish becomes "no va" or "it doesn't go," and General Motor's "Body by Fisher" translates as "Corpse by Fisher" in Japanese.

. . . but the business owner may face difficulties

2. *Cultural differences:* Physical and social differences among nations are substantial. Product standards, such as the voltages and plugs used in electrical appliances, also differ. Cultural values and preferences may require different marketing approaches in different countries.
3. *Legal differences:* business, patent, antitrust, tax, and other laws differ substantially among nations. For example, price fixing is a criminal offense in the United States, but it is legally acceptable in Europe.

The successful exporter is aware of these practical barriers among nations and is also able to deal with fluctuations in exchange rates and in the availability of foreign currencies. A variety of organizations, described in Figure 20-2, provide assistance to exporters and importers.

Recent Developments in World Trade

GATT and . . .

In 1947, the United States and 22 other nations reached the General Agreement on Tariffs and Trade (GATT). The central purpose of GATT was to reduce barriers to international trade by encouraging bilateral and

20-2 Sources of foreign trade assistance to businesses. A variety of private and public organizations exist to serve exporters and importers.

Organization	Services Offered
Commercial banks	Large commercial banks maintain hundreds of branches throughout the world that provide financial advice and services as a routine part of their banking activities.
The Export-Import Bank (Exim Bank)	A U.S. government agency, the Exim Bank, was formed in 1934 to provide credit to American exporters when it was unavailable from commercial banks or when foreign governments provided loans to their exporters at subsidized rates. Today, the Exim Bank makes large quantities of credit available to individual exporters.
Bureau of Foreign Commerce, U.S. Department of Commerce	The Bureau of Foreign Commerce maintains lists of foreign buyers and distributors, credit and other data reports on individual foreign companies, product information on export opportunities, and other valuable data related to international business. This information is normally available free of charge.
The State Department	Several hundred *commercial attachés*, employed by the U.S. State Department, live and work abroad. Commercial attachés provide data on foreign economic developments to the U.S. government and are also responsible for helping American firms conduct foreign business activities.
Foreign trade zones, U.S. Customs	*Foreign trade zones* are geographic areas near major American and world ports in which producers may manufacture, process, or store goods without paying customs duties. Businesses located in foreign trade zones can import foreign parts without paying American customs duties, placing them in an excellent position to export the finished products.
The U.S. Tariff Commission	The Tariff Commission is responsible for determining whether foreign exporters are dumping their products into American markets. The Tariff Commission also determines whether normally priced foreign imports are damaging a specific American industry. An industry that has been harmed by excessive imports is eligible for technical assistance, government loans, and tax relief, and its employees are entitled to complete or partial federally funded retraining.

multilateral negotiations among nations. In 1962, President Kennedy signed the Trade Expansion Act, giving the President the power to reduce U.S. tariffs up to 50 percent in exchange for tariff concessions by other nations. Subsequently, the United States and other GATT members negotiated a significant reduction in tariffs, popularly known as the "Kennedy Round" of trade negotiations. To date, the result of GATT-sponsored negotiations has been a substantial reduction in international tariffs. It is not yet clear whether the political-pressure groups favoring protectionist legislation in the mid-1970s will weaken future GATT negotiations.

The current international tariff reductions have been accompanied by the formation of economic communities, the most successful of which

... the EEC have
helped to expand
world trade ...

is the European Economic Community (EEC). The "Common Market," as the EEC is frequently called, was founded when France, Italy, West Germany, Belgium, Luxembourg, and the Netherlands signed the Treaty of Rome in 1957. The EEC's basic objectives have been: (1) to achieve complete economic integration by 1970, and (2) to work toward political integration. Great Britain joined the Common Market in 1973, and most other nations in western Europe have applied for full or associate membership. The population and the economic potential of the EEC now rivals that of the United States.

Although political unification has not yet been achieved, the economic integration of those nations in the Common Market is virtually complete. Tariffs no longer exist between EEC members and cooperation is advancing rapidly in other economic areas ranging from antitrust regulation to social-welfare programs.

Where GATT regulations permit, the EEC has erected high external tariffs against foreign nations, including the United States. Consequently, commercial transactions among EEC's members have increased even more rapidly than international trade agreements in general—the very result the EEC hoped to achieve by levying high external tariffs. Rather than exporting directly to nations in the Common Market, many American businesses have avoided the EEC's tariff walls by establishing their own plants in Common-Market nations. The Latin American Free Trade Association (LAFTA) and the Central American Common Market (CACM), composed of nine Latin-American and five Central-American nations, respectively, have also sought economic integration, but have met with less apparent success than the EEC.

... but not always to
the benefit of
the American exporter

Foreign Investment and the Multinational Corporation

The concept of international business—the view that the world is rapidly advancing toward a single integrated economy—has been supported by an unprecedented expansion in trade among nations. Even more spectacular, however, has been the increase in the flow of investments across national boundaries. Foreign investment is normally of two types: (1) long-term investment in plant and equipment abroad, and (2) portfolio investment. *Investment in plant and equipment* abroad involves the operation of production, service, or marketing facilities in a foreign country. A business that is engaged in this type of investment is said to be involved in *international operations. Portfolio investment* involves the purchase of the bonds of foreign governments or businesses, of stock in foreign companies, or of other types of financial instruments, such as mortgages, that are issued by organizations located in a foreign country. One indication of the movement toward an integrated world economy, especially in non-Communist nations, is that portfolio investment in foreign countries has become far simpler and more common in recent years. Today, most American brokerage firms could quickly purchase stock in an Australian copper mine, a German bank, or a Japanese conglomerate. Arab governments now invest billions of dollars in American stock and bond portfolios as a matter of course.

For businesses, direct investment abroad is far more important than portfolio investment. Recently, direct foreign investment in the United States has begun to grow rapidly, and U.S. direct investment abroad has also increased.

Foreign Investment in the United States

Direct investment; building facilities abroad

In 1959, Olivetti, an Italian typewriter firm, entered the American market by acquiring Underwood, a U.S. manufacturer that had lost $14 million that year. Six years later, Olivetti's acquisition became profitable. In 1970, Olivetti opened a new plant in Harrisburg, Pennsylvania, that employed more than 1000 workers. As a result of the devaluations of the U.S. dollar that occurred in the early 1970s, Volkswagen announced plans to begin producing cars in the United States before 1980. The activities of both Olivetti and Volkswagen represent a development that has been accelerating for the last quarter of a century—the invasion of America by foreign firms. Direct foreign investment in U.S. industry totaled more than $25 billion in 1975.

U.S. Investments Abroad

A reverse process of even greater magnitude is also occurring; direct American investments abroad during 1975 exceeded $100 billion. Many well-known American businesses are dependent on foreign sales. For example, Exxon, the second largest "American" industrial corporation, derives two-thirds of its sales from foreign markets. Colgate-Palmolive, Singer, and Massey-Ferguson are other prominent firms with higher foreign sales than domestic revenues. In fact, the growth in American plant and equipment expenditures abroad has exceeded both the increase in U.S. exports (see Figure 20-3) and the rise in domestic plant and equipment expenditures (see Figure 20-4).

U.S. industry in Europe: a world power?

The rapid growth in American investment abroad, especially in Europe, has been described by French journalist and politician J.J. Servan-Schreiber. Schreiber states, "Fifteen years from now, it is quite possible that the world's third greatest industrial power, just after the United States and Russia, will not be Europe but *American industry in Europe*." As Schreiber notes, U.S. investment in Europe has been especially heavy in the highly technological, rapidly expanding industries. The reasons for this are not hard to understand. The high external tariffs that have been

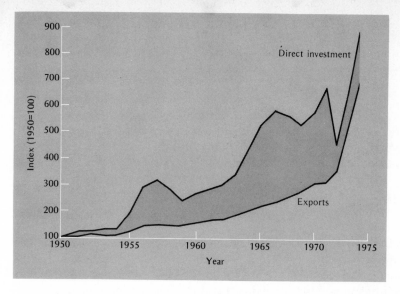

20-3

U.S. private foreign direct investment and exports.

established for some products by the Common Market make exportation to Europe difficult. European sales of many products also promise to increase more rapidly than American sales. For example, computer sales are expected to grow much more rapidly in Europe than in the United States, where most organizations that use computers have already secured them. This makes Europe especially attractive to corporations like IBM, Burroughs, Control Data, and Sperry-Rand.

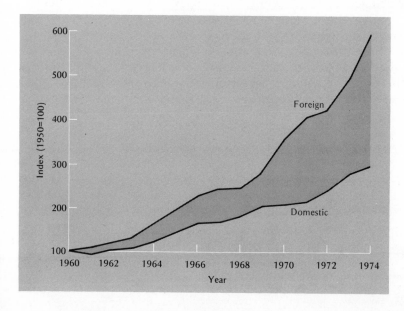

20-4

U.S. plant and equipment expenditures: foreign and domestic.

The Multinational Corporation

Projections indicate that sometime between the years 1990 and 2000, about 200 giant firms — two-thirds of them American in origin — will control more than half of the productive output of the private sectors of all the free-world economies. These *multinational corporations* will produce and sell in every major international market, will be owned by citizens of many nations, and will possess more economic power than most governments. They will be able to disregard national borders much as large American corporations disregard state lines. Their decisions will be based on comparative prices and costs — and not on national loyalties.

Multinationals operate in several countries . . .

✔ Benefits of multinationals. Even though experts disagree on the meaning of "multinational corporation," the most common definition is that a multinational is a corporation with plants in at least six nations and with operating facilities in countries outside the one where its main plants are based that are responsible for at least 20 percent of its total production. The major advantage of multinationals is their ability to respond to international market and cost differences. A multinational may locate some operations in the Far East to take advantage of inexpensive labor, while its research and development activities may be based in the United States and Western Europe. Its storage and marketing facilities may be in South America, Europe, Japan, and the United States to be near the corporation's largest international markets. Multinational corporations also try to secure capital in nations where interest costs are low; many multinational corporations are able to show high profits in countries where business taxes are low.

. . . present economic benefits . . .

✔ Risks of multinationals. The climate for multinationals deteriorated during the 1970–1975 period. One reason was a rise in nationalism throughout the world. A frequent aspect of nationalism is the desire to control most activities within a country's borders. Foreign-owned plants

---

HOW WELL DO YOU KNOW THE FOREIGN MULTINATIONALS?

From time to time, the list of the largest non-American businesses (nearly all of which are multinationals) changes. Below is a current list of the 15 largest industrial corporations operating outside the United States. Do you know the countries in which these corporations were originally founded and the types of goods that they produce?

1. Royal Dutch/Shell Group
2. British Petroleum
3. National Iranian Oil
4. Unilever
5. Philips' Gloeilampenfabrieken

6. Cie Française des Pétroles
7. Nippon Steel
8. August Thyssen-Hütte
9. BASF
10. Hoechst

11. ENI
12. ICI (Imperial Chemical Industries)
13. Siemens
14. Volkswagenwerk
15. Bayer

For the answers, see page 537.

and multinational corporations are particularly vulnerable during a nationalistic upheaval, since they represent powerful, foreign-dominated economic interests. Thus, the facilities of many multinationals have been *nationalized* — taken over by foreign governments with or without compensation to the multinational corporation itself.

. . . can see
their facilities
nationalized . . .

Multinationals are also attacked in their countries of origin. Rather than investing in their "home" countries, they send valuable funds abroad. Rather than creating jobs in the domestic economy, they are accused of exporting jobs to foreign countries.

Multinationals must also face the normal business risks of any foreign investor. A multinational may invest in a country only to watch the value of that country's currency decline — along with the value of its investment. Foreign nations may also change tax laws or impose exchange controls, both of which can disastrously affect a multinational's profits in that country.

To counter these risks, multinationals are obtaining more funds abroad and are employing more foreign nationals at higher organizational levels. By selling its stocks and bonds locally, a multinational can make it difficult for a government to nationalize its facilities at the risk of antagonizing its own citizens. Many multinationals have also sought to avoid nationalization in countries where it is viewed as a serious risk by *licensing* — selling technology to another company for a fee.

✔ **Political issues and multinationals.** In the absence of effective international regulatory bodies, multinational corporation present a number of problems. Who, if anyone, is to regulate such complex enterprises? What does the existence of multinational corporations imply for the sovereignty of nations that have less economic power than the multinational enterprise? To what extent should the local operations of multinational corporations conform to the customs and the political policies of their host nations?

. . . and are politically
controversial

Although multinationals raise many key political issues, their potential political benefits are also great. By using world resources wisely, multinationals contribute to higher living standards and to greater political stability. Multinationals also hasten world economic integration. As nations become more economically integrated, we can hope that political cooperation will be one by-product.

The United States in the World Economic Community

After World War II, the international position of the American dollar was unchallenged. But from 1971 to 1975, the U.S. dollar declined in value in comparison to other currencies. To understand this change or devaluation, we must consider: (1) the international trade position of the United States; (2) exchange rates; and (3) international financial institutions.

The United States and International Business

Historically, the United States has been a net exporter: the dollar value of its exports normally exceeds the dollar value of its imports (see Figure 20-5). Major U.S. exports include agricultural foods and grain, American-made machinery and equipment, American-made manufactured goods, and chemicals. Major imports to the United States are petroleum and petroleum products and foreign-produced manufactured goods, machinery, and vehicles.

The difference between the monetary value of a nation's exports and its imports is called that nation's *balance of trade*. When its exports exceed its imports, a nation is said to be enjoying a *surplus* in its balance of trade. When the opposite occurs, the balance of trade is deficient, or has shown a *deficit*.

The *balance of international payments* or, more simply, the *balance of payments* of a nation is a balance sheet representing all of its international economic transactions. As such, the balance of payments includes the balance of trade plus other expenditures like foreign aid and tourist pur-

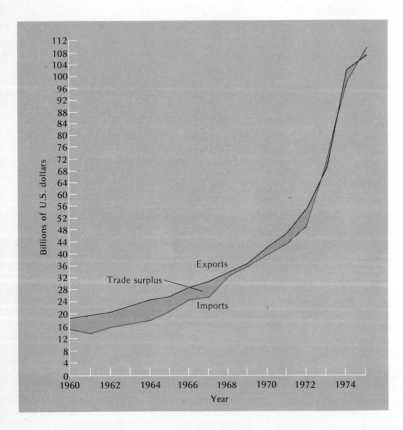

20-5

The U.S. balance of trade, 1960–1975. Most experts believe that the surplus of trade in 1975 will be eliminated as the American economy expands in the late 1970s. (*Note:* 1975 data have been estimated by the authors.)

THE 15 LARGEST FOREIGN MULTINATIONALS

Name	Country	Products	Sales*
1. Royal Dutch/Shell Group	Netherlands-Britain	Petroleum products, natural gas, chemicals	33,037,116,000
2. British Petroleum	Britain	Petroleum products, chemicals	18,269,240,000
3. National Iranian Oil	Iran	Petroleum products, natural gas, chemicals	16,802,000,000†
4. Unilever	Britain-Netherlands	Food, detergents, toiletries, feed	13,666,667,000
5. Philips' Gloeilampenfabrieken	Netherlands	Electronic and electrical equipment, chemicals	9,422,386,000
6. Cie Française des Pétroles	France	Petroleum products	8,908,563,000
7. Nippon Steel	Japan	Iron and steel	8,843,550,000
8. August Thyssen-Hütte	Germany	Iron and steel	8,664,021,000
9. BASF	Germany	Chemicals, petroleum products, potash, salt	8,497,038,000
10. Hoechst	Germany	Chemicals, pharmaceuticals	7,821,054,000
11. ENI	Italy	Petroleum products, chemicals, textiles	7,172,831,000
12. ICI (Imperial Chemical Industries)	Britain	Chemicals	6,911,813,000
13. Siemens	Germany	Electrical equipment, electronics	6,701,681,000
14. Volkswagenwerk	Germany	Automobiles	6,568,717,000
15. Bayer	Germany	Chemicals, pharmaceuticals	6,300,940,000

* In U.S. dollars.
† *Fortune* estimate.
Source: *Fortune,* August 1975.

chases. Since 1950, the United States has had a deficit in its balance of payments, because U.S. dollar outflows have exceeded the dollars spent by foreigners in America. The reason for this deficit is that the surplus in the U.S. balance of payments has been more than offset by federal military and foreign-aid expenditures, by the tendency of American businesses and private individuals to invest more funds abroad than foreign interests place in the United States, and by the large amounts of money spent by American tourists compared to the lesser expenditures of overseas travelers to the United States. In 1975, however, the U.S. balance of payments was again in surplus. It is not clear whether this economic trend will continue into the future.

Will the newly found American balance-of-payments surplus continue?

Exchange Rates

An *exchange rate* is the rate at which one nation's unit of currency is exchanged for another nation's unit of currency. For example, in August 1975, the exchange rate between the Canadian dollar and the U.S. dollar was one Canadian dollar equals $0.97 (U.S.). If the American dollar were to *appreciate* (increase) in value, a single Canadian dollar might be

An exchange rate:
comparing the values
of currencies

worth only $0.90. If the U.S. dollar were to *depreciate* (decline) in value, one Canadian dollar might be worth $1.02.

Fluctuations in exchange rates are vitally important to exporters and importers. For example, depreciation of the U.S. dollar compared to its Canadian counterpart makes American exports more attractive to Canadians, who receive more American currency for each Canadian dollar they exchange.

Students who travel to Europe are very familiar with the effects of the depreciation of the U.S. dollar. A candy bar in Switzerland currently costs $1; a dinner in Germany may cost $20 at a moderately priced restaurant. While European prices seem high to Swiss, German, and French consumers, the American traveler in Europe suffers an additional disadvantage. The American dollar has depreciated so rapidly in value compared to some European currencies that the exchange rate is extremely unfavorable (see Figure 20-6).

Exchange rates fluctuate because of changes in national balance of payments. For example, deficits in the U.S. balance of payments mean that

20-6

Foreign exchange as quoted in the *Wall Street Journal* for July 30, 1975.
Source: *Wall Street Journal,* July 31, 1975.

Foreign Exchange

Wednesday, July 30, 1975
Selling prices for bank transfers in the United States for payment abroad, as quoted at 3 p.m. Eastern Time (in dollars).

Country	Wednesday	Tuesday
Argentina (peso)	.03	.03
Australia (dollar)	1.3050	1.3050
Austria (schilling)	.0555	.0557
Belgium (franc)		
Commercial rate	.026100	.026225
Financial rate	.025	.025
Brazil (cruzeiro)	.1245	.1245
Britain (pound)	2.1645	2.1760
30-day futures	2.1566	2.1700
90-day futures	2.1441	2.1570
180-day futures	2.1241	2.1379
Canada (dollar)	.9702	.9699
China-Taiwan (dollar)	.0270	.0270
Colombia (peso)	.035	.035
Denmark (krone)	.1690	.1700
Ecuador (sucre)	.0407	.0407
Finland (markka)	.2665	.2680
France (franc)	.2294	.2303
Greece (drachma)	.036	.036
Hong Kong (dollar)	.1990	.1990
India (rupee)	.1180	.1185
Iran (rial)	.0153	.0153
Iraq (dinar)	3.41	3.41

Country	Wednesday	Tuesday
Israel (pound)	.1670	.1670
Italy (lira)	.001508	.001509
Japan (yen)	.003365	.003367
30-day futures	.003369	.003373
90-day futures	.003370	.003375
180-day futures	.003370	.003376
Lebanon (pound)	.4425	.4425
Mexico (peso)	.08006	.08006
Netherlands (guilder)	.3777	.3782
New Zealand (dollar)	1.2825	1.2825
Norway (krone)	.1859	.1862
Pakistan (rupee)	.1030	.1030
Peru (sol)	.024	.024
Philippines (peso)	.1325	.1325
Portugal (escudo)	.0381	.0382
Singapore (dollar)	.4065	.4050
South Africa (rand)	1.4050	1.4050
Spain (peseta)	.01725	.0173
Sweden (krona)	.2336	.2345
Switzerland (franc)	.3702	.3726
Uruguay (new peso)		
Financial rate	.3700	.37
Venezuela (bolivar)	.2335	.2335
West Germany (mark)	.39	.3916
30-day futures	.3909	.3925
90-day futures	.3931	.3946
180-day futures	.3964	.3979

Supplied by Bankers Trust Co., New York, N.Y.

foreign nationals accumulate more dollars each year than they wish to spend in the United States. Eventually, this surplus depresses the value of the American dollar. Similarly, Germany has had large surpluses in its balance of payments, so it is not surprising that the value of the German mark has risen substantially.

International Financial Institutions

Fluctuations in exchange rates are unsettling to international business. International trade that was once profitable can produce substantial losses. Contracts that once seemed reasonable to all parties can suddenly be grossly unfair if exchange rates alter the costs of future commitments. A highly desirable foreign investment can lose much of its value very quickly if the host country's currency depreciates rapidly.

Thus, exporters and importers often pressure governments to adopt *fixed exchange rates*—exchange rates that fluctuate only within a 1- or a 2-percent range of established norms. (During the early 1970s, for example, the British pound was expected to be worth $2.40 in American currency. The British government would intervene whenever the British pound fell much below $2.38 or much above $2.42.) To keep its exchange rate near the accepted norm, a government can either sell reserves (its stock of gold and foreign currencies) or borrow from foreign or international organizations.

Since 1944, when representatives of 44 nations attending the Bretton Woods Conference in New Hampshire founded the International Monetary Fund (IMF), the stabilization of exchange rates has been a matter of international cooperation. The IMF was established to perform two basic functions: (1) to serve as a referee in the establishment of fixed exchange rates, and (2) to assist in the creation of monetary reserves other than gold. In the 1970s, special drawing rights (SDRs)—a type of world currency created by the IMF to be used only in economic transactions among governments—gained wide acceptance.

Can exchange rates be governmentally controlled?

Today, a government wishing to stabilize its currency can intervene in foreign exchange markets by selling or buying its own currency. To finance such transactions, a government can use its own reserves of gold, foreign currencies, or special drawing rights, or it can borrow funds from the IMF. Nonetheless, fluctuations in exchange rates—particularly after 1971—were becoming so violent that many governments decided not to intervene in foreign exchange markets. This produced a system of *flexible exchange rates*. By 1975, most exchange rates were determined by a mixture of the demand for and supply of a specific currency on foreign exchange markets and occasional government intervention. While exchange-rate fluctuations in the current mixed economic system have been greater than before, most businesses have successfully adjusted to the increased complications that flexible exchange rates have introduced.

KEY POINTS TO REMEMBER

1. International business encompasses international trade, international investment, and the rise of a new form of business organization—the multinational corporation.

2. International trade is mutually beneficial in that it tends to raise the living standards of all participants.

3. Governments often encourage international trade for political as well as for economic reasons.

4. Major barriers to trade include tariffs, quotas, and exchange controls. Barriers to trade are often imposed due to the political pressures of special-interest groups who benefit from protectionist legislation.

5. Exports and imports can generate extensive profits for a business.

6. Barriers to trade have been significantly reduced in recent years as a result of the General Agreement on Tariffs and Trade (GATT) and the European Economic Community (EEC), frequently called the "Common Market."

7. International investment is growing more rapidly than international trade and will soon be more important to most businesses than international trade.

8. The multinational corporation treats the world as an international economic unit in terms of production, marketing, and finance.

9. The balance of payments reflects the entire range of a nation's economic transactions abroad.

10. Exchange rates are especially important in international business transactions and, in comparison with the past, have fluctuated by large amounts in recent years.

QUESTIONS FOR DISCUSSION

1. What reasons can you cite for the expansion of world trade after 1945?

2. What are the advantages of international trade to the American people? What are the potential disadvantages? What advantages and what disadvantages of world trade exist from the viewpoint of the business concern?

3. Textile imports in the United States have recently risen. What economically powerful special-interest groups would benefit from imposing trade restrictions? What regions of the United States would benefit from such restrictions? Which special-interest groups would tend to oppose such restrictions?

4. Suppose that the Arab countries, with their riches from oil exportation, decide to invest $200 billion in the United States. What would the consequences of permitting this be from the American viewpoint?

5. Define a multinational corporation.

6. Would you, as a corporate manager, prefer fixed or flexible exchange rates? Explain your answer.

SHORT CASES AND PROBLEMS

1. An American bowling-ball manufacturer uses U.S. dollars to build a plant in Great Britain for $2,400,000 when the exchange rate is one British pound equals $2.40 (U.S.). One year later, the exchange rate is one British pound equals $2.05. Ignoring depreciation and assuming that the value of the bowling-ball plant has not changed for other business reasons, how much is the plant currently worth?

2. A bowling ball cost one British pound to manufacture when the pound exchanged for $2.40 (U.S.). Bowling-ball production and marketing costs rose 10 percent in Britain the following year. Most of the bowling balls in Britain are exported to the United States, where bowling-ball production and distribution costs rose only 5 percent the following year. Is the British bowling-ball producer in an improved competitive position compared to the American bowling-ball producer, after accounting for the depreciation of the British pound mentioned in Problem 1?

In the Career Selection section at the end of Chapter 1, we discussed the five key steps in choosing a career. We will now turn to the four concluding steps in securing a position with a suitable organization: (1) job hunting, or how to be granted an interview; (2) preparing for the job interview; (3) the job interview; and (4) post-interview follow-up.

JOB HUNTING

The purpose of what we refer to here as "job hunting" is to be granted a personal interview. It is wise to schedule interviews with recruiters who visit your campus representing various employers. In addition, obtain lists of prospective employers who meet your career and geographical criteria from sources like the Yellow Pages of the telephone directory, Chamber of Commerce publications, and the *College Placement Annual*. Contact the nearest office of your State Employment Service, and talk to friends, faculty, and family who may be aware of prospective job openings. Check the classified section of your local newspapers. Pursue all employment possibilities. Don't get discouraged.

Once you have obtained the names of several prospective employers, send your résumé (see Chapter 5) and a covering letter to each company, requesting an interview or stating that you will contact each employer again by letter. Sometimes directly contacting a prospective employer without sending a letter in advance is more effective in obtaining a personal interview. When paying a direct, personal visit, be prepared to leave a copy of your résumé with the prospective employer, even though you may be asked to complete the company's job-application form as well.

INTERVIEW PREPARATION

After you have arranged the time, the date, and the place for the interview, doing your homework about a prospective employer *before* you are interviewed can pay big dividends. Be sure that you can correctly pronounce the company's name and the name of the person who will be interviewing you. Learn something about the company by reading its published material. Formulate any questions you may wish to ask *before* you arrive at the interview: as examples, you will want to know about the type of work involved, the nature of the company's training program, if any, what career promotional patterns are typical of the organization, and whether you might be transferred to a different location at some time. Try to determine if the specific salary requirement you have in mind is reasonable and what salary the employer is likely to propose if a job offer is made.

Write out the answers to the following questions commonly asked in a job interview:

1. Why is this specific employer of interest to you?
2. Why have you chosen the particular field of study or the particular career that you have?
3. What are your short-term and your long-term career objectives?
4. What special interests, activities, or qualifications can you contribute that might relate to the prospective job?
5. What do you expect of a job?

Take a pen and some paper for your own use after the interview is completed. Obviously, be neat and clean; use your own good taste in choosing what clothes you will wear. Make a point of getting to the interview five or ten minutes early.

THE INTERVIEW

Your own common sense is the best guide of how you should respond during the interview. Be friendly, honest, and sincere, and you will make a good impression. Try to judge how extensive your answers should be from cues the interviewer may provide. Don't answer all questions "yes" or "no," but don't talk too much. If you find that you are doing most of the talking, return the conversational lead to the interviewer by asking, "Are there any other questions you would like to ask me?"

Sit up in your chair and look interested—not bored, as if you are doing the interviewer a favor by being there. Look the interviewer directly in the eye frequently during your conversation. Don't go off on a tangent. Remember two important things: (1) you are there to obtain information about the company and the available job, so don't be afraid to ask pertinent questions; and (2) you are there to sell yourself, so get your good points across sincerely and without conceit.

Thank the interviewer for the time and consideration taken to interview you. Express your willingness to provide the interviewer with any additional information that might be helpful. Make pertinent notes about the interview after it is over.

POST-INTERVIEW FOLLOW-UP

Carefully note any further contacts your interviewer has suggested. Follow any instructions the interviewer has given you, but avoid unsolicited correspondence. If the interview seemed to go especially well or if the interviewer indicated that the organization would respond by a specific date, wait at least a week after the interview or the indicated date before checking with the company again. Then, briefly remind the interviewer of your previous conversation, express appreciation for the interviewer's time, and explain in a few words that you are still interested in the position.

A CRITICAL BUSINESS DECISION

—made by Michel Grinberg

THE SITUATION Michel Grinberg—a 17-year veteran with Gillette and manager of the firm's French subsidiary—was enjoying a peaceful summer afternoon on the beach at Lake Annecy in the mountains of southeastern France. After visiting a local razor-blade plant, Grinberg planned to meet a friend, Michel Dupont, a member of the family that owned the neighboring facility of S. T. Dupont.

S. T. Dupont, former photographers for Napoleon III, now manufacture lacquered cigarette lighters that sell for a minimum of $180. A business less related to Gillette's mass marketing of razor blades and shaving products would be hard to imagine, and Grinberg expected to spend a relaxing afternoon swimming and sunbathing. Yet, the conversation that ensued would profoundly affect both Dupont and Gillette.

Dupont casually mentioned that his family's firm had introduced the world's first disposable lighter, marketed by S. T. Dupont under the trade name "Cricket." French sales of the "Cricket" lighter were booming; S. T. Dupont could not keep up with consumer demand. The small French company had neither the financial resources nor the technical knowledge of mass production to match the explosive sales potential of the inexpensive lighter.

By 1970, when Michel Grinberg met his friend Michel Dupont, Gillette had become a highly successful multinational corporation. Its major international goal had been to establish good relationships with host governments while minimizing financial risks. "Unlike many multinational companies," Arthur Kirby, general manager of Gillette's European operations observes, "we've never been asked to roll back a price. The government's door is always open when we knock. And if local government respects you, you don't get a black eye in front of, say, 55 million Frenchmen. That's worth its weight in gold." To achieve good relationships with local governments, Gillette scrupulously follows local law and attempts to make its foreign operations a valuable economic asset to host governments.

To reduce financial risks, Gillette tries to borrow money not where it is cheapest, but from the countries where its foreign subsidiaries operate. "Since we have never considered the interest rate a factor in our borrowing policy," explains Gillette's treasurer Milton Gloss, "we have borrowed at extraordinary rates, as high as 24 percent in Brazil." This policy permits Gillette to reduce its potential losses due to changes in exchange rates, since both the assets and the liabilities of the firm's foreign operations are held in the same currencies.

THE DECISION Gillette desperately wanted to introduce the "Cricket" lighter in the United States, where—like the razor blade—the disposable lighter would have a strong, repetitive demand and could be sold through the company's existing marketing channels. But to acquire the "Cricket," Gillette had to purchase the S. T. Dupont facility—a difficult task in view of the French government's opposition to foreign investments.

Gillette moved quickly. Responsibility for negotiating the acquisition and for dealing with the French government was assigned to Grinberg. As a Frenchman, Grinberg undoubtedly soothed some French objections to the takeover, but the French government still required that Gillette agree to increase "Cricket" production in France, to export nearly half of the lighters produced in France, and to employ French workers. Once the acquisition of S. T. Dupont was completed and the French government was satisfied, Michel Grinberg, the new President of Dupont, still had a key decision to make: how could Dupont acquire the manufacturing and marketing expertise of its American parent company and still retain its identity as a French business?

QUESTION

What benefits do you think Gillette, Dupont, and consumers in the United States and France receive from the acquisition of S. T. Dupont by the multinational firm, the Gillette Company.

He that waits upon fortune is never sure of a dinner.

Benjamin Franklin

ECONOMIC GROWTH AND THE QUALITY OF LIFE

The British government recently conducted a search for a site on which to build a third airport to serve London. One location under consideration would have required the demolition of St. Michael's, a twelfth-century Norman church. Analysts decided to place a monetary value on the ancient church to contrast the value of the space in its present capacity with its value as an airport site. Based on the face value of the church's current fire insurance, the analysts assessed the worth of St. Michael's to be a few thousand dollars.

Placing a value on an 800-year-old church

When the basis of the calculation was publicized, one outraged citizen suggested another approach: take the original cost of building St. Michael's (say, 100 pounds sterling or about $210) and assume that the church has appreciated in value at an annual rate of 10 percent during the 800 years since its construction. That would place St. Michael's value at one decillion pounds (a decillion is a one followed by 33 zeros)! A public outcry arose, and the ancient church was spared.

The plight of St. Michael's dramatizes a fundamental problem that individuals, businesses, and governments alike must face: How important is sustained economic growth to improving the quality of life? Although we cannot give a definitive answer to this question yet, we can place the problem in perspective by identifying some dimensions of economic growth and of the quality of life and then by examining what their future implications are for individual Americans and for the American business system.

Relationship Between Economic Growth and the Quality of Life

Economic growth: a nation's expanded production

When economists speak of the *economic growth* of a nation, they are usually referring to its expanded production as measured by real gross national product. The fact that GNP can be measured conveniently in quantitative terms contributes to its wide-spread acceptance as a measure of the economic output of a nation. In this section, we will identify (1) the advantages of economic growth; (2) why economic growth is being challenged by people who believe it does not contribute to the quality of daily life; (3) the key factors affecting economic growth and the quality of life; and (4) the problems encountered when measuring the quality of life.

Advantages of Economic Growth

Comedian Joe E. Brown once observed: "I've been rich and I've been poor; and believe me—rich is better." These sentiments would have been echoed by the typical immigrant family in Boston in 1860. The father received an average weekly wage of $7 for a 72-hour work week. At birth, his children could be expected to live an average of 14 years, and they would spend most of their lives working in factories to help support the family. In contrast, the typical American wage earner today works 40 hours a week or less; in terms of real purchasing power, the average American's wages today are more than ten times the average wage in 1890, and life expectancy has increased from 14 to 72 years.

Thus, past economic growth has been enormously beneficial to the ordinary American. And, even in an affluent society, economic growth continues to provide advantages in the form of improved living standards for Americans:

Benefits conferred by economic growth

1. *Economic growth improves perceptions of freedom among families:* In a survey of American households with incomes above $20,000, families repeatedly indicated that they felt a great sense of freedom and satisfaction once their income passed a threshold of $20,000 or $25,000. "We no longer have to watch every penny" and "Now we can concentrate on the big things in life, rather than worrying over small purchases" were typical responses in this survey. Continued economic growth promises to place more American families beyond the $20,000 or $25,000 threshold.
2. *Economic growth is an efficient poverty fighter:* Obviously, if incomes are rising each year, fewer persons are suffering from physical want each year. Both the rich and the poor are getting richer.

IF THERE WERE 100 PEOPLE IN THE WORLD: A COMPARISON OF RICH AND POOR NATIONS

It is difficult to place the standards of living of people around the globe in the proper perspective. Michael D. Anderson has suggested an interesting example that achieves such a perspective. If the nearly four billion people on earth were represented by a community of 100 people, we would find that:

- Six would be U.S. citizens; 94 would be citizens of other countries.
- Six would own one-half of the money in the world, and 94 would share the other half; of the 94, 20 would own virtually all of the remaining half.
- Six would have 15 times more material possessions than the other 94 put together.

- Six would have 72 percent more than the average daily food requirement; two-thirds of the remaining 94 would survive on below-minimum food standards, and many would be on starvation diets.
- The life span of six would be 70 years; the life span of 94 would be 39 years.

These statistics highlight two important points. First, Americans in general are much more prosperous economically than people in most of the rest of the world. Second, the majority of the benefits Americans enjoy are traceable to the past economic growth of the United States.

More significantly, vigorously growing economies like those in Japan and Germany generate labor shortages and job opportunities for the unskilled. Some economists estimate that economic growth in the United States since 1960 has eliminated five or six times as many people from the poverty rolls as have all the highly publicized antipoverty campaigns.

3. *Economic growth helps to finance social programs:* Recent taxpayer revolts make it clear that it is difficult to increase taxes. In the absence of higher tax rates, desirable social programs can be funded only if taxes rise through the normal channel of continued economic growth.

4. *Economic growth promotes social stability:* In a growing economy everyone can gradually increase their incomes. In a stagnant economy, any one person's economic gain must be offset by another person's economic loss. This means that income must be redistributed from wealthier groups to poorer groups, penalizing those people whose hard work has provided them with more income. Hence, incentives to work hard and to be efficient may be lost. Periods of economic growth are also full of optimism, vitality, and opportunity — desirable conditions for most people.

There can be no doubt that the results of economic growth are highly prized.

Quality of Life: Economic Growth Under Challenge

But in the 1970s, the goal of economic growth began to be challenged by many Americans who asked if happiness were indeed an ever-rising GNP. More directly, Americans have now begun to question the traditional assumption that economic growth always contributes to the human *quality of life* which represents all aspects of existence: economic, social, cultural, and moral welfare. This controversy focuses on three major issues:

Quality of life: all aspects of a person's life

1. *Does increased production necessarily mean increased economic welfare?* Are the living conditions of the average family really improved if it has two cars but can travel only in traffic jams in polluted cities? Does consuming just "to keep up with the Joneses" really benefit anyone?

2. *Is increased production (or even increased economic welfare) a very important goal?* Today, the average American family has more than enough money to buy essentials like food, clothing, and shelter, and Americans are spending an increasingly larger portion of their incomes on nonessentials. Isn't it time that Americans recognized that humanistic, social, cultural, and aesthetic goals are more important than economic growth?

Controversial questions concerning economic growth

3. *Does economic growth have undesirable effects on critical noneconomic goals?* Are giant assembly lines—no matter how efficient—
really good for workers? Does new technology (say, deep-sea oil
drilling) always benefit mankind? Does it matter if economically
profitable construction projects are not aesthetically pleasing?

To many, the connection between economic growth and the quality of life
is no longer obvious.

Key Factors Affecting Economic Growth and the Quality of Life

Factors such as population, food, energy, and environmental
pollution affect both economic growth and the quality of life. In this section, we will examine each of these factors separately. Later in the Epilogue, we will show how these factors may affect Americans and American
business in the coming years.

✔ Population. In 1974, the earth's population was estimated to be
3.9 billion. Somewhere between the years 2000 and 2010, this population is
expected to double. An especially frightening aspect of our population
growth is that the populations of the richer nations—those with the higher
standards of living—are expected to grow at an annual rate of about 0.8
percent over the next three decades. In contrast, the populations of the
poorer nations are expected to increase at an average annual rate of 2.4
percent, and many of these annual rates are expected to be above 3.0 percent. Each year, the population of the earth increases by approximately 80
million people. And, as the gross national products of underdeveloped
countries rise, each additional person born claims a share and the living
standards of the people rise slowly if at all. An international official sums
it up simply: "The rich are getting richer, while the poor are getting
poorer, because the population now is increasing more than twice as fast
in the poor nations as it is in the rich countries."

**The world's population
will double by 2010**

✔ Food. In 1798, British economist Thomas Malthus observed that
"the power of population is infinitely greater than the power in the earth
to produce subsistence for man." Grim forecasts like this one earned economics the nickname "the dismal science." For the next 175 years, it appeared that Malthus had miscalculated. The human race contradicted him
by applying increasingly sophisticated technology to food production. But
by 1975, Philip Handler, president of the prestigious U.S. National Academy of Sciences, saw that rampaging population growth was outracing
technical advances in agriculture. His unpleasant conclusion: "Malthus
was right."

Was Malthus right?

U.S. Secretary of State Henry Kissinger also emphasized the
seriousness of the food crisis to the World Food Conference held in Rome

in November 1974. Kissinger noted that if current population growth rates continue, the gap between the grain that developing countries produce and the grain that these countries need will rise from 25 million tons per year to 85 million tons per year by 1985. In late 1974, world grain reserves reached a 22-year low: a 26-day supply, compared to a 95-day supply in 1961. A crop failure in North America today could mean starvation for millions. In fact, the increased demand for American grain abroad has already increased the price of bread in the United States.

✔ **Energy.** Modern civilization's thirst for energy is almost incomprehensible. Half the coal produced since the dawn of time has been mined since 1940, and half of all the oil in the world has been produced since 1963. Energy is important because it is essential to all economic activity. Not only is energy required to heat buildings and to power transportation vehicles; energy is also needed to produce food and to convert ores to basic industrial materials. The amounts of energy, measured in pounds of coal, needed to make one pound of various essential materials are shown below:

Material	From ore	From recycled material
Steel	1.11	.22
Aluminum	6.09	.21
Copper	1.98	.11
Glass	.36	.36

Alaska North Slope oil:
a ten-month U.S. supply

Thus, while some essential materials in the earth's crust are almost limitless, the energy to convert them is not. The lack of fuel oil in the mid-1970s partially reflects poor short-run resource planning. In the early 1970s, the Federal Power Commission checked the rise of the wellhead price of petroleum, discouraging U.S. oil firms from exploring for new deposits. But the long-term problem is that both natural gas and oil are becoming more and more difficult to obtain. In the 1930s, the American oil industry produced 275 barrels of crude oil per foot of exploratory drilling in the United States. But in recent years, this figure has fallen to 35 barrels, in spite of increasingly sophisticated geophysical exploration techniques. Moreover, the nation's thirst for oil has grown so large that a "major find" such as the 12-billion barrel oilfield on the Alaska North Slope will provide only a ten-month supply of the estimated U.S. oil needs in 1985. And such discoveries as the Alaska North Slope oilfield are rare.

✔ **Environmental pollution.** In 1970, the U.S. Congress passed the Clean Air Act, which set July 1, 1975, as the deadline for states to reduce pollutants like sulphur dioxide and solid particles in the atmosphere. Although impressive improvements in air quality were made by that time, the current Environmental Protection Agency (EPA) estimate is that three-fourths of the U.S. population are still exposed to higher levels of these two pollutants than are healthful. The EPA also states that a dozen U.S.

Clean air for Americans
is still years away

metropolitan areas containing one-fourth of the nation's population are years or even decades away from reducing automobile emissions to an acceptable level. Even seemingly harmless aerosol spray cans are suspected air polluters: some scientists believe that the fluorocarbons used as propellants in some spray cans are collecting in the upper atmosphere and breaking down the ozone layer that protects the earth from harmful radiation.

Solid-waste disposal presents similar problems. Americans discard about 400 million tons of trash every year, including about 125 million tons of garbage. Major cities like New York are simply running out of space — usually in the form of open landfills — in which to dump solid waste. Incineration is only a partial solution, since the ash residue from burning trash is also an air pollutant.

Increasing recognition is being given to the important tradeoff between cheaper energy and a cleaner environment. Automobiles can get more miles to the gallon if exhaust emission restrictions are reduced. Utilities can generate cheaper electricity if they are permitted to pollute the air with sulfur dioxide by burning coal with a high-sulfur content. Coal can be produced more cheaply if strip mining that scars the land is allowed. These are some of the difficult environmental choices to be faced in the 1970s and the 1980s. Some evidence, however, indicates that substantial progress has been made in recent years toward cleaning up America's air and water.

Measuring the Quality of Life

In Chapter 6, we stressed the importance of using a criterion or measure of success to evaluate the effectiveness of decisions. Business decisions are usually measured in quantitative dollar terms, while personal decisions are often based on qualitative measures such as health, happiness, and satisfaction. In many instances, personal measures defy quantification: What criteria can be used to measure a person's happiness? To evaluate the quality of life? To measure the innumerable intangibles that represent the quality of a person's daily life?

The federal government is considering social indicators

These questions are now being studied both by the federal government and by individual business firms. One proposal under consideration by the government calls for the formation of a Council of Social Advisers that will function like the current U.S. Council of Economic Advisers that assists the President. The proposed Council of Social Advisers would be responsible for designating appropriate measures of social and cultural welfare and for overseeing their implementation through federal, state, and local governments. Statistics on educational attainment, health, cultural achievement, the psychological state of the population, and other social indicators would be collected by the council.

Similarly, many business managers have begun to feel that their traditional reports — income statements and balance sheets detailing the financial condition of their firms — are too narrow to adequately reflect what they are trying to do. For example, how can these statements describe the social contribution of a company that assigns some of its top management to advise struggling minority business owners? What measures can be used to indicate that the installation of costly pollution-control equipment is a positive action and is not a drain on profits? How can the expense of hiring unemployed workers and educating them in company-financed training programs be reflected in a company's accounting statements? The Bank of America, which has begun to address itself to these kinds of questions, believes that methods for quantifying such social achievements will be developed in the future and that these measures will eventually become part of a firm's annual report.

Economic Growth, the Future, and You

In 1968, 70 scholars from nations throughout the world formed the Club of Rome, whose purpose was to explore the major issues confronting society. The group asked an international team of scientists working at the Massachusetts Institute of Technology to study the most basic issue of all — the survival of the human race. The MIT team summarized its findings in a 1972 book, *The Limits to Growth,* which assesses the worldwide impact of a continuing stress on economic growth. Although these findings are extremely controversial, the book does examine what the future will be like.

Compound Growth

In our discussion of economic growth rates, we have used such phrases as "5 percent a year" and "10 percent annually." It is this concept of *compound growth* — in money, in GNP, in population, in pollution — to which we often fail to pay real attention. Consider the well-known story of the child who talked his parents into giving him a penny on the first day of the month and then into doubling the donation every day: two pennies the second day, four the third day, and so on. In this problem, which involves a compound growth of 100 percent per day, the parents must contribute more than a million pennies on the twenty-first day.

Because we are a part of a growing economic system, we may fail to see the implications of such compound economic growth. *The Limits to Growth* cites a French riddle that illustrates the suddenness with which compound growth approaches a fixed limit:

> Suppose you own a pond on which a water lily is growing. The lily plant doubles in size each day. If the lily were allowed to grow unchecked, it would completely cover the pond in 30 days, choking off the other forms of life in the water. For a long time, the lily plant seems small, and so you decide not to worry about cutting it back until it covers half the pond. On what day will that be?

The answer: on the twenty-ninth day. You will have one day in which to save your pond! While most experts do not believe that the earth faces a similar situation immediately, they do believe that increasing emphasis should be given to using the earth's limited resources efficiently.

A Look at the Future

Answering "what if" questions about economic growth

The MIT research team used a computer to answer "what if" questions. They analyzed compound growth trends in five areas—population, industrial output, food production, pollution, and resource consumption—and linked these factors together mathematically to reflect their interrelations. Thus, human population cannot grow unless people have food to eat. Since much of the earth's best land is now cultivated, rapid increases in food production require the widespread use of tractors, pesticides, and fertilizers, whose production depletes scarce energy and other resources and adds to pollution. This pollution, in turn, eventually interferes with both population and food growth.

What if present trends continue?

One analysis by the computer assumes that in the future there will be no great changes in human values or in the population and resource systems that have operated during the past century. The results suggest that food, industrial output, and population grow steadily until the rapidly diminishing resource base forces industrial production to slow down. Thus, the MIT team concluded that if present compound-growth trends were to continue, a resource crisis could halt population and industrial growth within the next century: the world could literally exhaust its key resources.

Protection against the dangers of expanded economic growth

Many experts feel that this outlook is too grim, and believe that technological breakthroughs will make energy, material, and food resources much more accessible in the future than they have been in the past. Yale economist Henry C. Wallich argues that the market system can provide powerful safeguards against the hazards of economic growth if it is allowed to function effectively. For example, if a firm were required to cover the social costs of its pollution in the prices it charged its customers, the free enterprise system would demand less output from the firm because of its increased prices. In this way, the products and services demanded by society would eventually become low-pollution items (walks in the local park rather than car trips to the lake).

Economic Growth and You

These experts hope to alter current economic growth trends and to establish an environmental and an economic stability that can be sustained far into the future—but the sooner action programs are initiated, the greater the chances of success will be. For example, London has reversed its pollution trend in the past 15 years. Pollution has been cut by

85 percent, doubling the hours of winter sunshine in London and increasing the number of fish species in the Thames River from 0 to 55. And U.S. energy experts are advising that the 4.8-percent energy growth rate the nation hit in 1973 be reduced to 2 percent. The difference between the compound U.S. energy growth rates of 2 and 4.8 percent over the next 25 years is equivalent to 1,000,000 oil wells, or 14,650 new coal mines, or 1055 new nuclear power plants, according to one oil-company executive.

But how can people be persuaded to reduce their energy consumption to alter such trends? Not by asking them to voluntarily cut back, according to journalist and author Berkeley Rice (see ''Social Traps: The Individual Versus Society''). Rice notes that individuals are generally more concerned about their own immediate welfare than about action programs that are in the long-range public interest. Society's goal must then be to recast economic decisions, providing people with incentives to behave in the short run in a way that is best for society in the long run. Thus, we no longer see Oregon pleading with its citizens to put their throwaway bottles in trash cans. Instead, by banning throwaways and by attaching a refund value to returnable bottles, the Oregon legislature has reduced littering up to 90 percent in some areas. Oregonians now have a personal financial incentive *not* to litter their beaches with returnable bottles.

People are motivated by personal, short-run incentives

In September 1975, Federal Energy Administrator Frank G. Zarb identified a number of ''energy truths.'' These truths affect all of us di-

CAN A SNOOPY CARTOON HELP TO CONSERVE ENERGY?

In the summer of 1974, electrical utilities across the United States became concerned that an excessive use of power might cause brownouts or blackouts across the nation. In an attempt to counteract the possibility of a series of electrical power failures, these utilities launched several promotional campaigns to encourage Americans to reduce their power usage voluntarily. The central focus of one such campaign was this Snoopy cartoon poster.

During wartime, the federal government and some large corporations have called upon Americans to reduce their consumption of goods and services—and even to produce and recycle certain necessities. During World War II, for example, many Americans voluntarily grew their own vegetables in ''Victory Gardens'' and saved tin cans and grease to support the war effort.

But, in general, how effective do you think such campaigns are? Did you respond to Snoopy's or to someone else's appeal to conserve energy during the latest energy crisis? Would you respond now? Why?

For one person's answer, see the text and the discussion ''Social Traps: The Individual Versus Society.''

© 1958 United Feature Syndicate, Inc.

rectly. For example, one truth is "the energy crisis is real." Another holds "there is no easy way out." One of Zarb's solutions is that Americans reduce their reliance on imported oil by more efficient consumption and by learning to fulfill more of their own fuel needs. The goal is to do this without sacrificing economic freedom, largely by letting the price mechanism allocate resources more efficiently. For example, the increase in gaso-

SOCIAL TRAPS: THE INDIVIDUAL VERSUS SOCIETY

Shortly after taking office, President Gerald R. Ford asked the American people to help fight inflation by driving less, saving more, spending less, planting gardens, working harder, and conserving electricity. This was the essence of the President's "Whip Inflation Now" (WIN) campaign. But journalist Berkeley Rice observed that few Americans would follow the President's suggestions merely out of a sense of patriotic duty. The reason for the lack of support: no realistic reward could be earned by responding to the WIN campaign. While most Americans were opposed to inflation, they did not belive that their individual efforts would do much to counteract it, and so they didn't bother trying. This behavior demonstrates a fundamental principle of human nature apparent to historians, psychologists, and politicians alike: in general, people are more concerned with their own immediate welfare than they are with action programs that are in the long-range public interest.

In recent years, social scientists have coined the term "social trap" to describe the plight of people who face a conflict between their immediate best interests and their long-run best interests as members of society. For example, air-conditioner owners are warned not to turn up the dials during a summer heat wave. But individuals conclude that they will have little or no impact on the total demand for electricity and turn up their air conditioners anyway. When enough people decide to act in their own short-run best interests, the circuits become overloaded and a power failure results that leaves everyone sweltering.

Berkeley Rice has condensed most of the "social-trap" theory into three axioms to be used when directing people to follow long-range, general-welfare goals:

1. Immediate rewards are generally more effective than long-range consequences.
2. Rewards to the individual are usually more effective than rewards to the group.
3. The ideal way to reinforce some desired behavior is to reward those who do it while simultaneously punishing those who don't.

A striking example of the effectiveness of a carrot-

stick combination of rewards occurred several years ago when the managers of San Francisco's Bay Bridge tried to reduce daily commuter traffic by making public-spirited appeals to motorists to form car pools. There were no rewards or penalties attached to these appeals. The predictable result: nothing happened. Finally, Bay Bridge managers offered a reduced rate of one dollar per month to car poolers, which, compared to the regular toll of 50 cents a day, represented a savings of about $10 a month. Car poolers were also rewarded with a special reserved lane, which enabled them to bypass the jammed toll gates. The result: the number of rush-hour car pools doubled within several weeks. (There was, however, one minor problem: a few car-pool passengers turned out to be department-store dummies masquerading as typical commuters!)

Journalist Rice concludes that in changing a person's economic behavior, "buttons and slogans will never work as well as realistic incentives." And did President Ford learn this lesson? Probably. In 1975, Ford concluded that the most effective way to reduce gasoline consumption was to let the price of gasoline rise. Millions of Americans are now using their cars less than they were when regular gasoline cost only 28.9 cents a gallon.

line prices from 1973 to 1975 has already had such an effect. Sales of more energy-efficient compact and subcompact cars rose from 41 percent of the market in 1973 to 54 percent in 1975. And the average mileage for new cars increased from 14 to 17 miles per gallon during the same period. In this way, personal incentive can directly influence Americans to conserve the country's limited energy resources by driving more efficient cars, putting up storm windows, installing attic insulation, and so on. Limited resources will undoubtedly influence the thinking and actions of Americans in the late 1970s and 1980s more than they have in the recent past.

Economic Growth and the Challenge to Business

It seems unlikely that Americans will abandon their desire for improved living standards or that the needs for a better quality of life and a less polluted environment will diminish. Attaining the most acceptable combination of these often conflicting goals will require all the skill and imagination of America's great institutions: its businesses, governments, labor unions, universities, professional groups, and other organizations.

Business will inevitably play a vital role in this effort to regulate economic growth for three reasons. First, as we learned in Chapter 1, business accounts for about 60 percent of all American economic activity; hence, very little real change is possible without the active participation and support of business. Second, many scientific and technical skills essential to achieving lasting change are found predominantly in the private sector. For example, no enduring solutions to projected fuel shortages are possible without the assistance of the thousands of scientists, engineers, and technicians employed in private energy-related industries. Third, and perhaps most important, much of the managerial skill necessary to implement America's basic goals resides in the private sector. Because of their skills "on the firing line," American businesspeople will undoubtedly be called upon to resolve many of the problems posed by continued economic growth. This will involve some difficult choices. For example, to what extent, within the limits imposed by law, should an automobile engine be designed to reduce pollution when the price to be paid for added emission control is the increased consumption of gasoline?

Can business satisfy our noneconomic needs?

The prospect of becoming a leader in shaping the environmental forces to which it must also respond places American business in a fundamentally new role: in an affluent society, business institutions must become as sensitive to people's nonmaterial needs as historically they have been to people's economic needs. Based on its past accomplishments, the private sector in the American economy should be fully capable of meeting its new responsibilities with wisdom, imagination, and foresight.

GLOSSARY OF BUSINESS TERMS

acceptance An acknowledgment by the party to whom an offer is made that the terms of the offer are satisfactory and that he or she is willing to be bound to a contract.

account The title given to all accounting transactions of a particular type; for example, the sales account includes all sales made by a firm.

account executive The account executive or stockbroker at a brokerage firm who deals directly with investors or financial institutions that purchase securities.

accounting The functional area of business that deals with the collection, organization, analysis, and presentation of financial data.

accounting equation Assets equal liabilities plus owner equity.

accounting journal A journal or ledger in which accounting transactions and summaries of accounting transactions for a given period are recorded by hand.

accounting transaction Any activity that has an immediate and measurable financial impact on a business, affecting its physical or financial capital or its financial obligation to outsiders.

accounts payable A liability that includes obligations owed to creditors, usually arising from purchases of goods and services on credit; accounts payable are due in less than one year.

accounts receivable An asset that includes obligations owed to the firm, usually arising from its sales; accounts receivable are due within one year.

action item A specific task assigned to a committee member and targeted for completion by a particular date.

actuarial table A table listing the probabilities of an event (such as the death of an individual); commonly used in the insurance industry to compute risks, premium rates, and so on.

ad valorem duty A tax on imports that is a fixed percentage of the market value of the commodity in the importing country.

advertising Nonpersonal communication between seller and buyer that is conducted through paid media under clear sponsorship.

advertising agency A firm that specializes in providing promotional services to other businesses for a fee. Services offered include development of advertising copy, selection of advertising media, and placement of the advertisement.

advertising appeal A theme intended to trigger buying decisions or to project a better company image in the target market.

advertising copy The communication that a prospective buyer actually sees or hears.

advertising media The broadcast or print vehicles through which an advertisement is communicated—such as radio, television, magazines, newspapers, and billboards.

affirmative action program EEO (equal employment opportunities) legislation that requires employers who deal with the government to provide equal job opportunities for women and minorities and to demonstrate that they are aggressively seeking to identify and train qualified persons in these categories.

agency A legal relationship in which one party (the agent) is authorized to act on behalf of another (the principal) in transactions with a third party.

agent A person or organization authorized to act on behalf of another.

alternatives The factors over which a decision maker has control in making a decision.

analog computer A machine that solves problems by translating physical variables into related electrical or mechanical quantities.

analytic process A production process in which end products are obtained by breaking down more complex materials.

antitrust laws Laws designed to prevent or control economic concentration.

arbitration An attempt to settle labor–management conflicts through the intervention of a third party neutral to the dispute whose decision is binding. *Voluntary arbitration* takes place when the parties in a dispute agree among themselves to submit the dispute to arbitration. *Compulsory arbitration* takes place when the parties are forced into arbitration by an outside organization, usually the government.

arithmetic-logic unit The device in a computer that performs addition, subtraction, multiplication, and division, compares the relative sizes of two values, and senses positive and negative values.

assets The resources that a business utilizes in attempting to earn a profit.

auditing The process of verifying that an organization has properly recorded and reported its financial data.

authority The possession, either legally or informally, of the right to decide or act on a given matter.

authorized stock The number of shares of stock that a corporation is permitted to issue (make available to potential shareholders); this number is usually stated in the corporate charter.

automation The production of goods by self-regulating machines; also the process of making machines automatic.

bad debts Uncollectable accounts receivable.

balance of international payments Accounts, usually issued by a government, showing the flow of monies into and from a nation; these accounts are arranged according to certain broad categories such as exports and imports.

balance of trade The accounts that show the values of a nation's exports and imports.

balance sheet A statement of the overall financial condition of a business at a given date.

bank acceptance A draft that is backed (accepted) by a bank. Initially, a commercial bank provides a letter of credit indicating that the bank will accept drafts (in effect, checks) up to a designated amount drawn on the bank by a business. When ordering goods, the business writes a draft on the bank for the required amount.

bankruptcy A condition that exists when a business is unable to continue to operate because it lacks sufficient funds to meet its financial obligations to investors, creditors, employees, the government, and other groups to which it owes money.

batch process A production process in which the manufacturing time for an item is sufficiently short that the tasks of workers and machines can be changed frequently to manufacture different products.

batch processing A method of computer data processing that involves accumulating a volume of work and then processing it as a group.

bid rigging An agreement by competitors to divide up business contracts. For each contract, one producer is designated to submit the lowest bid; competitors bid a specified higher price in exchange for the opportunity to be low bidder on some other contract.

bidders list A list of vendors believed to be qualified to supply a given item to a firm.

bill of lading A document that lists goods shipped, times of shipment, and the destinations of the goods; it is signed by an agent for a common carrier (for example, the captain of a ship, a railroad or trucking company agent).

binary arithmetic A system of counting that uses only two digits (0 and 1); the binary system is the basis for all present-day designs of electronic digital computers.

board of directors A group appointed by the stockholders of a corporation to assume responsibility for overall direction of the business.

bond A fixed obligation of a business in which it agrees to pay interest plus a specified sum (the principal) to investors.

bonus A form of compensation in which employees are given extra pay when they perform outstanding work or when the business has a good year; the amount of payment may be varied by the firm.

boycott The refusal to use a product by a group acting in concert.

branching The step in a flow diagram or computer operation that involves taking one of two alternate paths.

brand A name, term, symbol, or design (or a combination of them) used by a business firm to identify its goods or services and to distinguish them from those of competitors.

broker The marketing middleman who performs services, such as obtaining and transporting a commodity from one location to another, for a fee.

budget A planning statement that shows the projected revenues and expenses of an organization.

buildings An asset that includes the structures housing the firm's business activities.

business Any privately owned and operated organization primarily devoted to securing profits or other benefits desired by its owners or managers.

business ethics Values relating to what is right, good, or moral in business relationships.

business forecasting The assessment and development of projections of the future that are likely to be of value in corporate decision making.

business interruptions insurance A form of insurance that protects a firm against disruptions in its activities arising from natural disasters like fires and storms.

business law All statutes, codes, rules, regulations, and court actions that regulate business behavior and relationships.

business life insurance A form of insurance that protects a business against the loss of an executive vital to its operations. Also called *key executive insurance*.

business model A systematic portrayal, usually in mathematical or graphical form, of the operations of a business or a subunit of a business.

buying motives The reasons that consumers buy specific goods or services.

callable security A security that may be redeemed before maturity by the issuing organization on terms specified at the time of issue.

capital Funds invested in a business. On a national basis, financial capital refers to the totality of all funds available for business, consumer, and government investment; physical capital refers to the plants, machinery, equipment, residential homes, and governmental installations.

capital budgeting Decisions on the allocation of financial resources that are typically not converted to cash within a year.

capital gain (or loss) A change in the value of an asset. A *capital gain* occurs when an asset appreciates in value over time; a *capital loss* takes place when the asset depreciates in value over time.

capital stock The part of owner equity that includes capital contributed by stockholders.

capitalism See **private enterprise system**

card sorter A piece of unit-record equipment that automatically places a series of punched cards in numerical or alphabetical order and sorts out cards according to the holes punched in the cards.

cartel A combination of firms in an industry that agrees to achieve a common objective, usually price fixing.

cash An asset that includes currency, checking and savings deposits in commercial banks, cashier checks, bank and postal money orders, and bank drafts.

cash budget A planning statement that indicates the ability of a business firm to supply those cash needs that must be met on time regardless of sales revenue.

cash flow The total funds available to a business during a given period. Cash flow is approximately equal to the firm's earnings *plus* the depreciation charges included in its accounting statements. Depreciation is included because it is not a "real" expense of a business in the sense that there is an outflow of funds to another party.

caveat emptor A principle in business that holds that without a warranty on a product the buyer assumes all risks; literally, "let the buyer beware."

cease-and-desist order An order by a government agency, particularly the Federal Trade Commission, requiring an individual or business to terminate a business practice that has been deemed unfair or deceptive.

central processing unit The portion of a computer that includes the memory or storage unit, the arithmetic-logic unit, and the control unit, plus the operating console.

certified public accountant A person who has fulfilled all the legal requirements of a state that entitle him or her to obtain an official certificate as an accountant.

channels of distribution The various ways that goods flow from manufacturers to industrial customers or ultimate consumers.

checkoff procedures A union requirement that employers deduct union dues from workers' paychecks and send these monies directly to unions.

choice-selection method The approach used to select an alternative solution to a problem that reflects the alternatives and the uncertainties identified for the problem.

civil service A permanent government staff whose positions are based on merit as measured by entrance examinations or recommendations and by periodic examinations for promotion.

closed shop A stringent form of compulsory union membership in which employers agree to hire only union members.

collateral Physical or financial assets used as security in obtaining a loan.

collateral trust bond A bond obtained by securities held in trust by the issuing firm.

collective bargaining The process of settling disputes between unions and management.

commercial bank A financial institution that receives checking and savings deposits and other funds from savers and lends funds to businesses, consumers, and governments. Commercial banks are the only financial institution in the United States that is currently permitted by law to offer checking account services.

commercial goods Goods used by a business in the administrative activities required for its continuing operation.

commercial paper Short-term unsecured promissory notes issued by a business, usually in multiples of $25,000.

commission A form of compensation in which employees are paid a fixed percentage of their total sales.

commodity market A building or organized meeting place where raw materials and agricultural products are bought and sold, for either present or future delivery.

common law The unwritten law, consisting of customs and past court decisions that may serve as precedents in future cases.

common stock Certificates of ownership in a corporation entitling holders to receive any dividends and to exercise other stockholder rights.

communicating The management process by which ideas are transmitted to others for the purpose of effecting a desired result.

communism A system of central direction of the economy in which the government owns and operates the bulk of economic institutions.

compensation The total wages, salaries, and fringe benefits received by employees.

competition The process of determining the price, quality, and available quantity of an item through the impersonal interactions of numerous firms.

compound growth Economic growth—in such areas as GNP, population, and pollution—that is analogous to the compounding of interest on the sum of the original principal of an investment and its accrued interest.

computer Broadly defined, any device that calculates, reckons, or computes. Today, a computer is more narrowly defined as an electronic device that processes data, that is capable of receiving input and producing output, and that stores instructions to solve problems quickly and accurately.

computer hardware The physical equipment used in a computer system.

computer program A sequence of instructions used by a computer to solve a problem.

computer programming The task of writing a computer program.

computer simulation Programming a computer to answer "what if" questions.

computer software Problem-solving programs plus other computer instructions designed to simplify the programming process.

concentrated marketing A marketing strategy in which a firm concentrates on one or a few profitable market segments.

conglomerate A firm that produces many types of goods and services.

conglomerate merger The acquisition by a business of one or more firms producing dissimilar products.

consideration In a contractural relationship, the exchange of something of value (usually money, goods, or services) by each participant in the contract.

constraints In a decision-making situation, the restrictions placed on potential solutions to a problem by the nature and importance of the problem; these restrictions usually involve time and costs.

consumer behavior How people make buying decisions.

consumer goods Goods that are destined for use by ultimate consumers (individuals or households) and that are available in such a form that they can be used without commercial processing.

consumer movement Activities aimed at giving consumers greater say about the products, prices, and information they receive. Also called *consumerism.*

consumer sovereignty The principle that a private enterprise economy and the business and government institutions in it exist to provide goods and services that consumers want.

containerization Placing goods to be transported into a large box or other container. When the goods are shifted from one type of transportation to another, the entire container is shifted.

continuous process A production process in which the manufacturing operation remains essentially unchanged for extended periods of time, often months or years.

contract An agreement between two or more parties that is enforceable by court action.

control unit The portion of a computer that directs the sequence of operations, interprets coded instructions, and initiates proper commands to computer circuits.

controlling The management process by which actual results are compared with planned performance and corrective action is taken when necessary.

convenience goods Goods that a customer characteristically purchases frequently, immediately, and with a minimum of effort in comparison shopping and buying.

convertible bond A bond that can be exchanged for other securities, usually a specified number of shares of common stock.

convertible preferred stock Preferred stock that can be exchanged for common stock in accordance with terms specified on the stock certificate.

cooperative A business chartered under state law that seeks the economic betterment of its members through the achievement of common goals. A cooperative is owned by its members, each of whom has a single vote; profits are returned to members either in the form of lower prices or as rebates given in proportion to a member's purchases from the cooperative.

corporation A form of a business ownership distinguished by three characteristics: (1) ownership may vary from one individual to several million people who purchase stock in the company; (2) the company is managed according to written principles set forth in the corporate charter; and (3) the owners are exposed to limited liability and at most can lose only their investments in the business.

corrective advertisement An advertisement run by a firm at the request of the Federal Trade Commission to correct misleading statements in the firm's advertisements.

cost of goods sold The direct material costs incurred by a firm in producing its products.

cost-of-living escalator An increase in hourly or other wage payments to keep pace with rising consumer prices.

countervailing power The theory that economic power at one stage in the production of a good or service creates offsetting economic power at other stages of production.

craft union A labor union that represents a single profession.

credit policy The conditions under which a firm extends credit to its customers.

credit union A financial institution that collects funds from and lends funds to members.

creditor A person or organization to whom money is owed.

cumulative security A security that entitles the holder to recover dividends or interest omitted by an organization in previous years.

current assets Highly liquid assets that are converted into cash within a one-year period.

current liabilities Obligations of a business that must be met within one year.

current ratio Current assets *divided by* current liabilities; the current ratio is one measure of the liquidity of a business.

custom manufacture The production of goods by a firm according to a customer's specifications.

debenture A long- or intermediate-term fixed obligation of a business.

debt Any legally binding obligation of a firm to pay a fixed amount of principal or interest for a specified period.

debt financing Obtaining funds for a business by borrowing from creditors and agreeing to repay a stated amount of principal and interest within a designated time period.

decentralization A principle of organization that states that decision making should be moved to lower levels of an organization that are independent enough to have their performance measured objectively.

DECIDE process A process of systematic decision making in which each letter of the word DECIDE represents a specific step in the process (see Chapter 6).

decision box An element in a flow diagram or a computer operation that involves answering "yes" or "no" to a specific question contained within the box; the two alternative answers to the question give rise to branching and looping.

decision factors The controllable and uncontrollable variables that together determine the outcome of a decision.

decision making The process of selecting among alternative courses of action.

delayed-action advertising Advertising that seeks long-range effects such as improved brand awareness, increased product preference, and more favorable company image.

Delphi method A business forecasting technique that relies on surveys of experts rather than on the use of past data.

demand curve A graph showing the relationship between the price of an item and the maximum quantity of the item that customers will buy.

demand deposit The checking accounts maintained at commercial banks. Such deposits can be withdrawn on demand—that is, at the discretion of the depositor.

demand factors Determinants of the intensities with which customers desire and are able to pay for goods and services.

demography The science of human populations and their characteristics.

departmentation by groups A principle of organization that states that people and activities may be grouped together in an organization when they have similar functions, have the same objectives, or need to be coordinated.

depreciation The deterioration of plant and equipment over time, whether the production facilities are in use or not. In accounting, the useful life of an asset as well as its original cost and salvage value is estimated; depreciation is then calculated as a normal business expense.

differentiated marketing A marketing strategy in which a firm designs separate products and marketing programs for each market segment.

digital computer A machine that processes discrete (as opposed to continuous) values by a sequence of instructions stored internally.

dilution A decline in the quantity and quality of downward communication in an organization; also a reduction in the rights of owners in a corporation when, for example, additional stock is sold to the public.

direct-action advertising Advertising that seeks immediate sales to customers.

direct material The purchased raw materials, semifinished parts, and finished parts that are incorporated in a final product manufactured by a firm.

directing The management process by which the performance of subordinates is guided toward common goals.

discount A reduction in the price offered to a customer for prompt payment or for buying in large quantities.

discount rate The rate of interest the Federal Reserve System charges member banks that wish to borrow funds from the system.

discretionary purchasing power The amount of disposable personal income available for nonessential expenditures. This is equal to total disposable personal income *minus* essential expenditures and fixed commitments (rent, mortgage payments, insurance, and so on).

disposable personal income The amount of personal income available for personal consumption expenditures and savings. This is equal to total personal income *minus* all personal tax and nontax payments to federal, state, and local governments.

dissolution In antitrust enforcement, the breaking up of business into smaller units so that it will lack power to reinstitute a violation in restraint of trade.

diversification The development of a multiproduct business in which several products are manufactured in order to moderate the effects of a decline in sales or in profits associated with any single product. In financial investing, the process of purchasing a number of different types of securities in order to moderate the consequences of a decline in value of any specific security.

dividend A cash or stock payment to the owners of a corporation that is based on the number of shares held by the individual owner.

division of functions The division of activities assigned to federal, state, and local governments.

doubling time The time it takes a quantity growing at a fixed rate to double in size.

dumping Selling goods, especially in international trade, below their production costs (or, under some international trade laws, below their domestic prices).

earnings per share Net income after taxes *divided by* the number of shares of common stock outstanding.

economic concentration Control of an industry by one or a few businesses.

economic growth The expanded production of a nation, as measured by its real gross national product.

economics The management of resources to produce goods and services that satisfy human wants and needs.

electronic data processing The analysis and summarization of data by electronic computers.

embargo The suspension, usually by a government, of trade with another nation or nations.

eminent domain The right of government to confiscate private property, usually real estate, for just compensation as determined by private negotiations or by the courts. Some privately owned utilities have been granted the right of eminent domain.

end-product goods Goods incorporated by manufacturers in their final products and ultimately destined to be a part of consumer or industrial goods.

equipment loan An extension of credit for which a firm's machinery or equipment is pledged as collateral.

equipment trust bond A bond that uses equipment as collateral. The holder of the bond owns the equipment and leases it to the issuing firm through a trustee. The trustee receives the lease payments from the issuing firm and uses them to pay interest and principal to the bondholder.

equity See **owner equity**

equity financing Issuance of common or preferred stock by a corporation to obtain funds for use in the business. In the case of a sole proprietorship or a partnership, equity financing involves obtaining additional investments from owners or partners.

exception principle A principle of organization that states that decisions on routine problems that recur frequently should be handled by lower-level personnel; only unusual, nonroutine problems should be referred to higher-level managers.

exchange controls Regulations regarding the use of foreign exchange imposed upon nationals under a government's jurisdiction. Exchange controls usually prohibit the use of scarce foreign exchange to purchase consumer goods and luxury goods.

exchange rate The ratio at which a unit of currency of one nation may be traded for that of another.

excise tax A sales tax levied on a selected set of specific products, such as furs, cigarettes, cars, and so on.

expected value The average payoff (in dollars or other terms) that a decision maker would receive over time if he or she selected the same alternative repeatedly under similar conditions.

expense A cost of doing business.

experimental data Data obtained from experimental studies in which two essentially similar groups are identified and each group is exposed to somewhat different factors, one or more of which is being evaluated.

export controls Government controls regarding the kinds of goods or services that can be sold abroad.

external financing The acquisition of funds through additional contributions by existing or new owners of a business or through borrowing from banks or other financial institutions.

external secondary data Secondary data obtained from outside the organization in which the data are to be used.

external transaction An accounting transaction that involves an exchange between a firm and an outside party (for example, sales to a customer).

extrapolation The use of information to extend past trends into the future.

face value The issue price of a security.

featherbedding The process of attempting to retain unneeded jobs; usually engaged in by labor unions in order to provide job security for their members.

feedback In automation, the process by which information about the output of a machine is repeatedly transmitted (fed back) by an automatic control device so that discrepancies between the machine's actual performance and its desired performance can be corrected; in a flow diagram, a looping step that returns to an earlier stage in the sequence.

fidelity bonds A form of insurance issued by bonding companies to protect a business against dishonesty among its employees.

fields Single columns or groups of columns on a punched card that collectively have a special meaning.

filtering An intentional sifting of the information transmitted to higher levels in an organization to place the sender and the message in a more favorable light.

finance The functional area of business that involves obtaining and using funds effectively.

financial institution An organization that receives money from savers and lends funds to consumers, businesses, and governments.

financial intermediary A financial institution that receives savings and makes funds available to consumers, businesses, and governments. Financial intermediaries provide such services as diversification, expert advice on investments, immediate or quick access to funds, and so on, to the saver. In return for these services, the saver accepts a lower interest rate than could be achieved by direct investment.

financial leverage The dollar value of a firm's debt expressed as a percentage of the total investment in the business.

financial ratio A measure of the relationship between two or more financial components of a business that provides insight into the quality and the prospects of the business. Financial ratios discussed in the text include the current ratio, return on equity, return on sales, and earnings per share. Also called *accounting ratio*.

financial structure The specific percentages of external or internal financing and debt or equity financing used by a firm and the maturity dates of its debts.

first-line supervision See **operating management**

fixed assets The property, plants, equipment, and tools owned by a business.

fixed exchange rate The relationship between one currency and another that is kept constant by government intervention in international exchange markets.

flexible exchange rate The demand and the supply of various currencies that establishes the relationships between the prices of currencies. Since demand and supply conditions for currencies (say, American dollars and British pounds) usually vary on a daily basis, the cost of one currency in terms of another also varies frequently.

flow diagram A graphic representation of the sequence of steps required to solve a given problem.

foreign trade zone A geographic area, typically located near a port, to which goods or services may be imported or exported without being subject to tariffs.

franchise Permission granted by a manufacturer or other organization to a retail firm allowing the retailer to sell its products or services in return for a fee; also a document issued by a local government permitting businesses to carry out activities over which the local government can exercise control.

fringe benefits Employer contributions to workers in addition to basic wages or salaries.

functional area A special operating area of a business, such as accounting, finance, or marketing.

functional organization A type of formal business organization in which workers report to a number of different supervisors, each of whom has an area of technical competence.

futures contract An agreement providing for the delivery or purchase of a commodity at a specified price at some future date.

Gantt chart A method of charting and scheduling various kinds of management and production activities.

general partnership A partnership in which each owner is exposed to unlimited liability for all actions of the business.

general-purpose computer A digital computer programmed to process data for a wide variety of applications.

gobbledygook Written or verbal statements containing so much technical jargon that they fail to communicate the message effectively.

grant-in-aid A program under which a central government transfers some of its revenues to local governments to help finance public projects.

gross national product The money value of all goods and services produced in a nation during one year.

gross profit The difference between a firm's net sales and its cost of goods sold. Also called *gross margin*.

guaranteed annual wage A form of compensation in which workers are paid a stipulated minimum annual income whether or not the firm has sufficient work to keep the employees busy throughout the year.

guideline An instruction from management that enables members of an organization to make decisions that achieve objectives more quickly, easily, and consistently.

health and accident insurance A form of insurance that protects individuals against illness and accidents; generally includes all or part of hospital, medical, and surgical expenses.

hedging The purchase of a contract for the future delivery of a commodity in order to offset business risk.

horizontal merger The acquisition of a firm by a competing business.

income bond A bond that does not pay a guaranteed rate of interest; payment is usually made out of the earnings of the issuing firm.

income statement An accounting statement that indicates the profits or losses sustained by a business during a given period.

indenture A document issued at the time of a bond's initial sale listing the conditions and terms of sale.

indirect material Equipment and supplies that are needed to manage and operate a firm but that are not incorporated in its final products.

industrial goods Goods sold to industrial firms for incorporation in a final product, for producing other goods, or for use in the administrative activities of the firm. Also called *producer goods*.

industrial revolution The replacement of hand tools by machinery and the factory system that began in England around 1760 and in the United States around 1790.

industrial union A labor union that encompasses all workers in a plant, whatever their occupation.

inflation An increase in price levels, often measured by the annual change in consumer or wholesale prices.

inheritance tax A tax on the individual receiving funds from an estate.

injunction A court order decreeing that a person or an organization either take or refrain from taking an action. Those who violate injunctions are held in contempt of court.

inland marine insurance A form of insurance that protects a firm against damages or losses in the shipment of goods by truck, railroad, barge, or air over land.

input device The unit in a computer designed to bring processable data into a computer.

insurance A contractual agreement in which for a fee (insurance premium), one party (the insurer) agrees to pay another party (the insured) a sum of money specified in advance if the second party sustains a loss under conditions indicated in the written contract (insurance policy).

intangibles Assets deriving value from the rights they accord the holder; patents, copyrights, trademarks, and franchises fall in this group.

interchangeable parts In mass production, parts so similar in physical characteristics as to be indistinguishable.

interest group An association of persons or organizations that is devoted to promoting common goals, usually by political or educational means.

internal financing The acquisition of funds through earnings retained in the business (after taxes and dividends are paid) and through monies made available by depreciation.

internal secondary data Secondary data obtained from within the organization in which the data are to be used.

internal transaction An accounting transaction that involves an exchange within the firm itself (for example, the consumption of previously purchased supplies).

international reserves Government-held gold and other assets used in international financial transactions.

international trade The exchange of goods and services among nations in the form of exports and imports.

inventories In manufacturing, stockpiles of raw materials used in producing a product and of partially or completely finished goods kept on hand by the firm; in retailing, goods available for sale to consumers.

inventory turnover Cost of goods sold *divided by* average inventories held; inventory turnover measures the rapidity with which a firm's inventories are depleted and must be replaced during a year.

investment bank A bank that assists or controls the placement of business securities—particularly the stocks, bonds, and notes—for individual investors or organizations who wish to invest funds. Also known as an *underwriter* or *security house.*

invoice A document issued by a seller to a buyer indicating the types, quantities, and prices of goods and the total amounts due.

job analysis An evaluation of a position in an organization to determine what detailed tasks the person holding that position should perform.

job description A written statement describing the duties and responsibilities of a particular position in a firm; the job description is developed by the personnel department in consultation with the manager who supervises the position.

job specification A written statement describing the skills, work experience, and education that a prospective employee needs in order to perform a given job satisfactorily.

knowledge industry A sector of the economy that produces information rather than a physical product; examples are education and scientific research.

labor union A group of workers who join together to achieve common goals related to their employment.

land An asset that includes land employed in the business.

legal department The section of a business that handles routine legal matters and most litigation in which the firm is involved.

liabilities The financial obligations a business incurs in acquiring resources.

liability insurance A form of insurance that protects a business or an individual against damages resulting from negligence.

license A document issued by a local government that gives the holder the right to engage in a designated business or economic activity.

life insurance A form of insurance that provides financial protection against loss of life, with benefits payable to dependents, heirs, or the insured's estate.

limited liability The legal obligation of the owners of a firm to be responsible only for the loss of their individual investments in the business in event of the firm's insolvency.

limited partnership A partnership consisting of one or more general partners who are personally liable for all debts incurred by the business and limited partners who risk only their own investments.

line-and-staff organization A type of formal business organization characterized by (1) unambiguous supervisory authority and (2) specialized technical support from staff personnel.

line-of-credit arrangement An agreement between a financial institution and an individual or organization entitling the latter to borrow up to a specified amount as a matter of right and at the time of the borrower's choice.

line organization The simplest type of formal business organization in which each position has general authority over positions below it in the managerial hierarchy in accomplishing the firm's objectives.

liquid assets Assets that can readily be converted into cash.

liquidity The speed and cost involved in converting assets to cash. Highly liquid assets (for example, U.S. Treasury notes) can be exchanged for cash quickly and at low cost. Illiquid assets (for example, used machinery) may take many months to convert to cash and often must be sold at a considerable loss.

lobbyist A professional who seeks to influence government through personal contacts, information-gathering techniques, political contributions, and letter-writing campaigns.

local The smallest unit of a labor union.

lockout An economic weapon of management in

which the firm discontinues all operations until a settlement with a union is reached.

long-term investment   Any asset held exclusively for investment (not resale) longer than one year.

long-term liability   An obligation of a business that need not be met within one year.

looping   The step in a flow diagram or computer operation that involves taking a path that leads back to an earlier stage in the sequence.

Machiavellianism   A leadership style that justifies using any technique—no matter how deceitful—to manipulate and control people.

machinery and equipment   An asset that includes tools used in the business.

main frame   See **central processing unit**

make-buy decisions   An evaluation by a business of which parts in a final product will be purchased from outside vendors and which will be fabricated by the firm itself.

management   A group of people who direct effort toward common goals by using available resources; also the process by which a cooperative group directs actions toward common goals.

management by objectives   A method of management control that seeks to define each person's area of responsibility in terms of the results expected, using observable and measurable job-related criteria.

manager   An individual who specializes in knowing how to run a business.

managerial accounting   The process of collecting, organizing, and analyzing the financial data of a business in a manner tailored to a particular managerial decision.

manufacturing   The process of converting purchased materials into useful products according to plans and specifications developed by the firm and then transporting these products to the buyer.

markdown   A reduction in the original retail selling price of an item.

market division   An agreement by competitors not to compete in one another's assigned sales territory.

market order   An order to buy or sell a security at the existing price. Thus, the investor who orders 100 shares of General Motors at market will pay the going price for GM stock and the brokerage firm's floor trader will obtain the stock at the best price that can be negotiated, keeping in view that the investor's main objective is to acquire or to sell the stock at whatever price can be secured.

market-product grid   A diagram used to analyze a market on the basis of the characteristics of potential consumers.

market segment   A group of potential customers who are similar in some respect, such as in demographic characteristics or in volume of product use.

market value   The price of a good, service, or security as determined by demand and supply.

marketing   That area of business that directs the flow of goods and services from producer to consumer in order to satisfy customers and to achieve company objectives.

marketing channels   See **channels of distribution**

marketing concept   The principle that stresses shaping products to meet consumer needs rather than attempting to mold those needs to the products.

marketing mix   The blend of the four basic marketing activities (product, place, promotion, and price) that a firm employs to reach its target market effectively.

markup   See **gross profit**

mass production   A system of production that involves (1) the use of specialized machines to make interchangeable parts feasible; (2) the replacement of human and animal energy by mechanical power; and (3) specialization of labor so that workers are assigned a specific set of tasks at which they are skilled.

maturity date   The date at which a security becomes due; at this time, the principal and any remaining interest must be paid in full.

mean   The number found by *dividing* the sum of a set of numbers *by* the total number of items in the set. Also called the *arithmetic mean* and the *average*.

measure of central value   A number that summarizes a whole set of numbers in a single value.

measure of success   A standard used in judging whether a proposed solution to a problem is satisfactory. Also called *criterion*.

median   The number located in the exact middle of an entire set of numbers when they are arrayed from lowest to highest. The median is the most typical of all numbers in the set in the sense that half the numbers lie above it and half lie below it.

mediation   An attempt to settle labor–management conflicts through the intervention of a third party neutral to the dispute who makes recommendations to unions and management.

memory unit   See **storage unit**

merchandise inventory   An asset that includes all goods purchased for resale or produced by the firm.

merger The combination of two or more businesses into a single firm.

methods search In problem solving, an investigation of how other individuals have solved substantially the same problem.

middle management Managers between top management and operating management in an organization.

middleman A marketing firm (usually a wholesaler or retailer) between the manufacturer and consumer in a channel of distribution.

mixed economy A system of resource allocation that combines elements of several ideologies (for example, capitalism and socialism).

mode The number that occurs most often in a set of numbers.

modes of transportation The basic methods by which goods are moved to customers: air, pipeline, rail, water, and highway.

money GNP The total production of goods and services in an economy, valued at current price levels.

monopoly The domination of an industry by a single firm such that it can control prices and prevent potential competitors from entering the industry.

mortgage bond A bond that is secured by a claim on real assets—land, buildings, equipment, or machinery. In event of default by the issuing firm, the bondholder can sell the pledged assets, using the proceeds to recover the principal or interest due.

mortgages payable A long-term liability against which specific assets are pledged as collateral.

moveable assembly line A production process in which incomplete products are carried past workers and machines in fixed positions who perform specified operations on the products before they pass to the next stage.

multinational corporation A corporation, usually owned by citizens of many nations, that produces and sells goods in many major national markets.

municipal bond A bond entitling the owner to receive interest exempt from federal income taxes. If issued by a local government in the same state as the bondholder, the exemption extends to state income taxes as well. Industrial aid, industrial revenue, and in some states pollution control bonds are tax exempt.

mutual fund An organization that pools the contributions of many individuals or organizations for the purposes of investment, often in security markets.

natural monopoly The presence of a single seller in an industry where competition would raise the costs of serving customers; natural monopolies are subject to government regulation.

near cash Interest-bearing assets that can easily be converted to cash.

net income The profits that a business realizes from its operations.

net operating income Gross profit *less* operating expenses.

no-fault insurance A form of insurance in which payments for damage are made by the company issuing the insurance according to a fixed schedule of fees established by a government, regardless of which party is responsible for the damage.

noncallable security A security that cannot be redeemed by the issuing organization until it becomes due.

noncumulative security A security that does not entitle the holder to recover dividends or interest once they have been omitted by a firm.

nonpar stocks A stock that does not have a par value printed on the stock certificate.

nonparticipating security A security that does not entitle the holder to receive profits beyond the fixed dividends or interest due him or her as an owner of the security.

nonprofit organization A nongovernmental organization that does not seek profits as a major business objective.

nonvoting security A security that does not entitle the holder to vote on matters of corporate business unless dividend and interest commitments are not met by the firm.

notes payable A liability that includes promissory notes owed by the firm to creditors.

notes receivable An asset that includes promissory notes on monies owed the firm by other individuals or businesses.

nutritional labeling Giving information on the labels of food products in common household units (per bowl, cup, or glass) describing the proportion of recommended daily requirements of vitamins, minerals, and proteins contained in the product; intended to assist consumers in judging food value.

objective A goal that a decision maker (or a group) seeks to achieve in a problem-solving situation.

observational data Data collected by watching how people or machines behave, either through mechanical means or through direct personal observation.

ocean marine insurance A form of insurance that

protects a firm against damages or losses in the shipment of goods across the seas.

odd pricing A retail strategy of pricing a few pennies below the exact dollar on a low-priced item (for example, $17.95 instead of $18 for a pair of shoes) or a few dollars below an even hundred on a high-priced item (for example, $495 rather than $500 for a sofa).

off-the-job training Job-related instruction obtained by attending courses, seminars, or workshops offered by the firm or by an outside organization or educational institution.

offer A proposal by one party (the *offeror*) to enter into a contract with a second party (the *offeree*).

oligopoly The domination of an industry by a few powerful firms.

on-the-job training All instruction given to an employee in the course of the day-to-day job.

online processing A method of computer data processing that involves immediate input–output access to the computer whenever a user wishes to obtain information.

open-account credit A grace period (often ten days) during which a customer may pay for merchandise or services at a discount price. If the supplier's bill is not paid within the grace period, a further period (often 20 days) is extended, during which the customer still receives a discount for payment (although less than during the initial grace period). At the end of 30 days, the full bill is due.

open dating Giving the date a retail item was produced by the manufacturer or received by the retailer; intended to assist consumers in judging product freshness.

open-market operations The purchase or sale of U.S. government bonds by the Federal Reserve System in order to alter the money supply.

open shop A shop or business establishment in which employees may voluntarily decide whether to join a union.

operating expenses All nonmaterial costs of conducting a business.

operating management Supervisors whose major job is the immediate direction of people performing clerical or shop work.

operation box An element in a flow diagram or computer operation that involves taking the specific action contained within the box.

organization chart A formal diagram of the authority relationships in a business firm.

organizing The management process by which the structure and allocation of jobs is determined.

output device The unit in a computer designed to translate electrical impulses into usable form, such as printed copy or punched cards.

overtime pay A form of compensation in which employees are paid at a rate higher than the normal hourly rate for working more than a minimum number of hours per week, usually 40 hours. A typical arrangement is for employees to be paid one and a half times the normal hourly rate for overtime during the work week and double the hourly rate for overtime on Saturday and Sunday.

owner equity The portion of assets owned outright by the firm.

par stock A stock with a par value printed on the stock certificate.

par value The nominal value of a stock at time of issue, as stated on the stock certificate.

participating security A security that entitles the holder to receive returns (in addition to the fixed dividends or interest due him or her as an owner of the security) when the company's earnings rise above an amount specified in advance.

partners' capital In a partnership, the portions of owner equity that include capital contributed by the partners.

partnership A form of business organization in which two or more persons are associated as owners but in which no stock is issued.

payoff table A tabular framework that relates the alternatives available to a decision maker to the uncertainties (or outcome states) that must be faced.

pension plan A plan involving contributions by employees or employers that provides income to workers during their retirement years.

per capita Per person; for example, per capita money GNP is the gross national product of a nation *divided by* its population.

peripheral equipment All hardware in a computer not associated directly with the main frame; generally includes the input and output devices plus auxiliary memory or storage units.

personal income Total income from wages, salaries, business, professional, and agricultural receipts, dividends, rent, interest, and government payments to individuals.

personal selling Any personal communication between seller and buyer that is performed by salespeople operating inside or outside the firm.

personnel management The business function that involves (1) recruiting new employees; (2) assisting them while they are employed (for example, by providing on-the-job training); and (3) sometimes assisting them after they leave the company (such as with retirement benefits).

piecework A form of compensation in which workers are paid in accordance with their output (for example, 5¢ for each rim placed on a tire in a tire factory).

place The element of the marketing mix that involves finding appropriate channels of distribution, including retailing and wholesaling institutions, to get the product to the target market at the right time and in the right place.

planning The management process by which a manager anticipates the future and designs a program of action to meet it.

plans The means by which an organization's objectives are achieved.

policy An understanding by members of a group that makes the actions of each group member more predictable to other members.

portfolio investment Investment—especially investment abroad—in securities rather than physical plant and equipment.

practice The usual mode of handling a given problem.

preemptive placement A method of obtaining funds in which existing owners are given an exclusive opportunity to purchase new securities issued by the firm.

preferred stock Certificate of ownership in a corporation entitling holders to receive specified dividends that are not directly based on the earnings of the firm.

price The element of the marketing mix that involves establishing a monetary value for the product that gives value to the customer and adequate revenue to the producer; also the money and goods exchanged for the ownership or use of some assortment of goods and services.

price discrimination The practice of charging customers different prices for products of like grade and quality.

price fixing An agreement among competitors to set prices at designated levels.

primary data Data collected for the first time for the immediate purpose or project at hand.

private enterprise system The dominant institution in the American economy, displaying four major characteristics: (1) private ownership of business; (2) private property; (3) freedom of choice; and (4) limited role of government.

private placement A method of obtaining funds in which a firm offers its securities exclusively to a single investor or to a small group of investors, usually banks, mutual funds, or other financial institutions.

private sector All economic institutions that are not owned by the government—business firms, foundations, cooperatives, and so on.

procedure A system that describes in detail the steps to be taken in order to accomplish a given task.

procurement policy Standards set by an organization to determine the basis on which goods and services will be purchased.

product The element of the marketing mix that involves developing the right good (or service) for the target market; also a physical item or service that satisfies certain customer needs.

product development An aspect of production that involves generating the designs, models, and prototypes necessary to build final products.

product line The array of products offered for sale by a business.

production The functional area of business in which people and machines design new products, buy and convert materials into finished products, and supply these products to customers; also includes the activities of product development, purchasing, and manufacturing.

production control A manufacturing activity that involves the identification, scheduling, and monitoring of the stages in the production process in order to insure the timely delivery of an item in the right quantity and specified quality.

production goods Goods used by manufacturers in the production of other goods.

productivity Real output per worker hour, usually expressed in percentage terms as an annual gain or loss.

profit maximization Achievement of as high a financial return as possible.

profit sharing A form of compensation in which employees receive, in addition to their regular pay, a share in the company's net profits.

profits The difference between the revenues and costs of a business. Profits are available for investment in the business or service to provide dividends and other income for the business owners.

program budget A planning statement that organizes expenditures according to the basic missions carried out by an organization.

promissory note A signed agreement between two parties (either two individuals or an individual and a financial organization) in which the borrower states in writing that the principal and any outstanding interest due on the loan will be returned to the lender at a designated time.

promotion The element of the marketing mix that includes the use of personal selling and advertising to facilitate sales by communicating information about the product to customers.

property insurance A form of insurance that protects a firm against fire and other natural disasters, usually applied to buildings and equipment.

proprietor's capital In a sole proprietorship, the part of owner equity that includes capital contributed by the sole proprietor.

proprietorship See **sole proprietorship**

prospectus A document describing a new stock issue.

protectionist An advocate of the view that barriers to world trade are desirable.

protective tariff A tariff created with the primary objective of placing domestic industry in a competitively favorable position with regard to foreign competition. This objective is accomplished by taxing imported goods or services.

public offering A method of obtaining funds in which a firm offers new securities to the public.

public sector All government activities, federal, state, or local.

publicity Favorable news coverage of a firm or its products that is obtained without overt initiation or payment by the firm.

publicly owned organization A business established by the federal government or by a state government to achieve goals felt to be for the public good.

purchasing An aspect of production that involves buying the right item in the right quantity at the right price and making it available to the firm at the right time and place.

pure competition An industry in which (1) a large number of firms produce identical products, (2) each firm is free to enter or to leave the industry as it chooses, and (3) government interference is absent.

quality control A manufacturing activity that involves the inspection of an item at various stages in the production process to insure that the final product meets the specifications set for it.

quality of life The economic, social, cultural, and moral welfare of the daily lives of individuals.

real GNP The total value of goods and services produced within an economy in a given period of time, valued at the prices that prevailed during a previous base year or years. By valuing GNP at constant (base) prices, the effects of inflation are removed from GNP comparisons.

reference group A group of people who influence a person's behavior either because he or she is a member of the group or because he or she aspires to be in the group.

register A listing of all accounting transactions involving a given category.

regulatory agency A federal, state, or local government unit that is empowered to review the activities of businesses in industries designated by law.

remote input–output device A computer terminal that is some distance away from the central computer but linked to it electrically.

reserve requirements The proportion of a commercial bank's demand and savings deposits that must remain in a Federal Reserve Bank. Raising reserve requirements for commercial banks makes less money available for loans and decreases the money supply; lowering reserve requirements produces an increase in the money supply.

resources All tangible and intangible items used in producing goods and services.

retailer An establishment that purchases only consumer goods from manufacturers or wholesalers and sells them to ultimate consumers.

retained earnings The part of owner equity that includes all profits that have been kept for use by the business.

return on investment The total return, or profit, obtained from a project *divided by* the amount of money invested in it.

revenue The financial receipts of a business.

revenue tariff A tariff or tax on imports primarily designed to raise funds to finance governmental activities.

right-to-work laws State laws that give an employee the right to join or not to join a union. Under right-to-work laws, unions cannot require union membership to obtain employment or force an employee to pay union dues.

risk management The functional area of business concerned with controlling unexpected variations in the outcomes of business decisions.

risk–return relationship The connection between the amount of risk involved in an investment and expected profits. Normally, the greater the risk associated with a business activity, the higher the return on investment that can be anticipated.

rivalry Competition in industries that are characterized by oligopoly (few sellers). Because the sellers in such situations are usually large and financially sound, reductions in price are typically avoided. Rivalry, then, usually takes the form of nonprice considerations—more advertising, differentiation in product quality, and so on.

rule A statement of precisely what is to be done (or not to be done) in a given situation, without deviation.

salary A form of compensation in which employees are given regular weekly or monthly payments for each period worked.

savings and loan association A financial institution that receives savings accounts, but not checking accounts, from individuals and organizations and largely places the resulting funds in home mortgages and other real-estate investments.

savings bank A financial institution that receives savings deposits, but not demand deposits, from individuals and organizations and makes the resulting funds available as business, consumer, or government loans.

scalar principle A principle of organization that states that authority and responsibility should flow in a continuous line from the highest person in an organization to the lowest.

scientific management A school of management thought developed by Frederick W. Taylor that emphasizes ways to increase productivity through careful planning.

secondary data Data pertinent to a current problem that have been collected by another individual or group for some other purpose or project.

secured loan A loan for which some physical or financial asset is pledged as collateral.

security market A building or organized meeting place where stocks and bonds are bought and sold.

self-insurance A form of business protection in which a firm meets risks by absorbing losses itself, rather than by seeking insurance coverage.

seniority system A reward system that assigns employees important work privileges (such as protection against layoffs) on the basis of their years of service.

shift premium A form of compensation in which employees are paid more than the normal hourly wage for working the evening or early morning shift.

shop steward The union member designated to represent a small group of workers within a plant. Also called *business agent*.

shopping goods Goods that the customer, in the process of selection and purchase, characteristically compares on such bases as suitability, quality, price, and style; these goods are fre-

quently unbranded or, if branded, the names are not very important to the consumer.

shrinkage Losses of a business firm due to theft, spoilage, or breakage.

social security The Old Age, Survivors, and Disability Insurance System, commonly known as social security, that provides retirement benefits, disability benefits, and makes other insurance-related payments to recipients. The program is administered by the federal government and financed by taxes paid by both employee and employer.

socialism The view of traditional socialism is that government should own the basic industries in the economy, such as automobiles, iron and steel, and the railroads. An alternative view of socialism is the welfare state, in which large tax collections finance such programs as social security, medical care, unemployment compensation, and welfare benefits; these programs are made available by the government either free of charge or at a nominal cost.

sole proprietorship A business owned by one person who often manages it as well.

span of control A principle of organization that states that there is a limit to the number of subordinates who should report to one superior, since a supervisor has only a certain amount of time, energy, and attention to devote to supervision.

special-purpose computer A digital computer tailored to a specific application.

specialization The division of labor in which each employee concentrates on a specific task or set of tasks in the production of a product instead of on the production of an individual finished product. As employees become skilled at their specialities, their output increases.

specialty goods Goods with unique characteristics and/or brand identification for which a significant group of buyers is habitually willing to make a special purchasing effort; such goods are generally branded, and the brands are important in the consumer's buying decision.

specific duty A tax on imports brought into a country that is based on a designated monetary charge for each physical unit of the good imported.

specifications A detailed description of the materials, dimensions, and performance requirements of all items comprising a finished product.

staffing The process by which managers select, train, promote, and retire subordinates.

standard manufacture The production of items by a firm in accordance with its own specifications.

standard parts See **interchangeable parts**

standards In mass production, tolerances or limits from which a given part cannot deviate.

statistical inference A method used to generalize from a small collection, or sample, of items to a larger collection of items.

statistical methods Techniques used to provide meaningful summaries of many numbers or to analyze and interpret these summaries.

statutory law Written constitutions, codes, statutes, and regulations enacted by the people or their elected representatives.

stock dividend A payment to the existing owners of a corporation of stock that is normally newly issued by the corporation; this payment is either made in lieu of or in addition to any cash dividend paid by the corporation.

stock right A document that entitles the holder to purchase shares of the common stock of a firm according to terms specified on the document.

stockholder A holder or owner of stock in a corporation. Also called *shareholder*.

storage unit The device in a computer in which data are stored and from which they are obtained when needed.

straight-line depreciation A formula for calculating depreciation that allocates the difference between the purchase price of an asset *minus* its salvage value equally over the number of years of the asset's estimated life. The annual estimated depreciation is then treated as a business cost, even though the firm has not experienced a direct cash payment to any person or organization.

strategic planning Planning to achieve general organizational goals over a long-range period (two years or more).

strike An economic weapon of organized labor in which union members collectively refuse to work until their demands are met by management.

subordinated debenture A bond that is an unsecured obligation of a business; in the event of liquidation, general creditors and holders of debentures must be paid in full before claims of owners of subordinated debentures are recognized.

substitute product A product that may be used in place of another product to perform substantially the same function; an example is the wide line of copiers offered by the Xerox Corporation.

supplies inventory An asset that includes accumulated supplies purchased for use in production.

supply curve The relationship (in graph form) that indicates what quantities of a good or a service suppliers in an industry will produce at various selling prices.

supply factors Determinants of the quantities of goods or services that producers will place on the market.

surety bond A form of insurance issued by bonding companies that protects a business against nonperformance by an employee or by a party with which the firm has entered into contract.

survey data Data obtained by asking people questions, through either personal interviews, telephone interviews, or self-administered questionnaires.

synthetic process A production process in which final products are built up or assembled from basic parts.

tabulating machine A piece of unit–record equipment that adds, subtracts, multiplies, and divides and prints reports based on information fed to it on punched cards.

tactical planning Planning to achieve organizational subgoals over a short-range period (less than two years).

target market The specific group or groups of customers to whom a company wishes to sell its products or services.

tariff A tax or a fee paid on imports; usually paid at the import's point of entry into a country.

tax-exempt bond See **municipal bond**

term life policy A form of life insurance that provides protection for a designated period, after which the insurer can refuse to insure or charge higher rates.

term loan An extension of credit by a bank or an insurance company for a period of more than one year.

time sharing A method of computer utilization that involves linking many remote input–output terminals (usually teletypewriters) to a central computer with a large storage capacity.

top management The president and vice presidents of a firm.

trade acceptance A draft (in effect, a check) drawn on the buyer for the amount of the buyer's purchase and signed by the buyer; the trade acceptance typically designates the bank or other financial institution to which the draft is to be presented.

trade credit An extension of credit in which a supplier allows customers several weeks or months to make payment.

trading area The geographic region from which a business draws most of its customers and obtains most of its sales revenue.

transfer payment A government expenditure for which no goods or services are received in return; social security and welfare payments fall into this category.

transportation A manufacturing activity that provides for the inbound movement of raw materials and parts and the outbound shipment of finished products.

trustee A person, usually a representative of a financial institution, who is responsible for protecting the rights of the bondholders of a business; the trustee also carries out much of the paperwork involved in paying interest and repaying principal on the bond.

tying contract The sale of a product to customers only in combination with another product; tying contracts are prohibited by federal law.

uncertainties The factors over which a decision maker has no control in making a decision.

underwriter A firm or group of firms, usually representing the investment banking community, that is responsible for pricing, promoting, and selling a new stock or bond issue.

undifferentiated marketing A marketing strategy in which a firm manufactures only a single product and attempts to attract all buyers with a single marketing program.

union contract A written agreement between labor and management that specifies in detail the rules and procedures to be followed by both parties.

union shop A shop or business establishment in which management is free to hire nonunion workers provided that they join the established union within a designated period, usually 30 days.

unit pricing Giving retail price information on a cents-per-ounce or cents-per-pound basis; intended to assist consumers in making price comparisons.

unit–record equipment Mechanical data processing equipment utilizing punched cards.

unit–record processing The consolidation of all information relating to a particular system into a single (or unit) record that can be used and re-used in the preparation of reports.

unity of command A principle of organization that states that no member of an organization should report to more than one superior.

unlimited liability A legal obligation of the owner of a firm to use his or her entire business and personal wealth to pay off any accumulated debts of the firm.

unsecured loan A loan that does not involve the use of collateral.

value analysis Systematic appraisal of the design, quality, and performance requirements of an item in order to reduce purchasing and manufacturing costs.

vertical merger The acquisition by a firm of one of its suppliers or customers.

voting security A security that entitles the holder to vote on matters of corporate business, such as election of the board of directors.

wages A form of compensation in which employees are paid at a fixed hourly rate or in accordance with the number of units (or parts) of commodity produced.

whole life policy A form of life insurance in which premiums are paid throughout a person's lifetime, with the full amount of the policy payable upon death.

wholesaler An establishment that sells to retailers, other middlemen, or industrial users, but that does not sell in significant amounts to ultimate consumers.

worker compensation insurance A form of insurance required by state law and paid for by employers that protects employees while they are engaged in the employer's business; the amount of the claim is stipulated by law.

working capital management Decisions about the uses of current assets and short-term debt.

REFERENCES

Chapter 1

Pp. 5–8. The material on Chester F. Carlson, the Haloid Company, and xerography is based on John H. Dessauer, *My Years with Xerox* (Garden City, N.Y.: Doubleday, 1971), pp. 21–87.

P. 7 The material in the box "One Face of Success: Persistence" is based on John H. Dessauer, *op. cit.*, pp. 45–48.

Pp. 15–17. The discussion of the four revolutions is based in part on Robert A. Brady, *Organization, Automation, and Society* (Berkeley: University of California Press, 1961), pp. 6–13.

P. 17. The quotation by Wilhelm Moberg in the box "Why in America?" is from his book *The Last Letter Home* (New York: Simon and Schuster, 1961), pp. 100–101.

P. 22. The 1970 projections by 120 experts are based on *Prospectives for the '70s and '80s* (New York: The Conference Board, 1970).

P. 25. The Critical Business Decision in this chapter is based on "Xerox Tries to Capture Some IBM Territory," *Business Week* (October 12, 1974), pp. 28–29; "The Office of the Future," *Business Week* (June 30, 1975), pp. 48 ff.; and "Xerox to Stop Making, Selling Basic Computers," *The Wall Street Journal* (July 22, 1975), p. 2.

Chapter 2

P. 27. The information about the Manoogians and the Masco Corporation is based on Allan Sloan, "Manoogians' Faucet Empire," *The New York Times* (July 14, 1974), Business Section, p. 1.

P. 36. Data on the control of large corporations are taken from R. J. Larner, "The Two Hundred Largest Nonfinancial Firms," *American Economic Review* (September 1966), p. 781.

P. 43. The assessment of the costs of concentration to the American economy is from F. M. Scherer, *Industrial Market Structure and Economic Performance* (Chicago: Rand-McNally, 1970), p. 406.

P. 51. The Critical Business Decision in this chapter is based on Margaret Rudkin, "The First Twenty-five Years," *The Pepperidge Farm Conveyor—25th Anniversary Issue*. Copyright © 1962 by Margaret Rudkin. Used by permission.

Chapter 3

P. 53. The information about the regulation of radio stations is based on Keith H. Bacon, "Federal Commissions Are Masters of Delay on Cases Before Them," *The Wall Street Journal* (October 13, 1974), pp. 1 ff.

Pp. 60–61. The discussion of four consumer rights is based on Warren G. Magnuson, "Consumerism and the Emerging Goals of a New Society," in Ralph M. Gaedke and Warren M. Etcheson, eds., *Consumerism: Viewpoints from Business, Government, and the Public Interest* (San Francisco: Canfield Press, 1972), pp. 3–7.

P. 64. The quotation by David Merrick appears in Jonathan Kwitny, "Wherein a Consumer Attacks a Big Firm—and Attacks and Attacks," *The Wall Street Journal* (June 6, 1972), pp. 1 ff.

P. 64. The quotation by Virginia Knauer is from her speech to the U.S. Jaycees, Metro Chapter Conference, Indianapolis, Indiana, January 14, 1972.

Pp. 65–66. The ways American business has responded to worker dissatisfaction and the quotation by Richard C. Gerstenberg are taken from *Business Week* (May 17, 1973), pp. 141 ff.

P. 72. The quotation by Theodore Levitt is taken from his article "The Dangers of Social Responsibility," *Harvard Business Review* (September–October 1958), p. 48.

P. 74. Some of the examples of corporate social programs are drawn from "How Business Tackles Social Problems," *Business Week* (May 20, 1972), pp. 95–103.

P. 79. The Critical Business Decision in this chapter is based on "Why Should My Conscience Bother Me?" by Kermit Vandivier, from *In the Name of Profit* by Robert L. Heilbroner *et al.* (Garden City, N.Y.: Doubleday, 1972).

Chapter 4

P. 83. The information on Henry Ford and on Alfred P. Sloan, Jr., is based on Peter F. Drucker, *Management: Tasks, Responsibilities, Practices* (New York: Harper & Row, 1973), pp. 380–84 and 520–

23; and Max Ways, "Hall of Fame for Business Leadership," *Fortune* (January 1975), pp. 66–68.

Pp. 83-86. The definitions of management and the six functions of management are adapted from Joseph L. Massie, *Essentials of Management,* Second Edition (Englewood Cliffs, N.J.: Prentice-Hall, 1971), pp. 6–7.

P. 85. The material in the box about George E. Johnson is based on "A new Black Cosmetics Magnate," *Black Enterprise* (June 1973), pp. 71–73.

P. 92. The information on Exxon planning is taken from Max Ways, *op. cit.,* p. 72.

Pp. 94–96. Gilbreth's bricklaying analysis is described in Allan C. Filley and Robert J. House, *Managerial Process and Organizational Behavior* (Glenwood, Ill.: Scott, Foresman and Company, 1969), p. 12. The discussion of Taylor's four principles of scientific management is adapted from Filley and House, *op. cit.,* p. 13; and W. Warren Haynes and Joseph L. Massie, *Management: Analysis, Concepts, and Cases* Second Edition (Englewood Cliffs, N.J.: Prentice-Hall, 1969), p. 6.

Pp. 100–103. The traditional principles of organization are adapted from the discussions by Filley and House, *op. cit.,* pp. 281–97; Haynes and Massie, *op. cit.* pp. 91–110; and Massie, *op. cit.,* pp. 64–72.

P. 101. The material in the box about Edwin H. Land is based on "Personal Management Styles," *Business Week* (May 4, 1974), pp. 43–51.

P. 109. The Critical Business Decision in this chapter is based on "A Negro Integrates His Markets," *Business Week* (May 18, 1968), pp. 90 ff.

Chapter 5

P. 110. The information about Andrew Carnegie is based on Max Ways, "Hall of Fame for Business Leadership," *Fortune* (January 1975), pp. 66–68.

Pp. 111–22. The material on the staffing function is based on Wendell French, *The Personnel Management Process: Human Resources Administration,* Second Edition (Boston: Houghton Mifflin, 1970), pp. 220–50; and John G. Hutchinson, *Management Strategy and Tactics* (New York: Holt, Rinehart, and Winston, 1971), pp. 317–30.

P. 112–13. Some of the ideas on job hunting are based on Nancy Axelrod Comer, "Job Hunting Now: The Employee Employers Look For," *Mademoiselle* (September 1972), pp. 146–47 and 193.

P. 114. Much of the material in the box "Would You Hire the Following Men?" was provided by Judith Furrer of Inver Hills Community College.

Pp. 115, 129, 135. The material in the boxes on the management styles of C. Peter McColough, Henry R. Roberts, and James P. McFarland is based on information reported in "Personal Management Styles," *Business Week* (May 4, 1974), pp. 43–51.

P. 118. The quotation on cheating on personality tests is taken from William H. Whyte, Jr., *The Organization Man* (Garden City, N.Y.: Doubleday, 1956), p. 449.

P. 122. The discussion of the Peter principle is based on Laurence J. Peter and Raymond Hull, *The Peter Principle* (New York: William Morrow, 1969), pp. 9–36.

Pp. 123–24. The bases of effective communication are taken from William F. Keefe, *Listen, Management!* (New York: McGraw-Hill, 1971), p. 44.

Pp. 124–27. The information on barriers to communication is taken from Herbert J. Chruden and Arthur W. Sherman, Jr., *Personnel Management,* Fourth Edition (Cincinnati, Ohio: South-Western, 1972), pp. 363–70; and Joseph L. Massie, *Essentials of Management,* Second Edition (Englewood Cliffs, N.J.: Prentice-Hall, 1971), pp. 97–98.

P. 124. The Second World War aerial gunnery incident is described in Mason Haire, *Psychology in Management,* Second Edition (New York: McGraw-Hill, 1964), p. 91.

P. 125. The plumber incident is cited in Stuart Chase, *Power of Words* (New York: Harcourt Brace Jovanovich, 1953), p. 259.

P. 123. The material in the box about Catherine Cleary is based on Wyndham Robertson, "The Ten Highest-Ranking Women in Business," *Fortune* (April, 1973), pp. 80 ff. Used by permission.

P. 126. The example of simplifying a gobbledygook passage is taken from Robert Gunning, *How to Take the Fog Out of Writing* (Chicago: The Dartnell Corporation, 1964), pp. 9–11.

P. 126. The reference to the 26, 911-word message on cabbage pricing is found in Dennis Murphy, *Better Business Communication* (New York: McGraw-Hill, 1957), p. 15.

Pp. 127–28. The discussion of the Hawthorne studies is based on F. J. Roethlisberger, *Management and Morale* (Cambridge, Mass.: Harvard University Press, 1941), pp. 10–11; and Allan C. Filley and Robert J. House, *Managerial Process and Organizational Behavior* (Glenwood, Ill.: Scott, Foresman and Company, 1969), pp. 18–23.

Pp. 131–32. The discussion of Machiavellianism is based on Richard Christie, "The Machiavellis Among Us," *Psychology Today* (November 1970), pp. 82–86.

Pp. 132–33. The quotation on leadership is cited in Robert Townsend, *Up the Organization* (New York: Alfred A. Knopf, 1970), p. 99.

P. 132. Ideas on leadership patterns are taken from Robert Tannenbaum and Warren H. Schmidt, "How to Chose a Leadership Pattern," *Harvard Business Review* (March–April 1958), pp. 95–101.

Pp. 136–37. The guidelines by John Lasagna are taken from his article "Make Your MBO Pragmatic," *Harvard Business Review* (November–December 1971), pp. 64–69.

P. 137. The material on Parkinson's Law is taken from C. Northcote Parkinson, *Parkinson's Law* (Boston: Houghton Mifflin, 1957), pp. 2–12; and *The Law of Delay* (Boston: Houghton Mifflin, 1971), pp. 3–8.

P. 141. The Critical Business Decision in this chapter is based on Rush Loving, Jr., "Bob Six's Long Search For a Successor," *Fortune* (June 1975), pp. 92 ff. The descriptions of Six's four potential successors are reprinted directly from this article, with editorial amendments approved by the author. Used by permission of the author and the publisher.

Chapter 6

P. 143. The Lincoln story is based on "Lincoln in Illinois," *Minneapolis Tribune* (February 10, 1974), Picture Section, p. 2.

Pp. 148–50. The dot, match, and river–crossing problems are adapted from Martin Scheerer, "Problem Solving," *Scientific American* (April 1963), pp. 118–28.

P. 158. The information about toy testing at Fisher-Price can be found in Jim Hyatt, "At One Toy Company, the Guys in Research Are Three and Four Years Old," *The Wall Street Journal* (December 20, 1971), pp. 1 ff.

P. 169. The Critical Business Decision in this chapter is based on "Gibson's L'il Ole Billion-Dollar Business," *Business Week* (March 20, 1971), pp. 60 ff.

Chapter 7

P. 173. The story about Dick Woolworth appears in Stephen J. Sansweet, "Dick Woolworth Builds a Better Mousetrap—and Falls on His Face," *The Wall Street Journal* (September 24, 1970), pp. 1 ff.

P. 174. The definition of marketing is adapted from E. Jerome McCarthy, *Basic Marketing*, Fourth Edition (Homewood, Ill.: Richard D. Irwin, 1971), p. 19.

Pp. 176–79. The discussion of target markets and the meaning of product is based on McCarthy, *op. cit.*, pp. 37–45.

Pp. 180–82. The discussion on changes in consumer population is based in part on "America's New Look, As the Census Sees It," *Changing Times* (August 1971), pp. 13–14.

Pp. 184–85. Some of the material on the changes in consumer attitudes and values is taken from "What Makes the New Consumer Buy," *Business Week* (April 24, 1971), pp. 52–58.

Pp. 188–89. The information on the use of colas and beer is taken from Dik Warren Twedt, "How

Important to Marketing Strategy Is the 'Heavy User'?" *Journal of Marketing* (January 1964), p. 72.

Pp. 189–91. The discussion of undifferentiated, differentiated, and concentrated marketing is adapted from Philip Kotler, *Marketing Management*, Second Edition (Englewood Cliffs, N.J.: Prentice-Hall, 1972), pp. 182–87.

P. 197. The Critical Business Decision in this chapter is based on Susan O'Neill, "There Is a Young Lady Who Lives in the Shoes," *Generation* (March 1971), pp. 47 ff. Data also taken from "Men Enjoy It! Says 28 Year Old Woman President," *The AMBA Executive*, Vol. 3, No. 1 (May 1973), p. 1 ff, and used by permission of *The AMBA Executive*.

Chapter 8

Pp. 200, 207. The definitions of place and price are derived from E. Jerome McCarthy, *Basic Marketing*, Fourth Edition (Homewood, Ill.: Richard D. Irwin, 1971), pp. 371 and 596–98.

P. 203. Information on the costs of producing and marketing a record is taken from "A Prosperous Turnaround for Records," *Business Week* (July 27, 1974), pp. 72–76.

P. 212. The Xerox pricing strategy is based on John H. Dessauer, *My Years with Xerox* (Garden City, N.Y.: Doubleday, 1971), pp. 125–27.

P. 221. The Critical Business Decision in this chapter is based on "Student Sells $1 Million of Magazine Subscriptions," *The New York Times* (August 1, 1971), pp. 41 ff.

Chapter 9

P. 223. The definition of promotion is taken from E. Jerome McCarthy, *Basic Marketing*, Fourth Edition (Homewood, Ill.: Richard D. Irwin, 1971), p. 513.

P. 226. The definition of advertising is adapted from Philip Kotler, *Marketing Management*, Second Edition (Englewood Cliffs, N.J.: Prentice-Hall, 1972), p. 663.

P. 226. The quotation by Martin Mayer is taken from his book *Madison Avenue, U.S.A.* (New York: Pocket Books, 1959), p. 22. Originally published by Harper & Row.

P. 231. The analysis of the two Honda ads is taken from Philip Ward Burton, *Which Ad Pulled Best?* (New York: Decker Communications, The Marketing/Communications College Workbook Series, 1969), p. 9.

Pp. 234–35. The information on trends in magazine ads in the 1970s is taken from William Tyler, "How Magazine Ads Looked the Last Five Years—The Trends and the Non-trends," *Advertising Age* (November 18, 1974), pp. 74 ff.

P. 237. The case history of the Xerox 914 advertising campaign is taken from John H. Dessauer,

My Years With Xerox (Garden City, N.Y.: Doubleday, 1971), pp. 145–46.

P. 238. The advertising campaigns of Rosser Reeves are described in Thomas Whiteside, "Annals of Television—The Man from Iron City," *The New Yorker* (September 27, 1969), pp. 47 ff.

Pp. 239–45. The sales categories and steps in the selling process are adapted from Allan L. Reid, *Modern Applied Salesmanship* (Pacific Palisades, Calif.: Goodyear Publishing Company, 1970), pp. 27–74 and 159–213.

Pp. 242–43. The four case histories illustrating the four steps in the selling process are from the following sources: *Benjamin Feldman:* Arthur M. Louis, "How One Man Makes $120,000 a Year Selling Insurance," *Fortune* (July 1974), pp. 133 ff; *Kenneth Dayton:* address at the College of Business Administration of the University of Minnesota on November 25, 1974; *Joan Thomas:* Roger B. May, "It Takes Luck, Savvy, and Drudgery to Sell Twenty Homes a Year," *The Wall Street Journal* (May 20, 1974), pp. 1 ff.; *Mehdi Fakharzadeh:* Arthur M. Louis, *op. cit.*, pp. 131 ff.

P. 246. Mehdi Fakharzadeh's five essentials of selling are found in Arthur M. Louis, *op. cit.*, pp. 131 ff.

P. 251. The Critical Business Decision in this chapter is based on "Pacific 'Fear of Flying' Drive Criticized," *Aviation Week and Space Technology* (May 8, 1967), pp. 30–31.

Chapter 10

P. 253. The discussion of Gene O'Neill's Wonder Whip is based on John A. Prestbo, "A Basement Inventor Scores a Big Success—With a Buggy Whip," *The Wall Street Journal* (October 25, 1971), pp. 1 ff.

P. 256. The material in the box "Serendipity: An Angel in Product Development" is based on John H. Dessauer, *My Years with Xerox* (Garden City, N.Y.: Doubleday, 1971), pp. 64–67.

Pp. 260–64. The sequence of purchasing steps is described in Dean S. Ammer, *Materials Management*, Revised Edition (Homewood, Ill.: Richard D. Irwin, 1968), pp. 19–37.

Pp. 262–63. The material in the box "What Bid Criteria Are Important in an Industrial Buying Decision?" is based on Gary W. Dickson, "An Analysis of Vendor Selection Systems and Decisions," *Journal of Purchasing* (February 1966), pp. 10–16.

P. 267. The material in the box "The Impossible Takes a Little Longer: American Production in World War II" is based on Alistar Cooke, *America* (New York: Alfred A. Knopf, 1973); and Alex Groner, *The American Heritage History of American Business* (New York: American Heritage Publishing Company, 1972), pp. 315–21.

P. 277. The Critical Business Decision in this chapter is based on "Polaroid's Big Gamble on Small Cameras," *Time* (June 26, 1972), pp. 80 ff.

Chapter 11

P. 281. The Edison incident is described in H. Gordon Garbedian, *Thomas A. Edison: Builder of Civilization* (New York: John Messner, 1947), pp. 52–53.

P. 284. The material in the box "The Income Tax People" is based on "The Troubles That Are Taxing H&R Block," *Business Week* (December 8, 1973), pp. 112–13.

P. 299. The material in the box "How Touche Ross Spots Fraud" is based on "The Touche Ross Manual for Spotting Fraud," *Business Week* (February 17, 1975), p. 52.

P. 307. The Critical Business Decision in this chapter is based on David P. Garino, "How a Big Company Controls Its Costs in Good Times and Bad," *The Wall Street Journal* (June 4, 1975), pp. 1 ff. Reprinted with permission of *The Wall Street Journal,* © Dow Jones & Company, Inc. (1975). All Rights Reserved.

Chapter 12

P. 309. The quotation by Irwin Friend is taken from his article "What Business Can Do to Prevent Recessions," *Problems in Antirecession Policy* (New York: Committee for Economic Development, 1954), p. 6; cited in J. Fred Weston and Eugene F. Brigham, *Essentials of Managerial Finance* (New York: Holt, Rinehart, and Winston, 1968), p. 14.

P. 331. The Critical Business Decision in this chapter is based on Charles J. V. Murphy, "Jack Simplot and His Private Conglomerate," *Fortune* (August 1968), pp. 122 ff.

Chapter 13

P. 335. The material in the box "What's New in Cash Management?" is based on David P. Garino, "Companies Gain Funds by Speeding Intakes and Slowing Outgoes," *The Wall Street Journal* (July 31, 1974), pp. 1 ff.

P. 356. The material in the box "The Insurance Company You Select Makes a Difference" is based on "They Are All Afraid of Herb the Horrible," *Time* (July 10, 1972), pp. 81–82.

P. 361. The Critical Business Decision in this chapter is based on Peter Vanderwicken, "When Levi Strauss Burst Its Britches," *Fortune* (April 1974), pp. 130 ff.; "Back to Basic Bottoms," *Forbes* (March 15, 1975), p. 80; and Milton Moskowitz, "The Levi Lifestyle," *The New York Times* (August 6, 1972), Business Section, p. 1 ff.

Chapter 14

P. 363. Information on the Home-Stake Production Company incident is based on David McClintick, "How Did Home-Stake Spend All That Money That Investors Put In?" *The Wall Street Journal* (August 29, 1974), pp. 1 ff.; and "Gulling the Beautiful People," *Time* (July 8, 1974), p. 45.

P. 373. The material in the box "Blipping and the Money Factory" is based on Barry Newman, "Moving Money: In the Back Office of a Bank, 'Blipping' Is Not Appreciated," *The Wall Street Journal* (June 6, 1975), p. 1 ff. Reprinted with permission of *The Wall Street Journal,* © Dow Jones & Company, Inc. (1975). All Rights Reserved.

P. 383. The material in the box "Financial Advice Isn't Always What It Seems" is based on John H. Dessauer, *My Years with Xerox* (Garden City, N.Y.: Doubleday, 1971), pp. 193–98.

P. 389. The Critical Business Decision in this chapter is based on John H. Allan, "Atlanta's Banking Wonder," *The New York Times* (April 21, 1974), section F, p. 7.

Chapter 15

P. 391. The McDonald's incident is based on "Hold the Stuffing!" *The Wall Street Journal* (April 24, 1975), pp. 1 ff.

P. 393. The data in the box "How Fast and How Cheaply Can Computers Calculate?" is from Donald H. Sanders, *Computers and Management* (New York: McGraw-Hill, 1970), p. 16 fn.

Pp. 391–97. Material in the section on the development of EDP and the computer industry is based on the following sources: Donald H. Sanders, *Computers and Management* (New York: McGraw-Hill, 1970), pp. 13–18; George Schussel, "IBM vs. REM-RAND," *Datamation* (May 1965), pp. 54–57; "Can IBM Keep Up the Pace?" *Business Week* (February 2, 1963), p. 92; and Gilbert Burck, "Computer Industry's Great Expectations," *Fortune* (August 1968), pp. 92–95.

P. 397. The definition of computer is adapted from Gerald A. Silver and Joan B. Silver, *Data Processing for Business* (New York: Harcourt Brace Jovanovich, Inc., 1973), p. 6.

P. 402. The quotation on "problem-plagued programming" is taken from Gene Bylinsky, "Help Wanted: 50,000 Programmers," *Fortune* (March 1967), p. 141.

Pp. 405–407. The description of the methods of utilizing computers and the quotation from the Armco Steel supervisor in this section are taken from "Business Takes a Second Look at Computers: A Special Report," *Business Week* (June 5, 1971), pp. 59–136.

P. 406. The quotation from the Ford Motor Company executive is taken from, "Minicomputers That Run the Factory: A Special Report," *Business Week* (December 8, 1973), p. 69.

P. 409. The material in the box "How a Wave of the Wand Computerizes Grocery Shopping" is based on Chris Barnett, "Why Supermarkets Are Going Bananas Over Computers," *Mainliner* (October 1974), pp. 41–43; "Bringing Home the 33900–10020," *Time* (December 30, 1974), p. 20; "When Food and Soft Goods Talk Different Codes," *Business Week* (March 30, 1974), pp. 64–65; and Jim Adams, "A Wave of the Wand Computerizes Groceries," *Minneapolis Star* (September 19, 1974), p. 6E.

P. 411. The incident on the computer that was "fired" in California is described in *The Wall Street Journal* (February 15, 1972), pp. 1 ff.

P. 415. The Critical Business Decision in this chapter is based on "Hewlett-Packard: Where Slower Growth Is Smarter Management," *Business Week* (June 9, 1975), pp. 50–58.

Chapter 16

P. 419. The information about small businessman Harry Marcowitz is based on Frederick C. Klein, "Launching a Business in These Risky Times Is a Frustrating Task," *The Wall Street Journal* (November 6, 1974), pp. 1 ff.

Pp. 421–23. The attractions and drawbacks of small businesses are cited in Wendell O. Metcalf, *Starting and Managing a Small Business of Your Own,* Second Edition (Washington, D.C.: U.S. Small Business Administration, 1962), pp. 1–2.

P. 422. The material in the box "A Common Small-Business Misery . . ." is based on Everett Groseclose, "You Have Problems? Consider the Plight of the Nation's SOBs," *The Wall Street Journal* (March 20, 1975), pp. 1 ff.

Pp. 423–25. The information on business failures is taken from *The Business Failure Record: 1974* (New York: Dun & Bradstreet, 1975), pp. 12–13.

P. 424. The quotation from Rowena Wyatt is taken from Frederick C. Klein, *op. cit.,* pp. 1 ff.

Pp. 428–29. The SBA case studies of small-business failures appear in Kurt B. Mayer and Sidney Goldstein, *The First Two Years: Problems of Small Firms' Growth and Survival* (Washington, D.C.: U.S. Small Business Administration, 1961), pp. 118–33.

Pp. 430–34. The case study of estimating a shoe store's sales revenue is adapted from William Rudelius et al., "Assessing Retail Opportunities in Low-Income Areas," *Journal of Retailing* (Fall 1972), pp. 96–114. The general method is adapted from *Retail Location Manual—Small Business in Low-Income Areas* (Chicago: Real Estate Research Corporation, July 1967), Vol. I.

P. 437. The Critical Business Decision in this chapter is based on Herschel Johnson, "Motown:

The Sound of Success," *Black Enterprise* (June 1974), pp. 71–80.

Chapter 17

P. 440. Information on McDonald's franchising arrangements is based on "Questions People Ask About McDonald's Licensing Policies" (Oakbrook, Ill.: McDonald's Corporation, no date).

Pp. 450–51. Information on financing that appears in the section on obtaining funds is drawn from Jack Zwick, *A Handbook of Small Business Finance*, Seventh Edition (Washington, D.C.: U.S. Small Business Administration, 1965), p. 53; and *Loan Sources in the Federal Government*, Revised Edition (Washington, D.C.: U.S. Small Business Administration, June 1968), p. 1.

Pp. 452–57. Much of the material in the section on operating a small business is based on Wendell O. Metcalf, *Starting and Managing a Small Business of Your Own*, Second Edition (Washington, D.C.: U.S. Small Business Administration, 1962), pp. 25–32.

P. 453. The material in the box "What Markups Do Retailers Really Use?" is based on "Ratios in Retailing," *Dun's Review* (September 1974), p. 93; P.I. Cifrino, "Cifrino's Space Yield Formula," *Chain Store Age—Supermarket Executive Edition* (November 1963), p. 85; and *Expenses in Retail Business* (Dayton, Ohio: National Cash Register Company, no date).

P. 463. The Critical Business Decision in this chapter is based on J. Anthony Lukas, "As American as McDonald's Hamburger on the 4th of July," *The New York Times Magazine* (July 4, 1971). Used by permission.

Chapter 18

P. 467. The description of Julian Granger's activities is taken from John G. Fuller, *The Gentlemen Conspirators: The Story of Price Fixing in the Electrical Industry* (New York: Grove Press, 1962), pp. 7–11.

P. 477. The material in the box "Blankenheim on Price Fixing" is based on Harry Jupiter, "Executive Tells of Price Fixing," *San Francisco Chronicle* (March 10, 1975), p. 48.

P. 495. The Critical Business Decision in this chapter is based on Steven Rattner, "The Elusive Promise of Profitable U.S. Mail," *The New York Times* (July 6, 1975), Business Section, pp. 1 ff.

Chapter 19

P. 497. The Homestead violence is described in Foster Rhea Dulles, *Labor in America* (New York: Thomas Y. Crowell, 1955), pp. 166–71.

P. 507. The material in the box "The Man in the Middle" is based on Lawrence G. O'Donnell, "As a Ford Foreman, Ed Hendrix Finds He Is Man in the Middle," *The Wall Street Journal* (July 25, 1973), pp. 1 ff.

P. 517. The Critical Business Decision in this chapter is based on Walter Mossberg, "A Union Man at Ford, Charlie Bragg Deals in Problems, Gripes," *The Wall Street Journal* (July 26, 1973), pp. 1 ff. Reprinted with permission of *The Wall Street Journal*, © Dow Jones & Company, Inc. (1973). All Rights Reserved.

Chapter 20

P. 528. The material in the box "Xerox and British Doors" is based on John H. Dessauer, *My Years with Xerox* (Garden City, N.Y.: Doubleday, 1971), pp. 141–56.

P. 532. The quotation by J. J. Servan-Schreiber is from his book *The American Challenge* (New York: Atheneum, 1968), p. 3.

P. 543. The Critical Business Decision in this chapter is based on Bro Uttal, "Gillette Swings a Mighty Blade Abroad," *Fortune* (November 1974), pp. 192 ff. Used by permission.

Epilogue

P. 546. The material in the box "If the World Were 100 People: A Comparison of Rich and Poor Nations," cited as coming from Michael D. Anderson, is found in Monte Bute, "War, Economic System Tied More Closely Than Appears," *Minnesota Daily* (May 2, 1972), p. 5.

Pp. 548–50. The material in the section "Key Factors Affecting Economic Growth and the Quality of Life" is based on the following sources: Ray Vicker, "Population Growth Is Still a Key Problem in Many Poor Nations," *The Wall Street Journal* (October 23, 1974), pp. 1 ff; "The World Food Crisis," *Time* (November 11, 1974), pp. 66–83; "Was Malthus Right?" *Business Week* (June 16, 1975), pp. 64–72; and Burt Schorr, "As Clean-Air Deadline Approaches, Pollution Is Still a Fact of Life," *The Wall Street Journal* (January 27, 1975), pp. 1 ff.

P. 549. Material on the energy crisis is taken mainly from Edmund Faltermayer, "The Energy Joyride Is Over," *Fortune* (September 1972), pp. 99–101; and "Metals: The Warning Signals Are Up," *Fortune* (October 1972), pp. 109–10.

P. 551. The French lily pond riddle appears in Donella H. Meadows et al., *The Limits to Growth* (New York: Universe Books, 1972), p. 29. The discussion of doubling time is also from this source (pp. 25–31), as is the discussion of computer simulation (pp. 88–184).

P. 552. Henry C. Wallich's comments are taken from his article "How to Live with Economic Growth" *Fortune* (October 1972), pp. 114–16.

P. 553. The material regarding the savings in reducing energy consumption over the next twenty-five years is based on Stephen B. Shepard, "How Much Energy Does the U. S. Need?" *Business Week* (June 1, 1974), pp. 69–70.

P. 554. The material in the box "Social Traps: The Individual Versus Society" is based on Berkeley Rice, "Fighting Inflation with Buttons and Slogans," *Psychology Today* (January 1975), pp. 49–50.

SOURCE OF ILLUSTRATIONS

Part 1: p. 1, *top*, Harbrace; *bot. l.*, Cities Service Co.; *bot. r.*, Harbrace; 2, *top l.*, Ezra Stoller © Esto; *top r.*, U.S. Dept. of the Interior; *bot. l.*, New York State Power Authority; *bot. r.*, Richard Swanson from Black Star; 3, RCA

Chapter 1: pp. 6, 8, Xerox Corp.; 10, J. I. Case Co.; 11, Standard Oil Co. (N.J.); 13, Ford Motor Co.; 14, Erich Hartmann/Magnum Photos, Inc.; 16, Culver Pictures, Inc.; 24, Xerox Corp.

Chapter 2: p. 28 *all*, Masco Corp.; 35, RCA; 39, Michal Heron/Monkmeyer; 42, Shackman/Monkmeyer; 51, Pepperidge Farm

Chapter 3: p. 63, Dr. Lillie Bruck; 74, U.P.I.

Part 2: p. 80 *top l.*, Raytheon Co.; *top r.*, Burk Uzzle © Magnum Photos; *bot. l.*, Univac; *bot. r.*, Foster-Wheeler from *Business Week*; 81, Nat. Education Assoc.

Chapter 4: p. 85, Johnson Products Co.; 95, Hugh Rogers/Monkmeyer; 101, Polaroid Corp.; 103, Cornell Capa/Magnum Photos, Inc.; 109, Fabian Bachrach

Chapter 5: p. 118 *top*, U.S. Dept. of the Interior, Edison National Historic Site; *ctr.*, Library of Congress; *bot.*, British Information Service; 119 *top*, Henry Grossman/Xerox Corp.; *ctr.*, RCA; 129, Conn. General Insurance Co.

Chapter 6: p. 150, Imperial War Museum; 169, Gibson Products Co.

Part 3: p. 170 *top*, General Foods Corp.; *ctr. l.*, Beetleboards of America, Inc.; *bot. l.*, IBM; *bot. r.*, Standard Oil Co., (N.J.); 171, Harbrace

Chapter 7: p. 190, Procter & Gamble; Colgate-Palmolive; Lever Bros.

Chapter 8: p. 199, Wm. Wrigley, Jr., Co.; 200, Harbrace; 204, Library of Congress; 205 *top*, Harbrace; *bot.*, Woodfield Mall; 206 *top*, L'Eggs; *bot.*, Rogers/Monkmeyer

Chapter 9: p. 223, Beetleboards of America, Inc.;

224, Harbrace; 225, Avon Products, Inc.; 226, Sibylle von Elbe; 230, Union Carbide; 231, Ross Photos; 232, Honda, Inc.; 234, Mercedes-Benz, Volkswagen of America, Inc.; 235 *l.*, Allstate Insurance Co.; © 1972, Volvo of America, Inc.; 240, Harbrace; 242 *l.*, Ben Feldman, C.L.U.; *r.*, Dayton-Hudson Corp.; 243 *l.*, Courtesy Joan Thomas; *r.*, Metropolitan Life Ins. Co.; 251, American Airlines

Chapter 10: p. 265, Wide World; 269, © Baron Wolman; 270, Cornell Capa/Magnum; 271, U.P.I.; 277, Polaroid Corp.

Part 4: p. 278 *top*, N.Y. Stock Exchange; *ctr. l.*, Wyle Laboratories, Electronics Dist. Group; *bot. l.*, National Cash Register Co.; *bot. r.*, IBM; 279, A. T. & T.

Chapter 11: p. 283, Harbrace; 284, H&R Block; 286, Arthur Lavine/Chase Manhattan Bank; 289, Wm. R. Devine/Chase Manhattan Bank; 297, Harbrace; 307, Harbrace

Chapter 12: p. 321, Raytheon Co.; 326, Harbrace; 331, J. R. Simplot Co.

Chapter 13: p. 348, U.P.I.; 352, Wide World; 356, Herbert Denenberg; 361, Courtesy Levi Strauss & Co.

Chapter 14: p. 366, Franklin D. Roosevelt Library; 371, U.P.I./Franklin D. Roosevelt Library; 378, Harbrace; 389, *New York Times*/Mike Keza

Chapter 15: p. 392 *top*, IBM; *bot.*, N.Y.P.L. Picture Collection; 397, MSI Data Corp., Costa Mesa, Ca.; 402, Arthur Lavine/Chase Manhattan Bank; 408, NCR Corp.; 409 *l.*, IBM; *r.*, Green Giant; 415, Jon Brenneis

Part 5: p. 416 *top l.*, Exxon; *top r., bot. l.*, Harry W. Rinehart; *bot. r.*, Jerry Soalt for ILGWU "Justice"; 417, Harry W. Rinehart

Chapter 16: p. 421, Harbrace; 422, Sidney Harris; 429, Harry W. Rinehart; 437, Bill Kelly

Chapter 17: p. 439, Harry W. Rinehart; 440, McDonald's Corp.; 452, Xerox Corp.; 463, McDonald's Corp.

Part 6: p. 464 *top l.*, Harbrace/Jacques Jangoux; *top r.*, U.S. Dept. of Agriculture; *bot. l.*, Harbrace; *bot r.*, Mobil; 465, New York State Dept. of Commerce

Chapter 18: p. 469, George Eastman House, Inc.; 470, Corson from A. Devaney, Inc.; 472, 474, U.S. Air Force; 477, *San Francisco Chronicle*; 481, A. T. & T.; 482, Harry W. Rinehart; 483, Jacob A. Riis Coll., Museum of the City of New York; 495, *New York Times*/Mike Lien

Chapter 19: p. 497, Brown Bros.; 500, Harbrace; 502, National Archives; 503, U.P.I.; 508, Harbrace

Chapter 20: p. 523, Roger Malloch, © Magnum Photos Inc.; 525, Standard Oil Co. (N.J.); 543, Gillette Co.

Epilogue: p. 548, Burk Uzzle, © 1969 Magnum Photos; 549, Exxon; 550, Elliott Erwitt, © 1970 Magnum Photos; 552, American Can Co.; 554, Harbrace

INDEX

ability-to-pay principle, 487
above-market pricing, 216
absolute advantage, 523
absolute ethical standard, 70
acceptance (contract), 56
accident insurance, 355
account, 287
account executive, 380, 385
accounting
    assets, 292–94, auditing, 297, 299; balance sheet, 288, 292–97; budgeting 300–303; classifying transactions 287–88; definition of, 281; depreciation, 287; income statement, 288–92, 295–96; liabilities, 292–93, 294; managerial, 285; owner equity, 292–93, 294–95, 296; ratios, 297–98, 300; recording transactions, 286–87; role in business, 285; types of, 283–85; users of, 282
Accounting Corporation of America, 441
accounting equation, 292–93
accounting period, 288
accounting transaction, 286
accounts payable, 294
accounts receivable, 290, 294, 324, 336–38, 447
accrued liability, 294
Active Corps of Executives (ACE), 458
actuarial tables, 349, 350
Adams, Richard M., 141
adjustment to sales, 290
ad valorem duty, 525
advertising
    affordable method, 228; appeal, 230; budget, 228–29; competitive-parity method, 228, 456; copy, 230–31; costs, 235, 236; definition of, 226; delayed-action, 227; direct-action, 226; direct mail, 226; goals, 228; measurement, 237–38; misrepresentation in,

61–62, 478, 479; objective-and-task method, 228; percentage-of-sales method, 228; retail, 456
Advertising Age, 234
advertising effectiveness (measuring), 237–38
affirmative action program, 69
affordable method, 228
AFL–CIO, 21, 498, 500, 526
after-tax profits, 486, 491
agency, law of, 57
agent, 57
AIDA, 248
Aiken, Howard, 396
Air France, 529
Alliance for Labor Action, 498
Allis-Chalmers Corporation, 467
allocation of resources, 40, 44, 522–23
allowances and discounts, 290
Allstate Insurance Company, 234
alternative (in decision making), 147
Aluminum Company of America (ALCOA), 213
American Express Company, 341
American Federation of Labor (AFL), 498, 502
American Home Products Corporation, 229
American Hydraulic Paper Cutter, Inc., 419
American labor. *See* labor
American Law Institute, 54
American Management Association, 121
American Medical Association, 21
American Motors Corporation, 74
American Stock Exchange, 377, 378, 383
American Telephone and Telegraph Company (AT&T), 20, 33, 69
Amtrak, 30
analog computer, 398
analytical engine, 392

analytic process, 269
Anderson, Michael D., 546
antitrust laws, 475–80
appeal (advertising), 230
apprenticeship (union), 505
arbitration, 511, 512–13
arithmetic-logic unit, 398, 399
Army Corps of Engineers, U.S., 21
Arnold Metal Products Company, 337
assembly line, 13–14, 266
assembly-line worker, 13–14, 505
assessed valuation, 489–90
asset management, 333–46
assets
    against bankruptcy claims, 58; current, 296; definition of, 293; fixed, 296; intangible 294, 296; long-term investment, 296; and small business, 445–48
Atomic Energy Commission (AEC), U.S., 482
auditing, 297, 299
authority, 100, 102, 103, 104
authorized share, 315
automatic merchandising, 15, 204, 205
automation, 16, 268–69
automobile insurance, 352–53
Avis Rent A Car System, Inc., 122
Avon Products, Inc., 225, 239

Babbage, Charles, 392, 396
Babson's Investment and Barometer Letter, 383
bad debt, 290
Bailar, Benjamin Franklin, 495
balance of payments, 535–36, 539
balance of trade, 535
balance sheet, 288, 292–97, 445–48
Bally Manufacturing Corporation, 382
Bank Americard, 341
bank charter, 365
banker's acceptance, 334

County and City Data Book, 155
court injunction, 469, 480, 508, 513–14
craft union, 497, 500
credit. See intermediate-term financing; short-term financing
credit-life policy, 357
credit manager, 336, 338
creditors, 282
credit policy, 336, 338
credit union, 374–75
criterion. See measure of success
current asset, 296
current liability, 296
current ratio, 298, 442
custom manufacture, 269
customs duty, 524–25
Customs Bureau, U.S., 430

Damm, Alexander, 141
data
    business forecasting, 88–90; computer, 399–401, 404–406; control group, 158; experimental, 151, 158; external secondary, 151, 155; internal secondary, 151, 154–55; for managerial accounting, 285; observational, 151, 155–56; primary, 151, 154, 155–58; secondary, 151, 154–55
Davis, Kenneth, 327
Dayton, Kenneth, 242
Dayton–Hudson Corporation, 74, 205, 242
death duty, 490
debt financing, 313–14, 450–51
debugging, 402
decentralization (in organizations), 100–101
DECIDE process, 143–65
decision factors, 147–48
decision making, 85–86, 132–34, 143. See also DECIDE process
delayed-action advertising, 227
Del Monte Corporation, 175, 177
Delphi method, 89–91, 434
Deltona Corporation, 311
demand, 207–209, 213
demand curve, 207–208, 211
demand-oriented pricing, 213–14
Denenberg, Herbert S., 356
departmentation by groups, 100

Department of Commerce, U.S., 206
Department of Defense, U.S., 472
Department of Justice, U.S., 467, 479
Department of the Treasury, U.S., 365
department store, 15, 204, 205
depreciation, 287, 444
depth strategy, 192
Dessauer, John H., 6, 8, 256, 528
Dewey, John, 145
Diamond International Corporation, 477
Dickson, Gary W., 262–63
differentiated marketing, 190–91
digital computer, 397–98
Digital Equipment Corporation, 415
Dillinger, John, 114
dilution (in communication), 125
direct-action advertising, 226
directing
    definition of, 84, 127; leadership styles, 130–34; worker motivation, 127–30
direct mail (advertising), 226
direct marketing, 200, 201
direct material, 260
direct sales representative, 239
discount (bond), 319
discount catalog showroom, 204, 206
discount house, 15, 204, 205–206
discount rate, 371–72
discounts and allowances, 290
discrete values, 397–98
discretionary purchasing power, 183
disposable personal income, 183
Disraeli, Benjamin, 26
dissolution, 480
diversification, 384
dividend, 316–17
division of functions, 468
dollar averaging, 384
double-entry system, 287–88
Dow Jones average, 379, 383
Drucker, Peter F., 83
dumping, 528
Dun and Bradstreet, Inc., 298, 337, 338, 423, 424, 441, 452
DuPont de Nemours and Company, E. I., 257, 259
Dupont, Michel, 543
Dupont, S. T., 543

earnings per share, 300
Eastman Kodak Company, 477
easy-money policy, 371, 372
Eckert, J. P., 396, 397
economic concentration, 475–76
economic growth, 545–55
Economics Laboratory, 191
economy, colonial, 9–10
Edison, Thomas A., 13, 114, 117–18, 165, 259, 281
EDP. See electronic data processing
Edsel, 88, 148, 230, 257
Educational Subscription Service, Inc., 221
Eisenhower, Dwight D., 162
electromechanical computer, 396
electronic data processing (EDP)
    computer components, 398–401; definition of, 391; development of, 391–92; future of, 410–11; growth of, 397; kinds, 397–98, 405–408; origins of, 392–97; and programming, 401–403; uses of, 404–410
Electronic Numerical Integrator and Calculator (ENIAC), 393, 394, 396
electronics and automation revolution, 16
Ellington, J. T., Jr., 495
embargo, 526
Emerson, Ralph Waldo, 172
Emerson Electric Company, 307
Emigrants, The, 17
eminent domain, 473
employment. See careers
endowment policy, 355
end-product goods, 186, 260
energy crisis, 17, 549, 553–54
energy revolution, 16–17
engineering. See production
ENIAC, 393, 394, 396
environmental management, 75
Environmental Protection Agency (EPA), U.S., 549–50
equal employment opportunities (EEO)
    ethnic minorities, 67–69, 74; goals of, 66; and the law, 69; women and, 66–67, 74
Equal Employment Opportunities Commission, U.S., 69
Equal Pay Act (1963), 69
equipment loan, 321
equity, 292–93, 294–95, 296
equity financing, 313, 448
estate tax, 490

Sherwin–Williams Company, 200
shift premium, 503
shopping center, 204, 205
shopping good, 186
shop steward, 499, 512
short-term financing, 321–25
short-term loans, 314, 323–25
short-term obligations (small business), 448–50
short-term profits, 37
shrinkage, 454
shutdown agreement, 508
Simplot, Jack, 331
simulation (computer), 410, 552
Singer, Richard, 307
Singer Company, 11, 532
single-line store, 204–205
sitdown strike, 508
situational ethics, 70
Six, Robert F., 141
skim-the-cream pricing, 214
Sloan, Alfred P., Jr., 83, 101
slowdown, 508
small business
  advantages and disadvantages of, 421–23; assistance for, 457–58; checklist, 426; definition of, 420; estimating revenue of, 432–34; failures, 423–25; financing of, 439–51; location of, 428–30; operation of, 452–57; performance of, 457; selection of, 421–27; trading area, 430–31
Small Business Act (1953), 418, 450–51
Small Business Administration (SBA), U.S., 320, 321, 420, 425, 428, 439, 450–51, 457–58
social institution, 72
socialism, 46–47
social responsibility of business, 38, 72–74, 555
social security, 357, 474, 490
Social Security Administration, U.S., 474
"social-trap" theory, 554
software (computer), 401–403
sole proprietorship, 30–31, 37
Sons of Bosses International, 422
sorters (punched card), 395
sources of financing, 315–25, 450–51
span of control, 100
special audit, 297

special drawing rights (SDRs), 539
specialization of labor, 94, 96, 266
specialized budget, 300–301
special-purpose computer, 405, 406
specialty good, 186, 430
specification (product), 256, 261
specific duty, 524–25
speculator, 382
Sperry Rand Corporation, 532
Spurgeon, Charles Hoddon, 332
staff (in organizations), 102–104
staffing
  definition of, 84, 111; appraising personnel, 119–20; compensating personnel, 120–22; definition of, 84, 111; miscellaneous activities, 122; recruiting personnel, 112–14; requisitioning personnel, 112; selecting personnel, 114–18; training, 119
Standard and Poor's average, 320, 379
Standard and Poor's Corporate Record, 297–98
standardization of parts, 11, 16, 266
standard manufacture, 269
standard-markup pricing, 215
Standard Oil Company (N.J.). *See* Exxon Corporation
standards revolution, 16
Starch Advertisement Readership Service, 231
state bank, 365
State Department, U.S., 530
Statistical Abstract of the United States, 155
statistical methods, 151–54
status differences (communication), 125
statutory law, 53–54
Steinem, Gloria, 66
Sterling Drug, Inc., 229
Stevens, Uriah A., 498
stock
  authorized shares, 315; buying, 379–85; capital gain and loss, 317; common, 315–17; comparison with bonds, 318; dividends, 316–17; issued, 315; and owner equity, 295; preferred, 317–18; prospectus, 315; right, 326; and security markets, 376–78; types of placement, 326–28
stockholder, 33–34

stock market averages, 379, 383, 384
stock markets, 364, 376–78
storage-unit (computer), 398, 399
stored program, 396, 397, 401
Strachan, John, 495
straight commission, 247
straight-line depreciation, 287
straight salary, 247, 503
strategic planning, 91–92
Strauss, Levi, 361
stress interview, 118
strike, 508, 509
strikebreaking, 497, 508
strike fund, 508
strike insurance, 508
subassembly, 266
subcontracting, 505
substitute product, 192, 208, 209
Sullivan, Leon H., 66
supermarket, 204, 205
supplemental accounting statements, 288
supplies inventory, 294
supply, 207, 209–213
supply curve, 210–11
surety bond, 354
survey data, 151, 156–58
Survey Research Center, University of Michigan, 183
synthetic process, 269–70

tabulating machine, 395
tactical planning, 93
Taft–Hartley Act (1947), 515
target market, 176–79, 187–91
tariff, 524–25
Tariff Commission, U.S., 530
tax accountant, 285
taxation
  and business decisions, 491; definition of, 485; goals of, 486–87; systems of, 485–86; types of, 487–91
tax base, 485
Tax Court, U.S., 471
tax-exempt note, 334
tax rate, 485
tax return, 489
Taylor, Frederick W., 15, 64, 95–96, 97, 103, 128
Teamsters Union, 21, 498, 499
Ted Bates Advertising Company, 238
Tennessee Valley Authority (TVA), 29, 467
term-life policy, 355
term loan, 320